THE NILE

The Life-Story of a River

EMIL LUDWIG

TRANSLATED BY MARY H. LINDSAY

1937

THE VIKING PRESS · NEW YORK

PUBLISHED IN FEBRUARY 1937
SECOND PRINTING FEBRUARY 1937
THIRD PRINTING MARCH 1937
FOURTH PRINTING APRIL 1937

THE NILE

The Life-Story of a River

TO
ELGA LUDWIG
the African

Thus do they, sir: they take the flow o' the Nile
By certain scales i' the pyramid; they know,
By the height, the lowness, or the mean, if dearth,
Or foison follow: the higher Nilus swells,
The more it promises: as it ebbs, the seedsman
Upon the slime and ooze scatters his grain,
And shortly comes to harvest.

Antony and Cleopatra, II, 7

FOREWORD

EVERY time I have written the life of a man, there has hovered before my mind's eye the image, physical and spiritual, of a river, but only once have I beheld in a river the image of man and his fate. When, at the end of 1924, I first saw the Great Dam at Aswân, its symbolic significance burst upon me with such force that I seemed to comprehend the River Nile forwards and backwards from this crucial point in its course. A mighty element had been tamed by human ingenuity so that the desert should bring forth fruit, an achievement which the centenarian Faust had attempted as the highest attainable to man in the service of his fellow-men. The thought of the end of *Faust*, as it stood embodied before my eyes in Aswân, fired me with the thought of writing the epic of the Nile as I had written the story of great men—as a parable.

But before I could tell the story of its adventures, and reveal their deeper meaning, I had to know the river from end to end, so that I might confirm or correct this vision in its detail. I had long known other parts of Africa. I loved that continent, because it had brought me happiness: even before the war I had seen on the equator the source of the Nile. But not until I set out to study it did it stand revealed as the most wonderful of all rivers.

This, the greatest single stream on earth, is yet by no means the most abundant, a fact which determines its whole life and that of its basin. It flows through the desert; for half of its course it receives neither tributaries nor rain, yet it does not dry up; indeed, close to its end, it creates the most fertile of all lands. In its youth it dissipates its finest powers, yet it arrives at its mouth with might. Though it flows along almost one-tenth of the earth's circumference, it maintains the simplest form of all rivers; save for a single loop, its course is from south to north, and over a

length of almost 4000 miles its maximum east-westerly deviations fall within 250 miles, so that, at the end, its mouth lies almost on the same degree of longitude as its source.

Its basin contains the biggest lake of the eastern hemisphere,
the highest mountains, the biggest city of its continent. Its banks
are peopled by the richest bird life of the northern hemisphere,
by nearly every animal species known to Paradise, by vegetation ranging from Alpine flora and the tropical forest, through
swamp, steppe, and desert to the richest arable land on earth. It
feeds hundreds of different races, men of the mountain and men
of the marsh, Arabs, Christians, and cannibals, pygmies and
giants. The struggles of these men for power and wealth, for
faith and custom, for the supremacy of colour, can be traced
farther back here than anywhere else in the history of mankind—
for six thousand years.

But the most wonderful thing I found was the realization that
all these phenomena, which reflect the power of nature, the activity of its creatures, the strivings of its human beings, agriculture and plants, animals and peoples, scenery and history, would
not have been what they were and are were it not for the river.

Since it had arisen before me as a living being, driven from its
radiant beginnings to its end in service, I could not but strive to
show the inward necessity of these adventures, arising from its
character, as in the lives of great men; to show how the river, like
the boy, emerging from the virgin forests of childhood, growing
in battle, fainting, falling, rises again to victory; how its distant,
gallant brother hurries towards it, how they glide together
through the desert, how at the height of its manhood it takes up
the struggle with man, how it is defeated, and, tamed, creates
men's fortunes, and how, in the end, it accomplishes more tragedy than in all its early wildness.

And since childhood and youth, as with every living being,
are chiefly determined by nature and environment, so here the
elements must work more vitally at the beginning, while later
life brings temptation and labour in the struggle with man. Out
of the confused simplicity of the wilderness, the Nile streams
into the complicated clarity of modern civilizations, sees the
great plan of its tamers jeopardized, and, in the end, wearied of

men's lust for gold, sinks into the sea, to be renewed in eternal resurrection.

The documents for the life of any river consist mainly of scientific works, or books of travel in which the writer travels with the reader. The new form of description here attempted demanded different groupings. In this, as in my former biographies, I had, for the sake of the *linea aurea,* to check the river at the five vital points of its career—on Lake Albert (twice), on Lake No, in Khartoum, in Aswân, and in Cairo. As my object was not to write a book of travel, but to tell the story of a great life, we, the reader and I, do not travel on the river. It is the river that travels; it is the river's adventures that enthral us.

It would, however, be vain to seek here either a complete geography or history of the four Nile countries, or an encyclopædia of their peoples, animals, or plants. They appear in fragments, which had repeatedly to be cut down, so that the river might flow on unhindered. Thus the long story of the discoverers of the Nile with which this volume opened had to be sacrificed; it may appear later.

The vertical line along the river from source to mouth had to be cut by historical horizontals, occupying a quarter of the first part and rather more of the second. For when I saw the elephants and lions on the upper course of the Nile, the camels and asses lower down, which come every evening to drink its waters, there rose again before my eyes the shadows of all those figures who had lived, ruled, or suffered here, an endless train. I saw the religious and racial wars in the deserts and steppes of the Sudan and in Egypt, the birthplace of occidental man.

In this book, as in my former biographies, I have sought to efface the evidences of the literature by means of which I deepened or completed my impressions. To show what I saw in its symbolic significance, to show the symbol in the visible event, seems to me more important than to parade with a host of names and dates that anybody can look up in works of reference. Here, as elsewhere, I sought to paint in colours what the expert presents in figures and tables. I had no wish to describe what is familiar in names, but to paint what lay before my eyes, then name it. Only once, at the crisis of the third act, where the problem of the dam brings the decisive moment of this Life, a few figures had to remain, to which I beg the reader to submit. Whatever else was absolutely necessary has been given in round figures, for 602½ miles from Lake No to Khartoum sounds less than six hundred. The transliteration of African names into European languages, too, is quite unsettled.

While in the later life of a river, it is character that proves itself in struggle, the physical environment, the landscape, exercises in its youth the determining influences which later will come from men. This thematic shift could not but be specially marked in the story of a river which in its age traverses the land that has seen the longest of all human histories: a century of history in the Sudan is followed by sixty centuries in Egypt. Thus while three-quarters of the first half of the book (on the Upper Nile) were devoted to nature, and only one-quarter to history, in the second half (on Egypt) they are about equal, especially since the landscape, flora, and fauna change relatively little between Aswân and the Delta.

In spite of this, the historical parts of the Egyptian half of the book had to be treated aphoristically if they were not to clash with the theme of the whole. In the same way as in my former biographies, pictures take the place of ideas. And in these pictures, social conditions take precedence of wars, and the feelings of men are more important than their state. Thus, in the Sudanese half, the feelings of the Negro or the elephant were depicted with more sympathy than those of the white man; in the same way, in Egypt, the attempt is made to show history, not as Pharaohs or Sultans saw it, but from the standpoint of the fellah, who has, from all time, lived in closer communion with the Nile than its rulers. For Egypt is the one land on earth in which every inhabitant lives at all times in sight of the river. Dynasties came, used it, and passed, but the river, the father of the land, remained. Six thousand years ago, the Nile, the begetter of water and grain, was as fateful to the fellah as it is today with its dams and cotton; hence this new attempt at a history written from below shows religion, temples, and carvings, in the main as the fellah saw them: for *he* is the people of the Lower Nile.

What will be specially missed here are big-game expeditions, in which I do not take part, and ethnological discussions. My distrust of ethnological theory was confirmed when I saw all the races of the Nile shifted about by zealous scholars and attributed to, and again withdrawn from, opposite racial groups. The whole learned dispute as to the Hamites and Semites, in the course of which fashion discovers new "circles of civilization" every five years, means less to me than the sight of a bedouin on the Atbara, in whose splendid limbs I could admire and honour a mixture of five or six races. Yet even if exact knowledge of such mixtures were forthcoming, it would be fruitless in a book in which the river holds sway. On the other hand, the social condition of the coloured peoples seemed to me important in an epoch which is preparing for them a new role in the life of mankind. All these things are perpetually influenced by the Nile, and, in their turn, react upon it. My only aim was to make its destiny clear, as a great parable.

*   *   *

On three other Nile journeys, between 1930 and 1934, I had studied the whole of the White Nile in Uganda, the Sudan, and Egypt, and the Blue Nile on a safari to Western Abyssinia which led me into the region of its sources, and, in the Sudan, along its lower course. The longest, central reach of the Blue Nile, from Lake Tana to the Sudanese frontier, even today almost unexplored, had to be sketched in by the notes of a few travellers who have seen it in part. That I could do all the rest at my ease by rail and air, steamer and sailing-boat, camel and mule, is due to the assistance and interest of the three governments on the Nile: the Egyptian, especially King Fuad I, who placed a steamer at our disposal; the English, which facilitated our travelling in every way; and the Abyssinian, which gave us a bodyguard of soldiers from Gallabat on.

The section on Abyssinia was finished before the outbreak of hostilities in East Africa.

I am deeply obliged to the following experts for advice in the reading of the manuscript: Major Barker, Director of the Zoological Garden, Khartoum, for the fauna; Marchese Gentile-Farinola, Varramista (Tuscany), for Abyssinia; Professor J. A. Yahuda, London, for Pharaonic and Jewish history; Dr. h.c. Max

Meyerhof, Cairo, for Arab and many other questions; Sir Harold MacMichael, Governor of Tanganyika, former Secretary of State in the Sudan, for the Sudan. These distinguished experts have preserved me from a host of errors. I am indebted also to the existing four volumes of the monumental *Histoire de la Nation Egyptienne* presented to me by the late King Fuad, to Miss W. S. Blackman's *The Fellahin of Upper Egypt,* and to the *Mémoire sur l'Histoire du Nil* by Prince Omar Tousson of Cairo.

Most of the photographs are by Lehnert & Landrock, Cairo. Others are by the British Royal Air Force, London; Karakashian Bros., Khartoum; and the Sudan Guide Book, London.

L.

MOSCIA
Summer 1936

CONTENTS

ILLUSTRATIONS

PHOTOGRAPHS

MAPS OF THE NILE REGION

Book One

FREEDOM

AND

ADVENTURE

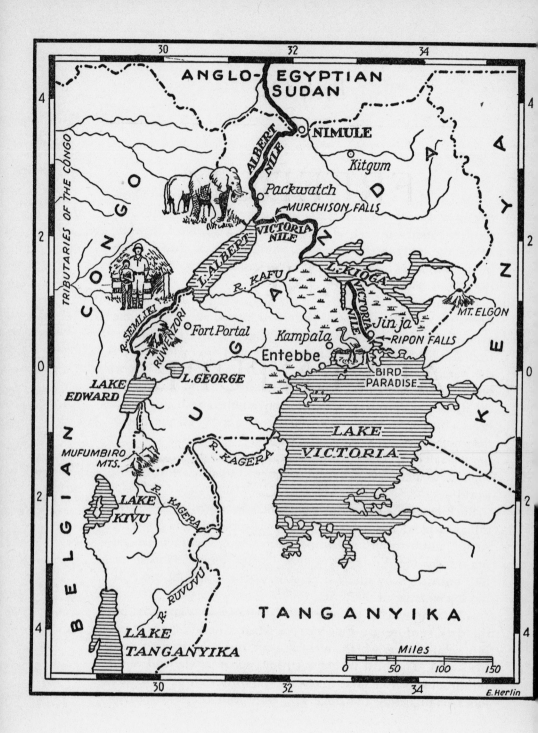

ANGLO- EGYPTIAN SUDAN

CONGO

TRIBUTARIES OF THE CONGO

ALBERT NILE

NIMULE

○ Kitgum

Packwatch

MURCHISON FALLS

VICTORIA NILE

L. ALBERT

R. KAFU

L. KIOGA

MT. ELGON

R. SEMLIKI

RUWENZORI

Fort Portal

Kampala

Jinja

RIPON FALLS

Entebbe

BIRD PARADISE

L. GEORGE

LAKE EDWARD

UGANDA

KENYA

MUFUMBIRO MTS.

R. KAGERA

LAKE VICTORIA

LAKE KIVU

R. KAGERA

BELGIAN

R. RUVUVU

LAKE TANGANYIKA

TANGANYIKA

Miles

0   50   100   150

E. Herlin

1

A ROAR heralds the river. Thundering, a shining sheet of water, radiantly blue, tense with life, plunges round the reef of a rocky islet in a double fall, while below, the spray thickens in a milky green vortex, madly whirling its own foam away to an unknown destiny. In such clamour, the Nile is born.

In a quiet inlet at the edge of the mighty fall, a gigantic maw yawns pink. Puffing and sluggish, the hippopotamus snorts and grunts as it raises its head above the water to squirt a water-jet from its nostrils between its pink-lined ears. Lower down, where the water grows calmer, bronze-green dragons, with black spots on their carapace and a yellowish belly, lie basking; to complete the illusion of fairyland, their eyes are rimmed with gold. Each bears a bird on its back, or even between its teeth, for the dragon sleeps open-mouthed. This is Leviathan from the Book of Job, the crocodile. It looks like some strange survival from the time when ferns and forests covered the earth and saurians ruled the world.

But above the primeval monsters, the world of feathered things soars, wheels, and swoops. All the birds crossing Northern Africa, and many from Europe, gather here, and their screaming drowns the din of the waters. On the bushy island in the fall, untrodden by the foot of man, at the source of the Nile, lies the paradise of the birds.

Soft white patches shimmering like orange-blossom from out the dark verdure are transformed, when a noise alarms them, into white egrets which fly away over the falls, trailing their black legs. The bird with the curious spoon at the end of his bill, from which he takes his name, the whitest thing in nature, looks small beside the huge grey one, who bears his heavier body with hunched shoulders and indrawn neck slowly through the air. Suddenly there is a splash in the hurrying water: a big, dull black bird has dropped from the wet brushwood of the islet; it is that notorious glutton, the cormorant; he stays submerged for minutes at a time, rises far off, and, with the struggling fish in his beak, disappears with the powerful wing-strokes of a sea-bird. Disapproving, a grave black and white bird looks on; he walks with drooping head; then, as if to display real dignity, slowly spreads the shapely bow of his yellow-striped wings in graceful flight. This is the ibis, the holy bird of the Nile.

Proud and solitary, like the princes of Arabian legends, mute and unapproachable, the cranes stand along the banks. One, silver-grey, with a noble gaze, who bears his rather too heavy head gracefully on his delicate neck, and holds his dark tail-feathers like a bouquet, at a single stroke spreads out a pair of gigantic wings and trails slowly away over the water, but his handsomer brother, whose feathers shimmer blue on tail and belly, carries on his head, like a peacock, a tuft of golden feathers; this is the crested crane, stately, gorgeous, and decadent like Van Dyck's royal portraits. Beside this prince, but slightly to the rear, as is seemly, stands the aged man of money. Ugly and comical, as in the fairy-tales, a picture of feigned repose and false dignity, unscrupulous and wary, shrewd and greedy, the black and white marabou is always to the fore if business is on foot, and takes everything that offers from the rat to the spider.

And among them the countless multitude of smaller birds flits to and fro over the source of the Nile, screaming, chattering, and piping: sun-birds flashing in water and light, turquoise-blue with orange feathers, pink and rusty red, iridescent, among blue-shimmering kingfishers, with gleaming thrushes darting over their heads. Bulbul, the oriental nightingale, invisible in the undergrowth, gurgles her melody, but close by her secret spot, the swallows from the north swoop past in softly twittering flight, seeking, like the German poets, the south and the oriental nightingale. And the rose-grey turtles coo in deep contralto, little opalescent blue-green starlings pipe their song into the screaming of the bigger birds, martins dip their brown breasts in the spray, and the wagtail, a Nile-bird like the ibis, the daintiest of all, warbles as it rocks. In a chorus of sound and colour, they whir round the inaccessible islet in the falls, as though they feared man more than the hippopotamus, more than the crocodile and the great birds.

Where are we?

The source of the Nile, the Ripon Falls, lying close above the equator, three hundred yards broad, called by the natives "The Stones," plunges between virgin rocks bare of any green growth save brushwood and wild flowers, on a treeless plateau, for the white men have felled the forest on account of the deadly flies. It is the most northerly point of Lake Victoria, near Jinja, where the mighty roar proclaims a mighty spectacle. Behind grey rocks, which form a kind of natural dam, on the other side of the bay, lies the lake with its many islands, great and small, the lake which sends forth the river, the great messenger from the heart of Africa, to bear wonderful tidings to a distant sea.

None guessed its origin. For thousands of years men sought this source and went astray. The strange river, they thought, must draw its strength from high mountains, and, like every other river on earth, be formed of little mountain torrents. One day, late in time, only seventy years ago, it was discovered that the Nile began its course with a gigantic waterfall: the child of the greatest of all African lakes, it showed its strength in the foam and thunder of the first day of its life.

Not all the breakers of these first hours will reach the goal. Wind and sun, rocks, animals, and plants will stop many, or dissolve them in air; nor will all the water that ends its course in the Mediterranean many months later come from this source, for the Nile has three sources, and, at the beginning, many tributaries. Yet there are many millions of atoms of water that follow the whole career of their river in its bed, from this fall which gives it birth, till at last they mingle with the salt of the sea.

Here, at the source, the veils of morning are rising from the lake, whose bounds no man can divine.

The growing light discloses hosts of islands, large and small, deep gorges cutting into the land, sandbanks far out, and, beyond, ranges of hills fading into the pale-blue distance. Broad, shimmering grasslands clothe the swelling banks, studded by single huge trees dividing light from shade in great masses, fertile, idyllic.

Even if all the islands and bays were not there to crowd the view, the eye could never reach the farther shore, for this lake is a sea, much bigger than Switzerland, with laws, forms, and dangers of its own, an unrelated element in this enchanted continent, a gigantic mirror for the sun of Africa, the frontier of a bucolic land which is called Uganda. It has been likened to Paradise, for here eternal summer reigns, without mortal heat by day, without sultry mist by night; rising from a level of three thousand feet, cooled by afternoon thunderstorms, by evening wind, almost without seasons, with an equal daily share of sun and rain, it is ever fertile, ever bountiful.

Behind the girdle round the lake, the last giants of a primeval world lie hid. For the land mounts terrace-wise from the shores of this silken blue sea, rising in the north-west to hoary granite peaks and volcanoes, to the sources of rivers all flowing to the one great stream, and yet higher to the snow-capped summits of the Mountains of the Moon. Like a loosely fitting armour, these heights enclose the domain of the blessed race of men who, in the lakeside uplands, reap much longer than they sow.

For the shores of the lake are a park, formed by nature and the sun-browned hand of man. Pastel-green, the liquid light flowing through their delicate branches, so that their shadow falls but grey on the grass, lofty acacias stand singly, their crowns spreading like open parachutes. Close above the ground, the thick main trunk branches out all round, dry, gnarled, and tender grey; much higher up, the finely articulated leaves begin to radiate, and the flowers droop in great mauve bunches. Above widespread roots, which rise above the ground, stands the dome of the ficus, as rich in timber and in shade as the royal sycamore beside it. The flaming red blossoms of slender flamboyants bow towards the lake, but the bright scarlet candelabrum of the coral tree thrusts its rigid fingers into the air. Thus each stands on these meadow slopes, almost motionless, the symbol of the landscape of a dream.

2

NO human being has yet dared to lay hand on this part of Africa to shape or subdue it, although many a plan has been woven round the source of the Nile. Yet the river has been bridged in the first moments of its life: a short distance downstream a grey iron bridge bears the train which connects the mighty lake with the Indian Ocean, the small sea with the great. Not until two thousand miles lower down, on the brink of the desert, will the Nile, completely transformed, know another bridge. Along this whole stretch through lands and peoples, save for one natural bridge, no one can cross the Nile unless by rowing; men and beasts have tried and lie buried in it: for long reaches the unbridged stream has proved a barrier between one fauna and another.

The young river takes no heed of the bridge: in a long series of falls and rapids, spraying and leaping, it drives its infant powers onward, foaming in the joy of life. A second fall, the Owen Falls, as broad as the first, but twice as deep, and still wilder, comes to lengthen the chain of rapids, and, calculating by the course of nature and not the other way round, these should be called the first and second Nile cataracts. Without pausing for breath, the young unnavigable stream foams and winds on northwards, but now it is no longer bordered by meadows and smooth plains. Since this region is uninhabitable owing to sleeping sickness, the river is here alone with the forest, as both were formed by the hand of their Creator, by vegetation and the erosion of centuries.

Living walls of trailing lianas here cut off the forest on both sides of the river, hiding from it the struggles and disasters of the great animals within, as we try to hide them from children, and leaving the river to its play all day. What goes on behind

7

these living walls belongs to a time when the earth was younger and life denser and more exuberant. In this luxuriance of careless growth, where the individual struggle for existence stands out less hard and bare than in the more sparsely provided regions of the north, life and death grow indissolubly united: plants and animals, which no human hand has touched, are, in their inmost being, mutually dependent, even though the animals fight. Under a dome of liquid-green gloom, which creates the jungle atmosphere, the roots of huge trees cling to their prostrate forefathers, while their crowns, like great and lonely characters, tower over the dense mêlée, to form above with others a community of sunny heights. What grew on them falls away, turns to fresh fertility in this zone of unquenchable life, for no one reaps the fruit of these trees. Steaming in the brooding warmth of love, nature lies free of all purpose.

Through the ages the floor of the tropical forest has steadily risen; a moist, spongy humus of vegetable matter begets roots and stems from the twigs of falling, still living giant trees. Out of dying plants returning to earth, and even out of the body of living and growing ones, new plants rise and bloom from sucking roots, in the fearless joy of growth, for frost and hail, the enemies of the northern forest, and rough winds from the neighbouring snow-mountains cannot penetrate these self-created walls, while warmth and water, the two great patrons of the vegetable world, reign in profusion. The only enemy who can force his way in, who is nearly the strongest of all, the creature from an earlier world who held his own while all the others dwindled, the elephant alone, is powerful enough to trample or break down with his mighty limbs whatever stands in his way. Without his huge tread, man would never have set foot in the jungle, for it is he who opened paths for the Negro, and it was these paths the white man followed much later with his roads.

And as the jungle grows together from above and below, as the ferns and giant grasses press upwards to meet the hanging lianas, a living wall arises, impenetrable, and multiplied a hundredfold in the course of time, for the virile ring of the tree-felling iron has never startled this humming world.

The density of the forest begets its silence: only the remoteness of the bird-calls can give an idea of its depth, and only of part of its depth. The grumbling of the monkeys, the whirring of insects, the sighing, creaking, and groaning of the giant tree-trunks, cramped for space and air, the croaking of frogs from the papyrus, the call of the oriole, the clatter of huge lizards, the silky gliding of the snakes, and again the whistling and rattling of the butcher-birds—it all sounds as muffled as the light in this forest, random and overloud, like children's voices raised in church, for in spite of all its wildness, the dimness and height of the jungle recall a cathedral.

Below, in the enormous trunks of the ficus, among drooping mauve orchids, deep niches have opened, as if in the columns of a cathedral, big enough to hold a man, while above, amid the blossoms on the branches, old baboons sit, still as black statues, bored with the capers of the colobus monkey, whose white tail and back stripes flash as he swings from one liana stem to the next. With its plant life hanging or standing weary and motionless, the sultry gloom of the jungle is quickened by the animals only in an eerie, secret way, so that the colours of the flowers sound louder than the footfalls and cries of the animals. Out of the mesh of creepers on the ground, part of a resting snake peeps out; the scream of a bird has a meaning only when the shadow of the white hawk flits by; and when parrots screech on the baobab, the elephantine tree with the wrinkled leather feet, even their noise is quickly overpowered by the mighty jungle silence.

But the burning cry of the coral tree, where its figlike branches catch the sun, falls from tips like a kind of giant bean; from out the feathery leaves of the acacias shine pink blossoms, big as a man's hand; bright blue convolvulus hangs in long festoons from the boughs of the sycamore to the flamboyant with its densely crowded, flaming red blossoms.

In the clearings, on half-cleared pools, where the tropical sun breaks through and the profusion of flowers is multiplied tenfold, their colours seem less audible. Here the animal is lord, for all living things gather at the water. From out the carmine convolvulus that muffles up the mimosa the turquoise-blue kingfisher, hanging close above the water, peers motionless, spying down to snatch the fish. Rocking to and fro on the flexible points of the palm-fans are the nests of the weaver-birds, who at these airiest points can elude the grasp of the monkeys and snakes. Down where the great ferns hang half rotting over the water, sky-blue swallow-tail butterflies with purple eyes flutter by, others white with bright green edges to their wings, and blue lizards with orange spots lie basking between swamp and water.

With grotesque movements, the hornbill utters his hoarse screech, as though every sound were born of inmost pain, but in the next tree a starling sits piping away to herself as if alone in an idyll, the born master beside the panting amateur. Yet both are outsung by the flute-bird, who sends his seductive, contemptuous oboe call from out the thicket, as though he lived on air and water, were flinging a challenge to the wildness of the jungle, and were mocking, in bold, melting trills, all the eager life and gravity about him, till a magpie screams down his song.

And far from this teeming and careless throng, or at any rate heedless of it, the great animals of the jungle live and hunt, mate and fight. It is they who emerge in the evening at the rapids of the young Nile, to lap its fresh water. The Negro who bathed and fished in some quiet cove all day has vanished, making way in the evening for the silent lords of the forest, for he fears them.

3

NOT for forty miles below its source does the young Nile calm down. It has grown familiar with its first surroundings; it has fallen six hundred feet through the long rapids and waterfalls. It has already embraced a few woody islands too, and seen on them naked human creatures who have built little huts to catch, fry, and smoke fish.

Yet at the point where it emerges from the rapids and enters on a broad, quiet reach, men surprise the stream with a new terror: boats are waiting there, and little steamers, and the young creature must for the first time submit to a rider. At first, it shakes him wildly, for there are still many stones and rocks in the river bed, but then it yields, for men were cunning and built flat-bottomed boats. For a hundred and twenty miles, the Nile is now navigable. Where navigation to the north begins, at 1° N. lat., the railway line to the south-east starts, leading to Kenya and the sea: it barely touches the Nile. Only at 13° N. lat., and twelve hundred miles from here, will a second railway approach the river on that second bridge; so long is the stretch of lands, still longer the course of the river, through regions which defy the railway-builder.

Scarcely has it taken the steamer on its back, when a new adventure awaits the Nile: the banks which bound its course retreat, it feels widened at every step. The forest which so firmly clasped it has gone. It is already six hundred yards broad, soon it will be many thousands: its waters are escaping its grasp, its form has vanished, it has poured into a sponge, seems to be losing itself there. As it broadens, it grows shallow; now it is nine feet deep, and still less at the edge of the swamp. At the same time its body is covered with flowering weed. The whole world round about seems to stand still, to sleep, the river's youthful valour is paralysed, its gaiety is gone. What has happened?

This is Lake Kioga, a broad, muddy sheet of water with four great arms, a swampy lake fringed with papyrus. And as the Nile flows through this lake for some sixty miles, it has to carry its vegetation too. For miles the river flowing through the lake is covered with a kind of water-lily, thrillingly beautiful, pale blue, with a golden heart out of which sometimes a second flower grows. They lie like carpets, hardly moving, an even pattern spread out over the lake which seems to have swallowed up the stream.

The first tributaries take good care not to flow into the great sponge: it would devour them. Not until the point at which the Nile leaves Lake Kioga, at its western extremity, does the Kafu discharge into it, like a younger brother ending his short life by bestowing his portion on the elder. When the Nile, once more a river, turns north, it has taken on the nature of the lake: it is a shallow, swampy, sluggish stream. A dreamy, indolent mood must overcome it.

At this point in the course of the Nile variations set in that might be compared to the cyclical variations in certain characters: in irregular rhythm, for hundreds of miles and for many months of its course, its character changes: it is by turns stormy and repelling, wild and weary. It is impossible to say whether the river takes on the nature of its surroundings, or the surroundings that of the river. For the present it drags along northwards, falling very slightly, in the rhythm of Lake Kioga.

Then suddenly it takes a sharp turn, quitting for the first time its northerly course, sweeps west, and is completely transformed. The rocky bottom it at last feels again gives it fresh spirit; it hurls the boat from its back: once more, as in earliest childhood, it is a mountain stream on which no man can travel, it grows narrower and deeper than it has ever been. Is this a new adventure?

The great African rift suddenly breaks through here in a curved escarpment. The region grows rocky, granite masses crowd together, a canyon narrows down. The Nile, whose first falls were no more than enlarged rapids, is suddenly faced with a great one: squeezed into a width of eighteen feet, it has to fall more than a hundred and twenty. The broad emergence from that inland sea is here compressed into a few foaming seconds: thundering, the excited river turns to spray as it falls.

These Murchison Falls, the first and last to plunge the Nile into such depths, first form its character. Here it knows terror, it dashes from one ledge of Africa to the next; this youthful experience, stormy as a passion, completely changes it. Here neither hippopotamus nor crocodile gambols, even the birds are rarer, for no fish will try the upward leap here. Instead of them, an everlasting rainbow, the immortal bridge between sun and water, hovers over the rocks. On the rocks, above and below, the light breaks into a thousand sparkling crystals, forming a glorious background to the mighty spectacle.

An hour below the falls, the foam on the hurrying water is still there to tell of the shock the Nile has suffered. Then it passes through bushlands into a rapidly broadening valley. And here for the first time the marvel of the antediluvian world comes into sight. Below the falls, the elephant, in the evening, comes to the river.

A giant, he still treads an earth whose creatures walk below him. The strongest of all, whom no animal and no tree can withstand, not even the thorn and the snake can harm him: like great men, he leaves his ponderous might unused, supreme in the consciousness of a strength which none need fear: neither vainglorious nor predatory, he is the most generous and shrewdest of animals. Gifted with an even temper and a sense of humour, yet terrible in revenge, or in the protection of his young against the attacks of crafty men, possessed of the smallest of eyes in the biggest of faces, the sharpest hearing draped with a huge flap, an organ half nose and half arm, and tusks that can tear anything, he yet seems to carry off only what is strictly necessary, seldom alarms and hunts animals, eats none, feeds, like a monster in a fairy-tale, on delicate grasses, barks, and juices, and when he strides the ground with giant legs, he seems to be taking his colossal body for a gentle walk. Nothing about this monster is wild or coarse: his gait, his grasp, even his look, is serene.

In earlier times, they were known to all the earth: nowhere have so many tusks been found as about the Bering Strait. They lived in Rome and Ireland, in Siberia and Northern Spain: the remains showing the African elephant everywhere are of themselves enough to prove a connexion by land between the two continents. But even in historic times the elephant was a European: a Phœnician traveller describes him in the neighbourhood of Gibraltar, and Hannibal's elephants on coins show the huge ears and sloping back which the Indian elephant does not possess.

When a herd comes out of the forest, hardly a twig cracks, so warily they move, and only the egrets ceaselessly wheeling above them betray where they are, for they live on the insects of the elephant's skin. These giants of the forest have learned to distrust man: he has too often tricked them from ambush: now they stand still, sniffing, for minutes at a time, with no sound but the flapping of gigantic ears. As they have a calf in their midst, they are on the *qui vive,* for they beat a soft retreat if they are unnoticed, but break out if they feel themselves watched; men, less noble, do the opposite. Now they emerge from the bushes, only two-thirds visible, for the high grass hides them to the knee. The calf moves under the mother between her forelegs, where the udders are, but first he throws back his trunk to take suck with his mouth. The others have already reached the water; they have sought out a little cove; they have trampled down everything, not in rage, but simply because they are big; they stand snorting in the Nile, squirting water over their sloping backs with their supple trunks, drinking now and then, and removing a whole meadowful of high grass, and as they can never be seen really chewing, as they never open a vast mouth like the hippo, it all seems to have vanished into the unfathomable.

As they return from the river, they look dead black against the yellow savanna, but their tusks, which the females have here too, shine the whiter. The bull leads the troop. The white heron resettles on his back, like the white genie in the fairy-tale which guides aged and great sinners, and the giant, refreshed, strolls towards the forest with his rolling gait, wet and happy, casually examining an acacia with his trunk to see if it is worth while stripping the bark with his tusks, casting a half-

glance backwards to make sure that his wife and child are coming. Thus he withdraws from the Nile into the dark green of
the jungle, of which he is lord, with his human intelligence,
which foresees, plans, and remembers, stronger than any other
living creature, serene and supreme, the last real king of nature.

Here, where the river steadily widens, is the first real home
of the hippopotamus and the crocodile, which have been counted
in their thousands below the Murchison Falls: here it is sunny
and flat, and these water-creatures seem to feel protected from
all dangers in the neighbourhood of a gigantic bathing-pool.

For now the Nile, for the first time, sees a great lake with
open water ahead, boundless like Lake Victoria, which it never
saw, for that lay behind it. Beyond the yellow savanna, which
spreads out like a delta, lies the northern end of Lake Albert.
The Nile, three hundred miles from its source, ceases here to
bear the name of Victoria Nile, and, powerfully reinforced
from a second source, becomes the Albert Nile as soon as a short
reach of the river has crossed the corner of the lake. On flat
islands and landspits, which lie before the shores as in the lagoons, the crocodiles bask in thousands, silvery fish leap in the
sap-green water of the coves, while the clear stream otherwise
flows blue and seems to suffer no swamp. On the banks, where
grassland alternates with forest and great clumps of trees approach the water, a herd of dainty antelopes moves: the reedbucks come slowly to the water, to the Nile, which gives all
creatures to drink.

In this clear lake the river cannot go astray, as in the Kioga
swamps: a powerful current draws it, the way lies clear ahead.
In the western distance rise the purple shadows of high mountains; there another great river flows, the Congo; it moves westward and the Nile will never know it. Its own course leads
northwards. Before following it, let us seek what feeds its second
source, the mighty water-basin of Lake Albert.

4

IN the wilful windings of rivers, their former existence stands revealed, uncertain as regards the passage of time and the details of their course, yet, as with men, discernible through the mists of memory, and neither to be proved nor ignored. In the land of Uganda, that prehistory is even more legible than history itself: the prehistoric world takes precedence of the historic. For what happened here to Adamic man has sunk back into the womb of time, because till yesterday he remained without writing and almost without tradition, but prehistory has carved its runes and signs on the mountains. The course of the primeval Nile can be conjectured.

Africa, a continent of shelves, the only one that can be called so, the continent without mountain ranges, has, on the ledge of the great lakes, made or suffered an exception. It happened when the crust of the continent was torn in two, when the huge rift was formed which runs diagonally through East Africa from Rhodesia to the valley of the Jordan, taking in the Red Sea. From the belly of the earth, raging fire burst forth, heaved giant clods into mountains, folded them back and laid the lower-lying land at the base of the new volcanoes open for the rivers and lakes to gather and flow away. To the south of the Nile basin, the rift branched, the eastern arm running to Kenya and forming Kilimanjaro, the western forming the three lakes to the west of Victoria Nyanza, which itself represents a subsidence of the plateau between the two.

However uncertain the intervals of time remain, it seems clear that the seven lakes of Central Africa are of recent date, that where Lake Victoria now lies, broad plains once lay, traversed by the feeders of the present lake. Later on, great water-basins

CROCODILE NEAR THE SOURCE

Photo: Karakashian Bros., Khartoum

ELEPHANT FAMILY

may have formed which, rising with perpetual rain, spread and broke through the flanking rim of hills. The water deepened, widened the gap, and forged its way to the plain: rapids and falls stand witness to this course of development.

Above the great volcanoes and small craters, which can be seen and heard to this day in the congealed lava, the earth tremors and hot springs, there rose in primitive rock a royal witness, the Ruwenzori, a range of snow-mountains higher than Mont Blanc. This is in truth the heart of Africa. The waters flow to east and west to feed the greatest rivers of the continent, the Nile and the Congo.

It is not the Ruwenzori itself that forms the watershed; it is a chain of volcanoes rising to a height of 14,600 feet, and running from about 2° S. lat. to the equator: of these a certain group, the Mfumbiro Range, now seems to form the exact watershed. In the course of that metempsychosis of the rivers, it has changed, and even today remains mysteriously uncertain: lines waver, the geographers and hydrographers perpetually renew their measurements. The names show where it is: the four lakes with the English royal names which have been so surprisingly transported to Africa belong to the Nile; those with the African names, Lakes Kivu and Tanganyika, to the Congo. Within these limits lie the sources of the two great rivers which quicken the ancient, strangely rigid continent.

But if the Nile takes all its water from the lakes, that does not explain what feeds the lakes. And if the lakes are fed less by rivers than by rain, that still does not explain where the rain comes from. These questions are still unsettled. At present the rain of the Nile basin is believed to come mainly from the South Atlantic. Evaporation and condensation caused by the tension between sea and land remains even on the whole, but not in the detail. Thus over this basin there goes on the tug-of-war of evaporation, the formation of rivers, and their departure for the sea. In this cycle, which holds a third of the rainfall of the earth captive, the depth of the basin plays an important part. As Lake Victoria is not three hundred feet deep, so that more water evaporates than is received, this constant diminution, as we shall see later, presents the Nile engineers with a very grave problem. In accordance with its configuration, the lake, as the source of the Nile, has a climate, and even a wind-system, of its own. The alternation of land and sea winds, the frequency of thunderstorms, the high temperature of the water, which reaches nearly 79°, the absence of dry months, and the evaporation from the gigantic surface are the basic factors of its climate.

Not its feeders. It certainly receives them from three sides, while it yields its waters only at that one northern point by Jinja; it also receives large quantities of steeply falling water from short rivers which flow from the isolated volcano, Mount Elgon, which rises to over 14,000 feet in the north-east. Only one of the fifteen feeders, however, is important, and it was this which was formerly called the Nile, since, by the logic of geographers, the greatest feeder of a lake must needs reappear in its greatest outflow, and this not merely in small lakes, where the current can be measured or seen, but even where the greatest distances intervene. If it is to be assumed that this western feeder is the original Nile, it takes two hundred miles by the shortest route through the lake to reach its outflow in the north. The only thing to support this idea, for it is an idea, is the name given to it by the natives, that is, "The mother of the Jinja river."

This feeder of Lake Victoria, the Kagera, is a mighty river, even without bearing the name of Nile. It is 450 miles long, drains the greater part of the western lake plateau, and at its three rather inaccessible mouths in Lake Victoria can be navigated only by rowing-boats, for these mouths vary according to the height of the plants which it carries down from the mountains. After a navigable stretch, which often broadens into pools, its higher reaches lie in deeper clefts, often thickly covered and swampy with papyrus, and, as we approach its sources, it is once more a wild mountain torrent.

There are three of these sources which, like the seven cities of Homer, dispute the honour of being the home of the Nile; all have fantastic names, but the one with the dark-coloured name Ruvuvu, after countless surveys, today holds the field as the source of the Kagera. Six thousand feet up, on Belgian territory, on the eastern fall of the rift between Tanganyika and Lake Edward, in the dense mountain jungle, lies the source of the Ruvuvu, and whoever likes may see in this most southerly tributary the top-head of the Nile.

5

IN a wide embrace, the Ruwen-
zori Range encloses the beautiful land lying round the western
lakes. The ancients called it the Mountains of the Moon, for,
as they could not explain the snow on its summit, the Negroes
said that the mountains had drawn the moonlight down to them.
And in its lofty isolation above the equator, it might well be
made of some unearthly substance where plants and granite
have come to an end and the eternal ice of its 15,000-feet-high
domes and peaks shines against the golden yellow sky of evening.
Lonely, a philosopher, sufficient unto itself in the feeling of its
height, this range long withstood the curiosity of man; for
months it veiled its head before three great explorers, so that
they began to doubt the Negroes' assurances, and many travellers
who today can seek it by the map at a particular spot never see
it. It is richer than all the mountains of Africa, for, as the rains
break against its rocks, it discharges a thousand rills which grow
into rivers, collect in lakes, and all, at last, form the other half
of the Nile. The Ruwenzori Range might be called the king of
this country, but it is the father.

This mountain range, along its sixty miles of length, ascends
in three impressive tiers: the first, that of the bush, at an altitude
of about three thousand feet, is the broadest.

The bush is light: an open, undulating country, traversed by
wide grasslands, bears the acacia in many forms: one, leafless,
thorny, greenish-white; another, white, with pale-green leaves
between the thorns; yet another, black and leafy, with dark
boughs; a fourth with shimmering red bark; and yet another,
the highest, with gigantic lavender-blue bunches of flowers hanging from it like grapes. Among them, darker and more massive,
the euphorbia, rising like a protest to heaven, is hardy enough

to live far up the heights. Everything about it, as about the elephant, looks primeval, shaggy, and strong; every tree might be a family with its head the huge yellow and red flower at the top. On the parched yellow veldt, tall mauve orchises and carmine amaryllis stand like lilies; close to the ground, thick-stemmed flowers like red powder-puffs grow in thousands. A marshy glint of dark green, with the birds wheeling above it, shows where the rivers are hurrying through the papyrus and denser parts of the forest. The strong giant grass, twelve feet high and as thick as the bamboo, tapering upwards with broad upstanding leaves, is called, here and everywhere along the Nile, elephant grass; it is overtopped by the reddish tree-heath, tall and thorny.

To the high plains streams of this lower region, the reedbuck crowds in troops, almost fearless. Greyish-red, hairy waterbucks raise their lovely horns, lay their nostrils upwind, sniffing the air, while the ungainly warthog, shambling along with hanging head, betrays less courage and hence less fear. Impala antelopes seem to float as they vault over the thornbushes: all are drawn by the green strip which promises water. Above the swarms of locusts sweeping by in long ribbons, marabous wheel in masses as if they were birds of prey; below them files of duck fly low over the papyrus swamp, startled by the sharp cry of a kite.

In the second, higher zone of the Ruwenzori, in the forest, among gorges and high valleys, where the rainfall increases, and with it the moss that covers whole forests, the mountains are girdled with a belt which can be clearly distinguished from a distance. Here a beautiful conifer pierces the bamboos; still higher, the lobelia stares open-eyed, a giant flower-candle like a lance, with strange grape-like clusters hanging from it. Like monuments in deserted graveyards, these great plants stand in the forest of eternal rain.

Pink and bluish, the tree-heath blooms near them, its thick stems bearded with cloudy mosses which grow, too, from below, green, orange-gold, even crimson. Generations of its dead ancestors lie about in heaps, and the bamboo, half broken, creaks on every side in the rain and the wind. In this landscape lie the crater lakes.

There are many of them, blinking dark-eyed from these forests, embedded between steep walls which show the soft formation characteristic of the crater. The dense quiet, the deep cooing of the doves, the bananas in cultivated spots in the forest, where a few huts hint at the presence of man, here and there a virgin mountain pasture—everything looks and feels like a park run wild, and only the game recalls, suddenly and terrifyingly, the dangers it harbours. Elephant and buffalo have been sighted up to 5500 feet; the lion, pursuing the wild hog, up to 7000, a few species of antelopes, baboons, and other apes, the great wild cats and the hyrax, a leaping hare, still higher; the leopard as far as the snow-line. Only one bird reaches the highest lobelia, a sun-bird, glossy green, seeking honey on the verge of the snow.

Along this third and narrowest zone, where an almost perpetual veil of rain and cloud is transformed into snow, a chain of snow-peaks stretches out, as in the Caucasus, running for over thirty miles. At this height, the last tokens of the Ice Age glitter through the millenniums like witnesses of a saga on the equator.

At the foot of these mountains where, to the west of Lake Victoria, in the basin of the Kagera, the land rises from 3600 to 10,000 feet, it reaches the eastern edge of that great rift which here suddenly drops to 5000 feet. The slope is so wild and intact that, save for the buffalo and the elephant, the game is suddenly faced by startling frontiers, and can go no further. This rift, broken and shaken by the not yet extinct volcanoes, has collected the waters in its depths to form the chain of lakes, and these lakes partly engender and partly receive the rivers. They dash down as strong brooks, but in the rift they are dammed, turn to sluggish rivers of the plain, and seek desperately for an outlet.

Lake Edward, which receives water from south and north, discharges the whole northwards into the Nile. Nearly all the waters draining from the Ruwenzori are carried to the Nile through Lake George and Lake Albert. All the water draining or raining in Uganda, rivers, lakes, and mountain burns, struggle towards the two Nile sources. Even what would fain escape is lost. The river Kafu, which first raced the young Nile, has not yet made up its mind. It has a choice of two directions: if it flows towards the swamps of Lake Kioga, it will fall into the arms of the Victoria Nile; if it goes west, the Albert Nile is waiting for it. In both cases, its little life will be swallowed up in the destiny of its great companion.

6
_____

THE two source-systems of the Nile have now met: everything flows together at the northern extremity of Lake Albert to strengthen the flow of the young stream whose length is yet unknown. The rivers have made many a twist and turn, for it is not so far, as the crow flies, from the source to this most northerly outflow of the stream in Uganda —a hundred and sixty miles, which can be quickly covered through hilly country on a good road. Between the two lakes, the Victoria Nile has flowed from south-east to north-west, and, strange to say, the three great tributaries which await it at wide intervals on the right all flow into the river in the same direction as it took itself from its first to its second source, like children following the first steps of a great father, without being able to keep up later with the many turns of his fate.

Lake Albert, which, though much smaller than Lake Victoria, is all the same eight times as big as Lake Constance, is the great receptacle for all the rivers, long and short, which stream down from the snow and rain of the Mountains of the Moon to feed the Nile. It actually fills the rift from 1° to 2° N. lat., and hence is framed by mountains along both its long sides. Owing to its length and extent, this lake even forms an animal frontier, and because here the locusts, or at least certain species of them, cease, the vivid speech of the Negroes has named it "Luta-nziga," that is, "The brightness which kills the locusts."

"The spirit of the lake," said a Negro king to a traveller, "can unchain frightful winds and capsize all your boats." To propitiate it, they gathered in the presence of the king and cast fowls and glass beads into the lake where the spirit had its dwelling. As there is only one real harbour, and the boats—or rather the curious rafts of papyrus stalks—are small, everything is in danger because the winds rise suddenly with terrific thunderstorms. On the other hand, the spirit of the lake has bestowed on the shore-dwellers great quantities of fish which, driven shorewards by storms, are caught with long lines or even in baskets, and the legend of monstrous perch found here by their ancestors is a commonplace of local talk.

The most important thing here is the salt. Victoria Nyanza, the great lake which looks like a sea, tastes sweet; Albert Nyanza, the narrow lake, is salty, and from it most of the Negroes of the region get their livelihood. The tall grasses which they use to wattle their huts are not as close at hand as over in Uganda: they have to tramp far to buy them, and they pay for them in the salt with which half Uganda seasons its food, as well as millions of other men and races far into the Congo State, where it is lacking. The fact that this salt remains in the lake, and that the Nile, on leaving the lake, tastes almost sweet, is destined to have serious results thousands of miles away in far-off Egypt. Thus the consequences of early experiences suddenly re-emerge in age from the depths of fate. Among mountains so steep as to prevent for miles on end any cultivation of corn, salt, the unfruitful, becomes the spring of human life. But the men stir no finger to get it. The women do everything.

It is a veritable witches' cauldron. At the north-eastern end of the lake, from deep gullies, from boulders and debris, the warmth of which the white man can feel through the soles of his boots, hot springs gush forth, and sulphurous gases rise, steaming, airless, stifling. From these hollows spurts clear hot water, saturated with salt. The women, working naked amid such vapours, build little walls of mud and water; an eerie sight, as though a village had fallen in ruins; and they dam up the hot, salty ooze in little channels. Between the little walls, each working-place separate, women and children crouch, scraping the mud from the water with native iron scrapers and filling little earthenware troughs with it, partly to collect it and partly to let it drip. The art lies in the mixture of earth and water. If rain has cooled the ground, there is no salt, therefore they dread the rain for which their brothers long. For this mineral, which they draw from the water, is as precious to them as that other which other men wash from other waters: salt is their gold.

The grey, bitter-tasting stuff is then packed by the men in banana leaves and laid in long, narrow sheaths of bamboo stems like models of Nile boats, which they carry on their shoulders, and now, equipped with a sleeping-mat and a gourd of water, they tramp naked for days on end to the market, where their brothers weigh up the salt and give them their treasures in exchange, papyrus, corn, beads, spears, a hide; everything they need for food, houses, clothing, hunting, and decoration they get for the salt which their women and children have scraped from the earth of their home amid fetid vapours. This astonishing industry, carried on by people who have never heard of a mine, in a land in which, till a hundred years ago, no white man had set foot, goes back, according to tradition, to very ancient times.

Yet close by there is a people far more astonishing, more ancient, whose physique and history are unique in the world. On the slopes of the Mountains of the Moon live the pygmies.

Here an African people can be traced from ancient times on the same spot, for Aristotle insists that he is telling no fable, that the dwarfs really live there in caves, and the only thing that has proved to be a legend is the pygmy horses he attached to them. In the course of ages, they appear to have migrated to these heights from the South African veldt, and, when the Negroes began to cultivate the land, to have been driven back, being the weaker, into the densest parts of the jungle; they still recruit themselves from the Congo forests, and continually sally forth, only to be driven back by the big Bantu Negroes. Thus the pygmies, generally called the Bakwa in these parts, perpetually beset, tough, wary, and inextinguishable, outlive the dominating races, with whom thay rarely mingle. Physique and fate have, here as everywhere, formed their character: in every way they recall the gnomes and brownies of Nordic tales, who themselves owe their existence to real dwarfs, whose bones have been found in deposits of the European Stone Age.

The pygmies are not handsome, but they are not really grotesque. Their body, brownish black or yellowish and very hairy, some 4 feet 4 inches in height, with a protruding abdomen and a navel like a button, bears a head which looks old, shrewd, and sad. Large quantities of hair, the long beards of the men, almond eyes, a big, thin-lipped mouth, at once distinguish them from their neighbours; their silence and thoughtfulness, their lack of Negro inquisitiveness and loquacity, a cleverer and shyer attitude, which recalls the big apes, set them apart. When they stand naked in the market, the women slightly clothed with garments of stretched bark, suspicious alike of Negroes and whites, the women more impudent, but shyer and wilder, the traits of the gnome stand out clear: they are masters of shrewdness and deceit, cruel and helpful, sympathetic and vindictive, cunning and grateful. Only the elders show signs of suffering: they know it was all in vain.

They could hardly have become otherwise in the struggle with other tribes which looked away over their heads and despised them as the bigger man of nature despises the smaller, especially in the midst of this densely populated part of the earth. All men about them lived on cattle or corn, hunting was a festival like war; they alone, in their smallness, a result of adaptation to their surroundings in the course of time, slipped into the jungle. Thus they lived through the ages as nomads, in tiny, swiftly woven huts in inaccessible haunts, which the Bantu Negro especially shuns in his superstition as the home of the dwarfs. There the pygmies guard the fire they cannot light— their cousins to the west of Mount Elgon do not even know it— roast meat and bananas on it, and make beautiful pots and baskets. They eat only what they kill, but they eat more freely of everything than other tribes—boar and gazelle, rats and locusts, fish and snakes; that is why men and women file their upper incisors and eye teeth.

Their life is strangely simple in the huts which they rarely share with others, creeping into them through little mouseholes; at home the women are always naked, without ornaments, tattooing, or necklaces. Thus they live, not only without a faith, like most of their neighbours, but without headmen or chiefs, and only from time to time do they recognize the best huntsman as a privileged being; they reject everything which might lead to state and community; each lives his own life, with a few

women of his own, a family man with a great love for the children whom the women have borne, not in the huts, but out
in the forest, biting through the navel-string themselves, like
animals.

As they have adopted from their neighbours neither vegetables nor the cultivation of crops, they meet them only for a
tribal or hunting feast. Then the pygmies are merrier and more
musical than all the natives of the region, sing choruses and
solos, laugh and tell tales, but drink little and are in every way
better behaved. Their only passion is smoking and snuff.

Just like the northern brownies, these goblins are thankful
thieves. When, at night, they venture out of their forest to steal
bananas, the food they like best because they have none at home,
they often leave under the pillaged tree a piece of meat from
some animal they have killed, or think out some still more elfin
way of payment; while their Negro victim sleeps, they creep
about on softly falling feet and weed part of his plantation, or
set up a trap to catch game for him, or drive the monkeys from
the bananas. But sometimes these cunning half-gipsies, these
shrewd half-apes, carry away a Negro child into the forest, leaving a changeling for the screaming mother to find.

Their greatest greed is for elephants. The biggest animal falls
victim to the smallest man just because he is small, as one of
their discoverers has described. Armed with sharp lances, one
of them slips under the animal, who is too short-sighted to hit
the mark with his trunk, and is doomed to fall into crafty hands.
There, round the quarry, they live long, till everything is eaten
up, but with the ivory they buy what they need. Even the fish
they ambush with impish cunning: damming up little water-
courses, draining off the water by canals, and catching the struggling fish with their hands.

Thus the little huntsmen became great smiths and warriors.
Despised by their bigger brethren, who mock the "men with the
span-long beards," they force them all the same to take in barter
the spears they have forged from pig-iron out in the forest, and
spearheads too, and iron rings for the women. Then one ruling
tribe uses them in war against the other, and when the dwarfs,
with their sharp wits, have become advisers to a chief, their

gratitude outgrows their malice, and, with the conservatism of all long-oppressed peoples, they cling to those who treat them well in order to exploit them.

But who are these Bantu tribes with whom the pygmies live in perpetual discord? Who are the lords of this land?

7

THE land of Uganda is richer and more blessed than all its neighbours because a gracious climate makes the fruits of the earth grow of themselves, and because a happy fate kept the white man away till eighty years ago. For hundreds of centuries, some millions of Negroes lived here, ignorant of the seductions of the east and north, and when Speke appeared here, he was the first to tell of a paradisial people which called itself happy. If a Buganda on Lake Victoria is questioned today, he has no answer save that he came from the land "where the moon draws fresh strength and its lovely white light from the summits of the snow-mountains." Or he points in the direction of the source of the Nile and says that that is the country of which the great river is born. But if he is questioned about time, he counts one year as two, for he reaps twice, and says: "The first month of the year is the month of sowing; the other five are for eating." They had everything before they were discovered—bananas, corn, and vegetables, fish and sheep, and have only been decimated of late by long race wars.

This race is believed to be a mixture of Bantu, Nilotic, and Hamitic tribes, but as nothing was ever written down, nothing is certain, and only one thing is sure, that here as everywhere the mingling of peoples has meant their happiness, and racial ambition their downfall.

The dominating Bantu Negroes, powerful, well-made men, round-headed, dark brown, with a satiny skin and strong frame, are the farmers: the pastoral peoples beside them, separated from them by the age-old jealousy between nomads and farmers, the Bahima, who are much lighter and handsomer, with a straight nose and thin lips, often look like the children of a white man and a mulatto woman.

Formerly—no one can say when—the Bahima pushed into the land as conquerors, perhaps from Abyssinia, and settled first on Lake Kioga, then on Lake Victoria too. They certainly lost their supremacy to the more capable Bantus, but because they are handsomer and more skilful, they look down on them. Although even the greatest anthropologists place many a question mark beside the conclusions they draw from the physique of the two races and from oral tradition, this early immigration offers the only explanation for the astonishing customs of these secluded Negroes.

For indeed, by incredible detours, the great civilization of the mouth of the Nile, Egypt, seems to have had an influence, a hundredfold diluted, even on these distant Negroes at the source of the river, just as a ray from some great mind illuminates that of men who never heard of its existence. As the Egyptians never penetrated up the Nile to Uganda, how did the straight-backed cattle with the giant horns come here, to wander to this very day among the Negroes on the equator just as they do on the ancient Egyptian frescoes? How came to the eyes and ears of these black chiefs the same harps, the same trumpets of antelope horn, as those with which a Pharaoh was wont to rouse the feeling of his might? Egyptian culture must have been powerful enough to impress itself upon those Hamitic-Arab tribes by way of Somaliland and Abyssinia, where its monuments survived; then, driven into the fertile land about the Nile sources in successive waves by war and famine, they brought it to black men who had never heard of, much less seen, those strange white men.

The people found here by the first Europeans in 1860, thousands of years later, cannot have taken its surprising culture from the three or four Arab traders who, about 1850, were the first to penetrate into the interior from Zanzibar to buy slaves from the great black kings. The first white man to discover them on the great lake was neither explorer nor missionary, but a soldier from Zanzibar who had fled from his creditors into the interior. The black king took a fancy to this man because he had a white skin, fine hair, and a fine beard; in 1857 he was still living with the king, surrounded by his three hundred wives.

These millions of men in Central Africa heard from an insolvent soldier of the existence of white races for the first time since, a few thousand years before, they had received customs and utensils from the most highly civilized land on the Mediterranean without even knowing its name. This oddest of all agents of civilization was followed by a few Arab traders and sheikhs.

And yet the king was by no means the most astonished man in Uganda. Anxious, flattered, and hurt, those Bahima who had grown steadily blacker by intermarriage with the Bantus, now, at the appearance of those first Arabs, swore they were their blood-relations, that their own ancestors had been much whiter, and had had long hair too. Now they feared that those strange men had come, as once their own ancestors had come, to take the lovely land away from them.

When, close on the heels of the Arabs, the first Englishmen, the real discoverers, arrived to find a people which, a decade before, had never seen a white man, what was the state of these savages?

From round, generally dome-shaped huts, skilfully wattled of high grass and banana fibre, stepping from a porch or gallery, there came to meet them men and women wrapped in skins or bark, whose first business in the morning was to stamp down afresh the mud wall which protected their dwelling from the daily rain. Through marshy stretches, they had made dikes of palm-stems; paths hedged by salvias led from one village to another in this densely populated country. The people were forbidden by their king, on pain of death, to go naked to market: only in war or in their canoes did the men take off their skins; save for house-building, their only occupation was war.

All the work was left to the women: they sowed and reaped, ground the corn between two millstones, cowering and singing, steamed meat and fish, wrapped in banana leaves, over pots they had made of clay without a wheel. Out of the narrow leaves of the date-palm they made baskets for the red coffee-beans which they grew outside the village, but they knew, too, how to dry hides in the sun, stretch them on a frame, make them supple with oil and cut sandals of buffalo-hide. So civilized were the manners of these Negroes that they washed their hands before meals, and again after, before they drank their coffee.

They might have lived on the banana alone, that gift of God, of which they grew some thirty species. The fruit of some they steamed to pulp; others they fermented, and added extracts of herbs to make wine and a sweetish kind of beer; the fronds were used for thatching the house, for their beds, and to protect the milk in the pots; the stems for hedges, or as rollers to carry the canoes overland. The pith they scraped out served for sponges, and from the fibres they made string and sun-hats. Except for meat and iron, the tree gave them everything—a true tree of life.

When no war was on hand, the men made iron fish-hooks or their lines of aloe fibre; they dug deep pits for the elephant, which they killed afterwards with the spear; the buffalo was caught in snares of thorn, the little antelopes with nets, and even lions and leopards in traps of heavy tree-trunks. On the hunt, they set out by the hundred. They even invented a weapon which might be taken for a myth of Munchausen if it had not been described by the greatest experts on Uganda. They caught young poison snakes in the jungle, nailed them to a tree above an animal spoor, so that the creature, wild with pain, struck a leopard or some other game passing by instead of the Negro, who, hidden close by, could then easily kill his quarry. They wove baskets of bark, hung them at the top of high trees where they had seen bees, and the bees, glad to find a home, deposited their honey in them; the Negroes hurried up, smoked them out, and collected not only the honey for food, but the wax for a kind of candle.

A man might have as many wives as he pleased, for there were three times as many women as men—even today there is a super-fluity of women—because in their battles they killed all adult males after the victory, but carried off the women with them, especially the beautiful Bahima women. Therefore, in Uganda, women were always cheaper than anywhere else: formerly they cost only three oxen, later six sewing-needles or a pair of shoes.

Few children were born, and a man to whom a second child

was born of the same woman had the right to beat the drum for two months outside his hut to invite his friends to drink with him. They showed in everything so highly developed a feeling for form and so much tact that Johnston wrote: "All the Bahima are born gentlemen." To the approaching stranger they sent refreshments, and they let him rest in his hut before visiting him. In conversation they have chosen strange formulas of speech, saying to each other: "Thank you for enjoying yourself. Thank you for admiring my house. Thank you for thrashing my son."

And all that was felt and put into practice by a people untouched by a definite faith in God or moral doctrine, and acting only by the profound moral standards graven deep in the heart of man. Such was the state of these so-called savages when they were found in 1860.

The guardian of it all was the king, who had jurisdiction over life and death, surrounded by his court, which, like that of the Carolingians, included not only the minister, the cup-bearer, the harper, the flute-player, the watchman, the pipe-bearer, but also the executioner, the brewer, and the cook. One of these kings, who had more than seven hundred children, possessed, in addition to his lawful wives, many hundreds of concubines, some nineteen hundred of whom he sent to the market, thus levying a novel kind of tax by providing his subjects with sensual satisfaction. As the sole owner of land and cattle, he bestowed, like the medieval kings of the west, lands in fief on his "counts," kept them in good humour at the cost of the peasants and played them off against each other by their mutual jealousies: he, the apex of the pyramid of state, stood high above the base formed by the landless peasantry, just like the Tsar in Old Russia. As the king taxed every cow, the count was responsible for each single one, and if a lion or a neighbour broke in, he had perforce to organize a hunt or a war to recapture or replace the cows.

The last of these kings to wield kingly power, Mutesa (1840–1884), whom the first travellers visited here, showed all the qualities of his white peers, only that he was much wiser than many of them. In his palace, a hall ninety feet long, surrounded by drummers, banner-bearers, and lancers, he received the first strangers with a dignity worthy of the Grand Monarch; he treated these men approaching his throne, who must have seemed like gods to him, with graciousness and without curiosity, gave them help instead of murdering or forcibly detaining them, and when he sat there, robed in Indian silk, one leg stretched out before him, like the western kings on old prints, how could he know that grace and dignity make the real ruler? The great hall was of straw, but spacious as a marble hall in Rome. When he ate, many men and women of the court stood about him, only the minister standing at the door to avert every evil glance from the covered dishes, for he alone had the right to eat up what was left. But when the king spoke, the courtiers cried after every sentence: "Nyanzi-ge," which means roughly: "Thanks! Excellent," not otherwise than at court banquets in Europe.

And who had divulged to Mutesa that a king must weave fantastic legend about his father? "My father," he said, "fell ill in old age; every day, to placate the evil spirits, he had a hundred young men killed. But when he recovered, and, as of old, came riding into the open air on his prime minister, he fell down dead. Then he was sewn into a cow-hide and left floating three days in the lake, till three worms came crawling out of him; then he was brought home and forthwith turned into a lion. My grandfather was so strong that he would have lived for ever if he had not, after endless time, spirited himself out of the world to make way for the son who had been waiting so long."

And what did the ancestors of his father do? "I am the eighteenth of our dynasty," said King Mutesa. "The founder of our house came from far away as a famous hunter. He was so strong and handsome that the queen fell in love with him, instantly poisoned her husband, and made him king and father of the next king."

Three fine sayings of Mutesa have been preserved. When about to drag his war-booty through an unfriendly land, he sent its black king a hundred arrows and a hundred hoes. "If you desire peace," he sent word to him, "take the hoes and dig your fields with them; if war, take the arrows, you will need them."

The other took the hoes, and since then has borne the name of King of the Hundred Hoes. When an Englishman appearing before him apologized that his presents had been swept away by floods, King Mutesa said: "The great rivers swallow up the small ones. Since I have seen your face there is no other thought in my mind." And when Stanley explained to him by anatomical charts how the wrist and finger muscles worked, the king said: "Wonderful. I couldn't make anything like that. And yet I should not destroy anything that I cannot make." Shortly afterwards he showed his royal displeasure with a subject by having his ear cut off.

It is wonderful that the Buganda should pay divine honours to the Nile, which they see only in its wild infancy, and of whose deeds and destiny a thousand miles away they know, or at least knew, nothing. But even on the islands in the lake, spirits live, and to secure safe transit for an American traveller the king beheaded seven medicine men who were believed to be evil demons of the lake. At the great Nile festival, to celebrate the rites of the source, King Mutesa issued, preceded by the great band, with flutes of reeds, trumpets of antelope horn, and a harp made of wood, animal-hide, and gut strings. If the melodies they played were diatonic, their ears heard the half-tones, hundreds danced along after the band, but the king came sailing in full ceremony over the lake, his boat loaded with wine and women, and ordered his rowers to keep their heads down so as not to see the women, so shrewd was King Mutesa, king or emperor of Uganda. His grave is built like that of a hero, fenced round with protecting spears, lances, and arrows.

In this way a gifted savage people has proved, in its constitution and customs, that the state of paradise can of itself develop forms not actually inferior to those elaborated with difficulty in the countries of the whites. The age-long struggles of the white man for God seem doubly terrifying in their purposeless obstinacy when we see these blacks, without writing and without priests, acknowledging a divine being which created the world, but wise enough to reject any religious ritual. When the first travellers questioned them, they gave the great answer that that being was far too high to trouble himself about the doings of men.

The vagueness of such a faith, combined with a definite moral code and organization, in a primitive people untouched by outside influences, proves that none of the great religions, and none of the great colonial, so-called ruling peoples, was necessary to establish order and beget community, and that while savagery may lead men to war, idleness need not lead to brutality. The state of Adam had here advanced only to the first stage of civilization, but men were happier before knowing the splendours of the white man's life, for, to achieve them, they had to work. Other Negro peoples, exposed for centuries to the influence of European religions and civilizations, have all the same remained, to this very day, half animals.

What, then, could the happy people of Uganda, at the source of the Nile, acquire from the tardy whites?

8

IN a deep, green park which knows no drought, on the northern shores of Lake Victoria, pretty houses, like a fantasy of Puvis de Chavannes, lie in the shade of ancient sycamores, surrounded by gardens in perpetual flower. Between them, on smooth roads of red earth, the motors glide by to the golf course, past high acacias with big yellow blossoms. Two Negroes are rolling the course with an ox harnessed to the roller, which clatters faintly, its handle-bar sometimes flashing silver in the shining brown hand that guides it. That is how the lords of the earth live in Entebbe, the little Washington of Uganda. But in its more northerly New York, Kampala, there is a hum of traffic; from seven hills rise the churches of almost as many Christian sects; and the tropical helmet becomes the bearded Carmelite Brothers just as well as the nuns, who wear it over their coifs, and have left not one of their voluminous petticoats at home. Beside the white saints, the white man's aeroplane, on its flight from London to Capetown, lands once a week; the English hail it with excitement, the natives do not even turn their heads.

Yet the planters live not only on the lakeside; far up, in the midst of the jungle, in Fort Portal they have built handsome tropical houses: in their gardens they grow strawberries and violets, narcissi and crocuses, just as if they were in Devonshire. Here, to the south of Lake Albert, on the Congo frontier, where the great motor roads cross, conquerors and natives, on certain days, meet in the market. Almost completely muffled up in their shrill-coloured robes worn Greek fashion, the Buganda approach, carrying on their heads gourds with delicate necks or earthenware pots in Cretan forms; many of the women stand still as statues; their hair is dressed in plaits, after the fashion of the

Roman empresses, and all of them seem to have something classic about them. The half-naked shepherds beside them look less civilized as they stand leaning on their crooks, as the shepherd has stood for thousands of years. Naked pygmies stretch out their hairy arms towards the little bundles of salt which the others hold hesitatingly out to barter.

With his inscrutable and avid eyes, the Indian, offering Europe's treasures for sale in his corrugated iron stall, dominates them all. And while the Negroes tender him the English silver that they have earned in hard labour on the farms, he gives them in exchange oil-lamps, tea-kettles, umbrellas, banjoes, safety pins, old tires. But the lord and master of the Indian is the white-clad Englishman, who, rolling by in his Ford, is still a demigod—for how long?

When, in the sixties, the first Englishmen discovered the country, and in the nineties began slowly to exploit it, everything went well until the Negroes began to rebel against the missionaries: why should they have only one wife and not half a dozen? That was all very well for the poor man who could afford only one. Could it be immoral? They did not know that in Europe a man can have only one, but can take his neighbour's wife unpunished, while here they have many, but can take none unpunished. They knew only that people wanted to rob them of a custom on which their social system was based, and so rebelled and fought. At the end of his life, King Mutesa regretted having let the missionaries into his country, for the Catholic Carmelite Brothers, being French, opposed the British Anglicans. And the people disliked a great many other things which the treaty of 1890 with the English government imposed on King Mutesa's son. Yet, when he began to fight, the king was defeated and deported, and a phantom of a royal life was arranged for his son, who today resembles his forefathers as much as a captive eagle resembles a wild one. Since 1905, the country has been quiet.

Thus, really without war, the English could win the precious land only by taking over as many forms and names as possible, by leaving to the chiefs a superficial jurisdiction and a feeling of participation in the government, and yet reserving their right of veto on the humblest policeman, like the Holy Roman Emperor at the nomination of the medieval bishops. And just as King Mutesa supported his counts in their struggle, the English secretly back up their missionaries in theirs, so that they may give the Negro schools and sanitation, but exercise no religious compulsion. The reward of so much shrewdness and perseverance is rich enough. They hold a land which completes their trade and air routes. They raised 200,000 Negroes in the World War and used them against their German neighbours in East Africa. Their English goods have found a new market, and 90 percent of the most important products, representing a value of $10,000,-000 are disposed of in the Empire. The Uganda budget has for some years past shown a surplus of over a million pounds.

But, it may be asked, have they in return enslaved these three million Negroes? On the contrary, here is a list of the benefits conferred on the Negro since the discovery and occupation of the country.

Two hundred thousand children—exactly the same number as that of the forces raised in the war—the sons of those who for centuries had no writing, now learn Swahili and English and a trade: a good many become chauffeurs. The white medicine man rescues many adults and children from death, and since large tracts of jungle have been closed or cleared, the death-bringing fly, and with it sleeping sickness, is dying out. If the Negro wishes to migrate, it is no longer a matter of months: he can try his luck over behind Lake Kioga, for the white man's steamer is there for everybody, the fare is small, and he can come back richer than he went. The herds of elephants break into the plantations more rarely than they did, to destroy all the crops in an hour or two; the government can keep down their numbers, watch the herds, and stop their breaking in.

The life and work of the Negroes have grown more refined. Their huts are of clay instead of fibre, their beds are broader. The fruits of the earth grow today as they always grew, but there was a time when the sugar-cane grew wild, and they merely tore up a cane in passing, bit into it, sucked the juice out, and threw the cane away. Now the canes are cut regularly from the fields and rolled away on railway lines under the corrugated iron roof of the sugar factory, and to induce the Negroes to come tomorrow, and yet again, the master has set up their pretty huts near by. While they used to smoke wild tobacco, they now cultivate it in even rows, and buy with their earnings the fabulously beautiful cigarettes of Europe. While once they went to the wild coffee bush, gathered the red berries from the ground, roasted them and drank the juice, now they crouch under the even clusters, pick them, collect their fruit first in baskets, then in sacks, till the truck comes, weighs it all up, and carries it off.

In the trunk of a tree with yellowish-green fruits their fore-fathers had of old made gashes to collect a sticky sap, like the red Indians whom Columbus saw playing with a big black ball which to his astonishment bounced marvellously. Now the Buganda has learned to plant the rubber trees in regular rows, to whet his knife, to cut at fixed places at a fixed time, to a fixed depth and in a fixed direction, and then to return with his little pail early in the morning when the sap flows most abundantly. In the neighbouring factory, he sees the machines first cutting, then pressing the quickly curdled milk in strips or sheets and wonders at the ingenuity of the white man.

For he has shown him new things too in his old land. Once he collected raw iron ore for arrows, and still does so; but at the white man's command, he seeks and finds in the mountain a love-lier metal, which shines in the sun. The white man calls it gold and seems greedy to get more and more of it. But he looks almost as greedily on the little green shrub with the fluffy fruit which he brought from far off, and which has here increased to millions. He gave the Negro the seed free, urges him to take care of the plant, plants fields of a quarter of an acre to five acres for him, and when the truck comes to fetch the sacks the pay is good. Here the Nile first makes the acquaintance of cotton, at first on its banks, then on the decks of the Nile steamers. Through all the centuries it did not know it. A fateful connexion has here been opened up, and no man knows whether it will curse or bless.

To produce all this for the white man, nearly half a million natives, an eighth of the population, have turned labourer, 90 percent working on the land. Though a far-sighted government may prohibit forced labour, and lets the majority of the Negroes work on their own account, yet it was white enterprise that first turned savage people into labourers. The wages are twelve shillings, or three dollars, a month: only a few artisans and chauffeurs earn as much as ten dollars. As a bushel of bananas costs ten cents, and sweet potatoes five, he has, even when his wife helps, a dollar a month over.[1] He cannot earn more, for the rubber belongs to the white man, coffee and sugar for the most part to the Indian, and the cotton brings in less every year. If he wants to send his son to the high school, his profit is nearly eaten up; if several women work with him, he can buy something. He goes to the village, where a Negro sits at his sewing-machine, has himself measured for a shirt and trousers, sits down on the steps, and waits for his suit. And he can buy a hat too, a pocket lamp, and, if the policeman is not looking, a glass of whisky.

But he has been picking cotton in the sun for eight hours, his wife has stood for ten swallowing dust at the ginning-machine, hunting is almost a thing of the past, and if he wants to sleep off a late night, he is wakened or punished. He is certainly free, but where are the times when he sowed for a month and reaped for five? Now the world is so full of things that he degenerates if he has nothing to do but cut off a bunch of bananas in the morning. The care-free life of his fathers, interrupted only by war, has gone. What the Christian padre tells him, that there are gods, his grandfather had told him long ago; it is the same thing as with the coffee; it was there before, only now it is tidier. And in exchange, his daughters do what they like; since they can no longer be sold, because it is immoral, they are no longer safeguarded as sound young merchandise, and since the white men levies hut-taxes instead of the old poll-tax, the family crowd together in one hut, and nobody knows who is his bedfellow.

If the white man awakened the Negro, well and good. Perhaps he awoke more quickly than was expected. The grandson of a cowherd who never even heard of books and writing now acts Horatio in the school play at Kampala, and the white ladies in the hall applaud. It is hardly to be expected that he will ignore the newspapers. He can pick out the places he learned in the

---

[1] These prices are given in American currency. The monetary unit in Uganda is the East African *shilling* (worth approximately $.25) which is divided into 100 cents.

geography lesson; he thinks it all out and one evening explains to his father, sitting in front of his clay hut, why the white men have looked so worried of late, why there is less planting and less pay, why, over in the coffee field, the berries lie rotting on the ground, why the rubber trees are running wild and creepers are throttling the aloe. For in the last few years the forest has begun to encroach on the clearings made thirty years ago. The jungle is taking its children back, and why?

The young Negro can tell the old one. Sorting letters in the post office, he has read the papers and learned that, in the last seven years, the exports of Uganda have doubled, but their value has decreased to half. Can it be that the white men are hard pressed? He reads too that the white artisan earns two hundred dollars a month here, while his black mate, for nearly the same work, earns only ten. The white man certainly needs more, he is lord of the world. But does he need twenty times as much as the black man? And can the Negro help feeling a certain pride in himself when the white man, who would hardly eat at the same table or play a game of football with him, serves him standing behind the counter and, when the black hand pushes back a piece of stuff, forthwith hauls down another which the customer may like better?

And what if the interesting post-office clerk were one day to examine more closely the revolver that his brother, the policeman, has learned to fire, reckoning the while that only two thousand whites live in this great land, scattered among three and a half million Negroes who know how to hunt the elephant and the leopard and have won many wars? Perhaps a savage race with so much strength and natural culture will one day spread slowly over the lands cultivated by the white man, and will take back its children—just like the jungle.

9

————

AT the source of the Nile, close
by the falls, there lies a block of grey granite bearing a tablet:
"Speke found this source of the Nile in 1862." A long road
through the virgin forests of history led to this tablet.

How many nations have laboured in the exploration of this
river! Of the five great discoverers, Speke, Grant, Baker, and
Stanley were British, Emin a Jew. How much strength and suffering these figures mean—how much fate, how little happiness!
And yet, nearly all who strove returned, or wished to return, to
suffering and danger. A magic power seems to dwell in this continent as in no other, an invisible magnet which, however, acts
only on men with iron in them. Not all who went were weary of
Europe, but none returned weary of Africa: most were seduced
by the personal freedom which no white land can offer, many,
too, by the sexual freedom which is very rarely mentioned.

How varied were the occasions which turned these men into
Nile explorers, their character and motives, their end and their
fame! Only their struggles and their sufferings were alike, and,
in the solitude created by an age without telegraphy and wireless, heavier and darker than those of an explorer of today could
be. The enterprise, the adventures, of those who achieved less
spectacular results than the five great discoverers were not inferior to theirs, for when a man sets out for unexplored Africa,
abandoning his home and his family, his career and his money,
merely to explore a remote river at its sources, everything about
him becomes interesting, his motives and his aims, his public
bearing and his secret self, his temperament, his outlook, his relations with white men and black, with missionaries and orientals, and, when it is all over, the reports he writes, which reveal
more of him than he meant to divulge. One was driven forth

44

by restlessness, a second by curiosity, a third by ambition, a fourth by discontent, a fifth by eagerness to discover new plants and animals. Many were moved by a misanthropy which subsided only in the presence of the Negro. For all of them defend the Negro. Stanley was the only one to prefer the company of white men to that of black.

Is it a wonder that all these men, in their passionate years, utterly alone, without any standard of comparison, cut off from the joys and sorrows of their fellow-beings, their eyes fixed immovably on one goal lying somewhere in the jungle, should lose their sense of proportion? Would it not rather be a wonder if any of them should keep it? Forced perpetually to sing their own praises, even when they do not exaggerate their adventures, it is the best of them who feel embarrassed as they write, and the born writers among them by no means keep the best diaries. An ironic Englishman like Speke remains an exception by the simplicity with which he expresses feelings magnified by others into heroics.

It is the sense of proportion they lose: even the best of them distort their achievement by a kind of megalomania.

What bitterness they knew when the armchair scientists contested their results! They had lived for years among wild animals, learned to bear with the superstition of every chief, with the mockery that a man should suffer so much to find the source or the course of a river, the configuration of a lake, but when they reached home, the same disbelief awaited them. Speke, on his return, saw professors proving with upraised finger that the sources could not lie where he had imagined he had found them, and even why they could not lie there. Whole societies were founded to prove him wrong. *Punch* celebrated him, but the Government gave him neither office nor reward, nor the knighthood he would have liked; a crocodile and a hippopotamus in his coat of arms were the reward of the discoverer of the source of the Nile.

Baker, the most favoured by nature and fate of all the Nile explorers, the one whose gigantic physique overcame every hardship, who went hunting in England when he was over seventy, the great pioneer in the struggle against slavery, was reduced to silence when, after his departure, he saw the suppressed slave-dealers restored.

What disappointments awaited Stanley, who had made the greatest conquests! When he found Livingstone, he was first regarded as an impostor, and the letters he brought with him were branded as forgeries. But when no discoverer could deny the discovery of the Congo, people began to talk of his cruelties, so that this great journalist should not enjoy his fame. And Stanley, the most ambitious of them all, had not Speke's serenity to find peace simply in the consciousness of his achievements. Even Stanley died bitter. All, moreover, had to see their maps constantly corrected by later travellers: the map of the lakes forming the source of the Nile varied widely between 1850 and 1877, at first showing them lying far apart, then with the distance growing smaller, coming nearer, as when a telescope is slowly adjusted.

If only their fame had lived! But where is it today? Each country knows the names of those of its sons who achieved so much, but practically nothing more. The only immortality the discoverer can attain, his name on the map, lives on only in hidden corners, but is written nowhere in letters of flame on mountains, rivers, lakes, or springs, where it should stand. A few tried to ensure their fame on a small scale by giving to new species of animals and plants their own Latinized names. The great discoverers could not do that: they chose the names of kings and queens, of presidents of the geographical societies which had sent them out, and only the childlike Stanley had imagination enough to name the Congo, when he had discovered it, the Livingstone River, and the Mountains of the Moon, the Gordon Bennett Range, and both names soon vanished.

The chivalrous Duke of the Abruzzi, who was the first to climb the summit of these mountains, named its three highest peaks after the three great discoverers of the Nile, but these names stand on no general map, and nobody knows them. A town on the Congo is called after Stanley and a fine grey crane too; a gulf on Lake Victoria after Speke. Nothing bears the name of Grant or Baker. But the importance of the kings after whom the great lakes were named has long since faded, and when the Italians say Lago Alberto, they think of Carlo Alberto, but who

Albert was, even today, outside of England, the crowd does not know.

And was it not for the crowd, for humanity, that these great men plunged into their adventure? The names of the source of the Nile and its great falls, Ripon, Owen, and Murchison, called after a minister and two professors, have no meaning save for the scholar.

What lay behind these men when their eyes closed in death can only be felt by those who have read their diaries and compared them with their own little adventures in jungle and bush, where mere fever or the failure of a hunt raises the question of life or death. That situation, magnified to enormous dimensions, can give some sense of the sufferings and achievements of these men. For what did it mean to seek the source of a river in those lands? Did it mean, as it does today, to seek and map a route, equipped with money and weapons, presents and provisions, maps, compass, and instruments, after a careful study of all the relevant literature?

It meant to assemble the men every morning, to distribute the baggage among a few hundred men and animals, to provide for water, to examine every saddle-girth, to point the way, to coax, convince, or cajole the Negro, who shrinks before the most trivial detail. It meant in heat, storm, and plagues of insects to be tirelessly lord and master of a hundred primitive men, whose obedience depended on the look and gesture of the white man, to heal the sick and bury the dead, to command even in sickness. It meant to recapture and punish deserters among the porters, to negotiate with crafty chiefs for grain, and to bridle their lust for gifts. It meant to be taken prisoner and to have the wits to escape, to struggle at midday with a stream in flood and in the evening with leopards in the camp. It meant losing chests of bullets on which life depended at the passage of a river, then sending out boats in search of a white man whom rumour spoke of, who might have bullets to spare. It meant living for years without women, or only with black women, and at the same time being cut off for years from all news of home.

Such were these men, struggling continually against men, animals, and the elements, criticized, yet adored like gods, helping everybody, solving every problem, without a pause, without a rest, moving without a port through pathless jungles and bush for months, for years at a time. The wonderful river, to whose discovery they sacrificed their lives, gave them in return struggle and sorrow, the joy of the wilderness and the disillusion of the homecoming.

LAKE KIOGA COVERED WITH WATER-LILIES

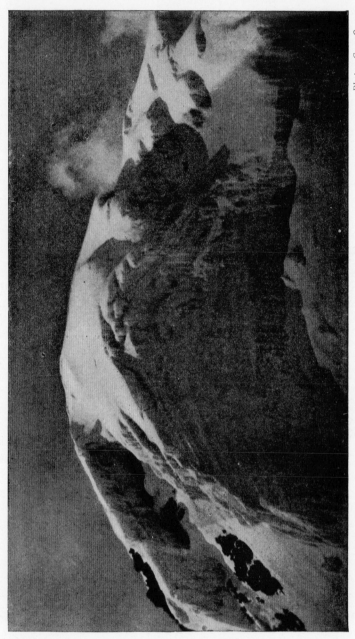

Photo: Geo. Ouzer

RUWENZORI

10

IN mild radiance, the morning star stands over the yellow-grey expanse of Lake Albert at the point where it narrows down into the river. Just as time, in its perpetual flow, links up great and conspicuous events, nourishes them, and in turn is nourished by them, many rivers seem merely to flow from lake to lake, yet often bear along in their narrow course stranger hazards than on those radiant surfaces whose broad sheen dazzles the eyes of men. The Victoria Nile, on its way from the great falls, traverses only a short corner of Lake Albert: with all its youthful might the river rushes through the lake, takes up its wealth of water, and, its substance doubled, hurries on northward.

But in the twilight before the dawn it seems to stand still: oily and motionless, the flood reflects in silhouette the life on its banks. While in the east, by the great falls from which it comes, a bulwark of tender pink piles up, and a few cloudlets are already tinged with gold in the middle of the pale blue-green sky, while the silence around is audible, awaiting with bated breath this quivering hour of dawn as if it were the coming of a great man, the western sky towards the Congo still shimmers to the water-blue zenith in pale pearl colour. Suddenly, within a few seconds, with the rapidity of all equatorial light, the east flames yellow-red, then crimson, like a brook flowing behind the rigid outlines of a parasol acacia.

The light has broken the silence. A few geese cackle, flying up from a dune to the east above the lake-head, but the white egrets sit motionless in the ambatch. Yonder a solitary grey heron, who has spent the night standing on one leg, makes the first move, draws in his long neck, stretches out his pointed beak, spreads his wings, and flies away low over the water. Soon there is movement everywhere. Sideways-twisted horns sway slowly on a few black heads, suspicious eyes peer into the new light, while a few tufts of hair twitch behind them—it is a buffalo family, velvety dark, broad-browed, and threatening.

Not far away, at the edge of the forest, half covered by the high grass, the white rhinoceros is leaving the river. This is the third in the company of the three jungle giants: as big as a young elephant, with smaller eyes, but more monstrous than either elephant or hippopotamus, light grey in colour, slow-moving, crowned with double horns, one on the snout and one a little farther back, like a fabulous king crowned in a nightmare with a fearful crown. The trapezoid head with the two enormous pig's ears, the broad nose, the ridge along the clumsy neck, the stumpy legs—everything is ungainly, even to the little peering eyes which see so badly, making the whole apparently as helpless and dull as the elephant is quick and clever; the rhino seems more than any of them to be a relic of an earlier world, and as he moves on in a slow trot, dragging his amorphous mass among the delicate feathers of the acacia, it is as if a shadow of hell had fallen on the bright soul of a fragile human being, for even this monster feeds only on ethereal things, on twigs, bark, and herbs.

With the growing light, the apparent rigidity vanishes too from the surface of the water. In majestic breadth, still a lake and yet already a river, the Nile has left its second source-lake, crossing the great sandbanks which would fain stop its course, powerful and resolute like a man fully armed, marching on to fresh battles. In the west, on its left bank, it sees the green, spreading forest of the Congo region, in the east the yellow bush. Soon it feels once more firmly bedded; after a stretch of some ten miles, it narrows down into a broad peaceful stream with open water.

And now it has been christened a second time: this stretch of a hundred and fifty miles is often called the Albert Nile, and that patron well suits its clear, navigable course in the parklike land it first flows through. For even when it narrows later, and the swamps begin to attack it on both sides, it maintains its open character. Gradually the banks begin to approximate to the river: from the plain, reeds and rushes advance; farther off, green strips show little backwaters which the swamps hold fast, not

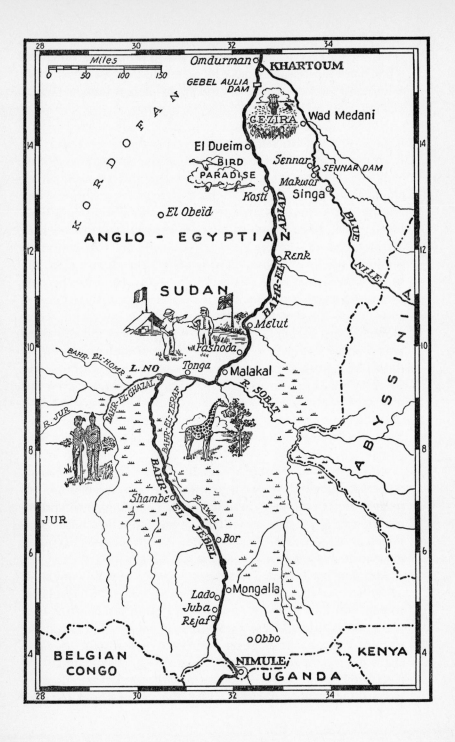

letting them discharge, but even where the valley narrows, the river remains clearly bounded and never disperses.

Where the land by the river is cultivated, it might be the Thames: grey-blue with green pools, coves and islets in the ever shallower stream, little lakes spreading out, a clump of forest in deep shadow behind the reeds; the bittern, the kingfisher, even the sycamore bear none too strange a shape. But the human beings coming to the water are naked, and most of them may well be so, for the Madi, who live here, are built on classic lines, men and women both, as long as they are young. They have a special costume, no apron, but only a bunch of fresh leaves tied on behind, waving like the tail of an ostrich and always clean, for it is picked and bound on fresh every morning. When the young men come down to the water, they lay aside their spears, and, with a cautious movement, put their short shoulder-skins beside them; then, first pushing aside the water-weeds, they wet forehead and mouth as if in a ritual act, and when at last they stand completely in the water, they do not grunt and shiver, like the white man, but maintain a kind of shapely repose. Then they come out, stick their heads through the short skin, which they throw over their shoulders, take up their spears, and leave the Nile.

And women bearing jars come to the river, while others carry off fish; a naked black man lies rowing in a black dugout, with a long black spear beside him. Against the tall ficus the shepherd leans in silence, but the cattle here are not the long-horned cattle of Uganda, the huts coming into sight beyond look poorer, the banana plantations more sparse. Farther to the north, where the forest nears the river, and the land rises gently to the west, towards the Congo watershed, where hills advance, the antelopes too come to the water, and herds of red-brown congoni run along the banks.

Suddenly the river narrows, once more granite, that enemy of broad and easeful river-life, approaches, once more the ships must stop. The rocks force the yielding stream into a narrow pass of two hundred feet, tear it at Nimule from its eastward flow through a sudden, sharp angle of ninety degrees to the northwest, and plunge it into a new chain of rapids. Once more, as in its childhood, the Nile feels transformed into a narrow mountain

torrent, a second river comes hurrying from the east to strengthen
and inspire it, the river bed cuts deep like a mountain river, and
from this point at Nimule, that is the name it bears, Bahr-el-
Jebel, the Mountain River, for about 450 miles, as far as the
ninth parallel. Once more, with all its waters, immediately below
Nimule, it is squeezed into falls sixty feet wide, and in the succeeding cataracts it never exceeds a width of 450 feet. In splendid
isolation, irresistible and unresisting, like a character somewhat
at odds with itself, the Nile pours downhill, a turbulent river.

And, as if to give expression to this stretch, a natural bridge
has grown at Nimule, such as hardly another river on earth possesses in this form, consisting of rank water-plants, so strong that
it bears the elephant from one bank to the other, and so powerfully rooted that when floods have destroyed it, it closes up again
of itself.

These spurs of the ranges from which it comes are the last
mountains it sees; the Nile takes leave of the mountains, of the
storm and folly of its youth. Reason and gravity, the plain, begin
to govern its course, it turns into a slow-flowing river and, as if
to erect on its banks a symbol of its vanishing youth, a monument
of the mountains, there rises in Rejaf, exactly at the point where
the river, now calming to the plain, again becomes navigable, a
solitary conical hill, strangely abrupt and as steep as a pyramid.
The earthquakes which sometimes shake it are explained by the
natives in their vivid way: the hill, which once stood farther
downstream, flew through the air and buried the human beings
at this spot; the cattle took flight; now the men are stirring, they
are trying to get out, they are still seeking their old cattle.

Here the Sudan begins. At the foot of the pyramid, the last
foam-wreaths on the water show how stormy was the time the
river has lived through. Laden with alluvial substance from the
mountains, it deposits these last evidences of its youth along its
banks: by doing so it raises its level, and, the rain co-operating,
it endangers those banks, floods and backwaters arise, and the
memory of a stormy past lays its heavy hand on the Nile's present

From now on, downstream from Rejaf and Juba, though the
Nile again becomes navigable, and remains so from 5° to 18°,
for about twelve hundred miles of its course, none but master-

pilots can navigate it, and they are rare. For not only must they
follow the meanderings of the river through all the swamps and
lagoons, among all the islands and sandbanks; they must steer
with the steamer the boats which accompany it on either side
and, in addition, three cargo-boats fore and aft, a regular flotilla
of boats all fastened together like a gigantic raft that only certain Dongolans or Nubians from the north, natives of Aswân,
can steer day and night.

The wave which leapt the falls in the morning at the sudden
bend by Nimule can flow past the Rejaf pyramid by evening. It
can see the sun sink, tinged with the smoke of the burning bush,
vanishing behind violet-grey clouds, reappearing below them,
shimmering orange, like love after temptation. In Venetian colours, pink and blue and black, then pale-green and salmon-pink,
mauve and velvet black, sky and water gleam and darken. Then
the sun casts its last red ray, girdled like Saturn by flat black
smoke-clouds, by rings. Again as in the morning, long files of
wild duck fly across its disk northward, racing the wave. White
herons wing away over the ever calmer river, ibises in their flight
stretch their legs out far behind, their heads and necks far ahead
into the sky, which now shines saffron-yellow, then begins to
veil itself in bluish shadow. In the greying world, with the scream
of the homing geese, the first great star begins to glow.

The wind swells a little, the low reed-grass on the banks ripples
in longer waves, the frogs strike up their monotonous chorus,
from the darkness comes now and then the grunt of a hippo heaving its fantastic body from the water, for now it goes feeding.
And only now, when all the world is dark, when all the antelopes
have gone home from their evening drink, the last creature of all,
the lion, creeps up and drinks the water of the Nile, waving its
long tail.

11

WHEN the new day dawns, the wave finds itself caught up into the great combat between water and land which began in the night. The Nile has entered the region of the swamps; for a long stretch from 5° to 10° N. lat. they determine its fate and that of the whole country; over a distance about the same length as that of the Seine the Nile could sooner be called the main artery of a swamp than a river.

Sluggish rivers of the plain succumb more readily to such a fate than rapid, cold, mountain streams, and if the Nile came to an end on the tenth and not on the thirty-first parallel, that end would be forced but comprehensible. But when the giant river leaves the swamps, it has only a third of its whole course behind it: thus it meets with this adventure astonishingly young. It has no greater one to face, so long as nature is its enemy. But later, when it is older and stronger, men can learn from this battle of the water with the land; suppose it should occur to them to imitate in stone the dams which here are made of plants?

Into this battle between land and water, the third protagonist enters, the wind, the ally of neither, merely an *agent provocateur*, egging them on to still greater violence against each other. Even in this battle, it is hard to say who began, whether it was the windings of the river which made it possible for the swamps to form, or whether the river winds more tortuously under the pressure of circumstances. Certain it is that the river, beset by strong trade winds, first loses its bank in the east, and that its broad bed narrows almost suddenly into funnel-shaped coils. As the plains on both sides lose all their incline, and the tributaries, unable to discharge, form pools and lagoons, instead of a clear river-system, a watery wilderness is created which, without co-

Photo: Egyptian Ministry of Public Works

JUNGLE

VALLEY OF THE BAHR-EL-JEBEL, FROM THE AIR

herence and almost without a current, at the mercy of the winds, disperses itself in countless channels.

And as all anarchy, provided it has a central point, of its very nature spreads and strengthens, the battle of the water with the land finds its centre in detached masses, in new islands. When a river which once ran a firm and contained course between its banks suddenly loses itself in a maze of channels, all the laws which govern water in the domain of land are dissolved, as is land in the domain of the sea. When the swamp has first formed in the shadow of grasses and reeds, this loose mesh of plants is multiplied a thousandfold, and day by day, and year by year, the whole chaos must become more and more impenetrable. That is what has happened on the Upper Nile in the course of centuries, and just as the dry jungle checked every horseman, this jungle arising from the waters seemed to resist every ship. Nobody has yet counted the animals and men who have perished here in the fight with the swamps.

This chaos seems to have been formed in the first place by the expansion of the main stream, which has no banks, and of its two big tributaries, the Bahr-el-Ghazal and Bahr-el-Zeraf, the Gazelle and Giraffe Rivers. All this region, covering an area of about 25,000 square miles, an equilateral triangle with Mongalla in the south, Malakal and the junction of the Jur and the Ghazal in the north, lies for the greater part of the year under water. How great is the anarchy of the elements in this region, which is half as big again as Switzerland, is most clearly seen in the vagueness of the maps. In many parts, say between Lado and Bor, between 5° and 6° N. lat., the geographers alter their lines year by year. Or, faced with water-courses in perpetual change, they dispute as to whether the Arab has a second mouth, or whether it is the problematical Bahr-el-Homr, or whether certain islands are stationary or floating, and here it is a question of rivers and islands hundreds of miles in length. There are water-courses which, sometimes open and sometimes choked with plants, suddenly vanish and discharge into one of the great tributaries. As whole stretches are inaccessible, it has only in recent times been possible to ascertain by means of air-photos how a great water-course shifts about in the course of a decade.

Once the water has attacked the land, and, by flooding it above and hollowing it out below, has detached masses, such masses seek to find a home elsewhere, turn against the water, and, at breaches and landslides in the banks, even dislodge it. When such a mass again finds terra firma, and is no longer hollowed out from below, aquatic plants take root in it in ever-increasing numbers, and the swamp begins to grow, like the jungle, from above and below at the same time. In a few holes, moss settles, soaks up the moisture, and fosters the growth of new mosses, which, mingled with the coarse grass, soon invade the pools. Laden with a thickening surface of overgrowth, the mass of land settles in more and more firmly, the water is ousted, the pool disappears.

These vegetable blocks or dams, the barriers which the Arabs call sidd and the English sudd, gigantic masses of floating vegetation, compacted by the strength of the current, work their way with the river to narrow points, especially to bends, block up the main stream, force its waters to take detours through shallow side-channels, till the current in the real middle ceases and mud settles on the roots, in which they can luxuriate at their ease. Instead of a river, there lies a firm vegetable path. And now where is the river—where is the Nile?

Like a creature enchanted, it is here and there at the same time; the water from those great lakes in the country of the Mountains of the Moon disperses and runs away into a labyrinth of channels, inlets and lakes, lagoons and ponds, extending over a breadth of miles. While the river covers as much as fifteen miles, the channel proper shrinks to about six yards. These water-courses, overgrown with springy turf and covered with dense masses of weed, form paths so elastic that the animals do not feel the danger: the heavier they are, the more readily they sink, and the antelope or buffalo which sets foot on it sinks into the depths; their narrow feet kill them, but even the elephant, for all his wit, has sometimes succumbed to these treacherous paths. The ant alone is cleverer still, building antheaps three feet high so as to save them from high water. But the Negro drives the game into these regions, just as the northern hunter decoys it into the bogs.

These carpets of matted vegetation, like the fabulous seaweed fields of Columbus, recall the frozen rivers of the north when the ice breaks up at the banks and lumps drift downstream, piling up till they block the current, but then the spring sun comes and thaws away the obstruction that here yields only to an occasional gust of wind. If such a mass is torn from the whole, entire herds are cut off; even the hippo has been seen starving to death on phantom islands of grass.

This is done by the wind, the eternal revolutionary, ever stirring up anew this battle between water and land; in a single night it can drive the grass islands of a lagoon into the main stream; the next night, its hostile brother from the opposite quarter may redistribute the whole, and suddenly clear the river. It can press floating islands upstream, back into the open water they left behind, and thus bring them to a standstill. In distant mountains it can multiply the rainfall tenfold, so that the Nile and its tributaries overflow. What yesterday was a sea is today a meadow, and tomorrow, literally tomorrow, a sea again.

If only these barriers, in their chaotic heaps, would sink! When, at the same place and the same time the papyrus is renewed in everlasting growth above and below water, when mud and rotting debris, piled up by the water oozing among the roots, blocks every channel, and a storm suddenly breaks through such a bar, the uprooted masses are violently hurled against the next bar, to thicken and strengthen it still more. Countless dead fish and even suffocated crocodiles and hippos are washed up onto these huge nets. Thus the elements contend, among plants as among men, when in a general anarchy the lower orders decay and the upper run to seed and drift. In such catastrophes, the grass-dams pile up to a height of fifteen feet. And yet in this exhausting struggle of a thousand little enemies against the one great river, nature has provided for a positive result. The river ploughs the land, for the dry earth constantly sinks, then refills. A phenomenon which elsewhere takes centuries, the shifting of a river bed, is quickly carried out on the Mountain Nile and is constantly repeated.

For two thousand years, men had spent their strength in vain struggling against this element; wind, water, and land, all ene-

mies of each other, seemed secretly agreed that man was to be
held off; from Nero on, every expedition proceeding up the Nile
came to grief against these plant bars and could advance no further. Just as the invincible river has changed its domain at its
own free will, it has in centuries completely altered its course.

But in Emin's time, man mastered the river. After frightful
deluges of rain, which in 1878 flooded even Khartoum and dev-
astated Egypt, after communication had been cut off for two
years by these giant barriers, Marno, the Austrian, succeeded first
in cutting through after six months' work with a hundred men,
but not until after 1900 did the English succeed in mastering the
primeval barrier. To make the Nile navigable, to overcome this
elemental world of mud and the vegetation of ages, gun-boats
and mission-steamers united, power took for its ally religion,
which prepares its way.

Even in the technique of this struggle, a parable lies hid. First
the engineer, steaming up from Khartoum, must find out where
the river is and where the bank, otherwise he might waste his
strength on masses which are not islands. If he attempts to set
fire to them, so that he can break them up more easily, he must
reckon with changes of wind and danger to his steamer. When
the attack proper begins, he rams stakes into the grassy surface,
ties ropes round them, and fastens the ropes to the steamer standing with its head upstream: then the engines are set going, slow
at first, then quicker, half steam, full steam, then reverse: thus
he can pull lumps of the bar away just as dentists draw teeth.
Sometimes the plants are stronger than the stakes, even when
eight men hold them: the art lies in the playing of the ropes.

But if the grass island is too old, or too heavy, or the swamp
too deep, or if the current pressing against it is too weak, the
engineer tries to map out the land he has to destroy in squares,
first has the grass mown with short swords, then the roots hacked
in pieces. Then a hundred naked Negroes stand in the breast-
high morass, striving to get the better of the weeds with knives
above ground and with spades below, dripping with sweat and
slime; but if a strong current comes, they must cling swimming
to the stouter stems of the papyrus, and fasten the ropes to them,

till the steamer tears the half-cut squares loose and sends them drifting away downstream, while the men quickly loosen their stakes, clamber up the sides of the steamer, and collapse exhausted on deck.

Night means danger. While the world rests, a half-loosened square is detached upstream; perhaps driven by the wind, it drifts against the steamer, and in the morning the fortress is besieged. Or the river discovers its strength in the night, itself uproots whole masses, presses them against the steamer, and the steamer against the boats behind it, anchors break, chains snap, wheels bend, the helm is put out of action, and all that in a country where nothing can be replaced. Or a few conquered barriers meet, as in politics, and drift together to form one block. Struggling against such powers and dangers, the English cleared five miles in three months with five steamers and eight hundred Nubian prisoners, without communications, surrounded by excited tribes, among mosquitoes and fever.

And yet even today, the vagaries of this long stretch of the river, which, with its banks, has lost all its bearings, cannot be foretold. A few years ago, an unexpected flood detached great fields of lightly rooted plants from the lagoons, washed them together at the bends, and thus blocked five miles of the river for three weeks at Shambe. What was to be done? A sixty-mile canal was dug to connect the Nile with the Zeraf and thus save water from being lost in the swamps: it was so quickly choked that only a channel of twenty-four feet can be navigated. Other canals are completely choked in twenty years.

Why did a certain shrub suddenly luxuriate in little forests after a very dry year in places where it formerly grew only in single plants or in groups? Where lagoons and open water had once lain, the seed of the grass, in this year of drought, had been able to settle and to grow so high that its head was above the water when it returned. Now, as it had breathing-space, it could live on in the water and grow in thickets.

Thus the secrets of growth confront the navigator yearly with new and confusing problems, but the great river, beset by a thousand little enemies, can overcome the dangers of the swamps with its inexhaustible life force. Though it does not succumb to them, and in the end takes flight into the desert, yet it loses so much water in this great sponge that its whole future is determined by the loss and with it the future of Egypt.

12

SOLITUDE broods over the lagoon country of the Nile. Man, penetrating to the river only at a few dry places, animals, their habits disturbed by waters and shallows, can live here only in certain groups and species and along certain reaches, but fish, birds, and reptiles are in their element.

In the southern half, perhaps as far as Shambe, where solid land lies in compact masses, life is more active, as the quiet river, flowing with a fairly strong current in a wide bed, keeps within its banks even at flood times. Soon, however, it is dotted with broad, low-lying islands, and while beyond the banks rich savannas cover the land, and the palms decrease so rapidly that a group of three palms is marked on the ordnance map, in the river itself, about at Bor, swamp sets in in bed and valley, the higher land retreats westward from its channel, the islands broaden, and the river begins to wind about over the three to six miles' breadth of the valley. The silhouette of an acacia, of a doum-palm, even the dome-shaped top of a great sycamore, shows where dry land lies. There the yellow spots of the Negro huts glimmer near the river or farther off inland, the cattle are driven to the water, the native fishes, harpoons, and hangs in the sun to dry the flesh of the hippopotamus he has killed.

Below Bor, with the swamps, the great solitude begins. For three hundred miles, northward to Lake No, swamps dominate. Even from above, there is nothing distinct to be seen. From the aeroplane, a red-brown undulating surface seems to be held together by a white slime, but everywhere backwaters, pools, and marshes come and go, green and brown, in gently heaving shoals of reeds and papyrus. From the west, where the swamps begin lower down than in the east, a strip of wooded uplands touches the stream at one point only, a low ridge which keeps the waters about six miles away from the river, and forms a kind of water-shed between the Nile and Ghazal swamps. As the latter come from the Nile-Congo watershed, the separation which governs half the continent is here caused by a swell six feet high.

Here, in the swamps proper, nourished by a boggy soil, fertilized by the remains of coal and ashes from the yearly bush fires, the grasses flourish.

First comes the papyrus, for on its fibres immortality was first recorded: it has survived for six thousand years, and is no more perishable than the granite rocks in which the same kings hewed their deeds, good and bad. From the banks of the Nile arose the rustling stems in whose shadow slaves rowed the war galleys of Egyptian kings, and when the pith had been cut in strips by the hands of other slaves, crossed, pressed, and rolled into a fibrous sheet, a third group of superior slaves chronicled on it the glory of those Pharaohs, while a fourth carried the rolls to the tombs, from which they were brought to light in later ages by the curiosity of white men and deciphered by their genius. Of this grass was made the first of those patient pages on which the rulers of the earth, not content with their daily pleasures, sought to secure immortality in fame.

These tall papyrus grasses, rising sometimes to a height of eighteen feet, form miniature dark-green forests, whose eternal rippling lends the whole surface softness and melody. When, at the water's edge, from out and from under the older plants, the younger, lower ones grow, pale green, shut, the crown not yet spread halo-wise, and still attached to their elders in the dark green jungle gloom below, something of herd life seems to emanate from these ever-moving, ever-whispering groups whose gentle murmur swells with the wind till it rustles and creaks.

In comparison with the papyrus, the elephant grass, with its stems like bamboo, looks stiff, ungraceful, male, its pointed upright leaves and brown feathery crown piercing the air like a challenge.

The thick, long-haired pale-green fur, with soft curved sheaths, covering the land in clumps, is the um-soof grass, the um-suf of the Bible, which the Negroes call "the mother of cotton," growing by the deeper water where the ground is flattest.

Above them all, a fourth plant towers from the water, forming whole groves, a shrub rather than a grass: growing more rapidly than all the other swamp plants, even more rapidly than the rising Nile, it shoots up eighteen feet above the water, always overtopping the highest level of the water, as thick as a man's arm, conical in shape, yet tapering again towards the root, with spongy wood with a fibrous pith, and little, imperceptibly curved thorns, sparsely clad with leaves like the mimosa, overhung and festooned with huge, blue-flowering convolvulus. This is the ambatch, six inches thick, of which the Negroes make their rafts, so light that a man can shoulder them, but strong enough to bear eight men.

And this grassy world of the lagoons, rippling or stiff, soft or jagged, is held together by blue and mauve water-lilies, by yellow ottelias with candle-shaped pistia plants and water mosses, so that whole ponds look like meadows and whole rivers like starry ribbons.

In the green monotony of this flat landscape, the calls of the birds and the big animals sound less loud than that eternal creaking or hissing of the grasses which answers the wind day and night. Where the swamps begin, an island below Mongalla is inhabited by an elephant family which, for at least fourteen years, has not dared to cross the stream, though just at that point it is narrow. Strange guests of the Nile! Once there were two of them; now they have two young who have eaten down this great island and made it flat and transparent, and placidly watch the weekly steamer pass, voluntary prisoners in a kind of natural zoo, unique in the world.

Farther downstream, in the lagoon country, only a few, strange creatures dwell.

Here is the home of the eerie race of the white ants, *fatalis* by name and by nature. Whatever they reach, they gnaw to pieces, and in order to lay hold of it, they first darken it, like certain politicians. The things they set out to destroy to their advantage are first undermined by subterranean passages, or covered over with earth: thus branches and tree-trunks, to the topmost twigs, fall victim, and not only these, but baskets, chests, and bales. Whatever is left over is armoured in earth heaps, rising to a height of twelve feet, which only dynamite can destroy. This nocturnal organization only collapses when the leader is killed, and to make the whole thing more romantic, the leader is a woman. When the queen is dead, and only then, the whole state dissolves.

And yet these clever creatures have enemies who are certainly more stupid, but craftier than themselves: as the natives are exceedingly fond of them as food, and have noticed that the young ones creep out of the anthill in time of rain, they drum softly on their domes and spheres, and the termites think that rain is falling on the anthill; then, when they emerge, the natives shovel them into baskets by the thousand, and the future hope of a state ends in the earthenware pot of a Negro family, whose porridge is spicier for once.

In holes by the river, though not in the water, lives the protopterus; making its way through the mud to spawn, it darts hissing on men and animals like a snake. Not only the natives, but even the experts are still in doubt as to whether it is a fish or a reptile. On dry landspits giant lizards lie basking, and poisonous snakes startle the natives and the monkeys, who especially dread them, yet few men are killed by snakes and many by crocodiles.

Here it lives happy, the crocodile: like a member of a Conservative club it spends its days for years on end mostly dozing on the same dry landspit, and yet it is ready every second to glide soundlessly into the water, for on land it is always frightened, in the water always frightful. With their jaws open for minutes at a time, their pointed snouts pressed against the earth, their little eyes half veiled by heavy lids, they lie like stones side by side.

If the crocodile has wandered from the Nile and is pursued, it hurries, defending itself, straight in front of his pursuers to the maternal river, quicker than a camel. It has finer hearing than all other reptiles, can defend itself earlier, and perhaps that is why it grows so old. God has given it time, for it grows with incredible slowness from one to nine feet; man increases his height only about three times. Hated with genuine passion by the native, and even by the dog, who realizes the danger, it is the enemy of all animals and all men, hunts and kills camels, asses, and even cranes; only the three primeval giants are safe, but they do it no harm, and keep to their grasses. Apparently invulnerable, it bears all kinds of wounds and even burning coals nearly all over its body; it seems indestructible and hence loveless.

Lonely and unsociable as these few animals, there lives and moves in the land of swamps the oddest of all birds, silver grey, with greenish and blue shadows, its head armed with an enormous beak rising from an indrawn neck. This is the shoe-bill, which the Arabs call "the father of the slipper," and which, on the Nile, lives only here and at the source. With its melancholy, silent figure, always misanthropic, always alone, sudden in all its movements, whether it twists its head through an angle of 360°, or spreads its heavy wings for a moment, or opens the huge pouch which serves it for bill, the whole phenomenon is in harmony with the motionless life of a gigantic swamp quickened by sudden winds, and quite especially so is the fact that it stands on one leg. For all the birds stand on one leg in the swamps.

This motionless silence hums, murmurs, and mutters away to itself, and its sounds resemble its smells. Into the chirping of the insects, the real masters of this region, into the soughing and silken rustling of the grasses, there falls at times the hoarse cry of a misanthropic giant heron, flying low over the papyrus in alarm, or the shrill scream of a hawk, and the stuffy, indistinguishable smell of rotting roots and fish rises from the forest of green stalks.

In the evening the south wind drops. The bush fires, which sometimes catch parts of the sudd, glow from the distance, the sun sinks dirty red in this thick air. Now the water-birds begin to wake up and take their evening flight to the interior of the swamp, the kingfishers and cormorants drop from overhanging grasses into the water, great silver fish leap out of the golden-red surfaces of the lagoons, the Nile geese fly northwards in long files. The grunting of the hippos grows clearer as they prepare to seek their supper inland; single goat-suckers utter their flute-like cry, and fireflies suddenly quicken the loose thicket of the papyrus, already in myriads.

Now, when the evening light has faded to purple, the frogs strike up the long bass-chord of the swamp night, but the creaking sound of the papyrus has sunk to a secret soughing, from which the elfin voices of the night insects rise in higher octaves. Now the swarms of mosquitoes stand like great cloudlets in the yellow gloom of the fading sky, bats dart about among them, and the last swallows, anxiously chirping, seek shelter from the night. Motionless, the egrets stand by the swiftly darkening water of the river. Where do the birds of prey sleep? Do they find some old tree in this infinite swamp, or must they fly to the far mountain ranges? Now the crescent moon is mirrored in the still water by the bank. Over the dark heaving mass of the papyrus, the stars wend their way of light, over the red flickering horizon of the fires of Africa.

13

THE men stand like the birds. Through the ages they have adapted themselves to their surroundings like these birds of the swamp, with their gaunt limbs, thin necks, small heads, and stiltlike legs, which they use in turn, standing for hours in the swamp with one foot supported on the knee of the other leg; stalk men, crane men, lonely in the Nile lagoons.

What kind of man is the Negro? Is it possible to ask what kind of man is the white man? The character of the dark peoples and races runs through a gamut of a hundred colours and shades, just as their skin varies from deep black to light brown. And yet it should be possible to determine in one group of Negro peoples the colour of the character which separates every Negro tribe of the Nile from the white man. It is best to take the heathen native of the Upper Nile, who, through the centuries, in spite of all the impressions received from white travellers or conquerors, has preserved the nature of the savage better than the Waganda on the equator, with whose innate culture these peoples form a contrast as great as that between animals and men. All the tribes living on the Nile and its tributaries, from 2° to about 12° N. lat., in a region much bigger than France—and there are many millions packed together outside the swamps—show some traits of the savage which neither administration nor navigation, nor the efforts of missionaries, nor even the slave trade, has effaced. Such traits are graven into human groups of similar colour by the pressure of time in widely distant parts of the earth, like the signs and runes which the countenance of the earth bears on its virgin rock.

The peoples, of whom examples are here given, belonging to the so-called Nilotic branch of the Sudan Negroes, are of very impure and mixed stock. From 2° to 6°, that is, from Lake Albert to the beginning of the swamps, these are, in particular, the Lur, the Madi, and the Bari; then, farther downstream to Kosti, the Dinka, the Nuer, and the Shilluk.

All these heathens naïvely reveal the light and dark sides of human nature: their organization is loose, they are guileless, unreflective, and very emotional. These are the jungles of the human soul which the ax of civilization, through the centuries, has never attacked, to lop and sever. In this unpruned thicket of primitive feelings, which, under sun and rain, between sky, steppe, and stream, in the even, dull warmth, grow, succour, and fight each other like the plants in the jungle, the clash of human instincts comes out more clearly, the colours jar more fiercely, or are at least more visible than in the character of the white man, whose ground-tones are only too often painted over. Here we see something like the man of the Garden of Eden, without concessions, qualms, or prejudices, moved to every selfish action by naïve lust, checked, according to his physical strength, by fear of spirits or the chief, and yet urged by sympathy and generosity to love his fellow-men far oftener than the white legend of the black man tells.

"The Negro is bad," wrote Baker, who knew the Nilotes better than most explorers, "but not so bad as the white man would be in similar conditions. The passions inherent in human nature affect him, but he has no exaggerated vices as we have. The strong man robs the weak, the tribes fight: what else do we do in Europe? They enslave each other: how long is it since we and America ceased to keep slaves? They are ungrateful: what about us? They are crafty and untruthful: does nothing but truth prevail among us? Physically they are our equals: why should we not educate them to be our spiritual equals too? A black child has a keener intelligence than a white, but soon it runs wild like an unbroken horse."

And as man really loses his innocence, not by knowledge of the other sex, but by the knowledge of gold, guile and greed ruin the simplicity of the rich Negro. If he is a passionate gambler from childhood, losing first the pebbles in the sand, and later his freedom with his cattle and his hut, he does not lose heart all the same; but the powerful and the rich man—for that is the same thing among the Negroes—no longer plays with pebbles or dances, no longer dons devils' horns; he turns solitary, suspicious, and malicious, brooding in revenge, greed, and dread of murder, exactly like a luckless white dictator, only that he coins no phrases and keeps no priests and professors to prove how patriotic are his aims. And, like most dictators, the chief, who can have no other culture than the slave, is pre-eminent only in the art of speech.

Each would like to become a chief for the same reasons as obtain among white men: he gets his beer for nothing, and after the hunt, the best piece of meat from the breast, the skin of a leopard, and, above all, an elephant tusk; moreover, when he goes travelling, an empty hut stands ready for him somewhere. But even here at the lowest stage of class conflicts, the curse of possession is seen, for the rich man—that is, the king—cannot enjoy all that is his and restlessly seeks to cheat death by bequeathing power. Since they are polygamous only out of greed, for wives mean labour, and since, heedless of Malthus, they beget as many children as happen to come, the great ones welcome fratricidal wars among their heirs, which kill off whole families, and tribes make war upon each other so that a few hundred head of cattle shall move from one village to the next. Thus, in the history of the Niam-Niam, who are cannibals, there figures one man who had one hundred and twenty-one grandsons, and another is recorded "with six brothers who were murdered by the Gambari."

In such anarchy, which is mitigated only by slavery, the herdsman can hold his own better than the husbandman, who does not know if he will reap what he has sown; thus the communistic tendencies of the nomad govern even the agricultural people. Even when they live without rights or property in a kind of slavery, they nevertheless unite as a mass, pasture and hunting belong to all, and when the population of entire villages, every few years, seek the new, still virgin land which lies beyond these boundless steppes, there arises outside of and below the autocracy of a king a herd-community which might be compared with that of Tsarist Russia.

The cannibals stand highest in the scale of culture: this remarkable fact is confirmed by all explorers here as on the Congo and among the Caribbees. The Niam-Niam, south-west of the Ghazal, have very big, wide-set, deeply shadowed eyes, classic noses, and small mouths with broad lips in a round face. These tribes, which their neighbours call the "great eaters," are hunters, eat no domestic animal but like the flesh of game, which each man cooks alone at his own fire, like a gourmet preparing his own pleasure. They are the best porters far and wide; they are most carefully painted with flower and star signs, which they renew every other day in red-brown colour; they have the oldest institutions, show the greatest interest in Europe, are frank in social intercourse, show great dignity, while their hospitality is famous. The king receives the stranger in his dead father's house, lays a bundle of lances at his feet as a greeting from the dead man, then invites him to a feast and never kills him. They punish theft severely, honour the mother of many children, punish a wife's adultery by cutting off her finger tips, and seduction by cutting off three of the man's finger joints. In every respect the customs of the cannibals are refined, and they cannot understand why they should not eat a man condemned by the oracle or a conquered enemy, or why they should not offer their guest a boiled human foot garnished with lugina, a kind of pudding.

"The Nang," so the West African Fergum, a tribe of cannibals, declared to an English explorer, "the Nang is everywhere, in us and you, it is the spirit of the invisible. But after death, it passes into one of our animals, never into a man. Therefore we never kill a cow. But when we eat a man, we need have no fear of devouring our own Nang."

And why should they be regarded as specially cruel, since their customs show so much tact and dignity? Is it not more natural to eat an enemy than to eat a pig or a fowl we have fed for years?

Photo: Egyptian Ministry of Public Works

PAPYRUS

Photo: Karakashian Bros., Khartoum

ARISTOCRATS

DEPARTURE FOR THE HUNT

14

THE customs of the Nile Negroes, practically uninfluenced by the white men and the Abyssinians, lead us into the virgin forest of human feeling: their contradictions are no more to be eliminated by explanation than those in the character of an individual. Undraped by the moral mantle of the white men, the contrasts stand out boldly.

If an old woman is suspected of evil-doing, they tear her gallbladder from her living body, for these Negroes, living far from the rest of mankind, place the seat of sorcery there just as Homer did, who was remote from them by thousands of miles and years. But the same men do not slaughter their cattle, which they reverence, and when a cow dies and is cooked among the Dinka the owner goes weeping aside, and does not partake. They celebrate orgies after a victory, but they care for the captured. Many leave their wives full liberty in love, but not in labour. They get a beating if the flour is badly ground, but not for their lovers; others, like the Bongo, who take no more than three wives, are faithful to them; among the Madi, a man must marry the girl who is with child by him; on the other hand, among the Banjoro, the wife can easily make up for adultery with a jug of beer; other tribes punish adultery by a fine equal to the value of the woman (a custom which cannot be too highly recommended to the white men). Even here they are superior in tact to the white races in that the women of chiefs and notables, who in Europe can do what they like, are, even among the tolerant tribes, forbidden the least sexual licence.

The Shilluk make a woman confess, after the birth of her first child, with whom she has associated beside her husband: each of these lovers must atone by giving the husband an ox, a new solution of the question of sexual honour. But if they were many,

and she is brave, she throws a handful of sand into the air, crying: "There were so many!" Then, quite logically, not her husband, but her mother has to suffer for bringing her up so badly.

A few tribes kill old women, in whom they see the witch;
others carry their reverence so far that the mother of the victorious hunter, at the feast after a great hunt, dances alone,
naked, in the midst of them, while all cry: "See the body which
bore the great hunter." The same human beings who, before a
war, set a child to roast, and decide, according to whether it lives
or dies, whether the war shall go on, nurse their children well,
and build them a kind of cradle, and what white father has ever
carried his adult son home for sixteen hours on end, as a traveller
saw among the Dinka? When the rainmaker, a mixture of magician and leader, does not allow the Nile to rise in time of
drought, they kill this fellow-tribesman with the righteous feeling that he has taken unto himself power over the elements and
hence gets more fowls and more corn than the others. But if they
honour a white man, like Baker, they throw the glass beads he
gave them as a parting gift into the lake to placate the hippos
which might otherwise capsize his canoe, and their brothers on
Lake Tanganyika, because they loved Livingstone, dried his
body, treated it with salt, and carried it for nine months through
the wilderness because they felt it should be given to the white
men on the coast.

Livingstone, it is true, never told them of the Redemption,
but only of the great Father who makes brothers of us all. Instead of teaching them strange legends, he showed them his
watch and his compass. "The Negro is not impressed by guns and
machines," he said, "but by continued kindness and benevolence,
and even this applies to only a few." He rarely punished, suggested to them no new needs, and made them Christians only by
making himself beloved. His mission of love bears nothing of
the curse of so many missions which, often unconsciously, are
really emissaries of gold and power. Why are all who really know
the Negro sceptical about the missionaries? Men without books
and pictures, tribes whose holy relics are preserved only within
the brown brows of their old men, must at a stroke learn to be-

lieve in some white god, so that cotton shares and the balance sheets of cotton firms may go up. Equally free from fanaticism and the business instinct, Livingstone took the Negroes as children, and since faith, here as everywhere, develops out of superstition, he used superstition as his starting-point instead of eradicating it.

Has any white scholar actually discovered more about the ape than the southern tribes on the Upper Nile which condemn to death any man who kills a chimpanzee, who once belonged to the human race? Many tribes so reverence snakes that they do not dare to kill them, even when they come into their huts, but drive them out, and most tribes are forbidden to kill the totem animal of their clan, even when it is a lion or a leopard.

Among the Bari, it is believed that many of the dead turn into leopards; among others, no one may shoot certain hyenas at night, because by day they live in their huts as men. These tribes, like most savages, dread evil spirits which bring sickness, death, storm, and drought, but know no good ones. They have no idols, as in West Africa, but sometimes carve household gods in wood. Loma, the Greek Tyche, means good and bad luck, fate, whether self-created or imposed. "Loma made him sick," or if a hunter returns empty-handed, "he had no loma."

The savage, more exposed to sickness and the elements, needs a magician to whom he attributes omnipotence because, in his turn, he wants to demand everything from him. The relationship is quite European: the rainmaker rules as dictator, now guiding, now terrifying the chief; he threatens hunger, drought, war, in order to extort more taxes, entertains the people with dancing and beer, ceremonially sprinkles certain magic stones with blood, and his only overwhelming distinction lies in his oratory. In the company of other rainmakers, he even tells the truth. "I never think of making rain," said one of them to Baker, "until they have given me corn, goats, fowls, and merissa. They have threatened to kill me? Not another drop of rain shall fall in Obbo. I will make their corn wither and smite their cattle with plague." Thus the black dictator talks himself into a power in which he does not believe. But the Negroes, like many white tribes, honour even the leader they have finished with: the Madi at any rate, when they burn their rainmakers, collect the fat dripping from the body to heal their wounds.

How near we are to their world of feeling! But the meeting with the whites dazzles the Negro as if he had entered a brilliantly lit hall, while in the Negro the white man meets the sun. It is this, rather than the lust of power, which has drawn white men who have lived many years in Africa back to it again as to a paradise which they cannot regain as a whole, but in which they can breathe the freshness of the breath of nature, ever renewed. The hardships and sicknesses of Africa shorten the life of the white man, but the contact with its natural forces strengthens his soul. Even the poet and the scholar, whose days are spent among eternal things, find it harder to flee the confused din of the daily tomtoms in Europe and America than the explorer, hunter, or planter, and this purifying influence does not come only from the daily danger, from the battle with the elements, but rather from the Negro's eyes, from the winged or plastic gestures of his hands, which are paler within, like a sign of greater depth of soul, from his childlike, inquisitive ways, from his dignity and realism, from his untragic being.

If the Negroes are to be compared with children, then, on the Nile at any rate, they must be compared with happy children, whose cynical innocence lives on in their cruelty. They may kill each other in anger, but they know nothing of the perversions of the white man; everything that darkens white life, hatred and contempt, ambition and jealousy, above all the curse of gold, is absent from the daily life of the Negro as a spur to crime, and appears only in the relations of chiefs of different tribes. Even here, as among the whites, the feeling of hatred and revenge is invented by greedy chiefs with respect to other tribes, so that their subjects may be brought to slaughter each other in war.

What the white man brought the Negro was at one time no more than the string of beads with which he cheated him out of his ivory. He took only one thing from him, his delight in his own handiwork, for, confronted with the white man's marvels, the instinct of imitation died. Why, with endless labour, make a sharp blade for a knife, when a splendid knife could be had from the white man for a lump of rubber? The Egyptians treated the Negroes they reached on the Upper Nile just as the Church treated the people: they did not even teach them to use the potter's wheel, so that the art of the armourer decayed on the Nile and withdrew into inaccessible swamps and distances. The white man can teach the Negro the so-called blessings of labour only by seducing him with unknown pleasures, by decoying him with the gifts of civilization, because without their cheap labour he can make no money here, and so he expels them from their paradise of idleness.

He can the more easily do so because part of the men are already in a condition of slavery: not all the work is done by the women, part is done by prisoners of war and the poor, the social organization being varied and not clear. Expensive pleasures are few, the rivalry of the whites for costly clothing, houses, or food is almost unknown, for no one wishes to seem what he is not, hence the great class differences of the whites vanish. Rich or poor, the Negro gains and loses by his contact with the whites: first he loses the freedom of idleness and gains sewing-machines, lamps, and whisky; then, having lost his right to vegetate, he gains self-consciousness; once awakened, he seeks to make himself independent in state and constitution, and in the end strives for a different kind of freedom, the phantom freedom of the whites. Today no white power need enslave the Negro: he has himself become the slave of civilization.

15
_____

THEIR bodies tell whether **they** are herdsmen or husbandmen. Beside a young Shilluk, the white man nearly always looks clumsy and dull. With the naïvely seductive beauty of the Greek adolescent, he sits there slender-legged, still, proud, and naked, with nothing but a skin over his shoulders, his hands held nobly, a bronze Dionysus. They bear their beauty consciously, for everywhere in Central Africa it is the well-made peoples which go naked, like the handsome herdsman tribes of Uganda even today, while the smaller, thick-set agriculturist wraps his body up even when he is poor.

The natural grace of the shepherd, whom patience and leisure have ennobled throughout the world, is enhanced in these Nilotic tribes not only by their nakedness, but by the curiosity with which they follow the appearance of the white man. They do not disfigure themselves with mouth-sticks and nose-rings, many of them have not even the branded signs of class: their childish mind is satisfied with hair and headdress. It takes months for the Loatuko—the handsomest man on the Nile—to weave the elaborate network of his natural helmet with horse hair, thread, and bark, and when he has bound it along the thick lower edge with copper plaques, and added shells and ostrich feathers, he may well display his dazzling teeth when the stranger gazes at him amazed.

Or one of the chiefs sits smoking: first he takes up his pose, leans his right elbow on the arm of his chair, crosses his legs, grasps the pipe with his left hand, takes a deep breath of smoke, returns the pipe to the slave with a proud gesture, and only then puffs out the smoke slowly between his teeth.

But they need not be kings, they may be mere shepherds, possessed of nothing but their strength, and still they offer pictures

such as only Africa has to show. A group of young Dinka, graceful as antelopes, with a shoulder-skin for their sole covering,
with the lithe strength of the cheetah they have killed, stand
shoulder to shoulder in a row, hardly moving, and when the
younger gives the elder a cigarette—no one knows where he has
stolen it—the latter, with the languid ease of Egyptian kings on
frescoes, stretches out his hand for the much-desired magic weed.
Another, with a reddish skin cast about him like a Greek chlamys,
stands behind, leaning on a nine-foot staff, silent and waiting,
all three motionless and at rest within themselves: a noble existence, raising their hands, not in work, but only in their fine,
virile handclasp or in hunting, when they are threatened or
hungry.

Since they do not know shame, they always expose their bodies,
and are as vain of them as the white man of his clothes, but their
object is by no means to be as white as possible. Their dark-
brown ground-tone deepens to darkest black or pales to light
iron-grey: there are colours like chocolate, coffee, light havana,
brown-yellow leather, and only the tribes which anoint themselves with ashes and iron oxide falsify their colour. As a long
skull is regarded as beauty, the princes press and bandage their
children's heads to make them fine and long. The ugly branded
signs are tribal designs, forming a kind of badge, but they are
also proofs of courage, like the scars on the faces of German
students, and the women are proud of lines which are branded
in a specially painful way as tokens of love. When the Negroes
wear necklaces of animal teeth, they have at least killed the
animals themselves, and the white man, buying their bracelets
and spearheads, cuts a shamefaced or comic figure beside them.

As hunters too they are superior to the white man in skill,
courage, and dignity. As they seldom possess firearms, they must
grapple hand to hand, for life or death, not only with the leopard
and the lion, but even with the three primeval animals, and thus
restore hunting, which the white man has degraded to the safety
of sport, to its prehistoric element. With his pitfalls, the Negro
reduces even the rhinoceros to helplessness, but to give it its
quietus, he has to attack it with his spear from a tree, or direct
with his sword. He can, it is true, scare away the hippopotamus

with fire and noise, but if it has to be caught, the Negroes here fight at close quarters with the harpoon, and often even with arrows. The crocodile, which they fear and hate more than even the biggest animals because it drags man and beast into the river, succumbs to their harpoons and a system of ropes, just as in ancient Egypt, but the death-stroke in the back, generally delivered with the lance from a boat, is again a test of extreme courage. After such communal hunts, they fall, themselves like animals, on the dead foe, cut pieces out of it, and, rending them raw with their teeth, seem to wreak vengeance on it anew.

Most tribes hunt the elephant less eagerly: often they burn down whole forests, and the females and tuskless young perish too. As the elephant practically never attacks, and as, in these latitudes, unlike Uganda, there is little cultivated land which he can destroy, he is not hunted out of hate or revenge, but out of greed for ivory, at the command of the chief, to supply luxuries for the white man. The struggle with wild animals is a constant menace, hence they have concentrated all their skill on their weapons: for their five-foot bows, they have invented arrows with cunning barbs on their iron points, have sharpened spearheads for their long spears, and have discovered the sap of a certain euphorbia with which to poison the heads.

In all tribes, the women are inferior to the men in looks, conduct, and intelligence. As love is nowhere an art, but a woman everywhere a unit of labour, neither sex sees any reason to indulge in taste or fashions, and the disfiguring sticks and braids which they stick into their lips are seen practically only among the women. Moreover, a white woman, who plucks out her eyebrows and eyelashes, has little cause to laugh at the dotted lines tattooed on the face, the iron hoops hanging from the ears, of her darker sisters. Love itself is a more moral affair than among the whites in that no girl marries a man for his riches, but each one chooses the man she likes. When her breasts are as big as her fists, the Luri girl is left alone in a special tent with the man of her choice, and when the child comes, he must buy her. If they see each other for the first time at the marriage feast, among the Bari the mother follows them into the hut while the feast is

BELLE

Photo: Sudan Guide Book, London

SHILLUK TRIBESMEN

going on, asks whether he is pleased with her, and then rejoins the company with screams of joy.

In modesty they are superior to the white women: while the latter discard more and more of their clothing as they grow older, among most of the tribes on the Upper Nile, only the girls go naked; among the Bari, the women wear an apron after the first child, some wear a tail of beads behind, others bind on daily a kirtle of fresh leaves, the prettiest of all fashions. The Jur women are even called "tailed" by the Arabs, because they wear on their kirtles a tail of fine leather strips. If the woman is barren, she can be given back and her price reclaimed, but in many tribes, the wife can withdraw if the man is at fault.

As the woman represents a capital bringing in interest in work, whose fruits can be sold, the Negro on the Nile thinks of her much as a white man thinks of a share of stock. If he can acquire one hundred cows by marrying off ten daughters of the same woman, he can have these one hundred cows herded by other children. Hence the Bari welcome a daughter more than a son, but regard twins as a bad sign and a reason for giving back the woman.

16

IN the swamps dwell the giants, not farther from the dwarfs than is New York from Washington. Beginning west of the Nile on the southern Ghazal, they spread on the right bank to about the twelfth degree; but the meaning of their life lies in the swamps. For while the dwarfs on the Ruwenzori shrank more and more in the thousands of years of their life in the undergrowth, the Dinka, the aborigines of these lands, probably the tallest people on earth, grew ever taller, because they had to spend their lives standing like storks on the lagoons and landspits of the swamps. While the pygmies dwindled to 4 feet, 3 inches, the giants grew to 6 feet, 7 inches: a Dinka of 6 feet, 3 inches, is merely of medium height. This height, as well as their flat feet and their lengthened heel and neck, show how animals and men approximate each other under similar circumstances. The Homeric battle of the pygmies with the cranes finds here its symbol, and perhaps its legendary prototype.

When they stand motionless in the swamp, literally for hours on end, on one skinny leg, the other foot supported either in the knee-crook of the standing leg or against its shin, without net or fishing-rod, far from their herds, generally leaning on a long staff, yet by no means asleep, but on the watch and merely still, without passion or thoughts, without aim and apparently without feelings, visible for miles in their endless watery plain, they offer the legendary contrast to those dwarfs who, in the undergrowth on the slopes of their volcano, live their clever, dark, invisible ant-life, always busy, wary and watchful. A spare body, which looks from behind as if it had been planed down, a slender waist, an elongated skull with a long arched nose, thin lips, fine wrists and ankles, make the Dinka, as they stand on one leg in their wonted posture, look like the long marabous, cranes, and storks, just as the pygmies seem to shrink into moles.

Their thinness, which makes them look even taller, is at least partly the result of their absolutely unparalleled laziness, for they will often rather eat grass soup than take the trouble to fish. The laziest of all, the Nuer, do not even bury their dead. The whites, striving to overcome natural predispositions of this kind under moral pretexts, because they need the working power of these millions of men, stake their hopes on the flies, who have decimated their herds and may force them to till the soil. And, indeed, fertile stretches of immense extent could be turned into arable land here, if "the Negro would learn to know the value of work." But as the demand for labour is decreasing throughout the world, the Dinka may with luck outlive the period of forced labour in the white world and preserve to themselves the state of paradise out of which their brothers were so recently startled after thousands of years.

Most of the Dinka tribes are herdsmen and cattle-breeders; the poorest have four cows, the rich up to a thousand; herds of three thousand have been seen. Therefore they have declared their possessions holy, just like the white man, only that their calves are not of gold In the morning, the leader of the herd is driven forth with a prayer; at festivals, it is wreathed with flowers; the fine, light-grey, short-horned animal, with its big hump, is sprinkled at milking time to keep off the flies; at night it is guarded against the lions in folds of thorn or euphorbia. The cowherd sleeps beside his favourite ox; once a month the cattle are bled with the spear. This passion for cattle was exploited by cunning slave-dealers, who bartered cows for men, and cattle-stealing is the cause of all wars and hostile enterprises. Their imagination and legends are peopled with cattle; and they believe in sacred kine which the Nile spirit guards, only letting them pasture at night, bound to stakes, when the mist veils the banks.

If drought comes, although drought is only a relative term here, and their miraculous plains are eaten down, they transfer the cattle with great ceremony from the right bank of the Nile to the left. Then the women and children stay behind in their light, swiftly wattled nomadic huts of elephant grass, while the men cross the river in a few hollowed tree-trunks. They drag a few calves into the water with ropes, the lowing of the frightened animals attracts the mothers, who follow them half swimming, and finally the bulls follow the vanishing cows. The sheep are carried over the Nile in boats, the dogs swimming alongside heedless of danger. Thus the livestock is ferried across the Nile by families in two days, and the medicine man, smeared with ashes, stands on the bank and exorcizes the crocodiles, who snatch their booty all the same.

On the Ghazal, some of these tribes are neighbours of their cousins, the Niam-Niam, and thus vegetarians and cannibals observe and despise each other, the more so as the vegetarians do not only live on milk and millet, and the cannibals not only on men: the hate between half-enemies is always deeper than between opposites. They jeer at each other for "gluttons" and "stick-men" because the Dinka seldom appear without long staffs. When the Dinka, the blackest men of Central Africa, with their filed teeth and ugly, red-dyed shocks of hair, with their headdress and plume, stand beside the cannibals, with their more refined forms of civilization, the moral scale of the whites seems quite ridiculous.

But if the cannibals look down on the "savage Dinka," because they worship cattle, dislike hunting, and have no etiquette, the Dinka in his turn looks down on another neighbour, the "savage Jur," who has to forge his iron. As they are dependent on the Nile and its shifting swamps, as well as on the deposits of iron, the Jur change their habitat and cross the river in the spring. Then the wilderness begins to live. They stack charcoal and crumbled ore in layers in their little, skilfully simple kilns, and although this black smith has only a stone for an anvil, a square lump of iron for a hammer, to which his own arm serves as shaft, and a split stick for tongs, he can, by stout hammering, make his iron hard.

Meanwhile the women are busy with eel-pots and fish-baskets, gourds and pottery, and the naked gipsy camp in the forest is broken only when they have collected enough iron to make arrowheads, lances, and ankle rings for the Dinka.

Thus the black tribes on the Nile strive to heighten their self-respect by despising or envying each other, just as if they were Europeans.

17

WHERE the swamplands end, towards 10° N. lat., is a flat lagoon, just like the others, only that its end cannot be seen. This is Lake No; here a new epoch begins for the Nile. Here the river, on 30° E. long., touches the most westerly point of its course (only the Third Cataract will again lie so far to the west); here it regains a firm bed, which it keeps to the end; in and near the lake it receives three great tributaries which affect its volume. The course of the river through the lake is visible, for it deflects sharply to the east, and flows in that direction for 75 miles, resuming its allotted north-south course only at Malakal. It is as though the mighty river had to strike athwart its wonted course in order to take up three ministering streams which come to swell its power.

As the river alters its direction and its character, the landscape slowly alters too. Now the banks grow clearer and broader, because they grow drier; the river again reaches a width of a hundred yards and more, the papyrus decreases, acacias spread their parasols, little round huts are grouped in villages, grey cattle, surrounded by little dogs, come to the water; motionless, the tall Dinka sit smoking round a fire, watching their women wading knee-deep in the Nile, filling their blue pots with yellowish water, then, on the bank, heaving them onto their heads and carrying them deftly to the village. When a Dinka stands solitary on one leg, he looks like the wading-birds standing close by on another bit of mud.

In this landscape, the Bahr-el-Ghazal falls into the Bahr-el-Jebel at the western end of Lake No, the Gazelle River into the Mountain Nile. Though the Ghazal is a servant of the Nile, it is itself a giant, with a basin stretching over ten degrees of latitude and nine degrees of longitude, and hence greater than the basin of the equatorial lakes, which beget the Nile. Here, as in human history, the mind revolts against the thought that the tributary should be stronger than he who receives the tribute. If the stronger is only a tributary because it discharges into the other, yet ultimately it is a question of greater vitality which decides as to who is the conqueror. The Ghazal has mighty adventures behind it, dramatic transformations and wanderings, by the time it nears the Nile, and is richer in water and in battles than any river of Europe. Even its own tributaries have lived the life of great rivers. Where they fell into it, the Ghazal River had seen broad savannas with gigantic trees, and later the tropical forest, stretching up to the Congo watershed. And then, on its lower course, it was faced with the struggle of water against land, just like the Nile.

But now it was clear who was the stronger: when it lost its bed, its direction, and its self-control, when plant bars and grass islands, lagoons, backwaters, and channels confused it, when the anarchy of the swamps set upon it, the Ghazal lost nearly half as much water again as the equally afflicted Nile, and thus the mighty stream, dispersed, discharged only through a kind of navigation channel, while the stronger character, triumphant over trials, received it with moral composure, ready to direct and to use it.

Even the life of the second of these tributaries, the Bahr-el-Zeraf, which falls into the Nile on the same latitude to the east of Lake No, has known adventure. It begins "somewhere in the swamp below the Awai," said the geographers, just as they might say of a foundling child. Its windings in the lagoon country, which lead to the conclusion that it arose from former swamps, its banks, if such can be spoken of, which seem to be formed of the root masses of earlier vegetation, and the jellyfishlike elusiveness of its course, make it look, seen from the aeroplane, like a frightful malignant disease eating into the flesh of the land.

The most interesting of the three, which falls into the Nile close below the Zeraf, at the point where the Nile again turns northwards, is the Sobat, for it is the first to carry down the strength of Abyssinia in the form of silt to the Nile, and hence to decide its future destiny. Dominating a gigantic basin, and originating only by parts of one of its tributaries from the plateau of the great lakes, the Sobat brings nearly everything it contains from the Abyssinian alps, from those south-western mountains which the few men who have penetrated so far have praised for their beauty. This river, and all the others which later flow into the Nile from these mountains, have, given the relative altitude, a long mountain and a short valley region to flow through, the opposite of all the rivers which come from the great lakes. Thus, impetuous and stormy, the river forges a virile course for itself, and conquers the seductions of its later life with the strength of its youth.

Although it thus stands the test of the swamps better than the Ghazal, which came from the west and was nearly lost, the Sobat must nevertheless forfeit a good deal of its water in the swamps which attack its tributaries. Since, even towards the end of its course, its banks remain somewhat higher than the surrounding country, the water which has overflowed in the rainy season cannot fall back into the Sobat, and thus remains lying on the land all the year round, unless the Negroes drain it for fishing. In spite of all these obstacles, and although the nature of the country forces it into swamps, this mountain stream is strong enough to deliver on an average 14 percent of all the water which the Nile carries down to Khartoum.

At the point where the river, after the last of these three confluences, turns northward, it receives at Malakal its fourth name; the Victoria and Albert Niles became in their turn the Bahr-el-Jebel and the Upper Nile, but now, as the Bahr-el-Abiad, it flows without tributaries straight to the north, until its most astonishing encounter will once more simplify its name.

18

NOW the tropics are conquered, the adventures of youth overcome, a river flows in manly gravity towards its fate.

Now it has time to recall all the surprises which befell it, lakes, waterfalls, and rapids, the manifold dangers of the swamps, the struggle with the lagoons. Even here the Nile is not deep, generally sixteen feet, at times only six, so that even the flat-bottomed steamers often run over sand; but it spreads out like a lake; at times, with an incline of an eighth of an inch to the mile, it seems to stand still. The vast plain, in which it now moves sluggishly northward, without obstacles or menaces, for 750 miles, stretches from the foot of the lake plateau to Khartoum, and is connected in the east with the slope of the Abyssinian mountains, in the west with the mountains of Nubia and the hills of Kordofan. Low undulations on either side of the river are enough to protect the land from floods and swamps, and to hold the stream, from now on, within firm banks, to keep it navigable. As far as this point, the Nile was known to certain peoples of antiquity coming upstream.

The landscape which conditions and permits all this is the bush: the Nile here receives a premonition of the desert.

The keynote of this broad land is the acacia, in vague colours, brown, green, silver-grey, sand-colour, red-purple. Before this belt lies a corn-yellow dry strip; close by the banks is a dark green border of grasses, generally um-soof, more rarely papyrus, and still nearer the water generally a strip of black mud. Sometimes, however, the bright light bush looks black, generally in March, when the acacias stand out like skeletons from the burnt land. The custom of firing the steppe is common to all the peoples on the Nile who do not live in the daily rain near the equator. It is ineradicable, and, although whole forests in this gigantic region are endangered, comprehensible. Otherwise the bush-grass would grow too thick and too high, and its juicy tips would be out of reach of the cattle.

Only a kind of winter sleep seems to hold the steppe in check; it only half dries up, but at high water is flooded over for a width of three miles. As far as Kosti, some rain falls all the year round. But the farther it spreads north the greater the difficulty which the bush finds in surviving the dry season; then the animals take flight, and the boundaries of the game are shifted.

Islands of gentle hills approach the river at all points, but the plain lies so flat that a difference of height of six feet determined the situation of the capitals of administration. In the next 500 miles the river falls only 36 feet.

Towards Renk, at 12° N. lat., more trees approach the river, and new varieties. The baobab, the pachyderm of the bush plants, broader than it is high, a demagogue of vegetation, impressive in appearance yet all but hollow, yields from the greenish skin of its thick, empty fruits an insipid lemonade.

In this region, and upstream to about Tonga, thousands of huts stand in a dense row. Here live the Shilluk, who seem, only some two centuries ago, to have been forced to the north from the Ghazal swamps; later whole tribes re-emigrated from this relatively small, fertile region on account of overpopulation, and settled as far south as Lake Albert under all kinds of names. Thus the half-nomad pastoral peoples of the Nile lands are cast hither and thither by flood and drought in the eternal battle of the river with the land.

This noble stock, resembling the Egyptian type as seen in the royal tombs, with an aquiline nose separated from the forehead by a deeper depression than in any other Negro people, with fine teeth and small feet, with slow movements and gestures like the Dinka, disfigure themselves by rubbing dung and ashes into their bodies and hair till they are an artificial red and grey, like their greyhounds. But their huts and utensils are skilfully made, and they make as much use of the acacia, of which there are eleven varieties in the Sudan, as do their brothers on the equator of the banana: boats and water-wheels, firewood, tanning material, gum, and fodder for livestock.

Now the animal of the bush and the desert, the camel, comes for the first time to the Nile to drink. And with him, on these latitudes, instead of the Negro a new kind of man, too, comes to the river, a man who will subdue it with more power than ever the Negro could foresee. The round huts grow rarer; square ones succeed them, but soon the first whitewashed houses are mirrored in the river, the bronze or painted naked figures vanish, women in gaudy garments wash their clothes in the Nile, the Virgin rides blue-veiled along the river on an ass, with Jacob and Abraham at her side, a white tent stands in the glowing sunshine, a man, no lighter in the face than the last Negroes, but muffled up in a white burnous, appears, and beside him a youth leads a splendid black horse with white feet.

Africa, the real savage Africa, where the Nile passed its childhood and youth, disappears. Arabia has dawned on the horizon, a hundredfold mingled and deflected by Nubia, and yet, with its thousand years of presence in this land, stronger than all the races whose civilizations preceded or followed it. The hippopotamus still rises from the river, but it grows rarer. Where asses, horses, and camels come to the water, where triangular sails spread over it, the spirit of neighbouring Asia advances to the Nile.

The river broadens and broadens, more and more white sails flash on it, casks and chests stand in heaps at the stations, thousands of sacks of cotton wait for the steamer, a flashing buoy betrays the conqueror, and suddenly, below a slight bend, a great railway bridge spans the river, the first bridge and railway since the birth of the Nile, 1900 river-miles away, on the equator. Corrugated iron houses and stone sheds, whistles, sharp words of command, and policemen, the rattling of trucks, the smell of oil, and the sweat of labouring men, a movement recalling the Mediterranean ports, everything in Kosti proclaims the advent of the new colonial empire, only that instead of a church spire, a little downstream, there rises the slender column of the first minaret.

And here, from Kosti on, lies a new paradise for the birds.

This is the second on the Nile, exactly in the middle of its course, while the two others lie at source and mouth. Here guests are more frequent among the natives than at either of the other points; for here, between Kosti and Khartoum, the migrant birds from the north have their winter sojourn. In floods of black and white plumage, they pour in millions over earth and water. As these countless hordes rustle and scream, flutter and swoop, eloquent even as they mutely settle on the green and yellow dunes, in the islands and embankments, in the creeks and bays of the swelling river, these smaller creatures draw eyes and ears away from the bigger animals, just as a large string orchestra can outshine the loud brass.

These guests from the north are no famished refugees: if merely cold and hunger drove them forth, they could find warmth and food nearer, and would not quit lands which are warm. Why else should the Egyptian swallow, which builds its nest in January, stay where it is, while the northern swallow flies farther and farther, up to the equator? A few species of duck from Lower Egypt migrate to Lake Victoria, flying over a tenth of the earth's circumference, the pelicans leave Egypt, some species, such as the corn-crake, even run on foot the whole way from the north, flying only when the sea compels them. What urges them all to leave their birch and pine woods for the acacias and bananas? Why do all migrate and none brood? Rest and food are their aim, but love and marriage are for the north, though they see others like them mating, brooding, and feeding their young.

Thus, by the thousand, they go staying with relations, but their hosts are as suspicious as human ones. The shrike with its quivering tuft, the honey-bird with its metallic plumage flashing like jewels, the oriole and the goat-sucker, seldom find their brothers on the Nile disposed to mix, fly, or play with them: they do not fight, but they keep themselves to themselves, the correct attitude towards uninvited cousins, and the water-hawk, visiting his brother the red-necked hawk of the Nile, is probably amazed at his smallness. Before the countless hordes of European storks, gulls, and tern, the native storks, gulls, and tern beat a prudent retreat to the south. Even the crested crane is by no means overcome with delight when, in autumn, there dawns on the horizon the army of grey and maiden cranes who, under pretext of moulting, devour fantastic quantities of corn. For that reason the peasant prefers the kestrel, who has perhaps nested on Notre Dame, for he is sensible and eats the locusts.

The life of these myriads of birds on the middle course of the Nile, free, or almost free of struggle, the distribution of these races, all different in size and strength, over a relatively small area, reveals a state of paradise which only the animal has kept, which the black man has half lost, and the white man lost for ever. The apostles of the heroism of war, always prone to take their stand on "nature red in tooth and claw," forget that man is the only animal to fight his brothers on the grand scale, but here they might see native and invading peoples, distributed in tribes, vegetating in harmonious freedom side by side.

The comic turn is provided by the pelicans: they fish, hunt, eat, digest, and sleep in common; at first sight they look like roughly piled walls of yellow-pink stone, as they sit with indrawn neck on low trees and bushes, half-asleep and motionless. Then, as they advance to the water, waddling along like stout old professors, now philosophically reflective, now screaming in argument, their huge, flesh-coloured feet rising and falling heavily, yet not clumsily, they gobble up whole armies of Nile fish, collecting them in the great pouches under their beaks, just as children bring home berries in their pockets.

As still as bronze statues, the stilt-birds stand with dignity on their long legs in the middle of the river on the bright sand of the islands or in the grass on the banks. Suddenly, a movement ripples through the rows, as if they had been awakened by a signal we cannot hear, and they rise in a rustling cloud, form long, slightly curved files, and disappear inland. Gliding mysteriously over the parasol tops of the acacias, over the dry spears of the rushes, they return from the fields as they flew away, wheel in flocks over their resting-place, and alight in groups to stand again on the islands and the banks, tall, distinguished, as still as bronze statues.

The great cranes arrive from the north with their light-grey plumage, with the fine arch of their backs sinking to the dark tail-feathers, with their small and proudly borne heads and their firm, energetic beaks, settling and drawing in their wide pinions in leisured movement. The domestic storks stand in groups beside them like town councillors. Black and white, and much less beautiful, yet sovereign in their flight, rows of northern spoonbills, busy with the water, form a white border to the bank, and among them the merry sandpipers and ruffs, rising in swarms, darting hither and thither close above the river, in odd slanting lines, yet never breaking their formation, look as if they came from Prussia. On the stones in front of the strip of sand the dainty wagtails rock, with the dumpy brown Nile geese swimming about in front of them like old-fashioned governesses in charge of schoolgirls.

The sacred ibises still wheel over their river with their shapely wings, stretching their necks far out, so that the peculiar curve of their beaks stands out against the sky. Water-fowl and duck have their haunts in the rushes by the bank, and swim peacefully about on the strange water in front of their more distinguished relatives standing along the banks. Little duck, big duck, striped duck, teal, northern and native duck are there, and over their heads the lovely swallows stream tirelessly all day long over water and land and rise buoyantly into the turquoise-blue sky, where the hawk hangs motionless over some prey until he drops like a stone to seize his quarry. Away over the ghostly pale-grey acacias of the forest, small light-grey hawks dart like silver arrows, for out of the tangled undergrowth of the acacias comes the everlasting cooing of the wild doves.

Snipe and lapwing, with their merry question—peewit, peewit?—run about on the narrow tongues of sand where there is no room for the big birds, but the hoopoe, the hudhud of the Persians, comes flying from the water, swells his fine comb, and spreads his tail, showing off in front of the others; a few seconds later, he departs to do his turn somewhere else, like a playwright following his play all over the world, and taking his call.

19

EMERGING from Moorish arches, the new god nears the Nile. The worshipper about to cross the river on his way east kneels, in his white robe and turban, on the green pasture, then washes his feet in the Nile, a solitary figure encamped before the blue and yellow desert landscape and sky, with sharp contours standing out against the pure, transparent air. Quiet groups on the bank, great herds of black and white goats, are watched by a few goatherds in fluttering white robes, among pastel-green dunes and hills. Camels stand in hundreds knee-deep in the water, or wait on the banks till those before them leave the watering-place; guarded by their mounted herdsmen, they stand hanging their heavy heads, lingering, without greed, oriental. Beside them the horses of the herdsmen drink the yellow water. It is still the same water, but its guests have changed: horses and camels on the Nile mean that it has entered middle age. All seem at rest here, and the long islands overgrown with bushes which split up the river, stretched out like goddesses at rest, create the impression of a life spent in idyllic breadth and leisure.

Little clumps of papyrus still come downstream like gently floating islands, the last witnesses of the great battle in the swamps, like the last belated prisoners returning after a great war to a world at peace, and unable to find a niche for themselves. They cannot recognize the tortured river they once knew, as it flows through fine, broad dhurra-fields, past neatly heaped pyramids of corn, as its water, now clear, stands out against the pale-green line of the rising cornfields and the bright yellow sand of the bush.

Every object, tree or house, man or animal, appears separate in the dazzling light, and so seems a symbol, an idea, an image of all trees and houses, of all worshippers and camels; only the sailing-boats drive swiftly before the wind, and the man at the high helm must keep a sharp lookout for the many and shifting shallows of the Nile. The coolness by the river is out of proportion to the heat of the desert climate, for the hot Arabian wind has been moistened by the magnificent stretch of water.

In this dreaming life of birds and men, this idyll of peace, everything seems happy save the father of it all, the Nile. Great dread befalls it just at this point, where the world of birds rejoices in its vast expanse. In summer, the Nile feels a check here, yet without knowing whence it comes; its adversary is invisible. The more widely the dammed-up waters spread, the more kindly the natives look upon them, for in autumn, when all the water has retreated, they will sow on the freshly fertilized land, and three months later they can reap. The stream is unaware of all this: according to the law of its being, it pours on with might, though the incline is but small, seeking to overpower its enemy. The farther it struggles on, the wider it spreads, the land already seems a lake, though not a swamp. In the distance it sees towers and buildings rise, higher and handsomer, more widely spread than ever it has seen before in its course. A town approaches, yet something else approaches still nearer.

As the opposing pressure increases, as its own forward urge is concentrated on smaller and smaller quantities of water, as towers and buildings grow higher, and men and camels, cargoes and boats increase, a swelling roar comes nearer, louder than it has ever heard. If this is a river, then it is a river like the Nile. A bridge, bigger than either of the others, is cast across it. It has bored seven double piles into the river bed, and trembles slightly when the trains rumble over it. A few waves on, then a huge river dashes to meet it from the right, as broad as itself, yet with a much stronger current, a wild, bold, foaming, dark-coloured river. These are the waters which dammed it up so long.

From under a bridge as long and high as its own, the stranger bursts forth, squeezes the broad White Nile into a narrow channel on its western bank, dashes against an evergreen, rustling island, then, on the level of a wooded tongue of land, casts its waters with frightful power into the other. But they do not yet mingle: even within the course of the elder, the wilder brother's dark, impetuous current dominates their common flow. This is no tributary, which, like the other three, ends at its mouth: this is a distinct character, a match for the Nile, free and proud, which seems to offer an alliance on equal terms, so that they may, from now on, traverse the world together. It brings gifts with it, memories of the high mountains of its youth, still invisible, but destined one day to become a life-giving element.

Thus, on the palmy beach of Khartoum, the White Nile meets the Blue Nile. Thus they create in a brotherly embrace one of the loveliest spots in the world. Thus they unite their fates, and, by their bond, lay the foundation of the fate of Egypt.

Book Two

THE

WILDER

BROTHER

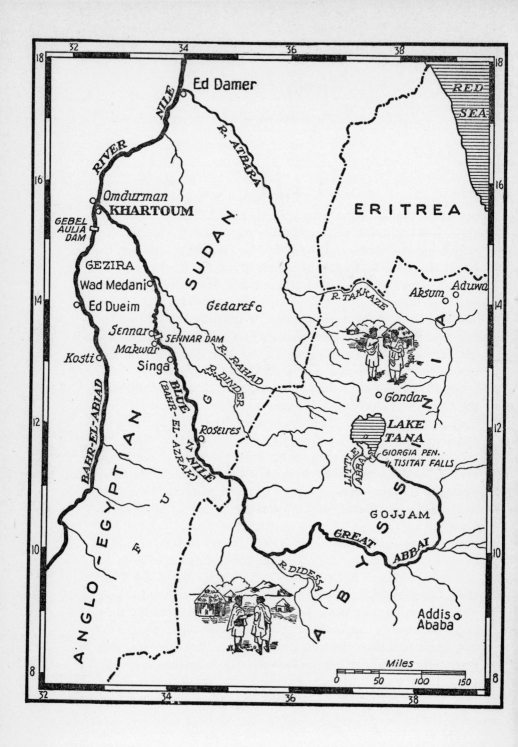

1

THE winds began it. If it were not for the monsoons, blowing at their appointed time from their appointed quarter, where would the rain come from? But the rain is the real mother of the Blue Nile, the mountains are its father. In the love-struggle of the elements, the bodily clash of volcanoes and clouds, the miracle of the second Nile is born. If Abyssinia bore no alps, if these alps were not volcanoes, if the winds did not break against them, to send the rain streaming from the sky, there would be no stream on earth to "hurry snake-wise to the plain," carrying with it metallic detritus from the mountains to fertilize the desert a thousand miles away.

For that is how the debris of the virgin rock became silt, and the silt became the oasis. Volcanoes and clouds, rain and winds, have created Egypt out of a howling wilderness, far away in space and time, and as here the elements have renewed their work for ages year by year at the same season before the eyes of men, this even ebb and flow gave birth to the first knowledge of month and moon, to the first questionings of sun and planets, to the first social order and the first law. Just as the farmer in other lands looks out for the rain, the eyes of this desert people scanned the distance, even as they do today, for the watery messenger riding in the bed of their one river, without whom they must perish.

The winds began it. Yet where do the winds come from? Even they, like great men, first bear fruit under opposition. In their war-time, when they jostle, and must yield to other winds, they bring the rain. As long as the wintry north wind blows, the north-east monsoon brings the rain from Asia over the Red Sea, and reaches the Abyssinian highlands nearly dry. But when, in spring, the south-west wind sets out from the South Atlantic, in its flight over Africa it adds to the sea moisture all the damp exhalations of the equatorial jungles, travels heavy-laden over the hot Sudan, till it suddenly dashes against the towering alps, and, after a flight of thousands of miles, discharges the vapour of sea and lands on their precipitous walls. Therefore, as the Abyssinian farmer says, the rain comes when the wind blows from the desert, and the Nile engineers say so too, for their calculations on the distant delta are based on these winds.

Thus African winds create the African river where it is to become fruitful, yielding only in autumn to their hostile brothers, the dry north winds sent over by India. And the winds and the mountains affect each other, the height and abruptness of the alps lengthen the rainy season, but the winds themselves have helped to mould their fantastic forms. And as here the rain determines the seasons, it turns them round: on the high plateau of the midlands, six to ten thousand feet up, it creates a dry winter which is never cold because the sun's rays, on the twelfth degree, slant relatively little, but it cools down the heat of summer. Thus temperatures are even, and their greatest yearly range is thirteen degrees.

But this rain, whose effects the Egyptian fellah enjoys every October, and the Abyssinian peasant rather earlier, visits the Abyssinian farmer in terrible guise: thunderstorms, heavier and more frequent than anywhere else on earth, cloud-bursts and hail, appearing and disappearing suddenly, like everything else in this strange land, destroy men, cattle, and huts. The number of thunderstorms has been reckoned at four hundred a year; hundreds are killed by lightning every summer, and not long ago the Emperor ordered services of intercession to be held because so many men had been struck down by it.

Though the rain arrives punctually, setting in, after a gentle beginning, with full force in the middle of June, as we know from Egyptian records which noted the beginning of the flood thousands of years ago, yet it varies greatly in strength and quantity. The mountains, the male element of this union, stand firm, and have probably not changed for the last few million years, but the sea, with its womanly passions, perhaps the jungle, too, with its secrets, these two most unexplored regions of the earth, load the wind with a quantity of moisture so variable that it cannot be calculated. So many peoples and generations of Egypt have studied this vital question through and through, and yet the height of the flood resulting from the rain has never once been successfully forecast for the following year. In close succession—in 1904 and 1908—one flood was twice as high as the other.

In its homeland, the rising Nile does not come in the guise of a liberator, as it does in Egypt, but appears like an angry god. Where it rises, in the region of Lake Tana, there rise with it two great tributaries, many small ones, and the Atbara, which flows northward alone. All these river beds run more or less dry in winter: the tributaries generally silt up, the Atbara always. Thus the peoples of these lands have had to turn nomad, spending the nine months' dry season where vestiges of water lie in the river beds, where men and beasts can find just enough to eat. The little, low-banked rivers which have inundated the country are often bordered with woodlands; the big ones, the Blue Nile and the Atbara, whose high banks generally prevent floods properly speaking, are separated from the plain and even from the desert by a narrow strip. Even along the driest brook, the acacia and even the palm grow, and the subterranean waters which so often in Africa proceed from the rivers nourish many springs.

With their camels and goats, with all they possess by way of women and children, these Arab nomads choose their camping-place in the dry, deep beds of these rivers, especially on the lower reaches where there is, after all, more food to be found than in the desert whence they come. There they knock from the doum-palm its dense clusters of fruit with hard kernels which can be ground into a resinous powder and cooked with milk as a cake; with poles they can shake down the seed-pods of the acacia, which yield a vestige of oil for the cattle, while the camel must be content with the dry thorns. Here they can repair their tents of leaves, and the palms supply them with mats and ropes. But the life-giving element is water, which lies here in pools.

In these pools, the crocodiles have forgotten the defection of their element; they half hibernate. A thousand doves and desert grouse drink at the pools where the crocodile sleeps, and even the gazelles, God's fleetest creatures, come punctually an hour before sunrise and after sunset to these most meagre of all drinking-places which the Nile has left behind.

Now danger haunts the springs, for not only men and cattle, but the beasts of prey too are attracted by them, and the Arab leads his cattle away from the water before dark, to leave the way open for the lions and leopards. The only stupid creatures are the baboons, who ought to be the wisest: the remains of dhurra-beer are left out for them, so that at times they have literally got drunk on it, and in that befuddled state have succumbed to craft. They are not half-men for nothing.

Suddenly, though the sky is clear blue, there is a rumble of distant thunder. All the thousands of men and women encamped in the river bed rush out, carrying their tents and their household goods with them, to take flight. A confused clamour arises—"El Bahr! The river!" Although these nomads reckon time by the moon and the stars, with their inertia, with the fatalism of the sons of the desert, they are always taken by surprise when the river dashes down from the highlands in the middle of June. In a few minutes, the rumble has swelled to a roar: that is the sign, dreaded and longed for. While, a thousand miles downstream in Egypt, hourly telegrams warn the engineer how far the river has travelled, how high it is, and how muddy, there is not even a camel-rider to tell the people who live in its bed what will happen the next minute. The thunder is the only harbinger.

El Bahr! A moving wall, the river approaches, fifteen hundred feet wide, pouring downward in brown waves, full of trees, bamboo, and mud, and so it hurries past.

And suddenly, as it came, the river awakens life on the banks. Already the rain is on its heels, and together they call forth buds, from the buds leaves, the buds overnight, the leaves immediately afterwards—they seem to unfold before one's very eyes. In the raging power of its youth, the Nile creates a green paradise where everything seemed to be thirsting to death. A few days, and round the pools where all the birds crowded for a drop of water to wet their throats, wild geese whir and mate and build. All the wild animals refresh themselves, wade and drink, and even the crocodile is joyfully startled, and thinks the drought was but a dream.

Even up in the highlands, thousands leave their homes and take refuge in the higher mountains, as men did in the Flood. All traffic is at a standstill in the rainy months, for nobody can cross the raging rivers, and even the poorest peasant going to the next village takes a kind of cape of papyrus with him to cower under when a fresh deluge overtakes him. The horses, who cannot cross the streaming valleys, stand unharnessed in the huts with the people, who pass the rainy months dully, perhaps sociably, but not impatiently. They all know it will not last long.

Only the nomads cannot linger where the gifts of God have enriched them. When the savanna greens, it at once becomes a swamp, a cloud of insects rises, the herds are in danger; even the most constant companion of man, the camel, flounders if its driver does not wait until the morning sun has dried off the surface a little. Men and beasts hurry to higher levels; the Nile creates wanderers. In three months, the greater part of the whole rainfall for the year has come down, and with it the flood. But in September, when the waters begin to abate, and men and beasts come wandering down again, the fat time begins. The whole earth is covered with rustling green, and the corn, which was planted in the soft muddy soil with a stick, ripens in a few weeks.

Permanent inundations such as those higher up on the White Nile are impossible on the steep slopes of the Blue Nile valley. For the rain has cut deep gullies in the volcanic rock, and in these narrow canyons river rapids and torrents have formed which all hurry westwards to the Nile. Thus the whole of the inner highlands looks rugged. Lower down, where the widened river enters the sandstone, it has eaten it down and reached the virgin rock. Here, where it has cut a deep, perpendicular bed for itself, and above, where it washes over volcanic strata, at all points it picks up minerals, which, in its rushing fall, it mixes with soil. Thus the silt is formed, a loose, unbound mass of feldspar, mica, and hornblende crystals, of chalky and ferruginous minerals, never two years the same, different on the Blue Nile and the Atbara, while its variations indicate differing sediments and the varying power of the river.

Man, too, has influenced this elemental downpouring. In prehistoric times, when the land was covered with forests, less water and less silt must have come down from the mountains, and the Blue Nile cannot have flowed into the White Nile at a time when a Mediterranean gulf is said to have lain where the Egyptian desert now lies. Man certainly began very early to fire the plain, and with it the forest, in order to produce fresh food for his cattle, and by deforesting the land, just as he does today in the steep highlands, he opened to the rain and hence to the rivers a free passage to the plain. In their turn, they washed the soil down with them, and now black masses of rock tower into the air, from which wind and water loosen millions of particles to enrich the yearly silt.

Thus Abyssinia, the "roof of East Africa," which lies so high that land up to 6000 feet is counted as lowland, by a unique combination of circumstances became the fountainhead of a life-giving element which has in its turn created a land without its like. Hephæstus is the father, for no country on earth has so many extinct volcanoes, and as these memorials of primeval time rise in ever new, fantastic forms, as ash-cones and lava-streams, hot springs and sulphur vapours, bear witness even today to the convulsions of the earth, this land will yield for millions of years to come the primeval substance which, carried away and deposited by the river, is transformed into new land.

Thus the winds, the rain, and the mountains of Abyssinia created, through their messenger, the Nile, that wonderful oasis in Egypt far away to the north.

2

LIKE its graver brother, the Blue Nile rises in a lake, but here there can be no doubt that the river first makes a brief passage through the lake, like a prelude to its song. In the high mountains lies the source of the "Little Abbai," the "Mother of the Abbai," that is, of the Blue Nile.

This mountainous country, lying 65 miles south of Lake Tana, on the eleventh parallel, gives birth to the river in the Gish valley, at an altitude of almost 9000 feet, which is higher than the sources of most European rivers. A sparse forest of cedar and juniper, of fig and euphorbia, is here interrupted by basalt rocks only half covered by the red soil. The high tree-heath does not bear fruit here, as it does on the equator, but it blossoms copiously, and beside it the white and pink balsam stretches out its red twigs. The golden-yellow flowers of the coreopsis and the purple patches of the acanthus lend colour to the grey-green of the mountain forest.

With the light the voices of the birds lend it life. When the goat-sucker has rent the night with its strange, hollow cry, the deep tuba tones of the helmet-bird begin before sunrise, the flute-bird tries its oboe, then the little starlings strike up, whistling an accompaniment to the morning song of the swallows, with the regular crotchets of the crickets fiddling the beat. But soon these tender sounds are drowned by the tussle of tropical screeching set up by the guinea-fowl and parrots.

In the middle of a moor, at the top of a steep slope, a palisade of bamboo has been planted round a hole rather more than a yard square. A moderately deep spring of very clear, very cold water, welling up quietly, flowing off without bubbles into a small runnel and then disappearing in an easterly direction behind the mountain forest, is the source of the Blue Nile, and only its volcanic origin can explain its extraordinary situation. Small and cramped, still and clear, compared with the heady, roaring fall in which the other Nile is born, it shows how little the first moments of a living being can foreshadow its later life. A great and grave character soon issued from the youthful turbulence of that other source, while from this still retreat an adventurer arises whose deeds amaze the world.

Yet the Blue Nile, with its first sound and step, reveals itself as the future eccentric. While the White Nile had to flow a thousand miles before it could be acclaimed as a wonder of the world, the Blue Nile, like the Prophet, is venerated even in its cradle. Here, too, the star appeared to a king in the distant east and prophesied to him that, far away in the mountains, a mighty creature had come to birth who should bear power and light over the desert even to the sea-coast. Christians and heathens pray at this source. The thatched hut with its surrounding gallery which stands by this and two other, smaller "Nile sources" is the Abyssinian State Church, and the bearded, ignorant man in front of it is its priest.

But the heathens who live almost untouched beside the Christians in these mountains take their shoes from their feet when they approach the rivulet. It flows through long stretches of little-known country, unwatched by present or past. The rain, which first makes the river important in the eyes of men, renders exploration difficult, just as, in the life of a prophet, the first years of withdrawal, a momentous epoch, are hidden from research.

Volcanic rocks in horizontal strata, bearing in parts traces of recent activity, and covered with vegetation, form a mountain landscape through which many small tributaries hurry to swell the stormy stream, till, having reached a width of about sixty yards, it settles into a flat alluvial plain. Then a great lake opens before it, it has reached the south-west shore of Lake Tana, to leave it again almost immediately.

This grey-green, heart-shaped lake, which the Nile quits like a great artery at its lowest point, lying at the same height of 6000 feet as the lakes of the Engadine, is flanked at a few points only by mountains of medium height: in general, the shores are flat, with palms and acacias, and poor thatched huts, the biggest of which, under the junipers, generally belongs to the "Ras," or prince, or is used as a church.

Today the lake is about as big as Lake Albert: once it was perhaps half as big again, but the rain made it shrink: decomposed lava, carried down for ages by its feeders, silted up the shores with mud, and thus hemmed in the lake. The lava and basalt on the shore, which show its volcanic origin, yield the first mud which the Nile takes up and carries away. Thirty rivers and brooks discharging into the lake are all smaller than the Abbai, and as this is the only outlet, Lake Tana must count as an important source of the Nile, and as such is more important to the Nile engineers than the Little Abbai, without whose inflow the lake would not lose much water: hence this lake may be called the source from a geographical rather than a hydrographical standpoint.

The crocodile has not reached the lake, but when the natives sail on its waters in boats of papyrus and reeds, they are exposed to danger from the hippopotamus which inhabits it. The thrilling hunt for this animal is so profitable that each man scratches his tribal sign on his harpoon: whoever strikes the animal first gets it, even though its body reappears above water only much later and far away. Thus the Caledonian boar was hunted by the Homeric heroes, and a tribal sign such as this on Lake Tana would soon have settled the epic struggle over Atalanta.

When the Abbai has flowed through the lake, visible and unmingled, for eight miles to the south—a stretch about as short as the course of the White Nile through Lake Albert—at the peninsula of Giorgia there lies a wide, deep bay: here the Blue Nile begins its real course. In the fields the coffee with its red berries still grows half wild, for Abyssinia is its home, and from here it migrated to Arabia. Red pepper grows near it; on long reaches the papyrus persists even through the dry season; and masses of yellow-starred flowers cover the slopes, a kind of prickly burr, whose black, barbed seed settles not only into the clothes, but into the skin, driving the traveller to despair. On the rocky islands fringing the shores oyster-beds and crabs are found, and egrets and wild doves nest there; the water is still, white and clear. It whirls out of the lake, falling only slightly at first, a hundred yards wide.

The course of the Blue Nile, which now really begins, shows how the river, like man, must, in spite of inconceivable deviations, yet travel its appointed road, and how it overcomes or circumvents every obstacle, so that it may irresistibly approach its appointed end in space and time. However clear the physical maps may look, indicating every hill as the cause of a bend, how is it possible to mistake the mysterious power which guides one river towards another through all hardships, through falls and deserts, through contradictions and ceaseless aberrations? If the whole course of a man's fate could, like that of a river, be contemplated from an aeroplane or on a map, its laws would stand clear before our eyes, and nothing would reveal the predestination governing the whole as clearly as the apparent fortuitousness of the detail. Only the man incapable of faith transfers his rationalistic scepticism to nature.

When it sets out, the Great Abbai seems to depart completely from the north-south course of the Little Abbai; to find its way north-west, it flows south-east, for the very range which gave it birth blocks its way to the goal. As beautiful in form as it is significant in symbolic strength, it streams round the Gojam Mountains, doubling its way to the White Nile, to which it was much nearer at its source. But when it enters the prairies of the Sudan, it is powerfully influenced, over a great distance, by the laws governing the stronger; here, where no mountains stand in the way, it takes, not the shortest cut, but the same north-westerly direction as that followed by the young White Nile and all its eastern tributaries.

From its first movement on leaving Lake Tana, the Blue Nile reveals the genius within it—a rashness which is yet fruitful. While it tears a huge gorge for itself through the rock, while it whirls down headlong so rapidly that in fifty miles it falls 4200 feet, yet from its earliest youth it brings with it the silt, the element of its later life-work, vital and productive from the beginning.

Where water and rock meet at the first cataract, the rocks are bare before the rainy season; later, when the flood has rolled away, and the river has sunk, they are covered with a flowery growth like sea-weed, with scaly stems springing from roots or

air-roots, and bearing a pink and green blossom which slowly
withers from its base until the rain, the next year, again washes
down the rocks. On these rocky walls, the fish lie in such heaps
that they can be caught with the hands, for, below, bigger ones
lie in wait for them, especially if they have injured themselves
against the rocks.

In the midst of the wilderness, close below the outflow, an old
stone bridge with many arches spans the river, lending it the romantic air of a copper engraving and speaking of ancient European civilizations, which are elsewhere alien to both the Niles.
This evidence of civilization certainly makes but a brief appearance, and only when the river, having passed through the utter
wilderness of its middle course, has neared its end through the
plain, is it crossed by another bridge, which is of a very modern
and very fatal kind. This first, basalt bridge, which the Portuguese built slanting over the river in the sixteenth century, takes
it through its middle arch, then the river quickly widens. Immediately afterwards, thirty miles from Lake Tana, the rocks narrow and force the Blue Nile, here in its very childhood, like the
White Nile in the far south, to pass through the adventure of a
great waterfall: this, too, is the only one in its life. The natives
call this fall Tisitat, that is, "Roaring Fire," just as the Victoria
Falls in Rhodesia are called "the Smoke That Sounds." The narrows in which the vortex breaks below simply look like a deep
hole, and it is inconceivable that the huge volume of water from
lake and rain can push its way through. Down there, they say, a
man in a battle dared the leap over the chasm, killed his enemy
on the farther side, and then achieved the still more difficult return leap.

Now the Nile is imprisoned in a canyon which, sliced into the
basalt, encircles the heart of the great mountains: for 500 miles it
is inaccessible, as the ravine sometimes drops to a depth of 5000
feet. Now it is alone, men flee not only the gorge, but the heights,
for a dense pall of fumes and suffocating smoke constantly rises
from the expanse of burning grass, and in it lurks fever for them
and their cattle. In the mountains, ten or twelve thousand feet
up, it is easier to live and breathe, and even the few explorers who
have ventured below lost most of their natives by fever, were able

to pay only brief visits to the bottom of the gorge, and have had to be content to represent long reaches of the river by dotted lines on their maps.

The only happy creatures on the southern Blue Nile are the animals. Here, where there are no harpoons nor spears nor bullets to startle the hippopotami and crocodiles down in their gorge, and the lions and leopards above on the banks, paradise has been preserved for them. Here all the wild animals live fearless, in heaps, pell-mell, more unmolested by man than in any other part of Africa. In delicious ignorance of the thermometer which, all the year round, even at night never falls below 100°, the wild animals live in brooding heat, and rich in the inexhaustible quantities of animal and vegetable food which the jungle lavishes on them.

Here, at 10° N. lat., winding about from east to west, inaccessible, so to speak, in its gorge, the Nile lives through the only long stretch of its course on which no face bends over it, no oar strikes its waters, no net catches its fish, no men bathe in it.

SWAMPS ON THE BAHR-EL-GHAZAL

GAZELLES ON THE STEPPE

3

FOR a hundred rivers and brooks water the animals on the higher levels before they, in their turn, plunge into deep chasms to reach the Nile below. In this ravaged land, where the mule can go no further, and the explorer has to climb 4000 feet down and up again to study the lower course of a brook, the Nile is often invisible from above, seems to be lost in its ravines and to flow on underground, but when it reappears, in spite of all its tributaries, it has not widened even in the rainy season. Evaporation, rapids, gravel, take away the water brought by the rather insignificant tributaries.

What increases is the silt, for as most of the tributaries flow from the heart of the mountains which it encircles, the countless mineral particles flowing into it darken its colour, which was quite clear when it left Lake Tana. "Bahr-el-Azrak," as the Arabs call it, means not only a blue, but a dark, or even black river. At low water, in the dry season, when it carries only 2 percent of solids, it often looks clear, and owing to the cloudless sky, blue, but in flood time, with 17 percent of solids, it turns reddish and dark, and billions of white ants, washed down with the water, swell the mud: some English scientists recently have even put forward the astonishing theory that it is the termites which throw up the fresh earth, and are swept away with it, and so become the true fathers of the Nile silt.

Up in the highlands, where men live, all the mineral deposits from the volcanoes are overgrown with a profusion of tropical vegetation. "The most beautiful country I ever saw," said Blundell, one of the few white men who were ever there, for here in the south of Abyssinia the land does not dry up so horribly even in the dry season as it does in the north, where in February it is impossible to understand how anybody could have placed the

Garden of Eden in so repellent a region. Here, to the north of the Abbai, the rain awakens a forest of magic colour.

The forest is shot with red and gold. From the immense baobab, which sometimes reaches a girth of sixty feet, from the huge euphorbias, hang the purple tufts of the loranthus; the dense hapericum bushes rustle in a sea of yellow blossom; beds of pale-blue clematis hang from the tamarisks; cascades of royal-blue salvias, festoons of wild vine, cover and sometimes kill what lives beneath them; for miles on end the gardenia shines through the green; the opalescent blooms of the protea cover forests of unknown extent; and the tree veronica forms tunnels so rich in flower that a caravan "could be buried in them."

High up in their mountain retreats, the natives can cultivate maize and wheat without difficulty: the earth and the rain do the work for them; they are less successful with the cotton, and even the coffee runs wild, as the vine once did in this region. With a plough such as Adam may have made after the expulsion, they turn up the soil anyhow, like the wild boars.

These lowest tribes of the land live as primitively as the Negroes on the Upper White Nile, but they keep a domestic pet whom they treat like a princely guest. Someone or other, whether a medicine man at court or some white man, when killing a civet cat, discovered the strong odour exuding from one of its glands—it may have been the three-hundredth concubine of the Emperor, who anointed herself with it, trying to infatuate her lord. In any case, the great ones of the land all at once began to seek this perfume, sent slaves through the country and found it here on the southernmost reaches of the Nile. Since then, the natives have caught these cats in snares. They keep them tame in their huts, give them beef for breakfast and porridge and milk for dinner. They even go so far as to warm their homes in winter in case the precious gland should be chilled. Then they scratch out of the gland a foamy white secretion which smells of musk, and collect it in ox-horns, and when the trader comes from the town, he gives them in exchange bars of salt and cloths, or silver money. Thus black men in the wild mountains of Abyssinia, who know nothing save hunger, hunting, and love, are made rich by the refinements of a distant court, increase their herds and fields, and in the end are no happier than their brothers, who empty no cats' glands.

Other animals are less familiar with court life. The gigantic grey baboon, which, in age, with its grey-black mane, is startlingly like a derelict tramp, breaks into the cornfields, but if he has been delayed, and arrives only for dessert, groups appear, gleaning in rows, more than ever like men, and the leopards, against which the great apes have set sentinels to protect their young, are doubly afraid. Not until the apes have gone do the leopards invade the villages.

Here, too, the elephants are the cleverest; they know exactly when the natives carry up the ripe corn on camels to their villages: then they charge, the camels cast their loads, and the giant gets what he wanted. Once upon a time, says the legend, a king invaded this country in order to subject the Negroes. As he seemed to these Negroes as terrible and wicked as the dreaded robber of their fields, they called aloud "Jan Hoy! Thou elephant!" The king had the word explained to him; being an oriental, he had a sense of humour, stopped his depredations, and promised justice and help to any who should call him by that name. Therefore later supplicants cast themselves at his feet in his capital crying: "Jan Hoy!" and in the end the word came to mean merely "O King! Your Majesty!" Thus an ordinary emperor of Abyssinia was invested with the honour and the title of the strongest and cleverest animal of creation.

In winter, the elephant retires to the wild south, scaling slopes that defy man. Here, where the Blue Nile receives the Didessa from the left and begins its great sweep to the north, the elephant is attracted by young bamboo forests. There hundreds of great trees lie prone: these are hegleek trees, of whose little sweet fruit the elephant is inordinately fond. Like many strong men, he has a sweet tooth, and so he stands shaking the tree with his trunk, but if nothing falls off, he simply overthrows the whole tree, and then stands picking up the sugar-plums carefully one by one.

Below that loop of the river, the highlands gradually fall away, the gorge grows milder: first a few miles of the stream can be seen, then comes the plain of the Fung province. Isolated groups of hills merge into the Sudan lowlands. Before it leaves Abyssinia, the Nile is confronted with a strange sight, which throws a far-reaching light onto the fate of the country.

At the mouths of the Didessa and similar rivers flowing into the Nile near the frontiers of the Sudan, a few hundred naked Negroes sit cowering in the water. What are they doing here in the torrid heat, whose fevers they generally shun? Others come out of the forest carrying a kind of hockey-stick and a flat wooden platter, with a little gourd hanging from their ear by a string. Then they crouch in the shallows, feel about along the stones with deft fingers, search their flat hands with a rapid glance, and throw most of the dross back, but what they collect on the platter glistens in the sun. When the day's work is over, they pour their takings into the gourd and carry it to the overseer, who weighs it up with little European scales.

By the deep erosion of the overlying basalt, the gneissic strata below have been so denuded that whole tracts are covered with gravel and flakes of quartz. That they contained gold was already known in ancient times, and the fate of the country has been determined by the search for gold and slaves. In many other places, the god of the subterranean fires, before heaving up the earth, mixed gold with it, and as it can be easily seen and washed out of the rivers, the princes of the country have worked it since prehistoric times. Once it was even believed that the land of Ophir lay here. At present, the annual revenue is said to amount to $400,000, but when have absolute rulers ever given accurate accounts of their revenues? And the Emperor straightway officially keeps half as a tax.

It is collected in quills, made into rings, and stamped, then sold. What is brought into the country in exchange? Machinery and arms. Who profits by them? The natives, cowering for ten hours in the river washing the gold from the volcanic debris for the kings, are slaves—Galla—who get neither salt nor silver, neither necklaces nor cows for it. Far away from them, where the glandular secretion of the civet cats is transformed into the perfumes of Addis Ababa, under the lights of a richly carpeted room, the gold glitters on the neck of some lady whose Byzantine eyes are hungry for the gifts of life, or it has been metamorphosed into a smart, well-sprung English car in the depths of which a ring-bedecked Ras reclines, brooding new desires and new revenge.

Just as he brooded three thousand years ago.

4

IN those days, the loveliest and most famous princess of Abyssinia adorned herself with gold and jewels to ride to Jerusalem, where, it was said, there reigned a prince as handsome and as famous as herself, whom she was impatient to greet in person. Actually, she was the ruler of the land which later bore the splendid name of Arabia Felix. Merchants had come from Palestine to Yemen to seek costly building-stones and to take them, whatever their price, to their lord, who was building a temple to the glory of his god, Jehovah. The mouth of that king, they said, was overflowing with story and fable, but most of all with songs of love, and none could say whether he knew more of wisdom or of women.

So the Queen of Sheba journeyed to King Solomon, and each found favour in the other's sight; but being a clever woman, she held him off at first and refused to lodge in his palace. When he began to pay court to her, she led the talk into the domain of wisdom, and he must perforce spend whole evenings philosophizing with the lovely woman, from whom he desired entertainment of a very different kind, for Solomon was a gentleman. When at last the day of her departure approached, and the caravan of the guest was laden with truly Jewish lavishness by the king, she became aware of the growing restlessness of her host, who, for all his wisdom, now felt very foolish, and she loosed the reins of her decorum, for, with feminine logic, she argued that she could, after all, leave the next day. So she plucked up courage and told the king that she would spend her last night in his palace if he would swear not to molest her, while she, for her part, would promise to lay hands on nothing that was his. King Solomon in his wisdom grasped the double meaning in her words, but just to make sure, summoned his cook and told him to spice the farewell meal as he had never done before.

Then the Queen saw that her host had understood her, and when at last she was alone with him under his roof, spices and wine had done their work so well that she only needed to say to him:

"I will release you from your vow, O King, if you will give me to drink."

The courteous king fulfilled her wish in every way. Her departure was postponed. Now he was more than ever reluctant to let her go, and she seems to have put no difficulties in his way. But when she was with child, and, as the months passed, her state became obvious to the whole court, she decided to depart, and with the Song of Solomon he seems then to have sung his swansong. It was high time for her to go, for on the way she gave birth to a son, whom she called Menelek ibn Hakim, that is, the Son of Wisdom, and he was very handsome.

When he had come to the throne, the youth visited his father in Jerusalem, was received with great rejoicing, and sent away with great gifts from all the twelve tribes of Israel, with warriors and priests, who were to give the Abyssinians thorough instruction in the Jewish religion. But hardly was Menelek gone when dismay fell upon Solomon: the Ark of the Covenant, the tables of stone on which Moses had written down the commandments of the Lord, the most holy possession of the Jews, was gone! Later, Menelek declared that his priests had stolen it without his knowledge, but any king would say so in such a situation. That is what priests and ministers are for. One thing is certain, that his father, in his wisdom, swore the High Priest to secrecy and pursued the caravan himself, but it had vanished. As so often happened in those times, angels had protected the robbers, who made their escape by passages under the Red Sea to their royal fortress. But Solomon had the tables copied by a good forger, and none of the Jews ever knew that from that time on the Ark that they worshipped was a fake.

So busily have Arab and rabbinical legends spun their enigmas round the figure of the Queen of Sheba as Biltis and Sibyl that she even had to prophesy the cross of Christ. To this very day, the Abyssinians cling to this legend, and have painted it a hundredfold on the walls of their churches. Today they have it printed in

Paris or London and distribute it broadcast over the country, and the lovers lie first in two beds, and then in a somewhat modern single one. But the Song of Solomon is obviously too gallant to have been addressed to the mother of their race: they declare that he laid it in the lap of one of Pharaoh's daughters, and strive in vain to forbid their young women and priests to read it, since they might read it together.

In this amorous fashion, a dynasty was founded which, in historic times, from 800 B.C. to A.D. 800 ruled longer than any other on the Mediterranean. No wonder that a clever prince, seeking in our own time to establish himself as ruler of this land, proclaimed his descent from this royal house of Solomon, and took the name of Menelek.

What has happened since at this edge of Africa is to be understood only through the mingling of the races and cultures which approached Abyssinia over the Red Sea and through the Nubian desert: the Abyssinians know that, and have themselves called their country Habesh, that is, the mixture. Every state in Europe might bear the name of Habesh.

For the conquering and trading peoples of antiquity were always drawn to the land which contained gold, ivory, and slaves. Which races supplanted which, how far the Hamitic peoples pushed the Semitic southwards—such things are uncertain, and are merely a parlour game for professors. The Ethiopians seem only once to have invaded a foreign civilization when, about 730 B.C., they conquered Egypt, bringing back with them later many Egyptian gods and customs. The Greeks, who called this country and its neighbour Kush by the general name of Ethiopia —the name it again bears today—became mixed with Jewish and Arab elements: Aksum, the remains of which were recently excavated in the north of Abyssinia, for a long time ruled Arabia too. To complete the confusion of cultures, a Jewish-Arab king about A.D. 300 called himself "Son of Ares": this scion of the Greek gods was the first to be baptized, obviously in expiation. Thus the Son of Ares wore the legendary three rings on his finger before the legend came into being. For the Abyssinians became Christians long before most of the white peoples, and the curious fact that these brown races possess today a Christian cult fifteen

TRAVELLERS

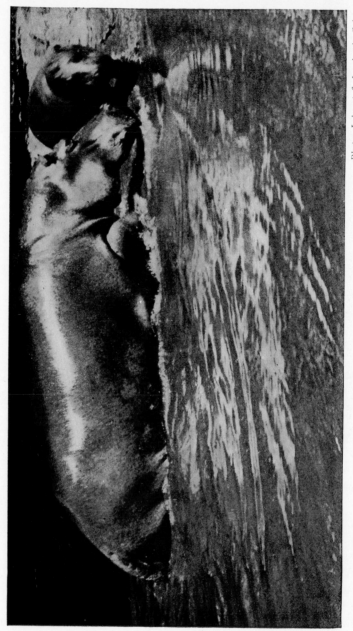

Photo: Lehnert & Landrock, Cairo

HIPPOS

centuries old provides a unique opportunity for inquiring how far they have reached a higher stage of moral development than their heathen and Mohammedan neighbours.

Beset on both sides, the young Christianity wavered. When the Abyssinian Christians threatened Mecca, they were repulsed in the very year of Mohammed's birth; soon after, they had to withdraw from southern Arabia on account of smallpox, one of the few cases in history in which a pestilence has involved world-wide political consequences. At that point the struggle between the two religions began. Meanwhile, in this Greek-Arab-Christian chorus, the Jews raised their voice, and endeavoured from the sixth century on to re-establish their religion in Abyssinia, long after the Greek Ethiopians are believed to have embraced the Jewish faith. This was carried out not by missionaries, but by the influence of nomads transmitting their customs to other nomads. While they called themselves "Falasha," that is, "the misunderstood," the Jews grew strong.

In the ninth century history took an ironic turn, for which documentary evidence again exists. A Jewish princess in Abyssinia drove out the dynasty descended from Solomon, which had later become Christian, and, under the name of Queen Judith, made herself mistress of the north. Not for four hundred years, till about 1260, did a Christian prince of the south, who traced his descent from Menelek and Solomon, succeed in conquering the descendants of Judith, and the new king draped his lust of power and his jealousies with anti-Semitic speeches, just as if he had lived seven hundred years later.

In bestowing upon themselves the title of Archpriest, these Christian kings made themselves no whit better than Judith. The kaleidoscope of their history, in the next few centuries, turns in bewildering pictures. Conquered queens were hacked to pieces and thrown to the dogs, and after their death the monks walked in public procession; there were chaste-living clerics who compensated themselves with wine and roast meat, invaded heathen chiefs, feasted with them, and then had their hosts slaughtered by their slaves, and all these were Christians, proud of their faith, who boasted of being the oldest sect.

5

AT first, Abyssinia was believed to be the land of Paradise, and even Josephus acknowledged the Nile to be one of the two Biblical rivers. But since, after the Fall, gold and power became men's chief motives, the nations came hither seeking gold and slaves: the land had no defence save mountains and rain. While in the plains of the Sudan, princes and dynasties, in the course of the ages, succumbed again and again to foreign marauders, the land of mountain fastnesses, like Switzerland, held all at bay: here the rain swept away roads and armies, for the land, save at one point, falls steeply even to the Red Sea, where, since prehistoric times, the commerce of the world has streamed past. Thus, of all the empires which flourished in Africa between 10° and 15° N. lat., only one remained, the country of the Blue Nile, a natural fortress.

From the ancient Egyptians to the traders of today, men came here seeking incense and ivory, gold and slaves; Abyssinian ivory goes back in Egypt even to prehistoric times; in the train of the merchants, three religions and four or five different civilizations spread light and chaos through these steep and narrow mountain valleys. But if they tried to conquer the country, mountains, precipices and rivers, men, and rain united to expel the intruders. Yet the same elements split this empire up into so many separate lands that no one has ever been able to rule it as a whole: the princes are perpetually at war with each other, and compel every man to be a soldier. If no one could conquer this strange empire from the outside, no one could govern it within: disunited and impregnable, encircled by desire and curiosity, the natural fortress rises like a humped shoulder at the edge of the continent, courted by the white powers which govern its neighbours, for it conceals within it the sources of the mysterious river which yet, as we shall see later, is innocent of all the legend woven round it.

Historical documents, stretching back thousands of years, tell of all the conquering strangers who were driven out of Abyssinia, from the oldest reports on papyrus of Egyptian journeys and landings on the Red Sea to the stone tablets recording the treaties of the Queen of Sheba; from the obelisks of the Ethiopians, which were raised a thousand years before Christ by methods we cannot even imagine, to Herodotus, who tells in a fable of the treasures of Abyssinia. Here Roman emperors caught elephants to perform for the amusement of the people, and Byzantine emperors bartered worthless things for gold.

In ancient history, one white people after the other penetrated into those inaccessible and pathless regions, yet none remained, and native princes ruled with hardly an exception from Solomon's day to our own.

Even later, the great sea-faring peoples succeeded only in establishing trade here. Venice drove the Arabs from the Red Sea coast, so that they had once more to carry the gold and ivory of Abyssinia through the desert on camels. The only memorial left behind by this strongest sea-power of its time was the bad pictures of an adventurer who was hailed here as a second Titian because he came from Venice; even today, the traveller is struck by the Italian style of their crude sacred pictures.

Once, in distress, an Abyssinian Negus, Emperor, and Archpriest recalled his Christian descent and called on the Pope for help against the infidels; the Pope confined himself to a fine Latin letter, which nobody in Abyssinia could read, and gave the pious Moors a church in Rome which, eight centuries later, is still called San Stefano dei Mori. Later, Abyssinian pilgrims in Jerusalem heard that the mightiest Christian of the time was the King of Portugal, but when the glittering embassy reached his court, he turned his back on the "Negroes," not trusting their Christianity. So deep was the darkness in which the Abyssinians lived three centuries after their entry into Rome.

Not until the next century did the Christian brothers embrace, and he who was powerful promise help to the oppressed. In the meantime, the Portuguese had not only heard that in that dubious Moorish land there were ivory and slaves to be had for nothing, but hearsay also told that the very earth there consisted of two parts of gold to one of soil, and though the king thought that must be an exaggeration, he hoped perhaps for one part of gold to two of soil. At first, the Portuguese had to pay dearly for their adventures. When they advanced from the Red Sea to help the king against the Arabs, who had spread over half Abyssinia from Egypt, converting it to Islam by force, not only was one of their noblest knights, the son of Vasco da Gama, captured and tortured, but his victorious enemy beheaded him afterwards with his own hands. The conquered Christians were castrated to a man. This happened in 1541. Centuries were to pass before a Christian king was to have a literal revenge—member for member. Two years later, the Portuguese were victorious and restored the Abyssinian king. How was King Claudius to show his gratitude now?

By way of thanks, he decided to have himself baptized in a slightly different form by adopting the Catholic ritual, and thus conjured up fresh struggles. Portuguese scientists and merchants remained in the country. The procedure of former kings had been never to let an ambassador go, but to pay him in women and treasure for advice of priceless value, and thus, in the most graceful way, to hold him prisoner. Then, north of Lake Tana, the Portuguese built the fortress and city of Gondar, with huge round towers and frowning walls like those in Toledo, which are the only bit of Europe, outside of the modern capital, to stand out from the Negroid architecture of the empire.

But it seemed the inevitable fate of this wild mountainland to be rent by religious warfare, whose storms tore as much away from the natural fortress as the rain and the Nile. Roman Jesuits, sent out by the Pope, went restlessly about the land in quest of power. On the confines of the Christian world, among half-Negroes, the struggle for the teaching of Christ began at the same time and with the same passion as in Europe. When the Mohammedan menace had disappeared, the Christians decided to fall upon each other. Why did these Arab-Jewish chiefs, whose churches were huts, and whose religious ceremonies were drums and shrieks, batter each other's head in?

Jesus was anointed by the Holy Ghost, but He did not need it.

Wrong, cried the antagonists, His dual nature was first made one by this anointment. Wrong again, cried yet others, he could fulfil the Redemption only through the Holy Ghost. At times all three sects united in the cry: "Kill the Jews!" Then they again fell apart and in the very year, 1630, in which Gustavus Adolphus, Wallenstein, and Tilly were driving Christians before their guns, each in the delusion that he possessed the true Christ, Coptic and Catholic priests in Abyssinia were setting loose their flocks on each other with sword and lance for the interpretation of the same doctrine.

In these sectarian disputes the empire fell apart, just as did the German Empire at the same time. The heathen Galla, a mixed race of Negroes, Hamites, and Arabs, invaded the country from the south; the capital shifted about continuously in rebellions and dynastic changes; the Negus in Gondar became a shadow; every prince ruled with his own mailed fist, if not with his own head. Two centuries of anarchy were brought to an end in 1850 by an adventurer, Kassa, who began as a bandit chief, like the Homeric heroes and modern dictators, and who, to provide for all contingencies, took the title of Negus Negesti, or King of Kings, and at the same time the name of Theodore.

This Christian Archpriest, who began by trading in cusso, the remedy for tapeworm, then rose as rapidly from robber chief to emperor as Napoleon from lieutenant to emperor, also recalls certain phenomena of our time in that he lost his head in gaining power, settled down to be a monster, killed all who stood in his way, and finally forced the Patriarch to consecrate him at the point of a pistol. The death of his second wife plunged him into gloom, and as his third was merely the daughter of a powerful prince, he consoled himself with a beautiful Galla woman. As both the slender women had to accompany him on all his campaigns, their tents stood at equal distances on each side of his scarlet imperial tent, but on the march, just to make sure, the rivals rode half an hour apart.

The only Europeans whom Theodore acknowledged were the English, because he wanted their help against the Egyptians. His friendship for two Englishmen was so intense that, to avenge their death in one of his battles, he had hundreds of prisoners beheaded. But as the Irish hunter and the Scottish consul were, after all, dead, he could see only one figure in England worthy of him, namely, the Queen. For she had just become a widow, and would assuredly be glad to strengthen her power over a number of dark races by a union with the most powerful emperor in Africa. In 1862, without further ado, he sent her an offer of marriage.

The incredible happened; the letter remained unanswered. It was hardly to be expected that the mightiest of emperors was going to suffer the affront. The Negus was beside himself, and had the English ambassador, Cameron, cast into prison and chained to a common criminal. Now, for the first time, a great white power took the field against Abyssinia: the English punitive expedition advanced, besieged the King of Kings in his fort, and demanded the release of the prisoner. But then the adventurer recalled his bold beginnings. He shot himself, and by this resolute gesture won the respect of posterity for his character, for at least he knew how to pay up.

6

IT was the mountains which made warriors of the Abyssinians; for thousands of years, the rain has interrupted every war. In Abyssinia, hate can flourish only from October to May. With the help of these two elements, this half-savage mountain people even made a successful stand against the second latest technique of warfare: in the seventies and nineties, they inflicted a crushing defeat on two peoples equipped with modern arms—first Egypt, three times, then Italy—driving them from the country. When, in 1885, the Sudan was in the hands of the Mahdi, Egypt fully occupied, and Abyssinia threatened by the Mahdi's followers, it was easy for Italy to assume the role of protector of the country with the object of securing, at the last moment, a precious lump of the great black cake. The embroilments of the great powers even then seemed to be deciding the fate of Abyssinia: no one believed it could hold out.

But when the last Emperor had fallen on the frontier fighting against the Mahdi, one of his most powerful vassals had proclaimed himself Emperor, and as he had, at that moment, good reason to dread the power of the Mahdists, he preferred to cede to Italy a certain amount of territory with a general protectorate. This remarkable man had learned from the white tribes that it is the proper thing to have a noble lineage attested by the competent authorities, and hence took the name of Menelek II, as the blood descendant of the first Menelek who, three thousand years before, had, like Euphorion, inherited the beauty of the Arab Helen with the wisdom of the Jewish Faust.

This second Menelek was, it is true, rather cunning than wise, and though he was handsome, all the same there was something of the lion about him. Neither Semitic nor Negro features distinguish him in his blondness from a Nordic type, and, if the big lower lip on his portraits is covered, he looks like some robust Scandinavian whose eyes might have been grey-blue. Less cruel, more rustic, more sensible than his countrymen and peers, thoughtful and humorous, his manners have little in common with those of his predecessors. His hands and handwriting were equally beautiful, so far as the Amharic letters can be judged.

In his youth, as the son of a mighty prince, he had sought to legitimate himself in every possible way. Having, at the age of forty-five, taken the reins of power into his hands, he made his rival his friend by giving him his daughter to wife, and turned for support to the priests, about whom he had no illusions. As the Negus is master of all the possessions of his subjects, a kind of reversed communism, he let the princes go on stealing as they liked, altered nothing at the head of the state, and very little below, and drew his innovations rather from his inborn common sense than from the imitation of the whites, from whom he adopted little except the army. He tolerated no prisons because "I will not have criminals fed at the expense of honest men, quickly forgotten and never seen." He had the less serious offenders flogged, the more serious mutilated on the face or the genitals, so that they should go about as a scandal and a warning. In his new capital, Addis Ababa, he would often, on a Sunday, entertain three or four thousand of his subjects, mostly soldiers, distributing among them ten thousand loaves, five hundred gallons of mead, and two hundred oxen.

Like all barbarians, and most white men, nothing impressed him so much as the achievements of technical science, but he regarded them with the innocence of a child and a soldier. When he was shown the model of a modern bridge, he refused to believe that it would stand firm, and proved himself right by breaking the model with his fist; a second, more solidly constructed, convinced him because he could not break it. He was the first to have gold coins minted with the effigy of the Emperor, oiling the minting machine with his own hands; when the first coins fell out, he wrapped them up in his handkerchief and took them home to his wife. He trusted his telescope more than his spies: having been warned against assassins, he mounted his tower, searched the streets and squares with his glass, and came down reassured. When the effect of the explosion of mines by electricity was demonstrated to him with puppets, he broke out indignantly: "That is the way you want to make war? What is the use of a man being brave if a coward can destroy thousands at a distance by pressing a button!" With this splendid flash of vision, a bold African warrior reduced to absurdity the white theory of heroism.

The decisive act of his life was perhaps due to a mistake, for when he concluded the Italian convention he seems to have overestimated the power of that state, and to have known too little about its greater rivals in Africa. It may be that he made use of Italy only in order to gain security and time to arm. In any case, he declared himself free to negotiate with other white powers, since in the convention he had only expressed his "right" to use Italy in his dealings with them. The Italians, on the other hand, argued that he was "bound" by the convention to use Italy as a channel for communication. Since a mere "right" would be pure nonsense in this case, it may be inferred that the whole thing was a trick by which he was trying to evade the treaty. His army was ready, the danger from the Mahdi past, the natural fastness, with the mountains and the rain, as impregnable as when the volcanoes were created. Thus he could venture on a duel with Italy and his victory was decisive. Now vengeance was exacted for that battle of three and a half centuries before: in good old fashion the Christian Emperor of Abyssinia had a large number of his Christian enemies castrated.

But it was not that outrage that made the cabinets of Europe tremble: a minister never thinks of the fate of his soldiers, otherwise he would stop making war. He thinks in terms of countries whose inhabitants are not present to his mind, a lack of imagination which has cost the lives of millions of men who showed far more imagination, since they believed in the ideals held up to them, for which it was a duty and an honour to die.

After the Battle of Aduwa, in 1896, the most far-seeing Europeans were gloomy. A great white power had suffered a crushing defeat at the hands of a coffee-brown tribe. Did that mean the rise of the coloured peoples, the revolt of the black soul? Had it been shown once for all that Abyssinia was by nature proof against conquest, like Russia? And had the source of the Nile, on whose possession the fate of two great countries depended, for ever slipped out of European hands? The Mahdists, though weakening, still dominated the Sudan, and the legendary "key to the Nile," stories of which circulated through an ignorant world, could decide who was to be master there and in Egypt. The victor of Aduwa, however, impressed his white colleagues by demanding from conquered Italy, when peace was concluded, neither more nor less than Bismarck after Sadowa, namely, recognition.

Menelek, the strongest African of modern times, was destroyed by a woman. Taitu means "The Mote in the Sunbeam"; in reality, she was a designing woman, who, in the then Prince Menelek, married her fifth husband: slender and fragile, she has nothing in common with the pictures of the fat old woman whose features spread all over Europe as hers. It was her white skin which had made her so much desired. As he remained without an heir, and appointed his daughter's son to be his successor, while she had fixed on her brother as Emperor, hoping to retain some share of power, she resorted to a method much in favour among the nobles of Abyssinia: she gave him poison; it did not kill him, although he was well on in the sixties. His mind clouded, his body paralysed, the miserable man, in lucid moments, grasped what was going on and once more appointed his heir.

Court intrigues darkened his shadowy end, but when Menelek died in 1913, in his seventieth year, he had united his empire after an anarchy lasting more than a century, and made one whole out of seven kingdoms and widespread colonies.

7

―――――――

TWO travellers are wending their way through the mountain gorge by the side of a half-dry river. The big man in front is the Apostle Peter, just as he stands on the mosaics of Ravenna, the bronzed face framed in long brown hair and a short black beard, with black, liquid eyes, and a headdress without shape or colour; in his hands he bears before him a great naked sword with a cross on the hilt, such as the Crusaders used to carry. Behind him, his slave, in his loose grey garment, bare-legged, without hat or shoes, is so bowed by the weight of the burden he carries that his face is hidden. Thus the real Abyssin-ian, far from the capital, journeys through his mountains, some-times by mule, often on foot, in the year of Our Lord 1930, though it might be 1130.

In the interior, it is impossible to distinguish the types, which on the coast show more definitely Arab, in the south more defi-nitely Negroid features. Here a predominantly Hamitic stock has been modified by overwhelming mixture, and darkened by blood and the sun, and it seems almost symbolic that nearly all the tribes have a yellow conjunctiva and yellow half-moons to their nails. An unexplained peculiarity is that they are nearly all left-handed, carry their weapons and use their implements with their left hands, and mount their horses on the off-side, while the only thing that these orientals regard as an exception, as something sacred, namely, money, they tender with the right hand.

The nobles look like the apostles. There sits St. Mark in a white cloak, with tight-fitting trousers and sleeves, his sword at his side, absolutely Byzantine in his woven chair, with slaves washing his feet. Others, in their clay huts, don gaudy, richly embroidered cloaks to meet their guests, while their bearing, their features, their bronzed skin, and splendid colours, make them look as if they had stepped out of a group by Tintoretto. This, and their dark eyes, their observant silence, and the weapons they never lay aside, give them the dramatic mien of prophets. The greatest of all, the Ras, with their silken cloaks fastened only at the top by a narrow band fitting closely to the neck, would look like Titian portraits if their lips were thinner; behind them, there gleams in the gloom a shield, a short sword, and a lance. In stature and colour they generally look healthy, and they live long in the pure mountain air.

Reserve seems to enfold the upper-class women with their almond eyes; they seldom go out, and only at home, where they are generally allowed to sit with the men, can the skill of their hairdressing be seen: this is their chief occupation, though their hair looks short, being deftly woven into many tight plaits, while the uncut hair of the men looks longer. The butter which both sexes rub into their hair smells rancid, but the women are so proud of their handiwork that they sleep at night with their head on a block of wood for fear of disarranging it. Like the savage tribes in Paris they pluck out their eyebrows, and paint arched ones in brown; further, their lids are painted black, their hands and feet red or brown.

Abyssinia is a theocracy, and as such has no real religious feeling: everything has petrified into rites in this medievalism without mysticism, which is sunk in superstition and ruined by trade. According to the accounts of the most observant travellers, the line of morality rises from the Christians through the Mohammedans to the Jews and the heathens.

With flowing black or grey beards, gigantic white turbans, and shoes turned up at the toes, with a cross of bone or metal dangling on their breasts, priests and monks wander through the country by hundreds of thousands. Many say millions. The upper ranks are men of learning and, like most of the Copts, have some knowledge of the world: they refuse to be enticed out of their cloud of wisdom, and threaten with the death penalty the translation of the Bible from old Ethiopian into living Amharic. By excommunication and other psychological methods, they have got possession of large tracts of land, which they farm out or have tilled by slaves; they lend money and hire out service, and in other ways live, like the medieval bishops, on their influence over the chiefs. The Archbishop, whose title is "Pope of the Copts and Abyssinians," and who is elected by the central Coptic synod in Alexandria, must be a layman of a low class. He is then carefully educated, solemnly consecrated, and sent out, but may never again leave Abyssinia. The prisoner of the Vatican had an easier life.

The mass of the priests have less difficulty in veiling their wisdom from the eyes of the people. They are completely uneducated, some cannot even read. Some man, too poor to live like a lord, too lazy to learn the use of arms, in his youth, by services rendered, by money or relationship, has won the favour of a higher priest, who has made the sign of the cross three times over him, breathed on him, and thus ordained him priest, much as the German princes used to become regimental commanders. Thus, for the rest of his life, he is provided for: he must be fed, for he can bless and give absolution; but he is despised and feared by all. These lower orders of the clergy may marry, but only once: if the wife of one of them dies, he is through with marriage. Idle and penniless, their numbers swelled by the dethroned, the disinherited, or by political criminals who find sanctuary in the cloisters, terrorized by menaces from within and without, monks and nuns live in sloth and sexual looseness and have forfeited all respect. This legion of mendicant monks has no occupation save lofty debates with foreign missionaries on the dual nature of Jesus, and whether He was baptized once, twice, or thrice.

When the priest celebrates the divine office in the fine highland church huts, as often as not wrapped in a sheepskin, for they are always cold, holding the cross and rosary in his huge peasant fists, neither he nor any man present must have looked at a woman for twenty-four hours, but the African howls of the faithful, men and women, the din of the drums, the braying of the asses and the lowing of the cows, recall an orgy. If piety could be measured by the number of church festivals, then the Abyssinian Copts would have no equal for piety: two-thirds of the days in the year are feast-days, every Wednesday and Sunday fast-days, and, considering the general laziness, it is difficult to say what is cause and what effect.

Thus the majority of the Abyssinians—there are no certain figures, four millions of the ten are said to be "pure"—live proud to belong to the oldest Christian sect, in a mental twilight, far inferior to the Negroes on Lake Victoria, to whom no faith and no dogma ever penetrated. Yet they have nothing of the divine innocence of the Dinka, vegetating in the sun, but only a spurious faith in God which gives them pride and deprives them of freedom.

The Mohammedans are more industrious; they are said to number only a few hundred thousands and live mostly in the northerly province of Harrar. Even though the fabrics they weave are not very good, they work hard, and although they misunderstand the precepts of their hygienic religion, they at any rate keep them. As the hippopotamus is called the river hog, they do not eat it because pork is prohibited. For their girls, they have invented or adopted—for it exists on the middle White Nile too—a device which even the Crusaders could not match with their gir dles: they sew them up with horse hair so that they shall enter marriage chaste. Jealous husbands have introduced the same practice among their wives before going on a journey. It comes cheaper than having them guarded by eunuchs, who are very expensive here.

As to the Falasha, the Jews, who, numbering about fifty thousand, represent today only about half of one percent of the total population, it cannot be definitely ascertained whether they came with their religion a thousand years before Christ, or only after the beginning of the Christian era. The Jewish monotheism, which then stood alone, early attracted the Arabs and converted the princes. Nowadays they know no Hebrew, do not believe in the Messiah, and do no trading. Moreover, in physique, they resemble the other Abyssinians in the African cast of mouth and nose, while on the other side of the Red Sea, on the same latitude, they stand out clearly from the Arabs. They are distinguished here only by their common sense and their high moral standard, which is acknowledged in all Christian and Mohammedan accounts: a German traveller even described them as the most useful inhabitants of the country.

They are the best artisans in Abyssinia, the only smiths, the most in demand as builders, chemists, potters, and silversmiths. Settled in the neighbourhood of the capital and round about Lake Tana, they sometimes own land, but are not rich and neither lend money nor hire out service. Their churches are very like those of the Christians, but they keep secret their rites, emblems, and books, which are in Amharic. They keep the rules of food and ablution and purify themselves after any contact with a non-Jew. They know nearly as little of the Bible as the Christians.

The influence of Jewish on Christian rites, though the Christians came much later, seems to be as strong as ever, despite the great decrease in the numbers of the Jews. The Christians have adopted from them circumcision, which they practise on both sexes, keep the Sabbath holy as well as Sunday, and reckon their calendar from the beginning of the world; their priests dance round the Holy of Holies, they build their churches on the plan of Solomon's temple, prefer the Old Testament, believe in the return to Jerusalem, and say in greeting: "The Sabbath be with thee."

The heathen Galla, who, in the fourteenth century, advanced from Mount Elgon in the south on account of the lack of pasture, and are numerous today all over the country both among chiefs and among slaves, are accounted the best soldiers with sword and bow and arrow, but use no firearms; they are splendid horsemen, and hence are much used as mercenaries by the chiefs in their internecine wars. In contrast to the Christians, they are described as hard-working, energetic, and temperate, but they have all the Christian cruelty and vindictiveness. It was they perhaps who first introduced the custom of castrating the enemy and hanging the severed organ as a trophy on their belt or on the dead man's door. If the wife lives with the victor without her dead husband being represented on the doorpost, the other women abuse her. The Galla are said to practise human sacrifice to their gods, lots being cast for the victim in time of dearth; at the source of the Nile, which they fear, they sacrifice cows and bulls. They worship the sun, fire, and trees, and three great stones on the Blue Nile which fell from the sun, but their customs vary from village to village, and when among them there appear vestiges of ancient Egyptian civilization, with its priest-king and holy bull, there rises before one's eyes a panorama of cultures such as only the Nile, in the whole western world, could produce.

CONFLUENCE OF THE TWO NILES, SEEN FROM
THE AIR

ABYSSINIAN SOLDIERS

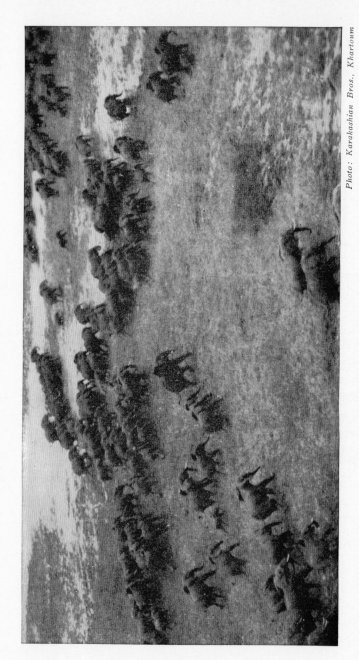

ELEPHANT HERD

8

THE narrowness of the gorges, the phenomenon of the rain, the size of the country, which is bigger than France and Italy put together, the difficulty of government in a land refractory to centralization and bound by no ancient sense of the community such as Switzerland's, the warlike spirit which hampers industry, the crowd of priests, whom all shun, the absolutism of a central power continually assaulted by individuals—all these factors would simply produce anarchy if the slaves were not there to form a foundation. Through them, any attempt at social reform becomes superfluous; the social question is solved in the simplest way, and if these people were not Christians, there would be nothing against it. The contradiction between power and faith is not greater, it is only more obvious, than among the white races of Europe.

It begins with the Most Christian Emperor, who, only thirty years ago, had five hundred concubines, twenty of whom he kept in the immediate vicinity of his palace. The strange fallacy of all these tribes, that a ruler must have as many sons as possible, seems to play a determining part in this question. In old Arabia, where grace was blended with dignity, and not only in the Arabian Nights, a sultan's mistress received lavish gifts. But the Christian Emperor regarded such a position as so desirable that every concubine had to bring a great dowry with her, cattle and horses, slaves and furs, or, as we sometimes read in the marriage-contracts: "Twelve cats to kill the mice." She had also to become a Christian. But, as the natural mother of the Emperor's son, she was better off than the Empress, for the legitimate sons were generally cast into prison at the advent of a new ruler. This relationship is a much superior one in the Koran, while above both stands the heathen Negro, who uses women as units of labour, and would not even understand the difference between legitimate and illegitimate children, the most immoral idea that the white races have produced.

The latest Emperor, who was crowned in 1930, is more modern than he will admit, although he ruled quite after the manner of a caliph. A single railway crosses the country, a single telephone line enters the capital, and beside Lake Tana lie the posts of a destroyed telegraph line. Though the Emperor dined off gold plate, the houses of his three towns were mostly of straw. He summoned his two "chambers," but their function was to nod their heads. And yet he was shrewd enough to marry one of his princes to a relative of a Japanese cotton-king when he granted large concessions to Japan in 1932.

When the Emperor gave one of his numerous feasts to keep his bodyguard in good humour, the whole spectacle was operatic: he and his court were separated by huge curtains from the great hall in which two thousand soldiers feasted. In front of the curtain was a scene from the Middle Ages, with kneeling courtiers, and a sovereign eating, drinking, listening to the minstrel, governing at the same time. Behind the curtain, the people squatted at low tables, with much noise and smacking of lips, to music usually consisting of trumpets and drums; among them hundreds of slaves carried about whole sheep and haunches of oxen, from which the guests hacked pieces with their knives, and basins of water and towels for them to wash their greasy fingers. Mead was brought in in barrels and beer in great vats, from which other slaves filled and circulated beakers and drinking-horns. When at last the curtain rose, all the assembled fell flat on the ground before the Emperor. In a single day, the loyal sentiments of as many as thirty thousand subjects were thus fortified.

The most worried man in Abyssinia was the Master of Ceremonies, for thousands of high officials were held in suspense by the award of rank and orders. How far the Emperor's chest might be bared, on the other hand how short the robe of a dignitary might be, how many drums and trumpets a functionary might have to precede him in the street, that is, how loud he might make his music, and how much softer that of the minor officials had to be, who might wear trousers like the Emperor's and who those like the ministers', who might carry a certain piece of metal on his sword-hilt, which favourites might use certain colours for their cloaks and sunshades—these were the problems which pre-occupied the upper classes. Here was the source of power, for such tokens of honour were the outward and visible sign of all the joys of life.

In this pyramid, as in all pyramids, one stone bore on the others, and as the apex was a single emperor, and the base millions of slaves, the goal of all ambition was to reach the highest of the intervening courses. And even when the Emperor, at the apex, strove for justice, he could not survey his country; the mountains stood higher than the pyramid, and the depredations of the mighty in the towns and villages of the highland valleys, on the rivers and on the pastures, and the medieval methods used by chiefs, nobles, and priests to feed on the subjects—such things have never been thoroughly investigated by a white man. As the pay of the functionaries and officers was non-existent or derisory, they preyed on the people, whom they despised as the people despised a poor officer or priest. It is told of a dying Ras that his last order was: "Bury me with one arm out of the grave, so that I may still collect taxes."

Who could feel any inducement to work in a land where nobody could save unless he was in government employment? Since everything belonged to the Emperor, since he bestowed land on his favourites only in order to extort high taxes from them, which could be wrung from the poorly tilled land only by robbery and slave-dealing, in the end no rich man worked: only the Mohammedan merchants, who were more cunning than the Christians, made a profit on the goods which the Emperor exported, ivory, coffee, wax, hides, to the value of thirty million dollars,[1] not counting the gold.

The coin which is known and current everywhere, however, is not of gold: it is a large silver dollar bearing the effigy of a distant princess, of whose life not even a legend has penetrated to Abyssinia. A hundred and fifty years ago, the Maria Theresa thaler was introduced into the country by the traders of the Austrian Levant, and has been minted ever since. Yet those who know the

---

[1] The Maria Theresa dollar was worth approximately $.33 in 1934.

country make it dirty before tendering it, for if it shines the natives refuse it. Baker ascribed the popularity of the silver empress to her décolleté.

The manners and customs current among the heathen Negroes in Uganda before they so much as saw a white man are still lacking in Abyssinia, which has been in touch with civilization for hundreds of years. It is not only that the people tear their meat raw with their teeth, differing only from the leopards by cutting off the piece between their teeth with their knives; even the rich, wallowing in gold necklaces and feathers, in spite of their contact with Europe, seldom think of teaching their children more than writing; the geography and history, the flora and fauna, of their own country are almost unknown. The skilful crafts of the Negroes, especially in the west of Africa, are here conspicuous by their absence. Even their music is confined to the monotonous chanting in the churches and to drums and trumpets, and there are no national dances. Dolls, the playthings of all the Negro tribes, are unknown; draughts and a kind of hockey are known.

9

HOW is this possible? A people, thousands of whom make the yearly pilgrimage to Jerusalem, still lives in huts of logs, brushwood, cow-dung, and grass, and often with the cattle in the same room, a thing few Negroes would tolerate; though the capital is in daily telegraphic communication with Europe, save for the one railway line, no passable road leads to the sea; though iron and marble grow out of the ground, they have no idea of felling trees, but burn them through close to the ground. It may be objected that these conditions of life are medieval, but why should they be so? Civilization and Christianity came to Abyssinia much earlier than to France, and yet barely eighty years ago, at the time of the English expedition, they invented a new way of killing an enemy, namely, by binding him and driving great nails into his chest. Here, as elsewhere, it must lie in the character of the people, and that character was formed, in this natural stronghold, by rain and wind, by mountains and rivers.

This wild mountain country, whose roads turn into rivers every summer, governed by nobles who are protected by armies of slaves and always at war with each other, could not but remain alien to culture, whether of the land or the mind. The peasant, not knowing who will invade his land tomorrow, tills his field perfunctorily, and prefers to seek out one of those rocky fastnesses with which the extinct volcanoes of Abyssinia still protect its people. Courage and cruelty have issued from this Alpine fortress, with a rude form of Christianity for their background.

The scars of many burns show how they steel their children's courage: the hero is he who can hold a burning straw or stick in his naked hand the longest. Tapeworm, which has become a national pest owing to the eating of raw meat and the dirt, is so customary that in many tribes it is considered a scandal never to have had one. The Negro, too, dreads sickness, but no Negro tribe has ever been known to do what Abyssinian tribes do, namely, to set fire to a house where the inmates have been stricken with smallpox, with the sick in it, driving them back with their spears if they try to escape. The Negro, too, hangs his dead enemy's skull in the market-place, but the custom of carrying the genitals of the murdered man on the belt like a cartridge-box is an original, if simplified, form of sterilization.

The Negro, too, eats raw meat, but only the Masai know the most cruel of all Abyssinian customs: at a feast the ox is led into the hall, and pieces are cut out of the living animal while the arteries of the head are skilfully avoided, so that the bellowing creature slowly bleeds to death under the eyes of the feasters. This custom, although attempts have been made to deny it, has existed for centuries, exists today, and is vouched for by all explorers and travellers. Which is the more cannibal meal—a dead enemy or a living ox?

Superstitions, under which cruel characters are apt to conceal their fears, come to swell the confusion of feelings. But they have fine gestures: ceremonial forms are always to be found among cruel men, who find a compensation for moral acts in æsthetic arabesques, and thus seek to restore the order they destroy. At night the Abyssinians roll themselves up to the chin in sheets; a married couple, rolled up together in a kind of bale, for fear of the evil eye, look like mummies. For they show respect by exposing their skin, and when two Abyssinians meet, and dismount from their mules preparatory to the gesture of ceremony, they raise the tip of their toga-like robe from their breast, and the higher they raise it, the greater the honour.

Marriage is a sacrament, which each man shares with as many wives as he feels like, but, in contrast to the Emperor, all the children of the ordinary man are legitimate, and any woman suing for maintenance wins her case. And in the midst of their medieval customs, they have a very modern institution—trial-marriage—with the motto: "See if she bears children." For their first marriage, which takes place in their eleventh to their fourteenth year, the girls are bound by their parents' will; afterwards, they are free to choose, and if a rich girl cannot find a husband, she keeps a lover, whom she pays and treats like a servant, calling him *"wotbiet,"* that is, "cook," who must live close by her and be faithful, while she is free.

The betrothed may not visit his future bride, and, if he enters the house, she must beat a horrified retreat, but she can receive other young men alone. The kiss is unknown in Abyssinia; instead, they rub the right nostril of the other with their index finger. The woman is bought as among the Negroes, and, as among the whites, married with great feasting and drinking: there is even a "great glutton" invited too, who, before the eyes of all, must drink anything up to three gallons, and eat a corresponding amount. The beer, which resembles the mead of the Germanic tribes, is not, as there, glorified with the names of eagles, lions, and kings, but is called Galla beer, the "drink of slaves."

The priest, who is of no importance in the ordinary marriage ceremony, comes into his own at a birth: all other men shun the house of the woman in labour, and run away from the pursuing laughter and shrieks of the young mother's friends. The man is allowed only to stick his lance through the door to make the newborn brave by the touch. The conviction, strange among Christians, of the uncleanness of women, is also shown by the fact that the women are forbidden to bake the communion bread. The woman addresses the man with the formal "you," he calls her "thou." Marriage may be dissolved as quickly as it is concluded. The man sells his wife, the brother his sister, in order to get money. She revenges herself by doing whatever she pleases.

10

IT was Noah's fault. Probably he was still drunk when he cursed his son Ham, condemning him to serve his brother, and thus vindicating all slave-dealers for all time. He did not know what he was doing, for Ham was no worse than Shem, and the anti-Hamitic struggle as foolish as the anti-Semitic. But the Jews, despite all persecution, have nevertheless made better progress than such of Ham's posterity as have spent their lives in chains or as chattels and have remained slaves to this very day. For the persecuted can struggle and conquer, his self-confidence grows with resistance, and even when he lies bound on the earth, his heart is swelling with the joy of the revenge to come. But when he loses his freedom, the slave is deprived of the noble feeling of revenge; when the chain has been dragged from generation to generation, such feelings atrophy like an unused organ, and, in the course of generations, die out.

This is probably the reason why seven thousand years of human history have so few slave revolts to record. For the history of the slave is longer than that of any other class except the priests, and in it the greatest philanthropists figure as slave-dealers: Solon the wise and Lycurgus the just. Cæsar ruled an empire two-thirds of which consisted of slaves.

The Mohammedans were no better, but their argument is difficult to refute. Mohammed felt the inward contradiction no less than Justinian not long before him, but ventured as little as he to shake the foundations of the national economy and only prescribed lenient treatment of the slaves. He subjugated the infidels instead of converting them, and to this very day, in slave-owning countries, the Mohammedans take good care not to convert the Negro, for only because and so long as he is an infidel can he be a slave. Fellow-feeling is no tenet of that creed: no one

GAZELLES IN THE DESERT

Photo: Morhig, Khartoum

SANDSTORM OVER KHARTOUM

claims that all men are equal. Allah is great, therefore let us sell the unbelievers into exile! The leniency recommended by a legislator in the application of his Draconian laws has never been practised by his successors.

Slavery under the Most Catholic King of Spain, which lasted in his country till the sixteenth century, and the cant with which it was surrounded, showed how much farther this religion had moved from its founder than that of Mohammed from him. When the Portuguese, even before Columbus, began to enslave Negroes on the west coast of Africa, soothing their conscience with the colour of their victims, when they began their man-hunts, and when they shipped thousands in pens to South America to mine the gold and reap the tropical fruits for them, they created an artificial migration of the peoples involving graver consequences than the natural one. Men went out of Africa, money came out of America, the planters grew rich, the Negroes decayed.

As the Mohammedans had sold the Christians, the Christians now sold the heathens. A great Father of the Church called slave-dealing a work of piety because it gave those poor pagans the unexpected chance of becoming Christians. Popes declared it a necessity and held thanksgiving services. Then England, by convention, supplied slaves to America, and even though the first Quakers were Englishmen, America must always bear the credit of having roused the world. Clarkson roused the English, but throughout the nineteenth century the Christian capitalists made use of their Mohammedan colleagues to deal in men, and, about 1900, the products of certain Negro states are quoted in school textbooks as: "Ivory, ostrich feathers, and slaves." All men in Abyssinia not wearing the monk's cowl or carrying the sword are slaves.

As Abyssinia, since the eighth century, had been surrounded by Mohammedans who, in their conquests, had taken Christian slaves, the Christians can hardly be blamed for doing the same when they came into power. They would have had to be better than their white brothers to act otherwise. That went on for a thousand years. About 1850, missionaries described how Portuguese Christian slave-dealers, under their very eyes, laid waste ten villages and slaughtered fifteen hundred men in order to capture fifty-two women. The price of a handsome Galla girl in the northern market stood between twenty-five and forty Maria Theresa dollars.

As long as they could, certain scholars tried to defend this trade in theory, proving that there was nothing against slavery in the New Testament, and declaring that the principle of the equality of all men in the eyes of God was only a "qualification." The moral impetus of the French Revolution, which attempted to put that principle into political practice, was as ineffective as the work of the Quakers in putting an end to slave-dealing: the end was not to come till the triumph of the machine, which made so many human hands idle, reduced the price of men, and then only of certain male slaves. When, with the falling price of slaves, moral indignation grew cheaper too, it was used by white capital, which never ventures into the rain without a moral raincoat, to draw a distinction between slave-owning and slave-dealing, so that it might indignantly condemn the former, which brings in no profits, while carrying on the latter. How should the Abyssinians, whom it is the duty of their brothers in Christ to supply with European civilization, acquire it save with ivory and human souls? The term "black ivory" seems to have been coined only in the last century. Man-hunts, in comparison with the sixteenth century, have been restricted, but never abolished. Such a solution consorts well with the pernicious notion that armaments can be reduced, while a new order can begin only when they are abolished. "They are under a spell," wrote Speke of the slaves, "and know as little of their strength as the domestic animals."

It was even proved by the white Christians how unhappy these poor, dependent creatures would be if they were suddenly emancipated, how the weight of responsibility would demoralize them, as they had never known anything of the kind. Captive animals which have been set free have returned to their cages, but their young, born in freedom, have never yet been seen to do so. An isolated example of kindness in a slave-dealer, which its defenders use to beautify the trade, proves as little as traits of generosity prove anything against the violence of a dictator. Certainly, there are many whose masters look after them better than free servants, for the latter represent no capital; thus, in many tribes of Abyssinia, it is considered unfair to sell a slave after long service, but the menace hovers over them constantly.

In this respect, the Mohammedans are described as more generous than the Christians. Christian priests do not free their slaves, but the Mohammedans declare a slave woman free if she has borne her master a child. As the Koran prescribes not more than four wives, a master can in any case rarely marry the slave who has been his concubine. Sometimes the slave is protected by the law: if his master knocks his eye out, he becomes free—a diabolical exchange, more frightful than the right to kill.

But what becomes of the emancipated slave? Forthwith, having got work perhaps as a sailor, he considers himself everybody's equal and calls the Africans savages. If he has earned or stolen money, he at once buys slaves, refuses to work, and generally begins slave-dealing. As the master rarely liberates a slave from moral motives, but only out of vague fear, the result is immoral, for in the long run the motives of human actions work themselves out in their consequences. Dissolute, lazy, and overbearing, the emancipated slave tries to conceal his past, and so destroys his future. If he is stranded, he returns to his master and embraces his knees. Neither the ancient crime of enslaving a man on account of his birth, nor the modern crime of depriving him of his civil rights on account of his birth or his faith, will be eradicated by leniency or exceptions but only by the breaking of the spell.

11

IN the eighties, a cardinal moved through Europe, calling upon men to free the slaves. The lords of the world vied with each other in banquets and speeches, but hardly anything was done. At that time, slavery had only been abolished in America and Russia for twenty years, and the movement spread. That Christians were being made slaves in Abyssinia, not only in effect, but in form, troubled the administrators of the Pauline inheritance. Even the Archpriest and Emperor John had endeavoured to put a stop to slave-dealing, and when a French traveller told Emperor Menelek about the revolt of public opinion instigated by the cardinal, he took three days to think it over and then promulgated an edict against the Mohammedan dealers; moreover, every prisoner of war was to be set free at the end of seven years; later he showed that a few thousand had been liberated. With great solemnity, he entered the Brussels anti-slavery convention which demanded in a hundred paragraphs precisely what some of its signatories were trying to evade.

But no more than a year after that edict, Menelek was again allowing his officers to keep slaves, and when he saw knowing officers having slaves "presented" to them, he himself accepted the same kind of presents from his officers. Moreover, as he had need of the Mohammedan merchants to sell gold and ivory, he closed an eye. And if "immorality" was going to go on in his empire, he wanted at least to have a share in it, and exacted two dollars' tax for every slave sold. With this stroke of genius, he restored the harmony of his world.

It might be imagined that conditions would improve when the nations united in a league and hence founded a kind of moral police above the frontiers of race and creed. What did the League of Nations do?

On November 11, 1918, when the white flags were hoisted on all the battlefields of the world at the end of four years of war, Menelek's daughter, then Empress, fearing a turning-point in the history of the world, signed an edict prohibiting slave-dealing. It was as powerless as the first. The natural fortress blocked the view of the authorities: in their solitary highland valleys, the chiefs laughed at a prohibition which was to curtail their revenues, and the dealers found plenty of hidden paths, just like the smugglers in any mountain country.

But since slavery was not forbidden, but only slave-dealing, and this, without exception, led to Arabia, so that the goods had to cross the Red Sea, surely the white steamship lines and parts of all the fleets of Europe sailing past were stronger than those dark dealers, and should be able to catch them? What if a police force were established to watch two or three of the slaving-ports? Did not Lincoln, much earlier, have a much harder struggle in his own country? While the white men were doing nothing, the Empress learned from her envoys that she was not counted in the commonwealth of nations; the "right thing," according to white standards, was to be represented at Geneva. But even here, as usual among the white tribes, trade was more important than civilization and religion; and as the Empress seemed disposed to abolish the slaves, she declared in her solemn application to Geneva that slave-dealing had already been abolished, while slavery would soon disappear, "save in case of war," which, however, can always be arranged in this country.

Instead of keeping Abyssinia out of the League until slavery was abolished, the diplomats sought for a formula under which it could be admitted. For eight years, from 1923 to 1931, experts were busy in meetings, commissions, reports, speeches, debates, articles, minutes, lunches, and banquets, trying to find the "formula." The Commission confirmed the Abyssinian statement that, "where slavery exists, the slaves are in general not unhappy," in general, too, "they are not ill-treated." The Commission further admitted that the Government would run the gravest danger by abolition, as powerful chiefs could prevent it. A general emancipation would have "disastrous results." The very words of the Tsar's ministers, of the Southern States, of the landholders, of the upholders of armament today. The Commission issued a warning against plunging Abyssinia into difficulties of a political, social, economic, and financial kind—the Commission indulged in stylistic opulence. *"En attendant, on doit souhaiter que les puissances . . ."*

The experts of the League did not venture to publish in its entirety the report submitted by their delegate, Lord Lugard. The revelations contained in that report correspond to the observations of travellers and explorers: the imperial edicts for the liberation of the slaves stand on paper, the sale of many thousands of Abyssinian slaves is noted in that report of 1925 as being "of recent date," and the priests especially are held responsible. "We will die rather than give up our slaves," said one of the most influential chiefs to a traveller. In the capital, slave-dealing goes on under the very eyes of the white ambassadors, according to a French Government report, which points out with irony that two dealers were actually hanged. According to two recent British writers, the state of things since Menelek's death has been made worse by civil wars, and, judging from their accounts, there must be five million slaves in the country. After a lapse of ten years, one of these writers found whole districts, formerly flourishing, desolate because the inhabitants had been sold, and just when the Englishman was in the capital, the Emperor received "as a gift one hundred and forty boys and girls between six and fourteen years of age, as well as women with infants at their breast."

And the years passed, and not a country stirred a finger: one country only, and a small one, New Zealand, sought to save its honour by energetic appeals. While nearly half the inhabitants of a country were forced into the position of old Egyptian slaves, receiving every gift on their knees or lying prone, were not allowed to drink from a cup but only from their hollowed hands, and were cast into chains at any attempt at flight, the descendant of Solomon, the Lord's anointed, like the sultan in Weber's *Oberon,* had his torches borne by slaves when he travelled, and kept a choir of eunuch boys. But the Commission of the League of Nations was of the opinion that the Church "would have" to create the atmosphere, the clergy "would have" to liberate the slaves first. "The Commission has considered whether warships have the right to investigate suspicious vessels. The Commission declines any competence to answer this delicate question, but expresses the burning wish that it may be inquired into."

Confronted by such actions, the Abyssinian Government could see how seriously the white Christians took the matter, and amused itself with a new law, by which anyone selling or giving a slave away would be punished in the same way as a slave-dealer, that is, not at all, for no one punishes him. Yet meanwhile, so as to have something to show in Geneva, the Abyssinian delegate in 1930 submitted a document containing the names of 298 slaves who had been set free the year before. Five millions remained slaves.

Meanwhile, all the slave-markets vanished. Slaves were not paid for; a gun or some cartridges were given in exchange, and the stranger was hoodwinked with the same graceful objections: it is mere consideration for the captives which prevents their liberation. In the whole country, agriculture would decline as it did in Cuba and Haiti; famine would invade the land, as it did in Eritrea when Italy liberated the Egyptian slaves there. Nobody reflected that the famine would soon be over, while slavery doomed generations for centuries. Nobody admitted that the Emperor did not pay his officials and soldiers, and that taxes could be paid in slaves, which came cheaper as long as they were allowed to breed properly. Nobody explained that the Junker makes war and goes hunting because he has learned nothing else, whether he be brown, white, or yellow.

In the Red Sea, where fashionable steamers pass nearly every day, with the ladies refreshing themselves, after their strenuous day, in the faint evening breeze on the upper deck, on the latitude of Jidda, white sails glide through the hot gloom and the officers on the bridge follow them through their glasses, grin perhaps, then look ahead again, for that does not concern them. When an English man-of-war once pursued such a boat, the captain threw all the slaves overboard, thus forcing the English to rescue them, while he made away. Later, after telling his story, he asked: "Why do the *chawadja* (foreigners) love the slaves so much that, to save a dozen, they let a fine *zaruk* (sailing-boat) like mine slip through their fingers?"

Others anchor their boats on one of the rocky islands in the Red Sea, and hand over their wares to another, which carries them to the Hejaz, for in Jidda there are no human markets to-day, in Mecca there are, and hundreds are smuggled over to Mecca as pilgrims. The League of Nations knows all about it; excellent French reports appeared in 1930, all the authorities know, the consuls on the coast know the names of the dealers, and even if they get no money, there are middlemen everywhere who have plenty of money to spend, for a fine boy of twelve or a girl of fourteen brings in as much as $600, and a pregnant woman, who can regain her beauty, is really even cheaper, for the child is thrown in.

The markets which, until 1913, were held publicly in the capital, have been replaced by depots, especially in the Harrar province, which was particularly subject to the Emperor. There whole villages live on hush money, for which they haggle with the leaders of the caravans; every house is a hiding-place, for the only dangerous time is that between the capture and the desert. There the captives sleep in ditches, which are covered over, till the migration to the sea begins. On these desert roads, today as long ago, lie corpses of human beings who have fallen exhausted by the way; others, that is, more than half, succumb still earlier to the effects of mutilation, which is carried out without doctors or sanitary measures.

The great raids made by Abyssinian slave-owners and dealers to the west and south of their country, into Kenya and the Sudan, are reported by the British authorities, who cannot always beat them off. These raids seem the more justifiable to the Abyssinians in that they are only trying to make up by them for the flight of slaves over the border, since neither the Italian nor the English Government gives them back. The British officers in Gedaref, eighty miles west of the frontier, take the fugitives in, give them work, and find the women suitable husbands.

But the slave-owners on the other side of the border feel themselves wrongfully robbed, and when a rich man sends a messenger across the frontier begging for the return of his escaped property, his letter to the British officer at the frontier begins: "May God grant that thou shalt know the blessings of justice. The protector of the poor and their property is the Government. It is a fact that all the slaves of our district have run away to Gedaref. That is the way we poor men are oppressed, for it is hard for us to work without slaves. Therefore I am sending my son, that you may help him in this matter. A thousand thanks."

12

THE Blue Nile has reached the Sudanese plain and is striving in a north-westerly direction towards an unknown goal. The adventures of the canyon over, no longer protected by rocks and forests, gliding through the dully glowing plain, its course has quietened, yet it is still young enough to suffer no boats. Not until Roseires, 400 miles from its mouth, has it grown too broad and deep to defend itself. A white steamer mounts it, and the untamable, wild Nile must perforce bear a burden. Yet even now its swift current and dark colour, and above all, the silt it carries with it, distinguish it from its graver brother, although, by their breadth, a certain resemblance begins in their outward appearance.

An evergreen park fringes the broad stream, and the formative hand of the English has very little to check, but the motor road on its left bank shows what kind of a land it has entered. The fortress-like building of Singa passes by, and the two guns in front of it tell of what happened there not long since; villages in well-kept enclosures succeed each other, half hidden by the natural park on the banks, or standing in the open dhurra-fields. Here peace, or at least quiet, reigns. Life is governed by a new phenomenon, which lies downstream.

For now the Blue Nile encounters the same thing as the White Nile encountered above Khartoum. Its breathing grows laboured, then stops. With terror, it feels widened, an invisible obstacle is damming it up. Suddenly it runs against a wall built athwart its course ninety feet high and almost two miles long. For unknown reasons, invisible hands have stopped its career, only letting it foam on through stone gates, which sometimes open and sometimes shut. It is the dam of Sennar, gripping and regulating it. A frightful experience! The splendid horse, galloping in freedom, suddenly feels the rope round its neck; then comes the trainer to force it into fixed movements at fixed times. The surprise is so great that even the steamer cannot go farther, for the dam has no lock and another steamer has to wait on the other side.

Soon, on the right bank, two great tributaries discharge.

The Rahad and the Dinder have been true brothers their life long. They rose close to each other in the same high plateau west of Lake Tana; they were fed by the same network of a hundred rivulets, have flowed in the same direction, first north-west, then parallel to the Blue Nile; they are of about the same length and the same volume. The only difference is that the Rahad in its deep bed runs through richer silt than the broader and longer Dinder. Both reach the Nile in summer, while a third, still farther to the north, sometime shares the fate of the Atbara.

The Atbara, too, rises near Lake Tana, close to the two tributaries of the Blue Nile. A little, wild mountain torrent, it is at first clear, dashing and free. Here is a being which is completely transformed in later life by the influence of its subject brothers; the great quantities of silt which then determine its career are brought to it only by its three tributaries. The longest of them rises in a volcanic hot spring to the east of the lake, the two others plunge to meet it from the mighty veins of the western mountains; then the Arabs can in all truth call it Atbara, which means "the black." It is especially on the lower reaches of this and the two tributaries of the Blue Nile that the nomads live, and are taken so fearfully by surprise when the flood descends.

For in January, the Atbara is helpless and dry. All it carries with it evaporates, the desert swallows the river. Fifty miles above the Nile it is a dry bed of stones and mud. One of the few rivers of the earth which so silt up that they cannot discharge, it looks at times like a man subject to fits of madness, whom his family leaves behind till he comes to himself. But then it hurls itself with furious energy on its more constant brother, bringing it more help in the three months of its real life than others throughout the year. Two hundred miles below the Blue Nile, the Atbara discharges, as long as it discharges at all, in the middle of the desert into the united Nile.

By that time, both Niles have passed through many an adventure. The Blue Nile quickly overcomes the crisis of the dam. It certainly feels that part of its water flows off in unknown channels, but soon it has grown broad and deep again, flowing on steadily between firm banks, calmer, yet with a lively pulse, and not even at the end relapsing into the sluggish habit of the White, even though, in this plain, the gradient is very slight. Throughout its lower course, from the dam onward, the Blue Nile sees and hears on its left bank the railway carrying off the cotton.

Then the towers which astonished the graver brother rise before it at the same distance. But the Blue Nile feels no hindrance, no check, for it is itself the one that hinders and checks. In wide enclosures the cattle graze day and night, and the light wooden fences show that the nomads have been left behind. From the desert plain rise a few tiled houses, with young trees protected by wooden palings against the goats; then come the white posts of football fields, a pergola with palm trunks for pillars—all signs of a town, things which the nomad, the child of nature, when he first approaches the capital, can understand as little as the Blue Nile flowing into the desert from the forests of its home.

Shortly before Khartoum, a great railway bridge with huge piles and arches stands waiting, and over it the railway runs to the capital. The green mantle which the stream has worn spreads out into an evergreen town with white houses, some of which are palaces. Some stand in the shadow of phœnix palms, in whose tops the great ospreys nest. From the midst of the plain rises the splendid town.

Having left the bridge behind, it sees on its left bank a castle with guns and troops in bright-coloured uniforms, looking like the guard of honour of some great lord. Fine boats, and splendid horses with brilliant carriages, stand at the gate, and when, not far away, the great doors are opened, a few hundred brown youths come trooping out to enjoy themselves on the palm-grown beach. This is the residence of the British governor, and the college in which three hundred Nubians are educated. A mile farther on, and the second giant bridge appears, with the startled, grave, broad White Nile below it.

Now, just before the end, does the Blue Nile, bold and childlike, suddenly realize with terror that it is itself only part of a greater whole? Does the pale, slow stream appear as a tributary which it must receive for good or ill? Neither betrays a trace of such rivalry.

These are two brothers, embracing, neither superior, neither subject to the other. In this embrace, the river is doubled. It is as though it must gather up all its strength to face the second half of its life. From now on there is only one Nile.

Now comes the struggle with man.

Book Three

THE

STRUGGLE

WITH MAN

1

AN aeroplane hovering over a camel-rider: that is the design on the Sudanese postage-stamps. If this rider were to set off on the left bank of the Nile, slightly to the west of Lake No, he could ride across twenty degrees of latitude—that is, about 1300 miles as the crow flies—to Cairo without crossing so much as a brook. On the right bank, from the mouth of the Atbara, riding in a straight line towards the mouth of the Nile, he would meet neither rivers nor rain. This waterless stretch of twelve degrees of latitude extends across the continent to the west coast over nearly fifty degrees of longitude. It is the Sahara, and even though it goes by another name east of the Nile, it is still the same desert.

Yet at this very part, where no mountains can check it, the Nile leaves its destined north-south course, and, for the first time in its life, describes a great loop. While railway and aeroplane, and even the camel-rider, cut off this loop by a straight line through the desert, the river, feeling some obstacle in its way, paints a gigantic S in the ochre-yellow sand of the Sudan.

If it perished of thirst, if it dried up, who could wonder? Imagine a solitary man, riding through a desert without vegetation, half as big as Europe, with neither brother nor friend to bring him water, exposed day after day to a glare which only night mitigates; imagine this rider, anxiously hurrying to reach the sea, his home, and the ports, suddenly stopped by granite bars and forced to make a detour hundreds of miles long, will he and his failing camel not collapse before the goal is reached? But the Nile has streamed for centuries through the desert glare to the sea, helped by no friend and no brother such as brought it water in its youth; stopped by granite bars, it flows round them, wins from them defiance and daring, quickens by their contact its

161

flagging flow, carries boats, struggles with the boats on its back, struggles with the men who fain would shackle it, and do shackle it, yet neither loses heart nor runs dry. The Nile forces its way through the infinite sand as once it overcame the swamps; it bids defiance to the curse of the drought as once it bade defiance to the greed of the lagoons, for both seek to suck up its substance, and thus actually reaches the country which it has watered and created by its flow since the beginning of time, reaches the delta and the ports, reaches the sea, the primeval home of the rivers. What a river!

The element with which the Nile takes up this new struggle is neither tableland nor mountain: it is an immense rolling expanse, where sandy plains rise into glowing hills of stone, where whirlwinds burrow holes, where pyramids and boulders, apparently created out of nothing, with their wind-whetted edges, crumbling recesses, and battered arches, betray the wind as the fanatical creator of their amazing forms. And just as, in unfathomable characters, a female element mingles with the male, the desert shows, in the churned expanse, where the camel sinks in up to its knees, hard hills of quartz, on whose sharp edges it loses its footing. The desert has often been compared with the sea, but only a sudden spell could make the ever-moving element like the dead desert. In the sea lives that strange, other world of plants and creatures, whose depths only the eye of the diver can penetrate. In the sea everything is movement, change, anarchy of forms; in the desert everything is rigid, for when the sand has once stormed over the dead land, its motionless forms rise again.

The only thing in common between sea and desert is their unreality, which is also shared by the appearance of glaciers. Man, accustomed to the steadiness of life about him, is startled in the presence of the elemental, and can no longer feel that sea or desert, or even the glacier, is really alive. That which oppresses the common run of humanity—simplicity in the place of the accustomed diversity—sets the inhabitants of these three regions, in their bare intercourse with sky and water, sky and sand, sky and ice, apart from all others and makes them all alike: all of them are silent and devout.

And are they mute? The mountaineer follows the whistle of

the marmot up to the highest crags, and over desert and sea alike rises the cry of some bird of prey, wheeling over a fish in the water, carrion in the sand, and screaming perhaps only from sheer vitality. But through all three roars the voice of the storm, and it is that voice that strikes terror to the heart of the boldest on glacier, sea, or desert.

How manifold is the desert! From rocky labyrinths rise mountains of granite and porphyry over six thousand feet in height; they are said to have been formed by the collapse of the rift at the Red Sea. Black rocks are immediately succeeded by light ones, and when fragments are struck off by the hammer, the marble inside is as white as Carrara's, or veined in red or black. Even into the Libyan desert, to the west of the Nile, long dry valleys run, stretches of fissured rock called *wadis,* looking like rivers petrified by a curse: rivers which may have flowed to the Nile at the places where these menacing valleys descend to it today. The light varies like the forms, though no clouds shadow it: on misty days the sun hangs pale blue over the yellow sea. Then the bedouins sing songs which liken the sun to the moon. Sometimes that is a premonition of the storm.

Suddenly the bright glare of day is darkened; a dull yellow glare suffuses the air; mighty brown mountains, like a palpable chain, roll through the air: no wind, heavy silence, the "thick darkness" of the Bible. The sinister cloud approaches, a voice with it, rolling in the distance. When the storm breaks, blustering, smoking, breathing heat, carrying grains of sand and stones with it, men and beasts cast themselves on the ground, for it strikes and kills them. Tents are overturned, the dry ropes break, but no one notices: all creatures tremble, cast to earth by the weight of the dark, devouring storm, and when the wind-god surveys the earth, he thinks perhaps that a terrified congregation of men is lying before him in prostrate supplication. At such moments, of what avail is it to the white scientist that, in his tranquil Oxford study, he was able to explain the south-west storm by the clash of the cold clouds with the overheated desert? In his deadly fear, must he, too, not think of the *jinn,* the evil spirits of the Arabs, which they dread as the creators of these rolling pillars of sand?

Often the storm subsides as quickly as it burst, and when men and beasts, their lives spared, stand up half stunned, some dead bird, a bunting perhaps, lies on the earth, for a few birds venture into this arid world, and when the pale-grey desert-lark has found refuge in the fold of a tent, it rises singing. Nothing is more moving in this desert than the trill of the lark which—Allah alone knows what it lives on—has ventured far from the oasis, like the gulls which follow the ship though land is days behind.

Still more unreal than the wind in the desert is the water. Capriciously, without rhyme or reason, as sudden as comets, the springs bring life into the rigid desert landscape, creating mild green spots, infinitely small, rising like points of rest in this formless, flattened waste. There are, it is true, ancient roads, on which the caravans move from spring to spring, but out of the whole, the springs break forth as freakishly as the submarine currents in the sea, as the crevasses in the glaciers, and shift as they do. From the depths of the deepest valleys, as from the depths of the deepest hours of human life, rises the life-saving water, and forthwith the land around turns green; a few thorny acacias, a parched palm appear, like a gift of the gods; men and beasts fling themselves to the earth to drink the great elixir which saves them from the burning sun. El Bahr!

Or again, life and soul have been parched for days by a gentle, glowing wind: the wood of the tent-poles warps, the ivory knife-handle splits, the roll of paper cracks, the rug sticks to the blanket, the woollen shirt crackles as it is unfolded, electric sparks fly from the hair under the comb. Then a group of acacias, which has appeared and disappeared for hours past, promises water—no, there is no oasis, and no spring to quench the thirst of the exhausted traveller. Yet they hurry to dig the subterranean water with their last strength, for it must be there to nourish the tree. As the spades crunch through the sand, the naked tree crackles above: it is the dried resin on its branches.

But how is this water to be preserved? To keep himself alive, the bedouin has invented slightly porous earthenware pitchers, more precious than a vacuum flask: the lukewarm water turns cool in them, at night it becomes icy. If the pores of the pitcher are clogged, terror stares him and the white traveller in the face.

Perhaps he has packed lemons in tin boxes to keep them juicy. Then he takes out his last, apportions himself the segments by his watch, if it is not sanded up, and sucks one every half-hour. In that way he may be able to struggle on to the next oasis, but one of the camels, which have to look after themselves, has fallen after all, and the scream of the vulture tells that within an hour it will be no more than bones.

Like milestones, the skeletons of dead camels mark the desert road, often six or eight to the mile. Their shadowy, bleached bones, quickly cleaned of flesh by sun and vultures alike, are the cleanliest remains of organic life, and, if they stood upright, would look like some carefully prepared model in a museum. Lying there, its outline still complete, in its ghostly, airy shape, with its visible ribs, this skeleton might be the Platonic idea of a camel. But even the bones are consumed to powder by the burning sun and turn into desert sand. The way of all flesh, dust to dust.

And the wind of the ages blows over it and the sand of the ages covers up all tracks of all men, from the governors of the Pharaohs to the British conquerors, from the worshippers of the sun to the faithful of both Mediterranean prophets, an endless train of men who have thirsted to death, whose bones have been bleached by the relentless blue of this cynically smiling sky, ground by the wind, turned into dust by the power of the sun, reduced to orange-yellow desert sand, through which the descendant of those sons of the desert rides on his camel, not knowing whether he will reach the end, the bush and the river.

How manifold are the gods upon whose names men have called in supplication in the whirlwind! When the aborigines crossed the desert, to bring tidings from the bush, or to drive a herd of cattle to the river, ignorant of foreign conquerors or priests, they worshipped the heavenly bodies by whose course they reckoned their road; no one knows how many, asleep on their beasts, lost their bearings and their way and, with their animals, turned into white bones for the wind to mingle with the sand. But when the conquering prophets of new doctrines invaded the prairies from the Red Sea, and the bedouins turned first Greek, then Christian, then Mohammedan, there arose to heaven a strange confusion of names, Hercules and Pan, Isis, Jesus, and Ares. To this day, in their inmost hearts, they have remained star-worshippers. Arab writers tell a strange tale, that the sons of desert and prairie believed in an immortal god, but they believed too in one who was mortal, and who had no name.

When the slaves of gold-hunting Egyptian kings, whose discoveries are recorded on their tombs, moved through the hills of this desert, great armies with their slaves, generals with their men, perished in whirlwinds, and the vultures made but one carrion of them. The temple of Thebes has preserved only the name of some king's son, of some great potentate who, in his last agony, may well have cursed his greed of power. Once Greeks came down, sent by Cambyses, but none followed them, and they left behind on the Nile only the tale that none of them returned. Sand and sun have hidden even from history the last traces of that insolent inroad, and there is not even a monument or a statue round which legend could grow into poetry. Like the bones, the names fell away to dust, so great is the power of the desert.

2

IN the bush, all the shapes are softer, granite and basalt rise more rarely, colours and lines look gentler, but the thorny, transparent outline of the leafless acacia, which dominates the whole, lends the parched yellow expanse a ghostly appearance, such as a dry cactus has in its small way. In this belt between the rainless desert and the region of the tropical rains, up-Nile from about Dongola to Malakal, that is from the Fourth Cataract to the beginning of the swamps, in this bush-land which goes by different names according to the varying degrees of visibility, the nomad prays fervently to the rain which, like the desert sun, can yet destroy him if he goes to his flocks under cloud-bursts. But in two days it creates the miracle of the grass, on which his flocks live, with the same magic swiftness with which it can vanish in a few hours. The very grass which threatened to choke the life out of the Nile in the swamps becomes, not far away, on both sides of the river, the greatest blessing for man and beast. After a few hours of rain, tiny feathery leaves can be seen unfolding on the acacia: the camel stands waiting for them, millions of little organisms come to birth, and all life feels that it has been saved from thirsty death. Within a week, a thousand dry branches have swelled anew, the humps of the camel distend, for the yellow plain has turned green.

Yet forthwith it arms itself afresh: the ripened grass pricks, cuts, tears cloth and leather; a green world begotten by water draws red blood from every traveller; and while the herds grow fat, the explorer waits impatiently for the time when the nomad burns the bush to destroy by fire what he had so fervently prayed for from the water. Thus the elements alternate and rage against each other in lands where the even measure of sun and rain must yield to the exuberance of both, like the ecstasies of joy and suffering in which monomaniacs consume themselves.

In the rainy season, the dhurra cereal has sprung up on the plain; the doum-palm has grown green, soon it bears fruit; and when the sudden sun destroys the corn, the nomads grind the palm-nuts, making their flour from the fruits of the tallest trees. All this takes place in the hundred gradations by which the so-called bush-zone links the steppe to the desert.

Now the elephantine baobab gains an importance unforeseen at the Creation: the giant tree, more like a giant mushroom with its dome and spongy wood, is used as a barrel after the rainy season. The soft wood of the trunk, which branches out quite low, can be easily hollowed out and made water-tight in the middle. With its diameter of almost fifty feet, it can hold as much as five thousand gallons of water. If only a thin rind is left, the tree grows and greens again. Some botanists assert that trees of this kind are five thousand years old. In the Nile bushland, the botanists are bolder than the historians.

Under the ghostly void of the transparent acacia, the browsing camel appears; it is incomprehensible that the huge creature can be satisfied with such thorns and tiny leaves. Though it is considered frugal, it is not humble, and though it is praised for its endurance, it is vicious and cowardly. It certainly serves man, but it neither loves nor knows him; stupid and defiant, it is terrible in rut, and seems to feel affection only for its young. Its strange and monstrous shape, for which it seems to have taken the giraffe's neck, the pig's head, and the cow's tail, contributing only its grotesque hump on its own account, makes it look like the embodiment of loneliness among the animals. It first came to Egypt in Roman times, when sheep and goats, cattle and horses, had lived there for thousands of years.

No other animal knows such tragi-comic moments. When, after much shouting and beating, it kneels for the load, it folds up its hind legs in three parts, like a mechanical toy. When the camel walks, it swings along with an ambling motion that makes riding difficult. When it gallops, it shakes its rider, because its hind foot strikes the ground a quarter of a second before the fore foot. The strongest species can carry seven hundredweight, and the fastest can cover a hundred miles in twenty-four hours, but not one is as trustworthy as a broken horse. It flies without warning into frenzies of rage, bites everybody, even its master, is thrown into panic by the remote howl of a hyena, and in its rage blows a great bubble out of its mouth like the soul which the old artists painted flying from the mouths of the dying.

Its whole life long it is a beast of burden, even on its day of triumph. Then it carries the bride and hundredweight-heavy trappings of brown leather, shells, and little bells. Perhaps one of those clean skeletons bleaching in the desert sand once moved in rich array through the streets of Khartoum to the wedding of a princess.

The ostrich, whose Latin name (*Struthio camelus*) betrays its kinship with the camel, is of course a faster beast. It is akin to the camel not only by its long legs and ungainly movement, but by its stupid expression. With its scraggy neck and crazy-looking head, it reminds one of some deranged idealist, running away as soon as the world runs counter to his dreams.

Once the ostrich could fly. But, the Negroes say, one day when he was arranging with a bustard for his bath in the Nile next morning, he forgot to add: "Inshallah—if God will." The next morning, as he was flying towards the sun, Allah punished him for his presumption by singeing his wings so that he fell dead to earth. Since then, the idealistic ostrich has flown no more.

Nor has Allah protected the ostrich from the bedouins. They catch this fleet creature by pursuing it on horseback, always in twos, taking it in turns, with camels bringing water in the rear, and at last, when the hunted creature flags, they stun it with blows on the head. Then they cut its throat. But why? It has little flesh: any gazelle, which is easy to shoot, has more. But it carries white feathers on its body, ten to fourteen of them, which the wives of the white pashas love to carry as fans. Actually the feathers grow better in captivity, like the voices of some birds and poets. But if they are hunted wild, their feathers must not be stained with blood: death, as in patriotic songs, must not be made visible, therefore the hunters quickly ram the big toenail of an ostrich foot into the wound. Now the swiftest two-legged runner in the world lies dead in the sand so that some lady in St. Moritz may flaunt a feather fan. An ostrich has fallen for the sake of a goose.

It is still more purposeless to hunt the giraffe, the most picturesque of all the bush creatures, for it is dangerous to nobody and has not even a hunting trophy to bequeath. A creature without enemies! For as their sight, hearing, and sense of smell are equally keen, and as they are several feet taller than all other animals, even than the elephant, they move about in celestial herds, browsing on the leaves and tenderest twigs of the highest trees, always on the lookout, yet not really timid, with the composure of very tall men who look away over the heads of the rest.

Hence their childlike ways. When two giraffes affectionately lay their necks together, and rub them together, it looks as if a giant toy had come to life. When they raise their heads and run, they are a miracle of grace; but when they droop their heads, they look as pedantic as professors of philosophy. As they can see everything, they are incorrigibly inquisitive to discover the cause of every noise and run into danger through sheer curiosity. When moving slowly, they look awkward, for they have no ambling pace; scarcely less swift than the ostrich, they are doubly amazing because they never gallop like the other animals of the bush. As their forelegs grow up to more than six feet, a man could walk under them with head erect, provided he were not a Dinka.

But how is an animal eighteen feet tall to drink from the river? The giraffe can reach the Nile only with legs asplay, and while all the other animals merely bend their heads, it has to perform the comic turn of the snake-man in the circus. Therefore, in the rainy season, it prefers to lick the damp leaves at the top of trees. Considering the superiority of its physique, nobody can blame the giraffe for not wasting its time with the white men, and yet there is one product of civilization which fascinates it. A few years ago, a new animal made its appearance in the bush, running more swiftly than all the others, more swiftly than the giraffe itself. It had four circular legs, and in other ways was not a proper animal. If the giraffe spies a car, it runs up and races it to see which can go faster, and if, by the end of half an hour, motorized man has won, can it be regarded as a triumph?

But the real life of the steppe does not come from the three running animals, but from the bounding game. There are thousands of creatures who, in utter freedom and fearless of each other, leap before the eyes of the rider in the bush, and as the plain is boundless, the number of moving specks on the horizon is countless.

If, in the invisible distance, a lion approaches, the rider can detect it miles away by the change in the direction and speed of a thousand bounding creatures, all of whom, following a leader or their own instinct, rush off in a remote, wild gallop, looking, at this incalculable distance, like rows of fleeing horses. Among the running ostriches and giraffes, antelopes vault over the parched yellow grass, no one knows whither, no one knows where they will take refuge from the invisible pursuer. A hundred shades of brown and white, striped, speckled, spotted, crowned with horns so various that an artist might have sketched them on one of his good days: the ariel and the dama, to mention only two of the prettiest names, great waterbucks, little reedbucks, dainty bushbucks with their big ears, and a swarm of different species of gazelle which, with the loveliest legs, leap most fleetly, whose veins are visible under their skin, an inexhaustible metaphor for Arab poets praising the slenderness of their beloved and the delicacy of her skin.

Less rich in small bird-life than the rainy countries, the bush has cultivated the tree-hoopoe, which always lives in company, chattering, screaming, even mourning with others when one has been shot, and living in strict monogamy (faithful husbands are the most talkative). The black rhinoceros-bird is a different matter: he enjoys himself on his own, but has invented a system of his own for the mother-bird and her young. Till the young birds are fledged, he walls them up with their mother in damp clay and feeds them from the outside. If he dies, he has, like an Indian prince, the glorious feeling that his wife must die with him. Of the bigger birds, the bush is inhabited by the red-necked hawk, sitting in the duhleb-palm, as swift and bold as his northern brother, and the hooded eagle, spreading his crest for hours in the sun on the naked boughs of an acacia, opening, closing, opening it again.

But the lord of all, the great air-policeman, is the vulture, who leads the dance of death in the desert and the bush, with his heavy, drooping wings, his heavy, drooping head, his straddling gait, his cruel, piercing eyes. No hygienist could invent a better means of preventing the development of poisonous gases in these temperatures from the decay of dead bodies. Yet the vulture is not guided by chemistry or the sense of smell; the vulture sees, and as, with his powerful wings, he can quickly fly over long distances, the fallen camel, the dead gazelle, cannot escape him for an hour. No one has ever smelt a corpse in these regions: hardly is a creature dead when they are there, as quick as heirs. With their long necks, they burrow into their prey, fight, vulture against vulture, for some bit of guts they have torn out, and, before the eyes of travellers, have left practically no trace of a dead dog within five minutes. But a year after they have been stuffed and filled with camphor, they are still odorous in the scientist's study, and yet fugitive and famished slaves have been seen to eat vulture flesh.

Over the plain, over the river, the bowl of the sky fills at evening with tender light. In the west, a piercing yellow appears, then a narrow misty belt of grey-green. Then the palest mauve-pink begins, deepening quickly to a massive dark mauve spreading up to the dove-blue of the zenith. Towards the east the sky is lightened by flashes of reflected red mingled with pearly blue, violet-grey, flamingo-pink, till, a minute later, a hard, steely blue touches the reddish-yellow hills of the desert. In the east, the light turns colder, the pink greyer.

Meanwhile, in the west, the lowest strip has deepened to a vicious sulphur-yellow. The river, over which a black bird glides in slanting flight, has turned yellow again, with grey-blue ripples, thrown into a chaos of light and shadow by the play of the little waves. Soon the yellow strip to the south-west is drowned in a sunset orange spreading from the brightest point at its centre, which quickly turns grey and livid towards the east. Meanwhile, at the very point where the sun set, a strange blue bay has swelled in the form of a chalice: it cuts flashing into the yellow tones, which now have turned more reddish. For, meanwhile, the night, rising from the east, has taken possession of the west and overcome the red-yellow belt at that proudest point where the light of day sank. Now the night has conquered, the colours die away.

The voice of the stream sounds louder: the Nile flows northward into the night.

3

_____

ONLY a nomad can be master of desert and plain, for to live on his herds he must lead them from pasture to pasture, following the vagaries of the climate and the river, and, above all, the belts of rain. Kingdoms stretch lavishly in front of him, belonging to nobody, and even though he has not to conquer them, he must constantly seek new ones before returning to the old.

It is not only in this respect that he puts into practice the old farmer's saw which grants the field its rest when it has borne fruit. There are other transitions to the farmer, and the Arabs to the south of Meroe, moving about as half-nomads with their flocks, sow corn at the same time, move on after the sowing, leaving it to the mercy of Allah, return only for the harvest, grind the corn, eat the bread, and again move on. The dhurra, like the camel, makes no demands and gives the highest yield, bringing forth five-hundredfold, and half of all the cultivated land in the Sudan is under dhurra. Other tribes leave behind in the oases to cultivate the corn selected families, who, in the end, settle, and in a few generations even degenerate into traders.

In every respect the nomad proves himself a king, the farmer a serf, although he grows richer than the king. Living on the river or in the oases, some of which, it is true, can extend to provinces, his eyes fixed anxiously on the earth, desolate if the weather lays it waste, the farmer unites in communities to protect himself better from the wild animals and the elements, but his greatest dread is the nomad, who lives on the confines of the steppe and regards the cultivated oases as outposts, to be besieged and plundered. The farmer distrusts the nomad just as the sober citizen distrusts the adventurer; shut up in his security, which is none, trusting to laws which totter, and all the same helpless in face of the vagaries of the river and the rain, which no community can dominate, he loses his beauty.

Beauty is with the nomad. Although the tribes of the Sudan have become hopelessly confused owing to the lack of mountain and river boundaries in this flat land, certain characteristics are common to all tribes. The intermingling of these aboriginal Ethiopians with the Arabs, who have crossed the Red Sea these four hundred years, has only gone to reinforce their character- istics as men of the desert. Camels, cattle, sheep, goats—it is reckoned that there are seven million of them in the Sudan— tents and huts, wife and child, the springs, the wanderings, the absence of fixed hours of labour, the sheikh as leader, the duel which at once decides the quarrel, insecurity, faith and supersti- tion, a land without frontiers, freedom without bounds: must not ages of life in such conditions make man draw nearer to Allah, grow more comely?

Tall and lean, gaunt and bony, a man that has always eaten rather too little, a bedouin of the plain stands beside his camel, bronze-brown, yet with a bloom over the golden shimmer of his satiny skin, with finely jointed ankles and limbs. The short, clipped beard looks like a prop to the oval of the face; the big ears, lying close to the head, like those of antelopes, the aquiline nose, which makes the aristocrats of all the world akin, the fur- rowed brow, jutting over deep-set, hunter's eyes, the narrow mouth, patient and silent, well-marked, but not salient lips, make a whole eloquent of the courage and prudence, the dignity and simplicity, of the man on his own resources, always in close con- tact with fate, perpetually dependent on its freaks. A man whose whole life is spent like the youth, at most, of interesting white men, a man who bears the laws of the stars in his being and the marks of the sun on his body—"looking burnt," Herodotus said— a being whose self-confidence is born of his body, who translates the power of his eyes, which are three times as keen as the white man's, into the strength of his soul, a man whose ancestors always chose the handsomest for their kings, whose court, when the king had lost the use of a limb, at once sacrificed the same one. Such truly royal customs were recorded by Strabo; most have survived till today.

In these latitudes, among these tribes, battle is still a necessity and hence magnificent; here man still stands up to man; the rules of combat, mercy, and sacrifice are still written in heaven; generosity is a virtue, like vengeance. These heathens could still interpret and mould to their own use the creed of Mohammed, but Christianity remained alien to them. They still have many a custom in common with the nomads of the Old Testament: revenge, reverence of age, the casting up of dust in danger, the rending of their garments. There are pilgrims, too, among these nomads, Negroes from the west coast of Africa, who cross the whole continent to see Mecca, earning their living on the way, remaining often for years here between the White and the Blue Niles, founding families, and reaching the tomb of the prophet twenty years after they set out, a feat of pious valour such as no sect of the western world has been able to record to this very day.

But that is quite alien to the native nomad. He knows no *suras*, no Koran; of Mecca he knows only its orientation, for he has learnt to set his rug in the sand that way before he prays.

Even the women he treats with more freedom than the surrounding religions and customs permit: the bedouin understands love. As the women do not live in a harem, there are romances and battles: an English explorer a hundred years ago found the power of the women in a tribe of the Djalli Arabs between Sennar and Kordofan so great that on marrying they stipulated in writing for one free day in four, so that on the fourth day they could present their suitors with chartered rights. Even today there are in these regions witches who can make a man impotent, restoring him his manliness rarely and then, very cleverly, only to their own use.

The laxity in love of these bedouins is consistent with their ideas of succession and inheritance, which are reckoned through the female line. Without house or land, this wanderer on the face of the earth has as his only certainties God and the moment, not answers to the questions of paternity. "Whether the husband be the father," says an Arab writer of the Bisharin, the handsomest bedouins, "is never certain, but one can be sure of the mother." Hence one's own sons are excluded from the heritage, which is passed on to the sons of one's sister, in whom the succession by blood is beyond doubt. This right of inheritance in the female line determined the succession in the royal family of Sennar till its extinction a hundred years ago.

In the course of the year, the day comes when the bedouin cleans up his land. Then he sharpens a stick of the "fire-tree," one of the leguminosæ, makes a notch in another, fits the point into the notch, and works them about until a smoky-smelling powder is produced, which begins to smoulder. With that he sets fire to the dry grass in the direction of the wind; in half an hour the plain is on fire. Then the gazelles take to their heels, the snakes seek shelter, insects, trying to find a refuge in the bushes, fall victim to the bee-eater, the snake-buzzard catches everything that flies, while the leopard takes flight instead of pursuing prey: there is a wholesale scamper through the bush.

Only the bedouin regards the fire with satisfaction, for now he has cleared his pasture.

OLD AND NEW

JOURNEY THROUGH THE STEPPE

4

MISQUOTING slightly an old Arab scholar, we might say that the Nile flows four months through the wilderness (jungle, mountain, and swamp), two months through the land of the blacks, and one through the land of Mohammed.

"When Allah made the Sudan, Allah laughed," says an Arab proverb, but one may wonder at which part of the Sudan he laughed, for it is a world in itself, with blooming and arid provinces. The Sudan stretches from the tropical forest into the desert; it is called "the land of the blacks"; it is five times as big as France, but has only six million inhabitants; it runs right across northeast Africa, hence it cannot but vary greatly according to the river and the rain. A land of lowlands and flat hills, with a single volcanic region in Darfur, falling gently from three thousand feet in the south, flanked by mountains to south and east, and partly in the west too, rising as a whole from west to east, in the direction of Abyssinia, the rain reaches it with varying strength and at different times, so that it shows no uniformity of flora, fauna, or men.

The rainfall, which, in the neighbourhood of the swamps, amounts to forty inches a year, and at Khartoum to six, stops entirely from 18° N. lat. on, about Berber, and only begins again close above Cairo. To the south of the Tropic of Cancer, where the trade wind is interrupted when the sun reaches the zenith, that is, where the rising air cools down over the hottest area, it falls again as rain in the months of June to August, because at that time the sun rapidly reaches and quits the zenith on the latitude of Khartoum, a scanty summer rain which brings forth grass and tamarisks, thornbushes and little acacias. On the other hand, farther south, owing to the greater distance from the tropic, there are two ill-defined rainy seasons, and complete drought from May to August. In September, when the sun dries out the sodden earth, the air is like a Turkish bath.

Nubia denotes only the part of the Sudan that stretches roughly from Khartoum to Aswân; Upper Nubia, which belongs to the Sudan, reaches as far as Wadi Halfa. In the west the Sudan is bounded by the white powers, but not by nature, for there the desert stretches straight across the continent, and sand and wind blow over the helpless stakes which at wide intervals attempt to divide the unity of the desert into British and French dominions.

This land above Wadi Halfa was called by the Egyptians and in the Bible the Land of Kush; by the Romans, Ethiopia. Of its provinces, the only name known to the world today is that of Kordofan, for gold and rubber have long come from there; the world knows too that the Northern Sudan was Christian for several centuries and has been Mohammedan since the fourteenth century, that Semitic and Hamitic peoples with a strain of Negro blood live in the north, Negroes with a strain of Hamitic blood in the south. Nubia, the name we may adopt for the Sudan to the north of Khartoum, has preserved its ancient customs better than Egypt, with its flood of foreigners, for here civilization penetrated from the north only in very ancient and in very modern times: in between the Arabs came over the Red Sea, for, long before the white races had ever dreamed of it, they had sailed to Zanzibar.

Here, too, the Nile determined the course of history, just because it did not form a constant waterway. At the First Cataract, by Aswân, Mediterranean civilization ceased. With galleys rowed by native slaves groaning under the whip of the conqueror, all the civilized powers, from the Pharaohs to Mehemet Ali, attempted to pass the rapids, either on the river itself or by dragging the boats along the bank.

In this huge country, there was no attempt to achieve unity until a hundred years ago; it was first achieved in our century, and it may well pass away before it is fully consolidated. Of what was accomplished by the peoples of antiquity on the middle Nile there remain only brief flashes. In the interior, great empires rose where the trees of the south stop and the bush begins, for a king can no more survey the savanna than a giraffe, for which reason both moved into the bush.

But these kings, some between the Blue and the White Niles, some in Darfur on the White, knew little of each other, for they, and other smaller dominions, differing in tongue and creed, were connected only by a river which was not navigable. The Fungs, who founded their dynasty when Cervantes and Leonardo da Vinci were flourishing in Europe, held part of Upper Nubia together for three hundred years; they entered history because great scholars from Arabia and Baghdad sojourned at their black court. Perhaps they will survive in legend only in the person of that gallant but sensible king who had thirty-three rooms built for his thirty-three wives, and had three hundred and sixty-five goats and a quantity of beer brought into the courtyard of his palace so that he might have his peace for a year, then locked the door, admitting his chancellor once a day. This excellent monarch— perhaps it was no mere hazard that he reigned in the European eighteenth century—by ruling half an hour a day certainly made his people happier than his conquering fathers. All these native kings of the Sudan lost their power about 1800, but the Fungs died out only in 1916, and even today their distant descendants are to be found in neat huts under the palms at Singa on the Blue Nile, where, as the last scions of mighty princes, they perform the coffee ceremony with dignity.

A hundred years ago, the capital of the Sudan was born of a camp of tents. A conquering prince from Egypt realized the vital importance to world history of the point where the two Niles meet, and named it Khartoum, after the trunk-shaped peninsula formed by the confluence, for Khartoum means "elephant trunk." Lying vertically below the source and above the mouth of the Nile, in the middle of the White and at the mouth of the Blue, it is the mathematical and dramatic centre of the wonderful river, where thought would make a halt even if there were no town. As it lies there, it extends from the fertile double Nile to the edge of the plain, linking the profusion of tropical gardens with the sands of the desert, an image of the river which created it. Lying where the Nile divides the desert, sketched in like a whim of God, the town is the meeting-point of all the roads connecting the two oceans on this latitude. A thousand pilgrims and a thousand traders crossed the Nile long before the bridges, in hope and prayer, or fleeing from persecution, to hide themselves in the desert beyond, and if all the ghosts of all the slaves were to arise here, who were driven from Kordofan to the Red Sea to end in the unfathomable depths of Arabia, their train of suffering would take weeks and weeks to pass, and the mountain of gold their sellers gained by them would be big enough to choke up both Niles and so to flood the land that no one would ever need to be a slave again—but Egypt would dry up.

Where the two Niles embrace like brothers, there lies a palmy island formed by the branching of the Blue Nile; on its rich soil fruit and vegetables grow. Where bridges and railways, motor boats and aeroplanes, speak of our century, the water-wheel, which made its appearance on the last reaches of both rivers, turns even today.

Here at Khartoum, the island of Tuti is the first piece of land on the White Nile to be fertilized by the silt of the Blue. In splendour and profusion, watered by a hundred water-wheels through days, years, and centuries, the bold date-palms, the huge baobabs, rise from the gardens of the governor and the high officials, whose palaces and stone houses speak here of England. From these rulers, a carefully graduated scale descends through Greeks and Syrians to the Sudanese, who in no wise appear here as the lords of the land.

Where the row of gardens ends, close to the confluence and the second bridge, lies the strangest zoo in the world: formed and kept with the greatest skill, it contains only animals native to the country. Here the gazelles walk fearless, flirting for the first time in their lives with the lion, who looks out from behind his bars with the sad eyes of the captive beast of prey. And beside the gazelles, the shoebird struts about with its comic gait, the egrets bathe, the cranes flaunt, the humped dromedary glides over the grass, and the young hippopotamus, behind an apology for bars, displays his huge pink mouth: they might be vague imitations of what is going on outside, a pretty parade instead of a war.

But when the master of the garden comes, the major who loves beasts and men, a great expert on this fauna, they run to meet

him, the gazelle nuzzles him in the back with her sharp horns, for
she knows he has his pockets full of food, and Jane, the lovely
cheetah, sweeps her bars with feline grace to greet him. A look
at this miniature Africa, with its animals, some tame, some half-
enclosed, stirs strange thoughts of the taming of the six million
inhabitants, who, taken from their state of nature, were trained
to become workers in the cotton-fields, teachers, and bank clerks,
and nobody can say for certain whether they are not savage still,
like the half-prisoned animals in the zoo.

Beyond, on the left bank of the Nile, they have their own town,
three times as big as British Khartoum. This is Omdurman,
founded only fifty years ago on a vacant beach, a white counter-
fort to the red-tiled city of Khartoum. There are no ramparts
here now; they are replaced by the masses huddled together in this
second largest town in Africa. Will they always submit? At the
turn of this century, they made themselves masters of the Gothic
palace on the other side.

This densely crowded oasis is flooded with desert light, a radia-
tion such as the sun creates elsewhere only on glaciers. In this
light, street and markets swarm with arts and crafts. Saddlers sew
gaudy leather to make cushions, or hammer shining nails into
saddles, smiths grip the iron with work-torn hands, silversmiths
hold silver in their tapering fingers, balances are held aloft to
weigh the silver rupee, spirited horses, gloomy camels, wise grey
asses, neighing and braying pell-mell, are bought and sold on
land, boats and sails are bought and sold on the beach, and men
and beasts scream each other down. The turban and the fez, the
well-groomed mane of the bedouin and the shorn head of the
Egyptian trader, fly-blown melons looking like meat, lumps of
mutton looking like enormous melons, children and priests,
shouts and protests, carpet-sellers and brothel-keepers, sheikhs
and mountebanks, officials, coachmen, and camel-drivers, dark-
brown Negroes with gaudy tufts of feathers, swarthy Syrians, slim
Greeks in tropical suits, huge Kordofanese in red silk garments,
squat Persians covered with furs to sell, half-castes with Negro
hair, red eyebrows, and an aquiline nose, planted here by some
Alexandrian prince in the Middle Ages, or by an English noble-
man a few years ago, all pushing their way in the incredible noise,

in the relentless smells, through the low white streets, and the tram-driver displays the iron nerves of a dictator, for he brings his tram, crowded inside and out, to the bridge without losing a man.

But where the cloudless glitter of the sun is reflected in the embrace of the rivers, an old man, led by a naked child, glides along the quay. He hears the noise of his brothers, can even smell them, but Allah has taken from him Africa's greatest gift, light.

5

IN a little Paris café, among white-coated waiters, among men and women trying over their bock at their wooden table to shout down the braying phonograph, two men are coolly playing billiards in the circle of light shed by a hanging green lamp. They are in shirt-sleeves, for sometimes it is an acrobatic feat to reach across the table with their long cues: city clerks, perhaps, who have spent their day adding up figures or sorting samples. Now, in perfect silence, they strike the ball, which rolls noiselessly along the fine cloth to the rubber-lined edge of the table, so that, by the rules of the game, it shall strike two other balls. At that same moment, at a few thousand other tables, a few thousand other intent and skilful players are at the same game, generally in the evening, in cafés or clubs, and they are nearly all men. Since billiards was invented four centuries ago in Italy, it has been a game for individualists; the crowd, playing golf with its arms or cards with its head, finds billiards, which requires both, too exacting.

To make these three balls, which the two men knock about on the green cloth every evening, the hugest animal of the earth, the last of the primeval giants to reach into our shrunken dimensions, has had to fall, for its two tusks yield eight or ten balls, the ammunition for three billiard tables, that is, for six men in shirt-sleeves under a green lamp. The various articles made of these tusks even today (the Romans made artificial teeth of them)—combs and fans, slide-rules and chessmen, jewel-boxes, piano-keys, and umbrella-handles, rings and buckles—are mere by-products compared with the billiard balls, belong without exception to the world of play and decoration, and are easy to replace, both as regards form and beauty. The balls alone, with their peculiar density, could not, in former times, be produced from any other material: everything else can be made more beautifully of costly bone and wood; and when the lady at her harpsichord, who till that time had delighted in the gleam of her white hands on the black keys, adopted white keys in the eighteenth century because the black made her eyes swim, at least one command of the muses came to reduce to order the scattered hazard of the industry, for, with ivory keys, the piano was better played.

Not only the elephant, but the native elephant-hunters on the Nile were ignorant of all that: they only saw Arabs and Turks bringing chests of splendid things on their camels and boats and asking nothing in exchange but an elephant tusk. Even today the Negroes cannot understand why the white man does not prefer a hippo hide, from which whips and saddles can be made, or congoni horns, which can be carved, or the juice of certain herbs, which can be used for poisoning arrowheads. They certainly carry all these things away with them, but their real passion is the elephant tusk, and a Dinka chief whose father made provision for the white man's folly and buried a hoard of tusks on the Nile, can buy what he likes with them and becomes lord of the world.

The native hunted the elephants only when they broke into his fields, and even then as rarely as possible, for he could get his meat more easily from a hippo and the great fossil tusks were good only for stakes to bind the oxen. And as the elephant, unlike the lions, leopards, and crocodiles, neither attacks nor carries off men or other animals, the Negroes hunted it less than the other animals, and could even manage at times to scare it out of their fields with howls and yells. No Negro saga makes it wicked, and many make it wise.

Certain mighty kings had long used ivory for their adornment; but only when the white man, the "Turco," made his appearance, long ago to the north of Khartoum, but no more than a hundred years ago on the Upper Nile, did his desire convert the elephant into a first-class object of trade; and the vision of glass beads and rifles, which the white man offered in exchange, at once made elephant-hunting popular. The same thing happened to the elephant as to the "hereditary enemy" of a state: he was the victim of a catchword, and now everybody set about hunting him.

This mightiest and most quick-witted of animals can be conquered by so small a creature as man only through cunning and fear: they dig pitfalls near the water, which they strew with elephant dung, then spear the helpless animals in them to death; they encircle the bush in thousands, set fire to it, narrow the circle by advancing with the flames, which dazzle and confuse the animal; they pursue it in hundreds, driving it towards other hundreds hidden up in trees, who drop spears on it from above, chasing it through the undergrowth from which long spears protrude like crowbars to rend and twist open wounds in its flesh until the colossus sinks to earth. Only the famous Baggara, to the north of Khartoum, hunt it chivalrously on horseback: with long lances of male bamboo, two of these Nubians gallop towards the herd, single out the elephant with the finest tusks; one keeps it in play on horseback while the other dismounts and, standing, drives his lance deep into its abdomen; then he mounts and gallops off and the other repeats the manœuvre.

When the hero has at last succumbed, men stream out of their hiding-places, howls of joy ring through the bush, the prize is two fine tusks, white and heavy. And far away, nine balls are rolling on three green tables, set in motion by six men in shirt-sleeves.

He was not easy to kill. Nature has protected her masterpiece, especially in this continent. For the brain of the African elephant is so situated on a bony plate over the roots of the upper molars that a bullet passes over it when he raises his head, as he always does when confronted with his attacker; thus even a grazing shot sits fast in the stiff bones and cartilages which contain the roots of the tusks. For the roots had to be placed three feet deep so that the huge head might keep its balance and support the strain when he uses the tusk as a lever to uproot a tree.

The African elephant is in all ways superior to his Indian brother. The arched back, the gigantic ears, which, thrown back, cover the shoulder, and, erect, are frightful to see, the convex forehead, and the well-marked back of the skull, all these details make his thrust more powerful. As he grows to over ten feet, so that the female is of the size of the Indian male, as he lives more on trees than the Indian, who eats grass, he requires more powerful tusks: in the Sudan, several together have been seen uprooting trees a hundred feet high, some using their tusks as crowbars, others tugging at the branches with their trunks. Thus armed, and, moreover, more active in the open bushland than the other in the Ceylon forests, they are not to be killed by a frontal attack: at most they can be turned by continued fire from the biggest calibres.

Even in beauty of outline, the African is superior; this beauty resides in clarity, as in the Egyptian statues: the head and trunk and ears form a more perfect whole in the Sudanese elephant than in the Indian. The light footfall of this heaviest of animals is incomparable: in excitement, he merely shakes his gigantic legs, just as men of self-control, in moments of growing suspense, merely shift from one foot to the other. Altogether, he is the pattern of a spirited, yet childlike, and hence cheerful being.

But now he lies dead on the plain, with a hundred black men round him, eager for his flesh, for his tusks. The myriad wrinkles on his skin tell the story of the forest and the steppe, of storms and insects: it is an atlas of whole countries, with smooth, as it were untouched, spots between them, as there may be on the soul of an aged man.

But when the black hands have at last hewn the two curved white trophies from his jaws, they by no means form a pair. Often the elephant uses one tusk more than the other, as men use their right hand, or one has been broken, or a hard deposit has formed round some old spear head or a bullet in the tusk. As the tusk has been built up in rings, like the trunk of a tree, but with the youngest inside, for a hundred years maybe, as it has continued to grow even in old age, it is not uniform even in colour. In the same way, after the death of a great man, criticism and analysis set to work on him, although, but a short time before, he stood harmonious, a living whole. But now they are already hacking off the huge feet from the corpse, for the chief demands four feet with every two tusks, to protect himself from being cheated.

Many a native king on the Upper Nile has collected hoards of ivory as his forebears collected hoards of gold: to this very day, four-fifths of all the ivory comes out of such hoards. Less is used today, for the balls can be made so well of synthetic materials that, of the genuine sort, only the hardest West African kinds are used for preference, as being most like the artificial ones. Critically compared, the synthetic balls are not as beautiful as those taken from the living tusk, but then the living elephant looks finer than the dead one. Since, moreover, the aeroplane has discovered the haunts of the great herds on the Upper Nile, since the English have imposed a tax of $250 for every elephant shot and have created vast reservations, ivory is now dealt with only in the same way as diamonds or radium—rarities, the value of which is controlled by a world market price.

Today, in the Antwerp market, there is a whole scale of colour, strength, density, grain; the tusks are bleached for piano-keys, for in nature, pure white is rare and hence looks unnatural; a pair of enormous tusks weighing four hundred and fifty pounds was presented as a wedding-gift to King George, who had no idea where to put them. The scraps cast off by the machine in turning the balls are shaken into a sack from which, as from a magic box, there issue buckles, handles, inlaid work, polishing powder, and even edible jellies. Even today, ivory is exported from Africa to the value of $5,000,000, and the native king on the Upper Nile who has hoarded anything up to a thousand tusks, a black capitalist, is no better than the white manager of a London factory who has never seen the Nile, and, in his armchair, with his list in his hands, shows that his present stock contains thirty thousand assorted balls. For those balls, three thousand elephants have died, and any one of them was, in strength and beauty, worth more than the manager.

6

ELEPHANT - HUNTING
turned into man-hunting. The later history of the Nile and the
development of the Sudan, which was completely dominated by
the slave-trade, would have been different if there had been no
billiards. Many thousands of men, living in a state of paradise,
became the captives and eunuchs of men living in its contrary
because two city clerks in shirt-sleeves needed three balls for their
green table.

In the beginning, some trader of genius had discovered glass
beads as a means of barter, and gave the delighted Negro or
Sudanese five big beads for a tusk. Was that cheating? Were the
five-cent pearls less beautiful than real ones which would have
cost as many hundreds of dollars? Was the value of billiard balls
not imaginary too, seeing that they were so soon to be imitated,
like the pearls? What fixed the value of diamonds, their beauty
or their rarity? Many a cheap, half-precious stone has a more fantastic effect. The arbitrariness of such valuation is revealed by the
rich woman's habit of wearing, instead of her real pearls, a row
of gaudy glass beads round her neck, quite in the taste of the
Negro, while her feet move to the rhythm of Negro dances.

So the Negro was not cheated, but his greed was awakened;
the glitter of the tawdry stuffs and stones with which the cunning
Arab bewitched the great sunburnt child made him want more,
and fired him with the joy of barter: he was expelled from his
paradise. Now he compared his hoard of beads with his neighbour's, sat for hours beside the strange trader in front of his chest,
fingering many a glittering stuff which he would have liked to
steal, if the trader had not had rifles. Buy—yes, but with what? His
ivory had run out, and until his whole tribe met for a new hunt,
which would, after all, bring in only four to six tusks, much time

might pass. Besides, it was the rainy season, the Nile was high, the western rivers made hunting difficult. What could he, a poor naked Negro chief, offer the great pasha? He possessed nothing but cattle and slaves.

Slaves? Supposing the trader were disposed to take on a few more hands? The trader nodded, that was what he had been waiting for. His own fathers had dealt for a century in slaves from Abyssinia, and had grown rich by providing slaves for Arabia's insatiable slave-hunger. This was a piece of luck! Here, at the end of the world, in a country without laws, without control, protected by his rifles, armed with the glitter of his beads and cloths, there was business to be done in men, which no rise in the price of ivory could reach.

The idea was new to the chief: it appealed to him. Till that time no slave-trade had developed on the Nile, as it had on the west coast of Africa, from the capture of enemy men, and especially women, who were used for field-labour and hence regarded as a kind of war-indemnity. But now it began, and since neither force nor law could check either whites or blacks, the new custom spread with the rapidity of bush-fires. There was another chief who needed thirty women for field-labour and thirty cowherds, but shunned war with his neighbours out of fear, laziness, or advanced age. Now he saw a few hundred men in his great Arab friend's pen. Supposing he were to offer him a tusk from his hoard for every three slaves?

By such barter, in ever-changing forms, which the oriental loves, the ivory-dealer of the last century became a slave-dealer, the slave-dealer a slave-hunter, and the slave-hunter in his turn an ivory-dealer. Man- and elephant-hunts vied with each other on the Upper Nile. From Khartoum, Arab business men concluded treaties with Negro chiefs through their emissaries, played them off against each other, and made them sell their subjects, just as the Elector of Hesse once did in Germany. What possibilities for those bold, ingenious spirits, one of whom first made his way through the swamps to the Bahr-el-Ghazal, found lost tribes there, caught and bartered them, and even became an agent of civilization by opening up unknown peoples on the Nile! Then East Africa, too, became what has been called the house of bondage. But no trader would have penetrated through all the dangers of the Nile and the Negroes to 3° N. lat. if he had not been drawn on by the lust of ivory to where it was to be found.

Some fugitive or adventurer, some Ali, would find a rich man in Khartoum ready to be inveigled into lending him a few hundred pounds in order to get it back with a hundred-percent profit in ivory six months later. Then Ali would collect a few dozen shady helpers, buy boats, rifles, bullets, and a few hundredweight of glass beads, which had been blown into existence by the pale mouth of some glassblower on the Venetian lagoons. The men would get five months' pay in advance, fifteen Maria Theresa dollars each, and the promise of double at the end of the river-pirate's raid. Each got a slip of paper to keep his accounts, and promptly gave it back to Ali, who was the only one who could write. They went up-Nile in December, as far as the Shilluks, even as far as the Dinkas, where friendship would be sworn with some chief, who got a few rifles and went off forthwith to make war on his enemy, his neighbour. Meanwhile Ali and his men would attack a village, burn it, kill most of the men, hack off their hands for the sake of their bracelets, and drive away the women, children, and herds. Then Ali would rejoin his new black friend and make him a present of cattle and a beautiful girl.

But now the savage king, greedy for more cattle, would drag his hidden ivory into the camp of the stranger, whom he regarded as a pasha, a god. The men would get part of the spoils, even some of the slaves, because the slave-markets began even here, and everyone would buy as many as he could. Ali wrote everything down on the little slip of paper, to dock it off the pay later. Then the men would parade a captive in front of his wailing wife or his father, and give him back for a few fine tusks.

The last act: a quarrel with the allied chief, whom Ali would plunder or kill, so that his wife and children became slaves too. And when the crowded boats set out for home, some of the men would stay behind to carry on the game, and to sell the trader the fresh spoils the next year. Before Khartoum was reached, the goods would be disembarked and distributed among middlemen, to prevent the authorities from finding out how rich Ali had grown. The slaves were driven through the desert, over the Red

Sea to Arabia, even to Cairo, each one in the *sheba,* a fork round his neck with a long handle touching his outstretched arm: if he let his arm sink, he was throttled by the fork. That was the worst moment of his fate. Ali would bring his backer the promised ivory, in good years up to twenty thousand pounds, to a value of $20,000 in Khartoum. As he paid his men in slaves, wages cost him nothing, and he had a net profit of a few hundred slaves worth twenty-five to thirty dollars each. Ali, like many a white man of business, had made his fortune with a by-product.

Thus the slave-dealers became a political power, and in the south were more powerful than the government, often allying with native chiefs against it. The Egyptian officers, often paid in slaves instead of in money, officials, small and great, the Pasha himself, lording it in Khartoum, all speculated as if in a Wall Street boom. From 1840 to 1860 forty to sixty thousand men are said to have been sold yearly, and the number of dead is incalculable. As the whole business had to be carried on underhand, it all had to be done by bribery. Commerce on the Upper Nile, which had begun with ivory, became a state necessity, brought about a state crisis, and in the end even led to the decline of Egyptian supremacy.

7

ONE day, a Frenchman appeared before the ruler of Egypt, bearing a strange gift—a bag of seed. Cailliaud, the explorer, had brought cotton-seed with him from the Sudan, had shown specimens of its peculiar fruit, and inspired the Khedive with the idea of cultivating it in the fertile delta. Mehemet Ali had probably not read Pliny, for he had been trained as an Albanian soldier, but he certainly knew of the tradition of Egyptian cotton, and as he was no hereditary king, but a conquerer, he was intelligent enough to grasp at once the value of the hint. There will be plenty to say about that later on. It was about 1820 when the botanist's report came to supplement and give final confirmation to the earlier ones made by civil officials and military commanders.

But the attentive Pasha picked up other things from the Frenchman's tales, and true and false were mingled as in oriental tales. There was gold in the Sudan, which the old Pharaohs had worked, there was ivory to be had from countless elephants, there was incense in Kordofan, and as for the diamonds, tidings of which had come along the Nile from olden times, they were certainly to be found below the eighteenth parallel, since they had been found in other places on that latitude in Africa. Cailliaud brought a glass of water from the confluence of the two Niles, for he was both an expert and an enthusiast, and just on that account impressed the enterprising spirit of the ruler. And the Frenchman spoke, too, of the source of the Nile, which an ambitious king should discover. What would Europe have to say against an Egyptian conqueror if he were to appear in the guise of a pioneer of science?

Mehemet probably betrayed no word of his political musings to the scientist with his glass of holy water. Gold would be good, diamonds too; still better to get rid of the last Mamelukes in Cairo, with whose brothers he had had a momentous quarrel, to occupy his idle Egyptian and Albanian troops, to attract trade from the Red Sea to Egypt—above all to get soldiers! To get soldiers from that hot country, the dream of all dictators, even if there are already so many that they are looking for something to do—soldiers, that means slaves set free to be re-enslaved. How long had these Nubians been owing their taxes? And if the tax-gatherers had pocketed them, all the more reason for inventing a tax which would bring something in—and that meant soldiers! If this cotton really grew wild, what if it were to be cultivated there on a large scale and brought down the Nile? And gold, and ivory, and the glory of discovering the source!

Mehemet Ali, with whose expeditions, between 1820 and 1840, the written history of the Sudan really first begins, this astonishing creature, of whom we shall hear further at the mouth of the river, paid dearly for his boldness. His son, a twenty-two-year-old general who had subjected the tribes in a rapid march up to the eleventh parallel, finally fell into a trap. In Shendi, below Khartoum, on the Nile, he had exacted as tribute from the mighty Mek Nimur a thousand oxen, a thousand young girl slaves, a thousand camels, sheep, and goats, a thousand camel-loads of corn, and a thousand camel-loads of straw. Mek Nimur bowed, saying: "Your arithmetic is of a monumental simplicity. A thousand seems to be the only number you know."

When all was gathered together, and the straw heaped up round the camp, the Mek invited them all to a feast in his house, vanished late at night, set fire to the whole, and destroyed the young conqueror with his officers. A frightful revenge was taken. Shendi was burnt to the ground, a thousand women and children were slaughtered on the banks of the river, and only the Mek escaped to the desert.

In spite of all the atrocities which filled these campaigns, exploration went hand in hand with conquest. There was a king in Sennar whose favourite dish was human liver with beer; the ears of prisoners were sent to the Viceroy in Cairo; yet at the same time Khartoum was founded, and light boats reached the Dinkas, who had never been reached before. Later, the Pasha came in person into the Sudan, and won immortality by a new form of tax-proclamation: on the middle tree of every village, he hung a sack of camel dung, and the village had to pay as many dollars as there were balls of dung. In the end, peace was restored to the accessible parts of the country—the peace of a graveyard. But in the south, robbers had followed the discoverers, just as they do today, when they call themselves explorers.

The exploitation of these quite unguarded regions set in with this questionable conquest; the greed of the traders was drawn up-Nile abreast of the explorers' efforts. Missionaries advanced and were forced to withdraw: for the Pope, Africa became a "vicariate," for a Sardinian consul, a "base." Up there on the Nile, where the path of Egyptian and Nubian traders and robbers crossed that of Austrian missionaries, the former out for ivory, the latter out to win the Negro for Jesus, where remote great powers could conceal their aims under the message of one prophet, just as others concealed their slave-hunts under the message of another, one thing could not but grow, in these lost corners of the world—the hate of the Nubian for the Christian, the attraction of the Christian to the Negro.

Later, when Ismail, the successor of Mehemet Ali, saw his strength broken by his good intentions, and the great slave-dealers defiant like kings in their keeps, determined to pay only such taxes at such a time as the strength of their private armies made necessary, when he was harried by debts and enemies, he called in a foreigner to help in the Sudan, the first Egyptian to do so; as Governor, Christian, and Englishman, this man was to get his teeth into the problem. It was a man with splendid teeth that came.

Samuel Baker was forty before his mind turned to Africa. Till then he had been merely the wild hunter of Ceylon, a restless wanderer through the world, who declared that in England he wilted like a plant in a dark room. It ran in his blood: on the coast of Jamaica he had seen his father's sailing fleet sail off with sugar for England. A young giant, all lungs, eyes, and arms, he flung himself into panther-hunting in Ceylon, and when he wrote it all down in a book, nobody cast any doubt on his traveller's tales. Something prehistoric emanates from him, as he stands half-naked leaning on his spear, and it is easy to understand that he needed a "battery of rifles."

Baker was in no sense of the word brutal: he understood and loved animals and children, reared a little slave boy, and nearly despaired of life when three of his own children died within three years. Hot-tempered, but soon appeased, as strong men often are, born to command, but generous and hospitable, independent owing to inherited wealth, above all, blessed with radiant health, he seemed to be born to adventure. The only thing needful to such a man was war.

He arrived too late for the Crimean War, but there, when his invalid wife was dead, he found the companion he needed. With this lovely Hungarian, he went bear-hunting in Asia Minor till he grew tired of it. In those days, in 1861, the English hunters and adventurers could speak of nothing but the Nile. There was another kind of elephant there, different species of game from those in Ceylon, and hunting without end, but there was a victor's crown too, a goal, a fulfilment worthy of the toil. There was the struggle against slavery, which was just rousing the men of the west, which meant freedom, humanity, and glory.

Then Baker, always accompanied by his wife, discovered the second source of the Nile in three arduous years, a story of greatness and courage, of renunciation too. From that time on, the fame of Samuel the Lion-Hunter had spread through East Africa.

But now, five years later, when he returned as a powerful official, hate and distrust awaited the famous friend of the Negro. Why did he come disturbing the circles of the dealers? Who told this Christian to overthrow the beautiful screen, the Koran, in whose shadow the Moslem could enslave the black pagans? What had a struggle in Christian America to do with African Mohammedans who knew how to treat their slaves properly, if only because they were worth twenty-five dollars apiece? And was not the long war between the southern and northern states of America the proof of how necessary, how pleasing to God, the institution was? What was Mr. Baker doing on the Upper Nile in the gilded uniform which the Khedive had presented to him in Cairo?

In gloomy moments, Mr. Baker may well have asked himself the same question. He had come to slay, after all his lions and ele-

phants, that great serpent, the slave-trade, which was rapidly deci-
mating the land he had learned to love on the Upper Nile. Not
slavery. He laughed, in his resounding bass, at the declamations
of the English Anti-Slavery Societies, and taunted them, saying
they would do better to look first to the sufferings of their white
brothers in the coal mines.

Baker loved the Negro and distrusted the Arab: all his successors felt and acted in the same way. But he did not love the slave
as Tolstoy loved him, nor wish to set him free, like Lincoln. What
he wanted to fight against was the *trade* in men. Among his fel-
lows, the slave bore the lot of the worker: once carried off, he became a piece of goods, a maggoty fruit, often with a brilliant exterior, and in the harem, a creature for lust or laughter: the
difference lay less in the question of human happiness than in
the question of human dignity. The dark dealings in human flesh
were repugnant to him as a gentleman. He had seen the fat pashas
in Cairo driving out, accompanied by running *sais* in gilded
jackets, and still playing at Arabian Nights. He had heard the
whispers of the informers, showing their master, with obsequious
cunning, the footprints of their escaped comrade, skilled in every
toe-mark and every smell. Before his eyes, Negro boys had been
laid on the sand and castrated with a knifestroke, while the bleeding of the wound was stopped with molten lead. Coptic monasteries lived mainly on the preparation of eunuchs, always a matter
of life or death. Of such things, invented and practised by Mohammedans and Christians, the black heathen had remained
ignorant.

Baker, the big-game hunter turned explorer, developed, as
Governor, from an explorer into a ruler. In the country he had
begun to explore ten years earlier he founded a province. But
he was an isolated individual, and all the Nubians and Egyptians
who should have worked for him cheated him, and among his
highest officials he discovered traces of the slave-trade. The power
of the great slavers seemed not to be overcome.

Among them were men of Napoleonic genius. A Nubian adventurer, without knowledge or money, who had risen by cor-
ruption, Zobeir by name, had established a slave-farm on the
Upper Nile, had formed his own troops to guard it, had built a

kind of citadel with widespread huts, in which he resided surrounded by rugs and silver, and, to impress his visitors, kept a lion chained at the door. He had nothing to fear from the weak governments in Cairo and their English governor in Khartoum, but he feared the warlike Shilluks, who sought continually to attack him, and the sudd, which might choke up the Nile and cut him off. He might have called himself King Zobeir the First, but his son, an heir to greatness, like the sons of the coal magnates who get into the peerage, was the first to assume the title, calling himself "Suleiman, Lord of Bahr-el-Ghazal, Bor, and Mataka." This wholesale dealer in men was invisibly allied with the pashas in Cairo and the officials in Khartoum: they were one in hating the Englishman who came to spoil their business.

Who did not hate in this country? The Negro hated the Arab, who took him by surprise, robbed and sold him; the Arab hated the Turco, saying: "In the footsteps of the Turco, no grass grows." The Turks, scenting their greed for the fruits of the land, hated the Europeans whom the extravagant Khedive had to leave in the country to enable him to cover his debts. Taking another cross-section, the heathen hated the Mohammedan, whose prophet allowed him to enslave the unbeliever; the Mohammedan hated the Christian, whose prophet forbade him to keep more than one wife. This gamut of general hate ran from black through brown and olive to white, but it by no means took the same way back. For the white man felt closer to the Negro, just as a highly intelligent man prefers the company of children to that of all grades of the half-educated.

Amid this glowing lava, Baker stood alone, rather like the pacifists of today. At the end of four lost years, he returned home embittered, and might well regard it as a miracle that he returned safe and sound even from this expedition. Ten years later, when the London "Foreign Anti-Slavery Society" was celebrating at its jubilee the end of slavery, and invited Baker to be the guest of honour, he said, more brusquely than was his wont: "With this horrible and disgraceful picture of cowardice and cant before me, I do not understand the meaning of a jubilee in England."

A single bold saying such as this often ensures an honest man a more lasting place in history than all his deeds.

8

HIS successor was in every way his opposite. The huge, heavy, and bearded hunter, the warrior and ruler in weight and weapons, was followed as the Khedive's Governor in the Sudan by a small, slight, and active man, with a delicate complexion and hair, very fair, his moustache already half grizzled, his step light, always on the move, his uniform never according to regulations, with any hat on his head, half sarcastic, half naïve. His boyish slimness and purity, the healthy colour of his skin, which did not seem to tan in the very midst of the desert, his ease and mobility, would have ensured him no great authority among black and brown men, if his steel-blue eyes had not pierced men like an arrow. "He saw with wonderful clearness, though not very far," a friend said of him, and that was borne out by the pure, yet keen look which characterized his being.

Such was General Gordon, whose character is marked by purity and inward light, while he lacked the robust self-assurance with which Baker shot elephants, discovered lakes, and, in the end, saved from Africa the life Gordon lost there. There may be a general tendency to overrate a man's virtues when his end has been tragic, but they should be used to interpret his nature, for even Gordon, in the last resort, fell as a result of his character. What inspired him, and kept him productive amid all his doubts, what gave his heart that confidence which speaks in his clear gaze, was a truly romantic relationship to God, which was not unlike Cromwell's, though it was less sombre. While other African explorers, by their constant association with Mohammedans and heathens, were in no way strengthened in their Christian faith, Gordon's never wavered, for he was, beside Livingstone, the only real believer among the Anglo-Africans.

When uncertain whether to advance or stay where he was, he

asked the Prophet Isaiah's advice; finding no water in Darfur, he noted an appropriate text from the Second Book of Kings. It seems that he read the Bible every morning for ten or twenty years. His generosity, a direct result of his faith, led him to let an enemy like the cunning Suleiman depart, and the manner in which he gave his money away all his life should be enough to dispose of the stupid popular canard about the meanness of the Scot. Once, when he lacked money for the sick about him, he sold the gold medal presented to him by the Emperor of China.

As a commander, such a character could not but be subject to serious extremes of leniency and harshness. After a victory, he confided to his sister, to whom he wrote long letters for half his life, his sympathy was with his fallen enemies. As he was too trustful, he overdid punishment when he was cheated, had his subordinates hanged when he found them corrupt, and took for his confidant a Negro who imposed on him. In the very midst of battles and journeys, he, on whom every move depended, would forbid anyone to enter his tent for a whole day at a time, while he consulted the Bible and searched his heart, meditating: "What is moral? What is the freedom of the slave? What is fame?" That he thought about fame so deeply and so long, with so much feeling and so much irony, would be enough to make Gordon lovable.

This Highlander, whose Bible bookmark was a ribbon in the blue, green, and yellow tartan of his own clan, was in reality an officer of the Engineers, but his faith stood so clearly written on his brow, he was, even in youth, so like St. Michael, standing supported on his faith and his sword, that, when a new Messiah arose in China, Captain Gordon was promoted general out of hand to annihilate the false prophet: he did so, and some said later that he had saved China. Between jobs in Constantinople and commissions in Jerusalem, he always returned to England, built a fort there, went abroad again, apparently never looking at a woman, yet with anything but the unctuous look of a "saint." With his fine, reddish colour, his regular, cheerful features, his splendid eyes, he might have been regarded as a flower of Scottish beauty if he were a little bigger. He was forty when he entered the Sudan.

It is easy for a pure spirit to be more tolerant towards the criminal than a man of the world, just because crime is so alien to it. In 1874, when Gordon was sent to the Upper Nile by the Khedive Ismail as Governor, so that the country might at last be conquered for Egypt, he was more interested in opening it up than in the struggle for the slaves. He wanted rather to win the Negro than to fight the Arab, and once, when he swam across the Nile at the Juba rapids, fearless of the crocodiles, holding his rifle high in his left hand, he won the reverence of the Negroes, on whose lips the saga of the great white swimmer with the rifle sped along the river.

But two years later, when Gordon had been promoted to the position of Governor of the whole Sudan, the contrasts there came out just as powerfully as under Baker. Zobeir, the slave-king, who had been powerful enough to drive out the kings of Darfur after five centuries of rule, had, like many an adventurer, weakened in face of the sirens of the legitimate rulers, and was lured to Cairo, where a firm hold was kept on him. When Gordon was trying to make his weaker successor Suleiman see reason, what did he do? He did not summon the rebel to his court of law or invite him to his house. Nor did he set out against him with strong troops and big guns. He consulted the Bible and acted like a Christian, not like a governor. He rode through the desert with two hundred men, urging on his camel sixty-five miles a day through the blaze, so that he appeared alone, ahead of all, in the presence of his enemy. Then he laid on his golden armour. Slowly he rode into the camp of the slave-dealers and robbers, trusting in his golden cuirass and in God.

Could savages understand such a thing? They did him no harm, the slave-king promised to punish the guilty robbers. When his men arrived, they were given a feast. For a moment, Gordon could believe that justice and order were conquering the sin in the world. But the savages thought him mad. Hardly had he gone when they were at their old tricks. Gessi, a courageous Italian, had now, with genuine armed force and without a golden armour, to take the field against Suleiman, whom he defeated and killed. He liberated the Negroes, but too quickly, so that they soon grew insolent; he turned the Arabs out of the province, but they loitered about resentful and bewildered. The revolution came too quickly, the slave-trade and slave-dealers were annihilated locally, but not their cause. The excellent intentions of these men led to the fatal result that everyone in the Sudan who had wealth and power became hostile to the Egyptian Government, which had given these Europeans a free hand in the country.

Embittered as Baker had been seven years before, Gordon left the Sudan, and put his talents at the service of British aims in other countries. In the Sudan he had left behind him a country which, at the end of ten years of British reforms, instead of being purged and reduced to order, was more than ever torn by unrest in the struggle against the Arab Nubian on behalf of the half-freed slave. Every year, the Sudanese grew to hate more deeply a government which had deposed the native kings in order to secure a comfortable life by the extortions of its pashas, while it remained itself remotely distant at the mouth of the Nile. The rich managed to evade taxation, to make fortunes out of slaves and ivory, while the poor merely heard that the Christian dogs were demanding the abolition of the slave-trade from the bankrupt Khedive, and thus already suspected their freedom on account of its doubtful origin. The Egyptian Government took from the traders their rubber and wax, ostriches and rhinoceros hide, monkeys and parrots, and above all ivory, in order to monopolize the sale itself.

When the Khedive's soldiers reached the oases, they quartered themselves on the bedouin and stayed there till he paid; if he did not, they laid him in the dry river bed or tied him to a tree till his wife brought money or cattle. The soldier who had not had his pay for years had perforce to make something on the tax, and so did the chief, who demanded more from the tribe than the soldier from him. The half-nomads preferred to abandon their crops and fled with their herds into the pathless bush. The peasant, who had paid taxes on his field and on every member of his family, preferred to let all lie fallow, moved up the White Nile, and turned trader or robber of men and cattle. Everything was taxed—the water-wheel on the Nile, the source of life, the palms, even if they bore nothing, the circumcision of children. But a gold-greedy pasha, whom Gordon himself had already turned out, sat in Khartoum, and proceeded somewhat in the manner of one of his predecessors. He set up a gun, which he called the "Cadi," the judge: anyone seeking protection who was irksome to him was led before the Cadi, tied to its mouth, and blown to pieces.

Such was the state of bondage in the Sudan. The time was ripe for a clever adventurer. In 1880, all the conditions, national and social, necessary for the foundation of a party, were given. The only thing lacking was a popular leader, who should invent a mystic catchword, and millions fell as blindly victim to him as if they had been whites.

9

MOHAMMED AHMED was poor in his childhood, and had suffered humiliation in his youth. Like most upstarts, he had been lucky enough to begin with a failure, and to win strength from it by defiant effort. The son of a poor Nubian, who built palm-wood boats between the cataracts in Dongola, he had, as the pupil of a sheikh, learned nothing save to reel off the ninety-nine names of the Prophet; later he learned to read and write, so that he could carry on a trade in little talismans in the form of strips of paper against witchcraft and disease, which brought him in just enough to live on. One day, when he had turned on his teacher in disobedience, the latter, in a rage, threw him into the sheba, the pillory, upon which the young man humbly asked for pardon. The infuriated teacher would not relent. Then Mohammed left him and departed to serve his deadly enemy, the head of another Koran school.

In thus beginning his career as a renegade, he discovered, in his warm welcome in the enemy camp, three facts about himself which might come in very useful: his name was Mohammed, he had fine eyes and silky hair, while on his right cheek he had a birthmark and in his mouth a striking gap in his teeth. As he saw that his indignant and desperate people lacked a leader, and as he was himself a clever speaker, it seemed to him not impossible that he might play a part, perhaps a great one. First of all, it was necessary to become a saint and a hermit. But where could one be visible to all and yet live in the interesting retreat of a fakir? Where could one live lonely as a saint, with the world fully aware of the fact?

Then he called to mind an uncle who built boats, like his father, on one of the big islands in the Nile above Khartoum. This island was admirably situated for a hermit, being quite central and visible. There, where all boats passed, and many put in for repairs, where the Mecca pilgrims from the west, the slave-dealers from the south, passed by, Mohammed set up as a saint, eating nothing but fruit and vegetables, presenting his two wives as his washerwomen, filling up his time with reciting suras, tending his long hair, and anointing himself with precious ambergris, so that he delighted all the curious, especially the women, with his perfume. In a few years' time, the saint of Abba Island was known everywhere, children came to see the pretty birthmark and kiss his snow-white robe, women, to compare themselves with the wives of the saint, soldiers, to get talismans against the spears of the heathen, peasants, to save their cattle from the pest. When he distributed the gifts they brought him among the poor of the island, they called him "The Self-Denier," all unknowing that it was just the poor of the island who fed him. On the rare occasions when he crossed the Nile, to wander on the shore with his beggar's cup, softly singing or reciting, they called him "Father Gaptooth," and all bowed before him.

Patience, the great faculty of the oriental, which makes him a more astute diplomat than the nerve-ridden men of the west, and a silent observation of the growing unrest, of which news was brought to him by the boatmen casting anchor from all parts of the Sudan, made Mohammed quietly bide the day on which he would first announce to his disciples on the island that the Messiah prophesied by the Koran, the Expected Mahdi, would soon appear. For centuries past, whenever revolution broke out in the lands of Islam, there was always somebody to proclaim the Expected Mahdi, that is, the Prophet renewed in eternal return, and generally ready to take the part himself. The Mahdi will appear, Mohammed prophesied. The Mahdi will appear, all repeated. Who is the Mahdi?

The authorities in Khartoum suspected nothing. On the contrary, the Governor prohibited his steamers from taking wood from the island of Abba, ordered them to slow down in passing, and to call the travellers to prayer with long whistles of the siren, and when a high Coptic official landed, and was entertained with sugar-water by the handsome gaunt apostle, it seemed to him that his jug did not empty, and he related the miracle to the astonishment of the pashas.

When Mohammed discerned the stupidity of the authorities, the disputes of the party-leaders, and the growing distress of the masses all round him, when he saw that he needed only to believe in himself to make the others believe in him, he resolved to ordain himself Mahdi. One evening, gathering his disciples under the shade of the palms on his island, he told them of his vision of the night before. The Prophet Mohammed, in a shining green robe, had descended towards him; angels, in a radiant circle, had surrounded him, with all the saints and those in glory; and Mohammed had spoken to him: "Lo! Here is the Mahdi, the mighty one. He who does not believe in him does not believe in God and in me." The disciples lay silent and shaken before their saint. But Mohammed said:

"Know, my friends, that I am the Expected Mahdi!" These men and women were the first to kneel before him, for now he revealed to them that he was of the race of the Prophet and therefore bore his name, and that Allah had branded him as his Chosen by the scar on his face. Hundreds were ready to believe in him at once, but he needed a million to lead his party to victory. In Arabic, Mahdi means the "Leader." The Mahdi now abandoned his saintly pose, grasped—figuratively at first--the sword, and sent his disciples through all the country round about with letters and messages proclaiming his magian accession.

"In the name of Allah, the gracious and merciful, praise be to the noble Ruler and blessings upon our Lord Mohammed and his race. And this is written by the servant of his Lord, by Mohammed the Mahdi . . . to his beloved friends in God and to all who follow him to restore and increase the faith. . . . Know that God has called me to the Caliphate and that the Prophet has proclaimed that I am the Expected Mahdi, and has placed me on his throne above nobles and princes, and God has surrounded me with his angels and his prophets. . . . And he has also said: 'God has set upon thee the sign of thy mission,' and to show all peoples that I am the Expected Mahdi, he has branded my right cheek with a mark of beauty. And another sign he gave unto me, and that is, that out of the light a banner shall appear, to be with me in the hour of battle, which is borne by the angel Asrael, the angel of death, the destroyer of my enemies. And he has given me to know that he who doubts my mission . . . he who is against me is an unbeliever, and whoever makes war on me shall be abandoned and without comfort in both dwellings, and that his goods and his children shall be forfeit to the faithful. Therefore, choose! Peace be unto ye!"

Thus the Mahdi had not only invented his divine mission; he had at the same time threatened his doubters and critics, and all in the name of God. As the Koran is also a code of civil law, and as the sheikhs, its interpreters, are also lawyers, his creed backed up his politics, and the Koran, better suited to dictators than the Bible, forthwith provided the new leader with the desired commandment: "Slay them who would slay you. Slay them where you find them."

The steps taken by the Governor, Gordon's successor, were too timid and too tardy. To an adjutant, who was sent to the island to summon the Mahdi to Khartoum, the latter replied:

"I am the Mahdi. The Pasha shall believe in me."

"How can you prove that?"

"My time is not yet come."

"Soldiers will be sent out against you."

"The Nile will swallow them up."

When a steamer came up-Nile with three hundred men and a gun, and moored by the bank opposite the island, three officers were disputing the command; the troops, ignorant of the place, groped about before sunrise, while the Mahdi's disciples, who knew every stone, fell upon them; the gunner on board could at first find neither powder nor shot, then fired in the air, and the expedition, with half of its men, returned defeated to Khartoum. The news of the Mahdi's wonderful victory spread throughout the Sudan.

Now the leader set out to establish his party, as far as possible, with all ranks and classes. To the poor he preached communist doctrines, the breaking of the bondage of tribute, the extermination of the big landowners, the praise of the peasant—whereupon a number of rich men were killed and robbed. But at the same

time he was able to court capital on religious pretexts by de-
nouncing the Turks and Albanians, that is, the tax-gatherers and
governors, as unworthy Moslems, who therefore need not be
obeyed. By playing on national and social feelings at the same
time, the Mahdi was able for a moment to unite under his flag
warring classes and interests. The rich Nubians laughed at him,
but they joined him, because he seemed to be protecting their
property from anarchy; the beggars banked on his communistic
catchwords; the Arabs clung to the new permission for slave-
dealing; and the Negroes, who had soon grown discontented with
their white liberators, because they still had to work for them,
hailed as their liberators from the the whites their old enemies,
the Baggara, and their leader. In a general state of despair, new
hope had sprung in every heart.

The Mahdi's first concern was a new flag, for he, a half-savage
himself, fully realized its importance for half-savages. Its green
and red waved before him everywhere as he travelled through
the triangle between the Blue and White Niles or over to Darfur.
While his party swelled, promising everything to everybody, he
looked about for two helpers capable of wielding the sword and
beating the drum for him. Though at first he had conducted his
own publicity, now, adored by thousands, he needed a special
manager for it. Professions, however, not being highly specialized
there, he found both functions combined in a slightly pock-
marked bedouin with a big nose, Abdullahi by name, a man
rather older than the Mahdi who was, in 1881, only thirty-three.
Belonging, as a Baggara, to the boldest tribe in Nubia, uprooted,
with his kin and his friends, by the chaos of the last decades, a
failure, hence ready for anything, this warrior pledged himself to
the saint, the sword superseded the word, and the great Dervish
drum, which from now on rolled through the Sudan, provided a
natural transition from advertisement to arms by belonging to
both.

The Mahdi's next care was ceremonies and uniforms, the real
instruments of a popular movement among savages, white and
black. The Dervishes—thus the rapidly formed army of the party-
leader was called—wore white shirts, *jibbahs,* with gaudy patches
sewn on them; the oath to the leader was taken with folded hands.

Abdullahi, the Khalifa of the Mahdi, followed his friend and leader on all his ways with a black flag, praying aloud. This warrior cared for nothing but the war against the "Turcos," who had humiliated his tribe, and defrauded them of their herds by taxation. And while the Dervish drum was drawing men from their huts to join the disorder and swell the warlike movement, the Dervishes, breathless and beside themselves with running and shouting, cried the names of Allah and fell into a kind of screaming frenzy.

While, as a national leader, he preached the simplicity of old customs, Mohammed imprisoned all who did not believe in him, confiscated the property of those who did not support him, reintroduced the death-penalty by hanging, and saw to it that thousands of rhino whips should provide for greater zeal in the faith. At the same time he maintained his sainthood, and made hundreds of devoted priests spread abroad that he was the twelfth Imam announced in the Koran, for whom the Moslem world had been waiting for twelve centuries, sent to purify the faith and win the world for his teaching. The Holy War was proclaimed. And while the women were finding mystic signs on the eggs in their poultry yards, which the busy Dervishes interpreted as the Arab cipher of the leader, he himself contrived to shake his visitors with alternate tears and laughter, until later a Greek (according to Gordon's diary) declared that he had seen the pepper under the Mahdi's finger-nails by which, putting his fingers to his eyes, he could provoke tears at any moment.

Where the legend did not fit him, the Mahdi twisted it until it did. He could hardly command the Euphrates, which was to dry up at his appearance, revealing mounds of gold in its bed, but Mount Masa, in the Atlas, from which the new Mahdi was to descend, could be transformed into the Sudanese Mount Gadir, provided the visions were forthcoming. And here Mohammed actually went to the mountain, even though it was not the right one, accompanied by thousands, who camped on the slopes, an army with women and children, who, however, were not, as they generally are in the field, a nuisance, but fanned the flame of fanaticism with their screaming. The Mahdi himself had many beautiful daughters presented to him by his devotees as wives,

Photo: Lehnert & Landrock, Cairo

SECOND CATARACT

Photo: Lehnert & Landrock, Cairo

THE NILE AT PHILÆ

and their tents were grouped round his own on the mountain; all the same he continued to play the saint.

In the Mahdi's sermons on the mount, some of which were oral, some written, and in manifestos carried far and wide by the troops on their lances, he drew further attention to his descent and birthmark, the source of his moral power, proved that all the signs were fulfilled and even replaced the thousand-year-old cry: "Allah is Allah and Mohammed is his prophet," by a new one: "and Mohammed Ahmed is his prophet." This Mahdi was perhaps the first modern tribune of the people to recognize that a fabrication, repeated often enough, acquires the appearance of truth.

At the same time, like the Prophet before him, he appointed four caliphs, each of whom had sub-leaders under him, with a complicated system of multi-coloured flags.

While these ceremonies, sermons, and flag-wavings were going on, the Khalifa Abdullahi collected a gigantic army from the whole of the Sudan.

10

IN Cairo, the English had quelled the chaos in their own favour. During a revolt, they bombarded Alexandria, and, declaring that order must be restored, took the power into their own hands. After so great a victory, they seemed disposed to withdraw—that is, withdraw docile Egypt—from the Sudan. And yet it was a British colonel, then in Egyptian service, who, warned by his government, opposed by the majority of the Egyptian officers, collected an army against the Mahdi to liberate the Sudan.

From the outset, Hicks was lost. Ignorant of the language of the country, dependent for guides on bedouins, who led him astray, what good were his modern weapons in desert and guerrilla warfare? In the decisive encounter, the tokens of two epochs came out clear, for the Egyptians, with their modern arms, which, it is true, they did not all know how to use, charged an army whose leaders came galloping along in armour and coats of mail, in armlets and greaves, like the Crusaders, followed by screaming Sudanese, dancing and waving their spears, and by naked Negroes, casting their bows in the air. An English officer, in trim khaki, armed with the most up-to-date pistols, advanced on a Nubian prince, who, in gaudy festal garments, with a silk turban, spurred his Arab horse against him, brandishing a great scimitar, and every time the Nubian was the victor.

In any case, by the end of the fight, the Egyptian army lay beaten in the sand, while the heads of the leaders were taken as trophies of victory. Colonel Hicks was one of the last to fall. Three hundred are said to have escaped.

After the victory, the Mahdi had become the hero of all hearts, and master of nearly the whole of the Sudan. When he entered El Obeïd and crossed the Nile as victor, the rotting head of the

English colonel was borne before him on a Dervish spear, and lowered to kiss the earth before the horse of the cunning adventurer weeks after his death. The sword carried before the Mahdi, presented by the Sultan of Darfur, bore, though nobody could read it, the inscription: "Charles V, Holy Roman Emperor." Once it had belonged to some belated Crusader, who had perhaps fought against the corsairs in Algeria, had fallen at his death into the hands of savage tribes, and, by the ways of legend, had reached the deserts of the Sudan. Thus the weapon of the All-Christian Emperor, in the hands of a Nubian Moslem, triumphed over the Christian Pasha.

In the face of such triumphs, the Mahdi began to believe in his own mission. Adored by all, he forgot his caution, took his pleasure in growing numbers of women, and put on flesh visibly. In his swelling megalomania, he had a man punished for saying that Allah was above the Mahdi—it was true, but the tone was insulting. Now he wore a yellow silk mantle with his green turban, was mild or Draconian as the fit took him, while the Khalifa, a kind of prime minister, busied himself with still more patches on his uniform, and had an ivory horn blown before him when he rode out. Both men succumbed to temptation, the one of adoration, the other of physical violence. As long as the Mahdi was simply striving for power, he was a clever tactician who, turning to account the outward distress and inward mystic yearnings of his people, sought to achieve their rise from poverty and humiliation, and to rule with Draconian severity a mob blinded with promises. When, under the rustling of his own flag, amid the hysterical cries of the crowd, amid men prostrate and worshipping before him, he began to doubt his mere cleverness and to believe in his divine mission, he lost his balance, revelled in processions and ceremonies, in death-sentences and royal whims, in speeches upon speeches. Therefore Allah soon took his life.

It was in November 1883. Gladstone and Bismarck, Queen Victoria and Wilhelm I, Crispi and Umberto, Alexander III, Francis Joseph, Leo XIII, were ruling Europe. Save for Russia, all were interested in the partition of Africa; a considerable part had already been distributed. Egypt's collapse in money and military power had been the signal for a dash to East Africa. With

the exception of Abyssinia, a natural fortress, the whole continent lay open for the white powers to snatch; the only thing was
to get there first. It should be easy to dispose of the Arabs and
Negroes.

Suddenly a monstrous thing had happened. English officers,
Egyptian troops trained by the English, had been beaten by a
horde of bedouins and peasants, Nubians and Negroes, had had
their heads cut off and had been insulted even in death. Egypt,
for which England was in vain seeking to shift the responsibility
which her suzerainty involved, had been driven from the Middle
and Upper Nile, which she had had the power if not to rule,
then at least to dominate, for sixty years. For centuries, Christian
Europe had suffered no such blow from savage peoples. An Austrian and an Englishman, Slatin and Lupton, Governors of two
Sudan provinces, pashas by the grace of the Khedive, had not
only surrendered; they had had to kneel before the Mahdi, repeat his oath, renounce Christianity, swear the Holy War against
the Christian dogs. The sons of citizens of Vienna and London,
Excellencies in glittering uniforms, had become the slaves Abd-
el-Kader and Abdullah, and had to run barefoot by the side of the
decorated horse on which the Mahdi rode through bush and
streets. Would this not be the signal for other coloured tribes to
break the invisible yoke in which the white lords held them
bound?

Still, the prevailing feeling at the time was not yet one of revenge. The number of European prisoners was small, their per-
sons obscure, the news vague. Looked at from Egypt, where Baring
(Lord Cromer) had been High Commissioner for a year, the desert
lay between the troops and the revolt—and what kind of troops
was it that had just been defeated? Ill-armed, ill-trained, without
enthusiasm. Liberal influences in England, which were out to re-
strict colonial expansion, supported the aged Gladstone, who was
not interested in Africa. It was therefore decided to abandon the
Sudan and withdraw the garrison from Khartoum. That needed
a man who knew it as an officer and yet was philosopher enough
to withdraw ingloriously. Such renunciation could not be expected of Baker the lion-hunter. A rather crazier man had to be
found. Gordon was found.

But Gordon, like Hamlet, was but mad north-north-west. It was never certain what he would do at the critical moment, and it was still less certain whether he would obey orders. Yet just on that account he seemed the right man to a disunited government and an uncertain public opinion. "The Sudan," he said once, "is a woman who has separated from her Egyptian husband. If she wants to marry again, let her. Then something can be done with her."

Since his return from Khartoum, five years before, he had almost disappeared, had been busy again in China and India, in Cape Colony and Mauritius, had spent a year in the Holy Land, and in between, had repeatedly turned up in Scotland, his home country; years without outward experiences had been rich in inward experience, to which his letters bear witness. He was about to return to Africa, though not in British service, but in that of Leopold of Belgium to the Congo, to the opening up of which Stanley had just given fresh impetus.

But hardly had he been summoned from Brussels to London when he let his chances on the Congo go, accepted, in an interview, the commission of the nation, which was passed on from Baker to Gordon. Even now Gordon's advice did not sound like evacuation: the Mahdi in Khartoum, he wrote, on the contrary, would mean a relapse into slavery and a menace to Egypt. All the same, the very ministers who distrusted him appointed him, and even Lord Cromer, who did not want a former Governor to have to carry out the retreat, had to yield; public opinion, England's dictator, bore Gordon up. Only old Gladstone was invisible, having wired his consent in so vital a question at the instance of three ministers. The wishes of the nation accompanied Gordon's journey, as though he were setting out to conquer a country, not to abandon one.

What was in Gordon's mind when he accepted the commission? He had to bring the white people and the officials from Khartoum into safety, to withdraw the troops, leave behind him some kind of government, and be the last white man to turn his back on the Sudan. A few days before his appointment, he had publicly advised the contrary. It could not escape him, as an officer, that he alone, unarmed, and with the prospect of the very few troops there, was going through the desert into a country in which the native army, once he had passed the cataracts, could shut him up in his capital from the north, and hence shut him off from the world. As a politician, a man who knew the country, he knew the power of a fanaticized mob, the hate of the Christian, and of any messenger from Egypt.

But General Gordon was a Crusader, sustained by the Bible and the sword; he was a philosopher and a puritan, sustained by his spirit and his conscience, and even if he had the tolerance to recognize God in a hundred forms, he had, all his life, been moved by the thought of glory, which he fought in himself as too worldly, and rechristened duty, like many a Christian before him. He was now fifty. A life lay behind him, rich in deeds, diverse in form, and scattered over many lands. With worthless equipment, without a firm supporter in the Cabinet, half distrusted by Cromer in Cairo, wholly distrusted by Gladstone in London, Gordon, a General Staff man, engineer and Governor, an expert on the desert and the Nile, like all his predecessors, was drawn back to Africa, back to his work, his soldiers and Negroes, urged on to deeds, perhaps to death.

In Khartoum, after five years of absence, Gordon found that the moral and political power he and Baker had built up was destroyed. There must have been a plucky heart in the body of the man who all the same took no advantage of his Government's instructions to retreat as soon as he could. The endless telegrams he sent to Cairo, communicating his decisions, though the detail varied, all betrayed the fundamental determination not to surrender the country and the town. How was he to bring away nearly sixty thousand people, officials, troops, soldiers, women, without transport or resources? Or was he simply to abandon them, while they all looked up to him at his arrival as the saviour prophet of the Bible? Both practical and moral considerations made it impossible in every way to carry out the order. Gordon acted as an officer—he fortified Khartoum, completed a canal three miles long by which his predecessor had again attempted to connect the White and Blue Niles, so that the town lay on an island, the trunk of the elephant was cut off. On the islands he set up forts, took advantage of the rise of the Nile, which made it difficult to attack the town, threw out trenches, drilled troops, and kept them only by the promise of an army of reinforcement in which he did not himself believe.

In such a situation, the officer in him had to send the puritan on leave, rather as Cromwell had done. Gordon did not merely have the whips and irons used by his Egyptian predecessors and successors destroyed before his palace; he abolished the prohibition of slavery so as to deprive the Mahdi of a trump card. He even tried to bring back to Khartoum the slave-king Zobeir, who was still detained in Cairo, and in him to put into power the only Sudanese who could resist the Mahdi. But this truly statesmanlike idea was rejected in London because the Anti-Slavery Society —gentlemen who had never been among savages and who moralized instead of thinking—worked public opinion up against the slave-dealer. Gordon was driven to such paradoxes that he, the liberator of the slaves, in vain called for the slave-king to save the situation, much as Gustavus Adolphus, towards the end of his life, outraged the tolerance of his own church.

What was to be done? Proclaim that the country would be restored to its ancient kings? Too late. Go and visit the Mahdi in his golden armour, as he had once visited the slave-king? The crazy scheme hung in the balance, but then he might have run, a third noble slave, beside the Madhi's horse. First he wrote him a letter offering him the Sultanate of Kordofan. The tribune of the people knew how to counter such things with caution. In his refusal, saying that no mortal could offer him power, the new Mohammed quoted to the Scottish puritan what the Jewish King Solomon was said to have told the Queen of Sheba: "You bring me gold, but what God has bestowed upon me is better than your gift," and continued with the taunt: "You are a people which loves gifts. But I shall come with an invisible army and drive you from your town into contempt and misery." The Mahdi even attempted to quote Jesus, who is, after all, a great prophet in the Koran, but Gordon, sure of his Bible, declared that there was no such passage.

The Mahdi had added a gift to his letter—a poor Dervish shirt, trousers, turban, a girdle of palm-straw, and a rosary, and wrote: "This is the clothing of them who renounce the world and its vanities and look towards the world that is to come, towards eternal Paradise. If you really desire God and a blessed life, put on these garments and come to me, then you shall have eternal blessedness." The ascetic who wrote this then had a harem of over a hundred women.

Gordon smiled and noted in his diary: "It seems to me that the Mohammedan fears God just as truly as we do, and if he is honest, he is just as good a Christian. We ourselves are all heathens, more or less." So far the tolerant philosopher in private. But the Governor, in a solemn convocation of the last notables in Khartoum, read the Mahdi's letter, then threw the false penitential shirt on the ground and trampled on it with his soldier's boots.

After this parley, the two enemies took up their positions: the tribes north of Khartoum, feeling themselves threatened by Gordon in the south and the promised troops in the north, now joined the Mahdi for good and all, shutting off the capital from the north. Fifty thousand Dervishes cut off from the world a solitary Englishman with a remnant of troops, though not entirely, for the wire on the Nile was still guarded, and the wire had at last promised men.

Could relief reach him? The British Government was irresolute, the Egyptian powerless. Probably Gladstone bore a grudge against the man who had forced him into this military adventure by transgressing his orders, and a grudge against his colleagues, who had sent the man out in the hope that he would transgress his orders. While Gladstone delayed with the relief, to force Gordon to return, Gordon remained in Khartoum to secure the Sudan and, as he thought, Egypt with it for England. Not until August 1884, under the pressure of the London press, did the other wing of the Cabinet prevail, and the troops which, had they been sent out in May, could have saved the situation, left three months too late.

Gordon saw the delay, saw its fatal consequences approaching, and now he spoke the truth over the wire: he would, he wired to Lord Cromer, from now on act as circumstances required, and take the decision into his own hands; perhaps he would go to the equator, "leaving to you the ineradicable shame of having left the garrison in the lurch." In his diary he wrote: "We are an honest people, but our diplomats are conies and not officially honest." But as the man of reason judges the fanatic more equitably than the fanatic the man of reason, Lord Cromer swallowed the insult, and later praised Gordon for being free from a national vice which "if not hypocrisy, is closely related to it."

The Nile joined with Gladstone to prevent Gordon's relief. A detachment which Gordon sent down the river to Dongola was exterminated because the steamer was dashed to pieces at a cataract and all the survivors were massacred by the Dervishes. In autumn, the race between the black prophet and the white believer began: the Khalifa concentrated increasing numbers of troops round Khartoum, the Governor strove to turn the desert city into a fortress, had earthworks thrown up, stretched canvas across them, had bread baked of palm-bark and gum arabic, at the same time rationing all supplies and having money coined. Above all, he kept everybody's spirits up, for he and he alone was the hope of thousands who saw the circle round them drawing ever closer, and a dreadful death before them if the English came too late.

Over in Omdurman, on the other side of the White Nile, which he had taken in December, sat the Mahdi, and when he issued from his harem, which seemed to occupy more and more of his time, he could, from a terrace beside the dome of his white Arab house, descry away over the Nile the roof of the Gothic palace in which his enemy held sway—for how long? He may even have recognized his silhouette through his field-glass, for Gordon sat for hours at a time on his roof, the highest point in the town, always looking north, from which, an African Tristan, he expected the rescuing ship—or perhaps expected it no longer. Was he already in the mood of one prophetically inspired—*moriturus*—only half-heartedly desiring rescue? In varying moods, he passed every free minute of his day with his diary, more than ever since the telegraph wire had been cut, drew caricatures of Cromer and the ministers round the edge, lauded, an all-too-Platonic general, every cunning move of his enemy, and yet never let his energy flag when he thought of all those who were counting on him.

In the end, even the Nile betrayed him: by running lower than in former winters, it undermined the fortress wall; between the wall and the river a swamp arose which protected the besieged only until it dried up. Hunger grew: the streets lay full of the bodies of men and camels; the vultures screamed over the town; but no steamship whistle sounded in the lost fortress. To show the besieged that their chief did not fear the Mahdi's guns, Gordon lit up all the windows of his palace. In these last weeks of his life, his fine curly hair literally turned white. "This may be the last letter," he wrote to his sister a fortnight before the end. "The expedition has delayed too long. Well, God guides all. His will be done. I am quite happy. Thank God, I have tried to do my duty."

The little army from the north had bad luck on the river, and hesitated many days. The Dervishes, who knew every rapid, lay hidden in the bush and fired at the steamers, whose crews had to stop repeatedly to take water-wheels from the banks for firewood. Then, at the southernmost point of the loop, the English set out to march through the desert to Khartoum. When the Khalifa saw that the enemy was only a few days off, he ordered a storm on the town he had besieged for three hundred days. In the morning, from the roof of his palace, Gordon saw the Dervish army approaching.

Though he had once resolved to kill himself in such a situation, in the end he felt religious scruples—he must die a martyr. In superb composure, at the end, recollecting at the last moment the dignity he represented as the last Englishman in the palace, he put on his white dress uniform, took his sword and revolver, and when the first enemy broke down the gate, came armed and alone down the stairs. For a few seconds, the group of gaudy Dervishes stood before the white apparition, with a last remainder of respect for the Governor. Then one shouted: "Kill him, the enemy of God." The first spear came flying, Gordon made a contemptuous gesture. Witnesses later examined in court said he had come fighting, sword in hand, downstairs, carving a way for himself to the door, only then to fall before the swords and daggers. His head was brought to the Mahdi as a trophy and set up in front of his house on a spear for the people to pelt with stones. Then a great massacre began in Khartoum.

On the following day, the comfortable prophet came across the junction of the two Niles on Gordon's steamer, contemplated the headless corpse of his enemy, the streets which lay full of the bodies of the last white men and Egyptians, the women, tortured to betray the hiding-place of their buried treasures, slaves trampling about on the still living bodies of their masters, dogs soaked, along with their masters, in brandy and set on fire, a death-dance of delirious humanity which, for half a century of enslavement, took a revenge which swelled to madness. Among the captive girls and boys, the Mahdi had the first, the Khalifa the second choice. The latter had Gordon's bath-tub and looking-glass brought to his palace. For they all remained in Omdurman, their own town, while Khartoum sank in ashes.

Two days after the capture, Scottish troops, many of them kilted with Gordon's own tartan, reached the Island of Tuti, were received with gunfire, retired precipitately, and came to grief again in the cataracts. Only a few managed to escape and bring the news to the camp set up downstream, pale as the messenger at the end of a Greek tragedy.

The Mahdi, who had grown fat and bloated in the last few years, survived his victory by four months. Beside the house of the ascetic a whole row of women's houses had arisen, many full of gold and Maria Theresa dollars, while gigantic heaps of dhurra were piled up as if he feared famine, and among them lay the grotesque loot of the treasures of Europe—lamps, tinned food, printing-presses, and a magic lantern, believed to be part of the Christian sorcerers' stock-in-trade.

But what was the Mahdi to do with the conquered Sudan? He sent messengers to all foreign countries, calling on them to believe in the Prophet; at times he preached to the people as of old, but now it was a mere form, for he had long since succumbed to gluttony, let his Khalifa rule, and was more occupied with the lovely Aminta, whose father and husband had been murdered in Khartoum, than with the disputes of the Dervishes, who were quarrelling with the younger party-members for money and office.

In public, the Mahdi still wore his linen robe, but inside his house, he wore costly stuffs, and when he reclined on brocade cushions, a few of his wives stood behind him with ostrich-feather fans, others massaged him, and the nearer to him they stood, the more costly were their garments. To the faithful outside they sold the water he had washed in, and little sacks containing the earth his foot had trod, till he died, perhaps poisoned by his lovely Aminta, perhaps only of fat, after a death-agony six days long.

Faithful, bold, and noble, a knight *sans peur et sans reproche*, Gordon, upright and alone, had fallen amid a thousand lances. A bloated colossus, surrounded by women and gold, the cunning tribune of the people, followed him. One left behind him a curse, the other a legend.

11

THE Nile was in the hands of savage tribes which were trying to block it. What would become of Egypt then? And even if the river still flowed, even if the silt of the Blue Nile still fertilized the land, would these hordes not move downstream one day, like their fathers two or three thousand years before them, occupy Egypt, guard the Red Sea coasts, and keep the British ships away from India? Was anything impossible after all that had happened?

Europe, in terror, saw its plan for the partition of Africa become doubtful. In England especially, the imperialists now had a hero, for whose memory it was incumbent upon them to take up the struggle and exact vengeance. Gordon dead rose to be a political factor, the strength of which he had perhaps foreseen in one of those lonely hours on the roof of his palace. When a nation has been guilty of a dereliction of duty towards one of its subjects who has fallen in the breach, it tends to do rather too much for his memory so as to dispose of him once for all. All motives co-operated to bring on the campaign which England had neglected after the defeat of Colonel Hicks.

And yet much time was to pass. During the years 1885–1898, the Khalifa dominated the Sudan, or at any rate strove to terrorize it by despotism. The first act of the new leader was to assassinate at one blow part of the family of the old, which was in his way. Then he threatened Upper Egypt in the north, the Negroes in the south, Darfur in the west, Abyssinia in the east, and while he was thus fighting on all sides with varying fortunes, the white neighbours of the Sudan, England, France, and Belgium, could break off bit by bit without a struggle.

Not until eleven years after Gordon's death did an event force a decision in England. When, in March 1896, the Italians had suffered a crushing defeat at Aduwa from the Negus Menelek, even the Liberals in England realized that Great Britain would have to act, or else make up her mind to abandon colonies altogether. Two coloured states in East Africa, then at war, yet neighbours, and hence perhaps allies the next day, had defeated two white powers, England and Italy. Now the time to act had come: twelve days after the battle of Aduwa, the advance into the Sudan was decided in London.

It was a universal resolve. At that time Africa was as good as entirely partitioned. Whichever country took the Sudan could consolidate its colonial empire for purposes of trade and war, less for the sake of its products than to obtain a land of transit, France to the west, England to the south. England had reasons and pretexts enough to take care of Egypt, which she had seized shortly before with the obvious intention of not letting it go again. Thus a situation arose which allowed England to appear in a threefold chivalrous guise: as the saviour from anarchy, the protector of the Egyptian states, and the avenger of the murdered Gordon, while at the same time she could check the expansion of France or Germany from the west and south. Though it has lately become the fashion to cast doubts on English sagacity, and to speak of luck and chance, it must be recognized that here English statesmanship was far-seeing, and in that spirit the enterprise was carried out.

In the Sudan flowed the Nile, the source of Egypt's life, and if a high English official writes, even today, that England could not "expose Egypt to the danger of the occupation of the Upper Nile by a third power," such a statement merely reveals the desire for power inspiring all annexation on the part of a country which can still hope for success in colonial wars. Thus the British Lohengrin sallied forth to secure the Egyptian Elsa from her perils, yet at the same time to win the right of her hand, that is, to her beauty and her fortune, which is generally the way of such mythological knights.

England profited by her experiences: this second campaign in the Sudan was not to cost as much in men and money as the first, but it had to be victorious. This time Egypt, for whose salvation the whole thing was ostensibly undertaken, had to provide both men and money, and thus the new campaign cost the English only a tenth part of those thirteen million pounds which had been squandered in the fight with the Mahdi. Victories generally come cheaper than defeats.

In this case, the gods had literally set the sweat and labour of the day before the crown of victory. From the Egyptian frontier to Khartoum, from 22° to 16° N. lat., stretched the almost water-less desert. This had to be crossed by a railway, for to venture on the Nile, with its rapids, its shallows, and its great loop, was to plunge into the same danger as Hicks and Gordon. If the Nile was the objective of the campaign, it was to be an instrument of conquest too, but it could not be the route of advance. The only possible way was a railway through the desert. As there were here neither mountains nor rivers to be crossed, as neither tunnels nor many bridges were necessary, the building of the railway, being a test rather of energy than technique, was quite properly con-ducted by officers. The enemy to be overcome by these railway-builders was not the land but the climate, which only the iron will of the soldier at work could cope with.

The commander in the desert was a big, muscular, and de-cidedly smart officer in the middle forties, sunburnt, with a full head of hair and a serious expression, elastic in his movements, especially on horseback. Once one realized that his squint was not of mental origin, but was due to a paralysis of the upper muscle of the left eye, it no longer aroused suspicion, but his icy, misanthropic manner, his domineering muteness, did not, for all that, make him likeable, and whoever had once shaken hands with him remembered all his life the man who, in shaking hands, sought not to please, but to impress.

A lonely youth, a private education without school or club, had, at his first, rare meetings with officers of his own age, fired his ambition, and the unsociability which now wrapped him in had confirmed in him his serious conception of the service. Always solitary, whether drawing maps in Cyprus or designing bridges in Palestine, with a Prussian faith in duty, offended by the slight-est criticism, and at once at his desk to complain of his superiors in London, he was liked by few—even women—preferred to be feared rather than to be loved, and in his lifetime was defended

by few friends, but by them passionately. He had trained himself
as a soldier and horseman in many an African fight, and nearly
lost his chin in a skirmish on the Red Sea. When this born auto-
crat was later called inhuman in high places, he became still more
defiant and regarded with satisfaction the growing number of his
opponents. As he listened to nobody, he could make no use of
advice, only carried out what he had planned himself, and
brought it to a brilliant conclusion.

Such was the nature of the man who built the railway through
the desert, beat down the Dervishes, and conquered the Sudan
for his country. Kitchener, who, happening to be on leave, had
been present at the bombardment of Alexandria, had become
Chief of Staff at the formation of the new Egyptian army, and
had soon after tried everything to rescue Gordon by an expedition. Seen in the light of his later achievements, he might have
been the man to relieve Gordon, and the thought may well have
brought a certain confusion into his secret meditations as he
sat solitary on his camel beside his lengthening railway and reflected on the vagaries of a fate which had made him the avenger
of the man he had not been allowed to save.

Thoughts of this kind may often have moved him, for Kitchener was a fatalist, as far as fatalism is compatible with so great
an ambition. This natural bias seems to have kept him in the
East and to have been reinforced by his dealings with Mohammedans. This rigorous Englishman took from the Arabs, whose
language he knew fairly well, what was congenial to him: the
belief in fate, the refusal to enter upon any argument with his
men, and a naïve pleasure in the productions of oriental craftsmanship, which he collected and later, when he returned from
the market to his palace in Cairo, would carry carefully upstairs with his own hands. That and a romantic garden which he
laid out on an island in the Nile opposite Aswân were the only
relaxations his tense ambition allowed, and in later years, when
the mail came in, he would push everything aside to read first
his gardener's report of his island. He meant, as an old man, to
wander through dreaming rose-walks, still solitary, but no longer
at work. In 1916, a German mine killed him on his ship, in the

very midst of his greatest work, as he was setting out to save Russia for the Entente.

When Kitchener began his railway through the desert, the eternal experts in London declared the whole scheme mad. When he sketched his plan with a lieutenant in his tent by Wadi Halfa, a comprehensive training of the Egyptian troops, especially the Sudanese, had already been carried out, for he knew how the oriental is discouraged by the slightest setback, and everything in this enterprise depended on an enduring and steady morale. His railway battalion of eight hundred men, which seemed to be made up of specimens of every tribe in North-East Africa, fellahin and captive Dervishes, Dinkas and Shilluks, learned tie- and rail-laying as they worked; and as the first miles grew along a line which Kitchener the officer had ruled straight through the map of the desert, a number of black youths were sitting under two palms in Wadi Halfa learning Morse, soon to become telegraphists.

At first the railway advanced into the void. But soon it was inspiring its own plan and execution, and drawing strength for the future from its own beginnings, like every scheme which grows out of thought into reality. Once the first lines were laid, they could carry up provisions for the three thousand men, then more rails, more ties, above all, more water. And both money and time were short. The railway had to be finished before the winter, and at any moment bedouins, in the service of the Khalifa, might appear in the desert and wipe out the handful of white and black enemies, who never had more than three days' water supply with them. The Dervishes had once before destroyed the line which Ismail had laid along the Nile in 1884 as far as the Third Cataract.

Kitchener had sent a detachment up-Nile from Wadi Halfa to secure that part of the river while he himself endeavoured to reach the same river with the greatest possible speed, moving south-east from the great loop at Abû-Hamed, three hundred miles, the most difficult, most desert part of the line. Which was the way? Without a map, without telegraph or wireless, with a compass and the stars, these navigators of the desert steered their way through sand and rock, never sure whether the goal of their work was not occupied by the enemy, the engineers always six miles ahead, followed by fifteen hundred road-makers, then a thousand railway-builders. Every four days, the advance guard, both in the technical and strategic sense, advanced about six miles, still with coal from Liverpool, still with water from Wadi Halfa, which the first puffing train carried up behind them, like an anxious mother running after her boy with his breakfast. On some days, the railway advanced as much as three miles.

And round about, the Dervish spies, sure of every hill, every oasis, every camel, passed the word on to Khartoum—the fire-spitting dragon was coming nearer and nearer. They might well destroy it from the Nile side. They began to call it the steamer on wheels. A sandstorm came to their help: twelve miles of railway were destroyed in half an hour. Yet the white men's approach was irresistible, whether they were coming through the cataract on boats or hurrying on camels ahead of the railway through the desert. Who would get there first? And if the Khalifa's troops in Abû-Hamed were to defeat those journeying up the Nile, what would become of the fiery dragon? But the Englishmen on the Nile took the place, and soon their brothers, the outriders, arrived through the desert and greeted them, like tunnellers meeting from two sides at the appointed place. Allah is great! There was the Nile, there was water, and now they could help the advancing railway-builders from the Nile and prepare the next stretch, southwards to the mouth of the Atbara.

Autumn passed and March came before Kitchener arrived in Berber. He was regarded as a wizard and his construction inspired far more fear than his men. That was perhaps decisive. The magic powers of the dragon produced their effect, like destiny, by their enigmatic movements, and the Sudanese in Berber dragged along their sick to the engine to touch it. The day before, they had been healed by touching the robe that the Khalifa wore; today, by touching the dragon which came to destroy the Khalifa.

Meanwhile the Atbara had risen with the silt and the flood of the Abyssinian Alps, yet it had to be quickly bridged. The American firm that supplied the bridge completed its thousand-foot span in forty-two days. American mechanics and African labourers cast the bridge on which England was to place her conquering foot below the confluence of the two Niles.

When, on the morning of September 2, 1898, there at Omdurman on the left bank of the White Nile, eight thousand English and eighteen thousand Egyptians threw themselves with their modern weapons on the gigantic army of the Dervishes, the last romantic battle of history took place: there were cavalry charges and sword attacks, and death in duels, and the courage of the individual carried the day. There were heroes there, and scenes from battle pictures. That day was more like the battles of Frederick the Great, a century and a half before, than the battles of the Great War, which were to come only sixteen years later: its picture has been drawn by the master hand of Churchill.

Atonement, which men of all times and all colours demand, the atonement for the murdered Gordon, had been exacted. But what impressed posterity then as now was not that the whites had conquered here, and settled in this foreign country, but that its leader and dictator, with all his screaming promises, had brought his fellow-countrymen nothing but evil. Of eight million Sudanese, the wars and pestilences of those years had made two million: that was the balance-sheet of Mahdism. Why had those millions perished? Had their life—the question arises when a people has passed through such great adventures—been enriched by hope, intensified by pride? Had these six millions had a shorter, but perhaps greater life, and been raised from the tedium of their existence by the new ideals of their race? In a duel like this does the mass really gain? A single adventurer has multiplied his self-assurance, a few thousand favoured ones have helped him and themselves at the same time, but the others about have been victimized and disappointed, and the atonement which was exacted from the outside did not help those who had been led astray by the dictator, for they had long since fallen in struggles which did no good either to their souls or to their country.

But it was not only the repeating rifle and up-to-date guns which had drawn the railway into the heart of Africa; it was not only the discipline, courage, and experience of the British commander which won the day here; fourteen years had passed, in which the fires of faith had died down in the others, that faith which, irresistible as the bush-fires, had fired the country. It had died out; two or three times in the next few years, little Mahdis arose in vain. And after this dictatorship, as generally happens, those who had been coerced for their own happiness were glad when it was all over. Many tribes went over to the whites quickly, of their own free will and in friendship, and the Khalifa, who remained in hiding in distant provinces for a year when the English had at last surrounded him, sat down with his faithful followers on a great rug, looked his fate in the face, like a true Moslem, and let himself be shot sitting among his men with dignity, without resistance and without a plea. That was close to the island in the Nile from which the Mahdi had come.

As regards the Mahdi's remains, Kitchener took strong action, completely destroyed the tomb, so that there should be no pilgrimages, burnt the corpse and strewed the ashes in the Nile. Immediately after the victory, he and his troops, just like the victorious Mahdi thirteen years before, had rowed straight across the White and Blue Niles to the place where the ruins of the palace stood. Yet not one, but two flags, the English and the Egyptian, were raised above the troops in the square, the two national anthems rang out, then Gordon's favourite hymn, "Abide with Me." One account states that at the sound of it, the iron Kitchener could not conceal his emotion.

12

WHILE in this way one white power was playing the avenger so as to get the land of the blacks into its hands, a second, its great antithesis, had set out to arrive there first if possible. A desperate race began.

For twenty years past, France, backed up by Bismarck, who wanted to take her mind off Sedan, had been busy building up a colonial empire in Africa, yet at all points she had found herself checked by English claims. Even in Egypt, where France had enjoyed a supremacy hardly interrupted since the time of Napoleon, she had been ousted by England, and interminable legal disputes as to the use of loans had increased the tension. But when the Sudan became what statesmen call *res nullius,* without adding *albi,* France required a base on the Nile, and, from her Congo possessions, had sent advance guards into the upper Ghazal region. When, in 1895, this had been declared an unfriendly act in London, France could risk no decision, and when she finally offered her help in Kitchener's expedition, her rival politely declined. In such French minds as then thought in terms of continents, there was growing anxiety lest she should arrive too late at the partition of the world, like the poet in the song. Then a few men devised a fantastic scheme.

What about beginning a race to the Nile! If England was advancing from the north to the Middle Nile, France would have to advance from the west to the Upper Nile; the higher up she seized the mysterious river, the greater power she would have. If France were to sit, say, on 10° N. lat., she could worry England by dominating the White Nile from above, and even, by means of dams, dry her out, as England could not live on 15° with the Blue Nile alone, nor could she keep Egypt alive. In the midst of savage tribes, invincible swamps, bush, deserts, and lagoons, a decision of world-wide import lay hidden. France resolved to try this decision.

And yet she had lost the race on the Nile before she began it, for the victor here was not the one to arrive first and hoist the flag, as in a match, but the one to arrive in better condition, and powerful enough to stay. Could the French build a railway from the Congo to the Nile? With the exception of two or three explorers, had ever a human being marched through these regions? Was there even anything known about the peoples who had to be marched through? A colonel, a handful of natives without guns, was all that France dispatched to reach the Nile from the heart of the jungle, by unknown ways, more quickly and higher up than England, who was building a railway from a secure base so as to drive her own and the Egyptian army against the enemy, who, for all she knew, might have subjected the natives up at Fashoda.

"Colonel Marchand," so his minister describes him, "was supple as a rapier blade, with eyes like darts; he spoke tersely, everything in him was charged with electricity from the soles of his feet to the tips of his hair." He had not held out long as a subordinate clerk in a lawyer's office, preferred to serve as a private soldier in French Africa, became an officer, and now, at the age of thirty-three, set out to give the lie to the old superstition that France must always have bad luck on the Nile. He had to do this in a race against England, with twenty-three white men and five hundred Senegalese, without the full protection of his country, which, to provide for all eventualities, pretended to be merely financing an exploring expedition, so as to preserve good relations with Turkey in case of failure, although nothing of Turkish power could be felt as high as the tenth parallel. Here indeed a knight sallied forth, to carry through a bold enterprise against all the ill-will of destiny. Marchand—he should have been called Chevalier—was a son of Brian de Bois Guilbert, though a thousand years late.

Adventurous as the old Norman heroes, their romantic descendant advanced eastward from Loango through the jungles of the Congo basin. Like the knight of the epic, he fought with cannibals and savage beasts, who in turn ate his soldiers and porters. He knew very well that England was arming, building, advancing on the Middle Nile, but how far his rival was on his way to the same river, whether desert and sandstorms were destroying his men as wild men and lions were destroying his own, whether the army of the Dervishes was fighting in the north and hence—with the help of Allah!—leaving Marchand's road open in the south—of all this he knew nothing for weeks and months, and when news blew across his path, it was vague. All that urged him on was the will to arrive before the Dervishes were annihilated by the English. What the Frenchman dreaded was less the wild brown Mohammedan enemy of civilization than the civilized, white, Christian Englishman, for the latter had guns, Egypt, and his prestige.

And the way of the French knight dragged on, longer and longer. Why must the accursed Ghazal stand so low that year that the march was held up for six months? Everything seemed to be conspiring against the warrior, and yet he pressed on, unbroken, his men diminishing steadily. At last, in July 1898, he saw before him the river of his dreams. In Fashoda, a focal point, Marchand hoisted the tricolour with ceremony. France really stood on the Nile. He had been marching for three years. Where was the rival who was to outwave him with the Union Jack? Nothing but rumours, which, all the same, distort and veil everything in Africa like the mirage. The Frenchman sitting in 10° N. lat., on the Nile bank, did not know that down on 18° N. lat., at Berber, on the Nile, the Englishman had already won his first victory over the Dervishes. The Englishman did not know that on the same stream, 600 miles away, there was a white ally against the blacks, who was also his enemy.

It is true that what strength the Dervishes possessed up there was so small that they fled before Marchand, who was barely armed: he was able to set up a kind of "fort" on the river, conclude a treaty for the "protection" of the king of the Shilluks, and at the same time plant a few vegetables. But the reinforcements, munitions, communications with home, on which everything depended, were lacking. In vain he sought to get into touch with the French Congo in the west, with Abyssinia in the east: everything echoed into the void, he remained alone. Now he sat on the Nile with his last white officers, with a few rifles and a flag which, in summer months, drooped pitifully about its staff.

Meanwhile, invisible to the romantic Frenchman, the iron Englishman was advancing inexorably on his steel rails, driving the enemy before him, perhaps down to the neighbourhood of Fashoda. Who could know what was happening in this land of anarchy? Only the Nile could connect the two officers, but the Mohammedan enemy was still standing between the Christian rivals. Kitchener had nothing to fear. What he knew was enough —twenty-three white men and five hundred Senegalese had marched off three years before. Even though they were all alive, and all sitting up there on the Nile, they could not make an enemy.

Four days after the capture of Khartoum, a steamer brought the first news from upriver: a white man was in Fashoda and had made peace with the Shilluks. It was five days after the decisive victory at Omdurman, and this Englishman, who had already been on his feet for two years in the country, might well have rested on his laurels for a few days. Yet he realized what was at stake, sent the steamer back at once, and himself set off three days later, up-Nile, to visit the fateful Frenchman. For all eventualities, he took with him a few hundred Sudanese troops, a hundred Scottish Highlanders, and a few gunboats to give his guest on the Upper Nile an impressive greeting.

Nine days later, the English steamers stopped at the Fashoda station, where a huge tricolour was hanging on a high flagstaff. It was a Gilbertian meeting: two white officers, both in khaki, but with different badges, belonging to two neighbour empires living at peace with each other far away, met surrounded by a thousand naked Negroes at the end of the world, each with orders to drive the other to the other end of the world. With all due admiration for Kitchener's pluck, at this moment all one's sympathy leaps out to Marchand, who, without a railway, without troops, without any instructions from the capital such as Kitchener got by wire from Khartoum, here met the victor of the day before, armed with nothing but a revolver he might not use and a flag which would not wave.

A conversation between the two conquerors followed in Marchand's hut. First the Englishman congratulated the Frenchman on having come through, the Frenchman congratulated the Englishman, for in the last few days the great victory of the white man over the Dervishes had found its way on Negro lips to his rival. We know nothing of how long the pause lasted after the congratulations. We know only that Marchand declared firmly: "I have been instructed by my government to occupy the Ghazal as far as its junction with the Jebel, as well as all the Shilluk land on the left of the Nile."

"I have been instructed," said Kitchener, "to recognize no white power on the Nile and must object," whereupon he handed Marchand a document, for now he had to hoist his flag beside the French one. But then the gentleman came out; he sympathized with the feelings of his comrade, would not force him to lower his flag, for that might have led to trouble, retired five hundred yards and hoisted—the Turkish flag. Then he sailed up-Nile for a day, established a post on the Sobat, returned, left behind him a garrison of Sudanese troops and four guns, and declared to the Frenchman, with the same courtesy, that "the country" was now under the protection of the Anglo-Egyptian condominion: all transport of munitions on the Nile was prohibited. And now the two officers faced each other, not sitting, but standing.

"I am to take orders from my government only," replied the Frenchman.

"And if I were forced . . . ?" asked Kitchener, but he does not seem to have finished the sentence.

"Then I shall die here."

Everything proceeded according to the ancient rites of military honour. According to time-honoured custom, the comedy ended in Europe. These two soldiers, whose meeting was reported by Kitchener, were mere puppets in the hands of politicians and speculators; Paris and London threw themselves noisily on the problem, and actually brought the two countries to the verge of a war which was prevented not by England's wisdom, but above all by France's weakness: newspaper orgies of greed and hate accompanied the six weeks' negotiations between the Cabinets, till Paris had to give way and celebrate Colonel Marchand as the "emissary of civilization," in order to cover with painful laurels the retreat of the knight and the defeat of France.

Kitchener later declared that, by his victory over the Dervishes, he had saved Marchand from being murdered by them. In any case, the English Government at the same time won a bloodless victory over the French. France realized in these weeks how powerless she was without England, and completely changed her policy under this impression. She resolved to go with England.

Colonel Marchand, however, abandoned by his superiors, and degraded into a mere explorer, at first thought of disobeying the order to leave: he declared that he lacked munitions and provisions. When the Englishman put all he needed, and his steamer too, at his disposal, Marchand rejected this easy way home. On his luckier rival's steamer? Even on his new railway, and in the end with false laurels to France? Another Nile explorer refusing to be saved, not far from the spot where Emin, twenty years before, had refused to be saved by Stanley. Marchand decided to make his way through to Abyssinia, and in this way crossed Africa.

A Don Quixote *malgré lui,* a tragic figure, who found the world comic, the man who planted the tricolour on the Nile only to have to roll it up again after five months of useless waiting, had, like his medieval forebears, resolved at the end of the adventure to save his honour, if not the honour of France, for if France, he felt, had let herself be shamefully defeated, there was still his private honour, the honour of the lawyer's clerk and private soldier, now the colonel and unhappy conqueror, Jean-Baptiste Marchand of Thoissey.

Six years after his return, he saw the indirect consequences of his Nile expedition, the Anglo-French Entente, later fought side by side with the English in the Great War, then saw the new coolness between the two countries. Before he died in 1933, Marchand saw the African empire that France had built up for herself in the west.

But the Nile valley was no part of it.

13

THE flag that Kitchener had hoisted in Fashoda was red—it was the Turkish flag. Today the beautiful green Egyptian flag floats beside the Union Jack on all ships and public buildings: the condominion has lasted a generation, and may last for a long time yet, for it is contested only by the weaker partner.

Even this turn in the fate of the Sudan was determined by the Nile. England found a welcome pretext for occupying the Sudan in guarding the river for Egypt and regulating its upper course—the reason was even a real one, for at that time she practically owned Egypt. She had redeemed the country from bankruptcy in order to make herself mistress at one point whose importance seemed, so to speak, eternal. And now, ruling the source and the mouth of the Nile, was England going to abandon to a third power its middle course, the dramatic junction of the two Niles? And to whom? To the Sudanese, who had proved themselves savages under the Mahdi? To the Egyptians, who had ruined the Sudan in sixty years? Or perhaps to the French? If anyone was to annoy Egypt from the Sudan by means of the Nile water, it could be only England.

Even the Egyptians, who, in their weakness, could neither reconquer nor rule the Sudan, must prefer England as the ruling power in the Sudan to the Sudanese or the French, for England had too great interests in Lower Egypt to ruin it by a quarrel. Even if England had hoisted only her own flag after her victory in Khartoum, Egypt was then powerless against her; but Egypt had secret allies, with whose money and influence England had to reckon in Cairo. The war with France, which threatened in the weeks of Fashoda, was avoided not only by France's weakness, but by the English decision to raise the Turkish flag which

Kitchener had hoisted as a symbol on the old bastion on 10°
N. lat.; the idea of the two flags and of the prevention of war
seem to have interacted. Like all orientals, the Egyptians took
advantage of the quarrel between the western powers: though
they had lost the Sudan by their maladministration, they were
now to be joint rulers of a country which they had won back,
it is true, with their own soldiers at their own cost, yet only under
English leadership, and could hold only with English prestige.

Lord Cromer found the solution of the two flags which he
himself called "a hybrid form of government whose fate its
authors would not bewail if it should yield to a firmer one." If
this hybrid form has stood the test, to the astonishment of the
world, that is due to the unequal partition of all rights. If this
condominion is a marriage, then it is an oriental one, into which
the wife brings her belongings and later her children without ac-
quiring any rights save the right to live—that is, the water of the
Nile: she is certainly the legitimate, chief wife, who, adorned
with jewels, yet deeply veiled, rides through a triumphal arch on
great occasions by the side of her mighty husband. The Sudan
was the first mandatory power in history, founded twenty years
before the term, with its false ring, was coined at the Paris Con-
ference of 1919.

From the Governor-General downwards, all the high officials
in the Anglo-Egyptian Sudan are Englishmen, and if the King in
Cairo had ever refused to appoint the Governor recommended
by the British Government, he would simply have found himself
up against the British world empire. This Governor, whom the
King cannot recall on his own account, still has rights such as the
Mahdi had, for the Sudan still stands under military law, and the
Governor commands and executes justice in all important matters with dictatorial power. In the beginning, the Egyptian was
allowed to provide troops, and, with a contribution of $3,750,-
000, may now bear a good share of the costs.

And yet Egypt profits by it. If she had lost the Middle Nile to
England by war, she could, by the morality of history, plan revenge: in actual fact, by England's intervention, she returned to
the joint ownership of a country she had lost to its original
Nubian inhabitants by misrule.

The Egyptians feel as superior to those inhabitants as any white mandatory power to its Negroes. The Egyptian upper classes, the non-fellahin, who are as small in number as were the upper classes of Tsarist Russia, look down on the Sudanese, as the heirs of a five-thousand-year-old culture on cannibals, and classify them in tribes according to their aptitude for serving as grooms, cooks, and footmen in their fine houses in Cairo. At the time of the reconquest, about 1900, the Sudanese servant was nothing but the son of his enslaved father, who, in his turn, had been used in slave-hunts as a kind of hawk to swoop down on the encircled victim. Today, he can return home at the end of a few years, bringing with him the money, ideas, and pride of the quarter-civilized.

This feeling of superiority, the role of master which the Egyptian assumes before the Sudanese, has increased the latter's rancour in the course of the last generation. In the Egyptian, he does not fear his owner; he hates the pasha whom the Mahdi drove out of his country, the Turco who could be carried back into the country only on the shoulders of the white giant, and who today employs a few thousand of his young men to clean his shoes and his cars. What do these lords matter to him—the foreign ones or his own? Should the Sudanese not rather compare himself with the fellah, who, with the same ox, on the same river, turns the same water-wheel, whose wives grind the same dhurra on the same rough stones with their strong hands, and whose children climb the same palms for dates? Does the Egyptian fellah know one hieroglyph of that ancient wisdom which stood on the fibres of his papyrus, or one syllable more than the young Sudanese who is just learning to read?

Once more we become aware of the moral cycle between white power and black education, that cycle which must lead to the impotence of the whites. England has not ruled here with the rhinoceros whip, nor did she make her first appearance with a code of law and a tape-measure, but upheld from the outset her co-operation with the customs of the tribes, left the lowest courts in native hands, and today fills 55 percent of the lower administrative posts with Sudanese and only 23 percent with Egyptians, so that there are now in the Sudan twelve hundred native customs and treasury clerks, post-office clerks, and teachers. Altogether, three thousand Sudanese employees, among them judges, printers, engineers, mayors, railwaymen, doctors, have been trained from the alphabet upwards, witnesses of English civilization, and at the same time the first, not yet menacing but rapidly increasing, pioneers of a people that must, by the training given to it by its masters, develop into those masters' rival.

This rise of the Sudan will have changed the fate of Egypt and even of Abyssinia by the end of the twentieth century. In the nineteenth, the Egyptian conqueror could give the Sudanese nothing, and hence could not impress him: the northern half of the huge country had, too, the same faith as he, and this faith, which binds the individual more closely to God, fate, and the morality of the state than that of a Christian on the same level, had long given him a justifiable pride in his dealings with the white man. His thoughts have been thus expressed by Harold MacMichael, one of those who know him best: "These odd white men obviously mean well, but they have but a mean conception of religion, and many of their habits are wanting in good taste."

The people of the Sudan, enslaved, sold, oppressed, then, in savage revolt, tricked by its leaders, and trampled underfoot, to be conquered in the end by white soldiers, has suddenly been lifted out of its gloom into the brightness of the western century, and of all centuries, the present one. The son of a Sudanese who, with his family, as a troop and a circus number, was led through the zoos of Europe, fenced in like the wild animals of his country, to perform the dances and hunts of his distant people for the amusement of white spectators, now sits at the microscope of the research institute in Khartoum, or counts in retorts the microbes in the Nile water.

Certainly, the twelve thousand Sudanese who can read form but a fragment of those six millions which the population has again reached, but the knowledge possessed by these few spreads today more rapidly than the knowledge of those medieval monks who were, too, superior to their fellow-citizens in equally small numbers; and with knowledge realization spreads. Why should they regard the fellah of Egypt as their master? His progress was just as slow as their own. Does Cairo possess a school for the sons of peasants as brilliant and beautiful as the Gordon College? There, beside the palace on the Blue Nile, five hundred pupils in white shirts file two by two in solemn procession through the splendid gardens, like the knights in *Parsifal*. Training-colleges for the army, the post office, and medicine, in all about fifteen hundred schools for thirty thousand pupils, have been given them by the white men. As the rapidly increasing Egyptian population is outgrowing the food and resources of the Nile valley, so that, by 1950, all the land will be under cultivation, the superfluous Egyptians will migrate up-Nile to the good fields in the Sudan, their depot and branch establishment, which will not be as underpopulated as it is today. Did they not do exactly the same after the expulsion of the Ethiopian kings?

All this, combined with the national feeling in which the coloured peoples are beginning to imitate the bad example of the white, points to future struggles which the medium of the English is attempting to mitigate. "For two or three generations," said Lord Lugard, the last great Anglo-African, "we can show the Negro what we are: then we shall be asked to go away. Then we shall have to leave the land to those it belongs to, with the feeling that they have better business friends in us than in other white men." And Marshal Lyautey even said: *"La seule excuse pour la colonisation, c'est le médecin."* This is the mature wisdom of two pioneers of the conquest.

England's great achievements in the Sudan were facilitated by world history. Even at the beginning, the railway, which reduced the loop of the Nile from its six-hundred-mile sweep to a straight line of little more than two hundred, was more than merely a decisive factor in the war; today it carries the visitor from Cairo to Khartoum in a hundred hours. The aeroplane takes fourteen. Goods, on a second line, take only twenty-seven hours from the Atbara to the Red Sea; Port Sudan, established on the site of the useless old port, ships three million tons of exports yearly to a value of $25,000,000. The way from the Red Sea to the heart of Africa, which the peoples of antiquity sought, is now open; the Upper Nile is served by weekly steamers. Wells on the old caravan routes, oil tanks for the new flying service, the distribution of grain in famine years, more gum arabic than before, and hence more of the sweets they love, more salt, obtained by evaporation from the Red Sea, the doctor, the friend of man, and, above all, a resolute protection against slavery, which survives only on the long, unguardable frontier of Abyssinia, all these things cannot merely be regarded as the achievement of the century: they must in part be the achievement of the ruling power in the Sudan; that is proved by a comparison with other colonies. Even the crows profit by English civilization: they pick up in Khartoum the glittering caps of the mineral-water bottles, carry them off to the paved terrace, turn them about, and make patterns with them.

The best constructive work in the Sudan was largely done by officers, a proof that there are even men in uniform who have learnt something more than slaughter. The World War enriched this secluded country; the decline of Turkey, the creation of the new monarchy in Cairo, in actual fact strengthened England's hand. A few riots, led by former Gordon College boys, disturbed British rule for a few days only; there were mutinies among black troops under English officers which made serious-minded Englishmen realize the dangers of education. The question was what to do with the dangerous Egyptian elements in the army which were behind the rising, as they had been there since the condominion was founded. The murder of a missionary did not provide sufficient pretext for severe measures.

In November 1924, the British Governor-General of the Sudan, on a visit to Cairo, was assassinated by Egyptian nationalists. A second Gordon! This time England could act more promptly. Instead of thirteen years, it took only three days to produce an ultimatum which, besides fines and other punishments, demanded the expulsion of all Egyptian troops and officers. It was not only those nationalists who had set the Nile on their white flag as the goal of their policy who trembled then: every moderate Egyptian had to realize that the power on the Upper Nile was menacing.

With the Egyptian troops went the last vestige of Egyptian power in the Sudan until the summer of 1936, when by the new

ABU SIMBEL

Photo: Lehnert & Landrock, Ca

THE NILE BELOW ASWÂN

treaty they came back. Today the green flag again floats beside the red-white-and-blue one from the roof of the Khartoum Palace, and from the stern of the steamers ploughing their way through the Nile.

14

AS far as Khartoum, the Nile was
a piece of pure nature. For miles on end, only the stakes driven
into the embankments showed, by their running numbers, that
man was watching over it, and where villages brought life to
its banks, they spoke only of today and yesterday. But now, on
the second half of its course, columns and temples, hewn stones
and pyramids irregularly scattered, fringe the river, milestones
of history which the hand of man has raised through five thousand years as a memorial of his deeds; and always on the banks
of the great river which, below Khartoum, flows through the
desert in a very narrow oasis 1200 miles long. As not only the
perdurable granite, but the lighter sandstone too suffered neither
from rain nor thunderstorms, but only from occasional sandstorms, they would still be standing here as they have always
stood if man, fighting with man, had not done the work of the
elements.

Here, in Khartoum, where the brother pair of Niles, for ever
united, quit the only city which has so far risen on their banks,
to see no other for months, nothing seems to rise so high as the
gracefully curved masts of the great sailing-boats, for the domes
of the native town on the White Nile, among which the white
walls fade away into the desert, look as low as the towers of the
English on the eastern, Blue Nile. There is nothing here to recall the aspect, or even the outline, of old European towns rising
so proudly from the Seine, the Danube, the Thames, and the
Moskva. Here the double river reigns in such majesty that it
would outroar the life of a million on its four banks.

Along the right bank of the Blue Nile, and continuing along
that of the united river, the magnificent Island of Tuti rises,
sloping upwards, on which the silt lavishes greater wealth than

on most stretches of its course. Nowhere are the palms richer than here, nowhere does the dark green flaunt in richer shades from out the yellow of the plain, and from the spreading branches of the sycamores on the banks delightful coolness flows. Under dreamlike, heavy-shadowing trees, the so-called haraz trees, the island stretches more than a mile downstream to its high, wooded point.

Smaller islands, which rise near it from the junction of the two Niles, disappear in the weeks of high water, and when they rise again, owing to the deposit of sand and stones, near by, but not quite on the same spot, squabbles set in among the inhabitants.

"That was my island," shrieks Ahmed.

"It isn't. I dug it last winter," Mohammed screams back, and the judge is hard put to it, for the ordnance survey lies buried in the Nile, like Prospero's book of magic at the end of all his wanderings.

In heavy-laden boats men and goods are carried from one of the four river banks to another. As they glide across, penned in under the great sail, they look, in their white shirts, like groups from Tartarus, and memory goes back to those times, hardly past, when these boats, filled with slaves, were really wafted towards the underworld by the wind. The great Nile barks, which from this point to the mouth more often cross than mount or descend the river, simple house-boats with a cooking-stove built of clay at the prow, can be steered only from the high poop by one who knows the winds and the reefs; and the oars, which protect them from the rocks by means of two great outriggers, can be manipulated only by the hands of experts. But above, on the two curved masts, the great lateen sails swell, and to the rider coming from the desert, and not seeing the deep Nile valley from the distance, they look like giant birds flying slowly over the desert, close to the ground, solemn and unreal.

But now, though the Blue Nile, in its reckless haste, forces the White against its western bank, it can do so only for a stretch; then the steady strength of the elder brother regains its appointed space, and only when the Abyssinian rains create the great flood can the Blue dominate the current. In this war of the elements, there are small profiteers: the fish of the Blue Nile, startled by the immense swelling of the current, take refuge in a quiet, silent pool by the bank, all unknowing that the pelicans of the White Nile await them there to kill them. Thus the lackeys of great rivals scuffle and cheat each other long after their masters are reconciled.

Here in Khartoum, where the brothers embrace, the stream confirms in its appearance the saga-like glory of its name: only here and in Cairo does the Nile appear a king. That after all the adventures of its youth it became a king, that at the end, after the stony weeks of its passage through the desert, which are now only beginning, it will still remain one—there its secret, inner power is revealed.

Yet just as great characters, in the midst of their struggles with the world, fret in inward discord, the Nile too, where it takes up the struggle with the desert, is caught in its own whirlpools, for now the epoch of the cataracts begins. Like the swamps above, they too are set there by nature as enemies, as tests of courage and strength, and they bring its character face to face with momentous problems.

The short stretch which the Nile still has to flow through the bush below Khartoum before it reaches the mouth of the Atbara is already something like a farewell to nature, for soon the desert begins, only to end close to the sea. Here the babanus, the Sudan ebony, still grows, and the mahogany tree; the indigo is so prolific, without being cultivated, that it was formerly worked there in a kind of factory; and the acacia is so stout that the Turks make dockyards for the Nile boats of it. Among the latter luxuriates a tree with soft, corky wood, whose poisonous sap blinds the woodman if he touches his eyes with it, shunned by all the animals except the goats, which peacefully nibble at it without harm. The acacia has adapted itself to the ebb and flood by striking longer roots so as to live through both water levels. In this region, the water of the Nile is singularly cold, a fact which cannot be explained merely by the frequent coolness of the nights.

A few miles below Khartoum, the river narrows down to less than 250 feet, two basalt columns enclose a gorge, the first cataract begins. Geographers have called it the Sixth Cataract, because they moved upriver with civilization, and counted from Egypt. We must follow their enumeration, although the milestones of a river, like those of a man's life, should not be counted from the end. The Arabs, who count thirty-one cataracts, since several consist of manifold falls, have not denoted them with cold figures, but with fantastic names: Camel Neck, Coral, the House of the Slave, the Pardoned, the Muddy Ones, the Shakers. At this so-called Sixth Cataract, the highest on the Nile, the river begins the great loop, the only one in its whole south-north career, and only close by the end of the cataracts, at the lowest and First, does the loop end, so that the last lies directly vertical to the first: the Shabluka cataract lies on the sixteenth parallel, on the same degree of longitude as the Aswân cataract on the twenty-fourth.

Here in the desert, where there is no sign of living nature to check the river's flow, the antediluvian world, in granite form, has thrown itself across the path of the Nile and forces on the river the whole enormous detour of 750 miles. And yet it is just this new struggle from which the heroic stream draws the fresh daring and the fullness of life without which it would run dry between the two deserts. In its thirty-one cataracts, it is again put to the test, as it was above in the swamps, and again it stands the test.

All the rocky hills which squeeze round the Nile on this long stretch are of granite, gneiss, and clay slate, that is, of primitive rock. They prevent navigation, for even if men had succeeded in laying canals through the swamps, they would still have had to sacrifice billions on this equally long stretch to overcome the granite, and at the end would have mastered only the long arc of a waterway, the chord of which is already crossed by Kitchener's desert railway. Even today, the Nile is navigable only on three reaches, for 150 miles on its upper course, then for 1100 miles from Rejaf to Khartoum, and finally for 600 miles on its lower course from Aswân to the mouth. Leaving the Blue Nile out of account, which is navigable only on its last 400 miles, nearly half the giant stream is unnavigable, even though boats use short stretches between the cataracts. It is the fate of all the four great rivers of Africa, and a consequence of its formation in plateaux, that none has become a great highway of traffic like the rivers of the other continents.

Here, 1250 miles below the pyramid of Rejaf, where the rock again rises, crowding in and cramping the river, the phenomenon of the hundred islands appears, to reappear in every cataract. For more than ten miles, dissolved into rapids, large and small, the Nile, in the midst of the precipitous fall of rock, creates the world of green islands which, refreshed by the eternal spray of the rushing waters, offers to the naked grey rock, the parched yellow plain, the contrast of its green paradise of growth, shaded by broad, feathery acacias, huge sycamores, stiff doum-palms, all interwoven with lianas as in the jungle, and compensated with eternal green for the solitude in whose eternal spell they live, visited by no men and few beasts, in the midst of the hurrying waters. Thus, in a flower-filled garden, secluded women stand, placidly watching the eternal travellers of life pass by on their way.

But while the rock forces the Nile to quit its appointed south-north course and turn east, it is not only the way of the river that is determined by its stratification: the angle at which it falls determines the fate of the small strip along the banks. In these narrow, fertile parts between the deserts, fifteen feet of mud-covered land between plain and river can suffice to feed a village which erects its clay huts on hard eminences, so as to save every inch of the fertile strip for grain and a few palms.

Shendi lies on the edge of the plain and enjoys broader stretches of cultivated land on the flat eastern bank. Then the Nile enters the desert which it quits only at Cairo. But first the Nile receives the last tidings from the east, as a king receives the last couriers from home before beginning his great campaign; 200 miles below Khartoum, at the most easterly point of its whole course, it receives its last tributary, the Atbara, which rises in the same volcanoes of Abyssinia from which the Blue Nile came.

Crossing the Atbara in June on the great desert railway bridge —it is the fourth bridge across the Nile since the source—one cannot understand what it cost Kitchener to bore the piles for six great arches deep into the rock, for a waterless river bed yawns below. But returning in July, a river 1600 feet wide roars with such violence round these piles that its muddy waters are hurled far over its mouth on the western bank of the Nile, and it is easy to understand why the Arabs call it the Black River. As mad as the Blue Nile, its bigger brother, fed by the same rains, it carries down bamboos and tree-trunks, boulders and roots, parts of dead buffaloes, even of elephants, with its rushing waves, victims from a heedlessly vegetating world of animals and trees that it has surprised, seized, and killed, as a great revolutionary the placid burghers.

This is the last tributary of the Nile. The desert has come; from now on to the end, it is alone with its ancient waters.

On its journey through the great loop, the valley of the Nile is of three colours: the deep yellow of the desert on both sides, spreading into infinity; the deep green of the cultivated strips, sometimes a mile or so broad, generally narrow, at times not more than a hundred paces deep; and in between, the shiny grey of the wet granite which rises above the foaming river in the form of a thousand islands and rocks, forming the rapids. The sudden transition from the yellow desert sand to the green strip along the banks, the luxuriance of that strip, and the absence of half-desert zones, shows that what is here is no field, such as Allah blesses with more rain or less, but a garden, which the hands of men created in defiance of the desert by carrying the gift brought down by the river in its stony bed to the desert's edge.

The magician who accomplishes it all, and who, later, will create those cultivated strips in Egypt when the brief flood has passed, is the *sakia:* thousands of water-wheels accompany the river with their whining and creaking, thousands of oxen turn the water-wheels in their ten-hour, dull round, each pair driven by a man or boy who turns with it. These oxen are the remote descendants of animals, the boys the remote descendants of men who through the ages have drawn up the water of the Nile at the same place with the same wheels and buckets, and the palms that yield the wood are the remote descendants of those palms which Egyptians and Romans, heathens, Mohammedans, and

Christians planted along the same flat bank, cut in exactly the same way, and fitted with ropes and cogs to renew the circulation of water and fertility on the fringe of the desert.

In the thundering desert sunshine, the water-wheel wails its melody along the Nile valley, a thousand miles northward, and just as Hephæstus, the ugliest of the gods, puffing and sweating, made emerald jewels out of the secret treasures of the mountains, the old gnarled water-wheel, groaning and creaking, turns the fringe of the desert into emerald-green land.

On some such slope of the Nile bank, a vertical wheel of thick hempen rope turns close to the bank, touching the water, with a chain of twenty or more longish, red earthenware pitchers. It moves round a palm log, which is set horizontally in the hub. Below, each pitcher sinks into the Nile and is filled to the brim; above, when it has passed the highest point of the wheel's circle, it empties its water into a trough of hollowed tree-trunk which conveys it to a shallow ditch. The horizonal palm-trunk in the wheel is attached a few yards higher up to a solid wooden wheel, which is turned round a vertical shaft by the pair of oxen. The boy driving them sits behind them on a wooden board, and twice in every turn ducks his head under a third, supporting palm-trunk, or, with the ropes in his hands, he walks behind the oxen, and then need not bend so low under the obstacle.

But when the driving-wheel moves, the vertical palm-trunk turns in a wooden hub below, therefore it scrapes and squeaks continually. Therefore the water-wheels mourn through all Nubia and all Egypt, always along the Nile. For the poor man cannot cement stakes into the earth: he has no chalk and no nails to spare; everything is carved out of wood; the trunks, the hemp, the very dried palm-leaves which he sets up all round to protect him from the sun, all come from the palm, but the wood for the wheels is often acacia-wood. All he has to buy is the pitchers, but his fathers did so before him, and when one breaks, nowadays he can certainly find in the towns an empty gasolene can or preserved-food tin.

These tins, flashing in the sunshine, are the only innovations the water-wheel has undergone since the ancients. On the frescoes of the royal tombs, it turns just as it turns today, and when two, three, four flat wheels turn above each other on the sloping bank, each turned by a pair of oxen, the water of the Nile, within a few minutes, reaches a zone which lies thirty to sixty feet above it, rainless, void, awaiting the hand of man to receive the water and forthwith to grow green.

This is the ancient magic wheel by means of which the men of the Nile valley replaced rain during those eight months when the river itself is not carrying down the rain from the Abyssinian heights, and overflowing all the flat land along its banks. Here in Nubia, and later in Egypt, where the artificial and sudden irrigation forces on all the crops, and where three months, often only a few weeks, take the place of the natural cycle from spring to autumn, the plough has lost its meaning, and over wide distances has never been seen. The peasant makes holes with a little iron, or simply with his heel, and throws a few seeds in, knowing no manure save the weeds he has previously uprooted. Swiftly the blade springs up, shooting aloft sometimes to a height of fifteen feet, and the best species yield a white, big-eared, fine-husked grain. This is the dhurra, wheat and barley, but besides they sow and reap beans and lentils, pumpkins, melons and red pepper, tobacco and castor beans.

Here, in the land of the great cataracts, at Berber and Dongola, the sweetest dates of the whole Nile valley ripen and are multiplied in a peculiar way. As there are too few male palms, their precious faculties must be distributed as in a matriarchal state. In spring, the boys clamber up the male tree, pluck twigs with flowers, and with them fertilize the female trees, which they water with the water-wheel below. And when the hot wind blows, they give thanks to God, for the Arab proverb says: "The dates of Allah grow with their feet in the water and their heads in fire."

Bronze-brown, tall, gaunt creatures, all muscle and sinew, from whom the desert sand and glow have stripped every shred of fat, the Berbers stand under their palms. They inhabit the Nile valley in the loop and for long distances round about. They settled there thousands of years ago, although they once were nomads, and their brothers are nomads still. Fleshless as they are, they also shave their hair and beards, so that their cavernous eyes, between their receding foreheads and slightly arched noses, seem to be hiding under their bushy eyebrows, and, as the only point of life, dominate their whole appearance; but those eyes are vivacious and friendly, like the character of their owners. When the rich Egyptians send for such Berbers to be their couriers and servants, cooks and coachmen, in Cairo, they know well the loyalty of this tribe to its masters and the good nature which makes the Berbers the most hospitable race in East Africa. While they live on maize, cheese, and a handful of dates, often sleeping on a chest, and always cheerful, for a guest they will slaughter a sheep, send long distances for the best milk, even coffee, while at night they watch over his sleep or tell him tales under the stars. In their language, there are traces showing that they were once Christian. Thus these Mohammedans still call Sunday *kirage,* that is *kyriake,* the Lord's Day.

Dark green in the yellow desert, their capital Berber lies close below the mouth of the Atbara; today it is small, eighty years ago it was the biggest town on the Upper Nile, because the great sailing-boats came up as far as this point, for above it the great cataracts begin. It was the old market for ivory and ebony, for gold, above all for slaves, and the shady gardens of the old officials and merchants actually arose from the sweat and toil of men and beasts.

In this zone, the Nile finds a voice. Here, in the land of the cataracts, in the region of the loop which crosses four degrees of latitude, the Nile begins to rush and storm, and along some stretches to thunder. These granite ridges and bars which, in the primeval times before the Nile burst through, may have formed great inland lakes, and have yielded only after millions of years of the duel between the water and the granite, are polished, big and small, from one year to the next, from one hour to the next, and in the never-ending battle yield their strength to the victorious water only in the form of tiny particles, of gravel. For the noise of battle cannot but arise when the river, among a thousand islands and rocks, forges its way onward in mile-long rapids. A Roman writer declared that the inhabitants emigrated because they lost their hearing, but the mighty voices of the

Berbers prove to us today that necessity strengthens any organ, for their call carries over the rushing river from bank to bank, while white men can hardly hear each other at ten paces' distance.

And the ear, in these wild, romantic stretches of the Nile, is surprised in another way when the camel-rider approaches the river along some desert track, without seeing in the distance the tops of the palm-trees or the masts of the sailing-boats, for then only a remote roar rises to delight him, and he hails it in the desert as the Greeks once hailed the sea. Or again, as he rides along the river in flood-time, he can distinguish amid the roar the perpetual rattling of the little stones which the rising water loosens from the bank.

Forty-five miles below Berber, where the rapids form the Fifth Cataract, there are seven big and hundreds of little islands which strive in vain to check the river over a distance of more than six miles.

But near the twentieth degree of latitude, 250 railway-miles below Khartoum, the rock is stronger than the water, and the granite is so far master of the river that it forces its enemy to make a detour which looks like a retreat. The great sheets of basalt running through the desert here from east to west force the Nile—the only time in its whole career—to turn round and run a few hundred miles back to the south, as though it were trying to regain the beginning of its course. It does so to keep alive, but later, far from the granite enemy, turns almost as suddenly northwards again, in an unguarded moment, and, by a gigantic detour, finds once more its appointed course, like a man thrown off his bearings and cast back into them again by magnetic powers.

For this turning-point near Abû-Hamed lies almost vertically below Khartoum and above Aswân. Here, at the great elbow, one of the biggest islands in the Nile, twenty miles long and three broad, has been left standing as a witness to the struggle of the elements, while the river, under the pressure of the obstructing granite, narrows and widens again irregularly from six hundred to six thousand feet. On some of these giant islands the ancients sought gold and silver, and Diodorus raved of copper and jewels, but either they have been stolen or were never there.

There have always been robbers in this region, in which the Nile is the only trade-route between two deserts. When, below the elbow, an old fort rises, gleaming black on a steep rock, against which the river breaks below in fresh rapids; when, narrowed, cramped between shapes of gloom, it drives its swift course through unyielding darkness; when again a poverty-stricken hut clings to the rock wall above, nourishing man, wife, and children on the tiniest of strips; old pictures from the Middle Ages fill the mind's eye, the robber-knight, the imprisoned merchant, and the beggar peasant, and the happiest of all are the poor, as they are in folk-tales, for the peasants of this region assure the traveller that they know no sickness.

Still wilder than the Fifth is the Fourth Cataract, which the river has to encounter in the middle of that south-westerly stretch it has had to take. Here, besides granite and basalt, porphyry and syenite press upon it, ravaged, wild, and gloomy to the view; a hill nearly four miles long thrown right across its path, of formidably crowded black rock, through which the river bites its way. This is the most difficult part of all the Middle Nile, and only the most experienced of the natives can cross it. Upstream, the boats can only be dragged through all the cataracts, but there is so much good fellowship here that one water-wheel calls on the other, and its drivers help to pull to the next. All are first-class swimmers; and when the Nubian of these regions sets out downstream, he blows up his leather water-bag, or builds a pointed raft of dhurra-stalks, takes bread and dates in a melon rind, and then, steering with practised hands, drifts down the Nile for days.

He may be stoned from above on his journey, or kidnapped, like the handsome daughters of those Nubians on the banks when a famous black Paris was carrying on in these parts and bore off his booty to Kaab el Aabid, "The Square House of the Slave," the remains of which are still to be seen here on the banks of the turbulent river. He was really only a wretched slave who had carried away his master's wife and dragged her to the rocky wilderness, where he built her a keep and failed to become immortal with his dusky Helen only because no Homer was there to sing their story. Only Negro lips murmur the legend of this revolutionary and lover of women through the roar of the Nile.

For here, between rocks and island, it has turned wild again, as it was at its source. On these reaches, the hippopotamus and the crocodile again disport themselves, the lord and the robber of the Nile, and lie in wait for the swimmer. When the crocodile has burrowed itself into the sand, and struck a man with its tail, it plays with him like a cat, appalling the brothers of his victim on the bank. The natives here have fewer weapons and means of defence than the Shilluks higher up. They say, too, that the crocodile prefers the white man to the black, and thus the European, here at least, in the middle of the African desert, commands a respect which is as questionable as his superiority. It is a moot point whether the crocodile really pursues men on land: many explorers deny it, but the Nubians declare that it is true, and advise a victim to run in circles, the most likely way of saving himself.

The hippopotamus, on the other hand, conducts himself like a gentleman, for though at night, on land, he may trample down men and beasts from time to time, he leaves them lying, and capsizes the boats in the Nile only by mistake, because God made him too big and the boats too small. But he would never drag men or animals into the water. As he swims as lightly as the elephant walks, as he is good-natured, lazy, and always pleased in the company of his like, he sometimes makes less noise and raises less waves than might be expected of this little steamer displacing two tons of water. Basking placidly, olive-drab, he might be a rock in the river, if his five coy pink patches, eyes, ears, and snout, did not betray an animal presence, or suddenly a monstrous pair of jaws yawn in the middle of the rock, with an exhibition of crooked, broken teeth, slanting against each other, and revealing the history of vegetarian orgies, although at the moment they take only the tenderest flower of the poets, the water-lily, to let it dissolve on their gigantic tongues.

With his rather big eyes, which seem to have been laid onto his face, and not stuck in, like the elephant's, and with his little ears, he is quick to note the presence of his enemies, but as no one can overcome him, he maintains, except in the rutting season, the repose of a clumsy dragon. When water-plants are plentiful, he spends his night too in the water, but as a rule, he goes on land in the evening to feed and then everything takes flight before his deep, bass grunts, which sound as if they were issuing from a cave, for with all his peacefulness, it sometimes happens that he inadvertently tramples a pair of oxen to death at a waterwheel, and when he goes home, the field behind him might have been turned up with an iron ploughshare.

Then he glides back into the maternal river.

15

THE Nile has flowed far through mountains, swamps, and deserts without seeing a sign of the past on its banks, were it only a broken column.

Suddenly a field of pyramids arises below the Fourth Cataract, with more than forty stone tombs of men who once were mighty. Others soon follow, eight or nine of them round the foot of a hill visible from far and wide at the southernmost point of the loop. This place of death is called Sanàm Abu-Dôm, which means "the place where statues lie under doum-palms," and now, as the Nile once more turns northwards, statues and pyramids succeed each other at long intervals down to below the Second Cataract. Down to what shadowy depths of history does the hand of man grope in the desert? What conqueror, with his picture-language hewn in granite, written on papyrus, first preserved the names of savage Negro tribes for posterity? Who but those Egyptians, whose greed for gold and slaves urged them up their own river, the oldest race on the Nile and in the western world!

And yet it was again the Nile which stopped their advance. It set the cataracts across their way, and just as the priest withholds from the worshipper the sight of the holy image, the mysterious river seemed to withhold from the stranger an insight into the solitude of the water he lived on. Whether they came up on their own boats, or built new ones between the cataracts, we do not know. The desert was waterless, and the Nile only in flood-time high enough for strangers to venture upriver. Only small groups advanced, dependent on the goodwill of the natives, and lost if they could not get it. In thousand-year-old sagas, curiosity urged the suspicious adventurers onward, fear held them back.

And Ramses the Great came up the river, founded cities and

temples, settled the land with a colony of peasants and craftsmen, and glorified his own achievements, up there in Nubia, in statues and pictures. Queen Hatshepsut had frescoes painted showing Negroes bringing her cattle and giraffes, lion-skins and golden rings, with the gestures of the conquered. Remains go back into the fourth millennium B.C.; about 2000 B.C. the Pharaohs once penetrated as far as the Blue Nile; and it is known that from 1900 to 1100 B.C. they ruled as far as the Fourth Cataract, and carried away gold and slaves.

But the Nile always rescued its children, or such as the strangers did not carry off. It wrecked the strangers' boats, and the natives arose and slew the intruders. But often, under the whip of the overseers, they had to bore shafts into the hills, follow the windings of the gold veins in the mountains, make the rock friable with fire, and then hack it out with picks. Why had they begotten sons only to work in the flickering light of the lamps, to seize the broken lumps of rock, and crawl up to the surface with them, where the women and old men were waiting to grind them to powder on millstones, till the pieces were as small as the lentils they reaped on the meagre riverside strips in flood-time? Then, on slanting stone tables, the dust had to be washed until all the lighter particles had been washed away, and a pale, shimmering tinsel was left, which the strangers mixed with lead and salt and melted in earthenware pans for five days, and cooled down in the form of rings, plates, and tiles.

Thus, groaning in the glare, the most powerful tribes of Nubia were wasted away, till they rebelled and were beaten again, and their sons again bore the lot of slaves. When these mighty strangers tore the white ornamental feathers from the Nubian ostriches, flayed the skins from the panthers, and loaded them on their camels, when they killed elephants for their tusks or forced these sinewy sons of the desert to sail downstream with them, so as to stand as guards in their public places, wrapped in strange, gaudy garments—all that could be understood. But what could the mighty lord care for wretched flakes of yellow metal, that they should sacrifice thousands of their slaves, half of whom had been destroyed by the desert and the river before others arrived to brandish the whip and then hold the pan? The Nubians did not know that the Pharaoh, in the flower of his youth, built a sarcophagus and a funeral chamber which contained thirty thousand pounds of gold, and all of it from Nubia.

But Ramses, who in the thirteenth century glorified himself as "the king at whose name the gold issues from the mountains," had already laid his gold mines with such skill that they might be worked today; the cunning of these kings was as great as their greed. Their power was for a long time actually based on the gold of Nubia, the name of which means "the land of gold." And yet they had a premonition of the curse of gold. Priests warned the kings, for an inscription on the Lower Nile ran: "But gold is the body of the gods, and not your affair."

The curse came true. These Nubians, who, in their blissful life as nomads, had never turned downstream, awakened to anger and curiosity, unrest and revenge, and one day, when news came of a dispute among Egyptian kings, a Nubian king called Pianki set out with his army, with boats and oxen, crossed the frontier, struggling and conquering, and in 750 B.C. entered Memphis and Thebes, became master of Egypt, like his sons and grandsons after him. These stronger, more savage conquerors from "the wretched land of Kush," who looked like Huns to the refined Egyptians, rapidly and roughly seized the power; inscriptions relate that the king did not deign to cast a glance at the beautiful women in the palace of Heliopolis, but complained of the bad feeding of his horses. One of these Nubian kings actually marched into Palestine from the delta of the Nile to help King Hezekiah against the Assyrian enemy. What an impression must have been made by the temples and buildings, the astronomers and navigators, by all the useful knowledge, on these barbarians who, having invaded civilization in their savagery, were feared and hated there and driven out again, though laden with an enlightenment which had once reached them only in legend.

For the empire which, before and after these conquests, stretched from the cataracts far into the east of Nubia, generally called Meroe, with its capital Napata near the southern point of the great loop, this colony, never more than half subjected, had already raised to power Egyptian priests who had entered the country as refugees, prisoners, or scholars, and it was these priests

who seem to have prompted their less civilized masters to undertake the campaigns of revenge into Egypt. But now when the
conquerors returned to their Nubian home, they sought more
than ever to imitate Egyptian buildings and temples, customs
and laws. King Pianki, who lauded his own deeds after the fashion of the Egyptian Pharaohs or the dictators of today, called
himself, in an inscription on a gigantic temple, like all conquerors, "the Bringer of Peace to both lands, King of the North
and South, Sun of Suns, Lord of the Diadems," and had frescoes
painted on which the God Amon hands him a sword, while he,
in majestic progress, slaughters a dozen enemies.

For five hundred years, this kingdom between the Third and
Fifth Cataracts was bound to Thebes and Amon, who, as the
national god, intervened directly in the government of the state,
and centuries after their brief rule down on the delta the kings
of Napata still called themselves "Lord of Both Lands," just as
the Pharaohs still glorified themselves as Lords of Nubia when
they had long since lost their power over the country—the obstinate pleasantries of men in power who, on their statues, the
visiting-cards of ancient times, would not abandon their claim
to provinces long lost. But kings in those days were in the fore-
front of battle, and Thutmosis I, at the Third Cataract, stabbed
with his own hands the enemy King of Nubia.

In later centuries, their halo shrank, the priests ruled, Egyptian customs died out, the hieroglyphics, still no more than an
official language, again yielded to a popular tongue of Nubia,
which is only now being deciphered, the legendary King Cambyses came, no one knows how far, Greek writers praised the
land of wonder with an enthusiasm which was all the greater
because no one set out to find the facts, while, to make themselves
completely invincible, the native kings withdrew from the southerly point of the loop to the Fourth Cataract, where Meroe, the
new capital, protected by the Nile, was inaccessible. There,
Strabo says, the handsomest, cleverest, or boldest men were
chosen king. Later, it is true, weak kings, remote descendants of
those ruder ancestors, obeyed the priests, who called their machinations commands of the gods, and even went so far, in the
end, as to order the kings to kill themselves by divine decree, till

at last a king, thus theocratically condemned, pulled himself together and slew the chief priest, for disbelief and strength generally intensify each other.

Or else the priests would put a queen on the throne, at first as regent for her young son, though her rule continued long after he had come of age. But when, in the first century, one of these queens conquered parts of Upper Egypt and advanced as far as Philæ and Aswân, a new people was already ruling over Egypt, and stronger than she; the Romans sent an army up the Nile to vindicate the name of their Emperor, for the queen had overthrown his statues. They advanced as far as the Second Cataract; after them, with the exception of an Arab army, no army succeeded in doing so for two thousand years. There the Nile stopped them.

Thus hate, revenge, and the fortunes of war swayed between the two Nile countries, till at last the Emperor Diocletian abandoned Nubia in A.D. 300.

16

RICH in palms, the narrow strip stretches along the river, which is now once more striving towards the north; rustling oases lie on the long road to the Third Cataract, over 200 miles away from the Fourth. Where grain flourishes, the birds abound, and on many a narrow field children stand on little platforms, scaring the birds away with twigs the livelong, burning day, while the tireless water-wheels sigh and the huge oxen of the country, whose skin hangs down under their necks like cloaks, turn without a groan for ten hours under the same sun, drawing up water, water. What they feel, whether they think, nobody knows, and man consoles himself with the thought that his slave, man or beast, knows no better. If, beside them, we see the white chargers of Dongola, famous since ancient times, we weave a finer life about them, yet they, galloping by, always bridled, perhaps look with envy on the equanimity of the heavy beasts in their eternal round.

On this part of the loop, from the southern corner of which the caravans set out for the south, even in ancient times, the memorials of the ages grow more frequent.

In the neighbourhood of Dongola, a granite stone lies on the Nile bank, heedlessly thrown away when a clay hut was destroyed, which it had served as corner-stone when the Scottish troops lived there on their last campaign. Earlier, brown hands had used it to support a water-wheel whose history no inscription records. Those who made the water-wheel had taken it from an Arab grave, where it had, for a few decades, protected from the onslaughts of the vultures the body of a slave secretly buried there by some pious son. The slave's son had dragged it down by night from a fort which the Mamelukes had built to resist the advance of Mehemet Ali, and finally abandoned to his troops, but the Mamelukes had hacked it out of the corner of a mosque which Saladin had built in the twelfth century in the middle of the Nile valley, when, after a long peace, he had massacred all the bishops.

For over wide stretches of the Middle Nile valley, the cross ruled for more than six centuries, and the stone may well have been the corner-stone of a church that King Silko of Dongola had built to the glory of the saints. At that time, Crusaders in coats of mail had tethered their fine white chargers to a ring, whose trace the stone has never quite lost, before entering the church to pray for the Madonna's protection against the dangers of the next desert ride. Then the knight would unloose his war-horse from the stone, gently spurring its soft flanks, but holding the stirrup with his big toe only. Before the stone was built into the church, it helped to support the porch of that temple of Phthur whose red sandstone columns on the edge of the palm-forest still reveal in their ruins that Greek hands raised it there late in time, and probably dedicated it to Ares, whose Roman name too makes a fantastic appearance in this kingdom of Meroe. But the slaves who built the temple had taken the stone from the pedestal of the giant statue which has, since time immemorial, lain flat on the beach of Dongola, the statue of some Pharaoh whose name no one knows.

Thus they passed away, civilizations and religions, conquerors and conquered, and yet they had all worshipped light and power, under varying symbols and names, even those who saw power in pity. In fortresses and mosques, in temples and barracks, all had sought to magnify their own lives, had passed and fallen with the places of their glory, and only the stone, the eternal granite from the banks of the Nile, has outlived everything, the pressure from above, the work of the chisel, the holes for the ring, the water-wheels, the tombs, the ages. In primeval repose, it lies on the banks of the river, which rushes by in primeval movement, yet cannot break it.

Close below Dongola, the granite again rises to ward off the water: there it splits the river with the longest of all the islands in the Nile—Argo, which is some twenty-five miles long—and, where the river forces it to end, throws out a short row of islets and another spit of rock, which again churn up the Nile into roaring spray in seven rapids.

Here on the Third Cataract, 700 miles below Khartoum, the Nile valley changes, the plain grows milder, the river narrows, the hippopotamus grows rare, and the approach of civilization makes itself felt in the superior organization of the bands of robbers. Chains of hills approaching from the east, causing the sudden westward curve of the Nile, a higher mountain ridge, where it even occasionally rains in winter, and again the rocky chasms and gorges on the river itself, mingled from now on with green and red porphyry, the many twists and turns which make the river completely unnavigable—all this encourages the robbers to play their tricks on the traveller approaching on horse or camel.

Here the natives are less skilled in navigation than those higher up. Their rafts of four slightly bent palm-trunks, badly propelled by oars split at the top, often founder, for here, where the Nile sometimes narrows to a width of 250 feet, so that the practised Nubian can throw a stone across it, the whirlpools and rocks which squeeze it in prevent any navigation for more than a hundred miles in the rocky valley which the Arabs, in their plastic speech, call "The Life of Stone." There the Nubian has learnt to swim as no white man can swim: with his spear tied flat on his head, he swims across the river; on the steepest part of the bank he can reach his narrow field only by swimming, to stick a few seeds or beans in the muddy earth and to reap the harvest, which he carries over to his hut on his head. Only in the Arctic Ocean can life be so difficult to maintain.

If he has a hut, two oxen, and four goats, he already calls it an oasis in this region; a water-wheel is a token of wealth, a palm the sign of Allah's blessing. Among these most poverty-stricken signs of the life of today, mighty signs of past power rise from the splendid solitude, and yet the giant columns which Amenophis, Thutmosis, and Sesostris here erected to their glory, even then stood on no market-place and on no trade route. Between black rocks and the shrill yellow desert, in the heat and the glare, amid a poverty which even then did not look idyllic, the megalomania of the Pharaohs glorified itself by the labour of thousands of slaves; if they could thus dispense with awe-stricken spectators, if they realized that there were nothing but a few hundred naked cowherds and gaunt peasants to gape at the record of their greatness, they may well be credited with a feeling of their own likeness to the gods which made them think and build for thousands of years to come. The situation of such a monument tells us the astounding fact that in the time of Amenophis III the Nile bed was twenty-five feet higher; that is the work of the water in three thousand years.

Perhaps only one inscription may have been interpreted to the naked brown men from generation to generation; it stood on the granite column just above Wadi Halfa, where the cataracts cease and the Nile becomes navigable. For there a Pharaoh thunders: "From this spot, to all eternity, no Negro shall sail down the Nile."

There at the Second Cataract, nearly a thousand miles below Khartoum, when this warning curse was pronounced, lay the southern frontier of Egypt, and there it lies today. This most magnificent cataract of the Nile, devoid of vegetation, volcanic, looks, in its confusion, like a maze. Approaching this wide picture of water and stone—the Nile has here once more become very broad—one could imagine it a collection of petrified hippos, whose wet backs, rising from the water, glisten in the sun, for the water has rounded everything, and a soft swirl round each of the blocks increases the illusion.

Seen from the rock of Abu Sir, which rises on the western bank, the whole looks more rock than water; in winter, three hundred and fifty rock islands have been counted, and even in flood-time more than one hundred rise above the water. More than fifty are inhabited by men in clay huts; there are, too, a few strong, old acacias, which have outlived many floods. The fields the inhabitants have rescued and sown with beans and lentils look like the children's beds in a garden. Their owners row or sail over to them twice a year to sow and reap.

Below, the little town of Wadi Halfa, which means the "grassy valley," stretches along the Nile bank, densely populated, with white house-fronts reflected in the water, and dominated by a hill on the left bank which looks like a sea-cliff. Palms wave, sailing-boats glide downstream, everything seems enlivened by the railway which begins, the navigation which ends, here, at the frontier of two countries. The green flag of Egypt waves with fresh self-assurance, for from this point downward, it waves alone.

The Nile has overcome its third adventure, the cataracts. Broad and slow, in a majestic mood such as it has not known since Khartoum, it enters Egypt.

17

THIS is not yet Egypt proper, for the country from Wadi Halfa to Aswân, known as Lower Nubia, stretching for 225 miles along the sharp easterly curve of the Nile, is the poorest part of Egypt, a desolate country in which the desert often borders the river, by which the cultivated patches seldom reach a width of more than a hundred yards. In these unfruitful stretches, the life of the Egyptian fellah resembles that of his brother on the cataracts; both are Nubians, both are dependent on the water-wheel and the Nile silt, only that here there are neither palms nor granite to be turned into houses, and the Nile must serve for the houses too. Hence the form of the pylon, which we still call Egyptian, and which was first created out of Nile mud, like the sand-castles the children build on the beach.

The ancient Egyptians saw in Lower Nubia merely a land of passage to the Sudan, from which they took slaves and gold, and since all later peoples could only move southwards up the Nile, many civilizations have left grotesque mixtures behind them. Shortly after Wadi Halfa, on the right bank, the ruins of a medieval fortress lie by the side of a rock temple in which early Egyptian reliefs are painted over with pictures of Christian saints: the ram's head of the god Khnum gazes out side by side with Saint Epimachus; on one wall, a Pharaoh is suckled by the god Anuket, on the other, Jesus lies at His mother's breast. A threatening Byzantine Christ stretches his hand from the roof, but close beside it King Haremhab stands in the presence of his god Thout. Beside the remains of a Nubian fort of the Meroe epoch lie the fragments of a Hathor temple, with graves of Moslems by its side. Further down, a Coptic priest, Abraham, in the temple of Derr, wrote amid the images of Egyptian gods that a Nubian king had made him raise the cross here: a medley of priests and kings, gods and slaves, saints and peasants, who fought bloody battles for the name and form of God, and now, recalled by Him, are all the same desert sand.

At varying altitudes, the two deserts approach the banks of the river in varying proximity, and their different colour is not merely an effect of the light: the western, Libyan desert is golden-yellow with brown mountains; the more rocky eastern one, the Arabian desert, is grey-brown. Between them, broad sandbanks hamper the heavy way of the steamers.

The steamers are white and shallow: their black coal has most likely come all the long way from Newcastle, and as, in this land without rain, the fireboxes stay half-open, the whole looks rather like a railway train on the river. At its side, the shallow-draught steamer leads a second, where the coloured travellers sit, but on both boats, the passenger thinks: "The other is second-class." Slowly the two linked steamers glide side by side on the river, a picture of the enforced community of white and brown men, for on the white boat is the engine, the brain which governs the journey, but the hands which stoke it are brown, like the passengers on the other boat; and it is this second boat that carries the products of the country northwards.

Forty miles below Wadi Halfa, where the heights of the Libyan desert run close down to the left bank of the Nile, between the hills and the water, there appear four colossal statues of yellow stone: each represents the same man, four times repeated, sitting in front of a temple wall, a god, a king—maybe a golem. There he sits, facing the rising sun, as he has sat these three thousand years since he was hewn out of the yellow rock—at whose command? Did some son here enshrine his victorious father for posterity, or a hero his protecting god? Did some queen here give immortal form to her heroic son? Or is it the monument of some ruler, whose people wished, after his death, to dedicate him to the gods?

It was none of these. It was Ramses II who here immortalized himself, and as his reign of sixty-seven years gave him time to attend to his glory, as he, in seven places in Egypt, erected the greatest temples to himself and his gods, among which this one,

near the southern frontier at Abu Simbel, looks small, he gave
the greatest examples of self-idolization known to ancient history, and would hardly be Ramses the Great today if it were not
for this highly imaginative publicity which, as a modern dictator has betrayed, lies in the perpetual repetition of one's own
name. Late emperors may have been presented to their people
by their priests as ambassadors of the gods, or by their scholars as
the fountain of wisdom, but how humble they look, how humble even our tribunes of today look, beside the king who hewed
his own statue, seventy feet high, four times out of the rock to sit
close beside his gods.

For it is really he, Ramses with the long nose of history, the
gentle face, and the crowns of Upper and Lower Egypt, and as
he turns his face directly east, without anger, with an expression
of repose, his hands on his knees, he looks like some giant, fearless of the sun's rays, who now, after the stillness of the night, is
looking down on the awakening life in the Nile valley. Before
his eyes, against the crude blue of the sky, a narrow green barley-
field stands out, with its water-wheel in front of it still whining
through the ages, turned by the slow-moving pair of oxen; a
woman in a floating black veil carries her earthenware pitcher to
the river: the water is blue, with ripples of silver in the morning
breeze, a white sail glides towards the bank, the boy clambers up
the mast to furl it, and downstream, where the river narrows, the
deep-yellow edge of the desert almost collides with the muddy
bank.

For however old and mighty the Pharaoh may be who had
himself gigantically enthroned there four times, the Nile is a
thousand times older and mightier, and from its eternal movement in this morning hour, through the year and through the
ages, Pharaoh received all his power. But look—in actual fact
there are only three of him left: the upper sandstone part of the
fourth has fallen at his feet, and the mighty king looks as if rebellious slaves had quartered him.

But what is that standing between the legs of the three and a
half colossal kings? They are his family, his wife and children;
one even represents his mother who, by a grotesque reversal
of nature. has come to stand between the giant legs of her son.

There, between his legs, Ramses has inscribed his name, and on his arms and his neck-ring too, but then the leaders and mercenaries of later peoples came by, wished to earn their share of glory, and inscribed their deeds on the limbs and pedestal of the old king, while below, we read: "We wrote this, Archon, son of Amoibichos, and Pelekos, son of Udamos." There they stand, poor, unknown lieutenants, who once came adventuring here, and have become more famous than the great king between whose toes they inscribed their doings, for many a wanderer in the East can read their Greek, but only a few scholars can decipher the hieroglyphics.

Inside the rocky cave, however, Ramses could proclaim by pictures on the walls what a demigod he was, while, to provide for all contingencies, he had himself sculptured again in a row of statues thirty feet high. Nowhere is the hawk-headed sun-god as big as the statue of the king, but even on the frescoes, where the king brings human offering, he holds towards him, at the same time, his own, idolized name in the form of a picture. Then he had himself represented with a god handing him a sword, or he is slaying an enemy, storming a fortress, shooting down from the battlements on the enemy imploring mercy, commanding his officers to count the enemy hands cut off in battle, or leading the conquered before his image.

At times, this self-idolatry rises to art. In Greek slenderness, the king is slaying an enemy, with his foot already resting on a conquered foe, or he is listening to a woman who has tenderly grasped his forearm, or two goddesses, in modern evening dress, each holding the key of life, are blessing the queen with upraised arms. Suggestion plays a great part in such impressions, when the rays of the morning sun strike through the door of the vault into the holy of holies, or the electric searchlight from the steamer lifts the whole out of its magic night into sudden vision. Since the whole is ten times over-instrumented, since all that these booming records have to tell has less appeal for us than the sight of their beautiful hieroglyphics, since the names of all these Hittites, Nubians, or Libyans reach our ears only like the distant surge of the sea, nothing would draw us to these documents of royal madness if it were not that they had preserved the life of their time in scenes which might have been drawn by the hand of a child.

There are soldiers and slaves, Egyptians and their enemies living in camp, feeding their horses; in the neighbouring temple of Derr, beside the same Ramses, refugees are carrying their wounded from the heights, while their people wait for them, mournful and still. Negroes bring monkeys and greyhounds, ostriches and giraffes, elephant tusks and gold, to the king; a woman carries a child in a basket fastened to a band round her forehead; one of the wounded is being led back to the village, where his wife is cowering by the fire; and on the fortress wall another is standing with her child in her arms. Why are all these scenes in the minor key more impressive than the strident major of the giant king who has become a god?

Perhaps the uneasy feeling that arises in us at the sight of the ruler's splendour amid this desolation comes from the river itself, on whose banks he set it up.

18

FOR now the Nile is urged on to
a new adventure, its fourth, and as it cannot now see the great
enemy, but only the consequences of his mischief, the feeling of
oppression grows. A pressure is brought to bear on the river
more terrifying than those at the great waterfall or in the swamps
of its youth, stranger than in the cataracts of its middle age: the
Nile rises steadily, and yet receives no rain! For 220 miles, counting upstream from Aswân, the Nile rises, and yet cannot feel the
great flood which the summer rain, in those distant alps, brings
yearly to the Blue Nile. No; it is stemmed by mysterious powers,
and if memory lives in it, it can recall no year in all the ages in
which it rose in winter, to inundate what had just been land, as
it has now done for thirty years. And what deepens the riddle is
that it rises at harvest-time, whereas in summer, when the flood
comes, it sinks.

The strips near the bank show clearly how rapidly it has
changed in winter: above the water rise palm-tops which cannot
have grown out of the Nile; the keel of the steamer glides close
by crumbling walls, as if Vineta had been submerged here, but
they were only poor clay huts, and the mud of which the peasants built them now returns to its father, the Nile. The tips of
water-wheels stick out of the water, islands form where palms
have fallen and collected mud, but they are no longer the floating islands of the upper swamps, and their former inhabitants
sail over in little boats to other, old islands, now under water,
and the boys climb on to the projecting palm-tops which still
bear fruit, although for nine months of the year they stand up to
the neck in the water.

But above, on the heights near the new bank, there stand new,
bald houses of mud, of stone too—granite again sets in here—

looking doubly blind in their new whitewash, like fortresses on old copper-plates; for they are windowless, the sun cannot light up their fronts; odd, serrated battlements make them look still more uninhabited, like the models of some engineer who tried here to change the face of the landscape. Women come down from the heights to sow their little green patch on the bank, and the solidified silt, which forms the edge of the bank, is like a firm quay, along which they ride on their little asses—always women, for the men are cleaning dishes or streets in Cairo: they are regarded as less intelligent and more honest than the Lower Egyptians, and since Kitchener's officers used them for orderlies, they have emigrated to the Sudan, though only for a year, after which they go back to their wives.

The fortunes of the peasants, between these steep, unfertile banks, rise and fall: the dam in Aswân has been raised twice; each time thousands of houses and homes were submerged. They were offered land in fertile Egypt, but they would not relinquish their old, tough earth of mud and stones, on which their fathers had walked and perished. Thus new dwellings constantly appear in higher parts, the old palm below is their own, and even though they can reach it only by boat, it is, all the same, the palm of their fathers, on whose dates they wish to live.

Hilly peninsulas have been formed, between which the river has run into little fiords, on whose edges the ruins of former villages still look out, to be inundated in their turn next month. Here, in February, there are green stretches of fifty yards—rare ones reach three hundred—but the Nubians have to hide their grain high up near the new houses, so that the winter flood shall not carry it away.

In the little towns which, standing rather high, have not yet been flooded, in Derr, where the great loop of the Nile really first comes to an end, close by in Korosko, above which the river is forced into a peculiar, quite short south-east turn, both lying on fertile land on the eastern bank, there, where a dozen palmtrunks spring from a single root, the people seem fresher, more healthy, the market is busy, the houses shimmer white from out the yellow acacias. Where once the camels were loaded which, with good luck, would reach Abû-Hamed in a week, on that chord of the Nile arc which was later followed by the railway, where the Mecca pilgrims once rode off to the Red Sea, the little Fords hoot through the narrow streets, and the last fine camels of Kordofan stand gloomily by the wayside, as if they knew that they are worth only $10 now, instead of $50, and that in Cairo they are even sent with humiliation to the slaughter-house, while their fathers bore General Gordon and Colonel Kitchener on their backs, and carried the first emissaries of civilization into the wild plains of the Sudan.

And the hampered stream widens and widens: on the frontier of Egypt proper, on the Tropic of Cancer, the Nile becomes a lake. It is a fantastic scene, without a plant, of grey stones, hills, and islands, with grotesque rocks, all polished, in round, strange heaps, the heavy stones towering up on the flat ones, here like columns, there like mountains. Thus here, above the First Cataract, the cataract of Aswân, the scenery of the Second Cataract is repeated, but magnified into measurelessness, for here there is no question of river banks, but only of distant coasts of dull red granite round about this half-petrified lake, from which the drowned palms raise their tops, like the drowned souls in a vision of Dante. No one would be surprised if this lake took fire, so unreal do the glistening, smooth sides of the rock look, rising from its uncannily swollen breadth, and even the white train, waiting over in Shellal, looks like a creeping dragon, lying on the bank, ready to pounce on the traveller landing from the lake.

Yet over the surface of this Nile lake, as if they knew no fear, the sails of the first pure Egyptians glide like happy birds, with gaudy Arab pennants at the mast and stern, sweeping by the tops of the sunken palms; the steersman, standing erect, with his upper arm on the great tiller, leans against the north wind, his white shirt fluttering back like the tunic of the Winged Victory, while the reddish rock behind him reaches to his hips, and the piercing yellow of the desert glides past his head in the background. But what strange capitals is his boat approaching?

Pylons and columns, ornamented with reliefs, painted and perfectly preserved, stretch their heads out of the middle of the colourless, petrified lake: the fragments of a fantasy rising from

the past, and forgetting the commandments of today, shadows
of faded memories of ancient gods, dream-pictures of a romantic
mind mourning for the defeated. Such are the thoughts which
flit round the mind of the traveller approaching the island of
Philæ by boat, in winter, when the water stands high, while on
the architrave of Osiris, close above the surface of the water, a
black and white wagtail rocks, a proud Pharaoh already bathes
his legs in the Nile, while only the crown of Isis can rise above
the flood. Softly the oar strikes against the rafter of a lower room,
but the pieces that have been hacked away show that here, too,
one god drove out the other, and that the jealousy of the priests
wrought more havoc than the flood into which the Temple of
Philæ has been sinking for only thirty years. Only when autumn
comes on, when the opened dam leads the Nile back into its
natural bounds, do the temples stand high and dry as once they
stood, but then a grey-green layer of mud has veiled the walls,
and transformed the festive halls into the dwellings of frigid
Undines.

When these temples still rose above the waters, Egyptians and
Nubians here, by the graves of their gods, swore solemn treaties
of peace, and now where the rock-martin builds her nest, the
lovely arm of Cleopatra may for a moment have rested on the
hand of a cowering slave. Then for a time the Greek gods held
sway here, and the Emperor Hadrian, who wished in any case to
stand well with the Egyptian gods, and here, far from Rome,
worshipped Isis and Horus, had the source of the Nile painted on
one of the walls: there the Nile god, with his snake at the foot of
a rock, sits pouring water out of two pitchers, with a vulture and
a falcon looking on at this romantic birth of the Nile.

And Isis still found a refuge here at the southernmost corner
of her domain, while Christ was already dominating the delta.
Then priests bore the image of the Madonna among the Egyptian gods, and after them the disciples of Mohammed overthrew
those images, putting in their place the text without an image.
And these graceful buildings, smaller, more elegant than all the
others, built in the decadence of the third century, unclassical
temples, gay and bright with colour, like a scene from *The Magic*

Flute, still stood here in the middle of the Nile, unscathed by the elements. They were still standing when the French chiselled their names into the Ptolemaic walls, taking care to place them high up, so that they can be seen on the eastern pylon from the boat: in the fashion of the Pharaohs, they praise their own victory of the Pyramids, and the generals had their names set underneath, but the name of Napoleon was scratched out by some excited English visitor. Then some son of Napoleon renewed it, and inscribed above: *"Une page de l'histoire ne doit pas être salie"*—a weighty lesson for zealots of our day.

If we climb one of the pylons by the iron ladders and now, towards evening, turn west, the beautiful colours of the temple are repeated in nature: the Nile lake looks pastel-blue, the few palms above it grey-green, the near mountains dark orange with blue-green shadows, the desert pink, the distant mountains violet. In the grey-blue western sky, a veiled moon follows the sun, while the northern sky spreads from its purple edge through a path of pink cloud to bright green light ending above, at the zenith, in the golden promise of an arrowy strip, hailing the last gifts of day. A few minutes later, and the light fades, the mountains turn dun, the boundless Nile lake sinks in shadow.

Suddenly a long row of lights flames up. Hundreds of lamps cut through the twilight like a knife, illuminating the huge wall they stand on. A spark has fallen into this dreaming, primeval world. A building has cut through it all, to destroy it. Chaos yields: an ordering will has flashed its way through in light and stone, the colours of the sky and the temple, the monsters of stone, have vanished; a fanfare has drowned all their sound. It is a grey stone dam, a mile long, which shuts off the lake to the north. Now the water, so to speak, reaches its neck, it just overtops it, like the pylon on which we are standing. On the other side of this piercing line, the eye discerns white waterfalls at isolated points, all of the same width, in a row, then again interrupted, revealing a system.

This is the dam, the culprit that spread unrest through a couple of hundred miles of Lower Nubia, that deprived thousands of peasants of their houses, driving them onto the stony hills, that drowned all the palms, and in the end the Temple of

Philæ too, on whose still unshaken columns we stand. This is the great construction by which men mastered the element, the bold invention which has determined the fate of the Nile upstream and downstream. It is the point at which its freedom ends.

It is the dam of Aswân.

19

THE struggle with man had imperilled the Nile along its middle course, but had nowhere changed it; it had been beaten neither in the swamps nor at the cataracts. In agony and wildness, it had withstood the temptations of the plain, broken the resistance of the rocks, had even eluded the hand of man, setting at naught his schemes for canals, his attempts at navigation. When, in Wadi Halfa, it had quitted the last cataract but one, with its biggest discharge it might have been some king among rivers which, mightier than those haughty Pharaohs, silent, with rare outbursts, had bid defiance to rock, swamp, and desert, and which had saved itself.

Then it had plunged into this last adventure, more terrible than all the others because the river could not ward off the invisible enemy; it had swelled and risen in dread, and, while it seemed to be spreading beyond all bounds, the river was appalled. For as, in its steady rise, it overflowed the banks of the desert, it could not but feel the whole as oppression, not as liberation, till a fearful wall stood before it, an inexorable stone bulwark, the great enemy which was not to be overcome because its strength was blended with cunning. While desert and rock had in vain striven to grasp and conquer the stream, men were wiser—they sought not to throttle, but to command.

In Aswân, the Nile has run to its end the adventurous part of its course; here the beauty of anarchy ceases, now it is tamed, it turns useful. Now the element which could not be broken by the elements is seized and bent by human hands in the way the brain of a single man has devised, the will of a single man resolved. The effect of the dam is so powerful that it does not merely govern the last quarter of the river, which begins here, but, by what it can and does do, it influences the whole Nile backwards to the source, more than 3000 miles upstream. Everything that it has lived through, that has been described, is given a new meaning by the dam of Aswân. What it does for Egypt, its Faust-like achievement, we shall consider in Egypt. Now the moment has come to consider the Nile upwards as an element, as what it is, as water. This is the only way to grasp why the turn of its fate should come in Aswân.

Where does the water come from that is dammed at Aswân? When and how abundantly will it flow tomorrow? The engineer in Cairo must know everything that nature in its vagaries betrays to him of the upper river before he can decide how much water he can pass through his sluices to the lower river, what he must reserve, when and how much. In his little room, the brain of the whole sits with pencils, maps, and logarithmic tables, and every morning the white tape oozing out of the telegraph apparatus reports the water-level on both Niles, up to Roseires and Malakal, and on these data he makes his decisions and gives his orders. Then he wires to Aswân how many sluices the engineer must open that day.

But if the measurements are taken upriver, why is no attempt made to master the element higher up, to dam the young and Middle Nile? Looked at from this fateful spot in Aswân, how does the youth of the river appear? What is the significance of the lakes, swamps, and cataracts, what is the significance of the duality of the two Niles, from the point of view of the great dam that controls all their moods?

In answer, we must change the tone and standpoint of our whole story. While up to now the Nile has dominated, and will do so again in Egypt, this interlude gives some play to the observer. We are standing on the dam looking upstream and considering, here on the Tropic of Cancer, what has to be done on the equator for the sake of this dam. The problems are new: the great dam has been standing for only thirty years, and many considerations must be left to the future.

Like the two Niles, the two lakes from which the White Nile issues are rivals as sources. The mountains in which Lake Albert has its home are an important factor; their system on the western edge of the Great African Rift, fed by the mighty alps of the

Ruwenzori, has an important influence on the volume of the White Nile. Calculating the combined area of these two source lakes of the White Nile together with their river systems, the result is an area of nearly 400,000 square miles of land, out of which is fed the narrow cultivated area of Egypt, which measures less than 12,000 square miles. In actual fact, only half of Egypt's water originates in the two lakes, and even this half comes only partially from the rivers feeding them.

For the basin of Lake Victoria is not filled by its horizontal inflow: with the exception of the Kagera, the tributaries are choked by papyrus and prevented for months from flowing into the lake. It is the rain from above that fills Lake Victoria; the old legends which told that the Nile came from Heaven revealed the truth under a metaphor. Lake Victoria, half as big again as Switzerland, combines the advantage of extent with the disadvantage of corresponding evaporation, so that the effects of its gigantic dimensions are neutralized. The gain and loss from rain and evaporation in Lake Victoria are about four times the gain and loss from feeders and outflows—symbols of a great character whose nature and destiny are ruled by powers beyond the earth and not by its fathers and sons.

To transform this huge lake into a reservoir which would safeguard its steadiness for Egypt, it would only be necessary to build a dam at its outflow, the Ripon Falls, and thus store up water for the low years. But then all the water thus stored would have to pass through the sponge of Lake Kioga and other swampy stretches, and would still lose relatively as much as now, when the outflow is free.

Hence, at the moment, plans for an upper dam tend to concentrate at Lake Albert. This much smaller lake, that has little swamp, forms, with its steep banks, an ideal natural reservoir, which with a dam only three feet in height could store 7 billion cubic yards of water, that is, more than in Aswân. As the banks are for the most part steep here, such a process would not increase the area of the lake and hence its evaporation: the dam might rather regularize the surface of Lake Albert. But then how could the young Nile be kept navigable, since it rises for the second time at the northern corner of Lake Albert? Hence arises the

question as to whether the dam should be built immediately
below the outflow from Lake Albert, at Packwatch, or only 125
miles lower down, at Nimule.

For the young mountain stream, along this first reach below
Lake Albert, takes up so many mountain brooks, and is so much
swollen by them in the rainy season, that by the time it reaches
Mongalla its volume is doubled. But the Nile is a real adventurer: it loses in one week what it won the week before. On its
passage through the swamps, it again loses on an average half
what it has just received, and would arrive, so to speak, empty-
handed, if the Bahr-el-Ghazal were not there to come to its help
at the last moment. This wasting of its substance in the swamps
is so great that of 18.3 billion cubic yards of water, 17.7 billion
are wasted in a few months, and with this waste Egypt could be
made two to three times as big as it is. Thus, in the end, the Jebel
and the Ghazal contribute only one-tenth to the total volume of
the Nile.

But since the tributaries have next to no slope on their lower
course, and all discharge into swamp, there comes into being
this strangest swamp-land on earth, where a single hippo, trampling down a path in the evening, can cause a bank to burst, and
so divert the course of a river. What is there to be done? A
"Pharaoh plan" has been devised, called after the Pharaoh
Menes, who once proceeded in a similar way on the Lower Nile.
It is the quickest and cheapest way of preventing the loss of
water in the swamps.

On the left bank of the Jebel, a stone dam would be erected,
thirty feet wide, six feet high, running from Rejaf to Malakal;
on the right bank of the Ghazal, a second would be built; in
this way, half of the present swamps would be cut off from the
Jebel water. The latter, compressed into half its area, pushed
against the Bahr-el-Zeraf, and hence rising, would swell the
swamps on that side. As the ground rises slightly here—that is,
towards the east—the eastern swamps would be further increased,
the western, on the Ghazal, reduced. These two Pharaonic dams,
550 miles in length, to be constructed in six years at the cost of
$5,000,000, would cut off half the swamps: if only half of this
half were saved in its turn, the loss of water in the swamps, which

amounts on an average to almost 20 billion cubic yards, would be reduced by a quarter, and that might be of great advantage to Egypt in bad years.

As long as this great plan remains unrealized, the swamps suck the Upper Nile empty, and Egypt depends on the water flowing into the Nile below the swamps, that is, first and foremost, the Sobat. This brings down a great deal of water from Abyssinia, and is thus dependent on alpine rains, being negligible in winter, swollen and turbulent in summer. A slight change of climate, and the last remains of the water from the great lakes might trickle away in the swamps: the Nile would then be a purely Abyssinian stream.

The waterless Nile, having lost its all in the swamps like a business man in some daring enterprise, is saved by the advent of the Sobat, which arrives close below the mouth of the Ghazal and Zeraf, at the moment of deepest distress. It is true that the Sobat has been reduced by its own floods on its upper course: thus its maximum flow is retarded till November, although its upper course begins to rise in April. Nevertheless, when it falls into the Nile, it is so abundant that it completely stems the scanty main stream in autumn, even throwing it back as far as Lake No. In actual fact, no Nile water flows to Khartoum in the second half of the year, but only Sobat water.

Meanwhile, the mainly Abyssinian water of the Sobat and its sons is creeping slowly along the bed and under the name of the White Nile to Khartoum.

Photo: Lehnert & Landrock, Cairo

THE ASWÂN DAM

THE FELLAH ON THE NILE

20

THE Nile seems to turn all the laws of nature upside down, yet, just because of that, nature can achieve her purposes. Flowing almost without a slope through deserts and swamps, it still does not evaporate; in summer, when other rivers dry up, it reaches its high-water level, reversing in Egypt the normal round of the seasons; less abundant than either the Congo or the Danube, it keeps going in much more difficult circumstances; crawling endlessly through rainless lands, it is all the same copious enough to supply the place of rain. To do this, nature has invented a trick—the double river, the brother pair.

Which of the two Niles is the main stream can no more be decided than which is the leading spirit of a pair of inventors. In the Curie couple or the brothers Wright, mathematics and imagination, intuition and research, clearly had to combine in order that the goal should be reached: thus these brothers too bear the palm between them. The White Nile is certainly the slower, but just because of that it saves Egypt, since, owing to the slightness of its slope, the water of the grave river is delayed and reaches Khartoum only from August to December, while the swift Blue Nile hurls its waters down from July to September. The White Nile would certainly never overflow its banks without the Blue, and agriculture in Egypt would be limited to the riverside strip and the water-wheel, but without the White Nile the Blue would let Egypt perish of thirst in the dry months when it carries only a little subterranean water. Nature has invented something wiser than an uninteresting "victory of the stronger." The elder of the brothers keeps life going, the younger is the genius.

The native intemperance of the Blue Nile is revealed in all the figures. While the proportion between maximum and minimum of discharge during the year on the White Nile is 5:1, on the Blue it is 500:1. While the water coming to Egypt can be reckoned in advance from December to May because it comes from the White Nile, nobody knows how high the flood on the Blue Nile will be in June, or what the alps and the monsoons will produce. A creative, yet moody character, the Blue Nile suddenly withdraws almost completely from the common work, and in return, does it all when it feels inclined, for in August and September, two-thirds of all the water at Berber belongs to the Blue Nile, one-sixth to the Atbara, and only one-sixth to the White Nile.[1] On a view of the whole water-discharge, the Bahr-el-Jebel might be regarded as the source-river of the White, the Blue Nile as that of the whole. And the White Nile, moreover, is never white, the Blue Nile never blue. The White looks green in spring, reddish later, and is not clear even in winter: the Blue Nile is chocolate-brown in flood, clearing later. The names only fit a general comparison of the ground-tones.

Yet the true genius of the Blue Nile is not displayed in the headlong rush of its waters, but in their composition: that it descends from volcanic mountains, transforming the debris of the Abyssinian basalt into life-giving silt, there neither the White Nile nor any river in Europe can imitate it. The people on the Ganges are well aware of the value of the silt, and if a great flood destroys the crops there, the Indians smile in Brahminical equanimity, for they know that the earth will be so much the more fertile next year. In Egypt, they knew five thousand years ago that the Nile silt had formed the delta, and that it created the harvest anew every year.

The White Nile, too, brings solid substances in suspension down with it; the percentage of the solubles is even about equal to that of the Blue Nile; but what it brings is mostly vegetable, because the swamps have acted like a huge filter, the slope is less steep, the long islands hold up the debris, and the clayey soil cannot be broken up. And the Sobat, which, as a half-Abyssinian river, carries silt with it, loses most of it up in its own swamps.

The solid substances, especially, which the White Nile and Sobat carry down have already been deposited along their flat

---

[1] The flood of summer 1935 was the biggest in forty years.

reaches and in the swamps, and as the Blue Nile brings them along only with the flood, 86 percent of all the solids in the Nile waters are carried through in the two months of August and September. In the cataracts, the Nile tears along eroded masses of basalt, granite, and chalk, and even thickens its silt with desert sand. But what is putrescent in it—for it contains 9 percent of organic substances—is destroyed during the desert journey by the dryness of the air. Thus the desert strengthens the power of its enemy, the water, and everything that is left stranded when the flood subsides—dead fish and all kinds of decaying bodies—is quickly devoured by the birds.

The Blue Nile, raging downwards, lays violent hold of tokens of its rush—as it were messengers from its country—and tears them along with it. When, for miles beyond the river banks, rifts and ravines, landslides and water-channels, are formed; when, from the walls, mud oozes down continually, and the river below swells to a torrent, its friable banks fall in and are dissolved; then all this earth rushes to the valley like a catastrophe. The debris of Abyssinian volcanoes, the soil from the collapse of valley walls, desert sand which, borne far by the wind, is mixed with the stream of silt, ashes from bush-fires which the wild Ethiopians have set alight to renew their pastures and keep off the elephants in the canyons of the southern Abbai—all this streams for months through the plains and deserts of Nubia, first black, then grey, to call forth much later from the soil of rainless Egypt the swiftest, at times the richest crops on earth, and the cotton-speculator in Manchester is dependent, in his calculations, on the whims of a wild river which no human eye has seen in its entirety from its source to its mouth.

This great natural spectacle has found a symbol in itself: the Nile silt contains gold; even today it is occasionally washed near the Sudanese frontier, but there is too little of it to tempt the prospector. But the pricelessness of the silt itself has been worked out in terms of gold by experts, and its fertilizing value assessed at $7.50 per acre in Egypt. The Nile silt has magnetic power owing to its high iron oxide content, while its fertility is further increased by the high temperatures.

Such is the nature of the great gift of the Abyssinian rains

—one might say, too, of the Atlantic. If the Nile silt is the male, fertilizing element, it finds ready in the Egyptian soil everything from which it can call forth life. The earth has cracked in the dry season, the air has penetrated into all the clefts which have elsewhere to be torn open by the ploughshare, and the unploughed earth, between the harvests, has received a quantity of fertilizing matter. Far below, the next flood can loosen what is necessary for growth, at the same time depositing the silt and diluting the salt contained in the lower layers.

Thousands of years before the silt had been transformed into crops by man, it had created the delta, and thousands of years before that, it had forged its way through the desert. And the first figures of its rise to have been preserved are older than any historical records of the western world: they go back six thousand years, and have remained, on the whole, constant, for the real revolution in the course of the Nile was made by the hands of men and begun only a hundred years ago.

In those days, just as today and yesterday, as we can see by the frescoes in the tombs of the Pharaohs, the seed was cast into the mud after the flood; two months later, the harvest was gathered in. We can see on these frescoes dams enclosing basins, just as they do today, and it can be concluded from signs and inscriptions by what statecraft the water, after the lapse of fixed periods, was conveyed from one basin into another, to carry the fertilizing silt farther on. Forty years ago, before the dam at Aswân was built, the day on which the first waves of the Blue Nile were leaving Abyssinia was still celebrated, just as five thousand years ago. Only the name has changed. Once the priests told the people that in summer Isis, mourning for her brother Osiris, shed her tears into the Nile, and so the river rose. Today the engineers wire from Roseires to Cairo that the flood has arrived, but even today, Christians and Mohammedans alike say that a divine drop falls in the night of June 17. No inventor has ever stifled the creative imagination of man.

As the high water comes to Lower Egypt in the height of summer, the parched fields could be fertilized by the silt; as the winter is mild without being tropical, the wheat germinates of itself. Thus the Abyssinian flood reaches Egypt at the most favourable moment, while Mesopotamia is flooded at the wrong time. How long a wave takes on its life-journey may be seen by the fact that high water sets in on the Upper Nile in April, but only in June at Aswân and in July in the delta.

For thousands of years, most of all this water was allowed to run off unused into the sea. Not until the dam in Aswân and its Egyptian brothers arose, not until our century, was it possible so to irrigate the higher land on the Nile that broad stretches now bear two and three crops, while behind them, the desert itself grows fruitful.

21

FROM time immemorial, those who live on mountain brooks have raised anxious eyes to their neighbour higher up, questioning whether he is using too much water, or whether he will divert some of it, and the laws of all lands protect the lower settler from the encroachments of the upper where both live in the same country. If the source of the stream belonged to the individual in whose territory it rises, irrigation would be impossible, for all property, all the wheels which once turned themselves, and are now turned indirectly by the turbines, would be in danger: the factories lie below on the roads, not up in the mountains. But what if a whole country were dependent on a gigantic brook, not only for its drinking water, but for the grain that feeds its inhabitants? What if the brook rose in a foreign country? Must not the thoughts of the ruler below on the delta search the mind of the ruler at the source, seeking to discover whether he will leave the young stream unmolested? And what will they do if hostility breaks out between them, and the settler above maliciously diverts the source? There is no fear of punishment to restrain him, for up to this day, the existence of an international irrigation law is as fictitious as the functioning of any real international law.

Thus the ancient Egyptians looked upstream just as anxiously as those of today to that distant, unknown Ethiopian people, into whose hands God has given the source of the Blue Nile, and with it the great waters of the flood and the fruitful silt without which Egypt withers away. Legends and inscriptions bear witness to struggles and parleys between those dwelling below and those dwelling above. This strange situation has created a fear bordering on folly.

Once, history tells us, in 1106, when the flood did not come to Egypt, and famine threatened the people, the Sultan dispatched a Prince Michael, Patriarch of the Copts, laden with gifts, to visit, as a Christian, the Christian Emperor of Abyssinia. Then the Emperor, moved by gold and pity, caused the little dam to be broken through by which, according to the story, he had diverted the Upper Abbai, and at once the flood plunged down to the Sudan, rising three inches daily. But Michael was received with great honour at the end of the flood in the delta, for he had travelled more slowly than the water. Thus the Sultan feared that the white Christians might deliver Egypt into the hands of their brother, the Archpriest, but at the same time that very Archpriest and Emperor feared that the Sultan might fall upon him so as to secure the Nile for ever. Thus the river, after all its swamps and moors, had to flow through the swamps of religious wars, half master, half servant of a world of thought as alien to its mission as the volcanic mud was alien to the teaching of the prophets.

In his silken tent—so we read of an audience in Cairo in 1488— the Sultan reclined on his divan, and the ambassadors of all the white powers kissed the ground twice before him. But the ambassador of the Negus was borne in on his litter, ignored the command to rise, and reclining on his litter like the Sultan, asked:

"Lord, will you have peace with your lord and mine, the Archpriest John?"

"My fathers were always at peace with that priest."

"Say not, 'that priest,' say 'my lord.' "

And when this preposterous demand had been repeated three times, the Sultan said slowly:

"It is my wish to be at peace with my lord, the Archpriest John."

Then the Abyssinian presented the Sultan of Egypt with a bow and six golden arrows, saying:

"It is well for you to say 'my lord.' In his hands lie your life and your death. You ask why? From our land comes the Nile. If my lord wished, he could cut off your water, and you would all perish of thirst."

"It is true," said the Sultan.

Such extortions were attributed, even by the historian Gibbon, to the trickery of the Copts, the pride of the Abyssinians, and the ignorance of the Turks.

But it was a Christian and an occidental who turned the ancient legend into fact. Alfonso de Albuquerque, so-called great, a Portuguese of high standing in India, desirous of getting the ancient trade-routes out of the hands of the Sultan and hence ruining Egypt, supported moreover by the Archpriest John, attempted to divert the Blue Nile to the Red Sea, and, according to his son's report, failed only for lack of skilled labour: otherwise he would have "cut through a little rise in the land and Egypt would have dried up."

Even today, more than four hundred years later, the most recent books describe the plan as well within the bounds of possibility, although we know that the greater part of the water comes not from a river which could be diverted, but from a hundred ungovernable torrents which reach the Blue Nile much farther down. Because it is a blessing and a danger, research with measurements and calculations set in much earlier on the Blue Nile than the White; such calculations were going on in 1930, and will be going on tomorrow.

For thirty years past, a dam at Lake Tana has been contemplated and even designed. As long as Abyssinia was independent, and, by means of slavery, could hold off the curse of foreign loans, it could not be forced to grant concessions. Garstin, whose calculations on the Nile still form the main basis of all questions of water-supply, therefore moved England, in 1902, to conclude a treaty with the Negus according to which the latter shall neither build nor allow anything to be built on the Upper Abbai without consulting England and Egypt. Italy acknowledged the privileged position of England in 1919 and 1925 in exchange for guarantees in West Abyssinia, should a dam ever be built—the modern form of stealing in colonies going under the name of "spheres of influence." For a long time France sought to fan the growing suspicions of the Abyssinian ruler; then, by the summer of 1935, she changed her policy.

When England, in 1927, proposed to supply the Abyssinians with money for a dam so as to increase the irrigation of her Sudanese cotton, the Emperor, supported by three Nile countries, took refuge with the Americans, and had a dam designed by an American firm. England saw the danger that American money might affect the Nile in the interests of American cotton-kings, and preferred to join forces with them. The world crisis put a stop to the whole scheme.

Thus every great power fears the dam on Lake Tana, which will be built all the same one day, out of jealousy of every other. The Abyssinians in the capital fear it, because with it the foreigner would enter the country, and no one knows when he would leave it again; the people on Lake Tana, led by their priests, say that the foreigners who came surveying there wanted to build a dam a hundred yards high, and thus overthrow their churches and divert the Abbai; the foreigners, they say, had already poisoned Lake Tana. The only people to regard the scheme with composure are those who once regarded Abyssinia with dread—the Egyptians, for they know today that a dam at Lake Tana can deprive them of no water, since only 3 percent of the Egyptian water comes from this lake; above all, it cannot deprive them of the silt they live on, for that does not come from the lake at all.

But a dam at Lake Tana would store 4 billion cubic yards of water for Egypt and at the same time for the Gezira in the Sudan. Once Egypt has built all the dams on the White Nile, all the water stored at Lake Tana could flow to the Gezira, and thus, except for flood-time and winter, the Blue Nile will one day be a completely Sudanese, the White Nile a completely Egyptian river.

The difficulty with the Blue Nile only begins far below the lake. As the highlands from which the water comes belong to Abyssinia, 85 percent of all the waters of the Blue Nile flow into it from the rising rivers and brooks of that country, and are much too diffuse ever to be dammed.

Given this situation, Great Britain preferred for the moment to take her water from where it belonged to her and to build a dam low down on the Blue Nile 200 miles above its mouth at Khartoum; this would raise the river bed, dam the river, and irrigate the cotton with the water storage. It was soon after the brilliant success of the Aswân dam, for such constructions set fashions, like books or dictators; people were rich and enterprising, the factories in Manchester wanted to get free of America, and tradition too was there, under whose shadow the English are prone to advance when they have to carry the prudence of their fellow-citizens over the dangers of an innovation. For on the Gezira, cotton had been planted for a hundred years. This solid land—called an "island"—forms a triangle with Khartoum at its apex, the two Niles as long sides, and the short side running through the plain from Kosti to Sennar: with its area of 5 million acres, it is half as big as Switzerland and nearly as big as the whole cultivated land of Egypt.

But this cotton grown by the natives was as poor as that growing half wild in the fields of Abyssinia today; it could never compete with the good species, for not only were skill and technology lacking in the Gezira, but water too. Uncertain rains watered the fields sporadically, in patches, at the wrong time and insufficiently. If the water from above, the sub-tropical rain, could be supplemented by water from below, the natural rain-showers between May and September would be extremely favourable; sesame and rubber once flourished here. At the beginning of the century, excellent crops were raised by means of huge pumps, and Kitchener, eager for fame and money for the land of his deeds, brought his decisive influence to bear on the Government to guarantee a loan so that a dam might be built in Sennar (Makwar). In 1913 it was designed, in 1914 it was to have been begun, it was postponed by the war, in 1925 it was finished. It was to have cost $15,000,000; it cost $67,500,000. This dam, a wall of stone, is two miles long; it takes a good hour to walk along it and back. This shows how difficult it is to achieve on a river the results a lake produces of itself. At Lake Tana, with a dam a hundred yards long and six feet high, three times as much water could be stored as here at Sennar with a dam thirty-five times as long and eight times as high. And yet even this quantity would be enough to supply London with water for two years.

But here the stored water is not, as in Egypt, passed through the sluices in fixed quantities: here a system of canals, unique in the world in its completeness, takes up part of the water and distributes it over a third part of the Gezira. The main canal, over 60 miles long, runs parallel to the river, but cuts off its bends, and, seen from the aeroplane, forms a logical, clear, straight line which looks as if it were trying to refute the romantic whims of nature. These canals, which are easily cut out of the stoneless soil of the Gezira, are, with the exception of the main canal, all narrow, and grow quickly narrower; the smallest can be jumped over, but they aggregate a length of 9400 miles, that is, twice the length of the White and Blue Niles together. All this water is taken away from nobody, for, until ten years ago, it flowed unused into the sea.

So accurately are these canals laid out that the engineer can fill the farthest, narrowest field canal on a definite day with a definite quantity of water according to the increase of the rain in the Abyssinian highlands. When, in the second half of July, the main canal has been filled from the basin to a level proportionate to the rising flood, it can then distribute its water over a period up to nine months.

It is a stirring picture. No scepticism about colonization with its manifestations of insolence and its disguised slavery, no reflections on the bliss of the man vegetating in God's sun, idle and serene, not yet turned into a factory hand by the machine, can lessen one's admiration for the brains which proved themselves a match for the elements. Here, in the Gezira, the Sudanese, for a thousand years a Mohammedan, for a hundred a cotton-planter, had been a slave of the Fung, the "Blue Sultan," and thus had long since been expelled from his Paradise. What the white man has done for him here must enrich him in every respect: even the young men realize that. It is true that the lands were blessed with dhurra in good rain years so that the Gezira was called the granary of the Sudan, but only one year in ten was a good year; in between we have seen these fields dusty and pitiful. The women were clever at cotton-picking, but the cotton grew only when Allah willed it, and that was not always.

When the native was told of the new forms his life was to take, he was startled; and when the Government, after years of work, had produced a kind of Domesday Book, assessing the peasants' rent per acre on a basis of the average for forty years, he grew really afraid, for as the land was squared out in blocks of ten acres, separated by canals, thousands could not find their old plots again, and many of the elders may well have turned bitter thoughts towards the bringers of their new fortune.

But then came the surprise. It may have been the children and the women who first curiously pulled the plug out of the hole in their canal to see what would happen and watched, laughing, how the water was watering their crops for them. Was it really flowing on to the roots of itself? They ran to the next canal, ten minutes off—there too it was overflowing, and now, when they sowed field after field with cotton-seed and grain, which the white men had given them in sacks; when, at New Year's, the plants bloomed and the bolls were cleaner and more uniform than before and fell into their hands like white wool, they sat down in front of their straw huts, the women learning how to clean the cotton better than their mothers had done, the men filling it into the sacks, one of them stamping it down firmly, the camels standing ready to carry two huge sacks each, one on each side, to the railway station which the white man had built close by; and then the cotton rolled away from the Gezira to the Red Sea, and from there, they said, far across the ocean to that other Gezira, from which the masters of the stone dam and the field canals had come.

The son of the woman who picked the cotton will learn in the elementary school what water-storage, dam, and canal mean, and if he is a bright boy, he can get as far as Gordon College, down in the big town of Khartoum, and a few years later, he will be measuring earth temperatures in the Gezira or working out flood tables. Then he will earn 150 piastres a month, live in a stone house, and drive his own car home at night. Since we always ask whether he will be the happier for it, we must distinguish him from his brother who has lived on in the tradition of his forefathers, afraid of work, and yet is made happier too by the dam, for now in harvest-time, he can earn in three days the three shillings that his father earned per month, and the next twenty-seven days to the next full moon he can lie about doing nothing or spend his time with the women. As it is difficult to get a number of these tribes to work, and the English are not slave-owners, labour has to be imported into the Gezira from the outside.

Here the Mecca pilgrims, who have crossed Africa to make the pilgrimage to the Prophet's tomb, come in exceedingly useful. Coming from the west coast, they are more used to field labour than the half-Arab cowherds here, and when they have deposited their tents and goats on the banks of the Nile, they are glad to stay six months in the Gezira to earn the money for the rest of their journey. For all their missionaries, the English find this heathen faith highly convenient, for the fanatical pilgrims are good workmen, and if they mingle with the native women—so much the better for the race which, here as everywhere, is freshened up by mixture.

The area which has been irrigated in the Gezira up to the present is only a third of the land proposed for irrigation. The cotton grown here amounts to only a fifth part of the cotton from the Egyptian delta, the species are different, and as for their quality, experts say in turn "much better," "much poorer." But the dry heat, the moderate rainfall in the early time of growth, the drought during the setting of the pods and at harvest-time, the ventilation of the soil, have produced a high-class "cotton soil," superior to that between the Euphrates and the Tigris, where the artificially irrigated cotton island is also known as El-Jezireh. In good years, four hundredweight and more per acre has been picked on the Blue Nile.

The first years after the opening of the dam were too good. The syndicate, which takes 40 percent of the proceeds, spoilt the Government, which receives 35 percent, like a young wife in an old-fashioned marriage when things go too well at the start and she can be as extravagant as she likes. The twenty thousand families, too, of the so-called "tenants," who, in the same way as in Soviet Russia, were turned from proprietors into partners in a community, were delighted with the sewing-machines and phonographs by which they sent their money back to England again, and the cotton kings came here into Central Africa to buy the cotton in the pod. Every acre yielded up to $150 net profit; the reserve fund grew, the Sudanese Government could transform $5,000,000 a year into schools, roads, sanitation; there was great haste to prepare further land for the water. The lack of labour was so serious that speculators, enraged by the god-like indolence of the natives, conceived the hope, which they went so far as to have printed, that the "gastric fever would soon destroy the cattle, and force the nomads to field-labour, and that the tsetse flies would soon kill the Dinka herds and thus send the children of the herdsmen of today cotton-picking."

But then, as in the Bible, the lean years suddenly followed, only that in our world crisis, they set in after only four fat ones. When, in 1929, the area of irrigated land had greatly increased, cotton prices suddenly fell, there were no buyers; instead of $150, the acre yielded only $35; the rain, which had once been so favourable for the grain, now struck the cotton too heavily and not at the right time, doubling the weeds and spreading disease.

For disease, in an uncanny way, followed the dam, the cotton, and the gold to which it gave birth. Bilharziasis, a severe parasitic affection, which had broken out before the completion of the dam in the Dongola province, and been carried to Sennar by western pilgrims, then ague, malaria, and smallpox—all spread, to the horror of the people, who saw their suspicions of the machines confirmed by Allah's wrath. In 1930, many thousands of sick passed through the Sudanese hospitals. Science and medical practice advanced vigorously from Khartoum against the pests; the locusts, which lay their eggs in light sand, were attacked by an army of chemists, policemen, and Arabs, who, by means of poison and rapidly dug trenches, endeavoured to keep the insects away from the crops. But when an aeroplane circled overhead, bringing fresh medicines from England, the natives looked up angrily and said that all the evil came from the aeroplanes.

Here lies the terrible warning that will again thunder towards us in Egypt. It is true that the world crisis, rain, and sickness have upset a reckoning that at first seemed good and brought in big profits. But what good is a new raw material to a country which, to export it, has to go without the bread which was its natural portion for thousands of years, and for the increase of which the dams and canals, the tractors and the engineers' brains, would have been admirably employed?

22

IN Khartoum, where the two brothers stream together, to which for the last time we must now return with cold figures, the wilder, younger of them, swollen with all the floods of Abyssinia, hurls itself against the other with such force that it stems its flow for three months, and even drives it back a short stretch, just as the Sobat did with the same White Nile. But this natural check corresponds exactly to Egypt's need, for just when abundance reigns there, the water from above decreases and a great deal can pour into the sea unused: the White Nile, oppressed by the reckless power of the Blue, cannot flow on, but saves its strength for those winter months of drought in Egypt. Then, when the other is exhausted, it will bring its help downstream. Such is the symbol under which the characters of the two brothers unfold.

The phenomenon of this natural water-storage has given the engineers the idea of turning the natural basin of the White Nile into an artificial one, much in the same way as is thought of for Lake Tana or Lake Albert—that is, to prolong the stoppage by a dam, and to hold up the water-supply thus saved for Egypt from winter till spring, when there is more need of it than in winter. At the same time, this would safeguard Egypt against the floods which have often caused damage there. The element, which is now too weak, now too strong, would in this way be released or restrained according to Egypt's needs.

This simple idea, put forward by English experts, has fanned to flame the passion of Egyptian national feeling. Their cry is that to dam the Nile in the Sudan would be simply to facilitate by mechanical means the old danger of thirst—it would simply tempt the owner to misuse. With this cry of warning, millions of Egyptians have been won over to the anti-English cause, whole elections have turned on the dam, the King and his ministers were accused of treachery to their own people for permitting the dam to be built and even promising to pay for it. This dam, it was said, would become the most powerful weapon in England's hands if ever a conflict should break out between Egypt, which is under English power, and the Sudan, which is under English rule.

The dam at Gebel Aulia, thirty miles above Khartoum, where a limestone dike running straight across the bed of the White Nile made building easy, is now under construction: it is to be ready in 1937. It will certainly be to Egypt's benefit. It might become a weapon in England's hands, but not to starve Egypt with. The excitement of people who see the key to their lives in foreign hands is not difficult to understand, but reason must in time cast out fear. Suppose war or the threat of war were to mislead England, with the approval of public opinion, to indulge in this kind of terrorization—quite an un-English thing—suppose even that England's interests in Egypt were not sufficient to restrain her from such an act of violence, then, by retarding or preventing the passage of this spring water to Egypt, she could do some harm to Egypt; but she could never cut off the river, for then the Upper Nile valley would be flooded, the spread of the water would bring disease with it, and agriculture would be hindered, not helped.

In 1926, when the Egyptian Wafd, the national party, interrupted the preparations for the dam at Gebel Aulia, their advisers declared that the raising of the dam at Aswân would have the same result, and that water could be stored there for Egypt on Egyptian territory till spring. Their distrust was increased by a certain eagerness on the part of the English, whose first thought is the profit they would make on the dam as its builders, and who cannot deny the advantage to the Sudan. In all treaties, however, the latest being dated 1929, England has given the Egyptians every solemn pledge not to undertake anything on the Nile which might adversely affect the quantity, level, or date of the arrival of the Nile water in Egypt.

After endless debates both things happened: the old dam of Aswân was heightened, but the scheme of the new one at Gebel

ASWÂN DAM

THEBES AND LUXOR

Aulia was taken up again, for the latter can work the whole year round without the risk of being silted up, since the White Nile leaves all its silt behind in the swamps. What is being built to-day is helping to secure Egypt's future.

Further schemes will be carried out in the course of the next twenty years. No river on earth is so intently observed as the Nile; hydrological research costs $500,000 a year, and the river becomes more important, and at the same time more difficult, in proportion as the statistics of its discharge, the census of its peoples, the demands of hygiene, and the research into its last unknown territory increase. Thus it has been calculated that even the dams of Gebel Aulia, Lake Albert, and Lake Tana cannot fully develop both Egypt and the Sudan at the same time. Further dams will be needed at the Nile sources or on the Victoria Nile; the Baro will have to be regulated before its inflow into the Sobat, and the whole system of the Ghazal too. And even then, only three-quarters of the reserve necessary for bad years could be stored.

Thus the Nile today resembles the treasury of a state which finds it ever harder to make ends meet as its population grows, because it has to import the greatest of all raw materials, water, and cannot increase by labour or any taxation of its inhabitants the quantity it has striven to turn to good account by continually supplementing and redistributing it.

THE Nile's struggle with man was decided in Aswân: only so mighty a work could conquer the mighty river. Everything about this greatest dam in the world is reminiscent of the Pharaohs—its rise, its use, its effect. If Napoleon had encountered an opponent of such calibre as has the Nile, we should take his outward defeat more calmly. But even the Nile, like every great character, really perishes by reason of its own nature, and the dam of Aswân can take advantage of the weakness of the element, that is, of the irregularities of the wilder of the two Niles.

When, in the nineteenth century B.C., a Pharaoh on the Lower Nile built a dam on Lake Moeris, he seems to have stored approximately as much water as the one designed at the end of the nineteenth century A.D. There are reports in classical times of similar works in China and India. The height of the dam at Aswân is exceeded by other dams, but no dam except the Gatun navigation dam in the Panama Canal can compare with it as regards the quantity of water stored: the great Soviet dams have other objects, and the Boulder dam in America is not yet completed. Outside of the Soviet Union, the biggest dam in Europe, situated in Spain, stores 264,000 millions of gallons; the Norris dam in America 1,174,000 millions of gallons. In Aswân, 1,323,-000 millions of gallons are stored; hence the backflow here reaches 225 miles upstream to Wadi Halfa.

Its purposes are as unique as its dimensions. A large number of all dams on earth are power-stations, and hence are constructed and paid for by contractors whose object is to produce light or power; only about one-tenth serve to regulate the water-supply. On the Nile, a work was conceived which would increase the cultivable land of a whole country by a third, later by a half, and would protect a people of fifteen million souls from the hunger due to threatening overpopulation. To this work was assigned the Promethean task of transforming the fringes of the desert into fertile land—a region which, with its 20,000 square miles, will be bigger than Switzerland. All that was and is feasible only because Egypt has no neighbours and because the land above Aswân, that is, the land of the artificial lake, is sparsely inhabited, so that its inhabitants can be compensated for being flooded out; the water will certainly submerge their homeland—an incommensurable quantity, like the beauty of the Temple of Philæ.

The idea of Aswân is as old as Egypt, but only the last century turned it into a practical proposition, and again it was no professional, but the amateur of genius who, with the simplicity of the layman, challenged the future. In 1867, Baker recommended the building of a dam in Aswân, exclaiming: "As nature has formed a delta, and is still forming it, why should not science, with its mighty powers, form a dam?" At that time, there were few of our modern dams in existence to make the problem look easy of solution: in this case the experiment was forthwith begun on the biggest scale.

Willcocks, a daring engineer, whose energy sprang from the faith in his heart, designed the work in the nineties, and, the British Government having turned the enterprise down, he and his friends contrived to inspire an equally daring financier. This was Sir Ernest Cassel, who, with the naïveté and pertinacity of the Englishman, combined the wariness of the Jew, and came, a second Joseph, to Egypt to develop the land as a foreigner. This man, who knew more about the power of money than about the power of the elements, to whom the wilderness and fog of the London Stock Exchange were more familiar than the wilderness of the cataracts and the miasma of the swamps on the Upper Nile, stood one day with maps and plans in his hands on the bank of the rapids of Aswân, and while the pencils of the engineers were busy with calculations of water-displacements, sluice-tables, and rates of discharge, he was adding up the costs dictated to him, and, as a sceptic of experience, adding 50 percent for unexpected eventualities. A shrewd business man, such as one-half of Joseph was, he left the parable of the other half to the dreamers at his side, who, in their imagination, already heard the water thundering through the sluices. Then he said: "All right. Go ahead."

And soon both banks of the Nile were teeming as in the times of the Pharaohs. The peoples here assembled, the colours, sounds, and smells rising to the pitiless sun of this rainless land, the accuracy of a construction which was to rise from the middle of the desert, incomprehensible to the thousand naked men making it, merely at the behest of an invisible king—all this renewed, after a lapse of three thousand years, the image of the building of the pyramids: the same naked workers, the same hard overseer, the same colossal stones, the same granite—only that the slaves were paid instead of being fed and that more ingenious machines took the heaviest of the burdens from human shoulders.

But here no god-king's illusion of immortality was satisfied, no tomb was built for an individual by the modern slaves who were no whit more mortal than that king. Here one man was working for millions of men, designing for them a construction which was to overcome no natural law, but merely tame a natural power and compel the ruling element to creative achievement. After three thousand years, those gloomy pyramids on the fringe of the Nile, in which the exaltation of lonely kings had sought to conquer death, were followed by a work of life, full of promise, which was to win new land from the desert, and bring to the old a threefold harvest. And yet the spectacle of the second work, as it rose, was as Pharaonic as that of the first had been.

Into the chaos of this desert of stone and water, there penetrated one morning the sound of the first oar-beat of the first boat, to reduce to order, as on the first day of creation, the world that was without form and void. It was in spring, the water was at its lowest. Strange sounds came from the boat to the shore: "Bab el Harun! Bab el Kabir! Bab el Sughair!" Those were three of the five great waterfalls which dominated the cataract, against whose dangers the natives had been warned from time immemorial. Now they were to set about surrounding the lowest of them as they surround the crocodile, which rarely appears down here, yet not with spears but with rocks, which they were shifting at its feet, with a substructure of stones, draining the first block of stone dry with pumps. Naked, a hundred men stood in the water to cement this first dry spot, for on it the great elephant was to be set up which would lift the hugest of the stones and carry them away. Through the middle of the chaos, it was brought along on a boat, and, with infinite toil, erected on the dry spot.

But now it began to shift with its trunk blocks of stone which, long ago, we do not know how, a thousand arms pushed before them inch by inch, day and night, when the Pharaohs, to their own glory, had obelisks cut out of the granite, one of which lies unfinished on the shore to this very day. But the iron elephant swung its supple-jointed trunk on all sides, raising and lowering it at the command of its master, creaking and rattling, yet with the same elastic power as its great model, which, far up on the young Nile, tears trees up by the roots to feed on their uppermost fruits. The crane was there, and a hundred cranes arrived, great and small, rolling onto the growing dam, and, like a colony of Cingalese elephants, they obeyed the will of their tamer who had calculated every detail.

For that first dam had only been a temporary one, *en miniature,* to shut off a single waterfall, Bab el Harun, but it had taken two months for the first pile to stand and nine yards of smooth surface to be laid, on which the first rails could rest. In their long white shirts, the men came on great black boats, tens of thousands of Nubians and Egyptians, different in colour and features, alike in their Mohammedan robes, heaving the heaviest stones on their bent backs, hampered at every step by their trailing trousers, which, in the evening, they took off and washed again in the Nile. The water they had set out to fight spent itself like a great lord on his enemy, for drinking, cooking, bathing, washing, making mortar, driving the machines.

Over on the right bank, in the blazing heat, rarely sheltered by thatched roofs, a few thousand Nubians sat hewing the white and pink syenitic granite—the ancient city of Syene once stood here—in great blocks out of the mountain, and beside them, the more skilful hands of eight hundred Italians chipped the blocks into shape, so that they should fit into the courses of the dam: it was the same mountain from which that Pharaoh had once brought the same stone down the Nile on boats for his temple columns. Then the Nubians dragged stones to the railway line, and rolled them on a narrow-gauge line to the river and to the place on the bank where other hundreds of hands cast them into the boats, which bore them with softly swelling sails to the beginnings of the dam.

The boats lie in rows under the lee of the newly fixed blocks, surrounded by naked bodies half out of the water—a single picture of rock, arms, and water. A hundred Nubians in white shirts, mournfully chanting, lift gigantic sacks of cement out of the boats, while a troop of Egyptians push iron rods upwards, and in a dark corner, guarded by a whip, a group of convicts from the prison haul along in baskets the coal to heat the cranes, which has had to be shifted by hand six times on its journey from Newcastle to the Middle Nile. Beside a troop of Sudanese, flapping their arms to keep warm, for they shiver till nine o'clock, the white engineer is fanning himself, for he begins to perspire at eight, as he works with his sextants, whose leather case the brown boy behind him fingers enviously, thinking what a fine pair of shoes it would make. While a nimble, busy pump ceaselessly draws sand out of a place in the river, bent backs carry sacks from the other side with fresh sand for the cement, and the men boring the troublesome stone under water ready to blast it away, no longer look at their brothers beside them dragging up blocks of other stone. A spectator not knowing that there is a creative will above the confusion could not but regard the whole as madness.

On the other side of the antediluvian silence of these stone mountains, above at Philæ, beyond the water softly lapping about the blocks, there rises, where the dam is growing, a confused noise—rumbling, shouting, the rushing of water: iron scratches as it is dragged across the freshly made surface; boring-machines, driven by compressed air, burrow into the rock; the cutting-machines whir and grind; there are sudden gusts of explosions; a thousand hammers echo and re-echo; little stones, on a sloping wood track, hop and rattle back into the water; the hinges of the machines scream like cats. In anxious wonder, a few ibises call warnings to each other, and as they fly away upstream to the capitals of the temple, their cries and the beat of their wings sound clearly audible through the din, for they have the charm of a slight irregularity, like all the sounds of nature.

And yet the whole displays no haste or excitement—on the contrary, it all looks serene: seen from a distance, a Pharaonic festival might be in preparation. The crowd shouts, as at most festivals, merely because a single man has taken it upon himself to declare that what he is doing is important. But he, the hero and king of the festival, is the snow-white engineer, and though his helmet is nothing but cork and linen, his shield nothing but a huge note-book, and his sword nothing but a compass, he still stands out as the master because he hauls nothing, does not get dirty, and commands in silence with a pointing forefinger; a great gravity, moreover, seems to separate him from the childish emotions of the crowd. The rock on which he stands—beside it lies his motor boat with the Union Jack—is now being examined for the third morning for leaks, to see how much water trickles through, and whether the little spring has really been sealed with cement so that the little drop of water that percolates through all the same will not eat away the piles from below, for here one of the great piles is to rest.

Thus a surgeon, with intent seriousness, swabs the ever-welling blood with cotton-wool pads, and wonders for all his experience whether he can sew the wound up today. Take care! The life and security of the whole organism, whether shaped by the hand of God or man, depends on this decision—perhaps the subterranean spring will take its revenge, for if one pile is unsteady, the whole work will tremble. There he stands in the midst of the thousandfold movement, which he has set going like a master conspirator from his quiet room; his gaze, fixed downwards, shows that his ears have ceased to hear, and if a telegram is brought to him, he stuffs it into his pocket and again fixes his eyes on that dangerous crack, that split through which he must divine the soul of the rock.

Nor does he see the rainbow which, slanting before him, links the fading chaos with the growing work, for here it appears everywhere, this familiar spirit of the waterfalls, as if trying to outshine with its magic all this creation of numbers. But the white Pharaoh sees nothing, jumps into his motor boat, points east, and ten minutes later is sitting in the little room where a hundred plans hang on whitewashed walls, finger-prints of nature, following the junction of every rock with its neighbour in the stony depths. Now, with abstruse figures, he works out the bearing-power of that very problematic rock which, if the crack alters it, can cause the towering pile to burst and with one wild wave destroy the meaning of the whole work. Then he decides to send down the diver to the root of the rock.

There is no time to lose, for eight piles must be standing before the next flood—that is laid down in the plan and the calculations, which, inexorable as the laws of the Pharaohs, have issued from the little whitewashed room, from the brains of half a dozen men.

For this reason, the work that is to tame the water obeys only the laws of the water, not those of the light, and while, after sunset, ten thousand men lie down on their straw mats in their tents on the bank, ten thousand others sail out into the radiantly illuminated night on little boats, on great lighters, and even roll on trolleys along the finished piece of the dam to prolong the festival of labour on into the night.

Now the great iron elephants loom up black on the growing bridge before the flashing bluish reflexes of the arc-lamps, and the indefatigable trunks gingerly raise sacks of hewn stones, then lower them into barges which, tied together to form a flotilla, are drawn off by a solitary little steamer into a dark corner of the night. Below, in the shadow of the quay-like bridge or wall, on a third of the river's breadth, a greedy dragon at the feet of the elephant seems to be protecting its brood, hissing, against the attack of the thousand arms, flashing faintly as its breast heaves: it is the cement-mixer, whose lid rises and falls with the sand, for it is insatiable, this dragon, devours sacks and chests of sand, and the water must now help to bind the cement which is to conquer it, for in the coolness of the night it mixes better with the stones heaped up in the daytime.

HORUS IN EDFU

PHARAONIC FELLAHIN

Where the first half-piers loom in the darkness like broken columns, like signs of a mighty antiquity, in a kind of defiant impotence, black figures hover on gently swaying boards in the growing gigantic windows, apparently cleaning the stones of the bridge close above their heads, as if the golden king were coming on the morrow with his glittering boat; in sober fact they are stopping up the still open gaps with grey asphalt, for after the last finishing touches, every pile must rest four months and all the sand from Aswân runs through the hour-glass of time. At his feet, a block is being drawn out of the dry river bed by shouting men, who have bound it about with ropes, as if it were a hippo they were dragging off to kill.

But over their heads, high above the surface of the bridge, a boy is floating in a rocking box on the trunk of the elephant; at every turn he has to reverse a lever, and seems to be playing with the arc-lamp near him. Nearer the light than all the others, freed from the law of gravity, master of the dam and the night, he is the true Pharaoh of the noisy festival.

24

THUS the great orgy of labour went on in the middle of the Nile for three years, more than a thousand days and nights, half interrupted only by the flood; and while the labyrinth of rocks and the uproar of the elements, of machines and men, were slowly transformed into the straight line of the dam, the designers and leaders of the work returned to their pretty new bungalows close to their work. Their gardens on the Nile bank, into which they contrived to lead the first silt before so much as one Egyptian field received it, rose under the hands of their black servants; and under the orders of their wives the desert was transformed as quickly into red and white oleander groves as the rock bed into the stone dam under their own.

When these lords of the new creation returned at midday from the glaring light into the coolness of their carefully shaded homes, the ancient drama of Venus and Mars was renewed, varied *à l'anglaise* with tea and sandwiches, which they could not dispense with even on the Tropic of Cancer. The romance which flourished in this oasis was born of a life endangered by heat and nervous tension, loneliness and friction, the life of a little community of a hundred souls surrounded only by elements and slaves. Contractors to whom part of the work had been allotted broke down because a rock fall destroyed their reckoning, and once, when the dam was heightened, a famous engineer was so much out in his calculations that, in his despair, he went to Alexandria, took a boat, and drowned himself at the mouth of the river which had given him its curse, but not its glory. For when the dam was finished, it was too low: the whole of Egypt was crying out for water in the spring, the gigantic basin was too small, and so, in 1912, and again in 1933, the dam was raised by a total of 50 feet, its height having first been reckoned at 130 feet. In the dispute over the costs, Willcocks, the expert, reckoned that the cost of $21,000,000 would only have amounted to $12,500,000 if the Government had built the dam itself, a striking refutation of the old capitalistic claim that private capital always works more cheaply than the state.

The dam gained in beauty as it gained in height; the piers were incorporated throughout into a stronger wall; the bridges above were so much widened that a projecting profile beautifies their line. As it was possible for the building to use the weaker pink granite where the pressure of wind and water is less, that is, in the north, the stranger approaching from Aswân sees it shimmering in the distance. In other ways, too, the inexorability of its main theme is softened by unexpected variations, for among its 180 sluices, separate groups of four are opened in apparently irregular succession, and there the water gushes out, foaming, like a four-in-hand which has been pawing the ground behind the gate. Only the engineer in charge, sitting in his white cell at the west end of the dam, knows how many sluices he must open, which, and why.

For while he keeps the sluices shut from November till January, so as to fill the basin after the flood, he must still provide for a certain flow of water to Egypt. Then, from April to July, by opening more and more sluices, he empties the basin, and in these three months sends almost 8 billion cubic yards of water to Egypt. Here supply and demand are balanced with such accuracy that on many a day the number and height of the sluices opened have to be altered as much as twelve times. It is true that each of the iron sluices can easily be moved from the dam with a wheel, a child can set loose the power of the foaming water and bind it again. But the artificial lake stands in eternal stillness on the other side of the dam, and only the levels of its surface would allow a spectator unable to turn north to guess what is going on on the other side: the higher the water rises on the inner edge of the dam, the lower sink the columns of the Temple of Philæ on the other side.

But on that July day on which the flood comes, and the engineer, within a few days, opens all his 180 sluices, the surface on the other side sinks instead of rising, and the columns of Philæ rise again with mud-dripping feet from their bath. Now the silt is passed down to Egypt, and thus the system of the sluices is protected from silting up. Egypt owes to the dam its perennial irrigation, with 7 million acres yielding two to three crops, while 1.2 million acres still live on the old basin system and reap only once.

In the midst of his figures and lists, tables and diagrams, the engineer in his cell is like the manager of a savings bank whose cashiers bring him daily the accounts of payments and withdrawals. With the nine telegrams from the White Nile up to Malakal, from the Blue up to Roseires, which he finds waiting every morning, he can calculate how much water will flow into the basin that day, that is, how much it will rise at the dam, for he knows that a wave of the Nile takes forty-four days from Malakal to Aswân; but at the same time the needy in the land are rattling at his cash-boxes, demanding water for the capital they have given in the form of taxes for the building of the dam.

And yet he too, like the manager of the savings bank, is dependent on natural events which may upset his plan. Thus the highest and lowest water levels in Aswân for the same months of 1913 and 1918 differed by 60 percent, and that was due merely to the White Nile, the steadier of the two brothers. What the wilder will be at when it comes foaming down in July lies on the knees of the gods.

For the vengeance of the conquered element still lurks in the subterranean rocks of the Nile. If man has ventured to lay his hand on the mysterious river, it must never tremble, otherwise the river will break loose. If the engineer in his cell, when the flood has run off, shuts the sluices too quickly, if he shuts too many at once, down in Egypt the embankments collapse, and with them the houses on the embankments. If the stored water, which nearly all comes from the White Nile, contains too much salt, the farmer in Egypt has to set about manuring like his brothers throughout the world, who may receive rain from above, but never receive silt from below. When the Nubian up on the margin of the basin, after the end of the flood, works his old field on the bank, it must grow quickly, before the basin has filled too high again, otherwise the water will flood out his crop.

In olden times the dam of Aswân would have been one of the wonders of the world. It is one today. A few decades after Baker, with prophetic vision, saw into the future, it all began to come true. "A time will come," he wrote, "when the world will gaze with admiration on a new Egypt, whose luxuriant cornfields will run over these desolate and sandy wastes into the far distance, where now only the camel can struggle with exhausted nature. From a few elevated points, men will look down upon a network of canals and basins, and will ask wondering how it came about that the power of the majestic river remained as long concealed as the secret of its source."

The height from which this spectacle unfolds is today reached daily by the aeroplane, which reveals the whole land of Egypt in its narrowness, even when flying low: between yellow wastes lies the green strip. But below it, as it whirs over the dam, a long, old boat is moving through the navigation sluice at the western end, recalling the tidings of his dam brought to Faust:

> And see, a stately boat advances
> Towards us on the great canal.

Faust went blind: he could not see it.

But we can see, as long as eye and heart can inspire us as gifts of God, how the old Nile, at the end of all its adventures, conquered yet wise, calm as an aged philosopher, becomes a source of help to the human beings swarming on its banks, and with carefully hoarded strength achieves more than was granted to it in the fire of its youth. We see the high sail, the same with which Pharaoh sailed on this river. An arch of six thousand years here spans myth and work, thought and legend, and the wonderful river now flowing down to the sea gains in the last part of its career the colour of all the time it has flowed through, the sounds of all the civilizations it has created and seen to flower and decay.

Book Four

THE RIVER

VANQUISHED

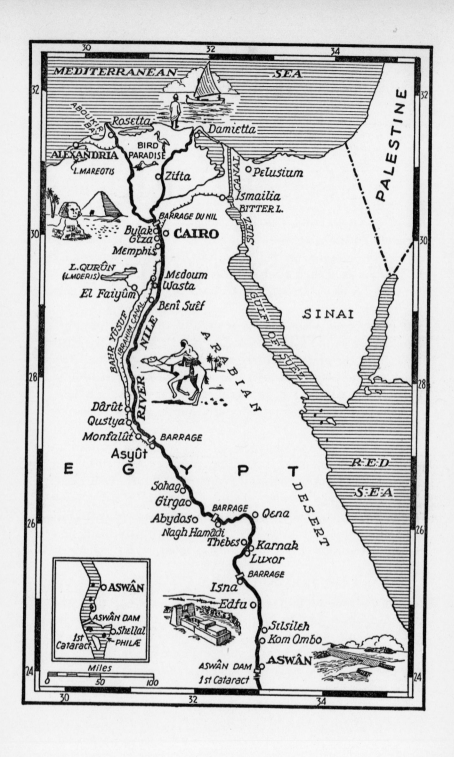

1

"THERE, an arid waste, lies a desert: on either hand it rises and between the heights lies wonderland. To the west, the range forms a chain of sandhills; to the east, it looks like the belly of a lean horse or a camel's back. This, O Ruler of the Faithful, is Egypt. But all its wealth comes from the blessed river that moves through it with the dignity of a caliph. Regular as sun and moon, it rises and falls again. The hour comes when all the springs of the world must pay their tribute to the king of rivers, which Providence has lifted high above all others; then the waters rise and quit their bed, and flood the plains, depositing upon them their fertile mud. Then all the villages are cut off one from the other; only boats can pass between them, and they are countless as the leaves on the palm tree.

"But then, in its wisdom, the river re-enters the bounds appointed by fate, so that those who live there may collect the treasure it has confided to Mother Earth. And thus, O Ruler of the Faithful, Egypt presents in turn the picture of a dry, sandy waste, of a stretch of silver water, of a swamp covered with thick mud, of a lush green meadow, of a garden rich with many flowers, and again of spreading fields covered with resplendent crops."

So vivid a picture of the lowest reaches of the Nile was created by no poet and no geographer, nor by any of all the artists and travellers, but by an Arab commander, Amr ibn el As, who, in the seventh century, conquered the country for his master, Caliph Omar. For a man all action and all eye can describe the goal of his glory as if it were a vision, just as many a poet can describe it as if he were its conqueror.

Two gods created the land of Egypt, and watch over it today as they have always done—the sun and the Nile; two male gods, they begot and fertilized the biggest, the greenest oasis in the world. But the Nile too was created by the sun-god, for Ikhnaton sang: "Thou didst create the Nile in the underworld, and lead it round about the earth, according to thy will, to nourish mankind." On no civilized country does the sun-god shine with such intensity, and as the dry deserts suck up all moisture, neither fog nor mist can rise from its surface. Thus sun and water, earth and water, earth and sun, stand apart in elemental purity, unmingled, unblurred, without transition; the air is clear, it suffers no germs, and the night, which brings no refreshment to the real tropics, bears coolness from the vast deserts to the oasis which, in the morning, is sometimes even covered with dew.

The products of all other climates, which the earth brings forth anew every year, are absent from this narrow strip of land running through the desert: it has no rain, therefore no trees, hence no wood or shade. When, in royal tombs, we find prehistoric skulls with retreating foreheads among bones of hippopotami and wolves, we can see rising from the deserts the forests of palms and euphorbias, peopled by buffaloes, lions, and hyenas, and naked man who hunted them. Later, this wilderness fell away into savannas, still later into grasslands, still later into deserts, while naked man turned nomad and peasant.

Yet he reached this stage much earlier here than anywhere else. First of all, no Ice Age intervened to shift the epochs, as in Europe. On the site of the great sea bay, which even Herodotus assumes to have reached up to Aswân, there lay a plain through which, as is shown by traces of former rivers, the primeval Nile traversed the Libyan desert, only later shifting eastward into the long furrow along which the sea had pushed its way. When man appeared, Northern Africa is believed to have risen slowly, while the Nile flowed through the primeval gulf. On the second of the terraces formed by erosion, the first traces and stone tools of those men were found. It was only later that North Africa became a desert.

At that time there was no forest left to make man live in fear and turn life into a ceaseless hunt. The wonderful river drew

men and held them together at such a time and in such numbers that they were united here much earlier and much more
densely than on any other spot on earth, save perhaps on the
other river-oasis, akin to the Nile, between the Euphrates and
the Tigris.

It may be that all civilization originated in such oases—civilizations such as even today form islands in the midst of the
human deserts, and if we were to deduce the history of these
greatest oases down to the present day from their climate, we
should find that even the most trivial detail of Egyptian culture
was determined by desert and water, was the gift of the two
gods, the sun and the Nile. Mesopotamia, that other, much
broader oasis, was exposed to many changes owing to the inhabited mountains and grasslands surrounding it. Egypt, lying
between two seas and three deserts, without a single neighbour,
unless we count the desert and the sea, rises in classical clarity,
with astonishing swiftness, simply and steadily from the womb
of time. Health came from the climate, want became wealth, and
regularity bestowed fortune.

The three metaphysical prophets emerged from the Arabian
deserts, but on the heavy, mud-laden earth of the Nile valley a
thoroughly material religion arose, drawn from life, transferred
to the dead, without twilight, of the earth and serene. The earliest customs and manners of the Egyptians are clear and dry as
their air, and since their whole environment forced realism upon
them, since the narrow space compelled them to live in dense
crowds, since each was dependent on each and no man could live
unto himself, they were, in all essentials, fully developed by
about the year 3000 B.C.

While for thousands of years the white men in the far north,
the black men in the far south, the former far beyond the sea,
the latter at the sources of the same river, were still killing each
other in lawless savagery, defenceless in their dull, dark virgin
forests against the anarchy of strength, in this narrow oasis of
the Nile a people was flourishing, swarming in dense crowds,
compelled to community by the river, already divided into fishermen and farmers, artisans and scribes. Even the records of all
they discovered were brought by the climate alone to the later

born, for the tombs and the papyrus which contain the history of Egypt resisted time only because of the dryness of the climate, and when we hold in our hands the almost perfect skull of Ramses III, it tells even today a vivid story of what he was and did.

2

IN the desert light a solitary man is moving, tall and dark as a god, doomed to dramatic destruction unless, on his swift-moving camel, he takes flight in time back to the oasis. But even in the Nile oasis the single man would perish if he were not united with a thousand others. All that the wild river did through the centuries until the last English dam arose, the power with which it flooded the land, casting its male seed, the mud, upon the fields—all this would be fruitless, or would beget the struggle of all against all, if men had not united, first to reckon the flood, then to distribute it, to dam it where they could, and by society and community, by rule and obedience, to take fruitful possession of the wild water and its gifts, which descend from the Abyssinian Alps, a thousand miles away, and from the Mountains of the Moon, to flow with mysterious power through the heart of the desert.

The Nile, which fell every year upon the oasis with catastrophic violence, was first transformed into its blessing by the ingenuity and skill of man. A land that receives the source of all its life, the water, from far away, a people that anxiously awaits every year the advent of this miraculous stranger, like those Eskimo tribes to which a ship brings the necessities of life every summer, could not but create a social order in its earliest days, long before the time of the hieroglyphics, so early that in its beginnings that order lacked even the name of state.

Since the whole land was, even by the protohistoric inhabitants, divided up into basins by dikes running at right angles to each other, in the hieratic picture-language a square still denotes a province. Necessity created on the Nile the first grouping of men, centralization, and obedience. It was the Nile that led Egypt's priests to observe the stars in order to calculate the time of the flood; the calculation of the height of the flood produced the measurement of height, the marking out of single fields with boundaries that were washed away every year gave rise to square measure, to the protection of property and the settlement of boundary disputes. It was the Nile that created mathematics, law and equity, money and police, long before any other association of people on the earth possessed them. What other people knew the zodiac before 3000 B.C., the calendar before 4000? It was the Nile that taught these things, and Napoleon said later that the Nile made the government of Egypt the most powerful of all governments, "for no man could, from Paris, influence the rain or snow falling in Beauce or Brie, but in Egypt, man could directly influence the consequences of the flood."

While this classical example, in a land without rain and almost without neighbours, proves the law of the soil to be omnipotent, the law of race is, at the same time, proved illusory before our very eyes. For as people after people later settled in this river land, all were remoulded by its soil and its enigmatic water, all became Egyptians. Even the cows, which are brought from long distances to the Nile, alter within a few generations the curve of their backs by a definitely Egyptian hump.

All this holds good only for the rainless oasis which stretches down to the latitude of the Cairo of today, once Memphis; that is, to the head of the Delta. There the wholesome dryness is troubled only in spring by the Chamsin, the hot south-east wind which suddenly darkens the earth: this is the plague of Egyptian darkness which spread at times over Palestine too, once, perhaps, at the death of Jesus. The poison wind, as the Arabs call it, suddenly raises the temperature of the air to over 118° F., the water to nearly 80, drying up the lungs of men and of plants. After the flood, too, the air absorbs all vapours, then the nose and mouth dry up, the lips crack, and wet garments dry in a few minutes.

The succession of changes in the weather-zones of the four Nile countries is shown by the annual rainfall figures: at the source of the Blue Nile in the Abyssinian Alps, over 50 inches; at the source of the White Nile, 48; in the Central Sudan, 20; at Khartoum, 4; in Upper Egypt, 0; in Cairo, 1.2; in Alexandria, 6.

It must indeed be a strange people that comes into being where the rainfall is nil, or little more, and where in spite of that the population is denser than anywhere else in the western hemisphere. For although Egypt, with its 350,000 square miles, is larger than France and Italy put together, the greater part of this land remains almost empty desert. Its 14 million inhabitants are crowded together in the Nile valley, that is, in a region smaller than Switzerland; hence they are crowded almost twice as densely as in Belgium: there are districts with 1800 inhabitants to the square mile. Such density, which, even thousands of years ago, obtained here in proportion to the total number of men then on the earth, could only create either a highly social, or a completely unsocial people. The Nile decided for the former.

Thus a people grew, trained—today as long ago, by the two gods of its climate—to love of life and frugality by the sun, to order and submission by the Nile. This was the state that made a god of Pharaoh, a necessity of work, an art of the technique of irrigation, a principle of rational and clear thinking; and though a few rich men, even more here than elsewhere, loaded upon the poor the burden of labour, especially that of watering, those who bore the burden bore it cheerfully, and hardly ever revolted against the rich. The sun seems to have dried up in this country even the will to revolt, just as the Nile, with its world of figures, has swamped the philosophic sense. The men we can see inventing so many great things millenniums before any others except for those on the Euphrates, who were as great in science as in mathematically calculated monuments, from which their very oldest statues are but little removed—these men full of practical enterprise could build up no transcendental world for themselves, and the world they created beyond death, with all its colour, was merely a copy of this one. The fear of the element, the Nile, made them godfearing, sociable, and conservative. The people that invented writing about 3300 B.C. never set down thoughts or songs in that writing such as were created by the fervour of the Jews, the profound philosophy of the Greeks, the mysticism of the Indians. They wrote rather to number than to sing, rather to record than to imagine. No mighty mythology or saga of the gods came to birth, but a tangle of many legends, all united in the one thought that dominated all these sons of the sun—the fight against death.

The strength of the Egyptian sun, the clearness of the desert air, the gift of the life-bearing river—by these things we can measure the richness of life on the Nile, for all its burden of bending and bearing. These things are the background of their souls. Canals are their epics, dams their dramas, the pyramids their philosophy.

3

THE first man that the dry air of Egypt preserved lay, no one knows for how long before historical time began, buried in the desert sand of Helouan. Lying there among urns and fragments of animals, knives and bracelets of copper and bronze, curled up like the unborn in the womb, he seems in some magic way to point back thousands of years, to the first mother, the first man, like those Arab storytellers in Egypt who sedulously trace back the pedigree of every wise man or caliph to Adam. Where did he come from? Where did those men come from before whose bones men have pronounced names which go back into the fourth millennium B.C.? Who were those upon whose daggers we find scratched elephants and panthers, hippopotami and snakes, giraffes and wild hogs, at a time when neither copper nor ivory was known even on the Euphrates? Did they come from the south or the north?

The question has never passed beyond the stage of academic dispute. In the same way, the students of literature pull the work of poets to pieces in the hope of finding what prompted the creative spirit, instead of trusting to the innate powers of his genius. And is not the question of race still more incalculable here in Egypt, where climate and nature hold undisputed sway, and have refashioned every man who approached the Nile? The Celts were the earliest race here, declared Sivrey. No, the Negroes, replied Volney. The Chinese, cried Winckelmann, but Jourès was for the Indo-Polynesians. All are wrong, pronounced Petrie, it was the Ethiopians. But then Rougé smiled and proved once for all that it was the Babylonians.

How little is proved by blood, how much by the soil, is shown nowhere so clearly as in Egypt, where all races, men and animals alike, became Egyptian in the course of centuries on this strange oasis. What enlightenment do the scholars bring us when, according to the latest fashion, they call the aboriginal Egyptians Hamites, related to the Galla and Somali, who later mingled with Semites immigrating into the eastern Delta? Let us rather look at the faces of the oldest mummies and the present fellah children: both show such clear traces of Asiatic length of neck and face beside the Negroid breadth of nose and lip, that the mixture has held good for over six millenniums, and proves that, here as everywhere, it was not racial purity but the mingling of alien races that created health and strength.

Nature and the river, the sun and the Nile, give, after all, the simplest answer. The Nile comes from the south, and as it has from all time borne boats on its back, they must, in spite of the cataracts, have sailed downstream since the beginning of recorded time. It was only later that Semites may have advanced through the desert and across the Red Sea from the east, those bearded soldiers and merchants whom the Pharaohs in their tombs are always shown beating or beheading. The peoples who landed in the northern, swampy part of the Delta, Aegeans and Phœnicians, Cretans and Persians, are all later than the historic Pharaohs. What is more natural than to find skeletons of Negroes on the Upper Egyptian Nile, of Asiatics on the Lower? If carbonized grain and vines have been found in the oldest graves, the former came probably, the latter certainly, from the Euphrates. And if the ram-headed Amon is to be found in African rock-drawings, why should not several neighbouring peoples have conceived this idea of the fusion of beast and god, and why, in the same way, should not the first fellah on the Nile have thought of drawing a line with a stick in the soft, muddy earth and thus inventing the plough?

What they knew, what they made, they clearly knew without being taught by strangers. Only one thing is certain—the first Egyptian idol was a goddess with the body of a hippopotamus.

To this people the Nile was at all times the measure of all things, whether six thousand years ago or today. "May men one day say of me, he was a Nile!" cried one of the Pharaohs to whom posthumous glory meant his share of immortality. Every man who stood before Osiris and the Judges of the Dead knew by heart the forty-two deadly sins from which he must absolve himself by sacred oaths, and one ran: "I have not sullied the water of the Nile, I have not stopped its flow in the good time, I have dammed up no canal." So holy did their river appear that the body of any man drowned in it was embalmed by the river-dwellers and buried with ornaments, "as though it were more than a human body." So completely did the river determine the law of the land that the god Amon decreed through his priests: "The land flooded by the Nile is Egypt, and any man drinking from the Nile below Elephantine is an Egyptian."

This too was realized most profoundly by the poetic mind. Homer used the word αἰγύπτος in the masculine for the Nile, in the feminine for Egypt. In this unemotional grammatical nuance, in the alternation between two letters, lies the symbol of Egypt. None of the Egyptian images of the Nile which are, for the most part, grotesque images of a bloated man with a flabby belly and breasts, no hymn in the Egyptian tongue, nor any of the graceful pictures of the later artists have grasped the whole myth with one word, as this stranger did, this Greek who, four centuries before Herodotus, beheld the river as a creative power.

The rocks of its bed, which distinguish the Nubian from the Egyptian Nile, had, in the form of six great cataracts of granite and quartz-bearing sandstone, so restricted irrigation and agriculture that along some 750 miles of its course, a breadth of only one to three miles was tilled. Below Aswân, where, geologically speaking, Egypt first begins, shell limestone dominates, and the Nile scoops out of its soft chalky earth its generally wide bed. Not until this point can it deposit the silt it has carried with it for more than a thousand miles; thus fertile land comes into being fifteen times bigger than in the Sudan. The Nile valley which, from Wadi Halfa to Aswân, is extremely narrow, and at some points does not extend beyond the actual river bed, now covers a width of between six and fifteen miles, and, if it were only as long as it is wide and not almost 700 miles in length, would be regarded as a normal, though big oasis in the desert.

But even as it is, the step from the green field to the yellow desert is literally often a step only, and anyone looking at the picture from above, flying northward over the river, can hardly believe that it is real: it is as if a model had been laid at his feet to show how water can conquer sand, skill conquer water, and the sun both.

4

EVERYTHING the Nile cre-
ated before entering Egypt seemed to belong to the world of
legend. Begotten by a gigantic lake, driven in torment from
swamp to swamp, delivered over helpless, without tributaries,
to bush and desert, then bolted in with granite bars, its long
course was like the life-story of some hero whose strength has
not failed him through hardship and battle, because he cannot
accomplish his appointed task until the sun is setting. So terrible
was the way of his ordeal, so steeled his soul, that towards the
end, descending from the mountain-tops of his suffering into
the valley of deeds, he has but to appear, his mere existence is
enough. So it is with the Nile: it has but to appear in Egypt in
order, without a struggle, without a purpose, simply out of
creative power, to beget a land.

And as it begets that land anew every year, the Nile takes its
own way too in the seasons of ebb and flow; in summer, when
its brothers are sinking or drying up all over the world, it roars
on in full flood, making the Egyptian New Year fall in July.
For three to four months, from June to September, it rises 13 to
14 ells in Upper Egypt, 7 to 8 in the Delta. In these hundred
days, the virile river takes possession of the expectant land, then,
every inch a god, withdraws into the unknown, leaving behind
it only the symbolic priest, who represents it and guards its
temples. Thus, as a god, it has been worshipped by all men dwelling on its banks, by all who have conquered it, down to our
own day.

This flood, which is transformed into bread, has been regarded by the Egyptians from time immemorial with curiosity
and awe, and as expectant mothers, in their time of waiting,
always wonder whether their child will be a boy or a girl, the

Egyptians, in the nine months of waiting, question signs and oracles, priests and engineers, to know whether the flood will be high. In olden times, Coptic monks used to expose a piece of potter's clay to the night air and weigh it in the evening and morning: if the weight increased, a high flood was predicted. Astrologers worked out the conjunctions of the planets. The Arabs, in the Middle Ages, predicted a bad flood when the river was coloured deep green because, for want of rain, it was supposed to have carried away all the vegetation from the lakes from which it came.

Today, when the engineers in Cairo and Aswân are informed hourly by electricity of the rise at a number of places on the banks of both Niles, the art of irrigation has become a hundred times more subtle, and what no Pharaoh, no Arab, and no Roman could achieve with his Nilometers, namely the daily calculation of the volume of water and its distribution, can be read at a glance from the tables. But if the hydrological experts are asked to forecast the height of the next flood, they can no more give an answer than the earliest inhabitants who raised the first dikes on the same banks, who with their own hands drew the first plough behind them and raised the water with the first pitchers, which even then may have whined through the Nile valley, so many thousands of years ago.

The explanations of the ancients went far astray, but their predictions were no further off than ours, though we know the origin of the Nile flood. The north winds, according to one Greek theory, cast the Nile back from the sea and prevented its discharging; it was the sea, according to another, that rolled round the disk of the earth, and from the sea came the Nile. It was the snow from high, distant mountains, said a third; and Herodotus mocked them all, but knew no better. "Mysterious in the full light of day, the veil of nature cannot be raised." Today that secret is the secret of the monsoons that break against the Alps of Abyssinia. No one knows their strength, nor can anyone reckon in advance the conditions of cloud-formation; hence neither the volume of the Ethiopian rain nor the force of the flood rolling down the Blue Nile and the Atbara can be known.

Once it is there, we can measure the flood exactly and distribute it according to the measurements, but so could the Pharaohs. Long before Herodotus, who travelled in Egypt in the fifth century B.C., men knew the numbers and prayed for 16 ells: that is the high flood, and that is the meaning of the sixteen "children" on the statue of the bearded Nile in the Vatican. Pliny expressed this with Roman terseness: "12 ells mean hunger, 13 sufficiency, 14 joy, 15 security, 16 abundance," and the "religious" background of his thoughts is revealed by his remark that the low water of the Nile in the year of Pharsalus showed how even the river was expressing its horror at the murder of Pompey. We may well wonder what would happen if the rivers of Europe, in our day, were to interfere in politics!

The measurements seem to reach back into the time of the Old Kingdom. The twenty ancient Nilometers which have been discovered between Aswân and Cairo must, according to the Arab story-teller Makrizi, have been in the form of marble wells on the bank with two copper eagles of both sexes on their margin. When, on the first day of the flood, the king and the priests opened the well with prayer, all listened to hear which of the two eagles would scream first: if it was the male, a great flood was predicted, and the first thing the king did was to raise the price of the yet unsown corn. The Pharaohs knew how to exploit their religious emotions in very practical form.

Later, under the dictators, even the geographers were frank. Strabo, writing in Cæsar's time, found "nothing in Egypt so useful as these Nilometers, both to the farmers, whom they show how much water they can count on and what they must save for their ditches and embankments, and to the government, which bases its taxes on them, since every increase in the volume of the river and the quantity of water means an increase of taxation." Girard, standing by the river with General Bonaparte two thousand years later, called them all, with the cynical innocence of his time, "holy relics, for the government was apt to exaggerate the coming flood in order to get in high taxes."

For the last 1350 lunar years, the history of the Nile lies before us in figures and dates which are more reliable than those of European history. How the Arab writers of the fourteenth

century later discovered the figures for their first six centuries
they do not say; their way of writing history was more artistic
than that of the legitimate historians of today precisely because
they did not reveal their sources. The fact that independent
lists tally proves them to be correct, and the comparison with
later centuries makes it possible to draw conclusions by analogy
to an overwhelming degree. From the Hegira, the flight of the
Prophet in A.D. 622, to 1935, we have the figures for all but 192
years: for 1122 years we know the height of the Nile flood.

Softly the tables murmur their numbers, like the priests their
prayers; the sound beats against our ears; average low level by
centuries—first century: 11.51 ells; ninth century: 12.52; thirteenth century: 13.90; average high flood by centuries—first century: 17.5; ninth century: 18.21; thirteenth century, 19.31—and
behind these figures Byzantines and Alexandrians, Jews and
Crusaders, Saracens and Franks, pass along the banks of the Nile,
caliphs and generals, emperors and cardinals, archæologists and
hotel-keepers, till at last the English arrived, to fetter the river
with their dams, and, by the subjection of African water, to
make the factories on their distant island independent of the
cotton of a third continent—to make Manchester independent of
Texas.

Yet behind this carnival of history, astounding knowledge
emerges from the cold figures, and, as on the Nile history happens in millenniums, there emerges from these lists drawn up by
Arab geographers and story-tellers one fact that is unique in human history. Since men knew the lowest and highest water-levels
for a thousand years, it was also possible to reckon the rise in the
valley of the Egyptian Nile caused by the yearly deposit of silt,
measured at four points between Aswân and Cairo. From the
second to the twelfth century there is a difference of about 36
inches at the ebb and 68 inches at the flood, so that in a thousand years, the earth level was raised by 52 inches. In the last
770 years (according to another reckoning 570) the Nile valley
has risen more than a yard.

When we are told that the light of distant suns takes thousands of years to reach us, we float on an ocean of figures like

nutshells, hugging the bank, and it means as little to us as the disputes of palæontologists pushing the youth of the earth backwards and forwards by a few hundred thousand years or so. Spectra and logarithms, crystals and skulls tell of spaces of time or light that no one can grasp.

But 770 years can be grasped. Since, 770 years ago, the Emperor Barbarossa entered Milan, fought and was reconciled with the Pope, planned and achieved, surrounded by German princes and Italian priests, by his sons and grandsons, and found his death bathing in a river of Asia Minor; since out of these Middle Ages, the flower of Italy arose, amid the struggles of a hundred kings and princes, shrewd marriages, and disputes for the succession; since cities and countries changed their flags, and nations bound themselves together and sought to destroy each other, from St. Louis to the Napoleonides, from Emperor Frederick II to the German Republic, from Dante to Nietzsche, from Giotto to Rodin, from the knight's charger to the tank— for these seven hundred years men fought for ideas in Europe, and caliphs and demagogues battled in Egypt—and seven hundred times the heavy clouds struck against the wall of the Abyssinian Alps, seven hundred times myriads of volcanic particles were carried down the Blue Nile, and seven hundred times the layer of silt was deposited on the banks of the river, and in the end, the rainless oasis was raised three feet. That we can grasp —literally grasp.

But one thing, in all these seven hundred years, never changed in the Nile valley—the subjection of the slave to his master, the dumb death of millions for the glory or shame of the few in whose name history is made. In spite of all the speculations of the powerful and the rich, the fellah lives, after seven hundred years, in the same Nile valley, in the same poverty as his forefathers under the first Pharaohs, only that, 5000 years ago, he lived twenty-odd feet lower down.

Like some spiritual conqueror, constantly enriching his sphere with fresh treasures of the mind from far away, accumulating them in the treasure-house of his life, the Nile, in its age, heaps up the fruitful substance it gathered in its youth and steadily enriches its world. If all the land tilled by the fellah is pure mud nearly forty feet deep, how rapidly, how richly, the crops must rise upon it!

At the same time, the land close to the river must stand higher than that farther off, for the latter receives only that part of the silt which did not infiltrate the former. The steepness and narrowness of the river, too, influence fertility: where the slope is steeper, the layer of silt is thinner. But as the Nile, from Aswân to Cairo, falls little more than 5 inches per mile, the gradual raising of the ground level has remained the same in Upper and Lower Egypt.

Yet here, as everywhere else, nature proves a cool and accurate calculator. Having brought fertilizing substance from Abyssinia to the soil of the rainless oasis, then, in the heat, cracked and split the clay soil so that the sun and the silt can penetrate it thoroughly, it spreads the next flood over fields which, even without the plough, are ready to bear fresh crops, and better crops, for in the depths the silt has loosened substances which promote their growth. Even the course of history was pressed into service, for the ruins of old towns and villages built of Nile mud were a rich source of manure.

At the same time, the Libyan desert advanced from the west, again stealing from man the land his fathers tilled. Thus the battle between land and water rolls up and down, as it has always done; giving and taking, nature sharpened the wits of the men she placed on the river banks: it was for them to devise irrigation.

The art of irrigation must have begun with the earliest agriculture on the Nile, but the first reports of canals comes from Sesostris, who had them dug by his prisoners of war about 3000 B.C. It was he, says Herodotus, with the naïve regret of the tourist, "who first turned Egypt into a land where nobody can ride or drive." Today we can do both, for the dams themselves have become the highways of the country, the motorist finds good roads, and the foreigner does not even know that not one foot of the precious, narrow valley would fall to his share to travel on if that road were not a dam that promotes irrigation.

Irrigation by means of basins, the Pharaonic method, is still in use above Asyût; to the north, roughly from 27° N. lat., where the cotton begins, the perennial system sets in, carried out by the dams. The technique of dams and canals is certainly more nearly perfect than it was under the Pharaohs and Caliphs, whose towns and villages, in summer, rose like islands out of the spreading waters, for the flood had turned the narrow land of Egypt into a lake. Today such islands are rare; the basins store the silt-laden water and keep it for forty days; then it flows, diluted, into a chain of descending basins.

The embankments, 6 to 10 feet high, between these basins, hold the water to a depth varying from 1 to 6 feet, according to the conformation of the terrain; from the middle of August till the end of September, it is left lying on the fields, and just as the safes in the big banks are guarded by policemen, soldiers are on patrol here all these weeks in case a fellah may kick an embankment down, or knock a hole in it with his broad, bare foot. The water in the Milanese rice-fields is guarded in much the same way. There is a special court for the water-thieves, but Allah has often made up to the fellah for his sweat and toil by making his wits sharper than the soldiers'.

Now everybody crowds to the river, like Germans crowding round the freshly opened beer-cask for the first, foaming mugs. For there is no "red water" for those whose fields lie farthest from the Nile and nearest to the edge of the desert, but the man who sows close to the bank can water his field with the *sakia* and reap twice.

The clear water is not the only trouble. There is the salt too. Up in the jungles surrounding Lake Albert, the Negro women scrape it out of the earth with their hands, for the pygmies want it and give meat and sharp arrows in return. But now the Nile, in its old age, has a superfluity of what it lacked in youth: from subterranean tributaries, salt water enters the fresh water of the canals, and recently destroyed a large number of neighbouring sycamores and apricots. Thus the Nile, which spent its whole life above ground, is, late in time, attacked by infernal powers; but then they bring it help—subterranean waters that help it to preserve the land of its age: some 1000 artesian wells and more than 50,000 water-wheels are fed by its subterranean waters.

Strangers could not but weave legends round a land so strangely nourished, and as it sent grain overseas, it was known throughout the world as the land of plenty. Could the land of the eternal blue sky be anything but happy? Sand had to be mixed in the soil of Egypt, wrote a geographer of the eighteenth century, otherwise it would be too rich: even the animals and the women were so fertile that the sheep lambed twice a year and the women generally bore twins.

Herodotus too seems to have encountered the same blitheness among the priests of the fifth century. "If you have no river in Greece to water the land," they said, perhaps smiling, "you may one day perish of hunger, if your god stops the rain from falling."

"Are you better off?" replied the shrewd Greek. "Today you take the fruit from the earth more easily than other men, without even needing to use a plough. But what if here in your Delta, the land should go on rising as you tell me it has done for the last nine hundred years? Are the Egyptians in the Delta not threatened with starvation as soon as the Nile can no longer overflow its banks?"

Such were the flights of fancy with which the priests of Amon, in their temple garden, entertained their learned guest, who believed in Zeus, and the rivalry of their national pride was expressed in gods and elements.

5

_____

TODAY the element is tamed. What that means, the river will tell us later. The dam of Aswân, and the four barrages below it have, in the last thirty years, transformed for the first time the age-old methods of irrigation in Egypt. To turn a grain-growing into a cotton-growing country, dams had to distribute the water throughout the year, that is, create a permanent irrigation; at the same time, however, an effort was made to fertilize the more distant parts, the fringes of the desert. Thus the new technique gave birth to two radi-cally different symbols.

The first was the levelling of the power of nature: an element which, from the beginning of time, had hurled itself down in full strength once every summer, and then run dry, became a reservoir; an adventurer was disciplined into a careful saver. The world is deprived of a mighty spectacle so that it may possess a few more million hundredweight of cotton. As men already had enough to make clothing for everybody, all that has happened is that portions of a product have passed from one hand to another, from the American to the Anglo-Egyptian.

And yet at the same time a second symbol, the great work of Faust, finds its most astonishing embodiment on earth: it was made possible to win new land from the desert, and becomes more so every year. The philosophy of the Egyptian dams does not reside in the cotton, it resides in that deep green into which the yellow desert sand has been transformed over an area of 1200 square miles.

Before looking at the pictures, let us look the figures in their cold face.

Of 11,500 square miles of cultivable land, 8500 are already under crops, and 3000 are to be added in the near future, while in Upper Egypt, 1200 are to be brought within the new irrigation system of the dams. In thirty years, Egypt will have reached its maximum of cultivation, though it will then have a population of 18 to 20 millions. Of the land now cultivated 70 percent yields double or treble harvests; in the region above Asyût —that means half the length of the Egyptian river and country, but, owing to the narrowness of the upper valley, only a quarter of the total cultivated area—half the land is still irrigated on the old basin system.

Let us once more consider where the water comes from. In summer, from February to August, the White Nile, carrying 80 percent of the whole, bears nearly all the responsibility; in some years, the Blue Nile dwindles to a trickle of 5 percent. In flood-time, the figures are almost reversed. But the total quantity of water is always an uncertain question; the low-water years, moreover, tend to occur in runs—for instance, 1781–1797 and 1899–1915. Hence the volume of water passing through the dam at Aswân fluctuates between 54 and 181 billion cubic yards. Before the dam was built, a low-water year could mean famine in Egypt; in 1913 it affected only the cotton crop.

Of the dams projected on the Upper Nile, none threatens Egypt, at least as long as there is peace. It has already been pointed out that England's power to turn the key and thirst Egypt out is a fable. But in case of war, the fluctuations in the quantity of water are big enough to permit the dam to become a powerful weapon in English hands. The highest dam, on Lake Albert, could, given the steepness of the lake-shores, easily raise its surface of 2000 square miles by a yard and hence store 6.5 billion cubic yards. But as the loss of water in the swamps amounts on an average to 25 billion cubic yards, the only remedy would be the canal in the swamps which has already been discussed. The water would then require 55 days to go from Lake Albert to Aswân.

The Gebel Aulia dam, just above Khartoum, which is now under construction, is intended to protect Egypt from the danger of inundation.

The dam which has been planned for the last fifteen years at Lake Tana could store still more water than Lake Albert, namely 9 billion cubic yards, five of which would remain in perpetual storage for unforeseen catastrophes, while four would irrigate the Gezira cotton in spring. The basin would then be empty, but Egypt would lose not a drop, for nearly all the water of the Blue Nile, which flows into the White at Khartoum, gathers far below Lake Tana in the frontier plain between Abyssinia and the Sudan.

Of the three Egyptian seasons, Nili, Shitwi, and Sefi—flood, winter, and summer—summer and flood merge, for though the flood sets in from June on, it reaches its height only at the beginning of September, when the basins in Upper Egypt are full and the canals can spread enough superfluous water over the land parched by summer. Later, part of the land becomes free for fresh sowings which yield a very meagre winter crop. The day after the grain has been reaped in April, and the last sheaves carried away on the canals, the water-wheel starts its work of reconciling the stubble-fields with water. Thus the soil of the Egyptian oasis is about 140 percent cultivated.

What can be cultivated is determined by the Nile, and the Nile-god has his whims, whereas, above it, the sun is a constant and lavish god. Little rice can be raised, for it needs most water and takes six months to ripen. For the sugar-cane, which must be watered eighteen times, there are pumps; but cotton, which needs ten waterings, is the great idol in whose service no toil is spared. The poor fellah works only what his arms and legs can manage with the help of water: clover for the livestock, watered eight times, but cut six times a year; maize, watered eight times; onions, beans, millet, vegetables, above all cereals—wheat, which he sows in the muddy soil in October, and he has only to water it three times to provide bread for himself and his family in April. Thus the water of the Nile, on the narrow strip above Asyût, today brings forth the same grain, in the same way, with basins and water-buckets, as under the Pharaohs; below, from Asyût to Cairo, a third of the soil is under cotton, but there everything is controlled by the dams on the so-called perennial system, and the humblest onion of the fellah sprouts under the supervision of the engineers of Aswân.

At all points the work of the dams is impressive. Since cotton has raised the value of every acre of land in this part of Upper Egypt by more than $36, men crowd more and more densely upon it, so that there are between two and three hundred more inhabitants to the square mile here than anywhere else. The density of the population even increases in proportion to the fertility of the soil: an increase of $10 in the value of a piece of land means the immigration of a family. The real work of the dam at Aswân appears only later, like that of great men: it sets in only 250 miles below Aswân.

A still more surprising consequence of the dams is the fear that the flood will be too high. It is true that, from the Pharaohs till yesterday, the Nile rose too high from time to time, but that happened so rarely that men always prayed for a high flood. To-day men fear that the flood may break the dams, for a generation that has bridled and carefully distributed the element must needs tremble before the destruction of its dams, like dictators before a revolution.

And just as money breeds greed, and thirst breeds thirst, the rich landowners of today complain more bitterly of lack of water than their forebears, who had none for months on end. Not until the new dam is built above Khartoum, a second at Lake Tana, perhaps even a third at Lake Albert—this plan has already been set forth—not until then, says the pasha in Cairo, will my cotton flourish as it should. But in his turn the poor man is dependent on the rich man and his water. Since the revolution of irrigation brought about by the opening of the dam at Aswân in 1900, nothing seems enough.

And little devils actually co-operate, here as everywhere, to frustrate a great idea. The contractor who helped to pay the heavy costs of the dams with his taxes, and dreamed of celestial cotton-prices in return, finds reason enough to complain. First, the storage-water has no silt, for until summer it comes from the White Nile; then it lies a much shorter time on his fields than in the basins, leaves less silt behind it, and yields smaller crops. And then how is he to get rid of all this water that flows down all the year round? Pumps are dear and not always reliable. But the fellah, standing beside the contractor on his field as his ten-

VILLAGE ON THE NILE

MOUNTAINS ON THE EASTERN BANK

ant, and generally as his labourer, is completely disconcerted. The salt brought down by the White Nile, which is rich in minerals, and the uneconomic methods of agriculture have to be counteracted by manure; for the first time since thousands of years, the fellah has to manure the soil of Egypt.

And what is the result? Since the richest grainland, the ancient granary of the world, has begun to export cotton, it has had to import cereals. While it has on the whole increased in wealth, it has become more dependent. As man's mental horizon widens, his inward peace is troubled. Goethe drew a similar distinction between action and thought: "Thought broadens, but paralyses; action inspires, but limits." If the *feddan* above Asyût yields only about $90, below, with its cotton, it yields as much as $140. Figures swell in the contractor's ledger, the population grows, but not their pleasures. The land that was kept healthy by its dryness breeds insects when it perpetually lies under water; new diseases, such as bilharziasis, rise from the widened Nile like Egyptian plagues, and from a thousand mouths rises the cry: "No more dams! No more water!"

With his heavy tread, the fellah returns to the water-wheel. It is familiar to him because his fathers knew it, and as no engineer could replace it except by pumps, which advance but slowly, the ancient wooden wheel still turns close to the concrete dam, slow, simple, and true, like the horse beside the motor.

It turns and whines. All Egypt is penetrated by two sounds—a scream and a complaint. Today as long ago these are the two messengers of Egypt's gods, the creatures of the sun and the Nile. High up above the river with its narrow green mantle, the horus falcon, the red kite, rises and swoops, hovers and darts, and when it happens to settle in the lonely temple court of Edfu, it cannot know that it is its divine ancestor, the stone horus, in whose crevices it is planting its talons. Its call, generally descending in seven half-tones with a drop of a fourth at the end, falls from the blue, generally from a great height—perhaps it is a mating-call, perhaps a hunger-cry, perhaps mere joy of life.

The answer is the whining dirge of the water-wheel whose wooden hub creaks against the beam. It is the same sound as the

Nile heard up in Nubia, but it is multiplied a thousandfold on this densely populated stretch. Here there are fifty, a hundred water-wheels in a row, and as they burrow side by side, they look like a battalion of archæologists let loose.

For what the dwellers in this narrow oasis dread is any rise in the land, though it were only a few feet in height, for the water must be carried uphill in a land where God neither allows rain to fall nor water to flow uphill. Nowhere is the rise more than 10 to 12 feet high, yet it threatens the food supply and life itself, and no dam can overcome it. Slavery began with the water-bucket, and even then many sought to flee from the deadly round, as many a papyrus vividly describes.

It is not always a wheel. At many places along the banks, two naked men—they stand in the mud, which they call "natal"—draw the most primitive kind of bast basket through the canal, and throw the water into the next basket higher up. Or else they stand at a movable scale-beam to which a bucket of goat's-hide or merely a basket is tied, fill it in the water, and empty it above: the balance weight is a block of Nile mud. This is the *shaduf,* and when three *shadufs* rise in steps above each other, the Nile water can cover the ten feet to the upper field within a few minutes. But the classical form, here as in Nubia, is the *sakia,* the water-wheel with its revolving buffaloes, and the boy driving them under the sycamore. And it is the *sakia* that sings throughout the land of Egypt.

Sometimes the nasal chant of the boys following the turning oxen mingles with the creaking and whining: "Come, little lamb, come and fill my money-bags," they sing, but they know that it is the money-bags of their master that their ten hours' round is filling. And their master has imposed his own *leitmotiv* on the song—an old oil-can that strikes the wood at every turn. By that sound, from his house close by, he can tell whether his men are really turning the wooden wheel without respite.

Thus, at a thousand places along the banks, the three melodies rise together: old hopes crooned by the dully dreaming slave walking behind the beasts or crouching on the shaft, the clinking of the tin spy, assuring the master of a return in the work of man and beast for his money, and between the two, strangely weeping, the sound of the ancient wood that once grew on the Nile itself, to be turned by a wooden wheel into a wheel, and later, in its turn to draw water—water—water—for other trees and crops.

6

NEARLY all the plants it calls to life were already known in Pharaonic times: in no other part of the world has the flora been known for 6000 years, because nowhere else did custom so adorn the tombs, and dryness so preserve them. Two hundred plants have been found in the tombs, most of them when the mummies were unswathed: laurel or a kind of lotus on the head, a sprig of myrtle or tamarisk in the hands, jasmine or mint in garlands round the neck. Rosemary, mignonette, roses, myrrh, and marjoram were laid on the couch of the dead, indigo was used for colours and henna for a soap lather to bleach the hair.

Then comes all the food they laid beside the dead, and all we see on the tomb-paintings and reliefs, like that delicate one on a kind of balustrade in Karnak, which shows both plants and animals. There in the rock the lotus spreads its chalice, the papyrus its nine-pointed heads: between them the dainty hoopoe and nimble thrush are feeding, the sand-piper runs about under the ranunculus, and beside the royal lily the ibis sits. All these creatures marvel at the rays of the sun-god, for long ago, when the artist brought his work into the tomb, he plunged them all into the night of a dark chapel till suddenly, three and a half thousand years later, the careful hands of an excavator brought them back into the light from which they, like their models, had come.

The most generous of all the plants was the papyrus. The bundles of stalks plucked by the slaves of the Pharaohs were used to weave mats, to twist ropes, to knot sandals, to bind boats; the papyrus could even carry a light roof; and its roots were eaten. Yet just as a high-bred animal can drag, yet think, imagine, and carry at the same time, this wise plant was universal too, and, having provided all that was necessary for rest, clothing, and travel, it retained a last, most subtle capacity. For when the stalks were cut into fine strips, laid out criss-cross, then firmly beaten and stuck together, the sheets thus made could be rolled up to await the records of wisdom and bear them down the stream of time, as the papyrus had already borne men in boats down the Nile. What should we know today of ancient times—and not only of Egypt—if it were not for this plant? Even as late as the eleventh century, blank rolls of papyrus travelled to Syria, and later to Athens and Rome, and stories and legends, philosophy and laws, were written on its flattened stalks to bear strange tidings of strange peoples into the world, and back again to the Nile, where it had grown.

Today the narrow Egyptian oasis has still less room for woods and meadows than it once had. Only the towns reserve the right to plant avenues, and here and there, outside of them, there are isolated sycamores, whispering tamarisks that look like conifers, broad-spreading mulberry trees or Nile acacias—all trees that need little water. The date-palm is lavish enough to make watering worth while, for here, as on the Upper Nile, its wood and leaves make houses, furniture, and mats, while its fruit, yellow, red, or brown, ripening indoors in winter like European pears, helps to feed the people. The doum-palm with its fans extends from the Sudan nearly as far as Cairo: the people eat its big nuts and even suck out the kernels of the glassy seeds. For the banana, Egypt is too windy. Cacti are grown in hedges; the fellahin eat its prickly pears in summer with or without the beautiful yellow flowers—and the cactus is eaten by the camel too, the waterless plant by the waterless beast of the desert, perhaps from a feeling of the kinship of want, of poverty, that equality of fate which in man so often breeds hatred.

On the Delta channels, the blue lotus blooms as in the days when they laid it beside the dead, and the white Indian water-lily, whose chalice opens above the green leaves, grows in lonely pools among the ruins; the nekheb alone, the true, sacred lotus, has vanished from Egypt.

The world of animals has changed more than the world of plants. This narrow strip of fertile land that leaves no space for the wilderness, no room for hunting, has been tamed today like the river—it was tamed before the river. When, in the earliest times the Nile flood pushed forward the bed of the river every summer, the primeval swamps bred countless animals and birds. Even under the Pharaohs, who adorned their tombs with hunting pictures and trophies, these animals dwelt in the river and along the banks, a living danger, as they are in Southern Nubia today. But now no lion approaches the Egyptian Nile in the evening, no hippo wallows, no crocodile basks on the bank—not even an Edward Lear could make crocodile rhyme with Lower Nile today, when a crocodile below Aswân is an event, and the last hippo, which was shot in the Delta in 1821, could not have roused more of a nine days' wonder on the Thames.

Nowhere on earth have animals been so sacred as here; nowhere are they so kindly treated today. "The people even regard all animals as sacred," says Herodotus, adding, with a knowing twinkle, that he will not give the reasons. In a hundred stories, obviously of popular origin, painted on the walls of tombs, the humour and good nature of the Pharaonic fellah plays on the animals. On one relief, a lion is playing draughts with a gazelle. On another, a leopard is herding gazelles and geese with its flute, carrying their young in its arms. A hyena is trying to stop a goose running into its mouth, a lion and a fox are paying a visit to a sick hippo, or a monkey, an ass, a lion, and a crocodile are giving a concert. A young lady rat, sitting on a chair with a flower in her hand, her rat slave-maiden behind her, is receiving gifts from a cat. Lions are standing petrified in front of a cat quietly ambling over the road. The hippo is sitting on a tree, while a bird is climbing up a ladder to reach it. Such things could hardly appear in a land where animals were not beloved, or among greedy, jealous men.

Every animal had its own keeper, and the pious man shaved his children's heads, sold the hair for its weight in silver, and had the keeper buy food for his sacred animal with the money. When a cat died, the family shaved their eyebrows; when a dog died, their whole bodies; they built tombs for them—the sacred ibis had its own cemeteries. Embalmed crocodiles and snakes have been found, and it seems to have been the cobra that God turned into a rod before the eyes of Moses. As the uræus snake, it adorned one of the Pharaonic crowns.

For Egypt, in its dryness, could not but become the paradise of snakes and bats, scorpions and mosquitoes. Up on a tree, the cowardly chameleon, with its tongue out, sits looking frightfully like certain politicians when they reach high places, and the waran, the dark-skinned giant lizard, lies below, screaming comically and shaking its head, like the voter who will not admit that he is afraid of the menacing creature above him. When the flood comes, the whole world of beetles and lizards are driven from their hiding-places, and the fellah, whose house they invade, struggles in vain to stamp them out. But the worst time of all comes when the plague of Moses' time is repeated, and clouds of locusts dim the light, destroying everything and multiplying furiously, in spite of all the pitch and oil with which the fellah attempts to destroy the eggs. The bonuses paid by the government for their destruction were recommended by Pliny 1800 years ago.

The Nile has kept its fish. The wonderful moonfish, which is caught today with nets, is the distant descendant of that moonfish which the slaves are cleaning and drying on King Mera's boat, while he leans back, drinks, and enjoys life, although he is sitting in his death-barque painted in his tomb. It is the same moonfish, tetraodon, that even today puffs itself up like a balloon, then goes rocking down the Nile, borne by its powerful back—a fearful sight, for it is covered with spikes. It can perform this puffing turn only because, like a dictator, it has developed in its interior a system of mysterious bones, valves, and plugs which make such distension possible. Oddly enough, this kind of dictator develops a voice only when it lets out air, a rare spectacle which brings crowds to the bank to see it collapse.

There is another wonder-fish in the Nile, the malapterus, which has the attitudes and length of a snake, the blow-holes of a whale in its skull, and the extremities and air-bladders of the amphibians. This is the electrical fish whose touch, according to Arab accounts, makes men tremble, then turns them stiff and heavy, whose mere breath electrocutes a swimmer.

When the Nile is not low, the buffalo-cow stands in it as in

Pharaoh's dream of the seven fat and lean kine, but the male buffaloes must be tethered, otherwise they escape through the water. The hybrid slughi, which also appears in the tomb reliefs and in the stories, is a fine dog, though dirty and wild; it fights with the jackals on the edge of the desert. Reddish goats with hanging ears and little pigs root about on the banks, but the most beloved domestic animal has always been, and still is the cat, which first became a domestic animal here; and its cemetery lies by the mosque today, as it once lay beside the temple. Cats and conservatism make the Egyptian akin to the Frenchman, but the Frenchman's oasis is broader.

Above, on the long, flat dam, a fiery little animal is trotting along, smoother and quainter in movement than the horse, swifter than the camel, which does not like to trot on paved roads. It is the one saddle-animal that Africa has produced, for the horse and the camel came over from Asia much later. But in Africa it galloped northwards to become the true Egyptian beast of burden. No one knows the donkey who has not ridden it in the Nile valley.

Obstinate, stupid, and lazy, the pretext for an insult, such is the donkey of northern lands; fiery, spirited, and handsome, such is the Egyptian donkey. Even in Spain and Greece, we learn to love him, but not one can compare with the Egyptian donkey, except that of the Hejaz, and if we ask why, the answer is the same as among men—a happy childhood, wholesome food, kind treatment, and comradeship made him lovable. In Egypt he is silver-grey. A good saddle-ass, dearer than a moderately good horse, as big as a mule, and really like one except for his ears, he stands blinking in the sun, powerful and slender, with a soft, smooth coat in which some amateur has cut pretty designs. He looks proud of his fine saddle, and in any case ready to prove his mettle. A giant of a man bestrides him, the sun beats on him from above, but he gallops along the dam, sweating less than his rider.

The cheap donkey of the fellah is not greatly inferior: he is hard-working, seldom intractable, and always intelligent. The female is the best of mothers. She has been known to rush into a burning stable to rescue her young. And when the donkey has been over a road once or twice, he knows it, and warns his rider by bucking and plunging if he seems to be taking the wrong way. His needs are few—nothing by day, clover by night, and everything the horse and cow reject, even thorns and thistles, almost like a camel. The only thing he cannot do without is pure water.

7

SOFTLY the white sail swells on the curved mast against the green of the oasis; behind, the irregular line of the desert runs along the sky, yellow on blue. Nowhere are these three colours so pure and deep as here, where they are born of the burning, cloudless light, the immaculate sand, and a moist, lush field. Red is the only colour that Egypt does not possess, and since the Turkish flag made way for the Egyptian, which could have been dyed no lovelier colour than the sap-green of the oasis, no sanguinary tint has crashed through the powerful, yet gentle harmony of Egypt's four tones. For even white is like a colour here, multiplied a thousandfold in the sails on the river, the houses on the bank, and placed in ever new relation to the three ground-tones.

In the evening, they break up and are dissolved. Then, near Aswân, the Nile turns pastel-blue, palms and acacias turn grey-green, the near hills orange-brown with blue shadows, the desert in the middle distance rosy, the distant mountains purple. All the boats seek the creeks; at night there is no light on the river. Streaks of cloud creep forth when the sun has vanished, pointing like arrows from west to east in the northern sky. And the sky itself, purple on the horizon, is brightened in the next strip by rosy clouds, then merges into pale green, while high in the zenith the last brightness gathers into a roseate promise, fleeting and innocent. A pale moon has entered the golden world like a messenger warning to departure. The desert mountains fade into dun, and the Nile turns grey, thinking of its age.

In the morning, illumined from the other side, the white sail again swells on the curved mast, which holds it higher than any tree of Egypt could; it consists of two or three rods bound together, and tapers at the top like a whip: thus it forms one of

the two lines that make the *dahabiya* so beautiful. The other is
the curve of the high poop, on which a man stands bolt upright,
his arm lying along the huge tiller, his white shirt fluttering in
the wind. Thus they pass to and fro, heavily laden with limestone or sacks of sugar, with grain and hencoops, while a family
crouches, eating and smoking, on the deck, and the fowls peck
about in the grain. As they glide down the Nile, man and beast
alike are nourished by what the Nile has begotten. Only the grey
donkey cannot eat the green fodder piled on his back, but he can
smell it, for he stamps and sniffs.

The remote ancestor of this fellah stood thus on the antique
boat with the same high prow, and the sails hoisted almost in the
same way, which sailed downstream and ran on the same sandbanks. Even the little boats that capsize now and then were
built in those far-off times, only that they were still more fragile,
for then they were made of papyrus. But what reward would
Pharaoh have given to the magician who presented him with a
swift motor boat? Most likely he would have killed him. The
mere fact that a river could flow in any direction but northwards
completely disconcerted the master of the Nile. When Thutmosis I penetrated into Asia, he stood aghast beside the strange
"water that flows the wrong way, so that boats go northward
when they sail upstream"; that was his description of the Euphrates, and the Persian Gulf was "the sea of the river that flows
the wrong way."

Throughout Egypt, dozens of high masts stand like signposts
at every one of the countless villages along the banks, showing
where the father of the land, the river, flows, but when they
glide downstream with sails spread, they look like its familiar
spirits hovering over it. Here is the source of life, and anyone
travelling on the river, in the heart of the green valley, with the
harsh desert threatening on both sides, feels like a man enjoying
plenty among the famished. Over in the caves in the western
hills the dead kings lie buried, but millions of dead fellahin fell
to dust in the desert sand, for the living could not feed here on
the river if the dead were not borne into the desert.

The boat often runs aground on the sandbanks, for there is no
chart of the shallows, and the river shifts its bounds at every

flood; even today it would be uncontrollable if it did not regulate itself, after the manner of great men. For the Nile scoops out its bed only to the depth made necessary by the changing rate of its flow; the size of its islands depends on the strength of the flood, its twists and turns are determined by the islands of mud it deposits everywhere.

In Aswân, it quits for ever the granite that gave the Pharaohs their statues and obelisks, and the English the masonry for their dam. It would be too far to transport the granite from the Red Sea, where it still occurs. Hence even in ancient times, the stones and water of the First Cataract, which is really the last, formed a fortification to the south. At the dam of Aswân, after the rocky, deserted stretch from Wadi Halfa, after the tragedy of the submerged palms, of the men who fled to the hills, and of the drowning temple, immediately below the confusion of rapids and the great waterfalls of the open sluices, the Nile valley opens, deep green, not yet wide, but brightened by white houses inhabited by Berber women, on which stone can still be spent. A fortress and a market, Aswân has been the real frontier of Egypt since the Pharaohs, for creeds and cultures broke against the unnavigable cataracts, and conquerors from north or south could not often cheat the river by going round it.

Here lies a little, dreamy island on which, in the shade of broad tamarisks and high palms, a garden blooms, purposeless, solitary, while everywhere else the rich soil must nourish grain and vegetables. It is no poet's vision, but the work of a general who dreamed of yielding himself up to romance here once his desert wars and journeyings were over, of Lord Kitchener, whose epilogue to battle was cut off by a German mine. Close beside this island of Elephantine, his Pharaonic comrades had set out on their Nubian campaigns, and even then it was called Yeb or Yebu, that is, Elephant Island, after the ivory that the Nubians sold here, and perhaps after the colossus himself, who may once have appeared here. The Nile must indeed have been terrifyingly low for him to be able to wade through it to the island. But perhaps the god Khnum helped him, for he lived on Elephantine, and even formed the first man here on his potter's wheel.

At this point, just before the Nile valley at last opens out, the sons of the desert approach their river for the last time. Under the name of Blemmyes they did so even in ancient times and, like other frontier peoples after them, were always on the side of the strongest, defended Theban against Roman gods, later Isis against Jesus, and sought with curiosity for the invisible Yahveh, whom Jewish colonists worshipped here. Perhaps Juvenal conversed with them, for even the first of the Neros banished men for telling the truth.

Even today they still emerge at sunrise from the tents in which Herodotus saw them living. Now they are called Bisharin, but their dislike of the Egyptian fellah is the same as ever: never will the nomad and the farmer, the bedouin and the peasant, understand each other, and even when they come into conflict—which can happen only here, for otherwise the bedouins live in distant oases—they can never stimulate each other like sand and water, the desert and the Nile, whose symbols they seem to be. The fellah lives in the most even temperature in the world; at night the bedouin experiences freezing-point in the desert and, like a professional boxer, goes nearly naked or wrapped in thick cloaks.

How should the eternal wanderers, always living dispersed, never in masses, understand the teeming crowd of men who never leave their fields? Changeful as the stars they believe in, their way is scattered through the desert, and since they desire nothing that the world does not offer, they remain cold-blooded and apathetic, proud and still, breaking their haughty silence only at rare feasts. What should they learn from the fellah, whose long garment mocks their slim nakedness, and what could they learn from the water-torture by which his daily toil wins his bit of bread from his tiny field on the bank, since he loses for it freedom and idleness, Allah's greatest gifts? To all eternity the noble adventurer will look down with scorn on the man chained to his home, nor will he imitate him even if he grows rich—at most he will rob him.

When they meet in Aswân, where the nomad sells his camel to the peasant, taking vegetables and eggs in exchange, though they speak the same language, they are greater strangers to each other than two Europeans who cannot understand each other. It is the spirit of the Nile that separates them, the green of its banks, the struggle for its silt on the one hand, the struggle with wild beasts in bush and desert on the other, and through all the nomads' poverty and danger, they are, in their silent renunciation, happier all the same. As they stand there together, haggling over farthings, both very poor, and neither far removed from their own domestic animals in the demands they make on life, they still look like lord and slave. That is predestined by the law of freedom and the soil.

What may the proud bedouin think when, in the quarries near Aswân, the hoof of his camel strikes an immeasurably long block of stone which it strives in vain to step across? Yellowish-grey, streaked with red veins, still half nature, and yet nearly art, it has remained lying where hundreds of slaves hewed it out of the mother rock forty centuries ago; we can still see traces of the mason's hammer and of the wet plugs of wood with which they contrived to blast open the syenite. It was an obelisk, and lying there, fragment and torso too, still bare of the hieroglyphs which were to express the glory of Pharaoh, it looks like some servant struck dead at his post, who never delivered his last message.

In its muteness, the recumbent half-obelisk of Aswân reveals the fate that would have overtaken the Pharaohs had not a Frenchman of genius, centuries later, succeeded in deciphering their language.

8

OUT of water, says the Koran, Allah created all life. But Allah also created its antithesis, the hills and the desert, so that the elements should try their strength in contest, as man does. Therefore, for one last time, he cramps the bed of his beloved river that it may once more know temptation. From Aswân to Edfu, on a straight run of 60 miles to the north, the Nile breaks through a sandstone barrier which may once have confined its water in a big lake: the river is less menaced and oppressed than the valley. Both deserts roll undulating up almost to the river banks—the Arabian desert approaches it so closely at one point that the railway has to pass through a tunnel on the eastern bank; it is quite short, but unique, and the Swiss engineer who built it must have thought he had been transported by magic to Lilliput.

Thus cramped, the Nile flows on for some 25 miles from Aswân; there a new adventure awaits it. Conquering hands had already been laid upon it, yet they had controlled only its speed; it was not forced into pipes to create power or light. Since it has plunged through the sluices, it imagines itself free—and it may well do so, for a long time will pass before it is dammed again. But now, for the first time in its old, free life, it is compelled to serve: in the midst of its flow, invisible powers violently rob it of its water on the eastern bank. Four huge conduits attack it below the surface, sucking away part of its power, and close by, a chimney-stack thrusts its black shape into the blue. Beside the chimney stands a sombre shed, but beside the shed stands a bright temple, and between the columns and the chimney, everything is green with palms. Behind the palms, a deep green surface stretches away out of sight.

If its spirit can remember, the ancient river knows that yesterday all this was not here. It all hangs together, the sucking and the green, before it began; the great stretch of Kom-Ombo lay in yellow stagnation: it owed its flat extent to the two wadis that debouch here from the Arabian mountains—valleys that bear the eastern desert down to the river. As they passed by on the river, the engineers of the Pharaohs may have regarded such a plain, rare as it was, with impotent rage—it lay almost 50 feet above the river and hence was inaccessible; such stretches could be watered only if they lay directly on the river bank. There too the little town of Ombos had grown up, and nothing remained of it but the columns beside the chimney.

It was not the dam of Aswân that created this marvel, but with the dam, the thought came to Egypt that the Nile might be pressed into service too; only fifty years before, the pashas had shaken their heads when a Frenchman spoke of building a barrage at this narrow point to water the wide expanse. Even in 1903, when the dam in Aswân was finished, hyenas and jackals ranged about and killed each other in this flat, desert expanse.

Today a green province stretches farther into the land than anywhere else in Upper Egypt. Forty villages lie on the fringe of the green land, 40,000 men move about here among sugar-canes and bananas, grain and vegetables, and in the little town in the heart of this ancient desert, servants are hurrying about, secretaries are telephoning, the teacher struts in front of the children and the bank manager in front of his customers, and where yesterday the wolves howled, the muezzin, five times a day, utters his cry to Allah from his high, round balcony. Thirty thousand acres, which had sent their sand whirling up to the sky since the Arabian mountains came into being, which the heavy foot of the camel had rarely crossed, are green now, summer and winter.

Two silent, grave, dark men, in white shirts, barefooted, cross the machine-room, where the little, shining pistons throb without respite; the fly-wheels roar, the hemp-ropes hum, the manometers quiver in their glass prisons, everything glistens with delicate oiling, it might be some temple built to serve the old, sweating pipe that has taken the Nile prisoner down in the cellar, and with ceaseless movement takes it prisoner ever anew.

Out of this pipe, the imprisoned water has turned the yellow plain green, carrying up the silt of flood-time with it through the pumps. During flood-time, the pump has an easier time, for then the Nile approaches to within 27 feet: it need no longer be pumped, but can be brought up by pressure. Thus it has gone on, here in the Arabian desert, since the machine was brought by the Swiss from their mountains thirty years ago; a piece of waste iron rusting in the green looks like a fragment of an obelisk, so quickly has it weathered in the artificial moisture, and the name of the Swiss firm on it might be hieroglyphics, whose meaning is only to be guessed. Looking at a driving-belt standing still, we see on this modern mummy-swathe on the banks of the Nile the name of the Swiss town of Schaffhausen.

But the black belt on the machine is made of camel-hair, and there is no need of coal. For the fuel used out here to make 30,000 tons of sugar from the sugar-cane of the ancient desert consists of the leaves of the sugar-cane. Thus children unite to press the life-blood out of their father, and burn themselves in the process. And there are children too standing beside the men not far from here, plucking the leaves from the cane, which looks sere and yellow as straw. The canes that now appear, some yellow, some red, are laid beside the leaves that are still green, which are used as fodder for the buffaloes. The whole is loaded onto gigantic shapes, which may be carts, machines, or even animals.

Those swaying shapes, so overladen that it is hardly possible to believe a living thing is there, are camels; even their legs and necks are not immediately distinguishable under the mountains of yellow sugar-cane straw. The little open trucks of the narrow-gauge railway also carry it out of the field; then it is piled up in front of the open boiling-shed in ragged stacks, and while a dozen men rake heaps together, four others stow these heaps into the burning maws of the boilers, where they vanish as rapidly as if the boilers were elephants' jaws. Thus the Nile feeds itself, while men force it to serve; its water has made the sugar-cane grow out of the desert; now the sugar-cane heats its water, so that it may itself drive the pumps that live on it. Thus great spirits are despoiled, yet pass on their way untroubled.

A few steps from the chimney the columns rise. The situation of the temples of Kom-Ombo, built under the Ptolemies as late as was Philæ, is as beautiful as that of Sunium in the hills, and far more beautiful than that of the confused old temples of Karnak. During the last hundred years, the Nile, in high floods, has swept parts of them away, making them still more romantic. And yet the eyes always wander away even from the ten splendid columns of the propylon with their leaf-capitals to that chimney which, hideous as Hephæstus, once brought to birth the lovely green background of palms and bananas. And when, in the third court, we see the "New Dionysos," the god-king who built this temple to his own glory, commanding a hawk-headed moon-god to inscribe the royal name on a palm-branch; when we read, here as in other temples, how the kings glorify their own conquests, we know that these sons of the Nile, with their sense of reality, would certainly have had the chimney painted too, and adorned with the key of life, if their engineers had invented the pumps and increased their fruitful lands.

This Faustian plain is never repeated. The mountains crowd closer and closer, without affecting the floor of the valley— twelve miles farther on, the Nile reaches its narrowest point: in Silsileh it narrows down to 260 feet. At this point, where it seems to have stopped in ancient times, forming a lake, it has, in the course of the centuries, gnawed its way through, forming rapids so narrow that for a time this point was believed to be the source of the river, and religious rites were performed here. According to a later legend, a chain here crossed the Nile. The rocks become yellow; the Nubian sandstone yields to the lime- stone of the desert mountains, out of which blocks were hewn for the temples. This region is so cramped and so poor that only one-seventh of the western bank from Aswân to the rock-barrier can be cultivated. These are the last narrows on the Nile. The western valley slowly widens, and then, some distance farther down, sinks into a little plain. Here stands the temple of Edfu.

It is the finest that has been preserved on the Nile; if it were not built of sandstone, it might be compared with the temple of Segesta in Sicily. For what can the fragments of Sappho or He- siod, or the colossal columns of Thebes mean to us, now that their forms have been so diminished by loss and collapse that they can be completed only by comparison and imagination? The romantic beauty of a torso, akin to that of a fragment, yet different from it, may, like a dream, transcend reality, yet only as a dream does. In this clear, burning light, half-ruined buildings rise from the blue and yellow landscape of Egypt with the horrible hideousness of mummies; even the impressiveness of the pyramids is due to their wholeness. Edfu, a thousand years younger than Thebes, built half in Greek form by Greek hands, in no way classically Egyptian, is all the same the loveliest of Egyptian temples today because it is perfectly preserved and because it stands in solitude: the same reasons bore Pæstum and the Peloponnesian temples into immortality. In our impression of buildings and of men, how can we neglect the landscape, the light, in which they appear to us?

The temple of Edfu, completed in the second century B.C., has come down to us in more perfect preservation than any Greek temple with the exception of the temple of Theseus in Athens, whose situation is commonplace. The high shoulders of the two pylons, which come into view from a considerable distance on the river, were adapted by the Ptolemaic master-builders to the ground-plan of the old temple in which Horus was worshipped here, for here, or a short distance downstream, he is said to have killed his brother and the murderer of his father Osiris. Even the heavy-laden camel mounting the short road from the Nile is Egyptian, and it is the *sakia* that whines its dirge close by. And it is Horus himself whose cry pierces the blue overhead.

Out of the sun, the ancient Egyptians bore their gods into the darkness, and the worshipper too, having passed the two great towers, moved out of the blinding light of the forecourt into the dimmer light of the first hall, then into the twilit hall of columns, then through a second into the total darkness of the sanctuary, or at least to the gate of the recess: within that the divine image rose in black marble. To find this image of the sun, the worshipper had to leave the sun, like the artist bearing the piece of the world he has seen out of the light and noise into his quiet cell to form its image there.

This great crescendo of shadow, swelling from the exterior

to the interior by means of diminishing skylights and wall-openings, the ever-closer ranks of the columns, the absence of any object built or placed in the temple which might diminish the majestic void, the darkening of soul of the man blessed by the sun till submission overcame him in the coolness of night— nowhere in Egypt has all this been preserved to our day in such compelling form as in Edfu, where from the outer walls of the court to the huge black sacrificial stone in the holy recess, everything is standing as it has always stood, and can stand for a thousand years yet, braving the only element around it—the sun.

The only sufferer was that late Pharaoh who, seeking to equal his great forebears' megalomania, had himself portrayed on the walls bigger than a hippopotamus, for still later Arabs, and Christians too, perhaps, seeking a refuge here among the heathen, drove huge holes in his body so that they might live in the cool corridors of the Horus who, after all, meant nothing to them. The roof overhead is blackened, and when foreign science and romance had driven the real heirs of the builders out of the temple, they left nothing behind them but the smoke of their fires. The holes scratched in the wall at certain places, which are still a subject of dispute among Egyptologists, clearly date from yesterday, for on the new bridges, the boys at play have made the same oddly antique cracks by sharpening palm-nuts to make tops.

On the steps an old lamp is smoking, its dim light alone guiding our stumbling progress, but on the roof it suddenly turns ridiculous, along with all the gods, snakes, and Pharaohs down below, for the light rolls and thunders over the huge flat roof of the temple. Now it is seen to stand exactly on the line of demarcation between the desert and the Nile valley, and the symbolism of its situation becomes still clearer.

At the entrance to the court below, the giant falcon Horus sits on its left foot, in the attitude of command, yet much more man than god; combining his gravity as a watchful bird of prey with his power as a son of the gods, he seems to be resting as he stands there in blue granite before his temple, crowned with his double crown. Can he hear the living falcon's cry? Can he see the shadow flitting along the walls of the court cast by the passing falcon flying low? It is striped with white, but the space within its wings is black, and so it flashes and darkens past, but, seen from below, it is pale blue like its stony image. It screams, for it is flying back to the Nile; it seems to be seeking something there.

9

BETWEEN the palms, two pylons rise out of the green. They may be ancient, but they are so small that they might be the model of a temple rather than a real one. Instead of growing bigger as one approaches, they shrink, for now they can be seen for what they are—these curious half-turrets on the fellah's house are dovecots. Still on green land, yet far away at the very edge of the desert, so as to take up as little fertile land as possible, a village stands—any village in Upper Egypt, the village which is the true, beloved home of the fellah.

The curiously unsteady look of the grey and white windowless walls—for it is the grey mud of the Nile that has made the houses here too—the cramped space within the village and the noise, the multitudinous clear, echoing sounds of men and beasts, the absence of any clatter of machinery, the sweetish smell rising everywhere from burning cow-dung—all this gives the stranger an impression of an organic, soft, and animal world, of a whole which has grown out of natural instincts. We can smell, hear, and taste the Egyptian village before we enter it.

In the early morning, the narrow streets are already swarming. Waiting at the coppersmith's door, the frisky donkey kicks its heels now and then, but its master is bent on selling the blue linen he rolls from the creature's back, and the smith does not say no, for he is no niggard, yet it will be a long time before he says yes. Time will pass, perhaps he will first hand himself over to the barber, whose brass shaving-dish he has made, and who is now shouting his way through the street in trailing slippers. There is no need to shout, for his regular customers are all around him, and they pay him for a year's shaving with a basket of beans or lentils. Happier than all three are the children and the fowls, playing on a heap of dried Nile mud, and the old man sitting on the ground close by telling his beads—whether they are Christ's or Allah's there is no means of knowing from a distance—and perhaps even the beggar who rides up on his ass dismounts to beg, counts his takings, then remounts, mumbling.

The village is swarming with all kinds of animal life. Fowls of every description strut about with the self-importance of army officers, as though the world were revolving round them, and we begin to understand how Egypt can export 200 million eggs a year. Dogs, which are regarded as unclean, are borne down by such a judgment like badly treated human beings; they turn vicious, and revert to the jackals from which they came. Is it the dog's fault if he grows dangerous, and what has the red and yellow cat done that it should sit blinking in the corner, plump and domestic, following the vagabond dog with its eyes, half in fear and half in contempt? The pigs belong to the Christians, but who knows behind what white wall the Moslem, flouting the hygienic precepts of his prophet, exchanges a good piece of his beloved mutton for a Coptic ham?

How the donkeys bray in such a village! That is part of their happiness, like the scolding and quarrelling of the women round the well in the middle of the village, out of which a whining water-wheel draws up the ground-water. They are disputing whether a neighbour will have any more children, for another neighbour gave her oilseeds the day her last was born; then they turn to the onion-seller, whose shouts are echoing through the village, and haggle over the price. If they lower their voices, they are probably speaking of the wealth of the quiet-looking man squatting in the open door of the café, smoking his *nargileh*, his water-pipe, whom no one would notice if it were not that under the sleeves of his grey cloak the splendid green and yellow stripes of a silk garment peep out, which must make him look like a caliph. His green turban shows that he has been to Mecca, perhaps only to get the right to wear it. If he looks across at the women, they draw their veils closer, especially over their hair, which is considered more provocative than their faces.

Now a great screaming is set up: a donkey, with a load six times the width of its body, has upset a pail into which a woman was milking her buffalo-cow, because the buyer in the street wants to make quite sure with his own eyes that she puts no water into it. The whole of the traffic stops, men and beasts crowd round, while a shadow falls upon them from a mysterious shape behind; with a heavy, high load of grain, unrecognizable at first sight, a camel has come along, stretching its gaunt neck like a skinny old Englishwoman sitting bejewelled at the opera. Now it has caught sight of a cactus at the edge of the street, and munches with composure, surrounded by the din of the impatient crowd. Into the general screaming another sound falls— it is the muezzin intoning the second of his daily calls from his high balcony.

But now the whole crowd suddenly turns to the other end of the street, for the fortune-teller from the town has made his appearance, and comes riding through the village on his ass. Now the women crowd round him, touching his silver amulets, scarabs, cats, and the images of the Madonna and Isis—he is equipped for all religions—lay them in the dirt, jump over them, kiss his robe, and anyone who can pay gets the seeds of the male palm to drink, so as to outwit the malice of other women, who are trying to prevent her having more children.

The house to which the young woman returns to cook—most likely the man built it himself—is surrounded by palms, and has a few pretty, shady straw seats outside it, for here all life, work and play, goes on in the open air. Here somebody has painted a pathetic camel, with the railway beside it; it is not the fine white train they see flitting four times a day along the Nile, but the curious old-fashioned one their father took on his pilgrimage to Mecca. There are fragments of blue earthenware let into the two turrets of the house: the pigeons like them, they stay there and give the precious droppings for which they are kept, for cow-dung is used for fuel.

The cool, dark single room inside is not a protection from the sun, but only from the night; low beds of mats and skins, copper pots, wooden dishes, earthenware pitchers, are there, and the thick smoke of burnt dung, for the light roof of dhurra-straw seems to obviate any necessity for a chimney. The dung has attracted dogs, fowls, and cats, and when the children are not at

school, they most likely roll about with the animals in this fetid
gloom.

In youth, the fellah woman is finely built because she is
healthy and cheerful. With broad shoulders and firm breasts,
her hair elaborately dressed and her face carefully painted, already a woman at thirteen, often married too young, in spite of
the law—they are quite ready to add a year to their age in front
of the cadi—a mother, too, before her time, her thoughts turn
solely on her sex-life, the more so because of the sun and the
fruitfulness of the land. But fertility is not everything. Jealousy
and passion never sleep, there are murders and poisonings for
a man whom one is bent on having and the other woman will
not give up. It is not only for the sake of money that the Mohammedan is nearly always monogamous. The sexual side of
life, like the Nile flood, is discussed in leisurely breadth with the
physician and the fortune-teller, as well as in the naïve instruction they give to the little girls. But as the moral level stands
much higher here than in Western Europe, for instance, divorce
and marriage are urged in every salacious case, and the law-
courts ring with them. Neither is eternal, for they can marry
each other three times before the Koran calls a halt, and even
then they can marry a fourth time if they have been married to
someone else in between.

As the soil of Egypt has, from time immemorial, bred superstition in all who were born of it, even the married man who
wants to marry his brother's widow—perhaps for the sake of a
plot of land—makes use of every known trick, and has his wife
bewitched by the fortune-teller to make her hate him. He hides
an egg, which was laid on Wednesday, inscribed with the name
of a spirit, in a grave, or pays the fortune-teller for some other
hocus-pocus, whether he is a Mohammedan or a Christian. The
surest method of getting rid of a wife is still sterility, and fertile
Egypt probably knows less of birth control than any land on
earth.

This attitude to sex works forward and backward, expressing
itself in great severity towards the girls and great reverence for
the mothers. A man's mother always comes first, even when his
own wife is grey—respect demands it. Little girls cannot go out

without their mothers; even a widow resumes her maidenhood and cannot enter a room alone with the men. It can still happen that a mother takes her erring daughter out into the desert and cuts her throat, or that a brother kills a loose-living sister. But a legitimate birth, especially the first, is a sacred event. The wife has already hung gaudy prints of handsome men on the wall to contemplate; just before the birth, she drags herself to the Nile and takes dry mud from the bank to eat in labour. Her neck and arms are hung with amulets to make sure of a boy, or in any case of a healthy child. After the birth of a girl, the mother is unclean for her husband for thirty days, after that of a boy, for forty. It is not known whether this is on account of the greater importance or the inferior cleanliness of the male sex.　.

Then she suckles the child, like so many Norwegian peasant women, for as much as two years: she can be seen sitting in front of her house holding the suckling child on her left arm, in her right hand the pipe of the nargileh she is sucking herself. In Egyptian, the same word denotes the last feeding with the breast and the last watering of the grain with the water-wheel—*el-fitameh*, the weaning. If the woman is expecting another child, she hangs a silver date round the older one's neck as a talisman to prevent its becoming jealous of the younger. Round her boy's neck she hangs something wrapped in cotton—it is a tiny Koran, complete. If a child is thin, and does not grow, she takes it to the Nile on the first day of the flood, gives it cakes and dates to throw into the water, and makes it cry at every throw: "As thou growest in depth, O Nile, may I grow in strength."

Outside on the field, driving the water-wheel, sowing or reaping, her husband stands all day long, for "fellah" means one who works on the land. The Egyptian fellah has been famous from time immemorial for his health and strength, and even today, of medium height, squat, with thick joints, he resembles a Pharaonic statue as he stands naked at the shaduf, throwing water to his mate with a basket. On the field, in a blue shirt and wide, short trousers, with a cloak of brown goat yarn that his wife has spun, generally barefoot, but with a low, thick felt hat on his head, he is, in gesture and physique, the silent, serious peasant, guarding the field of his fathers through the centuries. His head resembles that of his domestic animals: a firm, oval skull on a powerful neck, the forehead broad and rather retreating, high cheek-bones, a prominent nose with a sunken bridge, black, glittering eyes under long, straight brows, a big mouth with fine teeth, the chin square and often shaven, the head shaven too— a whole without Negroid features, and not prognathous, like that of other Africans. His body resists the machine as energetically as his soul, which takes generations to change a custom.

The fellah has been poor since the Pharaohs. As he makes up twelve out of the fourteen millions of population, he actually represents the Egyptian people, just as the peasant in old Russia represented the Russian people; he is the one who matters to those who consider the happiness of this people and how it is to be promoted. We may well ask why the fellah has always been poor. Is it because he is stupid or lazy? He is not: he is hard-working and, in youth, quick to learn, but he was kept too long in ignorance, and not until yesterday was any attempt made to educate him. He may be jealous and superstitious, but he has a good heart, and instead of growing quarrelsome in the cramped space he has to live in, he is as friendly today as he has always been. He may be hot-tempered, but he soon forgets, and when he has killed his neighbour for stealing his onions, the tears he sheds for him are sincere.

But though he lives in a land that hardly needs the plough, he cannot spend his life in blessed idleness like his brothers on the Upper Nile or his co-religionists in other oriental countries. That is because of the water-wheel that he must drive, the basket of water he must throw over his shoulder: the Nile does not give him its fertility for nothing. At sunrise he is carried over the river with his mates to the shaduf, and every morning the same round begins again, under the same sun, and generally to the same song.

> O ropes of palm-fibre, arms burdened with water!
> For thousands of years men must work at the shaduf,
> To haul up the water that falls not from heaven,
>   O Salih Zabadi!

In the pitiless glow of the shadowless sunshine
We stand hauling water to make the field fruitful,
And when our heart bursts there is none that will mourn us,
　　O Salih Zabadi!

Even ploughing, when they must plough, takes all their strength, for although the furrow need not, indeed should not, be deep, the plough is still the primitive wooden billet with the iron nose and the long shaft for the pair of oxen. Then the clods are broken by hand, the seed is cast, and even today is often stamped in by sheep. The fields, however, are small; every six feet there is a sign; the land is covered with tiny squares separated by low earth dikes which they open in flood-time with a little hole, or sometimes simply with a kick.

And the reaping? Is it really easier than anywhere else? In winter, grain, beans, and lentils ripen; in summer, maize and rice, and cotton and sugar-cane; then in flood-time, millet, rice, and vegetables. As these three harvests coincide with seed-times, and even overlap, for the seed is sown in the Nile mud at the beginning of November, there are actually in some parts of Egypt seven harvests in fifteen months. But the toil of watering is as great as the blessing of the sun, for the implements are still Pharaonic. The grain is still generally cut with the sickle, then gathered into heaps, and piled onto the camels, who carry it to the threshing-floor, where the oxen turn the thresher; then the heaps are winnowed and covered with palm-leaves as a protection against the wind. It is a long time before the donkeys can at last haul the sacks to the cone-shaped granary.

And for whom? Until a few years ago, twelve million fellahin worked for two million rich men. Even in the troubles of 1919, the fellahin only demanded half for themselves. But the bedouins who could read no leaflets, and had heard no speeches in their oases, suddenly appeared on the fruitful Nile with the determined cry: "Share and share alike!" For the theories of bespectacled town-dwellers are reduced to simplicity when they issue from the hard throats of handsome, naked men on the edge of the desert. Today the masses are slowly beginning to move. Small proprietors are appearing everywhere who, given the density of the population and the fertility of the country, can

still work all their own land with their children: there are even
tenant farmers who can keep 40 percent of the profits. Every
proprietor must pay taxes for the smallest plot of land on the
river, $15 or $20 for each feddan. But the ever-growing population, which has increased by half in the last thirty years, consists today, as it has always done, for the most part of day-
labourers. Many are already working in steam-mills and at
steam-pumps just as in Europe, but the majority work like their
fathers, and, like their fathers, are generally paid in kind; then
man, wife, and children carry the father's wages home on their
heads.

What a commotion there is outside the law-court when the
fellah rides into the nearest town to save himself from being sold
up! Since Kitchener's time, his last five feddan cannot be
pledged, but anything over, and anything he has bought, down
to the bits of silver on his wife's veil, is snatched by the tax-
gatherer from the man who has not paid his taxes, whether the
flood has been good or bad. And now he stands in the shade of the
acacias in front of the stone law-court, which exudes the same
chill as everywhere else on earth, trying to explain his rights to
the clerk squatting at his wooden desk; but beside him, ten
others are doing the same to ten other clerks. For here, where
justice is harvested, there are the same teeming crowds as on the
wheatfields, and the patience with which the clerk pokes about
in his odd-looking inkpot betrays his indifference as well as a
certain wily capacity to think out simultaneously the case of another, richer client. Suddenly everybody squatting in the shady
court stands up, the judge has arrived, and they all crowd
through the narrow doorway to get first turn.

Inside, the judge, in full view of the court, dons a black coat
and a red scarf before mounting his high desk; in the first row,
the lawyers sit laughing and chattering with the same self-
importance, the same show of cynicism, as on the Loire or the
Thames, the Elbe or the Arno; but only on the Nile do both
lawyers plead together, accompanied by the two squabbling fellahin, and while all four press forward, as if it were easier for
the judge to distinguish what is said by four voices when eight
arms wave in front of his face, the usher tries to drive them back,

until there is a sudden silence, and the man with the scarf chants from his high desk: "Adjourned for three months."

The fellah is very tired when he reaches home, whether from sowing, from the water-wheel, or from the law-court. The bread his wife sets before him is good—dhurra mixed with wheat, a sorghum flour which seems to preserve the teeth. He dips it into a warm mess of onions and butter, with cucumbers and horse-beans. He likes that, it is familiar, and because he has a good heart, he gives a cupful to the still poorer man lifting his hand towards him, for they are sitting in the street; even the cats have been waiting this long while. Onions at every meal, raw and cooked, lentils, and when he can get them, young vegetables—these are the things he likes, but his favourite drink is natural water—filtered, it seems to lose its taste—he prefers it with all its dirt. He believes in the Nile.

But how is he going to be relieved of his dirt, seeing that he and his fathers have lived in it for generations upon generations, that pigeon-droppings and cow-dung have rendered him faithful service, that he has shared his life with all these animals, and that rain has never come for 6000 years to wash man and beast, house and tools? He takes a generation or two to feel greater confidence in the healing power of the new hospital than in the old medicine-woman who strokes his aching limb with an ear of maize, reciting verses from the Koran the while, or, if he is attacked by trachoma, rolls back the eyelid and rubs a bit of sugar on it, or makes drops of onion-juice mixed with salt, or scrapes a wound with old shells and magic stones.

Creeds have vanished, the magician has remained. Perhaps this mist of enchantment is used as a foil to the golden light of an eternal sun. The fellah passes his life in the dread of the evil eye, and guarded by a hundred talismans which glitter on the necks of women, asses, and camels; in the evening the story-tellers come into the cafés where, with dramatic gestures, their right arm outstretched, their left hand, from time to time, curved round their ear as if they were listening to voices, they repeat what was handed down to them by their fathers but never written. In the reek of cigarette smoke, and the sweetish smell of the café, when the god has vanished in the west, there rise in cloudy vapours these stories of the night which shun the cloudless day. They are thousands of years old. It is told in the magic book of Thoth how once a son of Pharaoh dissolved the holy papyrus in water and drank it, thus absorbing all wisdom into himself; in the same way even today the Nubian cadi dissolves a word from the Koran which he has written in ink and, when a quarrel arises, gives it to both parties to drink to make them tell the truth.

But at all times, it is love and death which have enriched the life of the fellah with the greatest variety of superstitious forms.

The bride, however poor she is, comes riding along on a camel —today it is sometimes a Ford—then there is great merrymaking and a feast. The priest, even the Christian priest, lays a velvet cloth over the right shoulder and under the left arm of the man, then offers up a prayer, and collects his fee. Not until this chief ceremony is over does he remove the cloth, see that the pair slip the ring on their own fingers, and pronounce them married. At night, the dancers can see, and scare away, a troop of hyenas which have smelt the roast meat and crept up from the edge of the desert; they go on barking in the distance, while the jackals howl. Not until morning does the man go to the woman; he touches her with a stick he has made out of a palm-twig cut at the end. This custom is six thousand years old.

When a man dies, his shadow dies with him, for the *karin* or *karineh* is born with him, and is like him in form and nature. It fights with the *karin* of the other when their owners fight. Sometimes it grows vicious and creeps on him at night, so that he has to go to the sheikh to obtain protection from his own shadow. A bad-tempered woman's shadow can do harm to her own child if it is not over seven years old; a child over seven need no longer fear its mother's shadow. But when a girl is in love, she whispers shyly to her man: "My *karin* is good to me."

When a child dies, the whole house trembles to its foundations, sex and fertility feel the menace, all hurry to prevent worse happening. The child's soul, like that of every other dead being, is squeezed out of its mouth, but when that is done, the body must not be shrouded tightly, or the mother will bear no more children. Then an animal is slaughtered, loaves are fetched, and the priest, even the Christian priest, appears three days after the death and conducts the soul of the dead child out with incense. None of this is mentioned in the Koran or the Bible; it is, as it has always been, Egyptian.

Thus the life of the fellah rolls on, as it has always done, to the whine of the water-wheel, whether his happiness waxes or wanes, but he is always cheerful, and he owes his cheerfulness to the two gods of his country. They have made it fruitful, and his house is fruitful. That makes his happiness. He falls asleep to the champing of his ass eating its hard beans; he is awakened by the cooing of his pigeons.

KOM - OMBO

THE PHARAOH'S CRANES

10

ONE day, perhaps, he takes his little boy to see a royal tomb. The guide is a friend of his and lets him in with the other visitors. There the fellah sees, illuminated by electric light, what was once only to be seen in the fitful gleams of torches—frescoes in which the man who built this tomb had his whole life painted, his wars and his house, his dramas and his idylls, his wife and his children, officials and slaves, seed-time and harvest, hunting and games, and, if the grave has been recently opened, his tools, furniture, and utensils are still there. The fellah stands, his child's hand in his, silent beside the arguing foreigners; he cannot understand what the guide is saying in that foreign tongue, but he understands everything to be seen here better than the arguing foreigners.

There the fellah stands, amazed—so it is true, all that the sheikh and the magician and even the story-teller in the café have told him: it is the very same life! He bursts out laughing, and when he points with his right hand to the picture and notices that the boy below cannot see anything, he lifts him up and whispers to him the wonderful story shining there in front of them, and painted there thousands of years before the flight of the Prophet. For what does he find in this tomb of the Pharaoh? Everywhere he finds himself.

There is the shaduf, rising and falling on its hinge from everlasting to everlasting, to raise water—water—only that this shaduf does not creak or whine. All the land lies divided into strips between narrow ditches. The plough is a mere piece of wood guided by a rope; it has no iron nose yet, but there are the two handles, and there are the camels and asses too that he knows so well. Look how the boy is driving the sheep with a stick to make them stamp in the seed, while another entices the leader on with

grain. What are they doing there? Now look—that is the good
wheat that they are binding to the flail so that next year it will
be as good, and there is the priest too, receiving the firstlings,
just as he does at home. But why are they slaughtering the ox
there beside the new building? That is going to be the temple,
the one we take stones from when the watchman is not looking,
and they are making a sacrifice for it, as we do for the new steam-
pump.

The fellah is enjoying himself, nudging the child and pointing
—now to the other side of the same picture. There is mother—
can you see her?—weaving a basket of palm-leaves like the one
on the shelf at home. There are her wooden combs, there she is
painting her eyebrows, that is her veil—there the fellah is having
his own head shaved, and Ahmed is the barber. And now—oh
look!—they are mourning with unbound hair, the man is dead,
they are rending their clothes, burning incense—and there he is
again, the mourning Pharaoh, bidding farewell to his dead child.
And there—there is the shadow of the dead child, its *karin*. Suddenly the fellah feels doubly moved and presses his boy to him,
but then he laughs again, for there is a man, a clerk, branding
every ox, just as ours are branded, and there he is, writing down
how many sacks of grain he is giving us to sow. And now they
are pouring it all into the top of the granary that looks like a
cone, just like today.

How great were the possessions of the rich lord of the tomb!
The guide explains the inscription, and seeing the fellah's face
strained with attention, he whispers quickly in Arabic what
stands there. "Thou possessest 835 long-horned oxen, 220 horn-
less oxen, 760 asses, 974 sheep, and 2234 goats." Then the fellah
fetches a great sigh at the thought of all the labour, of all the
sweat that must run down men's backs till all these thousands of
beasts are cared for and fed. For the gauntness of the herdsman
driving the three fat oxen awakens a fellow-feeling in him. How
many horned oxen did the overseer say? There they are, with
the cowherd fattening them on dough—well, of course!

And the fellah gapes at the huge piles of grain on another
picture, and nods because even then they cut it knee-high, keeping time with their scythes, only that then one of them played

the flute to the reaping. Two sheaves are being caught at each end and tied in the middle, and now the troop of donkeys comes along, but even then the donkeys kicked against the load. How the boy laughs because somebody is pulling the donkey's ear, somebody else its leg, for that is what he does every day, and the sacks and baskets they are loading up are nearly the same as ours. Now one of them is beating, another pushing it, a third is watching to see that nothing falls off, but there is the clerk again, measuring, weighing, writing, just like the pasha's secretary from Cairo who lives among us.

They were good to the animals, these ancients, we can see that, for there among the fattened cattle the swan is allowed to have its share, and in the corner someone is even giving water to a crane. But what strange animals are these that the lord of the tomb has hunted? Lions and ostriches, giraffes and hippos—these the fellah has seen only in pictures. But the great men there sailing down the Nile with curtained cabins, reclining on skins, with girls making music and dancing—that is just like today. But what can they be driving up the fig trees there? What are those animals? The boy is quicker to understand: he laughs at the tame monkeys they have driven up the fragile branches of the fig tree to throw down the fruit. If only the painted figs were real!

Now the dream is over, all the visitors to the tomb are moving up the slanting steps to the exit, the little square of sky growing bigger and bigger, and when he stands again with his boy in the sun, which beats down on him today as it did on his father, the fellah is dazzled with all he has seen. It was almost too much for him to take in. How many horned cattle and asses did the lord of the tomb possess? Was he a Pharaoh or some rich merchant from the Delta? The fellah has a donkey too. It is tethered there, braying with impatience for home. Now, with its master on its back holding the boy in front of him, it gallops along the side of the road through the desert, while its master reins it in, for he has to hold the boy, and wants to think over all he has seen, and how the rich men, so many thousands of years ago, made the fellah serve them and sailed down the Nile in gaily decked boats.

If he wants to go to Luxor, the fellah has to pass the two monstrosities standing there in the sugar-cane field, which the sheikh calls Pillars of Memnon, though he calls them simply the bull and the cow. There they stand, the ridiculous monsters, the caricature of a Pharaoh who once sat enthroned there in front of his temple, with a few little ladies between his legs—probably his wife and mother, like Ramses up on the Nubian frontier. The fellah knows, and the colours show, that in flood-time Pharaoh must sit in Nile water up to his waist.

He has heard too that sounds issue from these statues but he would certainly side with Strabo, who was not going to be talked into believing anything, and averred that the sounds were made by his own men standing round the monument. Is it so hard to understand, he wonders, looking over at the sakia turning close by under the huge acacia. Who makes that sound? Not Amen-hotep who, in his Pillars, lost his immortality and even his name, not even the demigod whom Achilles slew, and who now sighs when Eos appears. What weeps by the pillars of Memnon is the old water-wheel turning behind the statue, as it turned behind all the Pharaohs' statues and temples, to raise water—water.

11

IN the green silence of the Luxor morning a clattering sound rises, sinking at intervals, then rising again, yet always soft. This river bank, where everything looks lush and moist, where the muddy earth can be smelt even when the foot treads the paved road, this luxuriant stretch where all vegetation seems to lie brooding in the silvery, trembling haze, is the true forcing-house of pleasure, more sultry, more enervating than any other part of the Nile. Is it the great tradition of the glory of Thebes, which, in these dark rustling gardens, in these white hotel palaces, continues to make life lavish of pleasure, as it was under the Pharaohs? Even if there were no huge columns rising close by, no wide gates, no endless avenues of crouching sphinxes, the stranger could not but place exactly here the site of the most brilliant epoch the Nile has lived through.

Here, for the second time, it sees men using it for other things than grain and vegetables, sugar and cotton; here it sees its water and its silt transformed into palm-gardens, as once before in Khartoum, the distant town on its middle course that it has long forgotten. Here, for a moment, it is no longer the condition of life for millions of men, but rather an element of luxury. It is like some great teacher who for once yields to poetic visions.

The penetrating, soft noise with its metallic clatter comes from the lawn-mower which the tall, white-shirted fellah is guiding over the deep-green surface with his dark-brown hands. For the soft, muddy soil which has been laid round the hotels, and the ceaseless work of pumps and pipes by which this luxuriance is created and maintained, has produced a neat model of a jungle, which must be kept within bounds by skilful gardening. Of the two gods of Egypt, the Nile alone seems creative

here, while the sun is rather the furious destroyer, and it is only
in the shade of the high palms that the flower-beds can deepen
to their richest colours. And just as Persian miniatures are separated from the roughness of the world by broad, costly frames,
these gardens lie behind high walls, but these frames are grey
and crude; they are built of Nile mud with *chevaux de frise* of
broken glass and cactus.

Here, where the foreigners indulge in the luxury they buy by
the day, they shun the spots where the sun shines in from above,
just as in dim cathedrals one shuns the harsh patch of light by
an open door. For from the shining, metallic rosettes of the
rhododendron, the dull purple of the bougainvillæas, from the
jasmine and oleanders, the light is refracted into the islands of
shade under ancient phœnix-palms: there all the colours sink
into a deep-green lustre, to scatter again in a scale of light and
dark greens.

Green is the colour of the Prophet. All the longing of the
desert wanderer is in it, the dreams of the nomad seeking coolness, of the pilgrim seeking in it the secluded quiet of his home
and the joy of his bed. The turtle dove of the Arab poets coos
from the mango tree, the hoopoe of Hafiz hops in the crackling
fan-palms; in the basin of the little fountain, rocking to and
fro, two wagtails are preening their wings, and in the golden
blue, Horus utters his brief love-cry, for below him the earth is
a garden, and above him the sky is a dream.

Outside, in front of the high mud wall, a young fellah is raising and shaking the leather band of the shaduf, singing the
while, three others are pumping and dragging hose-pipes about,
a fifth is watering the flower-beds. It is they who touch the wealth
of the lords of life, whom they see, hear, and smell all day. It is
they who watch the white lords and ladies, followed by black
servants, stepping out of the white train with the grey windows
that give protection against the sun, with the double blinds and
cream-coloured upholstery, who see them riding on their donkeys
to the temple, laughing, the women unveiled, and most of them
in breeches; it is they who see the white men and women em-
barking on the white launch, stepping close above the brown

hands which hold the wooden gangway from the lowest step to the ship's side, drinking coffee on board, ordering a slim native to stand still for a snapshot, or even brushing past a boy to feel his warmth with their bare arms; they see the women lying in their deck-chairs in the evening in silk garments worked with silver, beside the apparently cool gentlemen; lowering their voices, the women watch the sky to the sound of squeaking music —not that they know anything about it in the north, but they are looking for a new constellation to give them a thrill, for to them Egypt is merely one stage of that metempsychosis in which each was once Cleopatra, and is now seeking an English Cæsar.

The fifth fellah watering the flower-beds, who may be the brother of the one who visited the royal tomb today, and was perhaps summoned into the luxuriance of this garden life by the glance of a white woman riding past, is, in his turn, the distant descendant of another who, thirty-five centuries ago, watered the garden of some minister, summoned too to the power and splendour of life by a woman or some freak of fate. What did he see? How did the Theban Empire appear to this fellah, who served it in its flower?

There, at the same spot, the secheti, the Pharaonic fellah, stood under the ancestors of the same palm, listening to the noise of the great city beating against the walls of his gardens, for even to Homer, Thebes had seemed a glorious legend:

Thebes, where men's dwellings are rich, and rich the possessions,
Thebes of the hundred gates, from each of them riding
Twice a hundred warriors with horses and harness.

And yet Homer lived centuries after Thebes was in its bloom, and even Herodotus, four hundred years after Homer, saw here "nothing but a gigantic phantom."

But at the time when the secheti was watering the beds in the Vizier's garden, there was much coming and going, for on this part of the Nile the wealthiest metropolis of ancient times lay in its splendour. Through the noise the fellah heard two songs. Outside, where a few hundred of his brothers were hauling Pharaoh's grainsacks onto his boats, the men were singing:

All the livelong day we spend
Hauling sacks of spelt and corn,
Granaries are overflowing
Yet the sheaves must still be borne.
Sinks the broad ship in the river
With its heavy load of grain,
Though our hearts should burst asunder,
Haul and lift and haul again.

But when the raucous chorus had ceased, the fellah heard his lady, reclining on rugs in the thicket, singing her soft duet with her slave:

Drink till the senses reel,
    Pluck all life's joys,
Heed not thy neighbour's talk,
    Joy never cloys.

Yes, till the senses reel,
    Fill up the bowl,
Eighteen times brimming,
Till all my longing,
Nameless and burning,
    Is quenched in my soul.

The fellah listens in silence. He thinks more than his masters suspect, and secret papyri have revealed more of his thoughts to us than to them. Now he is feeding the water-fowl in the fountain, but his mates are already carrying along the little tables at which they will serve their masters and their guests from a big table. In the house the children are romping round their father, the dwarfs and fools too; dogs and monkeys are being held in readiness by slaves, so that the fun shall be fast and furious. In the evening, they all come to the pavilion, and between the house and the garden, laughter and feasting pass to and fro, and beer and wine and love.

For the wine from the Delta was rare, but beer, made of grain ground in stone mortars, then moistened, stamped in a cask, laid in a sieve, and kneaded till it dripped, was the daily intoxicant; it was kept in earthenware jars closed with plugs of Nile mud. The wine-jars bore little labels, the older vintages being more precious, and the labels read: "Good"; "Twice good"; "Eight

A PHARAOH

A CANAL IS DUG

times good." All the jars were decorated with the lotus, so was the table, and the women put lotus-flowers into their hair for the men to smell. Sometimes even a woman would vomit up the wine. Perhaps Aristotle was thinking of accounts of Egypt when he wrote that those drunk with wine used to fall forwards and those drunk with beer backwards.

As they sat there at the edge of the garden on gaudy papyrus mats, among braziers on which squatting cooks were cooking, first fish, turning them on skewers stuck into the fishes' tails, then a goose, the favourite dish of the Egyptians, then a quarter of an ox, and when, with the rapidity of these latitudes it had turned dark, then, before these great lords and finely dressed ladies, in the dim light of little oil-lamps, half-veiled dancing-girls and naked youths posed and danced and distributed perfumes to the endless melody of lutes, of seven-stringed harps, and of double reed-flutes. There the rich women lay in the filmiest of garments, which were held about them by shoulder-straps only for as long as they wished. They were always anxious about their hair, for it had been waved and dressed for hours, fastened with combs, treated with strange ointments to prevent its turning grey, rubbed with hippopotamus fat, and dressed with the essence of an ass's tooth powdered in honey, for they knew, or at least believed, that Eros dwells only in the hair, or at most in the eyes; therefore they painted their eyelids green and their eyebrows black, drawing them outwards to make the eyes look bigger and brighter.

All this was going on between the twentieth and tenth centuries, between Abraham and Homer, while the rest of the world, with the exception of the land of the two rivers, was in a state of barbarism.

12

THIS love of life, sustained by physical vigour, enhanced by perpetual imaginings of death, by bodily health and a countenance radiant in the glory of the sun, in the blessings of the Nile flood—these were the things the ancient Egyptians demanded of life, these the powers they brought to its living. And yet these things represented the limits of their feelings and their thoughts. Just as the Nile created a narrow, luxuriant valley, with the desert stretching to infinity beside it, these dwellers on its banks could not but yield themselves up fully and luxuriously to the joys of life, only to come to grief in that borderland where twilight leads to deeper knowledge. Beyond the sap-green of the oasis, beyond the creative power of their physics, where metaphysics begin for those peoples less blessed by the sun, arid deserts lay for the ancient Egyptians: the ardour of their cult of life is the premiss of their cult of the dead. A land without shade becomes a land without philosophy.

Hence it is not difficult to understand why a people that solved the greatest problems of invention, that even made the greatest invention of all, namely writing, that maintained its state not by war but by science, all the same won from their writing and their science nothing that could lead beyond time and space into the unknown—no moving poetry, no epic, no true religion. Once these limits and their logical necessity are admitted, we can have nothing but admiration for the achievement of Egypt in the dawn of national life.

Now that it has been made possible for us to read the documents, the native vigour of this people unfolds before our eyes in all its splendour, and even though it was only the great, the few, who enjoyed that life, it must not be forgotten that no form of social equality was known to man fifty, forty, and thirty centuries ago. Moreover, the slave-borne state was more logical in Egypt than among the later Greeks and Christians, whose moral doctrine stood in direct contradiction to it.

What generations of death-defying souls! When Ramses II was over eighty, he celebrated his rejuvenation at the feast of Set, repeating it yearly till he was ninety and more, and displaying his power of rejuvenation to the gods above in the obelisks he regularly erected as a memorial, which the aged Pharaoh decorated with electrum at the top so that their brightness should pour over both lands of Egypt when the sun was mirrored in them. When Mycerinus, one of the earliest of the Pharaohs, learned from the oracle that he had only six years to live, he defied that divine injustice by spending all the two thousand nights left to him in riotous living, and gave the gods the lie by living twelve years in that fashion.

And the physicians! The body that had to be preserved at all costs was studied in the earliest times, the foundations of anatomy and pathology were laid, a specialist was trained for every organ, and perhaps nothing about the Egyptians so impressed Herodotus as the fact that they were the healthiest men he had ever seen, with the exception of the Libyans, for he enumerates all the surgeons and all the purges, all disease being attributed to food, explains their health by the even climate, and again exclaims: "And the whole place is swarming with doctors!"

When these Pepis and Ramses boast of having lived ninety-five and a hundred years, when we read that one reigned for ninety-five years, the longest reign known to history, these figures, like those in the Bible, are not merely probable: they are recorded of men who remained hale till the end. Ramses the Great left, officially, one hundred and eleven sons and fifty-nine daughters, but in view of his harem, the figure is most likely an underestimate. And even in the midst of the countless intrigues set on foot among the waiting sons and grandsons of their hate-ridden wives and daughters, they managed to evade assassination; except for the great revolutionary, hardly one was murdered by his court.

They were not afraid. In the campaigns undertaken by a number of Pharaohs, they must have played a personal part, not because their inscriptions say so, but because then, and for a thousand years after the last real Pharaoh, the duel of kings was sanctioned and even prescribed by custom.

Even on their hunting expeditions against the wild beasts that have now vanished from the Lower Nile—for it is the life of the animals, not that of men, which has changed in Egypt—in the fight with the hippopotamus, which was stabbed with little lances, there were moments of physical danger, when not a hundred Nubian slaves could save Pharaoh if the huge creature attacked his boat. Crocodiles, decoyed by pieces of pig's back, then killed with a kind of harpoon, carried off arms and legs in its death-struggle, and when a Pharaoh boasts on his epitaph of having killed one hundred and eight lions, it is only the number that is exaggerated, after the fashion of hunters. Afterwards, the slaves would cut open the bodies of these Nile animals to see what they could find in their hard stomachs, and there is a later record of one fortunate who bought a dead crocodile and was made rich by the undigested jewellery of its victims. Just as in the tales of chivalry, there appear in the biographies of the great, which the tombs of these men really are, men who have slain lions and giants and won gold and glory by it. They set up their trophies everywhere, and even their silver table-ornaments reproduce the rare animals of the Nile and the desert.

Having thus given proof of their courage and cunning, they settled down to their wine and their beer, enjoyed the acrobatics of beautiful dancing-girls, or had a boat on the pond in the garden manned by "twenty women with the most beautiful breasts and backs, none of whom had ever borne a child; they put into their hands twenty oars made of ebony and gold, the handles incrusted with gold and silver, then cast twenty nets over the rowers." At the same time, a wooden mummy in a coffin was carried about, while a poet, a slave, sang to them.

> The body fades, its pleasures pass away.
>   Some are yet with us, others gone before.
> The pyramids enclose the gods of yore,
>   And those for whom thou mournest, where are they?

The great and good, who westward took their way,
   May not return to bring us tidings thence
To soothe our troubled hearts, which must pass hence
   By that same road the sun takes with the day.
Then laugh with us and cast aside thy sorrow,
   Put on fine linen, crown with myrrh thy head;
No man can take his pleasure with the dead,
   Rejoice today, for death has no tomorrow.

But this joy in life, which consists, on every painting, in every record, of wine, woman, and song, was never spiritualized by these great lords; draughts was the most spiritual form of amusement they achieved, and all the great things done by the priestly scholars were created and admired only for the sake of the state. It was the architect and engineer who became rich and famous, not the thinker or the poet. To have many wives, to beget many children—that was the goal of their lives. One Pharaoh was presented with three hundred and seventeen foreign women for his harem; another even set upon the head of his doorkeeper's daughter the uræus serpent, that is, the crown, for as long as he found her amusing; and on a relief of Ramses III, showing him with his harem, he and his women are clad only in sandals and necklaces. The same naked women later conspired against his life.

As the women, however powerful they were, could keep no harem of men, they made up for it by all kinds of natural, or, as Pindar relates, unnatural arts of love, although they exposed themselves continually to the danger of death in doing so, for a double morality, even then, threatened them for the very pleasures that good form made incumbent upon the men. The loves and marriages between brother and sister, in part imitations of the theocratic marriages of the Pharaohs themselves, hint all the same at perversion. In many legends the unfaithful wife is killed and cast to the dogs, and when the wife of the great magician Ubaner was frivolous enough to underrate not only her husband's sexual power, but his magic powers too, he had her lover eaten alive by a crocodile specially trained for the purpose, reserving for her the relatively urbane method of burning. Even then—this was in quite early times, under Cheops—feelings of revenge towards a wife's lover seem to have been more pleasurable than those towards the wife herself.

With the refinement of court life, the influence and intrigues of the women grew: they forced on new marriages in order to remove women who were their enemies, bastards were preferred before legitimate children, and the living memory of a single night could decide the succession and hence the fate of the kingdom. Often they worked hand in glove with the priests who, during a procession, would suddenly cause the statue of the god to flash fire—and there the bastard stood ready to become a Pharaoh, as the husband of a woman of the Pharaohs.

Later, there supervened an Egyptian Rococo, in which it was the fashion for the maturer women to intoxicate their lovers, or address them thus:

> Come with me to sunny waters;
>   Through my clinging robe so bright,
> Wet with oil and wreathed with garlands,
>   Gleam my limbs for thy delight.
> In the pool the goldfish glistens,
>   See, I hold it in my hand.
> Come, oh, come, the water dances,
>   Dive with me and leave the land.

But the youth, quite in the manner of some exquisite in an eighteenth-century court, longs to be the tiring-woman who disrobes her, or dreams himself into imaginary dangers:

> Far, far away my sister dwells,
>   The Nile between us roars,
> Upon the bank the crocodile
>   Lies opening hideous jaws.
> Yet nothing can my courage daunt,
>   I plunge into the Nile,
> And swimming, reach the farther bank,
>   And think of thee the while.
> Love's sweet enchantment steels my limbs,
>   But when thy face I see,
> I kiss thy trembling, open lips,
>   Drunk, not with beer, but thee.

13

POWER was the supreme form
of their happiness. The pyramid of state rose from the lowest
tax-gatherer, in a superb constitutional structure, to the apex
where the god-like Pharaoh sat. To be a stone in it, and to lie in
as high a course as might be, this was the desire that excited and
exacerbated their lust for fortune—that is, for gold and the reverence of the people, the two elements of power. Here in Thebes
where, a thousand years before the foundation of Rome, we find
assembled all the wealth of the Mediterranean peoples, whether
they were subject peoples, or visited by merchants; here in
Thebes, in the middle of the Egyptian Nile, where, even before
the year 2000 B.C., Upper Egyptian chieftains had usurped the
power over the whole land, in the dynasties of the Middle and
Early New Kingdoms there arose a hundred temples and palaces.
Round them were crowded storehouses, state workshops and
casemates, the villas of the rich and the huts of the poor, spreading to such a vast extent that we may assume it to have been a
huge city of a million inhabitants. But no house has remained,
not even a palace, for each Pharaoh had his own palace lightly
and quickly built for himself. Nothing has remained but temple
columns and tombs—the gods and death. The traces of living
men have vanished.

Everything required by this first metropolis of history was
carried by the Nile. From upriver the great sailing-boats brought
columns, bridges, and obelisks, granite and limestone for temples and palaces, while lighter craft carried birds, fish, and vegetables. From the Delta and Memphis, whole flotillas came up
with grain. Thus life went on from July to July, along the year,
in the perpetual round of harvests and labour, for what grew in
the neighbourhood of Thebes would just have sufficed to sup-

port a village. But now and then there came up from the Delta rare products of the Mediterranean islands, from the coasts of conquered or friendly states, from Cyprus and Crete, from Babylon, Syria, and Arabia, silks and metals, wine and fruit, while from the south came the Nubian woods and jewels, lapis lazuli and jasper, slaves and gold. But gold, the very source of their power and wealth, did not come only down the Nile from Ethiopia; it came up the Nile too, from the Delta, from Sinai, from Syria, from Tauris.

A thousand naked arms toiled through a thousand years at a thousand places on the bank merely to unload what the patient river bore on its back from the south with flood and current, only checked in its flow by sandbanks and islands, and from the north with the strength of oxen, camels, and slaves, and yet more slaves, towing the boats upstream so that the capital of the world might possess the wherewithal to fulfil the dreams of its lords.

They dreamed not only for their pleasure. If they were to maintain their power, to sustain their life, they had to feed all their dependents—not only the fellah, who bore everything, but thousands of prisoners of war, Midianites, Canaanites, Libyans, Nubians, who, though they were slaves, were foreigners too and hence unreliable; then came the hordes of scribes and reckoners, of officials, stewards, and policemen, who made the king's palaces safe, but ate them empty, and outside the countless herds of cattle, the thousands of oxen sacred to the god and hence to Pharaoh.

For he was himself the god, and in that fact lay the secret of the Egyptian Pharaohs. No contemporary king on the Euphrates dared to elevate himself to godship, as every king did on the Nile. A primitive period of clans with equal rights seems to have led to the distinction of the most capable or most cunning, who set up a holy of holies to himself and, with the help of privileged or terrorized priests, made himself High Priest. The last unarmed mediator between the people and the godhead having been abolished, the people could learn the will of the gods only from the strongest man; all he had to do was to divert supernatural power onto his own head and proclaim himself son and heir of Osiris. All this was introduced in the Old

Kingdom, even before the foundation of Memphis, and long before the year 3000, when Menes, who first united north and south, made his appearance as the heir of Osiris, king of the fruitful earth.

It is certain that Cheops, who built the biggest pyramid, was regarded as the son of Osiris, and at the same time as "Son of Ra," thus uniting heaven and earth. Pharaoh, as son of the god, having become priest and judge, war leader and magician, all springs and animals, plants and men, belonged to him. Thus in a land which had, in the earliest times, seen the bravest in the seat of power, but had required from him that he should render to his co-princes a half-yearly account of his spending, the very soil became the property of a god beyond control, and this determined the whole structure of society, even into the kingdom of the dead. What was not possible, not permitted, to the son of Osiris? Had he not read under the statue of his mother Isis in Sais: "I am all that was, that is, that shall be. No mortal has raised the veil that shrouds me." But he translated: "What pleases Pharaoh is just; what displeases him is unjust."

When the people threw themselves to earth before him as before the idol, when they counted it a special favour to kiss his foot instead of the ground before his foot, when the court, not daring to pronounce his name, said: "Obedience in the palace," or: "The god," or merely: "It is commanded," it was difficult for an heir, still more difficult for an upstart, to keep his balance. If Pharaoh's councillors wished to consult him about some well to be dug on a desert road, the Vizier would begin: "In all things thou art like unto Ra. The desire of thy heart comes to pass. If thou hast desired aught in the night-time, at dawn it is there. If thou sayest to the water, 'Flow up the hill,' the ocean bursts its bounds."

And yet the very Pharaoh who could not even fall asleep during this address would receive letters from friendly princes in Asia such as this: "Send me gold. Thy father sent me gold"; or again from his father-in-law, a distant prince in Babylon, wondering why he has received no gold: "All my other daughters, who are wedded to kings, receive my messengers and send me gold by them." Whereupon Thutmosis replied: "The kings,

thy neighbours, must be very powerful. But what are the possessions of thy daughter, who is here with me? Had she brought
me the veriest trifle from thee, I would send thee a fine gift now,
for I perceive that thou marriest thy daughters to thine own
profit."

So ran the correspondence between these sons of the desert
and the lords of the oasis, on tablets carried between them by
sweating runners.

Their theocratic dogma of royalty was superbly constructed.
But it was not the world of the real gods, which, beyond the
borders of real life, flowered and withered like the jungle. Creeds
and legends, the names and significations of the gods whose son
Pharaoh was, changed with the centuries, and, in the narrow
Nile valley, were given different names and meanings in different places at the same time. But as a general rule, the supreme
god was Amon-Ra.

The birth of Pharaoh, of a mortal woman, yet "of the Holy
Spirit," was invented three thousand years before the birth of
Christ. Up to this point, we can understand how the myth of
divine descent was used to work on the people. But it was not
the mere galvanization of some old, petrified priestly trick. On
the contrary, these upstart generals or petty princes who continually founded dynasties began to believe in what their sim-
pler, but shrewder fathers had used as a method of obtaining
power. There happened here what can happen only to men
without self-criticism, that is, without humour and philosophy—
they felt themselves gods, and their fathers and cousins, the gods,
gradually subsided into images of the Pharaohs. Priests to enclose
the whole process in religious formulas were speedily found.

Amenhotep III was probably the first to have temples built
to himself, and his *kà* worshipped in them during his lifetime.
The god Amon was made to give thanks to him, "his bodily son
and living pattern," crying: "I work wonders for Thy Majesty,
I turn my face to the south so that the great ones of Nubia shall
bow down before thee."

Thus their self-idolization went on through the centuries,
void of all reverence for their fathers, and even a Pharaoh who
was accounted so devout as Ramses II erased his forefathers'

names in the temples to put his own in their place. In poems, they compare the countenance of the gods with their own, so that men did not think and write of Pharaoh that he was like Amon, but of Amon that he was like the reigning Pharaoh.

14

IF the divine nature of Pharaoh was to be preserved in the eyes of the people, phenomenal stage-management was required. It did not need to go to the length of a victorious campaign: with the help of the priests, any of the frequent festivals of the year could be used to make the divinity of Pharaoh radiate in highly suggestive form. All that the kings of the Old Kingdom had done to create amazement was to gird on the tail of a lion and, thus equipped, to ride past in their manhood.

In Thebes, after the head of the procession, formed of captive slaves, priests, mountebanks, and all kinds of animals, had passed, the gaping populace saw a litter approaching along the avenue of sphinxes, borne by twelve soldiers, surrounded by men waving fans, preceded by outrunners who drove the people back with sticks and merely aggravated their curiosity. In the litter sat Pharaoh with a false, pointed beard, the golden uræus snake in his headdress seeming to rear itself on his forehead in defiance of his enemies, above it the double crown of both Egypts; in his hand he held the key of life and the whip, which, with Egyptian common sense, he used to keep off the flies. He was followed by the litters and carriages of his wives and the princesses, and a retinue such as that in *The Magic Flute.*

When the great royal barge sailed along the Nile, the huge sail skilfully fixed to the mast with strong ropes, Pharaoh sat under it in front of the cabin, while to make room for the cabin, the court, and the cattle, the rowers sat balanced on the boat's edge round the prow. At every festival, Pharaoh poured fresh life into the illusion, had himself gigantically portrayed on every temple wall, crushing his enemies, and when the Pharaoh was a queen, she glorified herself as a god-like figure, in all things divine.

We may well ask how many Egyptians really believed that such ceremonies were divinely appointed. In the Old Kingdom, simple people had revered in Pharaoh a god walking upon the earth, moving in the sight of the world, visibly rewarding and punishing. In the early morning, he robed, rode and drove abroad, inspected the quarry, ordered the building of canals, supped, slept like other men, and could even fall in battle, and yet he had eternal life because he was Horus, even when he himself was worshipping the god Horus.

But later, in Thebes, the constitution of the state and the priesthood was so complicated, and the knowledge of social conditions among the people so advanced, that Pharaoh had to lay far too much stress on his leniency, his care and responsibility for the people, and his services to the state, for everybody to accept him uncritically as a god. He seemed rather an open-handed monarch than a god when, on the day of the Nile flood, at New Year, he distributed silver chariots and his own statue in ivory, sphinxes with his head, armour and quivers, swords and mirrors of fine metal. And he was seldom a leader in war.

For in this oasis kingdom, war could not make history: the wonderful green Nile valley between the deserts, without rain and hence without neighbours, stirred the lust of conquest neither without nor within. It is true that the gold had to be brought from Nubia, and many things came into the Delta from the Syrian peoples. But for a very long time it was commerce that brought the oasis into contact with Asia Minor and East Africa, seldom war. In 2700 years, Egypt was only in foreign hands for 300. Ethiopians and Libyans possessed it for a short time only, and only in part: even the Hyksos, whose race is still a matter of dispute among experts, left little in Egypt except their war-chariot, the first to be drawn by horses, and the comic story of one of their kings who lived in the Delta, but sent a message to the prince of Thebes, high up the Nile, asking him to have all his hippos killed, for their roaring disturbed his sleep.

The three or four invading races left nothing behind, and Egypt's own conquests brought nothing of decisive importance into the country. Not even glory. For it was not the great conquerors, Thutmosis III, Amenhotep III, or Sethos I who made the name of Egypt immortal; only the historian still knows anything about the long struggles in which they penetrated to the Euphrates and to the Blue Nile. But the world still looks up with wonder at the temple columns of Ramses II, who, in his sixty-seven years' reign, made no conquests, abandoned Northern Syria to the enemy Hittites, and then made friends of them. Oases do not develop soldiers, and the lords of these oases recruited their armies from Nubian and Asiatic prisoners, who left nothing behind them in Egypt when they went forth to battle, not even the thought of the Nile.

In a folk-tale—a kind of school poem—the teacher tells the truth about the soldier as it was understood among the people. "And thou believest him to be happier than the scribe? As a child he is taken away and locked up in barracks, a blow on the stomach, another over the eyebrows, and he is already stupefied. Then they beat him out like papyrus. Shall I tell thee of his marches to Syria? He carries bread and water on his shoulders, like an ass, his back is bent. And the only water is foul. And when at last the enemy comes, he is like a captive bird, his limbs are like water. If he ever returns home, he is like worm-eaten wood, he is brought back on an ass, his clothes have long been stolen, his servant has run away. Therefore, O scribe Ennene, change thy saying and speak thus: 'The scribe is happier than the soldier.'"

The legend of the lion-headed war-goddess Sekhmet owes its greatness and its gloom to this dislike of war among the Egyptian people. Ra, being full of years, had sent her to earth to destroy mankind, which was plotting against him. She came and bathed a whole city in blood. But when Ra, in the morning, saw the blood-drenched place, he was appalled. "I will rather protect mankind," he cried to his servants. "Let all fields overflow with red, intoxicating drink." But when the war-goddess came, she mirrored herself in the fields, drank, and was drunken. Then she no longer knew mankind, and left it in peace.

It was not war that determined the history of this people.

15

IT was the Nile. The snake-like form it gave to the oasis made it difficult for any ruler to control, since the hinder parts could fall off like the snake's without the central organs being affected. In the attempt to put a stop to the endless warfare of the chiefs against him, Pharaoh sought to impose fear by means of his divine descent, and to secure control of the country by establishing a hierarchy. The mystic link with the gods and the realistic link with the bureaucrats became his instruments of government.

For in spite of all his power, which made all land and men his property, Pharaoh was in danger of losing everything between the Nile floods in the confusion caused by the element, unless he tamed it, distributed the water by canals, and hence increased the food-supply. All the forces that barbarian princes of other lands in much later times, and even in our own day, have turned to account in their raids and wars against weaker and richer neighbours, were refined into organization by the government of the Pharaohs. The Nile commanded them, thus early in history, to train the people not to fight but to till the land, to create not a military dictatorship but a feudal state, in which technique and science were invented to master the element, and in which the subjection of millions of slaves was sublimated into comradeship and mutual support. The Nile, for whose understanding the spaces of the heavens were mapped, for whose distribution the fields of the earth were divided and subdivided, strengthened, in the course of the centuries, both the mental power of the people and its desire for union in itself and with others.

When the fellah in Edfu saw the messenger arriving with the readings of the priest's Nilometer up at Elephantine, to have them entered for comparison on the king's tables, his confidence

in the wisdom of the government grew, and Pharaoh's claim to
be the son of Horus was still more firmly established by his skill
in forecasting the harvest. Pharaoh was bound up with the element, and the fellah watched with never-failing curiosity to see
how far it would obey him. "Pharaoh commands the Nile to
rise," the fellah heard in the temple, "and the Nile obeys him
at the dangerous moment when it is about to lose itself in the
abysses of the underworld."

Yet immediately afterwards, he heard the priest calling on
the god of the Nile in a very ancient hymn that had been preserved and written down in Thebes, and runs:

Hail to thee, O Nile, that risest from the earth, out of mysterious
darkness, to the light of day where men hymn thy coming: who
waterest the fields, whom Ra hath created to feed all the cattle, who
waterest even the desert, which is far from water, for it is thy dew
that falls from heaven. If the Nile is sluggish, men's noses are stopped
up, all men are wretched, the sacrifices vanish, millions die. If it
riseth, then the earth rejoiceth, every back laugheth, every mouth is
glad, every tooth is to be seen.

It is he that maketh the trees to grow and bringeth forth ships,
for none can be made of stone. Thou lavish one, who waterest the
fields and strengthenest all men, what man dare liken thee to the sea,
which bringeth forth no grain?

Comest thou in flood-time, we sacrifice to thee, slaughter oxen for
thee, fatten geese, snare antelopes in the desert, that we may make
thank-offerings to thee for thy loving-kindness. Therefore pray to
the nine gods. Fear the power that the lord of the world hath shown.
Thou art he who makest both banks to grow green, who makest man
to live of his cattle, and the cattle of the field. O Nile, thou greenest,
thou makest green, O Nile.

In this beautiful obscurity, the functions and symbols of the
gods are indistinguishably confused: a hierarchy of the gods
was alien to the Egyptian theogony, for they could not organize
the incomprehensible.

But everything rational, everything created by human skill
and political power, was built up into a superb pyramid. As an
element, the Nile was dark and terrible, but in the state it was
organized. Every basin was the centre of an agricultural province, every shire was dependent on its neighbour, every prefect

THE ASYÛT DAM

PYRAMIDS, SEEN FROM ABOVE

had to manage his water with a view to the next; all submitted
their petitions to the central organization, from which they took
their orders. Thus the Nile created absolute monarchy. It was
only when Pharaoh called himself the son of Hapis that he was
really the son of a god.

Hence of all gods, Pharaoh too feared Hapis, the Nile. On
the "Column of the Seven Years of Famine," one of the oldest
Egyptian inscriptions, said to be written before the pyramids, a
Pharaoh complains: "For seven years the Nile has not risen.
There is no grain, the fields are dry, no man buries his neighbour, everyone flees, to return no more, the children weep, the
young men faint, the old men wither. Their legs have lost their
strength: with folded arms they crouch on the ground." Yet if
the Nile rose too high, the disaster was just as great: therefore,
two thousand years later, a Pharaoh of the XXIII Dynasty writes:
"The whole valley is turned into an ocean, the temples are full
of water, and men look like water-fowl."

And yet even such a catastrophe rarely had the power to
trouble a hierarchy so skilfully constructed, for it was the most
astonishing organization known to the ancient world, and has
never really been excelled by the modern. It embraced every·
thing "that Ptah has founded and written in the skies. At the
top, the sun and moon and all the other elements, then the supreme beings, that is, the god and goddess, the king and queen,
the vizier of the king down to the officials in Thebes, province
and city, all men concerned with the temple, the law, finance,
and the army, down to the scribes and artisans, the engravers,
carpenters, and shoemakers of the king." Here the list breaks
off.

Such a scheme for the preservation of the state, stretching
from the sun to the shoemaker, and setting Pharaoh very close
to the sun to ensure his authority over a people of eight million souls, had certainly never been seen before in the history
of the world. Those who later regarded it all as a great example
were the born dictators. Here at last was a people that divinized
its kings, and it was not mere chance that led Cæsar and Napoleon to the sphinx. The first Greeks to approach the Nile ro-
manticized it; since then it has seduced all men who went there

into becoming Pharaonic, and the last of them were the English.

At the apex of the pyramid, immediately below the king, stood the priests. As a god, Pharaoh meant more than they, and prevented them from making themselves kings, as they did among the Assyrians and Sumerians. But they did not let him out of their sight; their power was often inherited in the direct line longer than was permitted to the Pharaohs by their changing dynasties, and they overthrew more than one Pharaoh. When Pharaoh, in the state of grace, moved to the image of the god his father, two priests held his hands, and when he looked up, two priests were holding the masks of the hawk and the ibis, representing Horus and Thoth. As the king knelt to exchange the ritual formulas with them, he was at all times under their spell, and when the most interesting of all the Pharaohs once dared to revolt against them, it was he who lost.

To amass great wealth, many cattle, and much land, was the passion of the priests; that alone secured them pleasure and power, for what poured into the temple and belonged to it was in fact their property. On lists such as are to be found in the tombs of the great Pharaohs, we read as priestly property in Thebes alone: 80,000 slaves, 420,000 head of cattle, 600,000 acres of arable land, 83 boats, 46 wharves, 56 villages, a hundredweight of gold, a ton of silver, 2½ tons of copper, 25,000 jars of wine and cider, 300 sacks of wheat, 290 birds. These treasures had been paid to the priests by the fellahin as the price of grain, and we still possess the receipts in duplicate. Goethe once wrote: "The priests managed their business as well in Egypt as everywhere else. They made a great to-do about the dead in order to keep a firm hand over the living."

For since they were in possession of all knowledge, being at the same time the real scholars and magicians, they were able, by means of mysteries, to use their power as a menace and their association with the gods as blackmail. Since the people, in a kind of Reformation, had developed the demotic script, the priests were at last able to stabilize all kinds of mysteries, and for some thousands of years they preached to the people the veiled image of Sais, under which, in the end, nothing was found but two crossed arrows.

At the same time, they kept control of the people by means of their school of medicine and their baths, by the sale of everything necessary for the burial rites and the mummies, by mass orders for statues—500 lion-headed war-goddesses for Karnak alone—and by their care of the sacred cats, cows, beetles, fish, and crocodiles, which were waited on by an army of keepers.

And above all by the festivals to which, in the New Kingdom, the cunning of absolute rulers lent a certain air of democracy, since the people were allowed to look, eat, and drink for nothing. When, at the greatest festival, that of the Nile flood, the sacred boat of Amon-Ra was carried about by a great procession of priests, preceded by the statues of former kings, with Pharaoh bringing up the rear, when thousands of lamps moved in fantastic night displays, and Pharaoh performed his symbolic washing with Nile water from Elephantine, the people, for a day and a night, thought themselves happy. But it was not the meat and the beer that had filled them with new hope in their life of bondage; it was the water, the Nile, that brought the flood they longed for, and approached the columns of the temple of Abydos as though it had come to carry off the ship of the god.

When the first waves of the flood reached Thebes and Memphis, when the canals were opened, the great popular festival turned into a feast of love, for the young men were inflamed by the idea that the Nile, on the opening of the canals, took bodily possession of its beloved, the dark earth. Under its influence, nights of love and marriages took place, and the young men sang:

> Light my bark upon the water
>   And my head is wreathed with flowers,
> Hastening to the temple portals,
>   And to many happy hours.
> Great God Ptah, let my beloved
>   Come to me with joy tonight,
> That tomorrow's dawn may see her
>   Lovelier still with love's delight.
> Memphis! full of sound and perfume,
>   For the gods a dwelling bright.

The maiden replied:

> Hear the holy waters flowing,
>   Ra is come, for all to see,
> But my heart is sick with longing
>   Till my brother comes to me.
> I shall see him when the waters
>   Hurry through the opened ways,
> Give him wreaths for wreaths of flowers,
>   Loose my hair for him to praise.
> Happier than Pharaoh's daughters,
>   When I lie in his embrace.

During the festival, the river, as the male element, was sym-bolically wedded to a maiden, as if to stimulate it to fecundate the earth. This powerful and primitive sexuality, suggested by the Nile, comes out in many a popular story. In the oldest representations, the Nile appears in two figures, male and female, but in such a way that the male too grotesquely represents fertility with its heavy breasts and flabby belly.

Sometimes, during the anxious period of drought just before the flood, Pharaoh came in person up the Nile to Silsileh, where the river seems to vanish in the narrows between the rocks. There he sought to propitiate the Nile god with gifts, particularly a white ox, and if he threw a roll of papyrus with magic formulas into the water, the river was certain to rise again from the earth.

All these festivals contributed to the priests' social and political power. If the officials kept in with the priests, it was because they wished to clutch at the fringe of divine descent, whose centre meant supreme power. From Pharaoh, through the priests, down to those who sat at the receipt of custom, everyone clung to the tradition of divinity, in order to receive a certain piece of every ox slaughtered in the temple, or a jug of beer on processional days. These thousands of sinecures made it necessary later to appoint beside the "Director of Appointments" a "Real Director of Appointments," a "Real Judge," while other court officials bore such titles as "District Chief of the Nile," "Inspector of Horns, Hoofs, and Feathers," "Chief Deputy Hairmaker to Pharaoh," "Privy Councillor of the King's Stomacher,"

"President of the Secrets of the Morning Apartment," "Chief Inspector of the Bathroom of the Great Queen," "Director of All Beautiful Diversions," or, in more monumental fashion, "Commandant of the Desert."

But the real driving-power of the great organization was the scribe. His office, such as we see it in a tomb-painting, with clerks weighing grain, drawing up reports, checking accounts, dispatching and making notes with a chief clerk looking on, admirably symbolizes the administration, and in it the recently invented art of writing was used to the point of absurdity.

About the year 2000, Sesostris had distributed the land among all Egyptians in little squares, and if the Nile washed any of it away, the owner had to go to Pharaoh about it. Later, in the great time of Thebes, this organization had given rise to hordes of surveyors, hordes of tax-gatherers and water-inspectors. Then there were departments for the temples, for the canals, for fishermen, wood-cutters, cemeteries. Even the demons who, at night, drew the sun-boat through the underworld were departmentalized. Endless lists seem to have been drawn up simply to keep the scribes busy; the chests of documents and rolls of papyrus in their cases multiplied; record offices which filled whole houses were thick in the capital; and in the popular tongue, the scribe was likened to the donkey-driver, for he drove the other heavily burdened officials before him at his own sweet will.

By that time the numbering of the people had so far developed that the scribe was the most powerful man in city and province. One of the last native Pharaohs, the cunning dictator Amasis, then carried bureaucracy and state socialism so far that he commanded every man to give an annual account to his local police of his means of livelihood. Anyone not showing a proper basis for his support was put to death. Solon, who later introduced something similar into Athens, is said to have taken the idea from Egypt.

State control of this kind, which is again being attempted today, is at best tolerable only in a community of free citizens; in a slave-borne state, or in a slave mentality, it means nothing but power seeking to maintain itself by terror.

16

WHAT had Pharaoh to fear? First, sickness, which could put an end not merely to his life, but to his power. The only reliable evidence that the priests killed Pharaoh so that his soul should pass to a stronger successor comes from Meroe on the Middle Nile; today such ritual murders are tolerated by custom among the Shilluks on the Upper Nile. After defeat in war or a bad harvest, he was in danger of being deposed; in the Bible he is held responsible for the seven years of famine under Joseph and for the plagues under Moses, and yet, in such cases, his overthrow always remained a matter of legend. What Pharaoh really had to fear was his people.

We do not know which Pharaohs they hated, which they despised, for what history of the Pharaohs we have was inscribed in paintings and words on the walls of temples and tombs, and on obelisks visible from far off to all the people, in accordance with the dogma of divine descent and for reasons of state.

In Egypt, where thirty dynasties succeeded each other in the course of three thousand years, that is, ruled on an average only a hundred years, in spite of the shadow-show of divine descent and the custom of slavery, the feeling of distrust towards those deprived of their rights must have lived deep in Pharaoh. Given their contiguity, the dependence of all on the same river and its yearly vagaries, Pharaoh on the roof of his palace cannot but have admitted to himself that everything the river brought on its back into his royal city had really been borne on the backs of the worker and the fellah, had been hewn by their arms from the quarry, cut and threshed by their arms in the harvest; he must have seen the sweat trickling down a thousand legs as they stood echeloned up the Nile dam; he must have said to himself that they could not but feel Amon and Hapis, the gods of the sun and the Nile, to be a torture and a burden, condemned as they were their whole slave-life long to raise water—water.

The peasant was distinguished from the cattle only by his food and his thoughts; as regards the former, he was worse off because, as there were more of him, he was easier to replace; in the latter he was free, yet of his real thoughts not more has been written down than of those of the Pharaohs. The foreign prisoners of war were in the same plight as the natives: their work on the Nile, on the land, in the quarries and the tombs, meant the same toil by day, the same exhaustion at its end, and was branded with the same bondage of a lifetime, even though the subject was not called a slave. Everybody was in a state of serfdom except for a very small intermediate class of merchants and artisans. Their way was the way of their fathers, and the practical impossibility of improving their status was overcome only in the rarest cases. "The boy is begotten," says a popular rhyme, "only to be torn from his mother's arms. When he is grown to manhood, his bones are broken." He bore branded on his arm the stamp of the administration, just like the cattle.

And the shaduf was not even the greatest hardship. In the quarries, which had to yield up their colossi without machinery, it was he who hammered the holes in the rock, and before the great block of stone stood in the sepulchral temple of Khefren, hundreds of arms had to work for a whole year, for, with its weight of nearly 50 tons, it was 15 feet long; two others supporting a temple roof in Faiyûm were 25 feet long, and many an obelisk more than 100. Every sarcophagus of black granite had been hauled by the workmen along the desert road on a kind of wooden sledge. On the knees of a colossal statue, which was dragged to the tomb with ropes by several hundred men, a relief shows the little overseer, standing, shouting, ridiculous, commanding others to sprinkle the road with water to prevent the sledges catching fire from the friction.

Whether, or how far, the field belonged to him, the fellah never quite knew. Was the local count, the nomarch, the landlord, or Pharaoh himself proprietor of his land and his service? Since it was he who, together with his kinsfolk, worked and founded a village, he could, unlike the prisoner of war, call himself free: he was not sold by law, but only by custom. We seem to grasp the fate of thousands when we read on a papyrus, in one of those pithy popular tales, how somebody described the fate of the fellah.

The worm has eaten half the grain, the hippopotamus the rest. There are mice in the fields, the locusts have come, the cattle have broken into the grainfield, the sparrows steal. What was left in the granary fell into the hands of thieves. The cattle have perished of threshing and ploughing. And now the scribe comes in his boat to the bank to gather in the harvest. Woe to the fellah! The officials have sticks, the Negroes rods of palm. "Give up your corn," they cry. If there is none, they beat him, he is bound and cast into the canal, then he sinks. His wife is bound before his eyes, his children too. The neighbours flee to save their grain.

What may the brickmaker have felt when he saw the mason chiselling the praise of some hated, all-too-living governor into a tomb? "I have mishandled no girl of the people, oppressed no widow, imprisoned no shepherd, taken no workmen away from their taskmaster." What did the fellah feel when he saw the scribe landing from his boat at the village and announcing to the crowd that for Pharaoh, who was shortly to pass that way, there must stand ready on the bank: "15,000 good loaves of five different kinds, 14,200 other loaves, 2000 cakes, 70 pitchers and 2000 other vessels, 1000 baskets of dried meat, 60 jars of milk, 90 of cream, and wood for the kitchen, baskets of figs and grapes, and flowers and garlands to deck his table"?

While they were listening to this, the workmen who were building the city of the dead of the same Ramses were striking to enforce the delivery of their food. Six months of their history, which have been recorded in state documents, show how they first waited patiently, then came and shouted: "We have been starving for eighteen days. We have no bread, no fish, no herbs. We have a great word to say—verily at this point in Pharaoh's kingdom evil will be done." In this way they had to force 50 sacks of grain a month out of the scribes and the police, while the same administration was delivering 10,000 sacks of grain a year to the priests in Thebes alone.

They heard how Pharaoh presented one of his wives with the

EVENING ON THE NILE

HOMING HERDS

harvest of a whole district to pay for her shoes with the taxes, how he gave another the yield of the wine of Antylles in the Delta to pay for her belts and bodices, and at the same time, for years on end, they had to feed in Thebes the flame in which a kind of bronze was being wrought into the gigantic wings of the temple gates, or drag a monolith of 300 tons down the Nile —two thousand men working for three years.

Sometimes pungent satires rose from among the people and were written down by some scribe to amuse his master.

I saw the smith at his fire—he has fingers like the crocodile. Even at night he works more than his arms can accomplish. When the stone-cutter has finished his work, he sinks exhausted by the side of the stone. Late in the evening, the barber runs through the streets to find customers; he wears his fingers to the bone merely to fill his belly. The boatman who takes goods to the Delta works beyond his strength, and the flies sting him to death. The weaver in his workshop is worse off than any woman: crouching with his knees against his belly, he cannot even breathe. The messenger bequeaths his goods to his wife and children before he goes away, for fear of the lions and the Asiatics. The shoemaker curses all day and eats his own leather. The washer-man bleaches his washing on the banks, but his neighbours are the crocodiles. The fisher is still worse off—he is still nearer to the crocodile.

But once the fellahin and the workers of Egypt revolted against their masters; once their resentment burst out: a revolution dispossessed the rich men and the priests of Egypt of their power. It lasted a long time, probably from 2350–2150 B.C., at the end of the Old Kingdom, long before Joseph. This revolt may have been provoked by the dictatorship of a cruel nomarch Kheti, or, as some authorities think, by the marriage of a Pharaoh to a woman of the people. In any case, the doctrine, then new, of Pharaoh's responsibility to the people, must have been at the bottom of it, since the priests, from the fifth dynasty on, had, Protestant-wise, shifted his responsibility from heaven to earth.

This is the only revolution in the history of the world of which we possess only the records of the defeated. At that time, only the hieratic writing existed, there was no popular script, hence the victorious classes could write no account of their victory, but the conquered priests probably did not dare to set down any facts even in their own language; thus only lamentations have been handed down to us which, with their parables reminiscent of the Bible or Arabian stories, roll on in grandiloquent rhapsodies, remarkable for their beauty, but remarkable too for the power of their movement; they need only be transposed from the minor to the major of victory. A priest of Heliopolis writes:

The land is lost, the sun has ceased to shine. The Nile is empty, thou canst cross it on foot, the wild beasts of the desert drink from the Nile. Enemies advance from the east and see the land in mourning and in pain. Every man murders his neighbour, hate rules in the city, every mouth that speaks is struck dumb. The words of others turn to fire in one's own heart.

An official writes of the rule of the poor:

The poor triumph; they cry: "Let us put down the mighty!" Every man wearing a robe of linen is beaten, men who have never seen the light are rising into high places. He who will work must go armed. The Nile is rising yet no man labours, for each says: "We know not what will come to pass in the land." The flocks wander without shepherds, the crops are destroyed, there is no raiment, nor spices, nor oil. The granaries are in ruins, their watchmen slain, men eat herbs and drink water. The women refuse to bear children. The children cry: "Why did my father beget me?" Men flee from the towns, and build tents again, for gates, walls, and temples have been burnt down. . . .

He who had not where to lay his head has now a bed. He who found no shade sleeps under trees, and he who had shade flees through wind and weather. He who had no bit of bread to eat has now a granary. He who had not the wherewithal to paint his face has chests full of perfumed oil. The woman who could see her face only in the Nile has now a mirror. The man who knew not the lyre has now a harp.

But the great hunger and weep. All that was in the pyramids has been carried off, the mysteries are unveiled. Pharaoh's revenues are no more, yet grain, fish and birds, linen, bronze and oil, and all good things belong to Pharaoh. Even the Vizier has no servant, for there are no more servants. Those who once had their tombs built by others now work themselves. Where shall we find the resin to purify the dead, where the oil to embalm them? The dead are cast into the river, the Nile has become a city of the dead. In the temples, the gods are cheated, for men bring them geese instead of oxen. Insolent mouths say: "If I knew where the god was, I would gladly bring him my sacrifice." No man laughs, and the sound of laughter is still. Ah, if this world were at an end, that there might be an end of noise and confusion."

This, the first and only revolt of the Egyptian fellahin in the course of fifty centuries, will always remain a mystery: only a few brick tombs of the poor, built into the fine sepulchres of the princes of that epoch, speak with tongues of stone. Whatever else has been excavated or deciphered echoes the voice of the defeated rich, and it is unique in its melancholy. But the heritage of this revolt can be seen in the changes that now set in with the Middle Kingdom, that is, with the first Thebans, roughly the XI and XII dynasties, about the year 2000 B.C. Princes and priests, taking warning by the catastrophe that had fallen upon their fathers, admitted the people to certain privileges, let them participate in the religious rites, began to paint their customs and scenes from their life in the tombs, and even proclaimed every man immortal who merely performed the customary observances, for by the plunder of the temples of Osiris the people had come into possession of his mysteries. By this cynical pleasantry, they placated the menacing forces, comforting those who were weary and heavy-laden, two thousand years before St. Paul, with the promise of resurrection in God, when all should be equal; to make it clear, they allowed the officials and even the artisans to build tombs for themselves and hence partake of immortality.

Only once in the history of Egypt was a revolution created from above. This was the achievement of Ikhnaton, the only Pharaoh whose life would be worth writing. Ikhnaton was that Amenhotep IV whose portraits move us even today. When he had raised the sun to be Lord of the world, he wrote this hymn to it:

Radiant thou risest to the heavenly hill of light, O Aton, who hast lived since the world began. Thou dost arise and lead the world in thy beauty. Thou shinest high over the land, thou dost embrace all thy creation, yet while thy rays linger on earth, thou thyself remainest far off. When thou withdrawest from us to the west, the earth grows dark as though its end had come. Men lie heavily in their chambers and if a thief steals from them what lies under their head, they see him not.

But when thou returnest, darkness taketh flight, both lands rejoice in thy rays. All men arise, for thou drawest them. They wash themselves, clothe themselves, then raise their arms to thee in prayer, thou radiant one! The country goes to its work, even the cattle in the pasture rejoice, fields and herbs grow green, the lambs skip upon their feet, the birds flutter up from their nests, they praise thee with their wings. All ways are open because thou shinest, the boats ride up and down the Nile, the fish leap in the river, for thy rays reach far down into the sea. Thou makest the child to grow in its mother's womb, comforting it so that it shall not weep, then thou givest it breath. When it comes forth, a son, thou openest its mouth, and bestowest upon it according to its need. Thou givest air to the chicken in the shell, and strength to break the egg: it comes forth, pecks, and runs away.

Great is all that thou hast created. The earth with man and beast, great and small, all creatures that tread the earth and all that fly under the heavens, the lands of Syria and Nubia and the land of Egypt, and thou settest every man in his place and givest unto him according to his need. Different in tongue, in stature, and in colour, thou hast divided the peoples.

Thou didst create the Nile in the underworld and lead it about the earth according to thy will to nourish mankind, thou Lord of all. In heaven thou settest a Nile, that it may descend and roll in waves on the mountains like the sea and water the fields according to their need. Thou didst give the Nile in heaven to the mountain lands and to all cattle that go there upon feet. But the Nile from the under-world thou didst give to Egypt.

Thou didst make the distant heavens, that thou mightest rise in them and look upon all that thou didst make, thou alone. All men look up to thee, sun of the day. Thou livest in my heart: no man knoweth thee like thy son Ikhnaton. Thou hast made him privy to thy plans, thou, life through which we live. Since thou didst lay the foundations of the world, thou hast raised mankind for thy son, who did proceed from thee, and for his beloved, the queen, who lives and blooms to all eternity.

17

THE two basic elements in the Egyptian character gave birth to writing: it was the Nile that produced administration, and the desire for continued life that created records. Thus the greatest of their inventions was made very early, in the first three dynasties. All the distinguishing marks of the Egyptian character, clarity and sobriety, order and organizing capacity, are revealed in their writing on columns, bridges, and statues. Their writing is more beautiful than that of the Sumerians who wrote in stone, more beautiful than that of the Assyrians who made cuneiform impressions on clay. Since the Nile mud ran away between their fingers, the Egyptians wrote with fine-pointed bulrushes, that is, in fact, with brushes, first on wooden tablets in black and red with palettes and pots, and then on papyrus.

It is true that what they wrote consisted mainly of panegyrics, but how much of ancient historiography is anything else? A representation of Thoth, the letter-writer of the gods and the god of the scribes, as a monkey with white hair, is certainly popular in origin, like any outburst of humour in Egypt; there is no trace of humour among the Pharaohs. But writing itself created classes between Pharaoh and the people: the scribe, as an official, was mighty and high in honour, like the princes in the Old Kingdom. Of course, here as everywhere else in the world, he stood in opposition to the soldier, but it was only in Egypt that the pen was mightier than the sword, for this people remained until the end a writing people and never became a people of war.

But writing, and knowledge with it, always remained realistic and purposeful. Egypt possesses none of those universal anecdotes in which other peoples immortalized their philosophy or artistic sense. The Nile and its oasis turned all their thought and writing into calculation, and all their intellectual powers were concentrated on the practical solution of the problems of the Nile.

For æons these sons of the desert must have observed the stars, seeing that, a thousand years before the first Pharaoh, they had already invented the calendar. It has been proved that they possessed it in the year 4236 before our era. Since they divided the year into three parts, Flood, Seedtime, and Harvest, and into twelve months of thirty days each, a few days remained over every year, which had accumulated in five hundred years to such an extent that the Flood season actually fell in harvest-time. To eliminate this error, that is, to bring the whole year round to its starting-point again, it would take 1460 years; and in the epochs of Egyptian history, this "wandering year" first arrived in 2776 under Pharaoh Zoser, who built the step-pyramid, then again in 1316 under a successor of Ikhnaton, and still in time to find the Pharaohs in the Nile valley, but the third time the wandering year came round, it encountered Ptolemy, the greatest mathematician of his time, in 144 A.D.; the fourth time it met the Mamelukes, and there were still two centuries to wait for General Bonaparte. So great are the epochs of the people who invented our calendar more than sixty centuries ago. They are like the halls of some vast castle through which there sounds the hidden rushing of a river.

It was the river too that fostered the knowledge of the hours, in the lapse of which the water-wheel could raise a certain quantity of water. And the Egyptians invented the sundial for the daytime, and the water-clock for the night in the form of stone basins with the scale of hours marked on the inside. The hours ran through holes which varied in size according to the season and the length of the night. And since the courses of the stars were known, they were pressed into service too. Two priests would sit facing each other, due north and south, each with a sighting-glass and a table on which he had entered the stars for every night; thus each could calculate the hour from the position of the other relative to a star, measuring from his right elbow and left ear. What a majesty of repose! And what a turmoil of emotion if one of these priests, sitting and reckoning, hated the other!

While they calculated the moon and stars from the pylons of their temples, in their realism they sought no prophecy in the aspects of the stars, as the Babylonians did; at all times, they wanted to know simply what was, in order to act upon it, and though they used to trace the course of the stars in a dead man's tomb, they did so only for a fortnight in advance, the rest he had to do himself—he had time. They recorded the twelve houses of the zodiac and discovered and named five planets during the New Kingdom; later men took three thousand years to discover two more. To divide the fields on the Nile by canals, they invented the foot and the ell, and they are said even to have understood the decimal system, the advantages of which the English have not even yet managed to appreciate.

Since the Egyptians had more constructive genius than artistic sense, we cannot but admire these inventions more than their buildings; and in the buildings it is the technical execution that is incredible, even when we take the millions of slaves into account.

Though the Nile fostered the growth of all rational and communal institutions, it prevented the buildings from rising where there was stone to be had: everywhere in the Nile valley the temples stand where none occurs. This is one of the disadvantages that at once tells against them in comparison with the Greek temples; another is the material of which they are built. The limestone of Karnak is beautiful only by moonlight, while the Parthenon exposes its marble to the radiant brightness of the day, and its roseate patina deepens with the centuries. When the Nile enters the country at Aswân, it has left behind it the last fine building-stone, the granite, which is Nubian like the gold: neither occurs in the Egyptian oasis. The flatness of the Nile valley, moreover, in which the buildings stand, reduces their impressiveness, since we are accustomed to raise temples and palaces, God and the king, above us on the hilltops.

Their vitality, their desire for immortality, flames up in the obelisks they invented and hewed out of the virgin rock, those obelisks for which Nature herself seems to have supplied the model. Goethe, who read the ways of nature with the insight of a god, recognized and demonstrated this form in the course of his geological studies: it was the granite itself that brought them to it.

I have, in the course of very accurate investigation of the manifold forms in which granite occurs, discovered a feature which seems to be general, namely that the parallelopipeds in which it is found are often divided diagonally, so that two rude obelisks are formed. Probably this natural phenomenon occurs on a colossal scale in the mountains of Syene in Upper Egypt, and just as we set up some large stone to mark a notable place, the biggest granite wedges, which were rare even in those mountains, were sought for and set up in that country as public monuments.

What adventures these pillars of glory have passed through! Of the four obelisks on which Thutmosis III, one of the most powerful of the Pharaohs, inscribed his deeds to publish them abroad, one was taken to Byzantium by Constantine the Great, another to Rome, where it first stood in the Circus, then lay prone for centuries, till a Pope, about 1600, set it up in front of the Lateran. The third, which had also lain prone for a thousand years, was taken to England in 1880 and stands on the Thames Embankment; the fourth is in Central Park in New York. Thus the victorious Pharaoh, so many thousands of years later, still lauds his glory to the skies, but no one can read it, and when a late priest of Amon on the Nile read the inscription to a nephew of the Emperor Tiberius—the inscription which told of all his ancient victories over the Medes and Persians, his conquests of Syria and Lydia, the number of his war-chariots, the quantities of his gold and ivory—he called the great man who had thought to immortalize himself in it Ramses the Great, and even today the dragoman, in front of any great monument, tells the tourist: Ramses the Great.

In the finest squares of Paris and Rome, London and New York, motors now rush round the obelisks all day, and fountains play about their feet, a sight for which Pharaoh would have given half his fortune. Nobody understands their meaning, but at night they stand bathed in magic light rising from below, as if Osiris were still illuminating the glory of his son from the underworld.

The Egyptians seem also to have derived part of their sculpture from architecture. The cube (now in Berlin) bearing one big and one small head, representing a court official holding a princess, is architectural rather than sculptural. All the statues, moreover, are reposeful: crouching, sitting, or pacing steadily forwards, they know neither adversaries nor desire. All of them are clear-cut and firm, men slow of thought and rare of feeling, borne by others and sure of themselves. Since in a general way only the head is worked out, and the body remains an outline, they often look as if they were telling the one great event of a life, with its commentaries appended below in notes.

Thus the individual specimens from the Old Kingdom produce very varying impressions, chiefly determined by their size and material, since geometrical sculpture can be fully developed only on a monumental scale and in stone. The famous little limestone group (now in Berlin) of a man and his wife, their hands crossed in touching fashion, is thoroughly comic, for she is self-assertive and housewifely, he uneasily submissive: other little groups (now in Cairo) are almost grotesque, with their "figures of the donor," while the crouching naked kings of the Middle Kingdom, in their cubic outline, look like a mathematical puzzle.

The life-size Ranufer, on the other hand, rises before us in full splendour, in spite of all the four and a half thousand years that have passed over his head, athletic, without exaggeration, not unlike some channel-swimming woman of today, with his bare neck, his hair like a helmet, his eyes gazing straight ahead, but fully worked out, the fine mouth not too broad, with hardly a hint of thickness about the lips, and hardly wider than the wide nose; he is the type of a calm, resolute man. The over-life-size statue of Ti is similar, but more sensual, the eyes and nose more widely opened, the whole more expectant, younger. Just as characteristic is the head of Perhernegret, with its more intelligent, inquiring look, whose mouth is even not quite straight, or the delicious head of the nameless wooden statuette (Cairo, 2600) whose surprised, youthful eyes are clearly fixed on something. All are portraits: even Zoser, probably the earliest of al! the portrait busts, has such expressive ears that it is easy to fill in the absent eyes and nose. The primitive god Ptah, who created gods and things, was made the god of art, and the creation of a work of art was called "making alive."

Since the Nile had taught them to write, they became painters too, and thus these oldest statues of mankind possess the added charm of colour. As the climate of the Nile preserved them, so that they were often brought intact out of their dry sepulchral chambers, they show a life as blooming as it appeared to the eyes of both artist and model. A princely couple of the IV Dynasty, Rahotep and Nofrit, are seated on white thrones: she, cloaked and rounded, a healthy woman with very modern features, all white and yellow, with touches of green and red in her necklaces, her hair, and the hieroglyphics black, her eyes of coloured stones; the man in dark red, angular, a boxer type, guileless, stupid. The story of their days and nights, their children, their quarrels, and their happiness stands clear upon them.

How completely these builders lived in three dimensions is shown by the poor quality of their painting: they knew how to tint a statue, but rarely painted a man, for among all the thousand frescoes that have been preserved, few seem to be more than industrial products. In the chapels of the Sethos temple in Abydos, there are a few coloured reliefs of great beauty dating from the thirteenth century, with curiously little green in them. Among the pictures of the king's homage to Isis, there is one in which her robe, of a delicate pale blue, falls over her breast; the flesh is yellow, with a little red on the headdress, but the king below at her throne is all in tones of red, only his crown and hair are yellow. The life of the men in the sun and air is elsewhere similarly differentiated from that of the highborn, painted women.

In general, the Egyptians were great only in stone—stone alone was Egyptian; they did not live with wood, and even copper had to come from a distance. Their sense of style in stone became highly developed in the course of three thousand years during which no revolution, nor even a threat of one, troubled the monumentality of their sculpture.

But just as they set fragile chapels in their colossal stone temples—delicate canopies borne by a few papyrus stems—they adorned their heavy, four-square statues with the frailest of necklaces even in the first dynasties, about 3000. Later luxury expressed itself in a greater refinement of buckles and bracelets, and we can no more understand today how they polished the finest turquoises and cut the finest filigrees than we can understand the technique by which they raised their gigantic blocks for the pyramids.

18

OUT of the wilderness of ancient history oases rise, linked by untrodden paths known only to a few explorers of historiography; this is more than a metaphor; it is connected with the oasis character of these countries. Among them Egypt was and remained the biggest, and whoever came into contact with it entered history, for where would the Sumerians, Canaanites, Hyksos, Ethiopians of 3000–2000 B.C. be today if it were not for the Egyptians? Leaving the Babylonians out of account, only one people that crossed their path equalled and surpassed their fame, was even the first to attract the curiosity of mankind to the Nile, where it had lived for only a short time and without power. It was the Bible that brought Egypt into the literature of the world, and to this very day millions of people believe that Pharaoh was the name of a particular king because he appears thus in the Book of Exodus.

The Jews, who conquered nothing, and first appeared in the country in the form of a family, who were humiliated, not glorified as they multiplied, and in the end fled from the land that had enslaved them, did more for the name of Egypt than all the nations that invaded and became masters there. A few pages of a book written in a little-known language by its enemies conferred immortality on a people which figures in it only as the oppressor. And all that came about because two particular men conquered the imagination of the world by their minds, without weapons, or perhaps simply because a romantic-minded poet wrapped them both in the flowery mantle of fable. Distant peoples, thousands of generations who know nothing of Ramses and Amenhotep, know the story of Joseph and Moses in Egypt.

Today we know for certain that they lived, and that they lived on the Nile. Since the hieroglyphics were deciphered, legend has received its *droit de cité* among scholars: it was especially the brilliant researches of A. S. Yahuda that proved the historical accuracy of the Bible..According to him, Joseph lived in Egypt about 1850, and Moses left the country with the Hebrews about 1450.

There are, it is true, no documents, unless we accept as such the scarabs from the Delta that bear the hieroglyphic for Jacob. But comparisons between the customs shown in the tomb-reliefs and papyri with those in the Bible would be certain proof even if the names were not there; moreover, our knowledge of social conditions in the New Kingdom enables us to fix the date before which Joseph must have carried out his *coup d'état* in Thebes. Then there is the prison of Zaru near the Asian frontier, the dream of the kine on the Nile, to which the seven sacred cows of Hathor in the seven districts correspond, the Vizier's chariot preceded by criers, a custom which survived to Cromer's day, the Vizier's golden chain and the fact that Joseph appeared before Pharaoh shaved, and not with the unkempt beard of the Asiatic. There is the land of Goshen (Gessen), an oasis between the Nile and the northern end of the Red Sea, to the east of the Delta where Joseph placed his brethren, so fertile that a scribe of Ramses II's time cannot find words to describe its fertility. Joseph lived, in actual fact, in historical Egypt.

Everything about Joseph looked strange in Egypt. He was the imaginative Jew, equally charming for his grace and dignity, at the same time the distinguished youth who troubled the women because he was too "goodly and well-favoured" to be so well behaved, as the Bible tells us. Yet he was a shrewd and wary man of affairs, enriching his king without robbing anybody; and again the diplomat who could wear a mask, especially to cover his feelings; at the same time a man of patience, able to let his plans mature slowly; perfectly honest, but silent; friendly to all, but always on his guard. But for all the self-control with which he held his imagination and his intelligence in poise, for all the quiet self-confidence with which this child of fortune accepted the gifts of life as his due, at one point he betrayed passion—as a son and a brother—and in this unity of mind and heart, in this wealth of deep feeling and wise thought, he is the living symbol of the noble Jew, such as Disraeli was later. Joseph alone, and Joseph more than any later Jew, would suffice to disarm the enemies of the Jews.

His character, and his character alone, can explain his success. Achieved by a foreigner without patronage, without arms, even without specialized knowledge or capacity, it has remained unique in history. For what did Joseph accomplish? Out of the vagaries of the elements, the seven years' failure of the Ethiopian rain and the Nile flood, he made the ruler of the country, faced with revolution and overthrow, owner of the whole land. By hoarding grain for the seven plenteous years "until he left numbering; for it was without number," he calculated his dictatorial power in advance for the time when famine would come and the people would find Pharaoh the sole seller of corn. So they came and offered him first all their cattle, then their bodies, then their lands if he would only give them food. In this way Joseph "saved Egypt from starvation by foresight and wisdom, and at the same time put the king into possession of the land by an unprecedented speculation."

In these words, Goethe, who made his Mephistopheles do the opposite, that is, create a fraudulent inflation for his emperor, reveals the genius of Joseph, the Hebrew statesman and merchant. At one blow, he made himself master of three powers: the fellahin praised him as their saviour from the local princes who stood between him and Pharaoh, for he preferred to belong to Pharaoh, in whom he now saw more than ever the god of his salvation; Pharaoh had every reason to praise him; and the third element he had conquered was the Nile. Joseph was the only man who ever mastered the Nile.

A young man of thirty, he accomplished it all only because he knew how to learn from dreams and to turn them to practical use, because, as a realist, he trusted his imagination, and could progress from the singing of songs to visions of action. And yet in this masterpiece of state socialism, he developed his character as a philanthropist and a gentleman, not otherwise than Pharaoh, who placed so much confidence in a stranger.

Yet the stranger was a man of such innate distinction that his beginnings as overseer to a court official might well be forgotten. It was unprecedented for a Pharaoh to take a strange convict, and without hesitation to clothe him in vestures of fine linen, to give him his chain and his ring, and proclaim him "Feeder of the People," and all before he had put him to the test, before Joseph had even had time to prove himself, merely on the strength of a plan that the strange youth had woven out of a dream.

It was no wonder then that Pharaoh, for the first time, bowed his head before a man. Joseph's father had said, it is true, that he was one hundred and thirty years old, and hence was worthy of reverence. It was Jacob, the foreigner, who, at the end of his audience with Pharaoh, rose and blessed him in his foreign fashion. The son of Ra, the body-on-earth of the god, bowed his head to receive at the hands of the grandson of a distant shepherd chieftain, an unknown nomad, the blessing of a god of whom there was not so much as an image.

While Joseph had risen to master the Nile, and had overcome the consequences of its vagaries, Moses was a child of the Nile. For since he was to have been killed along with all the male children of the Hebrews, because they had multiplied in Egypt, and then was found in an ark by Pharaoh's daughter, they called him Musheh, sheh meaning pool, but also Nile, and mu meaning child.

Behind the graceful and happy figure of the prince charming, stands the horned prophet, a figure of gloom. After the stranger who warded the plagues of Egypt off the head of the Egyptian people, came the other stranger who called them down upon the country. In his lifetime, and by succeeding generations through the centuries, Moses was less beloved. As mediator between God and man, he is less personal, and his mission, with all its mourning and profundity, is much too symbolic to be true in the form we know. The anecdotic element which gives life to every tradition, and by that very fact guarantees its truth, ceases almost entirely after his death. Only one thing sounds like a reminiscence of a well-known event, that is the murder he committed in his youth. The blow with which a Hebrew slew the offender of his people reveals the younger Moses to us as a man of free will, saving the honour of his race from the insult of a scoundrel without any command from God, beside the later prophet obeying God's will alone.

It is true that Moses was faced with a different people than Joseph, for it was his own, and much more difficult to manage, seeing that it was to become really a people only through him. By rising as the national leader of an unruly crowd, this unknown shepherd, the servant of a foreigner, could not but awaken more enmity than Joseph, who protected Pharaoh's interests under Pharaoh's protection. But it was an oppressed people, grown strong in bondage and hate, upon which Moses laid his hand. Living there at the edge of the Nile Delta, the Hebrews were not the first people to serve the Egyptians: Babylonians before them and Trojans after them had been ground underfoot there. If the Pharaoh who had determined to exterminate them, yet would not let them go, was Amenhotep II—and there is a date in the Book of Kings to support the assumption—he was an utter sadist whose personal features show how closely he resembled a dictator of our day. He was the man who segregated the Jews in camps, who took away the straw with which they made bricks, yet demanded as many bricks from them as before, but who, when he had to let them go, shouted after them the impotent, echoing command of the tyrant: "Bless me also."

Everything that Moses did in Egypt reveals the violent heir of violent fathers. His education at court, or at least under court protection, the influence of Egyptian culture, of the tribe from which he took a wife of princely birth, left no trace in him. Moses, the "child of the Nile," retained nothing of his name, or of his childhood. He became a child of the desert, always solitary, always communing with his God, always devoured by his own expectation, always darkly seeking deeds meet for his strong arm. For years, the only news he had of his people came from caravans. At last he girded up his loins to lead his people back to the land of their fathers by the light of his desert meditations without direct contact with that people, and guided only by his visions.

But heavy and simple-minded as he was, he could have no conception of the astuteness of highly imaginative despots. The very Pharaoh who decimated the Hebrews by labour and ill-treatment, and killed every male child at birth, when the people he swore he hated rose to leave the country, refused to let them go, laughed Moses and Aaron to scorn, saying that this guest people had first learned agriculture and craftsmanship in the land of their hosts. Having just decided on their extermination because they might join forces with the enemies of the country, he kept good hold of those whom he had robbed of their rights. And with all the stupidity of the dictator, he added: "Behold, the people of the land now are many, and ye make them rest from their burdens!"

But he had not reckoned with the Hebrews' God, the conscience of Moses that could outdo malice with malice. The vengeance of the humiliated, which had moved Moses to kill a single Egyptian in his youth, now moved him to kill the firstborn of those Egyptians who had once killed the firstborn of the stranger. The thought of their father Joseph, who had once saved this people from starvation, must have strengthened the Jews in this struggle.

They may have passed between the Bitter Lakes and the Red Sea, or by way of Gaza, along the Red Sea to Sinai, then through the land of the Midianites and Moabites to the Jordan, or straight across the desert. Goethe has removed from Moses the reproach that, "though a powerful, resolute, and swift man of action, he allowed a huge mass of people to wander about for forty years in so small a space, in sight of so great a goal"; he even made fun of a French writer who tried to explain the forty years geographically, saying that he made "the caravans dance a polonaise." With perfect realism, Goethe concludes that, in the exodus, the Hebrew rearguard was formed of men who had been trained in the massacre of the firstborn. "In their way of fighting, this probably gave them the advantage of the terrain." In any case, the six hundred war-chariots of the pursuing Pharaoh were swallowed up in the Red Sea.

19

SLOWLY the columns of Karnak, witnesses of the Pharaohs, fade from the sight of the river. Everything that approaches the Nile below Thebes is older or younger than the Theban kingdom, for farther down, in the neighbourhood of Cairo, the fourth and third millenniums saw only beginnings. Later, however, when strange peoples came from the Mediterranean, all their power was concentrated on the coast, at the opening of the Delta, where today cotton and world traffic have finally drawn the threads of the world together. With the plain of Luxor, the Nile quits the place of its glory: what it founds lower down is certainly a world metropolis, but only once was Alexandria the heart of the world, like Thebes.

This last long reach of the river, 250 miles to Cairo, is dominated by the Arabian desert hills, which run west and force the Nile into an almost perfect arc, with Qena and Wasta at the extremities of the chord. Since these ranges run along the river for long distances, here as in Upper Egypt, the breadth of the valley and the cultivated land lie on the other bank, the left bank of the river, and that, in its turn, determines the situation of the canals.

Yet even this last epoch in the life of the aged river does not pass in Platonic composure. In Egypt the Nile stands under double pressure: not only the eastern, but the western hills too force it into many a twist and turn, and in the confusion of its rapid changes of direction, it deposits many an island, like the last cries and struggles of a man haled off to captivity. At the same time, men torture it through many canals and barrages. The vanquished river chafes noisily at the restraint, and, like a fettered giant, at least makes little, cunning man, its captor, feel its strength in thrusts from below.

The dams which reinforce the work of Aswân between Aswân and Cairo retain so much silt—about 58 percent—that the Nile must be continually dredged; nevertheless it forms islands which, in their perpetual going and coming, lend to its bed the eternal unrest of an erratic character. Thus at Girga, a big island came into being which had to be circumnavigated first to the east, then to the west; meanwhile it grew to such an extent that it can now be reached on foot from the east. As the Nile cannot be carried round the barrages, like our rivers, at a large number of places huge sailing-boats cast stones into the river, which are brought downstream 30 miles and more, and pave the river floor to a depth of four to six feet. Thus the struggle between man and the river continues here, and if the struggle is unequal, the river has at any rate the satisfaction of forcing men constantly to rearm against its power.

Since the density of life now increases steadily in the Nile valley, movement on both banks increases steadily too. Gliding onward, the river sees blooming on both banks the life it has created, and men ride and walk on the dams, which are roads.

On a little, nimble grey donkey, a tall man comes riding by bearing a huge sugar-cane, as comically armed as Don Quixote. An old Ford passes him, containing six Arabs in white turbans and floating scarves, for when they travel abroad, they must put on a great deal of clothing to keep up their dignity. Four camels, two asses, and a troop of children, all heavy laden, march slowly in front of a man and his wife, moving house—a turning-point of their lives—and hope and fear hover before the little procession like the *kà* of the two beings who have dared this step, or perhaps were forced into it. Two girls in black skirts are playing catch with their veils, and beside them a little boy is dragging a huge camel to the water.

Three young men are lying in prayer under a sycamore, their hands at their ears, their bodies moving; horses are grazing beside them, and all are like shadows against the saffron-yellow and turquoise-blue background of the desert and the sky. A man is coming down through the yellow sandstone from the mountain to the white quarry, in a blue cloak, infinitely great and solitary—Moses descending from Horeb. A file of men with baskets on their shoulders is outlined in profile against the sky and the desert—a frieze from a temple wall come to life. Something like the skeleton of a dead camel is lying on the high shoulder of the bank; gradually it turns into the skeleton of a boat they have left lying where they built it, till the rising river reaches it in summer: the Nile fetches its own boats. It has washed away the earth under the feet of an old, shady tamarisk low down on the bank; the tree stands there with naked roots. Where the chalk caves of the hills come close to the river, fishers are spreading their nets out to mend. A big man on a small ass rides slowly along the dam against the sun, a black figure against the green of the fields. And sails upon sails! A rowing-boat without sails rarely crosses the Nile.

In the middle of the field, three shadufs are drawing up the ground water, and making a well at the same time, for here a plot of land lies five feet below the basins; these six men will take forty days to make the well. They stand echeloned on the bank; the lowest has the best place in summer, but now in January it is cold down there, he has to stand in damp darkness. He is singing to make himself feel that he is alive. A herd of goats trips by, the goatherd running with all his might to keep up with them. Men and animals are ferried over the Nile in a huge boat; now they are stamping up the soft earth of the bank, the black-veiled woman on a trim-legged donkey, and now the procession flits through the narrow green to reach the yellow desert; they seem to be making for some oasis.

On a big island, covered with rippling sugar-cane, twenty camels are moving slowly down from the sakia to the bank; there four monsters are waiting in the Nile—freight cars on four boats with a little steam-tug. A few dozen naked fellahin are unloading the sugar-cane from the camels; others are wading to the boats with the load, for no boat can land on the shallow bank; then the steamer tugs the whole fairy flotilla downstream to where the cars can reach a railway line on the quay, to vanish in the neighbourhood of a sugar factory; built out of the stones of a ruined Ptolemaic temple, it now seems dedicated to the god of sugar.

Life begins to move more swiftly on the river too, the nearer it comes to Cairo. The boatman in his narrow boat at his evening prayer cowers slanting, for in spite of all the windings of the river he knows where Mecca lies, and as his friend pulls the boat round out of the current, he slews round again so as not to lose his prophet. Not far from the bank, women and children are sitting beside grazing donkeys, the man is fishing with a line, but he seems rather to be dreaming, the house is out of sight, they seem to be living in a legend under the evening twilight in the midst of the Nile. The slow-moving steamer stops in a lonely place, it is almost empty; a pioneer, holding up his long white skirt, lands with deliberation and drives a huge plug, three feet long, into the bank; two others come to help him. With huge wooden hammers, reminiscent of some fairy-tale, the stakes are driven home, and finally a canvas is drawn round the boat; then the traveller is ready to spend the night in this creek.

The flat hills which approach the river on the east rise in a superb triple structure: below, a double plinth, with beautifully artistic parallels; then a sandy, eroded middle part; and a rocky-looking summit. Lines run in a perfect vertical down to the plinth, forming elephant's hoofs in it. In the uppermost part, four to six horizontal lines run parallel to the plinth, while the absolute flatness of the tops emphasizes their lovely regularity—it is like a Bach fugue.

Where the Arabian heights come nearer to the river, at Monfalût and Qusîya, the geology of the landscape creates moving visions. As the limestone was deposited in strata, and has been eaten away by water and wind, the yellow mountains close to the Nile take on the shapes of beings mutable as the clouds: there stands a huge desert table six feet above the green and hence yellow and arid; here a pedestal all eaten away, blackened with Nile mud, like an aged human face ravaged by a thousand lines and wrinkles; there are ravines like the backs of elephants or the broken columns of huge temples; and between these giants of the desert lies a green spot of earth not a hundred paces long, not twenty broad, on which a fellah in his blue shirt is watering his beans with an old bucket, moving carefully and humbly to and fro from the river, up and down the bank, to raise water—water.

20

AT the point where the Nile takes its last sharp turn, not far below Thebes, at Qena, it approaches to within sixty miles of the Red Sea; according to a number of geologists, in earlier times it poured through the open gorge between the Arabian heights to the sea. If that is the case, and if things had remained so, the course of this ancient history, which was not then a Mediterranean history, would have been different: one thing is certain, that rounded gravel has been found in this ravine. Here in ancient times all men went to the sea, to Punt, to find incense. At this very interesting geological spot, the sculptors of the Pharaohs found their hard, dark stone, and hence put the place under military guard. Min, the god of the desert travellers, was worshipped here, and even today a pilgrim's road to Mecca here descends to the Red Sea.

Here are made all the millions of clay pitchers that raise the water. If the Nile is the god of the country, the pitchers are his priests, for they carry the spirit of the god to men. Even the Pharaohs knew the good clay soil of this muddy spot, and it was called Kene, the black country, in contrast to the yellow desert. Some derive the word alchemy from it. A certain air of magic still surrounds the men who, from father to son, have turned the potter's wheel for centuries to make these pitchers, without which the water-wheel could not live and great stretches of Egypt would bear no fruit.

It is shady in Qena; under the palms the women prepare the soft clay, generally with their feet, with water and chaff. But the creative act, the shaping of the pitcher, is, like sowing, left to the men. The man squats in a low, open brick room with a thatched roof, and as the wheel must rotate freely in the air, he turns it from below with his feet. When the spinning disk is wet, he puts a handful of clay on it, then smooths off a little—but never twice the same amount: none of the 3 million *ballas* and *gullas*—pitchers for the water-wheel and for drinking—that are produced here every year is exactly like another: at some point the shaping thumb leaves its mark in a beautiful irregularity. The pitchers from the tombs or on the reliefs, three thousand years old, look exactly the same, and it is quite within the bounds of possibility that the man shaping them today descends in the direct line from one who shaped them in Kene then: even then these artists of the pitchers formed the oldest dynasty in the world. But he himself sits in a welter of potsherds, the holes in the walls are stopped up with them, and the pitcher out of which he pours water steadily on to his wheel is broken off at the neck—the artist's fate.

When the pitchers have been dried for four days in the sun— in winter for eight—they are taken to the neighbouring town to be fired for twenty-four hours in the kiln; then they are skil- fully piled up in hundreds on a boat, and rush swaying down the Nile as if they were on the back of an overloaded camel. And in the end they are inserted into the rope-work of the water- wheels to raise water—water.

The pottery ovens are no older than those of the fowls, a little lower down, near Sohag, for the incubators, which seem to have come from China by way of Iraq, were admired by travellers here at all times: chickens were so cheap in Egypt that they were sold by measure. From ancient times this has been a specialty of a few villages whose inhabitants even today go into the Delta to attend to the ovens. An incubator of this kind, 25 feet broad by 80 feet long, is heated for only one hour morning and eve- ning; they call it "the fowls' dinner." Of the 4000 eggs that are put into the incubator simultaneously, 98 percent of which are hatched out by artificial heat in twenty-one days, the tenant gets half, the other half goes to the owner, who can carry through the operation ten times a year.

In the midst of this world of the fellahin, who live today with their pitchers and their fowls as they lived under the Pharaohs, three barrages have been constructed along 125 miles of the river in the last thirty years—in Isna, Nagh Hamâdi, and Asyût—

which water a number of provinces all the year round for the sake of the cotton; they are miniature Aswân dams, for even the barrage of Asyût, the biggest, with its 111 sluices, is not half as long as Aswân, and, since the latter was raised, only a third as high; the granite used in its building was brought nearly 200 miles down the Nile. In the middle of the Egyptian Nile, where the oasis widens to fifteen miles, thirteen of which are under crops, the four dams have watered the cotton in the driest months from April to September, and hence enriched the country. But even if the time should come when cotton is artificially produced, or its cultivation is abandoned on account of over-production, the new dams and barrages would be the real key to the life of the land, for they have opened up the future, as Champollion opened up the past. Invisibly the key of life hovers over every dam.

The river feels it, and its mighty, fettered forces foam and roar at the sluices which are opened for navigation at the side of every dam. At night, when the men turn the huge rings that move the iron gates in their hinges, they begin to sing, and sing ever faster, the faster they turn: it might be the remnant of some primeval song with which their forefathers sought to propitiate the god of the Nile. Then they stand out like gods against the starry sky, up on the stone dam, guiding the boat that is swung on two ropes from hooks in the wall. They look like knights of the boat, not of the river, for they are careful to prevent its rubbing along the walls. Growling like lions, the gates above have closed, guided by the dark, silent hands, while the naked feet press into the iron rungs of the ladders in the walls. In a few minutes the chamber has filled, then the two gates on the other side rattle open, groaning rather than growling, and when the boat has passed, they growl too. There is a hiss, and between the gates the water foams white with rage; that bit of white foam even prevents the two flat gates from completely closing: it is the last resistance of the vanquished element. Within the steamer, the stoker opens his stoke-hole, the flames leap out of the belly of the ship, and flicker over the green walls it has just left behind.

Thus the two tamed elements play round each other, both in

the hands of man, yet never completely, never quite reliable, always sending forth menacing flashes and hisses—fire and water.

Immediately below the last of these dams, the Nile, too old for adventure, sets to work on a curious piece of juggling. Since it has received no tributary since the Atbara, many hundreds of miles away, it makes itself one, and suddenly sends off a narrow, second Nile, separated from it by only eight miles, but following it for more than 150, though this second Nile is 50 miles longer, since it runs its course in vague windings imposed by no mountains or other decrees of fate, a decadent heir. This is the Bahr Yûsuf, which rises at Dârût, and is as it were the shadow or *kà* of the Nile: it is also called the Canal of Joseph and is linked in saga with Joseph, though the saga is belied by its tortuous course.

Even today the fellahin relate the Arab legend of the patriarch Yûsuf (Joseph): how the courtiers got tired of him as they do of every minister who has ruled too long; how they wanted to get rid of him, and hence spoke slightingly of him to Pharaoh. "Great Pharaoh, Joseph has grown old, his understanding is enfeebled, his beauty is gone, his judgment fails." But Pharaoh, who had never forgotten Joseph's *coup d'état*, determined to show them the great powers Joseph still possessed, and said: "Prove it to me. Make Joseph undertake some great thing and come to grief."

"Command him," said his enemies, "to drain the water of the Nile from the marshy land under the lake, to dry up the whole and water it anew, so that thou shalt possess a new province and more revenues."

Pharaoh nodded, sent for Joseph, and said to him: "Joseph, I have a favourite daughter, as you know. I wish to dower her well, but there is no land left. Could you not make a new province out of that old marshland over there? It is well situated, not far from my capital, and in the midst of deserts. My daughter would be independent there."

Then Joseph said: "When shall it be, great Pharaoh? For with Allah's help it shall be done."

"As soon as may be," replied Pharaoh, like all those set in authority over others. But then Allah, who is anticipated in the

Arab story, showed Joseph how to build three canals, one from
Upper Egypt, one from the east, and one from the west. With
these he drained the land; at the same time he felled a thousand
tamarisks and bushes, and when the flood came, the Nile entered the canal, watered the marsh and flowed out through the
other canal. The whole was completed in seventy days. Then
Pharaoh said to his dismayed councillors: "See what my old
Joseph has done with his enfeebled judgment in seventy days.
You could not do it in a thousand." Since then that land has been
called "the land of the one thousand days"—El Faiyûm.

In addition to this, a huge canal, the Ibrahim Canal, the longest in Egypt, runs from Asyût close along the left bank of the
Nile, with the railway running beside it; thus from Dârût to
Faiyûm there are three parallel Niles, two of which water the
latter oasis. These are the great arteries of Middle Egypt. Here
we can see with what wisdom the aged river dispatched its messenger to call the strange oasis of Faiyûm out of the very desert
probably many centuries before the Pharaohs, and in any case
before the English engineers who built the artificial canal beside it, which, together with the dam, regulates the supply of
water to that spot.

These canals, big and little, are never finished. Like the
Gothic cathedrals, which always have some scaffolding somewhere about them, they are always being corrected, built, or
widened, and, like the cathedrals, building goes on outside and
inside at the same time.

Dry or growing, the canals teem today as in the time of the
Pharaohs with hundreds of figures, for they are all dug by hand,
and the overseer points to the human antheap, saying briefly:
"Eight million cubic yards." The diggers, all born earth-workers,
each attended by three younger carriers, work twelve out of the
twenty-four hours, and much harder than at the sakia. At this
time the fellah eats only black bread, onions, and radishes.
Every other day, each group elects one to wield the whip. Each
man carries half a hundredweight at a time, thus carrying 4.5
cubic yards of earth daily in 125 baskets: 8.5 million cubic yards
of earth mean almost 250 million baskets. For that he earns one
English shilling a day; his sweat has never been measured. The

embankments and steps are entrusted to specially skilled workers, who earn sixpence more, for they can measure and write, they know where the embankments have to be walled up, at the places where the inrush of water, creating a whirlpool, would eat away the bank.

In winter, when they are empty, these canals are let out as grainfields in tiny plots, and the fellah knows exactly which plot collects most of the fertile silt; he takes it, and in such soil he reaps in May—just like the critic after the poet's death.

But like some aged revolutionary overcome late in life, the old Nile has still other ways of letting the last surges of its wild nature break out. Yet, though it may displace the big islands year by year, so that at certain places, for instance at Monfalût, the river flowed farther east a century ago, men strive to outwit it again. The river is betrayed by its own colour, for the boatman can see by it that with his 50-inch draught he will no longer be able to find a passage where he passed last year.

With his embankments, man affects the most essential laws of the river's being, for at curves, where the current is strong, he builds embankments of pointed stones to master the silt and relieve the land at the dams. The engineers, of course, dispute as to the form of these stones, and if the English build them in triangles with the points downstream, there is at once a quarrel, which promptly becomes political. Meanwhile, the vanquished river has taken its revenge for this new malice of men, and when, by dividing its course, they have split an island into three small ones, it deposits mud in the middle of its bed, so that the steamer runs aground all the same, and has to be pushed and pulled clear with curses and appeals to Allah and the sweat of hours.

The work in the desert stone close by is still harder; there some moraine from the Ice Age has been cemented with limestone and has to be blasted with dynamite. At night, when the men all cower together, only the fire holds off the jackals and hyenas, whose eyes flash in the firelight, and whose barking rends the dark.

The tortuous Yûsuf Canal, running parallel to the Nile, has created the most astonishing of all the oases which suddenly turn the desert green on both sides of the long Nile oasis: it lies near-

est to the Nile of them all. For the Faiyûm is separated from the
Nile by hills and desert, and the low Libyan chain which shuts
off the wide western valley in the neighbourhood of Benî Suêf
leaves only a narrow corridor for the natural canal to flow
through. Without this gap, which the train runs through in a
few minutes, this province, perhaps the most fertile one in
Egypt, would never have come into being. Since the natural
canal has less slope than the main stream, its length permits more
water to be stored at definite times.

El Faiyûm, which has come to mean "lake," both in Egyptian
and Arabic, required for the regulation of that long canal a special lake, once called Lake Moeris, now Lake Qurûn. This too
was believed to be artificial in ancient times, when they spoke of
a basin and a canal, while it is obviously a lake and a river that
created the Faiyûm. It appears that first nature, then irrigation,
reduced its size, and even in Strabo's time it took up the superfluous water during the flood, and when the waters had subsided,
returned it to the Nile. Sluices had been made to assist nature
in producing this double effect in order to measure the water.
Even the Greek called this "the taming of nature." In this
lake, the remnants of a civilization are hid, for certain knives,
polishing-stones, and scraps of household gear point to human
beings who lived by hunting, perhaps by agriculture too, six
thousand years before Christ, where fishermen live today.

How the art of irrigation developed out of Nature's wisdom,
perhaps out of Nature's vagaries too, abetting her secret purposes, is to be seen nowhere on the Nile so clearly as here, where
in the course of millenniums the lake was reduced and the canal
widened, where the Ptolemies turned swamp into grainland,
and changed from this point the agriculture of the Delta, so that
we can follow the tracks of time down to the great water-works
of our day.

It is a sinister kind of lake of greenish salt water, over which
the wild geese are swift to elude the hunter: the dark lush green
refreshes the eye and the spirit only here and there on the southern fringe of the oasis. It lies, too, 130 feet below sea-level. Ruins
of temples and cities, whose debris lines the shore, only make the
whole more sombre, and when we read that Ikhnaton once lived

here with his mother's court, it remains an idea, it never becomes a vision.

South of the lake, the rich oasis is beautiful: at this point it delighted Herodotus, and Strabo saw olives and vines here, but only here, and not farther south. With its hundred canals all originating in the one, with its most remote corners all growing grain and rice, olives and vegetables, El Faiyûm looks like the fat fields of a fellah's dream, though it no more belongs to him than any other strip of overflowing fertility in Egypt.

21

BROAD and calm, divided by huge islands, bordered to the west by a broad green land, oppressed on the east by mountains, the Nile approaches the capital of its life, the biggest city of its continent. At the same time, this is the point at which its single course ends, at which it divides into a network of many courses.

Long before this, however, in the latitude of the northern part of Faiyûm, it sees on its left a strangely formed building of stone rising from the midst of the green: it is the pyramid of Medum. And then, for the last 50 miles above Cairo, six groups of pyramids succeed each other at ever shorter intervals till the site of ancient Memphis is reached. The light is so clear, and the hills so low, that they stand out very distinctly, and the river may well catch sight of the last, which lie almost on the same latitude as the metropolis, before it sees the minarets, domes, and towers appearing on the other side at the foot of and on the slopes of the higher hills of the Arabian desert. These are the three pyramids of Gîza, the oldest stone buildings to have been prefectly preserved.

Even here, faced with these most famous products of Egyptian powers, our wonder is by no means aroused by their beauty, but by the basic qualities of the Egyptian character, the product of their climate and the laws of the Nile valley—clarity, accuracy, the cold smoothness of all these sun-soaked outlines, as well as the extravagance of this mania to conquer death by vast preparations for the other world—mathematics with grotesque aims, sublime clarity for absurd purposes. All the great things they discovered and invented in order to overcome their primitive element, to distribute and raise the water, everything that their reason devised or realized before other men, is here lavished on madness. These are no sanctuaries of the gods, no symbols of power, no buildings for life's joys, no secret places of love: here the megalomania and the fear of death of absolute rulers raise their smooth, pointed walls to heaven.

They shimmer light grey against the desert yellow, casting sharp shadows which lengthen in the afternoon, their slanting shapes emphasizing this geometrical rigidity; the onlooker, according to his mood, feels admiration, or irony, or both. For beside their monumental weight and simplicity, there rises the insistent thought of a purposelessness which ought to be beautiful, but is here only logical. The elimination of imagination and art, in this harsh light, strangles every dream, and all that remains is the purely visual astonishment caused by the effect of straight lines in the very middle of the rolling chaos of the desert hills.

Of the three kings who built these greatest of all sepulchral monuments, no deed and no thought, no idea, has descended to posterity other than this of making a people haul stones for a century so that their coffins should have stone cases of a height and weight the world had never seen. All we know of Cheops is that he found life tedious, and hence summoned a magician from Memphis, who told him stories and even offered to stick a severed head onto its body again.

"Fetch a condemned criminal," cried Pharaoh.

"Not a man, O King," said the magician. "Have a beast brought from thy stables." Then he cut off the head of a goose, set it on the neck again, and the goose fluttered away.

There is another story, very credible in the light of an existence so vacant: he hired his daughter out as a courtesan, and from each of her admirers, she demanded a stone for her father's grave, though, considering that it took 3¼ million cubic yards of stone, even a life of a hundred years in unimpaired health and vitality would have sufficed only for the tip of the pyramid.

Khefren, the builder of the second, had a better idea. Looking at his powerful but simple face—if the naked statue that bears his name is really he—at first one sees nothing but the giant blinkers of his headdress: it is Horus, the falcon, whose wings are magnificently worked into its folds. This Pharaoh too spent his life building his tomb, but the divine falcon did not help him enough, for to his shame, his pyramid is ten feet lower than his predecessor's. The third, Mycerinus, who was a slight improvement on his two predecessors and hence passed for a good king, was satisfied with a pyramid of half the height, and seems in a general way a more likeable figure, for he preferred to become his daughter's lover himself, though she hanged herself for grief. She is said to have been buried by her father in a golden cow, which Herodotus saw. Once a year they brought it forth, for the dying girl had prayed to see the sun once a year.

Such barbaric legends are well suited to men whose life-work was their tomb, and amid such ugly and grotesque stories this one voice praying to see for a moment the sun of Egypt brings the one note of humanity.

All the rest, instead of being superhuman, remained merely inhuman. For the oldest documents agree with the latest re-searches to prove that the three Pharaohs—or perhaps only two—spent more than a hundred years building their tombs. Three to four million men had to be mobilized for at least four months in the year, during the flood, to bring the stones to the Nile, then over the river, then to their place on a specially laid road to hew them into shape there and raise them aloft with unknown tools. All Egypt was enslaved, the temples were shut for a hundred years. And then came all the temples and statues that were built round about, which deprived them of the monumental solitude in which we now meet the monsters. Khefren seems to have set up twenty-three colossal statues of himself beside his pyramid.

And what remained?

The name of Cheops, the builder of the highest structure in the world, which held the record for so long; the other two names echo into silence in the outside world. But then, and for many centuries after their death, these kings gained nothing but the curse of a people which sacrificed its life for three generations to the stony whims of its king. A feeling as if they stood before devils and witches overcame the people even in the time of Herodotus, and merely to avoid pronouncing the hated name, they called the place of the pyramids Philitis, after a shepherd who pastured his flocks close by.

Yet even in the interior, which they had armoured so giganti-

PTOLEMAIC KING AND QUEEN

GATE IN CAIRO

cally, nothing of the Pharaohs was preserved. Tomb-robbers, cleverer than the builders, rifled and smashed the coffins; no name remained upon them; on the vaults, nothing stands but the mark of a mason in red on a block—a tally for his piecework in stones. In later times too, there still stood written on a wall that the workmen had eaten more than a million dollars' worth of onions, radishes, and garlic.

Such are the relics of the three Pharaohs, who were immortalized, or at least strove to immortalize themselves, in the biggest heaps of stone in the world: a shepherd, a stone-mason, and an onion bill have remained, and so, after all, the fellah triumphs over Pharaoh.

The three great writers of antiquity speak of the pyramids as one of the wonders of the world. Any man who knew the limits of contemporary engineering must have stood amazed before this masterpiece of the earliest engineers. And men too were misled by their astonishing form into a mysticism of numbers, not even ceasing their play when Champollion so blithely unveiled the image of Sais.

But not one speaks of the sphinx lying before the second pyramid. As it was often half buried in sand, it may well have been almost invisible in the century between Herodotus and Strabo. In any case it was just a thousand years before Strabo that Thutmosis IV unearthed the giant. As a prince, living in luxury, he is said to have fallen asleep by its foot while hunting. Then the Sphinx said to him: "I shall make thee Pharaoh if thou wilt dig me out of the sand."

To the Egyptians, who made the sphinx the symbol of Khefren, it remained, like everything else, without mystery, and since everyone puts just as much mystery into things as he feels in himself, the Greeks were the first to tremble before the sphinx. For within the area enclosed by the three frigid constructions of thought and number, a work of art arose out of the Egyptian desert, without its like in the world because it remained half nature.

There the royal lion lies at sunset, at first small by the side of the pyramid, then steadily growing as our eyes rest on it. A face profound and speaking, in spite of its silence and its wounds.

And its mutilation awakens no pity, as torsos often do: the expression is too sublime to admit of compassion with its earthly fate.

Without the royal cap, seen from the front, it is the head of a youth with a long neck, a narrow brow, outstanding ears, the bridge of the nose broad and flat, like that of the fellah, the fleshy underlip weathered to a greater asceticism than was intended; heavy and patient, the gigantic eye-sockets between wide-open lids alone betray unutterable longing in its lordly power.

Thou art greater than all that have stood before thee, for greatness comes to thee from them. Thou art the strongest, for thou art contained within thyself. Thou hast no need of signs of power or beauty; thou hidest thy strength in the shape of a beast. Thou growest with it in the earth that we must tread underfoot to cower questioning before thee. Thy speech is mighty, our knees tremble before the wind of thy great words. Thy voice is mighty through the spaces of the desert, though thy stern mouth is shut. Thou growest out of the rolling sands of the centuries, out of the solitude of the desert, beside the nameless graves of dead kings, living thy secret life between the sand and the sky.

Thou art a man. The ridge of thy brow, the weight of thy eye-sockets, the lean walls of thy cheeks, proclaim it—thou art an Egyptian, with thy high cheek-bones and broad mouth, growing here between the desert sand and Nile mud, and no god, for with the sudden fall of night, thou dost lift thine eyes to the stars, raising thy gaze to them from thy mighty beast's eyes, even as we. And as thy gaze rises to the signs above, we follow it, and cannot grasp the order that thou, behind the walls of thy brow, perhaps mayest comprehend in thy silence.

Book Five

THE

GOLDEN

MOUTH

1

_____

THE shadows lengthen, evening is drawing on, the loud waters of the mighty river roll on to their appointed end.

Yet Nature does not blot out her greatest creatures with a heedless hand, as she does the millions; she has summoned too much strength, too much thought, to the effort; she has put too much to the test. For, in Goethe's words: "Nature has her favourites, on whom she lavishes much. It is on the great that her protective hand is laid." To exhaust Alexander's strength at an age which befitted the swiftness of his career, she used his excesses; to fell Cæsar, she used a dozen enemy daggers; she used Nordic hordes to destroy the Roman Empire, volcanoes to lay waste the glorious orange-groves of Messina, and the evil wind of a desert island to break Napoleon, while to wrest the brush from the centenarian hand of the greatest of all artists, she had recourse to the plague. How could she take leave of this, the most wonderful of all rivers, without devising for it some new form, some unexpected denouement, which, in the last act, would do justice to the uniqueness of its career?

For a hundred and fifty days, the wave of the Nile has been travelling from the equator to Cairo; it has flowed through thousands of miles, more than thirty degrees of latitude. Is it going simply to pour into the sea like a wave of any of the thousand rivers which link the earth to the sea? Nature's last stroke pours fresh vitality, for the last time, into the Nile's creative power: just above its mouth, it divides.

But man, who mastered the Nile, turns Nature's whim to good account and commands the river, in its strange transformation, to create a new country, rich in crops. At the end of its career, when other rivers sink exhausted, this child of nature makes a fresh spurt, and in the last 50 miles of its course creates the most fertile land in the inhabited world. Its Delta becomes an idea; every delta in the world is called after the Nile Delta, as though it had been the first to conceive the idea of discharging its life-powers in a final act of creation.

But everything on this river verges on the incredible: just as the magic of the Nile, in the strange adventures of its life, was always illuminated by the clarity of natural law, here, at the end, reason arises over this astonishing triangle of earth and water and clearly pronounces a grotesque statement—this delta must be at least 13,860 years old. It is as curious a number as the light-years of the stars, yet, like them, it can be proved.

For in earliest times, when the Nile trickled away in vast swamps, running off in countless branches, this filter dammed the waters, and out of the wilderness of the jungle-swamps there must have risen a confused din of beasts and birds such as we can only dream of. But when man brought his skill and cunning to Nature, long before the Pharaohs, he began to regulate these swamps with dikes and ditches, and by his skill to turn them into fruitful land. Since man thus took Nature's play seriously, she willingly obeyed him, after the fashion of a god apparently yielding to the prayer of one of his worshippers; she allowed man to reduce the wilderness to order, until in historical times, the structure of the Delta was altered and simplified.

The Delta was sometimes called the biggest island in the Nile, but the two outermost branches, the Canopic and Pelusiac Niles, were much wider than the Rosetta and Damietta branches of today. At one time, three branches of the Nile were reckoned; Herodotus named five; Strabo, Pliny, and others saw seven; Idrissi, the greatest Arab geographer, speaks of six, and places the head of the Delta, the so-called "Cow's Belly," higher than it lay before or after. Aristotle even regarded only the western branch as natural, and all the rest as artificial, and the old maps show canals which have changed their course five times. Of all the changes which have reduced the area of the Delta in the last 1500 years, nothing has remained but the beautiful name of the seventh branch, which was called the "Bucolic," after a tribe of herdsmen who once lived their nomad life there.

But how was and is it possible, on this Delta which has been trained to serve man, on these fields wrested from the swamp, to keep the water lying long enough, since the ground-level does not rise in this alluvial country as it does in Upper Egypt? This question leads to surprising conclusions.

The oldest measurements on the Nilometer at Roda near Cairo agree with the latest in placing the average altitude of the Delta at about 60 feet, so that the slow and steady rise in the ground-level is measured from "sea-level plus 60." Since the Egyptian water system as far as Cairo has never varied, the rise in the ground-level from Aswân to Cairo must have remained constant throughout the long and narrow Nile valley, given its even width and the absence of waterfalls. The difference in height between the upper embankment at Aswân and Cairo is 235 feet, which, given the distance of 520 miles, means a fall of less than 5½ inches per mile. In the Delta, on the other hand, the incline is more than 7 inches per mile, so that the rise in the ground-level per year and century ought to have been less. And yet it was the same.

For although the water in the branches of the Delta rushes down more quickly than along the whole earlier course of the river, the rise in the ground-level is caused only by the spread of the waters which, in its turn, is dependent on their speed and length. The Nilometer at Roda records the rise in the ground-level for centuries. Thus men have discovered Nature's tricks in the structure of the Delta, since instructed intelligence once began to take measurements here over a thousand years ago: the results, according to the latest methods of research, show 700 years for every yard of rise in the Delta. Since the Delta, with its level of 60 feet, has risen in six stages, the formation of each stage of roughly 10 feet can be reckoned at 2310 years, whence we arrive at the mysterious figure of 13,860 as the minimum time in which the Delta can have come into being.

This is more than mere playing with figures, for there is nothing hypothetical about them; they have been taken direct from the oldest Arab records, and since it is precisely the figures for Lower Egypt that go back into the fifth millennium B.C., nearly half of those 140 centuries are already covered by history, and thus the imagination can be enriched with a map of the Delta as it looked about the time of the building of the great pyramids. Wall-paintings from tombs of the Old Kingdom carry on the tale into the succeeding epochs, with herdsmen, in rustic quiet, sheltering from the weather under woven mats, for here in the Delta, the fate of rainlessness, with its blessing and its curse, ceases; the laws of rain and wind are not the same over the sea as over the desert. On those paintings the herdsman lies sleeping at the edge of these half-swamps, his dog is on guard at his feet, its ears pricked up, the calves and oxen are being led through the water, and naked men are waving their arms to ward off the dangerous crocodile.

In the accounts of Greek travellers, these tender shepherds, it is true, have turned into brigands, living near the coast on islands and landspits, and almost inaccessible once they had landed from their boats: tall strong men with small feet and horsemen, riding bareback and shooting sharp arrows, called Biamites in the hiero-glyphics—the name really means Asiatics, foreigners—perhaps the last remnants of the Hyksos are to be found in them. The masters of Egypt sought in vain to get the better of these swamp-men in their natural retreats, for they constantly sallied forth on surprise-raids, under Marcus Aurelius as under the first Caliphs, and Bonaparte's men were still startled by their war-cry.

Even today, half an hour by air from the metropolis of Cairo, they form unmanageable tribes in distant islands at the eastern fringe of the Delta, sailing in boats with high, triangular sails, and bailing the water out of their boats with a pelican's beak. They have remained on a lower cultural level than the bedouins, with whom they have been compared, for they do not reckon time, like them, by the length of their shadow: they merely dis-tinguish morning, midday, and twilight. Even today they cure their fish in the way Herodotus saw them do it.

WOMEN CARRYING WATER FROM THE NILE

BETWEEN THE CANALS

2

OF those fourteen millenniums
through which we can follow the history of the Delta, only three
are opened up by national history, for everything that happened
in the Old Kingdom is conjectural. If the pyramids were not
there, the excavations in ancient Memphis would conjure up far
fewer pictures than those in the Thebaid high up the Nile. The
residence of the later dynasties did not return to Memphis till
about the year 1000 B.C. and only remained there till 300 B.C.

After having been the capital of the world for nearly a thousand years, Thebes perished, largely owing to the continual
changes in its ruling house, for in the rapid development of world-
traffic, Asiatics invaded it from the east, Africans from the south,
the former with merchandise, the latter with war-chariots, and
while the last ten Egyptian dynasties were rapidly succeeding each
other in the course of seven centuries, continually warring against
native princes, the weapons of foreign conquerors were flashing
outside the fortress-temples, strangers, light and dark, were washing their bodies in the Nile, costumes and customs, languages
and religions, were mingling in the narrow oasis, and still more
in the broad Delta which opened up more readily to the awakening Mediterranean.

For six centuries, until the Persian invasions, peoples pass on
the Nile whose names sound biblical or legendary, whose strange
doublets and weapons march through the reliefs on Pharaonic
walls. Philistines in copper armour, with long swords, round
shields, and big, feathered helmets; Achæans and Sardians, who
perhaps saw the Minotaur in Crete; the Sekal and other great
pirates with unpronounceable names, who descended on the
Delta like Vikings. And King Solomon came through the desert
to the Nile to take a Pharaoh's daughter to wife, for he had to

make peace with her father, who had invaded Canaan and was now paying the dowry in the towns he had just taken from his son-in-law. Solomon was too wise and too lustful to carry on his race, and a barbarous Libyan king carried off the treasures of this great lover of life and confessor of religion and of his invisible God.

The Negro King Pianki was stronger. He came riding down the Nile from Nubia, past the cataracts, on splendid horses, making it look as if, being himself the representative of Amon up in Napata, he merely wished to visit the god in his Theban home. The Pharaoh, who was still dreaming of Nubian colonies, like his fathers a thousand years before, was indignant. But the Ethiopian besieged him and killed men in the fortress until the Egyptian within, overcome by pestilence and the stench of corpses, mounted the walls and offered the conqueror an olive-branch in the shape of a fine horse. The barbarian standing below suddenly saw Egypt once more reaching to Ethiopia, but now it was ruled from the south, for the colony and the motherland had changed places.

But now the Assyrians advanced from the east, the Ethiopian fled up-Nile out of the strange country before the Assyrian, who conquered it. The victor advanced to Thebes, and in 661 B.C. destroyed the heart of the world. This time, however, he was no barbarian seeking for horses, but in his way an art-connoisseur, especially when it came to assessing the value of the gold objects: he showed future conquerors the way by carrying off fifty-five statues and obelisks, of which the electrum alone was worth 2500 talents.

While the two continents were fighting for Egypt, one of the contending native princes, for the last time, made himself king: Psammetich of Sais was banished to the Delta on account of an oracle. Then armed pirates, Ionians and Carians, landed there, took mercenary service under the exile, while the Egyptian princes fled before the new and terrible sight of men armed with iron, and abandoned to Psammetich one of the last Pharaonic crowns. His portrait is extant: with his pinched profile, snub nose, big-lobed ears, and sharp mouth, he looks plebeian. By rewarding the iron-clad adventurers with land in the Delta, divided by branches of the Nile to prevent their falling on each other, then turning them against his own subjects for his own protection, he revealed Egypt to the eyes of the Greeks who were sailing in the archipelago, and thus prepared the great conquest of his land by Hellas.

Only one of the Pharaohs of this period has descended to history, because he designed a great work of civilization in the interior: in 600 B.C. Necho began the Suez Canal, which was not finished till our own epoch. At the point where the Atlantic and Indian Oceans thrust out two great arms which so squeeze the land between them that they approach to within sixty miles of each other, both the Middle and the New Kingdoms had attempted to build a canal. But the constructive genius, the money, and the slave-labour by means of which those Pharaohs had mastered the Nile was not yet supported by the desire to spread beyond the oasis, to link up the element of their life with that of their sea-faring neighbours, the Nile with the sea. The heads and hands which had built the pyramids and obelisks, the temples of Thebes and the system of dams and canals, would have been equal to building the Suez Canal. But their vision could not reach across the desert to the sea. It was the oasis character of Egypt which always frustrated such efforts.

This latecomer Necho, who had seen the foreign conquerors in the land of his fathers, and had himself pushed its defence as far as Syria, was the first to grasp the spirit of sea-faring and commerce; he built a fleet and advertised it so well that the ladies of the court wore little brooches in the form of ships, which were found in our own day, twenty-five centuries later. At the same time, he designed a strong canal wide enough for two triremes to pass.

In the neighbourhood of the ancient city of Bubastis, this canal carried ships on Nile water in four days from the eastern branch of the Delta, through a valley which is still fertile, to the Ismailia of our own times, and was then planned to turn south to the Red Sea. Though it did not cross the isthmus, the passage from the Mediterranean to the Red Sea was nevertheless opened up through the Delta. Thus the Nile, at the end of its course, became the mediator between the two greatest domains of life, and at that time the only one: Phœnicians and Greeks could transport Chinese silks and Indian precious stones by ship to Memphis and Crete without having to unload and reload their men and camels.

Yet even this time the great idea was never realized. What stopped Pharaoh was not the trickling sand, nor the death of the 120,000 slaves who are said to have lost their lives during the building. It was simply an oracle: "Thou art creating this work for a barbarian"—thus spoke the priests when it was half finished, a purely practical consideration which prevented the completion of a great work of civilization, just as today the building of the Channel Tunnel between Dover and Calais is prevented only by the secret fear felt by both nations that they may be building for their barbarian neighbour.

A century later, the barbarian had appeared: Darius the Persian, the conqueror of Egypt, continued and perhaps even completed the canal; the half-ruined column on which he eulogized his deeds permits of more than one interpretation. According to Diodorus, Darius seems even to have contemplated piercing the isthmus, but to have abandoned the plan for the fantastic reason that it would swamp Egypt, which lay lower.

Every few centuries, in later times, foreign conquerors were attracted by the strategic advantages and commercial possibilities of a Suez Canal, yet the fear that the barbarian on the other side might use it too, in his bid for conquest, seems always to have prevented further developments. But none omitted to name it to his own glory; thus it was called in turn Ptolemy's River, Trajan's River, the River of the Emir of the Faithful, and may have changed not only its name but its course. In the eighth century, an Irish pilgrim, Fidelis by name, says that he sailed in the same boat from the Nile to the Gulf of Suez.

Here again, so-called international politics frustrated the natural communication between neighbours, for a revolt in Mecca caused the Caliph to block the Canal, in order to starve the city out. In later times, religion took a hand: Harun ar Rashid refused to restore the Canal because Christian corsairs might hold up the Mecca pilgrims in the Red Sea.

But today, a thousand years after the Caliph whose nights enriched the world with its loveliest stories, the world has not yet quite awakened to the light of day, for seventy years after the completion of the great work, it is again playing with the idea of closing the Canal, to prevent one colonial empire from threatening another. It is as if the heart were to threaten the head with cutting off an artery.

3

ONLY one Pharaoh, and he an upstart, stands out among those who ruled in the Delta. Amasis, having risen to be minister and marshal, took the occasion offered by a revolt in the army to overthrow, and later to kill, his king, and then to enjoy life in a long, wise reign. This Pharaoh was not afraid to record himself, on the inscriptions to the gods, as a former secretary to the treasury, and to declare to his subjects that he would reign only till midday, for a taut bow must be unstrung. He dismissed the judges who had acquitted him for his youthful follies because they had thus given proof of folly themselves; those who had condemned him he rewarded for their wisdom. He had a gold basin, in which he washed his feet, melted down and made into a divine image, and when the courtiers made obeisance to it, he told them how often he had spat into it.

His weak successor lost Egypt to the Persians. The new masters of the world appeared on the Nile in broad, embroidered cloaks bordered with fur, in high, broad-brimmed hats, in pointed shoes, and armed with long swords. But their kings, Cambyses and Darius, wore short cloaks, like the later knights, and white turbans, like the later Mamelukes. They were followed by archers with huge quivers on their backs, while others were armed with long spears, but all had beards and thick hair cut in soldierly fashion. They remained masters of the Nile for two hundred years, till Alexander came. The Egyptians, however, rose against the Persians in more than one great revolt, in which, from time to time, some native prince would regain shreds of power.

The last of them came from the swamps of the north-eastern Delta, from that inaccessible domain of the hunters and herdsmen, from islands which legend declared to float, from that wilderness of grasses and trees, from hiding-places in which refugees

446

had hidden since Isis, on her flight, had borne her son there. Here bold chieftains allied with Greek mercenaries and Spartiates who served anybody who paid them, and now, in the fourth century B.C., overran Egypt.

For one last time, all the vitality of the ancient Pharaohs gathered itself together in the founder of the last dynasty, the thirtieth, who built not only temples in Karnak and Philæ, but fortresses in the Delta too, and caught the great fleet of Pharnabazus in the closed and choked arm of the Nile. When the Persians all the same advanced to Memphis, the river turned on them. It rose mightily, forced the invaders back into the Delta, and then into a general retreat. Once more, the Nile had saved Egypt.

Twenty years later, when a great army of Persians succeeded in a third and victorious landing in the Delta, the descendant of those valiant old monarchs fled before them, carrying his treasures up-Nile to the Ethiopians. That was the end of the last of the Pharaohs. He withdrew into the African interior, fled from the silken cloaks of the Persian nobles to the naked, brown men up on the rocky cataracts of the Nile, as though in a last attempt to unroll the history of the river backwards.

Ten years later, the Persian Empire fell to pieces: all that the Persians left behind in Egypt was the peach tree, which Cambyses is said to have brought with him from Ethiopia. For a piece of a new Europe, brilliant and fiery, destined to carry an idea to victory, had arisen against that Asiatic power. That idea was called τὸ καλὸν κἀγαθὸν: with it the Greeks conquered part of the physical and the whole of the spiritual world, and if a schoolboy of today asks how it happened, we might explain by translating the expression as the union of the beautiful and the wise which gives birth to the good. The native Egyptians could hardly have been conquered by a people more different from themselves. The Greek soldier was as alien to the fellah as the Egyptian was to the Athenian citizen, whose popular songs jeered at the man who worshipped the ox instead of eating it and adored the cat instead of skinning it. If the Nile peasant had come into contact with the Greek peasant, they would have understood each other at once. But those who poured into the country were simply soldiers and merchants, and since they introduced, with their olives and new kinds of vine from Samos and Cyprus, Crete and Athens, their customs and their gods, since they founded cities in the Delta, since the Æginetans built temples to Zeus and the Samians to Hera, founding at the same time their free ports to avoid the payment of customs dues, the Egyptians were astonished by the idea that they should attempt to introduce new customs to a country with four thousand years of history behind it, while the foreigners could not realize how a people who could live together with their cattle could yet have priests who possessed supreme wisdom.

A democratic people could not comprehend a people educated to monarchy, nor an island people an oasis people, and although neither felt the other to be barbarian, the Greeks, who burnt their dead to ashes, could not but feel alien to a people which endeavoured to preserve them with all the resources of chemistry. Mental clarity and grace here met an inarticulate mysticism, freedom of thought revolted against the compulsion of tradition, scepticism against faith, the mentally swift against the mentally slow-moving, resilient beauty against massive fixity. A mountain country rich in springs and rivers here met the desert, and the spirit of the sea the spirit of a river.

4

WHEN Alexander the Great landed in the eastern Delta, he was twenty-four years old. We do not know whether his portrait-busts are good likenesses: the only thing we do know is that he was still handsomer. The story of his soul and his glory paint his true portrait; each one of us can conjure up his own Alexander from all the busts, coins, and paintings. In no other case has a man's physical beauty played such a determining part in his career; all the accounts of his contemporaries begin and end with it, a fact which at once sets him apart from the two later conquerors of the world. If ever personality left its mark on the world, it was here, where fame and beauty were not the attributes of a conqueror, but where both impelled him to conquer the world; they did so very early, since the gods had granted him so short a span of life.

Alexander's third incentive was his descent from the gods, from Achilles, the son of a goddess; he envied Achilles his bard, took poets on his expeditions, and kept Homer beside his sword at night, at his bedside in a Persian casket mounted in silver, which had once contained perfumes.

His leonine aspect was not only due to his hair, which stood up above his forehead and fell away on both sides of his face; it came too from his liquid eyes, which are mentioned in all descriptions of him: they seem to link him to the feminine, for it is not by mere chance that just such liquid eyes were attributed to Aphrodite. The fine mouth, on the other hand, was youthful and virile, full but not broad, and puckered, and its hint of sensuality was perfectly balanced by the eyes, for a slight bend of the head to the left counteracted any stiffness in their upward look to the right. The unequal structure of the forehead, with the prominent lower part characteristic of the athlete, and the will-power expressed in the chin, set him apart from the mere lovers of the muses, and mark him out as a master of warfare, not of music.

Yet in all these busts, it is Alexander after a victory that we see: Lysippus captured him in this mood in highly modern fashion. The mosaic portrait on Pompeii alone shows us the king in battle: with flying hair, for he has lost his helmet, he is fighting on his rearing horse, rushing on to the attack, his eyes wide open in the oriental oval of his face.

The greatest of his battles were just over when he arrived in Egypt: he had won the battle of Issus, Tyre and Gaza had fallen, before Gaza he had nearly lost his life. The Persian world empire was no more. This youth owned the world from the Black Sea to the mouth of the Nile. It was hardly likely that Egypt, the last Persian province he was to invade, would offer any serious resistance. Alexander came to Egypt with an easy courage, in the great cæsura of his young life: six years of conquest lay behind him, and premonitions that not much more lay ahead may as yet hardly have touched him.

Life was still streaming towards him, rich in fulfilments, and it was his good fortune to win them from battle to battle with his own right hand. He still trusted his friend, although he was already being warned against him. He still believed it possible to reconcile the enemy by the virtue of the spear he had received from Achilles his ancestor. He was resolved, against the advice of Aristotle, not to treat the conquered barbarians like animals and plants; he was resolved to take his own decisions, and in so doing, was guided by his master's words: "Genius cannot be ruled by any common law. It is like a god among men. The man who would try to impose laws upon it would make himself ridiculous." He lived according to that saying; Alexander's presumption was as boundless as his achievement.

Egypt received him like a god. After three centuries of a foreign yoke, it believed then, and even later, at each foreign conquest, that the new master must, of necessity, be better than the last. And this one seemed like a figure of saga; he had covered the distance from Gaza to Pelusium in seven days. Then he sailed up the eastern arm of the Nile and not an archer bent his bow; to the crowd he looked like the heir of the last Pharaoh, and not like a conqueror, as he brought his sacrifice to the god Ptah and the sacred bull, as he honoured the priests who had been humiliated by the Persians, and at the same time sent for the best athletes for the Hellenic games he held in Egypt.

The Egyptians could not but feel secure in the protection of such a youth. As part of an empire such as the world had not yet seen, they were at last released from the struggle of the Greeks against the Persians, all the Mediterranean coasts were Greek, so was the road to Asia, and when the new conqueror left strong forces behind in the land, they simply looked like the troops of a league of nations. The Persian satrap had at once submitted. The policy of Pericles, Egypt for Athens, had become a peace-making world policy.

By regaining the sea in the neighbourhood of the Rosetta of today through the western arm of the Nile, past the city of the Greeks, to which he wished to pay all possible honour, Alexander had traversed the second side of the triangle. The surprise only came when he reached the long landspit at the extreme western corner of Egypt which stretches between the sea and Lake Mareotis. What was he doing in the west when his mission called him to the east?

In this isolated arm of the sea, he at once recognized the great, wind-free harbour, and with it the point at which Egypt could be linked up with the sea. At the same time, this was the point at which the silt carried down by the Nile could not settle to choke up the harbour. This was the place to found a city which should stimulate the Greek exporters, make sure of the Egyptian harvests, and at the same time stir the imagination of the world, a place for the warrior, for the uniter of the world, and for his glory. Alexander himself designed the town which bears his name, like an American of today, fixing the site of the public buildings and the two main streets, which for the first time crossed at right angles and were called after the letters of the alphabet. At the same time he designed a mole to the isle of Pharos, and temples to Isis and Zeus, and created a super-national whole, penetrated with the spirit of unity. By founding this city, Alexander accelerated the movement which drew the Pharaohs from Thebes to Memphis: he made Egypt a Mediterranean empire, he even drew the Nile into his Greek sphere, at a time when Europe was just coming into being.

Legend tells that he had flour strewn on a table in the open air and drew the course of the streets and squares on it with his finger, to show his architect, but then the birds came and pecked the flour. "That means wealth and well-being for the new city," cried a wise man. And it was so.

Such were the visible events, but beside them the invisible was working with profounder purpose.

The plans of his city laid, Alexander rode west without delay, always retreating from his goal, to the most westerly point of his career. Accompanied by a handful of troops, he rode along the sea-coast for ten days, then turned through the desert to reach an oasis in which there was nothing to conquer but a saying. In that oasis there was an oracle; there were gods whom he did not summon to himself, but whom he went forth to see.

Deep thoughts must have beset him as he rode across the desert on his camel to question the priests of an unknown god. His mother had been a Thracian priestess who had raged through the mountains, a thyrsus in her hand. Had she not told him of the lightning that had struck her womb in a dream, and how her son had been born of it? Everything that had stirred his boyish passion, the repudiation of his Greek mother by his father, drew him to her and away from his Macedonian father, whom even Demosthenes had called a barbarian. And the Athenian satirists had jeered only a few years before at the bad taste of the customs he had brought to Greece with his Macedonians. Now they mocked no more, because they feared his sword. Only a short time before, the Greeks had built altars to Lysander, and proposed building one to Agesilaus. The times of divinization were not yet past. Yet no one conferred divine honours on Alexander, who had accomplished deeds so much greater.

What if he were to receive, in this most ancient country, in a mysteriously hidden temple, the sacred honours that Zeus of Dodona and Apollo of Delphi had not yet conferred upon him? And though it was a stranger god, what did that matter? Pindar had sung of the oracle of Amon which was more than a thousand years old. He would not be crowned Pharaoh in Memphis—that was too easy, it smacked too much of the rude homage of the conquered. But if he were blessed by the most ancient cult in the world, in the presence of only a few witnesses, in the shade of palms, in the midst of the desert, which till then no Greek foot had ever trod, how the imagination of the world would be stirred!

Hercules had questioned the oracle before setting out against Antæus, Perseus before he went out to seek the Gorgon. They were demigods, but where was the dividing-line? Heraclitus had dared to call the gods immortal men, and men mortal gods. All these thoughts, shrewd and worldly, romantic and mystical, the memories of his mother and his teacher, must have held Alexander's expectation tense as he rode on his camel to the oasis of Amon.

He knew too, for certain, that Aristotle's definition of the Greek godhead as "that which moves, being motionless, that which created itself," corresponded even in the wording to certain formulas of the priests of Amon. And so he knew that the priests in the desert were spiritually prepared for him, even though no messenger had announced the coming of the new ruler.

At last the outline of palms rose on the horizon. The court poet whom Alexander had taken with him, so as to be prepared for everything, tells us that he was surprised by the brightness of the sacred domain, with its surrounding date-palms, olives, salt-springs, and healing waters. Yet before the solemn procession of priests had time to move towards him, he entered the temple alone, greeted by the High Priest, who led him into the sanctuary. "After a short time," we read, "Alexander returned with a bright countenance, and said that the answer of the god had been according to his desire." Then he witnessed the procession with the sacred bark, and returned by the direct eastern route to Memphis.

None of the countless legends which, even in his own time, sprang up round this scene, the questions he is said to have put, the world dominion promised to him, and his own interpretation of the priest's greeting *"paidion"* as *Pai Dios,* by which he felt himself hailed as the son of the gods—nothing of all this can compare with the effect of these two lines, which, in their cool terseness, clearly represent the truth: a brief visit, a bright countenance, and the smiling answer of the great ruler: "All is well."

We can see him appearing before the startled priest, expressing a few wishes in the form of questions, and, on the assurance that he was indeed the son of Amon, for he was now Pharaoh of Egypt, quitting the temple for whose blessing he had sacrificed a precious month of his rapid life. In later years, when he was questioned by his friends about the oracle, he said nothing and denied nothing.

As the son of Zeus-Amon, Alexander left Egypt, never to see it again. He had made full preparations for leaving the country a long time without a ruler, had divided the military command among three Greek generals, put the internal administration into the hands of the Egyptians, provided for the protection of the priests, while the gold coins with his head show two little Amon's horns among his curls; if his deeds had not later conferred upon him the title of the "Great," the world might have called him, as the Arabs did later, "Alexander the Double-Horned."

What he took from Egypt was the desert oracle which proclaimed him of the race of the gods. What he left there was a world metropolis. His great successor, Napoleon, went so far as to write, at the end of his own career: "Alexander made himself more famous by the founding of Alexandria than by his most brilliant victories. It is a city which could not but become the heart of the world."

5

IN the first centuries after its foundation, the focal point of the roughly isosceles triangle formed by the Delta seemed to shift from its head in the south to this north-western angle. Memphis struggled in vain against its young rival, and while the whole world was trying to become Greek, it became Alexandrian. The Egyptian capital succumbed; even Heliopolis, which had seen Moses, Herodotus, and Plato within its walls, sank into a mound of potsherds, while Cairo first came into being in the seventh century A.D.

Alexandria rapidly grew into a world centre. A hundred years after its foundation, its million inhabitants not only made it the most populous city in the world, as Thebes had once been; owing to its situation it was more powerful than Thebes, and it made the Nile oasis more powerful by linking it to the sea. The foundation of this city exercised a more decisive influence on the fate of Egypt than any conquest before or after, for neither the Arabs nor the English created a new exit or passage for the Nile.

Alexander's city was described as the city which knew no idlers. "Some blow glass, others make papyrus sheets, others again weave linen, every man practises a craft, or pretends he does. There is work for the halt and the blind, no rheumatic goes idle, for the Alexandrians worship one god only—money." That is Emperor Hadrian's description. In a kind of gallery in the market-place, the people stood at their stalls crying their oil, salt, or strange woods, just as they stand today. The ladies displayed their charms in the public baths, hot and cold; dinner-parties were given in the water, and when all the Egyptians were later expelled from Alexandria, the stokers of the baths had to be retained. The whole was Greek, but it was colonial.

Yet there was not much room. Covering a narrow rectangle

four miles long by one broad, the shape of which was compared to an antique cloak, bounded by lagoons stretching away to Lake Mareotis, the city looked rather like an annex to Egypt than part of it. The harbours on the sea-coast and the Delta were linked up; warehouses were built at the eastern trading port, at present destitute of traffic; at this same eastern port the palace of the kings was rising, the museum and the library, the theatre, the race-course, and the circus were coming into being; and where the cranes today hoist bales of cotton onto the ships, the bales of papyrus then rolled into them. But the city's chief glory radiated in quite a literal sense from a huge lamp, shining on the light-house outside on the island of Pharos. The first concave mirror multiplied the light. Even today the name of the island of Alexander's choice shines through the night to the navigators of distant lands, the symbol of rescue.

The King of Egypt was now one of Alexander's generals, a Macedonian of the minor nobility, older than his master, and faithful to him, but he had come late to his high place, and was obviously less familiar with him than he was apt to claim, after the fashion of all satellites when their sun has died out. And yet even independent of his master, he seems in his way to have been eminent, and while born to be a Mæcenas rather than a ruler, he was strong enough to make himself powerfully felt in his royal function.

On Alexander's death, nine years after the foundation of Alexandria, when the empire was divided among his generals in the name of his posthumous son, this first Ptolemy had taken Egypt. It was not until he had been regent for seventeen years, and long after the death of the legitimate heir, that he crowned himself Pharaoh and assumed the name of Soter, that is, saviour. The dynasty descended from this relative mediocrity ruled for three hundred years, while Alexander's line died out with him. Genius is not hereditary.

The supreme stroke of the first Ptolemy was to get possession of the body of Alexander. Alexander dead, since he could not defend himself, passed from hand to hand, was first stolen on account of his gold coffin, then carried off by an elephant army, and later robbed of his gold coffin. Whoever possessed him, the

THE AUTHOR IN ABU SIMBEL

PICKING COTTON

god of this empire and this city, felt sustained by his spirit, but the house of Ptolemy, which possessed him for centuries, inherited nothing but his luck.

For this house, which was neither Egyptian nor Macedonian, but Greek in its thoughts, speech, and government, was in so far favoured by fortune that it could satisfy all its passions, pluck with extreme refinement the fruits of life, enjoy pride and revenge, pleasure and culture, without ever being teased by the question at whose cost they were living here, though strangers in the land. It was a court of muses and hetairas, of philosophers and criminals, where most men murdered their families, and where the finest temples of Egypt were designed. A love of life which at times swelled to madness made these men declare themselves gods, crown their mistresses with divine honours, exploit the children of an hour of love in the intrigues of the succession within, and foreign alliances without, or forge—even then—wills to establish their claim to power. The women killed one brother in order to marry the next; all held themselves scatheless, amid revolts and wars, by pillaged wealth, and at the same time assembled the greatest spirits of the time to goad the jealousy of declining Athens and rising Rome. The most astonishing thing about it all, however, was that many of these men and women were able to prolong a life of such intensity into an advanced age. As they rarely waited for their predecessors to die a natural death, and hence generally ascended the throne in childhood or youth, there were among them men who reigned thirty or forty years.

Perhaps women have never attained such legitimate power in the whole course of occidental history; it is unique too that, without reigning in their own right, and merely as the wives of kings, they had numbers to their names like the kings themselves, so that they might inherit the great name of some famous courtesan. With insatiable avidity they exacted and gathered in the spoil of distant lands, and when their statuettes, with their rouged face and short chiton, were dispersed among the people, their royal lovers laughed. But then, we are told, the king would suddenly stop to look out of the window of his palace, and speak with envy of the fellah eating his bread below.

At the same time, some of them had time and spirit enough to

undertake conquests after the fashion of Alexander, and the third
Ptolemy, with the help of a good general, advanced to the Euphrates, overthrew the Seleucid Empire, and became for a few
years the greatest man of his epoch. He was the first to have his
fat, flabby face reproduced on coins with the trident, the symbol
of his dominion over the seas, and amused himself by crowning
the curly head of Berenice II with the double crown of the Egyptian Pharaohs. At the same time, this adventurer was the friend
of scholars, and looked very grave when a successor of Euclid
pointed out to him, as he sat with his companions, the confusion
in the calendar, and, four thousand years after its invention, declared that the insertion of a day was an absolute spiritual necessity.

The next, Ptolemy IV, adopted the most pleasant side of this
science, as a pupil of Eratosthenes, by having himself rowed up-
Nile in a superb dahabiya as a votary of Dionysus, between his
favourite and his mistress; in Thebes, to his astonishment, he
found ghosts of the real Pharaohs, the native princelings who
ventured to reign up there for a few years on their own account.
His wife and sister, later murdered, then enshrined in a book by
the great philosopher, preceded his brother, who was drowned in
his bath, and his mother, who was poisoned.

From that time on, after the defeat of Carthage, the Ptolemies
began to ship Egyptian grain to Rome, and while, in their own
country, they declined in rapid decadence, in their foreign politics they became increasingly dependent on Rome. The struggle
between Rome and Alexandria was decided before it began. The
cloaks of the Ptolemies had grown too long and too fine, the hilts
of their swords too costly, their faces too fleshy, their mouths too
vicious, for them to be able to hold their own against the trim
armour, the hard heads, and the thin lips, whose owners came
over to demand tribute of them out of hand, as though Egypt
were already a conquered country. By this time the last Ptolemies,
suddenly remembering their patron, had assumed the names of
Alexander I and II: one was proficient in dancing, and gave
public performances, then tried to steal Alexander's coffin, and
was killed when taking flight; the other, who first married, then
killed his mother-in-law, was assassinated by the mob in the sta-

dium. But at the same time their Roman adversaries were conquering the Mediterranean. Jerusalem and Cyprus fell into their hands, and when Ptolemy Auletes, the flute-player, fled to Rome for help against his daughter, and found Cato governor of Rhodes, Cato did not rise, but merely asked the king to be seated

6

AND yet, in the three last centuries before Christ, it was Alexandria that was the cynosure of the world's eyes, not Rome. The opulence of its kings attracted men of mind and learning to their court; its refinement of culture brought women to their flower, and its bad reputation goaded the general curiosity, while its harbour linked up three continents, and no other did.

It was above all the mixture of different races that worked productively here. While in the eyes of the Egyptians, the kings played their part as Pharaohs, especially in religious ceremonies, to the Greek administrators and politicians they seemed brothers. In actual fact, nobody was taken in: the Egyptian priests despised these crowned upstarts who lacked four thousand years of history; the Greeks, looking upon them as Macedonians, half-barbarians, did not take them seriously; the Jews, who were powerful and rich in Alexandria, felt superior to all three as the Chosen People; and the Ptolemies imagined that, in any case, the world belonged to them, the successors of Alexander, and emphasized the rude origins of their fathers by high boots, soft felt hats, and a carefully cultivated Macedonian accent. But as Alexander, after all, had been half Persian, they also introduced to their court the table-manners of the satraps.

And nothing in the Alexandrian court was as important as the table and its banquets. There were kings who celebrated their birthday every month, driving through the streets in a chariot laden with grapes, from which wine gushed out among the people, but when the smell of the mob reached the silver chariot of the king, the lovely Arsinoë II drew back, offended. Then the giant galley lay in the harbour in all its pride: the world rang with its fame, for it was 500 feet long and could hold three thousand men.

When Ptolemy founded the library, he started it on a lavish scale with a hundred thousand rolls, and when it was burnt down three hundred years later, the greatest collection of books in the ancient world perished with it: the Ptolemies were so proud of it that one of them prohibited the export of papyrus when Pergamum was trying to set up a rival library. Like all parvenus to power, they contrived to attract the best minds from the older centres of culture by offering huge enticements in money: mathematicians, geographers, physicians, and sanitary engineers came, many to stay, and Epicurus, the wisest of them all, breathed here the air of life and wrote here his last, immortal letter.

What the first Ptolemy founded in this library was and remained unprecedented in the ancient world, because for the first time it represented knowledge for its own sake; a brilliant centre of learning was founded in truly royal fashion. While the full freedom of the republican school could not be enjoyed here, the first two kings demanded no sacrifice of conviction for their money, and everybody who counted crowded to this coast from foreign countries to learn and to teach.

To the persuasions of Greek culture, the Egyptians and Jews, before the Romans came, offered an obstinate resistance, though here as everywhere, those who assimilated were in the majority.

The standing of the Jews, who owned two out of the five divisions of Alexandria, was lower than that of the Greeks and higher than that of the Egyptians, a double injustice and a double source of later persecutions. Here the Jews began their wanderings; here they took the first step on their fateful course of adapting themselves to every strange people, while remaining themselves strangers, of abandoning now too much, now too little of the heritage of their fathers, of forming within every state a spiritual state without ever becoming a physical one. Greek among the Greeks in language and customs, enjoying Greek citizenship in large numbers, administering their own affairs, and undisturbed for long stretches of time, they became Greeks to such an extent that one of their High Priests tried to Hellenize Jerusalem. Cleopatra II had Jewish generals.

There were probably fewer Egyptian than Jewish prefects and generals. The Greeks seem to have regarded Egypt as a mausoleum of human and animal bones, which the visitor contemplates in silence, paying no attention to its custodians. Since they possessed the language, the power, and the country, they could afford to call their Plato a disciple of the Egyptian priests, but they prohibited intermarriage between Greeks and Egyptians. They spoke of Zeus-Amon, sacrificed in Faiyûm to Nemesis and Isis at the same time, kept a sacred bull in Alexandria, although in their eyes it was grotesque, allowed the priests to keep the proceeds of the exhibition of the bull, and paid for the costly linen swaths required at its death, but the priests had to learn Greek at their own expense. Spiritually, the Egyptian religion gained by the influence of the Greek, but as the two mingled, no clarity was achieved on the most delicate point of Egyptian doctrine, namely life after death.

To all the tribes and languages which flooded the Delta, the Egyptian people presented an unbroken front. Foreign lords came, bringing their own customs and vernaculars; descendants of the Persians and Assyrians were still settled on the Upper Nile; Syrians were already penetrating into the Faiyûm, Jews into the Delta, Thracians and Cilicians, Libyans and Galatians, were all crowding onto this most fertile spot on earth. But it was the Greeks who carried its fruits overseas, and filled the holds of their vessels for the return voyage with a host of superfluous fripperies which they brought to the Alexandrians as a greeting from the land of their fathers, but imposed on the inquisitive fellah as the marvels of distant lands. Here in the great port, where the northern sea met the Nile from the south, the Greek sailors sang:

> Oh, shipmates from over the rolling sea,
> Boldly adventuring, strong and free,
> Come, look at the freshwater lubbers here,
> Who paddle the Nile, who know no fear.
> Oh! it's a dog's life, the life of the sea!

But the eternal fellah could not but come to hate the Greek, who grew rich without labour. All he had to do was to sail to the Isles, buy, charter a vessel, load up, and then extort ten times the value of the goods from the Greek ladies. The Egyptian weavers worked too well and too slowly to supply such things.

But the gold and silversmith, the lamp- and vase-maker now worked at home in Egypt on Greek models, to adorn the tables of the court and the rich people. Wheels and factories rattled in the world city, and since, beside the slaves, there were thousands of paid workmen, syndicates were founded, wages were kept down and prices up by capitalist societies, and there were strikes and riots.

But the basis of all this trade, of all this life in the Delta, was and remained the grain, which the fellah had to sow and reap all along the Nile, just as he did four thousand years before. But before he could get his price for it, to earn a bare living for himself and his family, he had to pay the king taxes on every waterwheel and every muddy strip of soil; and although the new Pharaoh built embankments and canals with the proceeds, he nevertheless made a huge profit, for the Ptolemies are said to have had revenues amounting to $16,000,000. Still greater financial geniuses than the Pharaohs, they founded monopolies on oil and wine, and taxed every man who wanted to live—there were beer-taxes, professional taxes on hetairas and actors, even the roof of the house on which the exhausted people slept in summer after their day's work was not free: the Ptolemies invented the tax on air.

7

OF all famous women, Cleopatra probably lived the shortest life, and when she died at thirty-eight, none left a fuller life behind her. During this time, she had reigned for twenty years and loved for at least twenty-eight. The major part of both these periods was shaken by civil war, in her country and in her heart, but on both fronts she carried off the victory. She never surrendered; she was, perhaps, once humiliated. She fought all her battles as a woman, and, in all her boldness and her crimes, never turned mannish. *Non humilis mulier*, said Horace of her, but he did her less than justice, for she lived out her own nature with more genius than any other queen. In the very midst of the storms of her dangerous life, she did not hesitate to bear children. She was no more cruel than her fathers had been, was generous in little things and vindictive in big, a good scholar and linguist, and yet a creature of instinct. Her beauty gave her everything. When, for the first time, she felt her strength yielding before a man, she put a violent end to a life that had lost its inmost meaning.

Perhaps she was not as beautiful as her story tells; on one of the few genuine medals, she looks rather brave than beautiful. But metal was no medium for her charm: the subtlety of her conversation, the delicate and seductive modulations of her voice and her look beggared not only description but portraiture, and a great poet is really the only thing lacking in her life. But her victories over the three great Roman soldiers bear witness to her genius: they are the poets of her charms.

If we are to understand her cynical innocence, the ground-note of her being, we must see her as the product of a number of races: a woman of the Levant, drugged with the dangerous drugs of Egypt, the grandchild of a courtesan, the daughter of a bastard and a criminal, and, moreover, a child of that late Alexandria

IN THE COTTON

SAILS ON THE NILE

which was three hundred years old, and already on the wane, when Cleopatra died. Lying between the two hemispheres that Rome had subjected, at the meeting-point of three civilizations, close to the isles of Europe and to the frontier of Asia, and yet on African soil, still on the sea and yet already on the Nile, such was the background against which this city and this woman flowered. The feeling that the end of the world was at hand, the clank of arms in the streets and the palace, the mercenaries from all over the world landing in the Delta, fanned her youthful vitality into a passionate lust of life, and yet, from the middle of her life onward, she filched year after year of almost idyllic love from fate. Chance, such as comes once in a thousand years, drew the men of the mightiest empire into her country: they came to find grain for their voters, and found an enchantress.

Her father, whose insolent name, Neos Dionysos, had been turned by the people into Auletes, the Flute-Player, had returned from his flight to Rome, where he had not omitted to kill to a man the hundred citizens of his capital who had been sent to speak in its defence. After that, he murdered only his wife and her party leaders, then married his eldest daughter, Cleopatra, then fourteen years old, to her ten-year-old brother, in order to bequeath the crown to them both; he himself died in contempt. The man appointed guardian to the two royal children in the name of the Roman Senate was Pompey, whose character was an occasion of dispute in the Senate and of bloody fights in the Forum. The same thing was happening in the Forum of Alexandria at the same time in the fight against one of the court parties.

At twenty, Cleopatra encountered her first Roman, Pompey, who was then at war with Cæsar. In spite of his fat, unsoldierly face, he must have made an impression on her, since she sent fifty ships to his help, which never returned. At that time, Cleopatra VII, as the queen was called, was so hated in her capital that she had to flee from the party of her brother-husband. She collected troops on the Arabian frontier, where she spoke the language of the tribes, and was soon in the field against her sixteen-year-old brother, when a second Roman, who had just murdered his enemy Pompey, entered the Delta.

Cæsar, by the battle of Pharsalus, had just become sole ruler of Rome, and actually of the world: the only thing he lacked was money. That was why he came to Egypt, and he seems to have felt no curiosity whatsoever on the subject of the Amazonian queen who had supported his adversary. As he had arrived in Alexandria and at the palace before her, and had made a triumphal entry preceded by lictors, to the intense annoyance of the people, who could not suffer such displays, the queen was hard put to it.

She therefore embarked in Pelusium in disguise, slipped into the capital between the great galleys, had herself wrapped up in rugs and carried into the palace, where she knew she would find the conqueror and her brother-husband; Cæsar, expecting a gift, watched the unpacking of the roll. Cleopatra emerged.

Then her offended brother appeared and threw the crown at her. Cæsar had to decide between a furious boy and an enchanting woman. He endeavoured to placate the mob raging under the windows by restoring both the children to the throne in accordance with their father's will. But there was a Greek ringleader who was clamouring for a reward for having saved the king. The mob broke out. Cæsar set fire to the seventy-two Egyptian ships in the harbour, the conflagration spread to the shore, the library caught fire, 400,000 papyrus rolls were burnt to ashes. Below, in the vast square, a eunuch was proclaimed general of the forces.

But Cæsar and Cleopatra were sitting in the beleaguered palace. He was fifty-two, she twenty-two. It was enough for her in such a situation; their first rendezvous was illuminated by the flaming wisdom of the world.

At that time, Cæsar remained a year in Egypt, twice as long as Alexander. While the friends of his rival Pompey were assembling in Spain and Africa, the elderly gentleman with the bald head was sailing up-Nile in a luxurious boat; while the new world was rebelling against the new world-conqueror, he was studying the old on columns and inscriptions, and the young in the charms of the last female Pharaoh, who no longer thought of wearing an artificial beard. The troublesome husband, who had by this time grown into a youth insisting on his rights, was mysteriously drowned in the Nile.

At last Cæsar arose, defeated Pharnaces, and if he now wrote in his dispatch to Rome: *"Veni, vidi, vici,"* he may well have first heard that flashing word of love from the smiling lips of Cleopatra as he lay conquered at her feet. In any case, when he went, he left her three legions and the prospect of a son, whom she later called Cæsarion.

When she went to visit Cæsar in Rome a year later, she embraced in him a demigod, for that was the title he bore on his statue on the Capitol. She sat on the tribune when Cæsar, at his triumph, watched his defeated enemies led in chains across the Forum, and saw among them her hated sister Arsinoë. She could not but think that that would have been her own fate if she had not bewitched the mighty Cæsar in that hour of conflagration and siege.

Those two years in Rome were the perfect fulfilment of her dreams of ambition, if not of her dreams of pleasure, for there she could parade in the eyes of the world her happiness as the mistress of the world's ruler, whose wealth was probably exceeded by her own. Yet Cæsar was not careless of his wife's honour, for he made the Egyptian live and appear in public with her new husband, who was again a mere boy. As a guest of Cæsar, she held her court in a magnificent villa on the other side of the Tiber, and, with her Pharaonic ways, annoyed the old republicans of the Ciceronian kind; they said she was suggesting to Cæsar the joys of a crown.

Cæsar loved Cleopatra. When he came to visit her, he saw himself mirrored in the features of a two-year-old boy, who was so absurdly like him that the likeness was a living proof of the genius of the woman. He probably enjoyed too the pale fury of his stepson Octavius, when the latter came and had to admit that the child at play, his future rival, was charming. Cæsar refused the crown which Antony offered him in the Senate, but meanwhile he had a gold statue of his mistress set up in the temple of Venus, and caused a law to be framed which gave him the right to a number of legitimate wives. Everything seemed ready to make Cleopatra, the daughter of an Egyptian bastard, empress of the world, when Cæsar was murdered.

It was a miracle that she escaped with her life without actually taking flight, for she set out for Alexandria only a few weeks later, where her second brother-husband conveniently disappeared at the psychological moment. But now the masters of Rome followed her, as though the enchantress were drawing them to Egypt. Since Antony copied Cæsar instead of inventing a style of his own, he was determined to possess his favourite mistress too. For what else was there to take him to Egypt? To lay Cæsar's ghost, the last thing necessary for him was to see this Cleopatra, who had stirred his blood for two years at Cæsar's festivals, at last unveiled.

Antony, a soldier and a soldier's son, a plebeian, inferior to Cæsar in everything but youth, frequented women in orgies and dancing-halls, and could do nothing with his jealous Fulvia. A voluptuary in every feature, as co-heir of world-power he began to drink, perhaps thinking to emulate Alexander, for instead of making himself emperor in Rome, he preferred to have divine honours conferred on him as Dionysus in Ephesus.

But Cleopatra, whom he summoned as he would a criminal, did not go to Ephesus, and when at last he sat on his judge's seat waiting for her in the market-place in Tarsus, news was brought to him of a sumptuous ship that was coming upriver with crimson sails and silver oars. He could hardly maintain his pose. He went down to the shore, and helped the queen, who disembarked amid the perfume of flowers, to the sound of guitars, to set her tiny foot on land. When Cleopatra met her third Roman, she was twenty-seven, but he was not yet forty, and was not bald. As he was less ambitious and philosophical than Cæsar, as he had more time, as nature and habit had implanted in him a bias to the oriental, it was his fate that was decided in this encounter, while Cæsar had granted himself only an episode.

Then Cleopatra, in the same Alexandria, in the same court, before the eyes of the same courtiers, or at least of as many of them as she had not cleared out of the way, repeated her Roman adventure, but this time it grew into the great love-story of her life, and actually lasted ten years.

The greatness of Cæsar was not in his successor. When this Roman presented her with 200,000 rolls to found a new library, he may, in her eyes, have seemed meaner than the other, who set double the number on fire to illuminate their first night of love with a truly imperial torch. She seems, too, to have feared him less than Cæsar. But by prolonging his pleasures, she had time to draw a great comparison between the two roles, the two crowns glittering before her, between two men and two countries. It actually lay in the power of this one woman to decide whether Rome or Alexandria was to become the capital of the world. It is true that the decision did not lie solely with her. For when her new lover vanished after the first winter to marry Octavia, the sister of his rival Octavian, she had no idea whether he was going to come back. That was his great political marriage. She was faced with the necessity of devising some new, some unprecedented scheme, to keep her hold on him.

While he was yawning his way through his honeymoon by the side of his Roman virgin, Cleopatra bore him twins. "A little sun-king and a little moon-queen," she wrote; together with this news, she sent him a soothsayer's prophecy that, judging by the stars, he would be lord and conqueror only in the east. Such were her wiles. And the triumvir soon tired of his virtuous Octavia, with her straight nose and severe lines. He left her in Athens, where his Fulvia had already died of jealousy, using as pretext the hardships of the campaign against the Parthians, then sent for Cleopatra to meet him half-way, and since, out of friendship for Herod, he could not make her a present of Jerusalem, he presented her with a few islands and a piece of Phœnicia.

But ill-luck pursued him. Antony was beaten by the Parthians, while Octavian was garnering victories. When Antony demanded reinforcements from his brother-in-law, he was told he would get them only if he gave up the Egyptian. In the Roman world empire, however, there was no difficulty in finding a people by means of which he could restore his fame—this time it was the Armenians. And then back to Alexandria, where, in the presence of his Egyptian, who was now his legitimate wife, he too produced his triumph.

On a silvered tribune stood a gilded throne uniting the Roman war-lord and the Alexandrian queen, she, now in the middle thirties, in the costume and with the attributes of Isis, he as Dionysus. Opposite, on a smaller throne, sat their six-year-old twins, Philadelphus and Selene, and beside them a slim boy of ten, that Cæsarion whom she had conceived under the great sail on the

Nile in the embrace of her elderly, bald Cæsar. But the children wore Macedonian shoes, because the ancestors of their race had been carried hither by the barbarians through the genius of Alexander, their king, exactly three hundred years before. Below, the barbarian prisoners were led past in gilded chains, and perhaps the queen was offended that they did not prostrate themselves, but merely made sullen obeisance from below. The three children were proclaimed kings of Roman provinces.

That meant the breach with Rome, the signal for battle. Octavian challenged the new oriental and defeated him at Actium, in the presence, though not with the connivance of Cleopatra. If Antony had won that day, Alexandria would have become the capital of the world, Egypt its centre, and the Nile the river of kings, and not merely the king of rivers. The conquered army, for that matter, returned to Egypt at its ease, where Antony tried to open negotiations with the victor, even sending him his son with gifts; but Cleopatra sent the new master in secret the regalia of Egypt. She meant now to try her hand with Octavian.

This fourth Roman, however, was more Roman than his predecessors. He had no mind either to amuse himself, or to flatter himself with the possession of Cæsar's mistress. He meant to see her led in his triumph, to drag her through the streets of Rome, for he hated Cæsarion, the only man who, as the real son of Cæsar, could dispute Cæsar's world with him. And he wanted all the gold, the grain; he meant to drain Egypt dry, but he had no intention of sailing on the Nile, to fall victim to the radiant heat of the enchanted oasis and its mistress.

Octavian's ships cast anchor, the Roman troops arrived, Antony remembered that he was a Roman and fell on his sword. Dying, he had himself carried to her. She was hidden in her tomb with her daughter and her tiring-woman beside her. Antony died. His bloody sword was carried to Octavian as he landed; strangely enough, he is said to have wept at the sight, as Cæsar wept at the sight of Pompey's bleeding head. Octavian entered the city, pardoned the people "for great Alexander's sake and to give pleasure to my friend, Areios the philosopher." The first thing he did was to seek out Cæsarion and promise him his friendship.

A few days later, he visited Queen Cleopatra, who was living in the palace, and lay sick in her bed; she threw herself at his feet and handed over to him the inventory of her treasures. A court official, who knew the real amount, accused her of fraud. Octavian laughed, was courteous, and rejoiced in her health, for now he would be able to lead her to Rome, a prisoner.

And yet she outwitted even him. Always ready to side with the victor, she cast her last die with her fourth Roman; she did not succeed, but she got so far that he neglected to have her guarded. And while he was going up and down in the palace, gloating over the image of his coming triumph, his prisoner killed herself under the same roof, perhaps by the bite of an asp—every inch a queen, every inch Cæsar's mistress.

When Cæsarion came to pay him homage, Octavian murdered him. Thus at one blow the dynasties of Alexander's power and Cæsar's blood were wiped out.

8

UNDER the dominion of Rome, the Nile received the greatest honour in its history. Rome issued to all senators and *equites illustres* an edict prohibiting them from entering Egypt. So powerful was the seduction of the country that the highest office-bearers of the Empire had to be forbidden to visit it. This edict is unique, since it assumes that, in the hands of a powerful Roman, the granaries were the pledge of world power. At the same time, Diodorus pronounced the highest praise the Egyptians had received, for he called them the most grateful people on earth.

By their very nature, the Romans, who, at Cleopatra's death, made Egypt a Roman province and governed it as such for seven hundred years, could not but revert to its classical times, so that they might, here as everywhere else in the world, contest the Greek element. When it came to commanding, the Roman virtues resembled the Pharaonic, for Romans and Pharaohs were alike great in organization and discipline, in building and administration.

The Romans understood the Nile. A river that demanded ceaseless observation and measurement, an element that could be made profitable only by cunning and care, could not but reinforce in the Romans the traits which made them akin to the Egyptians and Americans. Canals and dams, signals for the beginning of the flood, reports and calculations, were quite in their line, and the emperors detailed legionaries to measure 14 ells' rise. "On September 20," wrote one emperor to his prefect in Egypt, "the Nile reached 15 ells: the commandant has informed me of this in his dispatch. If thou shouldst not yet know it, rejoice to learn it from me." Written from Rome to Alexandria, precise and sober, like a Roman, yet pompous as coming from an emperor. Even the opposition between the civil and military administration was here foreshadowed for our epoch.

About this time, the statue of the Nile came into being which represents a bearded man with sixteen children symbolizing a rise of 16 ells; its style shows in what practical form these realists regarded the wonderful river.

But now it was the river of gold, for it brought forth wheat for half Italy; the arrival of the Egyptian grain-fleet was a general holiday in the peninsula. The Romans could not but keep a jealous guard over the country. Special "architects" were appointed to regulate the smallest canal in the Delta, to clear away the silt, and to link up canals in order to provide waterways between the seven branches. Since they could find no play for their passion of road-building in the long, narrow Nile valley, they built roads in the desert. Trajan widened Necho's Suez Canal till even the big trading-ships could pass. All the fields were surveyed and surveyed again, every nerve was strained to increase the grain crop, every prefect turned robber to please his emperor; for the more imperial Rome grew, the more this province became the personal property of the ruler, and at the same time the model province.

Meanwhile, Egypt became the great cash-box into which the emperors dipped their hands to enrich their favourites: in certain crises, its possession actually decided the succession. Though the majority of the emperors never visited the Nile in person, all reckoned on its fertility without ever asking what kind of people were working for them there.

These Romans, however, did not follow the example of Alexander and the Ptolemies: they did not bury the sacred bull, they no longer allowed the Egyptians to swear by their gods, but placed the foreign priests under supervision, took away half their revenues, and the right to sanctuary with them, and while they still built temples in the old style, they did so only in order to figure on their walls in paintings and inscriptions as the successors of the Pharaohs. They imagined they could rule over this most ancient of peoples as they ruled over the Druids in Britain, and Roman tourists whistled the popular songs of Rome at the gates of the old temples, inside which they laughed at the sacred cats and ibises. When fashion later took up the Egyptian gods, they even invented a Horus-Cæsar, a Roman war-lord with a hawk's head and crown of rays.

Once the Egyptian godhead exacted vengeance for tactlessness so gross. When Prince Germanicus offered the bull of Hapis something good to eat, the sacred animal turned away and left the Roman standing. The fact that the story created a sensation shows how great the inward tension was.

The few emperors who came reasoned after the fashion of Hadrian, who called the Egyptians frivolous, rebellious, good-for-nothing, and abusive, or after the fashion of Caracalla, who took revenge for the Alexandrian lampoons in a bath of blood, and always referred to the Egyptians as clodhoppers. Egypt was good enough to provide them with grain, and with crocodiles and hippos whose fights delighted the mob in the circus. Marcus Aurelius was the only one who came to learn, who, in the Academy of Alexandria, sat at the feet of the scholars, or debated with Lucian, who held an official appointment there, and praised the Nile in the distich:

> Terra suis contenta bonis, non indiga merce,
> Aut Jovis in solo tanta est fiducia Nilo.

Their practical sobriety made the Romans turn this greatest academy of its time into a kind of technical college, where Hero invented the first automatic slot-machine, from which, on the insertion of a coin, a sacrificial offering fell out; others the first automobile, a self-propelling vehicle; the first steam-engine, the first guns; while one ingenious spirit even invented shorthand, the automobile of the scribe. Ptolemy the geographer, perhaps the last genius that Alexandria produced, who was the only man to suspect the secret of the Nile sources, seemed like a tardy descendant of the great scholars who had flourished here as long as the city and the land belonged to the Greeks.

In the excitable and witty metropolis of Alexandria, the Greeks, who had governed it for three hundred years, now sought in vain the charm of its former royal house, the brilliance, the extravagance, even the interesting crimes of the Ptolemies; they had nothing but scorn for the Roman governors, whom they saw ruling without geniality, without imagination, in their military fashion, putting numbers to everything and spreading an intolerable cleanliness over the whole city, moved by the sole desire to make their fortune in the colony and to reap their reward by breathing Roman air again. The Greeks, moreover, became poor, for honorary office was forced on them, and they had to bear the costs. Today we might say that it was the Prussian air which these Viennese of the ancient world could not breathe in their easy-going, artistic world.

The man to whom the Egyptian soil really belonged fell into utter contempt. The Egyptians, to whom the Ptolemies, as half or three-quarter Greeks, had been familiar long before their political supremacy, and hence had never really appeared as conquerors, became, under the Romans, subject enemies again; and the feelings of the conquered, which can at best subside from hatred to rancour, seemed to have lived on in them throughout the Roman centuries. "The Egyptian is not a human being," we read in a hundred dispatches and letters, and while the Romans prohibited for a long time any intermarriage between their officials and Greek women, the Egyptians, until the third century, could not even become Roman citizens or legionaries; while Romans and Greeks could fetch from the dust-heap some foundling which a poor mother had exposed on the chance that a passer-by might take it and bring it up as his slave, any Egyptian venturing to rescue a child of Roman origin was punished.

For centuries, however, gold flowed from the Nile Delta to Rome. In Alexandria, the greatest trading-port of the world, through which passed all the wares of the Far East, prices, especially of exports, were enhanced by the unity of the empire to which it now belonged. The Roman merchant reckoned in quite different quantities from the Greek traders; his ships brought spices and precious stones from India, and silk from China, in mass lots. While the ships brought to Egypt wine, Syrian horses, and clothing for the Romans in the capital and for the troops, they carried away glass, papyrus, and textiles, and the main cargo, grain, travelled as far as the Rhine. Perhaps Augustus's main object in contesting the rise of an Arab Empire was to prevent the weakening of Alexandria.

Deposits and drafts swelled as never again till the time of the

English; 16 to 24 percent was paid for ready money; and when the first troops of tourists arrived, to gape, like the decadents of today, at the stark hugeness of the ancient temples, pleasure-boats were organized on the Nile and night-trips arranged to increase the profits.

But then as now, the man without whom the granaries would have stood empty came off worst, namely the fellah, who had been "Hellenized" for three centuries, and was now to be "Latinized," processes against which his wholesome peasant instinct rebelled with equal force. There was nothing that the Roman Emperor did not command him to pay taxes on, just as Pharaoh had done long ago. Tiberius reckoned out at the end of the year how much money he wanted to extort from Egypt the following year: it was the business of his governors and prefects to squeeze it out, deducting their private profits. We can read in letters of complaint how the Roman soldiers, if the fellah paid only nine out of the ten taxes due, seized his camel and his asses, and even the clothes of his old mother, how every mummy was taxed, and every vine laid under a special contribution known as "the gift of Dionysus," for even the upstarts of that time were fertile in the invention of high-sounding names with which to plunder the people.

The famous Roman bureaucracy compelled the terrorized fellah to make a return to the local authorities of how many calves he meant to sell at market on a certain day. Every man had to dig a certain quantity of earth for new canals, and keep the old ones clear; the scribe was there again—he was always there! But the rich Egyptian bought from the Roman authorities some priestly office, or rented a village, where he oppressed the fellah at his own sweet will. What good was it to the fellah that the population rose to 7 million under the Roman order? He and his brothers formed the 90 percent of those millions who worked and fell, and could not rise, just as they do today.

There was only one right which the later Romans did not venture to tax—the fellah's right to carry his dead over the Nile to be buried in the west. The Romans left to the fellah his ancient right to die.

9

FOR seven centuries, Persians, Greeks, and Romans had ruled Egypt by force of arms. Then, for the first time, men came up the Nile without sword and armour, without spears and arrows, in small groups, and without even the desire to sell the fellah anything. What they brought cost nothing, nor was it to be grasped with hands: it was a new doctrine—it was not even quite new. While other peoples had taken grain and left the gods in the land, these men left the grain but brought a new God. From the second century on, Egypt became the refuge of the new Christians.

What drew them was the desert. Here was a land in which a step, literally a step, was enough to pass from rustling, fruitful life into the silence of sand and sun, into that great solitude which only the sea, the glacier, and the desert can offer. Except in the loneliness of a room in some vast hotel of today, it is nowhere in the world so easy to become a hermit as in the Egyptian deserts, for here, too, the two worlds lie side by side. What Jesus and John had, even in neighbouring Palestine, to seek outside the country, the first, that is, the real Christians found close beside their path, and though they did not seek an oasis, the great oasis of the Nile was all the same at hand; from it they could fetch the little they needed to keep themselves alive. Thus none of the anchorites remained in the Delta, but moved on south-west, generally to the Upper Nile, and the feet of many of them were winged by the longing to breathe the air that Moses and Jesus had breathed as children.

But just as man constantly takes flight from the order of the world to the wildness of nature, only to impose a fresh order on some part of it, even these pure souls did not long remain alone in their flight from the world. The cells, which had housed one, housed two, and only too rapidly swelled into communities. The saint became a monk, the cave a monastery, and with this change the most profound abandonment to God, the possibility of perfect union, had vanished.

Saint Anthony, in the third century, offers the great example of how a noble seeker of God, against all his intentions, is doomed to found a community, and in the end to intervene in the disputes of the world from which he has fled. The son of a rich Egyptian from the Thebaïd, he had sold everything for his soul's sake and withdrawn into the desert at twenty to kill the lusts of the flesh at the very spot at which, a few millenniums before, the Pharaohs had hunted the lion and the gazelle and, in the evening, gloated over the transparent dresses of their women. At thirty-five, feeling himself the victor, he withdrew to a ruined castle in an oasis, and twenty years of perfect solitude still lay before him. But then well-meaning weaklings, always in search of a pattern, urged him to become their master, and when he was seventy, the man who had spent fifty years alone with God founded the first monastery. He became the first abbot of history.

And just as the hermit had turned father, the father turned fighter and prophet. In the full tide of the persecution, he travelled to Alexandria to encourage the Christians there. But then he said to his disciples: "Fish die if they tarry on dry land; even so the monks that tarry outside their cells, or abide with men of the world, fall away from their vow of quiet. Let us hasten back to our cells." For this veteran realized in his strength how much easier renunciation is in the desert than in the city. What did it matter to his soul if the Emperor Constantine sent a humble message beseeching him to pray for the new Rome, for Byzantium, and no longer for the old? The greatest of his deeds was that all this hardly touched him, for men say of him that he was still beautiful, still serene, when he died in his cloister, over a hundred years old.

Had not his predecessor, Paul the Egyptian, followed his conscience in greater purity? After he had lived for ninety years alone by a spring in the desert, he left nothing behind him but his tunic, which he bequeathed to Anthony, who wore it only on high festival days, as the Romans used to put on an inherited piece of armour. For there was actually in Anthony's life between youth and age a difference as great as that between Pharaoh and the fellah, and though he himself bridged the gulf, how was it possible to the many thousands of monks who congregated in monasteries on the Nile in the fourth and fifth centuries, turned them into fortresses, formed whole cities, like that monastery near the Suez of today where ten thousand monks tilled the land, earned money, and assembled only in the evening to raise their hymn of praise, while actresses came sailing up the Nile from the Delta to see the misogynists at work? By the fifth century, 50,000 Egyptian monks were holding an "annual congress."

Thousands of these later monks were simply fellahin, and we may perhaps speak of millions of fellahin who became monks while remaining peasants on the fields of their fathers. For seven hundred years of foreign dominion, for three thousand Pharaonic years, their lives had been hard enough. For the first time in his age-old oppression, the slave of the Nile valley heard from the lips of passionately religious men tidings that had reached him only vaguely before—there was another standard of judgment in the beyond, and it was a pure heart and not a costly tomb that weighed in the balance after death.

And for the first time he heard the glad tidings in his own tongue. He hated the Greek of the Neo-Platonists, the Latin of the worshippers of Jupiter Capitolinus, or felt them, at any rate, as alien to him as the hieratic language of his ancient priests. The first Christians, who, being saints and refugees, were poor, lived at the desert's edge on a few beans and onions, like the fellah himself, had learned the vernacular of Egypt from him, and wrote it down in Greek script. The cities were far away; up in the Thebaïd, Greeks and Romans had penetrated much less deeply into the soul of the native than down on the Delta, and it was up there that glowing hearts taught the heavy-laden to bear a lot that was merely a prelude. No part of the ancient world succumbed more rapidly to the new teaching than the valley of the Nile.

But what were the old Egyptian priests to do? What was rumbling here might swell into a revolt of the poor against the rich, like that single revolt three thousand years before. Here it be-

hoved them to steer a middle course, to turn the whole move·
ment against the foreigners, and thus for the first time, Greeks
and Romans were denoted as heathens, not by the young Christians, but by the old Egyptians.

Thus not only peoples and languages, but religions too formed
an astounding medley on the Nile. On the little island of Philæ,
which can be walked round in half an hour, Jesus and Isis were
worshipped daily side by side as late as the sixth century; a mor-
tuary temple of the Pharaonic Queen Hatshepsut became a Greek
sanatorium, then a Christian monastery; on Lake Mareotis, a
Jewish community celebrated festivals every fifty days with Bud-
dhist rites taken from tales of Alexander's campaign; in a temple
of Karnak, a church was installed; and in Edfu, the new Christians even called the successor of Horus, Saint Apollo. On the
walls from which Ikhnaton had erased the names of his predecessors, and Alexander Ikhnaton's name, where the Semitic nose had
followed the Greek, ecstatic heads now appeared with a new form
of glory: instead of the key of life, a halo shone above them.

But the fellah heard the monks praying to the new God to cause
the Nile to rise; he heard them teaching that Christ, the God
with the halo, was but Osiris transformed, and so he did not even
need to remove the talisman from his neck. Ramses had written
on the walls: "This temple shall be a house of God for ever." And
it was so. The word was fulfilled, for the name mattered not.

But when this first ecstasy settled into an organization, when
religious fanatics became missionaries, and monks became bishops, the power of Rome rose against it. Were these men not teaching that all nations were equal in the sight of God, and were not
thousands refusing to perform their military service for the Emperor in Rome? An entrenched monastery had already thrown a
messenger from Rome out of its gates. All at once the emperors
began to take an interest in the despised bull of Hapis, and for
political reasons permitted sacrifices to the Egyptian gods, merely
because the faith in that strange Jew, who was alleged to have
been crucified under the Roman banner, was making them uneasy. In any case, since they had destroyed the Jewish temples,
they felt the growing hatred of the once so loyal Jews.

The persecutions, however, merely strengthened the Chris·

tian communities. Rich Greeks endowed the Church with their property, the Church itself founded export businesses and dispatched thirteen ships overseas, so that the Patriarch of Alexandria was soon believed to be as rich as the Ptolemies before him. There were still fanatics. A famous beauty, Euphrosyne, to the great scandal of the capital, left her husband to pray in a cell for thirty-eight years, dressed as a man. A distinguished young Roman, who was a friend of Marcus Aurelius and bore the highly suitable name of Titus Flavius, had not only been converted to Christianity in Alexandria, but had suddenly taken the name of Clement, and now, with all the experience of the quondam dandy, was preaching not only against short skirts, which expose the knee, but against trains which sweep the ground, and was thundering with such tender accuracy against fine linen and stockings, that for a time he fascinated all the drawing-rooms.

When, in the fourth century, Christianity was recognized from the outside, the strengthened Christians set up more violent persecutions in Alexandria than they had ever suffered themselves. The temples and inscriptions, the statues and wall-paintings of the Pharaohs, which no foreign people had touched for a thousand years, were destroyed by fanatical Christians; hundreds of so-called heathens perished, and Hypatia, the lovely disciple of Plato, who taught astronomy at the university, was cut in pieces as a creature of Satan, and her body burnt. But when they destroyed the sanctuary of Serapion, and still no thunderbolt fell from heaven, a bit of the ancient world perished.

Æsculapius, however, one of the last sages of Alexandria, wrote the prophetic words:

The day is coming when the world will know nothing of the faith of the Egyptians. Our land will stand desolate. Tombs and the dead will be its only witnesses. O Egypt! Naught but fables will tell of thy faith, and no posterity will believe them. Nothing will remain but the word, hewn in stone, to tell of the ancient gods.

10

THE Pharaohs on the walls had
been hacked in pieces, but the fellah rejoiced in the new creed.
God was closer to him than to his fathers, for He spoke Egyptian.
Since the monks read the new Scriptures to him in his own
tongue, which had gone on softly breathing under the splendour
of the priestly hieroglyphic language, he was glad, and it troubled
him not at all that they wrote it with Greek letters, for he could
not read the book in any case. From far distances, a native fervour had come to swell the fellah's heart.

Why, we may ask, was Rome not strong enough to resist the
Christians?

The Christians were young, the Romans old, and when they
committed their most fatal error of adopting the faith of the
enemies, they doomed themselves to destruction, for by that step
they robbed their philosophy of its sword, and laid it in the hands
of those whose creed rejected it. Here, too, in the same way as
in our own time, the political heir adopted the aims and methods
of the man he had so long combated on account of both: the
armed Roman Emperor became an armed Bishop of Rome.

Between the two ideas, barbarians without ideas clattered
through the world. Wild tribes, clad in skins, who broke out of
their oak forests, Teutons in the uniform of Roman mercenaries,
who were nothing but adventurers on their own account, spread
over the Nile, burning as they went. In Edfu, an inscription
speaks of Huns who had become Christians "housing everywhere,
unwelcome guests" (as a German scholar wrote recently). The
only people they spared were, strange to say, the Jews in Elephantine and the Faiyûm.

Under the boots of these hordes, who no longer found the iron
cohorts of Rome in their way, the dikes and canals of Egypt fell

into decay, the water-wheel stood still, the wheat and gold dwindled, the slaves increased, while only a quarter of the grain-fleet arrived in Ostia. A few leading families took possession of the fat Delta and the green earth between the deserts; they held up the grain-ships of their rivals as they came downstream, or blocked the enemy canals. Thousands of fellahin evaded the tyranny of the taxes which the new masters imposed in their pride, and turned bandits. Then, with the help of Teutonic mercenaries, they would break into the castle of some rich Greek, or plunder a monastery and steal its money and cattle.

Egypt, the land that requires order more than any land on earth, could not but perish by disorder. But Justinian, whose justice did not reach the Delta, fought at least the fight of faith, and had bedouins and Blemmyes, and even Negroes on the Middle Nile at Dongola, baptized shortly before the birth of Mohammed.

Such confusion could be mastered only by people born of the same climate, who did not succumb to the unaccustomed heat like the soldiers of Augustus before Yemen, and came bringing a state god armed with a sword, and not a god without one. The quarrels of the sects, the weakness of Byzantine rule, had again laid the way open to a fresh invasion of the Persians, and for ten years they held the capital. Then there appeared in the Delta a new people, which had always resisted the Persians, Romans, Assyrians, Egyptians, and the Ptolemies.

With a long sword hanging on their left side, and a short curved one stuck into their belts on the right, armed with round bucklers, the archers in long hose and low shoes, the cavalry in boots and short doublets, but all alike adorned with three gaudy scarves, round their waists, over their right shoulders, and on their heads, the sons of the desert and the sea, the Arabs from the neighbouring peninsula, entered the Delta and history. It was in the year 640, eight years after Mohammed's death, when a new and warlike faith was in its first bloom.

When the general of the Caliph's forces, Amr ibn el As, he of the hymn to Egypt, took the port of Pelusium, and Heliopolis and other Delta cities, he did so against the will of his master, who, upon a final consideration, thought his 4000 cavalrymen too weak. Seldom had disobedience so fine a reward. This headstrong move on the part of his general heralded nine centuries of Arab rule.

In Alexandria, the Patriarch and the Byzantine generals assumed simply that a few more wild hordes of nomads had come galloping through the desert, but that the real Arabs, who had, in the course of a few years, conquered all Syria and Palestine, still had their hands full there. Above all, they misjudged the feelings of the Copts, that is, of the Christian fellahin, who hailed the new conqueror with the same childish enthusiasm as their fathers had shown to Cæsar six hundred, and to Alexander nine hundred years before.

The new conquerors placed before the Byzantines an astonishing choice: either the Egyptians were to become Mohammedans, and live in peace with them, or they were to submit and pay tribute. Negotiations came to nothing; the Byzantine Emperor proposed an equally astonishing alternative—either the Arab general was to become Christian and marry his daughter, or the war was to go on. The Arab, always supported by the mass of the people, turned down the offer, marched on Alexandria, and besieged it for nearly a year without taking it. But in the end the Patriarch surrendered his unconquered and by no means famished city, promising tribute, but demanding religious freedom. It is difficult to understand why he surrendered Egypt. He may have wished to prevent a massacre. He could have had the city and the port relieved from the sea, since the enemy had no ships. Was this an act of cowardice or cunning, or was he perhaps so religious that he abandoned the city to save the faith?

A credible account states that the Patriarch soon afterwards died of remorse for having surrendered the city to the Moslems, for he lived to see the conqueror's deeds of violence. The fleet returned to Byzantium, as though from an unsuccessful expedition, and not from a dominion of two hundred years. A last attempt on the part of Byzantium to reconquer the city found the whole of Egypt on the side of the new masters. The fortress of Alexandria, which had been for three centuries the capital of the world, and then for six the biggest port on the Mediterranean, was razed to the ground. All the Christians were glowing with enthusiasm for the conquerors, who had expelled the Christian lords with their strange creed, for they left to the Copts their "homoousian" God, and no longer forced them to worship the "homoiousian."

Not far from ancient Memphis, at the head of the Delta, there rose a new fortress, El Fostat, which moved a little to the north in the course of the first centuries, there to become the capital of Egypt. The planet Mars was crossing the meridian during the first hours of its building, and the Arabs called their city, after the planet, El Qahira, the victorious, that is, Cairo.

11

A CLOUD of dust is rolling towards Cairo from the north-east. It rises from the great desert road which brings to the great city everything that comes from Syria, whether by way of Damietta on the sea-coast, or along the old canal that runs to the Red Sea. Here, under the walls of the city, the crowd swarms and jostles, and today the mob from the neighbouring villages comes to swell the throng, for tomorrow is the day of the great Nile Festival. For a day we have gone back to 1400, or, more exactly, to August 15, 1395, and it is afternoon; the horseman, reckoning the year by the flight of the Prophet, calls it 773.

The horseman is a stranger to us. He is a Turk who has fought in Barkuk's battles, without rank or fame, but certainly not less valiantly than many a one whom good luck has thrust into history. It may be that, like those great ones of history, he has robbed some dead Mongol under Tamerlane who, in these years of battle, faced him in single combat. For it is no long time since Barkuk, the general who paid him, returned victorious to his capital, where, though born as a Circassian slave, he had twice risen to power by courage and cunning, and was playing the part of Sultan of Egypt in a frenzy of energy and crime. This obscure Turkish soldier has followed him on his own account, in order to see for once with his own eyes the famous city which has now been growing and flourishing for four centuries. He has a rich friend there, and can be his guest. He will spend a month in Egypt, or perhaps his life, as Allah wills.

The journey was no hardship, the desert road was strewn with public *hans*, the inns in which pilgrims and couriers, emigrants and tourists, can find fresh food and water for themselves and their camels. For the Fatimids and their successors had built so excellent a road into Syria for their armies and messengers that a courier, finding relays at all points, could cover the distance from Cairo to Damascus in the record time of four days.

In a cloud of dust and heat, through the bellowing, jostling beasts and men, whose fatigue is aggravated by their excitement, the impatient rider manages to force a way, for he is travelling alone with his servant, a slave. From a distance, the two dusty wayfarers are hardly to be distinguished, but as they approach, the finer horse shows which is the master. He also carries more weapons.

What does the rider see? Nothing but a high, yellow wall crowned with many turrets, rising in the yellow-mauve haze of shimmering heat. Where is the famous citadel? Can it be that building rising a little to the south? Where are the domes and minarets? Where is the great Nile, of which he has heard so much, but has seen till now only the children and grandchildren —insignificant, narrow canals? Here there are towers and walls, just as in Asia.

But now the jostling crowd is near the Bab-en-Nasr, the Gate of Victory, which, with its square towers rounded to the outside, threatens rather than invites. Customs men, policemen, money-changers—the whole crowd, in a cloud of dust, screams, elbows, and even beats its way along, while, among the Moorish arches, swords and spears glitter from loopholes in the masonry, for at a gate like this, a surprise attack has before now decided the fate of a dynasty. And yet all who come in from the surrounding country are happy—there is shade. Under the towering walls, though they may glow with heat, the swelling, expectant crowd, rubbing against the dirt of camels' skins, in all the exhalations of sweat and hot breath, may snatch one shady moment, and a profound hope, a hope beyond faith, fills the hearts of all, that from now on they will have walls about them again, to ward off the heat of the sun.

And indeed the whole city looks like a vault, for the street that runs to the gate is narrow, like all the streets of the East, and to make the shade perfect, all the balconies are roofed over, rugs and sheets are stretched across to the other bank of the teeming river of stone, so that the newcomer sees nothing between the high walls but shade, a diffused, hazy light which blurs all the outlines. Often he can recognize what he sees only by its sound and smell.

Fresh vigour comes to the horseman now that he has reached his goal, and though his slave may groan for home, where he can at last lie idle, his master is determined to see the city first. A shouting boy has long been striving to drag him to a tavern. In this year 1400, coffee and tobacco, the two great refreshments of oriental life, are not yet known, and wine is forbidden. But when he has squatted tailor-wise on his cushion in the street, and waited awhile patiently, a sleepy servant brings him sherbet of sugar-cane or honey, a melon, or a few dates, while three water-carriers crowd round him, offering the stranger the water which trickles out of the grey-black goatskins on their shoulders down their dirty rags. At the same time, men of indistinguishable age creep up, half-naked beggars with matted beards; one raises the stump of his arm, probably the hand was cut off in punishment for theft; another limps along on one leg, displaying the gangrened end of the other; and both raise their voices in a nasal whine: "Praise be to Allah, who moves men to compassion. My supper must be thy gift, O Lord." But the slave of the inn kicks these low slaves of the street out of the way, screaming: "Son of a dog, son of a whore." And as the lame beggar hobbles off, he picks up a dry crust, and lays it to his forehead before eating it, and suddenly he has the aspect of a saint.

Now a procession, with drums and pipes, approaches the resting horseman through the narrow street, a few making music, while the crowd pretends to sing. Boys turn cartwheels, perhaps thinking to earn a coin, perhaps merely to show off. For every-body streams out of the open stalls and courtyards to the edge of the street, all agog to see a wedding, and even the women looking down through their wooden grilles, who must more often curse than bless their wedding-day, are excited, for a bride is always a beginning, a sacrifice, and a mystery.

Now a group with a fine horse has pushed itself between the band and the bride—poor folk who have hired the horse to make a show of their two boys, for the festival of their circumcision. They sit together, one hanging on to the saddle, the other to his fellow-sufferer, feeling that they, too, are to be a sacrifice today. They have been dressed as girls, to avert the evil eye, although the all-too-familiar show betrays their sex. For the barber's assistant, in a gaudy shirt, precedes the horse with its cluster of parents and relations, carrying a carved casket, while the barber, in white, walks along with his knife in his hand and a comical expression on his face, as if he were laughing at his own office. Only then, when the children have passed, does the bride appear, and in her litter, on her camel, she may be the victim of the same disquiet, while her friends scream encouragement at her and all the onlookers clap their hands, casting a tragicomic veil over it all.

When the street is free again, and the horseman, refreshed, has remounted, he sees through a courtyard two high towers, and when he points and questions, someone shouts: "El Azhar!" Soon he is standing amazed before the famous building which is known to every oriental as the oldest university of Islam. No one would think it was now four hundred years old, for it has been rebuilt since the great earthquake a century ago, but the horseman gapes at the height of the minarets, which seem to spring from the top of the walls.

In the gateway, where a few students are being shaved on stools, he takes off his shoes, for it is a mosque that he is about to enter; it goes by the name of "The Flowering One," and everything that is taught there, law and rhetoric, physics, algebra, and poetics, is as rigorously religious in its principles as the interpretation of the Koran itself, which fills up most of the time.

The men in the great court with its central fountain make no great show as they walk, squat, lie, read, chatter, or sleep in the ancient cloister. All are poor here, and think little of food and less of the future. How many nooks and corners, walled-up windows and secret doors, how many marks left by generations of learners, visible prints of fingers on the walls, invisible marks of the secret longings of all the young men who have ever crowded these halls to gather wisdom!

There they squat, twenty or more of them, round their teacher, who is sitting at a pillar on his straw mat, and expounding a verse of the Holy Book in his monotonous singsong. It has been more deeply studied than the Bible, or any other book in the world, for it gives the constitution of heaven and earth in one. And its study must be profounder than any other, for it can last as long as twenty years, which are often devoted to the one book; and any man knowing it by heart completely, and able to expound it, may teach it himself. Certainly most of the time they learn nothing, but they are there, and since the Sultan feeds them all, teachers and pupils, there is not the least incentive to hurry.

Now there is a great commotion in a gloomy corner of the court; the horseman hears curses and the sound of blows; and when he comes up, he sees men fighting with the air, like madmen. This is the chapel of the blind scholars, and, in the conflict between inner light and outer darkness, disputes are more frequent and more furious than among those who can see. But a voice is calling them; they hear the sheikh passing, stop their fighting, grope their way back to their familiar court with the vague, aimless movements of bats in the daylight, and when they have found a leader, they grasp their teacher's hand with their waving fingers and kiss it.

12

THE horseman has reached the bazaars which adjoin El Azhar; the first stalls are the booksellers'. As men and animals, in these narrowest of alleys, mix with the piles of goods in one pervading, fetid stench, as sweating camels jostle braying donkeys, creatures and things, in this airless, oppressive languor, seem to have been living there for centuries unwashed; the only thing that ever cleaned the bazaar was the fire that consumed it. Many dealers seem to have fallen asleep on their wares like old dragons, and the gleam of a copper pot, or the shimmer of a brocade, is more living than the dull eyes of their guardians. The rider can make nothing of the old Koran in Cufic script which is offered to him, but the weapons attract his attention, and as he sits on the buyer's cushion in front of the little stall, the centre of attraction as a foreigner, holding across his knee a bow with great yellow topazes at the ends, his thoughts may waver between slaughtered Mongols and lovely dancing-girls, but he has not made up his mind to buy; he goes on on foot, for in these narrow alleys his slave leads his horse behind him.

A dealer holds out a real turban towards him, measuring it against him to see if it will go seven times round his head, that is, whether it is long enough to serve as his shroud one day, if Allah will. But the horseman is more attracted by a great bowl of cornelian, a superb piece with nineteen facets round its edge; beside it, lamps of rock crystal and bronze door-handles glitter, and farther on, the colours of striped silk vests, gold-worked jackets and capes shimmer when the seller, with a weary gesture, releases them from the closely packed piles of beautiful things, like Allah releasing the enchanted bird in the story.

Suddenly the horseman hears a call from one of the smallest shops. Nothing but a perfume was wafted to him from this padded doll's house, but it drew the horseman in, and the magician of the perfumes raises now one, now the other, of his phials from the tiny shelves among which he has grown so old. He feels behind him without looking round, then softly draws the stranger's rough hand towards him over his tiny counter, rubs the palm with a glass stopper, and holds it up to his face for him to smell: jasmine; another, ambergris; another, clove; a fourth, musk. Then he shows him powders and crystals—musk, myrrh, incense—burns little bits of them in tiny candles, all in silence, and the horseman thinks of a certain slave-girl at home, whose bosom will flower with the perfumes of distant Egypt. The old man feels the thoughts of the huge stranger, and out of the vast stretch of time, he sees rise again the night in which he, a true Musulman, learned that perfume dominates the senses of love.

And as the rider passes on, copper vases from Bulgaria, held high in brown arms, flash in front of the stranger, Armenian silks flow in rivers through the hands of a tired old man, Frankish linen crackles in the fingers of a white boy, who probably sailed over with it, while the eyes of a veiled woman follow him from behind glittering glass from Cyprus.

But now he has reached the main street again. Water!—water! —the never-ending cry, and everywhere pious hands or bad consciences have set up fountains, for when Mohammed was asked what was the greatest act of charity, the son of the desert replied: "To bring water to men."

In this quarter, mosques and madrasahs are crowded together. The one over there has just been built by Barkuk, now Sultan of Egypt, to serve as his mausoleum, yet it looks as if he were content for the moment to put others to death. In another, built by Sultan Kalaun a century ago, a portal of black and white marble leads to the domed tomb with its mother-of-pearl inlays and the porphyry columns of its praying-niche shimmering in the gloom.

Suddenly the stranger sees slanting above him the walls of the citadel. In vain he struggles to make his way more quickly through the throng. At the foot of the hill, a huge pile of masonry draws his eyes—blocks of stone bigger than he has ever seen in his life— it is the high shoulder of the new mosque of Sultan Hassan, whose murder cleared the way for the present ruler. Divided into five long bands, the wall thrusts its yellow and mauve colours into the blue sky, decorated with gates, double arches, and triple bouquets of plaster, with a superb rosette in the middle. Outside, the eyes are confused by stalactite-groups, but inside, they come to rest.

For out of the brightly coloured marble floor of the huge square court, a huge fountain rises, borne by eight columns, under which many men are washing their feet. The regular succession of the side-chapels, the impression of space and height, calm the heart of the believer; the battlements crowning the walls steady the mind of the soldier. If his eyes follow the steep wall, they rise to the highest tower in Cairo; if he lowers them, he sees a web of fine iron chains swaying in each of the Moorish arches: on them the lamps will be hung when the festival begins. On one side only does the high, steep pulpit behind the inlaid dais show that there is a presiding spirit to it all, and the verse from the Koran running round the top of the court in a grey-white band of high relief shows it too. Over his head, the pigeons wheel in Allah's guard, till the great Horus hawk appears who once created Egypt; he is stronger, and drives the pigeons away.

At last the rider, once more on horseback, has reached the interior of the fortress; he has been admitted to the citadel through a menacing portal. Here, in this stony chaos of walls and towers, the power of Islam has been maintained for centuries, strengthened and transformed by each succeeding generation, always with an eye to the rapidly progressing art of siege, for on the other side, the hills of Mokattam, higher than the citadel, lie threatening. Hoofs and cries resound through the court, slaves hold broad stirrups for proud emirs in gaudy cloaks, who strike them with their whips at the slightest delay. A hundred hands are busy about a train of camels that has just arrived, unloading strange cargo that seems to trickle gently out of thick cloths. These are the camels which, since the time of the Fatimids, have brought fresh snow daily from Lebanon for the Sultan and his court, so that they may sip iced drinks in the heart of Egypt. They have been on their way through the desert for some weeks, but to make up for it, Allah has cooled their backs on this astonishing pilgrimage with the melting snow, and the cellar-master shouts in vain at the drivers because, as usual, only half has arrived.

Beside their horses and camels, surrounded by dark-eyed soldiers and spying policemen, stand the messengers from Kush and Nubia, from Gaza and Alexandria, from Baalbek, Beirût, and Sidon, all with letters from governors, friends and half-enemies. At the assembly-place in a farther court, four armed sentries stand in front of an emir's tent held up by two spears; and behind, there is a bay in the wall which opens onto Cairo.

Now, at last, there spreads before the stranger the sight that soldiers, pilgrims, and story-tellers have so often praised: steep towers and rounded domes, like male and female symbols above the roofs of the world-city, which stretches far away to north and south, sending up a steady roar in which the cries and sounds of the city mingle. Behind, in the east, rise the rocky shapes of the desert, but towards the west, where the sun is sinking, the greenest of valleys borders a wide river, hundreds of sails are swelling in the fresh north breeze where the river is flowing straight to the north, split by two long, narrow islands. For the first time, the horseman sees the full width of the Nile, and behind him, half transparent in the bluish-purple light, just beyond the margin of the green land, groups of stone tents stand in massive stillness. They are the pyramids of Gîza, with those of Sakkara beyond, indestructible milestones of history.

But now, when the horseman sets out to find the house of his friend, he has to pass through the poorer quarters, for in this world-city, poor and rich live cheek by jowl. He sees more huts than houses: they are built of unfired tiles, held together by clay. Beside the door, the unveiled woman sits in her blue tunic, and when she wearily raises the veil to her face as the stranger looks at her, the gesture is no more than a symbol. She is getting the children's supper ready—eggs and cheese, milk and rice—and inside, on the stove, which takes up the whole width of the single room, onions are frying—the rider's nose tells him that. In the winter, as he knows from his own home, man and wife sleep on the stove, which is stoked with cow-dung, while the children lie on mats on the floor.

At last he finds his friend's house. It is locked up, for its owner is rich, and as they are all Moslems, the rider has never known it otherwise at home in Damascus. It can hardly be for safety, because the master of the house is not strong enough to defend it, and a gate with iron bolts would keep out robbers. It is on account of the women that all the wealthy houses in Islam look like fortresses, for while the women are beings without rights, and seldom to be seen out of doors, they dominate life all the same. The armed caution with which the man surrounds his women makes every house look like a woman's face —the mouth and eyes veiled, and only a pair of eyes to form a link with the world. Perhaps Islam, the most virile of all religions, came to grief by these customs, and lost the world which seemed to be within its grasp by its humiliation of women.

The watchman sleeping on the ground by the gate is startled out of sleep by the sudden silence of the horses' hoofs; he jumps up, awakens movement inside, a gate rattles, a second watchman strides ponderously to the threshold with his lance, there are questions, shouts, and hurrying, the horses are handed over, the major-domo struts down the stairs, and, pointing first to the ground, then to his heart, then to his forehead, greets the stranger. The wooden windows above begin to rattle: whispers have reached the women that a strange man has arrived. Two, who were sitting in the court by the fountain, flit through a secret door, in and up, for everything belonging to the harem is upstairs. They need not have hurried, for to prevent any visitor looking into the court as he enters, even the entrance is carried round a bend. Everything the women would like to see is locked away, but above all, they themselves are locked away from the men, and even the muezzin, who calls the faithful to prayer five times a day from the round gallery of the minaret, is, as often as may be, blind, so that no woman may cross his sight in his bird's-eye view of some rich house.

Below, where the rooms of the men are faintly lighted by latticed windows, the windows are divided into a hundred little panes by a mosaic of wood, generally carved, since larger surfaces would warp in the heat. The divans running round the raised half of the room, with their mattresses and cushions covered with costly stuffs, are in disorder, for a number of men who were reclining on them have risen to greet the newcomer. The master of the house displays that blend of dignity and cordiality which only the Orient knows.

With his white shirt drawn over his trousers, with his short, sleeveless cloth jacket, with his gown of striped silk the sleeves of which fall over his fingers, and with his pointed shoes of red morocco leather, he stands before his friend the horseman, bearded and laughing, with only a skull-cap on his head; and while the slaves take off the stranger's shoes, and prepare water for him, as he sits dusty among the brilliant guests, nothing would induce his host to ask him whence he comes and where he is going; at most he will show him a gift the other once presented to him. Dignity is so great here, and the respect for the private life of others so perfect, that no one attempts to find out the home and the family, the past and the projects of a friend. And yet, as they sit together sipping sherbet, each tries in secret to probe the other, watches every gesture, his glance at the slave, at the door, reckoning up within his own mind his position, his fortune, his degree of security, but he betrays nothing of his private calculations, and speaks only of tomorrow's festival.

From above comes the sound of whispering and chattering, for since the women live, eat, and generally sleep together in the one big room, they live like girls of the west in an old-fashioned boarding-school, now frightened, now mischievous, lascivious and greedy, jealous and insanely inquisitive. There are never more than four of them, for that is the limit set by the Koran, but the slave-girls, who sometimes have the upper hand, are not counted. Generally the women in a harem are all alike, with a full face, rather short curls, their black brows drawn out with paint, their skin very white, because the sun can never reach them, with wide silk trousers tied below the knee, their bosoms half bare; their main occupation is the care of their toes and fingers. As they have been kept like dolls for centuries, and educated in the art of love and in nothing else, they take their revenge, like all prisoners, in a tornado of intrigues, and while they develop their refinements to the utmost, they are early ruined and, to the connoisseur, past their best at twenty.

Since no companionship can grow out of a life so artificial, even where there is only one wife, and since, after all, the women do not die at twenty, the interior of these houses is haunted by hatred and revenge, contempt and threats; and though the houses are, after all, not brothels, but homes in which children are born and brought up to inherit, the arbitrary will of the man knows no limits, and when he says: "I repudiate you," and returns a third of her dowry, he has fulfilled the law of the Koran as a pious Musulman. But he is not allowed to accuse her, for the man who accuses an innocent woman of adultery, even if she belongs to him, commits one of the six deadly sins, which do not include adultery.

So delicately are the threads of honour and faith woven here; and in these shuttered houses, where love has become a monomania and debauches every natural instinct, where, in a thousand dreams, every possible adventure is lived through, to be discussed with naïve perversity into every physical detail in the endless talk of the women, in these separate worlds where imagination ranges far more wildly than in any brothel, the only thing that matters is sole possession, actual and physical: it is guarded, revenged, defended, by the faith and by the sword.

13

THE next night, light pours over
the island of Roda, over the river-banks, over the river itself; the
whole city is out to hail the coming of the Nile flood. For on the
following day, the Sultan will command the Nile to burst
through the last dam. On June 17, two months before, they celebrated the "Night of the Teardrop," on which the tears Isis shed
for her spouse caused the Nile to rise, for the calculations of ancient and modern times agree in placing on that day the first fall
of rain on the Blue Nile, thousands of miles away, and all the
time it has been rising, in answer to the general prayer, the
Munadi-en-Nil, with his choir of boys, has been proclaiming to
the great city the joyful tidings of its steady rise. Today he has
announced 16 ells. No one knows if, this time, it is the truth, or
the government's trick to increase the taxes, which swell with the
water, but all rejoiced as he wandered through the main street
with his boys today, singing: "Allah is great! He hath awakened
the river from death to life! Allah hath shown favour to our
fields! The canals are overflowing! Praise be to Him who hath
given to Egypt the stream of water! Rejoice, O Faithful! Sixteen
ells! Allah hath watered the high fields!"

The Nile Festival has been celebrated for thousands of years.
Most of the foreign conquerors followed the custom of the Pharaohs, but never was the festival more brilliant than under the
rule of the Arabs.

In a long file, the melon-sellers run through the crowd, holding aloft their obscene, fly-blown fruit; they are never satisfied
with a para—if it is too little, they declare the coin is false. Soon a
ring has formed, screaming, jeering, and laughing, and in the
end some bystander limps off howling, for he has got a beating.
But already there is something new to see: the boys have torn the

turban off a sheikh who was riding by on his ass. "Exalt the crown of Islam," yells the crowd, and helps and laughs, and the face of the aged prophet brightens for a moment, for today the Nile is rising, and forbearance is doubly due.

Bawling, the crowd rolls along behind two half-naked fencers, who are carrying on a sham fight with long sticks, for on a day like this the mob wants to see its own habits turned to fun, but the frontier of the serious is never closed, and screams cut through the multitudinous laughter. All eyes have turned to the dervish at the edge of the street—can this be a joke? He has slit up his belly with a knife and taken out his entrails, and now he is putting them back again, as a sailor piles ropes in the stern of his boat, while the people, horrorstruck and delighted, throw him their coppers; one, more impudent, tries to stick his coin into the gaping stomach.

Now a company of fine folk comes along; they like to smell the people once a year. Helmeted horsemen ride ahead, followed by a eunuch in a flowing red cloak, an enormous turban crowning his flabby face; then, mounted on horses with gay trappings, reclining on padded saddle-cloths as on a well-cushioned divan, the veiled women ride past, their avid eyes drinking in all these strange doings; and behind them the slave-women carry the children aslant on their shoulders, beside the men on horseback, who hold their stirrups away from their horses' sides to proclaim their pride to the mob. Ragged boys, who have held out their hands in vain, snuffle scornfully after the cavalcade; to demonstrate to the streets the lavish waste of civet and musk in the clothes of the rich ladies, a half-naked little girl, tattered and beautiful, holds a rag in front of her dirty face, and imitates the darting eyes of the ladies; but behind her, a group of blind fakirs stumbles along, begging alms in a nasal singsong, and following a red flag carried ahead by one of them.

Plucking their tinkling instruments as they ride, a procession of minstrels comes up the street on frisky donkeys, and their jingle sounds louder in the gloom. Past the guard, they break into a trot, for even today the Mamelukes preserve their gravity, and the regular beat of hoofs is enough to spread a secret terror among the merrymakers. There they come, a hundred or two armed men, riding along in their wide trousers which nearly reach their shoes, three quite different knives stuck high in their belts, the veils of mail they have copied from the Crusaders hanging from their helmets, their great scimitars swinging. They are riding to the dam.

Just where a stone bridge leads over the great canal, the Khalig, a hundred yards before it discharges into the Nile, near the long islands, a few hundred slaves have thrown up an earth-dike, narrowing at the top. In June it stood twenty feet above the lowest level of the Nile, but only thirteen or fifteen above the canal, which lies higher. Meanwhile the rising Nile has reached its top. Today the dammed waters will be let loose. Between the dam and the bridge, they had built a cone-shaped heap of earth: that was the "Bride of the Nile," a symbol of the maiden once sacrificed here, but this bride yielded to the flood eight or ten days ago.

But now, as it is only a few hours till sunrise, the Emir commands the Mameluke guard to prepare the dike for the thrust of the river. The people crowd round in boats decked with a hundred lights in coloured glass, sailing down the river, ceaselessly singing and shouting, their passions inflamed by their growing excitement. For what happens here, when the hurrying Nile streams through the dike to fructify the waiting land, is felt by all, men and women, as a marriage, and for them, too, this night is a marriage-night.

But who are these that have been commanded to cut off the dike, so that the river's *droit de seigneur* may be fulfilled only symbolically? The grave-diggers have come; and while, with hundreds of helpers, they dig the dike away from the dry side, while other hundreds carry the earth to the banks in baskets, and yet others empty them up the banks, the thousands on both sides of the river and on both islands scream jocular encouragement into the hot, turbulent night; many dive madly into the Nile in their clothes and climb out again, spitting and puffing; others throw money into the water, and the stupidest of the boys who dive for it try to be the slyest, and take nets with them. The boats rock and capsize, screams rise from among the musicians; the girls dancing in the lighted barge inflame the men, who gape at them from little boats in the darkness; half-naked witches on the bank, where the fireworks are flashing, cry their aphrodisiac spices; dogs slink off with pieces of meat from the stalls, then howl under the whip; thieves are caught and beaten; dervishes in frenzy drive nails into their chests, stick burning palm-twigs under their arms or glass under their tongues as they dance along in procession, accompanied by snake-tamers, and by conjurers who have themselves tied up in sacks, and pretend to be drowned in the Nile—the whole mob reeling, shouting, sweating, until in the east, under the towers of the citadel, the sky brightens, first greenish, then yellowish, then dull blue, more rapidly than the eye can follow, while the entire crowd hurries to the dam, where a hundred dancers, in skirts whirling like parasols, call on the name of Allah, inflaming all to call on the name of Allah, who has appointed day and night, has commanded the water to rise, and created the father of all fortune, the Nile.

A magnificent silk tent has been set up, the place and a long avenue to it are held clear by the lances of the Mamelukes, for now the Sultan is riding down to the Nile in person.

The procession is arriving from the island of Roda, where they have rewarded the Nilometer, the octagonal marble column in their mosque, which has shown the height of the good and bad floods since the time of the Pharaohs. The prefect of the Nile and the canals had to plunge into the basin in his costly silk robe, and while he held himself in the water with his left hand, he rubbed the sacred column with a mixture of saffron and nutmeg dissolved in rosewater, which he poured out of a silver jug in his hand, half-swimming, without wavering. The whole court, the Sultan himself, looked on, but good care was taken that only a few initiates should stand near enough to read the real height of the Nile on the scale.

Now the ceremonial procession has reached the tent, a flood of colours rises to meet the new sun, all the brightness of shimmering seraglios, which at other times is displayed only in the shaded lights of shuttered palaces, flashing from a hundred costly robes, from the jewelled hilts of swords, and the Sultan, recognizable by his splendid horse, which none of his Emirs is allowed to rival, stands in the middle in the green turban of the Prophet. He gives the sign, the mob is still. Then the Vizier reads a solemn proclamation in which the Sultan returns thanks to Allah for his mercy, and to the Nile for its flood, and craves a blessing for Egypt from on high. Hundreds of slaves, who have thrown up the dam and destroyed it again with the help of the grave-diggers, raise their eyes, with hands outspread, to their god, the Sultan.

Now a spade is put into his hand; he throws it into the gap in the dam, and the boat, standing ready on the full side of the canal, pushes off, reaches the narrowest part which still seems to be standing in the middle of the dam—for the water has long since found its own way—rams against it, and bursts its way through, while a little waterfall threatens to swamp the boat, and it hurries to save itself on the new bank.

A hundred thousand voices rejoice to the morning sky, and as if to proclaim the opening of the way, the central firework is let off into the clear blue sky. It crackles loudly, but it has no power to dazzle: the symbol of the delirious night has vanished with the dawn; the women stand pale in the morning light, but the men have no eyes for them now, all are braced by the joyous, virile realization that the saviour of the country, the father of the grain, the Nile, has come. From above, the Sultan casts an open bag of money among the slaves. By the decree of Allah, it falls into as many hands as there are coins, and a frightful struggle ensues, for everyone fights for what he can get—only once a year does it rain gold! On the canal, boat follows boat through the broken dam, under the stone bridge, and all acclaim the Sultan with rejoicing.

But he stands above, knowing that his Vizier beside him is thinking the same thought: the taxes are safe. We told the people 16 ells; nobody knows it was only 14.

14

FOR five hundred years, Egypt lived under independent Islamic rulers. They had long ceased to be Arabs, nor were they subject to the Caliph in Baghdad; on the contrary, he repudiated them as anti-Caliphs. They felt superior in tradition and faith to those Arabs who had conquered Egypt about the year 640, for the Fatimids, who were the first to undertake a fresh conquest of Egypt after a lapse of three hundred years, attributed their descent to Fatima, the Prophet's daughter, and hence claimed to be of his blood. But as warriors they had nothing to support them but their own right hand, and when the conqueror who came with his hordes and founded Cairo in 969 was once asked about his descent—for there were many who doubted the Fatimid pedigree—he drew his sword and said: "Here is my race." Then he threw gold among the crowd and said again: "And there are my nobles!"

In the struggle with the Crusaders and the Normans, these North Africans had conquered Syria and Sicily. But when Moizz, of whom that story is told, landed in Egypt, he had already determined to stay in this, the most powerful country in his own continent, for he brought his father's bones with him to bury them there. His son must also have been a real ruler, for he wrote: "I would count myself happy if my people could attribute all they enjoy to my labours—gold, silver, and precious stones, horses, clothes, land, and houses." But his grandson Hakim was already no more than an heir to power; feared and full of fear himself, he was subject to moods of madness in which he raged through the city at night. As the son of a Christian mother, he first protected the Christians, then turned against them, made them wear signs round their necks, and burned churches till he vanished mysteriously in the Mokattam Mountains. His body was never found.

New peoples came, and all began as warriors; later they de-generated. The brilliant Saladin, always in the field, enjoyed but a few years in his city, and it was probably just because his power was so far away that legends gathered round his name. He built the citadel rather against his own men than against enemies; even the man he charged with the building was not a soldier, but a eunuch, who had a few of the smaller pyramids in Gîza pulled down for the purpose. Instead of rallying the people to build his tomb, Saladin ordered every boat coming down the Nile to carry a certain number of stones and unload them here. There were Frankish prisoners of war who knew how to hew them straight, and when the Sultan came home, he was so delighted with his building that he would watch the work for hours at a time, and even carry a stone himself now and then.

The difference in the destination of the stones reveals the re-ligious difference between the Pharaohs and the Mohammedans. The Pharaohs had worn out entire generations of men in the labour of carrying stones to the left bank of the Nile, so that they might themselves live for ever under their shadow. The Moham-medans had the stones carried almost to the same spot, but on the right bank of the Nile, to raise a citadel such as Egypt had never seen. Security in death or security in life: in both cases, a single man's dream of power cost the people its freedom, for the fellah remained the slave; it was his back that bore the stones.

And yet something new happened in Egypt then. For the first time, the slave himself rose to power. Not the fellah—he remained the poor native, a subject, a mere Egyptian. But from beyond in Asia, where the slave-dealers found the healthy, strong men they sold to the Nile, the word Mameluke, which means white slave, brought the unprecedented innovation in the career of the slave. Among the Mamelukes who ruled Egypt for nearly three hundred years (1254–1517), many were born in slavery; if their sons are reckoned, then all were descended from slaves. A dynasty of slaves —something unheard of in history. But the most astonishing thing about it was that they made no effort to conceal their descent.

For more than a millennium, in this land of divine kings, all its conquerors had had their likenesses hewn into the walls in the mask of the Pharaohs. Now men rose from the cellars of society to the palace, purchasable things, that had been chattels like a basket of figs or a silk gandurah. And yet they proclaimed their descent in the name of their dynasty. The first line of Mameluke Sultans even retained their nickname officially—they were called Bahri Mamelukes, after the Bahr, the Nile, in which their fathers had stood naked during the fortification of the island of Roda. Many of them preserved in the series of the royal titles the name of their first slave-dealer, as if they wished to perpetuate the memory of the man who had founded their fortunes. Proud of their own strength, like the Fatimids before them, some even decreed that the royal succession should not be hereditary.

For as they were always in need of soldiers, the Sultans bought slaves by the thousand. Kalaun is said to have acquired 24,000. The Viziers bought, the Emirs bought, the rich men bought, for they were not only looked after, spoilt, or flattered by their slaves; they flattered themselves in the possession of a handsome, or huge, or skilful youth; it was not by chance that the dealers went to the Caucasus to find boys and girls among the Georgians and Circassians, the handsomest type living even today.

With grace and cunning, it was not difficult for the slave to make himself indispensable. And if once he caught the eye of some dignitary, perhaps even of the Sultan himself, he would become his page; from there, with elegant malice, he could worm his way into the bodyguard, where he was generally declared free. If luck was with him, and he remained under the eye of his master, he might be made sword-bearer, or keeper of the ink-pot, and thus, even as a youth, become an "Emir of Ten," that is, he could reach the lowest grade of command. With that, he had taken a hand in the great game of hazard in the citadel, was already a partisan of the Master of the Horse, or of his opponent, and a partisan of the Head Cupbearer, and within the year he had slipped into some conspiracy, and everything was possible.

What a lust for life—that is, for rising in life! When his dealer's ship approached Alexandria, and he saw for the first time the flat coast on which his brothers, landing from the same boat, had risen to be Viziers and Sultans, the thought began to gnaw at him—how shall I get my freedom? They all knew about these freaks of fortune of recent centuries. Twenty years after he had attracted the attention of some dealer as a handsome boy in a village on the Black Sea, and been bought from his parents for little more than 20 dinars ($50), then packed onto a sailing-boat for Alexandria, and bought by an Emir in Cairo for 50 dinars, Barkuk became Sultan of Egypt. Twenty years after Sultan Barkuk had bought him, Muayyaid became Sultan of Egypt. But Kait Bey, who was regarded as a great Sultan, having won the favour of a powerful man by fencing and throwing the lance, and thus obtained his freedom, reckoned his descent so high that, as an old man, among all his sons, he named the son of a slave-woman his heir.

Even distant princes of ancient lineage had to negotiate with these slave-born kings as their equals. Sultan Kalaun treated with Rudolf of Habsburg. Bibars succeeded where even Saladin had failed: he drove out the Crusaders. Since the Mamelukes always sent for some genuine descendant of the Caliphs, so that the Caliphate should continue to flourish under them in Cairo, amid all the unrest and all the conspiracies, they remained lords of the Holy Cities, and retained the privilege of sending the Holy Carpet to Mecca every year.

All drew their strength from Islam. If Islam was powerful enough to convert the Christians in Egypt, where they had been received with such enthusiasm, if it became so strong in the course of thirteen hundred years that it could not be reconquered by the Christians, what was the secret of such success? It must lie in the logic which guarantees to Islam alone, of all living religions, the unity of power and faith, of state and mosque, for its founder had defended a powerful God with his sword, and no eternal contradiction weakens and confuses Islam as it does the Christian state religion. "The sword is the key of Heaven," said the Prophet.

The partial origin of Islam in Judaism, from which it took four of its six prophets, its early forms, and the virile principles it has developed up to the present day, is nevertheless relaxed by the tolerance which makes it regard itself as the true faith, but not as the chosen people. While the Koran permits the Moslem a plurality of wives, and proclaims an anti-ascetic life of enjoyment, it enjoins charity as one of its four chief commandments; while it sets good works and God's grace as doorkeepers of Paradise, it does not people that Paradise with angels contemplating the crown of the godhead: a tent of pearls, jacinths, and emeralds awaits the true believer there.

And yet, in spite of the worldly brilliance of this faith, the Moslem possessed the greatest of all virtues: the belief in predestination has schooled him in impassiveness, for everything that happens, happens according to God's will, and if he wears his shroud his life long wound round his head as his turban, when he dies in the desert he can wash himself with sand instead of water, dig a hole, wrap himself in his cloth, which shrouds him to his mouth, and wait for death. To cover his dead head, Allah will send a merciful wind through his desert.

15

FOR centuries, the Sultan on the Nile lived in peace with the Christians, broken by occasional quarrels. Who began a quarrel, we cannot decide even for yesterday. Yet it seems to have been the Christians who took up the struggle with their rivals in the conquest of souls. Did the Moslems insult the tomb of Christ? That can hardly be the case for He is the fifth of their six prophets; and at the beginning, Mohammed even declared the Jews and Christians true believers: it was only their Scriptures that were false. The Arabs and their successors had certainly not come to convert anyone in Egypt: their migrations, begun long before Mohammed, led them to fertile lands, and that was what they set forth to conquer. They wanted grain and tribute, not converts. In the first century of their rule, uncultured and ignorant as they were, they left the administration in the hands of the Copts, who were at any rate better arithmeticians than they, until Coptic riots in the Delta against high taxes led the Arabs to adopt a stricter policy. When, two centuries later, Arabic superseded Coptic as the official language, the Copts were the first to learn Arabic.

Thus, when Christian enthusiasts, moved at first by noble motives, set out to win back the Holy Sepulchre, it was a war of offence, and when Jerusalem nevertheless remained in the hands of Islam, only belonging to the Christians for 113 out of 1300 years, it seemed as if the war of the gods had been decided, too, for, as in Homer, it had been fought out in the heavens at the same time.

What happened during the Crusades was an intermittent persecution of the Christians by the Moslems, who carried it out as a revenge and a reprisal. Later Sultans persecuted the Copts, forbade them to ride on horseback or to keep Mohammedan slaves, ordered them to wear a bell round their necks when they went to the baths, branded the sign of the lion into their hands, and cut off such Coptic hands as were found without it. But the origin of such measures was never to be found in the fanaticism which had impelled the Christians under Diocletian to massacre and to destroy the venerable temples of Egypt.

About 1300, there was even a Sultan of Christian origin. Lajin, if we can trust the sources, is said to have been born on the Baltic, and to have entered the Order of the Teutonic Knights, to have fought first against the Slavs, then, in the last Crusades, against the Mohammedans, till he adopted the faith of his enemies, and in the end, when there was no one left to know his origin, he became Sultan of Egypt. We might regard as his counterpart that vase of Islamic beauty which, in the course of some Germanic raid, was carried out of the treasury of the Mamelukes, taken to Prussia, and now stands in the Marienburg.

The many thousands of Christians who went over to Islam did so neither under compulsion nor by conviction: their only wish was to avoid the high taxes, and the stream of converts of this kind was at times so great that the terrified treasurer, when the taxes dropped from fifteen to ten million dollars, begged the Sultan to close the gates of Mohammed's religion for a time; otherwise the state treasury, and hence his power, would be jeopardized.

That ushered in the long period of religious peace in Egypt: at that time, a Christian even became the Vizier of Sultan Nasir, as Joseph had once been the Vizier of a Pharaoh, the Copts could borrow chandeliers and rugs from the nearest mosque for their festivals, and on one occasion, when the Nile showed no signs of rising, all religions united in a pilgrimage to the river. Then the Sultan, robed in white wool, moved to the river, surrounded by the Caliph, the head cadis, and the sheikhs, followed by the Jewish rabbis and the Coptic priests, while the three precious books which had caused so many wars, the Koran, the Torah, and the Gospels, were carried side by side. In three different languages, in the name of three alien prophets, Allah was besought to allow the divine drop to fall into the river so that the land might grow green. Such things were possible in the Middle Ages, which men call dark and fanatical; in Egypt, the land of tolerance, such a scene might be repeated tomorrow.

Caliph Omar proceeded in more sagacious fashion when the Nile flood did not arrive. When Amr, the conqueror of Egypt, would not sacrifice a living virgin at the Nile Festival, and the river really seemed to be sulking, he asked his lord in Damascus what he should do. The Caliph sent him a letter with a message that he was to throw it into the Nile:

"From Abd-Allah-Omar, the Prince of the Faithful, to the Nile in Egypt! If thou flowest of thine own will alone, remain as thou art. But if Allah, the One God, the Almighty, causeth thee to flow, we implore Allah, the One God, the Almighty, to cause thee to flow again." In reply to this royal threat, which combines so much pride with so much humility, what was the Nile to do? It rose the following morning. This is the way the story is told by the great Makrizi, for in those days, geographers were still allowed to be poets.

Even the old Suez Canal was again brought into use under the Sultans: they used it to send grain to Arabia, but the Caliph closed it, like the Persian king before him, when he was threatened by revolution on the Egyptian side. Another had a wide canal built from Cairo to Alexandria in forty days, and by that means developed the south-western Delta; he speeded up traffic in the new district by means of thirty stone bridges, and the splendid castles of rich men, a hundred fellah villages, and fruit trees from Syria arose in a land which had just been desert.

All these things, the great trade-roads they made, the acacia woods they planted on the Upper Nile for the sake of ship-building, could be achieved by the Sultans, in the perpetual changes of the ruling house, only by the strictly hieratical structure of the army, which filled the gulf between the ruler and his subjects with weapons, but left no feudal lord between them, for no conquests were undertaken, and the officer had no personal dwelling. Since even the humblest emir had to provide his own contingent, that is, his troops of slaves, and not less than ten of them, while the Drummer Emir had forty to eighty, and the Commandant a hundred and twenty, since each had to keep his men out of his rations and his pay, a system of Mamelukes was created in which a powerful central power could secure the citadel, the city, and the country.

The Mamelukes might perhaps be compared to the Foreign Legion, so great was the medley not only of Turks and Circassians, Albanians, Greeks, and Serbs, but also of Southern Frenchmen and Genoese, who, in spite of all the royal prohibitions and papal bulls, were shipped yearly to Alexandria in thousands. The only difference was that these men were slaves, and went passively, like horses, from one rider to another; their name and origin were obliterated, they were kept in the name of their dealer and their master. Powerful viziers rose from their ranks who, after the fashion of the Frankish major-domos, bequeathed their power to their sons, instead of ascending the dangerous throne themselves. Could a power built up on such instruments satisfy a people in the long run?

They practised the delicate arts that they had inherited or conquered, Persian craftsmanship flourished in Cairo. Silks of such splendour were woven in Tinnis and Damietta that distant princes paid $500 for a robe and as much as $2500 for one woven with gold. Roger of Sicily's famous cloak came from this country.

When building was going on, the domineering irritability of the Mamelukes was never satisfied with the rate of progress. If slave-labour did not suffice, the people was whipped into service, and in thirty-six days and nights had to transform a quarry in the citadel into a sheepfold. The earnings of the craftsmen flowed into the coffers of the state, but the fellah remained far out of sight, standing somewhere at his sakia, raising water—water.

The state was embodied in the Sultan, and every time he died, fled, or was assassinated, the whole structure trembled. Yet that used to happen every five years. In the course of 260 years, 53 Mameluke governments, representing 22 families, succeeded each other; 13 died a natural death as Sultans, the others were deposed or murdered. In such a country, who could feel even the relative security necessary to any great spiritual or even financial enterprise? Even the administration of the Nile was kept up only because the Pharaohs had established it four thousand years before.

The Nile remained, but how distant the Pharaohs were! Their passion for divine immortality was succeeded by the warlike simplicity of the Asiatics, that, in its turn, by the spiritual elegance of Hellas, the dry prudence of Rome, the fanatical other-worldliness of the Christians. Now Egypt was in the hands of dark, wild adventurers, most of whom scrambled through life from day to day, and, so to speak, devoured their brief reigns in plots.

Who was ruling—the Sultan or his Vizier, the Sultan or his harem, the Sultan or his emirs—that was the perpetual question agitating the capital, and on it depended the joy or sorrow of all the great ones of the land. Nine hundred pages of a history of the Abbasids in Egypt relate little but this state of insecurity, and only the water-carrier with his skin, the fellah at his wheel, could be sure of seeing Allah's sun on the morrow, provided his heart was still beating. To approach the sun of the Sultan, to become visible to the circles of his satellites, was the goal of every man and every woman, but the nearer they came, the hotter grew the glow, and in the end most were consumed in the heat. Since it was only the humble who went on quietly earning their bread, while everyone else struggled for gold instead of bread, since all the gold and all the rights to it lay up in the citadel, a system of favourites developed, the like of which even Europe in the eighteenth century, even St. Petersburg itself, never saw, and whose last, feeble reflection is only today dying out in Cairo.

At that time, it had become the system of the Sultans to fatten up their favourite, and when he was fat enough, to slaughter him and distribute his hoard to new favourites. There were treasurers who plundered religious houses for years, and blackmailed the emirs, and nobody hindered them, least of all the Sultans, from diverting part of this gold through special channels into their own coffers. In the end, a fortunate of this kind would seem to the Sultan, who kept him under constant observation, rich enough to be good booty: one morning, he, the second man in the land, would be taken prisoner, bound naked on an ass, and led through the streets; then the executioners would find his priceless stuffs and precious stones and, by torturing his mother, brothers, and friends, would discover more and more secret cellars, while the Sultan had a merry day. There were Sultans like Nasir who inquired what tips the emirs had given their messengers, and there were viziers like Nashmid, who would borrow paltry sums from friends to make a show of poverty.

16

THE distant Nubian gold from the Middle Nile was still pouring into the cellars of the lords of Egypt. It was sought in the mines at night, so that the dust could be seen glittering in the lamplight. There the naked men would remain half asleep till morning. Then they loaded the sacks of golden sand onto camels to be taken to the well, and when it was mixed with mercury and melted down, it travelled on armoured boats through the cataracts to the mint in Cairo. For greed was the greatest of the Sultans' passions. From time to time, Allah provided another surprise for the greed of the Caliph or the Sultan who was ruling for him. In 1350, the great plague had come from China to Europe by way of Egypt, and while on many a day, as many as 20,000 human beings died in Cairo, while the dead fish floated on the Nile, the cattle broke out in blains, and the dates were full of worms, the Sultan gathered in all the property the succession of which could not be settled in the confusion. In fact the plague twice saved the rulers of Egypt from bankruptcy.

Yet they were generous, for when a people has made the most splendid hospitality the basis of intercourse, when the poorest Mohammedan is a sultan for his guest, how much more must the Sultan prove himself a Mohammedan! Like so many rich men, they would at times fling the gold that oppressed their consciences among the poor, who killed each other for it; they built baths and mosques, made presents to scholars and poets, generally as indiscriminately as they threw the gold on the streets; they would suddenly relieve a village of its taxes, load obliging emirs with weapons and hawks; and anybody whom they particularly wished to honour, they would present with the noblest gift the Arab knows—a fine horse. Sultan Zahir is said to have paid $75,000

for a horse. Another said to his vizier, who was also a great physician and had laid a book of medicine at his feet: "I will reward
thee more richly than Alexander rewarded his teacher," and gave
him great estates in the Delta, but when he felt sick, he declared
that the purge which the same vizier and physician had admin-
istered to him was too drastic, and had the octogenarian beheaded
the next day.

Cruelty was the second of their passions. When the powerful
treasurer Nasir Mohammed, who was, by the way, born a Christian, had not managed to squeeze enough out of a rich man by
torture, he had his hands wrapped in cloths, soaked in liquid
resin, and set on fire. Others were washed with salt water and
lime, then thrown on to cold stone slabs. It was not only the executioners who flogged and blinded, shod men with hoofs like horses,
or nailed them to the saddle. The Sultan himself would leap from
his throne and flog a high dignitary of state till he bled. Another,
enraged by the low taxes, called for a dozen living pigeons, and
cut their throats one after another, merely to be able to say: "Thus
I will slaughter you all." Not only was the head of an enemy
carried through the streets on a lance, but the headless body was
thrown into the drain so that the people might realize the power
of the Sultan, who could do the like to every great man in the
country. Once when Sultan Nasir had cast one of his favourites
into prison and condemned him to death by starvation, he sent
him, on the eighth day, three covered dishes; when the famished
prisoner, believing they brought mercy, opened them, he found
one filled with gold, the second with silver, the third with precious
stones. On the twelfth day he was found dead, the palms of his
hands gnawed away, and one finger, torn from the hand, still in
his mouth.

They were subject to sudden attacks of humility, and would
command the sheikh not to pronounce their names until he had
descended one step from the pulpit, or would pray without a rug,
touching the floor with their forehead, and if a conquered enemy
appeared, believing his life lost, they would raise him up and embrace him. All this was perverted cruelty.

Extravagance was their third characteristic. Then, as now, it
began in the harem, where a slave-girl who could sing to the

guitar would be rewarded with sixty pieces of silk, four precious stones, six pearls, and a turban which three successive sultans had had embroidered with jewels; at the same time her music teacher was given an estate. When one Sultan's daughter married, we read of gilded tents, of 11,000 sugar-loaves filled with confectionery, and when the emirs presented 311 wax candles, adorned with pictures, each weighing a hundredweight, he presented all the emirs of Egypt with three times their value. The same thing happened every time one of his eleven daughters married, while the treasurer sighed: "I spend my life collecting treasures for him, and he flings them all away." When Mohammed-en-Nasir made his pilgrimage to Mecca, four ships preceded him through the Red Sea, 600 camels in his retinue carried 1000 geese and 3000 fowls; pots of fresh vegetables and chests of flowers followed him through the desert, so that, in the end, he might pray in humility at his Prophet's tomb.

And yet each one lived in a perpetual tension of fear. Behind every curtain he suspected daggers; the rancour of unpaid Mamelukes meant the conspiracy of some favourite determined to capture and kill him. They had none of the serenity of the Pharaohs, who, after all, enjoyed life on the backs of the slaves and allowed their families to enjoy it with them. The general atmosphere of suspicion, the machinations of the eunuchs, who were insatiable in revenging the crime against their own bodies by crimes against those who had remained whole, the ruses of that eternally incalculable factor, the harem, all together formed an invisible web of terror, so that the Sultan would suddenly double his bodyguard overnight, close the arsenal, even prohibit the young men's archery practice, drive all the townsfolk of the great city into their houses at nightfall, and, on his travels, change his tent several times in one night.

Yet they could not elude their fate, the great *kader*, that Allah had predestined for them. Some day they would realize they were surrounded; only a few succeeded in taking flight. Sultan Yusuf, helped by his old nurse, smeared his face in the harem kitchen, and, in the guise of a scullion, fled beside the cook, with a dish in his hand, out of the very gate that had guarded his power the day before.

Confronted with a spectacle of such vitality, such boldness, such indomitable will, the later observer hesitates in his normal desire to see the memory of such a fighter obliterated by the triumph of justice which, in the end, killed him in just the way he had slaughtered his own enemies.

Fighting, cunning, and beauty, which play a more decisive part in this religion than in any other, have often led its devotees to live boldly, but at the same time implanted in them the belief in their predestined fate; hence the lack of any continuity in the sequence of events. Thus, of the confusing pictures of nine centuries, nothing remains but the flash of a sword, the scream of a tortured conspirator, and the bloodless victory of a slave-girl.

17

STILL less remains of the Turks
who came after. Like the Romans, they did not themselves live
in the land during their three centuries of rule, but reduced Egypt
to the rank of a province of a world-empire which lacked all
Roman discipline. What the long rule of the Turks (1517–1798)
left behind it on the Nile was less than any of the six conquering
peoples before them had achieved. The most the Turkish Governors did was to spread the fame of Egypt overseas by carrying away
its magnificent columns of all epochs to the Bosporus to support
the roof of their Seraglio, or to dye the nails of their wives with
powders unknown in Asia, for drugs and perfumes for the harem
were part of the tribute in kind which distant provinces had to
pay to the ruler of all the faithful.

Historically, the Turks were the normal heirs of the last Abbasids, for most of the Mamelukes who, from the Sultan to the emir,
had already had all the power in their hands so long were, after
all, Turkish slaves. In the course of the two centuries since it
had broken out of Anatolia, the aggressive Turkish nation had
conquered an empire as big as the Roman. The princes of the
Balkans, the Sultans of Algiers and Tunis, the Khans of the
Crimea, the Caliphs of Baghdad, the rulers of Mosul and Basra,
and all the land they held from Persia and the Black Sea as far
as the Moldava had been conquered by the sabres of these horsemen. Yet when this world-empire fell asunder in the World War,
no spiritual heritage remained, and even the Caliphate, which
the conqueror of Egypt had also stolen from its last ruler, no
longer had sufficient strength to send a current of civilization
into the conquered countries.

In the very year 1517 in which the Padishah, the conqueror of
Cairo, entered the great mosque, an obscure priest, in a little Ger-

man town, nailed to the church door a paper in which he declared a spiritual war on his Caliph in Rome. The one, by his curved sabres, established his dominion over a whole country for centuries to come; the other, by imagination and faith, founded a new spiritual community of the people. But what does Selim's name stand for now in comparsion with Luther's? It was even the priest and not the Caliph who left his mark on political life for half a millennium. It was no thinker, but the greatest soldier of all time who, in the end, declared: "The spirit and the sword rule the world, but in the end, the spirit will always remain the victor."

No idea bound these conquerors to the lands they conquered: all they wanted was to possess, to heap up treasure, as bankers accumulate shares of factories they have never seen. Selim's successors never so much as went to Egypt to look at it, and even the governors they appointed never took the trouble to go up the Nile; thus they saw neither the fellahin nor the temples which even then were attracting hundreds of tourists. In the sixteenth and seventeenth centuries, these pashas were still just strong enough to maintain the power of their distant overlords, for periods at any rate, and the Mamelukes, who shared the government afterwards as before, when they had murdered their Pasha, always waited, in a kind of interregnum, for the appointment of his successor. For that matter, they all delighted in appearing at the Pasha's divan, for then they could fill the huge courtyard of the citadel with splendid horses and glittering slaves, and beys and emirs strove to outshine each other with stuffs and rugs, jewels, pistols, and whips, all flashing in the sun as though they were the most brilliant men who had ever seen this fortress, and as though Allah had never caused hundreds of their predecessors to be thrown from this court into the cellars to be strangled. They were the glory and the terror of the city.

Yet the stream of gold had stopped flowing. Just before the Turkish conquest, only two years after one of the mightiest of the Mameluke Sultans, imagination and the spirit had, even in Africa, broken through the iron rings enclosing this mightiest empire without recourse to arms. When Vasco da Gama first sailed round the Cape of Good Hope, then anchored his three Portu-

guese vessels on the south coast of India, he destroyed the power
of Egypt and Venice; for all the silk from China, and all the calico
from India, that had travelled to the west for a thousand years
by way of the Nile Delta, the pepper and sugar, the nutmeg and
aloes, the pearls and precious stones, now travelled to their customers for three hundred years by the new route, and the Dutch
and English transferred the world market to Amsterdam and
London.

Those who were hurt by this in Egypt in turn simply robbed
the fellah, who always bore the brunt, whether the Nile forgot
to rise, or some foreigner, a thousand miles away, had discovered
a new sea-route. French consuls reported:

The greed of the Mamelukes is never satisfied until the fellahin
are sucked dry, and these unfortunates have no remedy against their
oppressors except flight. They flee from field and home, with their
wives and children, to try their luck in another village of the Nile
valley, and perish in the desert. The fellahin, the true slaves of the
soil, are not treated as the descendants of the real Egyptians, but only
as the scum of the country. Hopeless, their manhood crushed by their
humiliations, they can no longer revolt. Their masters treat them
like the cattle they use on the fields, without kindness and without
humanity, and have unlimited power over their property, even over
their lives, and the government encourages them in this. Some base-
less complaint is enough for the central government to send its men
to destroy whole villages with their inhabitants.

In Cairo, they slaughter men like beasts. Officers, who make their
rounds day and night, hold their courts in the street, condemn the
accused, and have them hanged at once. A man supposed to have
money is denounced by some enemy and summoned to the bey; if
he refuses to go, or denies his wealth, he is thrown onto the ground
and given a bastinado of two hundred strokes, if he is not executed
at once.

In the eighteenth century, when the power of the Pasha in
Cairo steadily declined, the real government was in the hands of
the so-called "powers," that is, groups, the number of which is
stated as having been anything from four to twenty. There were
triumvirs who led their parties against each other, dictators who
managed to postpone their murder for as much as ten years. One
Pasha after another sat trembling on his silk cushion; each was

soon busy trying to save his life, while the despot Ibrahim was terrorizing the city. Mamelukes fought their beys, the beys the kashefs, the sheikhs and ulemas the emirs, and all were descended from slaves, all had grown rich rapidly, and with their fine houses, the brilliant dresses of their wives, their private guards of janizaries, they were a thorn in the flesh of their opponents and a spectacle for the world. But the white slave-girls they collected were no longer as beautiful as the Arab girls had been, they merely had to be fat, "a face like a full moon and hips like cushions."

The Copts too had slave-girls, the rich up to eighty at a time, white, black, and Abyssinian slaves, but they could not bequeath their wealth to the descendants of their harems, for an hour after their death, the "powers" would seize it and declare them bankrupt. Even during their lifetime, they could not display their pride and wealth; in the Cairo of the eighteenth century, one of the most populous cities in the world, no Christian was allowed to ride on horseback; he even had to dismount from his ass if a bey, or even some old, pensioned eunuch from the Seraglio, rode past on his fine horse, and then each would think of what he had not got, the one of the splendid horse, the other of the splendid women.

While the despised Copt had remained as indispensable in business as the Jew, the dragoman, literally the interpreter, acquired increasing power; as the perpetual mediator in the perpetual disagreements between the Turks and the Europeans, he resembled, and still resembles, the family doctor who knows all the secrets of a marriage, tries to heal its breaches, awakens suspicion on both sides, but wins increasing confidence from both.

The first consuls were sent, though irregularly, by the English in the seventeenth century, but it was again an outsider whose intelligence was responsible for the most vital step. When Bruce returned in 1773 from his long adventures in the discovery of the Blue Nile, the Turkish Commandant of Cairo found him so ragged that he sent him a purse of gold in a basket of oranges. Bruce declined it, and when he was asked what could be done for him, as a famous man, he replied: "Give my fellow-countrymen the right to ship their Indian goods to Suez, instead of Jidda."

This privilege, which was granted, and soon proved itself invaluable, was first put into practice by Baldwin, a powerful merchant in the Levantine trade who at the same time submitted his ideas to the government in London in a series of reports: "We shall unite the Ganges, the Nile, and the Thames, and drink England's health on the top of the pyramids." But ten years passed before the English government realized the value of Suez as a port of transhipment, with only a short land route to the ships of the eastern Delta.

At that time England and France began their rivalry on the Nile. The French were more highly respected. The new consul sailed down the Nile from Bulak to Rosetta with the pomp of the Sultans in an illuminated dahabiya, the luxury of which Cleopatra would have envied. The end of the Bourbons was at hand, every official was hurrying to adorn himself with the lilies of France before it was too late. When the Revolution changed the lives of the great, even the beys in Cairo learned by it: like the rich men of Europe today, they declared themselves bankrupt as a result of the new rights of man, and finally ceased paying tribute to the distant Caliph.

Soon the Revolution was to land in unexpected form at the mouth of the Nile.

18

BONAPARTE'S campaign in Egypt begins with Leibniz and ends with Geoffroy Saint-Hilaire. Of these two great thinkers, who had nothing to do with the war, one was the inaugurator, the other the victor, in this outwardly abortive expedition.

An unknown philosopher of twenty-six, a clerk in the ministry of a little German principality, had devised a means of luring the powerful French away from the German frontier. This was in 1671, in the full glow of the Roi Soleil. The combined struggles of German and French troops against the Sultan had directed his attention to the ever-crumbling, but still unbroken power of the Caliph: it should be possible to break a piece off his big cake without his even noticing it. The idea was then in the literary fashion, yet nobody had ever put it clearly into shape as Leibniz did in his *Consilium Aegyptiacum*. He attempted to make his way to the Roi Soleil, with whom nothing could be done except in person, with a highly ornate personal letter from his Prince Elector. For in his practical idealism, he was a thorough-going German. What he really wanted to put into the hands of the French King was a Latin account of the conquest of a Turkish country. He waited in Paris in vain for four years, for the King was always at war or occupied with his ladies, and, like a true king, imagined himself far wiser than the philosopher.

The men who were to be united by an idea, a king and a philosopher, passed away, but the idea lived on, and quietly made its way. Discredited from time to time by the advocacy of all sorts of adventurers dreaming of Egyptian slave-girls, it was taken up a century later by a powerful man, the Duc de Choiseul, who, in his elegant exile in the garden of Chanteloup, passed it on to an obscure young abbé, for the duke was the first to recognize the genius of Talleyrand. Ten years later, in 1797, Talleyrand gave a public lecture under the caryatides of the Louvre, entitled: "On the advantages of new colonies for France, who lost important ones to England under the last kings." When he spoke of the East, it was familiar to all his hearers, for not thirty years had passed since England had succeeded France in the possession of India. But his reasoning, the way he presented his proposal, pointing to Egypt as the key to the situation, made the idea seem new and important. It was a magnificent speech; this cool-headed man spoke more warmly than was his wont, for he had just felt the charm of colonial life in the new America. A fortnight later, Talleyrand was Foreign Minister.

When General Bonaparte, holding court in Montebello, after his first victories in Italy, read the speech of the new minister, an electric circuit of old feelings and thoughts suddenly closed in him. The mathematician in him united with the visionary: he looked forward and backward, and the memory of Alexander and Cæsar, both of whom had found glory in Egypt, mated in his mind with the idea of injuring England. As a young philosopher, in the tedium of his years as lieutenant, he had read two writers on Egypt and India, famous at the time, and had even visited one of them. In the lieutenant's diary we read: *"Toute la gloire vient de l'Orient, comme le soleil."* Later he lost his glory in the east. As he was always ready to prove or dispose of his philosophy with gun-fire, after reading Talleyrand he wrote to the Directory in Paris that England could be beaten only in Egypt. Immediately afterwards, he was revolving great plans for the Mediterranean. "Why do we not occupy Malta? If we yield the Cape to the English in peace, we must at all costs get hold of Egypt. With 25,000 men, accompanied by eight or ten ships of the line, we could sail over and take it. Egypt does not belong to the Sultan." Later, this son of a Mediterranean island called the Mediterranean the main goal of his policy. For the moment, like all soldiers bent on taking something away from somebody else, he discovered moral reasons: the liberation of the poor Egyptians from the oppression of the Sultan. He even had the good luck to be able to exploit the French Consul's complaint of oppression by the Turkish government.

Five months later, he was in the midst of the preparations for a campaign which no European power had ever ventured. The secrecy that had to be preserved regarding his objective increased his haste, for now he set out on the great race of his life, by which he was to keep himself and his collaborators, France and the world, on the run for seventeen years. "There is not a moment to lose." He prepared the campaign in seventy-six days. For that matter, after an adventurous crossing, he landed in the Delta as comfortably as Alexander and Cæsar: not one of the three conquerors had to risk a fight at sea.

But Bonaparte was the first to come from the west to conquer Egypt: that was the first reason why he did not succeed. Gaul belonged to the Roman Empire when it took Egypt, but the Roman centre of gravity lay in the east. From the Mediterranean islands belonging to Rome, it was only a stone's throw to Alexandria; two thousand years later, it was, from Toulon, a sea-voyage of eight weeks without a port of call, straight through the enemy English. To defeat England in Egypt seemed as hopeless a task in 1798 as in 1915. The only success Bonaparte achieved in Egypt was that England occupied the Delta. The second reason for his failure was his ignorance of naval warfare; for, ten days after his French grenadiers had beaten the Mamelukes in the infernal desert heat of July, with a loss of not more than fifty men, he was beaten by the English at sea. The third reason was that Bonaparte, unlike Alexander and Cæsar, had to reckon with enemies in Egypt who came from the outside to its relief. Neither Cambyses, nor Alexander, nor Cæsar had had to fear an attack by strange peoples from the sea.

The fourth and deepest reason, however, was that he, a Frenchman, or at least half a Frenchman, was irresistibly drawn westward, when everything in Egypt was still unsettled, for Paris meant more to him than all the suras of the Koran. What was glory on the banks of this forgotten river? It was on the Seine that he must drink it! He fled from Egypt as soon as he scented power in France. The man who brought him the decisive latest news, two months old, from Europe, the newspapers reporting the defeat of France, was an Englishman: if it had not been for this delicate attention, Bonaparte would never have left his post, would never have stolen away in secret from his officers and men in the face of all discipline, and would not have been able to carry out his *coup d'état* at the psychological moment a few weeks after his return. He decided everything in a single night in Cairo, reading those papers.

The Nile was rising during the Battle of the Pyramids: it was at its height when Bonaparte climbed the pyramid of Cheops in September. The sphinx caused him no stirrings of the heart. We read only of the jokes he made, of how he teased Berthier, assuring him that he would not find his adored up there, and when some of them tried to slip away, for nobody would know in Paris later, he made them climb up. The only thing we notice is that he sent the others ahead. Perhaps he wanted a few minutes alone with the sphinx, like Alexander and Cæsar before him. A drawing by Vernon shows the scientists standing in a somewhat ridiculous posture on the head of the sphinx, letting down a tape to measure its height.

Yet Bonaparte understood the Nile as well as the Romans did, for he wrote the magnificent sentence: "In Egypt, the Nile, the spirit of good, and the desert, the spirit of evil, are ever present," adding that with hundreds of dams and canals, a new kingdom could be won from the desert. He studied the system of the canals, and even in St. Helena sketched barrages and plans: it was above all the Suez Canal that fascinated him. Bonaparte, in fact, was far more constructive than befitted a general. In exile, he was to dream of canalizing the Nile; as a lieutenant, he had made extracts from a book on the ancient Canal; and now he noted "the piercing of the isthmus" as one of his aims in the instructions he wrote himself. Then, at the risk of his life, he rode to Suez and discovered the ruins of the old Canal, alone with two guides while the others remained behind, followed its course for five miles, and lost two horses and one guide. The whole expedition to Suez was undertaken practically without baggage. The natives told later how each soldier had carried a loaf of bread spiked on his bayonet, and a leather bag of water round his neck, so ghostly had the Franks seemed to them. Bonaparte recognized the possibility of piercing the neck of land, and thus linking up the seas.

My plan [he said in St. Helena] was to prevent water flowing into the Canal except at the ebb: considering the distance of 30 miles to the Mediterranean it would not then have amounted to much. In addition, I would have had a number of sluices constructed in two years at a cost of 18 million francs. A thousand sluices would be enough to carry the Nile water to every part of the country. The huge quantity of water now lost in the sea would irrigate all the low-lying parts of the desert, in the west beyond the oases, in the east as far as the Isthmus of Suez. A large number of pumps and windmills would raise the water into canals from which it could be further distributed. In fifty years, agriculture would advance into the heart of Africa.

Goethe's enthusiasm for this plan was as great as Napoleon's. That alone was enough to keep the question alive, and seventy years later it was Eugénie, the wife of another Napoleon, who, by a symbolic gesture, united the two seas.

At first the fellah's feelings at the appearance of the French were the same as those with which he had regarded all his earlier conquerors: he welcomed them because he saw his oppressors, the Mamelukes, fleeing through the desert before his very eyes, and imagined that life could not but improve. He even saw these Frenchmen fishing for drowned Mamelukes in the Nile near the pyramids with bent bayonets, and catching literal goldfish, for on that day many a grenadier became a rich man. Then the fellah saw his new master celebrating the Nile Festival, heard that he had summoned a divan, and occasionally presided over it, sitting in the European fashion, and hence dominating the squatting Turks. He saw with some surprise that Christians went through the streets like lords, while, before, they had had to dismount from their asses. It disappointed the Cairenes that the Pasha should be so simple and only the most intelligent understood. "I am a poor merchant," said a rich merchant, "and have eleven servants. The general has only three. No wonder he beat the beys in the battle." Above all, there was justice for the fellah, or at least the intention of justice, as Desaix in particular showed on his expedition to Upper Egypt.

But what would the fellah have felt if he had known of the new Pasha's admiration for Mohammed and Moses, how he ranked them higher than Jesus, and laughed at the Crusaders who prayed instead of marching.

Of all the Napoleonic campaigns, none, not even the Russian, had the spectral unreality of the Egyptian, nor was it ever resumed. It was left like a fragment, written in a poet's youth like an unhewn block. All that had been established there by force of arms at once disappeared, and the upshot of the adventure was the complete capitulation of France to England. Bonaparte had foreseen this necessity at his departure, for he gave his successor permission to capitulate in case of extreme emergency.

Nevertheless, the enterprise sank deep into the historical romanticism of later times. To found a French colony on the Nile, Bonaparte required a thorough exploration of the whole country, but for spiritual reasons he aimed at more than what was merely necessary and useful. This was the reason why three years of doubtful French dominion left such profound effects behind them, while the 280 years of unquestioned Turkish rule left none. This young general, who celebrated his thirtieth birthday in Cairo, had taken out a spiritual insurance, so as to make at least a profit on it in fame. It was the scholars alone who saved the far from victorious general in the eyes of history.

For Bonaparte had conceived the new idea of taking an academy to war with him; none of his models had done so. The radiant dawn of an epoch of general ideas, the brilliance of a nascent glory, decided many great and elderly scientists to go to Toulon to join an expedition with an unknown goal. "Are there stones in this nameless country?" asked the geologists. "If so I am going." When they sat in their sailing-ship, 143 scholars and artists of all descriptions, systematically selected and divided into five groups, when their general opened the evening debate in the cabin on a subject he had proposed in the morning, and later, when they sat in the enchanted castle in Cairo or philosophized peripatetically in its orientally luxuriant gardens, when they saw their leader honouring the things of the mind so highly—for he always appeared at the meeting unarmed, while the men called the academy *"la maîtresse favorite"* of the general—they realized that this was no common adventurer or raw dictator, but a genius that was always anxious to learn, and therefore never missed one of their meetings.

At the first meeting, three weeks after the occupation of Cairo, he proposed the following subjects to his scientists: (1) On the construction of ovens, (2) Windmills or watermills? (3) The species of hops used in native beer, (4) The purification of the Nile water, (5) Are raw materials for powder to be found in the country? (6) How can justice and education be improved in accordance with the wishes of the people?

Once only, when he had consented to read a paper himself— he had entered the mathematical group but would have been just as much at home among the poets—Monge warned him very tactfully that he must never produce anything mediocre; Bonaparte relinquished the idea of speaking himself and thus gave an example of renunciation not followed by certain little Napoleons of today.

For three years, the scientists and artists collected data on all the Nile produced, flora and fauna, men according to class and history, temples and tombs, statues and inscriptions. It was Napoleon himself who carried out a hydrographic survey of the canals which nobody had done before him: lists of the canals, how far they could still be used, how far they were choked up, the extent of the area under cultivation—this was all magnificent spadework for the English enemy. It was not until just before Napoleon's departure that the Rosetta stone came to light: its importance was at once recognized by the academy, although they still had to mark the second of the three scripts "unknown."

All this precious material was within an ace of being lost, for when the scientists, after the English conquest of Egypt, were about to return home on English ships, according to the agreement, the English Admiral ordered them first to hand over everything they had. As always happens when the sword and the spirit clash, sparks flew, and this time not from the sword but from the spirit. To the Englishman sent to negotiate, the great Geoffroy Saint-Hilaire cried with fire: "We shall rather burn our treasures than hand them over to you, Sir! Glory is at stake, Sir! Think of the pages of history, Sir! This would mean a second burning of the library of Alexandria." With this superb retort, the scholar rescued all that remained of the campaign, and won a spiritual victory over the English at the very spot where English bombs had conquered the French.

Bonaparte's conquest of Egypt had taken twenty-three days from the landing of the first ship. The publication of the nine volumes of his Egyptian academy took twenty-three years; the last volumes were again presented to kings. When the scholars crept up to the light from the mine of their work to find the old kings on the throne again, they may have felt like a belated reveller seeing the dawn, and riding home sobered, his eyes dazzled, in the full light of day.

Thus the Egyptian campaign ended, as it had begun, with the gesture of a great scholar. What Bonaparte personally brought home from the Nile was a gigantic Mameluke who slept at his door, and a scarab from the finger of a Pharaoh.

19

THE Renaissance of the Nile set in with two soldiers. Those who at last discovered its sources in the nineteenth century were hunters and not scholars; in the same way, it was men of war and not engineers who, at the same epoch, discovered how to control its mouths. The titanic efforts of the five or six really great generals who have raised the war history of mankind out of its haze of blood and destruction into creative clarity have always brought them face to face with the struggle with the elements; sometimes they won. And whatever their motives, the results they achieved were humane. Thus the Nile also was conquered in a new and decisive fashion by Napoleon and Mehemet Ali.

If General Bonaparte had not fled from Africa to become Napoleon in Europe, he might have realized on and in the Nile what was revealed to him in the vision of his youth, and given expression to that side of his character which, even in age, always moved him to conquer the relics of chaos by the force of his will. Of no country did he dream as he dreamed of Egypt; it was for him what a woman may be for a poet. His successor in Egypt took up the idea which had hovered before his mind: the Nile was the great link between these two greatest rulers of their time.

That this is no mere hazard is shown by the inward dependence of Mehemet Ali the Turk on the Frenchman, or rather of the Albanian on the Corsican. For the two show this further resemblance, that both made their second fatherland great, though they were strangers to it. Born in the same year 1769, of the same middle class, both fatherless as children, but belonging to a large family, thrown on their own resources very early, they both learned as boys the value of the two instruments of power, money and arms, and while the one grew up as the son of a coffee-dealer in Kavala, the other as a lawyer's son in Ajaccio, from earliest childhood they heard no talk save of real estate, ships, and money, and of how they were to be obtained by party politics. At the same time these two sons of the Mediterranean both became soldiers and both attracted attention in the local disputes of their little countries. The remoteness of their homes bred in both their romantic guile, and the instability of the social order bred in both daring dreams in which everything was at stake and everything possible. Such mixtures produce a realism winged by imagination, and hence form a soldier and a diplomat in the same man.

The young Napoleon, however, could enrich his mind with the treasures of the past by reading; he was the heir of a thousand years of civilization. Mehemet Ali inherited nothing, and was already a king when he learned to read at the age of forty. The one was destined to put an end to ten years of revolution, the other was faced with the task of moving a paralysed mob; the one came to calm a delirious people, the other to awaken a sleeping one. Here lies the reason of the different rates at which they lived: in the feverish course of fifteen Napoleonic years everything had to be done, and everything perished, but Mehemet Ali was granted fifty years of constructive work, from the age of thirty to the age of eighty, during which, in spite of all his campaigns, he found time to develop Egypt. Every time Napoleon felt ready to proceed to constructive work, the shadows of his youthful victories drove him into the distance, while Mehemet Ali was turned from his conquests late in life to concentrate on work inside the country.

These fifth acts were determined by the different forms of their ambition. Not that Mehemet Ali's was less great, for by the time he was thirty-six he had risen from a tobacco-dealer and lieutenant to be a king; at the same age, Napoleon became an emperor. But while Napoleon took the crown from the Pope's hand to crown himself, Mehemet Ali remained the vassal of his Caliph, and for all his autocracy, he remained a vassal, never took the last step to independence, and died a Pasha or Viceroy. Yet both usurpers pursued one aim with the same personal passion—their hereditary succession.

Here the Moslem was happier than the Christian. Napoleon

was lavish in family feeling, but amidst all his brothers and sisters he was forty before he had a son; Mehemet Ali had a son when he was nineteen, and by the time he was an old man, he had a collection of ninety-five sons and daughters. He had no need of brothers and sisters, and could have all his later battles fought by his highly gifted firstborn, while he himself sat in Cairo and negotiated. For though he could not compare with Napoleon as a general, he was certainly his equal as a diplomat: he was, when all is said and done, an oriental. Victorious in his campaigns against Turks, Arabs, and Negroes, he never fought a European power and hence had to win by persuasion the powers conquered by Napoleon's sword. His mastery in the game was the more admirable since he knew none of their languages, and trained himself to read by their expression whether the interpreter was cheating him. Every visitor or negotiator fell victim to the personal charm of the little man with the beaming eyes.

The fact that Napoleon was keeping Europe busy was Mehemet Ali's great good fortune, for while both dictators reached the summit of their power roughly in the same years, from 1803 to 1813, it was the stronger sun that attracted the planets, in the western sky at any rate. Without Napoleon, Mehemet Ali might never have entered Egypt, and he would certainly not have conquered and kept it. No wonder that the figure of Napoleon fascinated him.

20

THE Albanians are said to be descended from the Macedonians, and when one of them follows in the footsteps of Alexander, he has double reason for saying so, even if he is not King Philip's son, but only the son of a coffee-dealer from Kavala. In any case, until recently, they were Turks, but so were the Egyptians; hence an Albanian could not conquer Egypt: the most he could do was to rule over it in the name of the Sultan. Thus the Turkish rule, which began in Egypt in 1517, actually lasted until 1914, but since Fuad, the first King of Egypt, was a great-grandson of Mehemet Ali, the self-made man from Macedonia became the founder of an Egyptian dynasty, namely the present reigning house. In the same way Ptolemy, who began as one of Alexander's generals, bequeathed to his successors three hundred years of power in Egypt. Genius triumphs, and remains untitled, while its weaker heirs, be they generals or bankers, win a crown or slip into the peerage.

Mehemet Ali drew a veil over his youth, and contested his first wife's first marriage in public only in order to establish the legitimacy of his eldest son. On his single visit to his old home, fifty years after he left it, he presented no colours, christened no regiments, and issued no medals: all he did was to found a school, the thing he had lacked in childhood. He first went to Egypt at the age of twenty-nine, as an Albanian officer in Turkish service, but General Bonaparte, against whom the expedition was directed, prevented a landing. The two men never saw each other, for in the confusion of the second battle of Aboukir Bay, Mehemet Ali fell overboard and was picked up by an English ship, whose captain could hardly be expected to know that this was a fish nothing could kill. A few months later, in the same year 1799, the one had made himself First Consul in Paris, the other Commandant of the most important regiment in Cairo.

533

In doing so, both attached themselves to those in power at the moment, both played off the political parties against each other to their own advantage: in Mehemet Ali's case, it was the Mamelukes against the English, who distrusted the Ottoman Porte and the new Albanian commander. During a riot, Ali became master of the situation, but created a terrible enemy in the Pasha he supplanted, who was to work against him in Constantinople for many years to come. The Albanian captured the citadel, and became Pasha by the grace of his impotent overlord.

Once more he used the Mamelukes to help him to beat the English, who returned four years later, but this time he was shrewd enough to turn his defeated enemy into a customer. At one stroke, the Albanian on the Nile had entered European politics. He was then thirty-eight. For his constructive work, he turned the "Franks" to excellent account, and relieved the Christians of all their humiliations.

Feared and therefore honoured by the Sultan, free of the European powers who were busy killing each other, Mehemet Ali soon made himself popular, for he had, from the outset, won the support of the malcontents, that is, of practically the whole Egyptian people, which was beginning to feel stifled. He declared himself "chosen by the people," and as he knew how to deal with them, they all believed him. The only power he had to break was that of the Mamelukes, who were still there, and still armed. He did so by having them all murdered in one day.

Even today, more than a hundred years later, history speaks more of that day than of all Mehemet Ali's other deeds. We are apt to feel more moral than Napoleon because he had the Duc d'Enghien shot, and a few plague victims killed in Jaffa. Such murders are generally judged more severely than the decimation of whole peoples, because in the latter case, the tradition of military glory seems to demand its traditional victims. And yet in the forced levies for the campaigns of Napoleon or Mehemet Ali, thousands of young men lost their lives, most of them for purposes to which they were indifferent or hostile, while on that day of March 1811, there perished in Cairo not more than 350 men, men who had enjoyed every form of power or pleasure at the cost of the happiness of half a people, and even if there had been more than a thousand of them, history knows of not a single Mameluke whom it has cause to regret.

Such an act of violence lay not only in the Turkish, but in the Egyptian tradition too. A year earlier, Mehemet Ali had defeated the Mamelukes in Upper Egypt, and when he declared that he possessed proofs of conspiracy among them, it sounds highly probable. He invited them all to the citadel, received them with ceremony in the great hall, and having trapped them by raising the drawbridge, he had the entire company of heavy-laden and armed horsemen shot, as they rode into the walled court, by his Albanian mountain troops. One saved himself by leaping from the wall on his horse, another, who had arrived late and found the gate shut, galloped away, and is said not to have stopped until he reached Syria. When Mehemet Ali's physician, a Genoese, presented himself before the viceroy and reported a complete success, Mehemet Ali made no reply, but beckoned for a drink.

This oriental form of *coup d'état* was necessary to Mehemet Ali's plans, but it was not characteristic of him. He seems never to have done anything else of the kind, even on a small scale, for instance in the Sudan. The murder was certainly a benefit to the country, which had borne the Mamelukes, groaning, for centuries, and the man responsible for it gave abundant proof later that it was not a mere transference of power.

When he handed over the command of the forces to his son Ibrahim, the world realized, with some astonishment, that a new and great military figure had arisen. Supported by this son, Mehemet Ali could have got free of the Sultan, could have become master of a huge Arabia, and made Egypt the centre of a new empire, like his compatriot Alexander. Why did he not do so?

In spite of all his rapid success, he seems to have lacked the ultimate daring. Like certain statues in front of the walls of ancient cathedrals, Mehemet Ali clearly needed the feeling of the great wall of the Caliphate behind him, and though he kept his back turned to the Sultan, he dreaded nothing so much as the collapse of those walls, the decay of the Turkish Empire in his time. Instead of seceding, although his son had twice won the opportunity for him in the field, instead of using his mighty prestige and authority as protector of the Holy Cities to declare himself Sultan and Caliph, as Saladin the Brilliant had done on the Nile seven centuries before, when he took Syria or Arabia he declared that his object was simply to extend his territory as a vassal of the Sultan, and hence to increase the Sultan's power.

But when the inevitable breach with the Sultan came, and Ibrahim, in a series of victories, penetrated nearly to the Bosporus, it was first Russia, then the five great powers, which saved the Sultan, because they could not but fear the terrible Albanian on the Nile as master of Islam, and desire a renewal of the weak and greedy Mameluke rule.

It was above all the English who were made uneasy by this Pasha, whose hand reached into the Armenian mountains and over to the Persian Gulf, but they had to have the ships of other powers besides to bring about the downfall of the eastern Napoleon before the very Acre where the western one was beaten forty years before.

Thus Mehemet Ali, at seventy-three years of age, lost the final bout. He had to surrender Syria, to pay tribute to the Sultan, abandon the Holy Cities to him, and part of his financial sovereignty as well. The only thing he gained by this treaty was the thing he most deeply desired—the vassal dominion in Egypt became hereditary.

As he had not grasped at the throne himself, like Napoleon, he lost the great chance of making himself independent; because he had grown-up sons and daughters, and lived to a great age himself, he won for them the hereditary throne which Napoleon lost. Which won most is open to question.

21

HOW did the fellahin live under the new master?

The Mameluke and his oppression had suddenly vanished, and with him starvation and worse troubles. That was a great event in the life of the Egyptian fellah. Even the bedouin raids became less frequent, the fellah's cattle was stolen less often, and if everything had gone according to the wishes of the new master, he would not have been flogged unjustly by the cadi. But however often the new Pasha might ride about the country, though he was at times generous and willing to help, he was, after all, a man of violence, and saw he could awaken this sleeping people only by compulsion, with the curbash. His model was Peter the Great.

Thus though the fellah might feel a heavier hand, he began to realize at the same time that he was no longer being starved, like his fathers, merely in order that strangers in the land might live splendid lives or kill their enemies; he felt that there was at last a man in the citadel who was working for Egypt. Though he himself was often dragged off in chains in the forced levy, and sent up the Nile to Nubia, or over to Anatolia, he saw at the same time that his son was being sent to school, was being fed there at the Pasha's expense, was taught and even paid. The fellah, under Mehemet Ali, gained a hint of what his fathers had never known —self-respect.

He could certainly understand nothing of all the Pasha was doing, but who did at that time? At first, it looked like robbery; actually it was a first attempt at state socialism. This Moslem, who could not even read the Koran, had certainly made someone read to him out of the Bible what Joseph had done as Pharaoh's chancellor. Thus he confiscated a large part of the cultivated land as so-called crown territory. The Mameluke's property was seized, but the tenants were expropriated with a compensation. Being now the biggest landowner in Egypt, Mehemet Ali made himself the sole tradesman, the sole producer of goods in Egypt, by building factories. He subjected the entire Nile valley to a compulsory organization, prescribed what was to be cultivated, threw a crowd of idlers out, forced the fellah to sell his grain to the officials at a fixed price, and paid part of it in molasses from his sugar refinery. Egypt became a single state farm with the Viceroy as its master, a hundred years before Stalin. The expropriated rich stood aghast, the fellahin were afraid, the middlemen cursed, but the country, as a whole, flourished, and after thirty years of a dictatorship which was, at least in intention, just, the coffee-dealer of Kavala could stroke his patriarchal white beard and, when he sailed up-Nile, say to himself that Egypt was flourishing as it had not done for centuries under any Sultan or Pasha.

Like the Mamelukes, Mehemet Ali took from the fellah his money and his freedom by forced labour on his buildings and canals, by forced levies for his campaigns, by the whip with which he collected his taxes; he fixed grain-prices which nobody could pay, sold hens, sheep, and goats for three times, six times, what they had cost before, but he put it all back into the country; provided that he himself received his Cretan cherries, his coffee and tobacco of the finest quality, that his castle was fit to live in, so that he could receive foreigners in it royally, he was satisfied. "In your country," he said to a German, "you need many hands. I work the machine myself. I have to be my subjects' teacher, and a severe one at that. I am the fellah's doctor, and he does not even know what is the matter with him." Mehemet Ali's work shows that a hundred years ago in the Orient a dictator could be a blessing.

Whatever he thought useful in Europe, he took, but he borrowed money only from commercial houses, often repaying as much as 70 percent in his own goods. He liked best of all to deal with the French, and it was probably his passion for Napoleon that caused his growing antipathy to England. When one of Napoleon's officers, who had entered Persian service, was passing through Cairo, he stopped him and empowered him out of hand to form an army: the Catholic Colonel Sève became the

Mohammedan Suleiman Bey. For the first time since the Pharaohs, an Egyptian army was created, and the fellah proved his worth on all fronts.

When Mehemet Ali ran short of sails for his fleet, he planted hemp, which had hitherto been used only as a drug on the Nile, built factories, and manufactured his own sailcloth. In every province he planted acacias for shipbuilding, and the avenue leading to his palace was guarded by hundreds of turrets to protect the saplings. In the Faiyûm he planted 30,000 olive trees for soap, at other places a million mulberry trees for silk. When a great cattle-plague broke out, he did not, like the Pharoahs and Sultans, call in the help of the gods against the Egyptian plague; he sent thousands of his best cavalry horses on to the land, and yoked them with camels, or forced the fellah to put himself in harness.

He did not love the fellah, but he seems to have loved Egypt in his own way. When Champollion, who deciphered the hieroglyphics, spoke to him in an interview of the misery of the fellah, whose life he had observed in the course of his researches, and, like a true philanthropist, repeatedly returned to the charge, old Ali always evaded the question, and asked about his work. This new Pharaoh wanted to learn from the only man who could then read the hieroglyphics what sort of men the ancient Pharaohs really were. Beside him—for he liked to show off in front of strangers —he had his tame lion, like Sesostris, but the Frenchman was not impressed: he merely appreciated the humour of the situation, and most likely Mehemet Ali saw it too, for he had a sense of humour, and relished impossible situations.

He would have liked to find gold on the Upper Nile, gold and slaves being the real object of his Nubian campaigns. Although he himself found hardly any gold, he had every Nile boat searched in the harbour of Cairo, and even carried off all the specie he found, paying in drafts on his own factories. Such was the high-handedness of the man who had the Code Napoléon translated, in order to introduce reforms by it, and was the first ruler of Egypt since the building of the pyramids to establish equal security for the life and property of all classes and all religions. And again, it was the same man who, when his Albanians revolted in summer, opened the canals and flooded part of his capital to drown the riot. Thus, for once, the Nile even saved a dictator.

But Ali had done much for the Nile. When he put 6000 new boats on the river, or 30,000 new water-wheels on its banks, when his son Ibrahim set up the first steam-pumps, to raise the water in Bulak, sending to England for coal to work them, they used forced labour everywhere like the Mamelukes before them. When Ali, on his way to Alexandria, missed a canal where it ought to have been, and the engineer, whom he summoned, asked for a year's time to build it, he gave him a bastinado of a hundred strokes and threatened him with three hundred more if he did not find it ready on his return four months later.

In the construction of the canal by which he linked up Alexandria and the Nile, 20,000 men are said to have lost their lives, but when it was finished, the harbour, which had fallen into ruin during the preceding years, again became the real mouth of the Nile, for in Damietta and Rosetta, the sand from the sea and the strong current continually reduced the size of the harbours. Ali named this great canal after his enemy and feudal lord, the Sultan, the Mahmudia Canal. The greatest thing he built was the first dam, for with that, the new epoch of the Nile began, half a century before the English dams. Ali discovered that the Nile had a golden mouth. No one had recognized this hidden possibility earlier and more clearly than Napoleon. "The day will come," he wrote, "when work will be put in hand to dam the two branches of the Nile at the head of the Delta, so that all the water of the Nile can flow through the one branch and the other alternately, and the flood can be doubled." This, and everything else about the Nile that he wrote on St. Helena, was known to Mehemet Ali, who had all Napoleoniana read to him; as an old soldier, he may also have realized that Napoleon was dealing with the hostile element exactly according to his tactics on the field of battle, which were to concentrate all his forces at one spot, so as to overwhelm the enemy with his troops, or inundate the land with water.

Ali's first, barbaric idea had been to stop up one branch entirely, and allow the Nile to flow only to Damietta, that is, to fly directly in the face of nature; but the Frenchman Linant showed him, first that the plan was not feasible, secondly that Alexandria would be left entirely without fresh water. When he resolved to dam both branches of the Nile, he first thought of using the stones from the great pyramids; it was no piety for ancient monuments of civilization that stopped him, for Mehemet Ali simply laughed at them; the transport was too costly. The construction of the "Barrage du Nil," as it is still called, was repeatedly held up: it cost no money, for the builders simply took the men they needed, but first the plague came, then the war with the Sultan, then a new engineer who was dissatisfied with the first scheme, but did not improve on it. The barrage was completed much later, and in a certain sense this old-fashioned dam remained the most important and certainly the most indispensable of all.

For dams on the Nile mean cotton on the Nile, and Mehemet Ali was the first to realize what two Frenchmen had pointed out, that Egypt must produce sugar and cotton, and would make much bigger profits on them than on grain. It was a great and daring idea, since its realization was favoured by the climate, but hampered by the water-conditions. The cotton plant cannot survive inundation, but needs regular watering in summer, when the Nile is low and there is no rain, even in the Delta. These existing conditions could be changed only by the dam, but, in addition, it was necessary to install a system of pumps and siphons, to deepen the canals, and, just to keep them clean, to employ an army of 27,000 men working a hundred days out of the year. The old coffee-dealer needed to reckon with only a few million pounds, and since the labour on the dam cost nothing, the sum worked out precisely. But what about bad harvests or world-crises? And what if the import of grain, which was now necessary, were to fail in time of war?

The old merchant, however, does not seem to have troubled his head with such questions. It was not until the end of his life, in 1847, that he laid the foundation of the barrage in its second or third form. At that time the defeat for which England was responsible had plunged him into alternate states of rage and depression: he never said "England," but only "that country," and in the midst of crises and reforms, he was seeking a way into the interior, since the way out was blocked. It was in these last years that Mehemet Ali became a real father of his country, and in his own way a great ruler. He sent teachers from old El Azhar to London to make them realize that there were other books in the world beside the Koran; he founded an Egyptian school in Paris; and when he ultimately sent a batch of princes to it along with the other pupils, he could not dream what consequences this Parisian education was to have for his grandson Ismail. At the same time he had useful books printed cheaply and distributed in Cairo.

And all the time he was revolving in his mind vast projects for the Nile. Fifty years before the English made their first plans for Aswân, he was planning to take the water from that very spot, and then to build two embankments along the Nile, running the entire length of Egypt! He meant to take advantage of every bend in the river to increase the cultivable land and set up his factories —Faust's work, dreamed by a king who had once sold coffee. He lived to see many things flourishing in Egypt, whose population had increased from 2½ to 4½ millions, in spite of the plague.

Just before his end, Mehemet Ali made a last pilgrimage, but not to the Holy Cities. He was not a religious man, and only his despair at his defeat abroad led him to spend a fleeting thought on Mecca. But his pilgrimage was to his feudal lord, the Sultan, to pay him homage after the long years of hate and discord. When he returned, making a triumphal entry into Alexandria, he wore the Sultan's likeness, framed in diamonds, on his breast: it was a display of vassal loyalty which, in so powerful a servant, was merely another form of pride, like Bismarck's obeisance before his young Kaiser forty years later.

In the end, the octogenarian Mehemet Ali fell into a kind of mental paralysis; in that condition he may not have fully realized that his son Ibrahim had died at the age of sixty. Much had happened between the two, the whole drama of father and son, of a king and his successor, had played itself out between them in oriental fashion. Great powers had never come to full fruition in this great son, and no man can serve a dictator for forty years without coming to harm by it. Appalling letters have been preserved. It is impossible to calculate what Egypt lost by the death of Ibrahim. If he had lived to be as old as his father, he might well have proved as much greater than this second Philip as Alexander was greater than the first. This powerful heir was no longer a Turk, no longer an Albanian—he had become in every sense of the word an Egyptian, while his own son and successor, in his turn, became half a Parisian.

When Mehemet Ali's mind was still fully active, he was visited by a man whom history itself might have called to pronounce judgment. This was Napoleon's son, borne to him by the beautiful Polish countess. Count Walewski, later Foreign Minister, was sent to Cairo in 1840 on a special mission and wrote of the King:

His first feelings may at times be dictated by vanity, pride, self-conceit, but his decisions are always taken as the result of long thought. His genius is greater in civilization than in organization. He has neither the eagle eye which sees men and things from above, nor the superior intelligence which permits a man to take decisions which at first sight look surprising, but he has a keen intelligence, perseverance, a strong will, and is astonishingly adroit. Had he been born a Frenchman, he would have become a Metternich or a Talleyrand rather than a Napoleon.

Genius and courage were obviously born in him, experience played a great part in his life, education none at all. Such a case is rare, and the mania of certain historians to break up into its component colours an inborn light here, of its very nature, becomes absurd. He once gave a delightful proof that he had never read any of the books which are supposed to train a man to command. As a true dictator, he had heard of Machiavelli, and so he grew curious to read how men become in books what he had become in a life without books. He therefore commanded his foreign minister to translate passages from *The Prince* into Turkish. The minister brought him ten pages a day. On the fourth day, Mehemet Ali said:

"In the first ten pages I discovered nothing great or new. I waited, but the next ten were no better. The last ten were merely commonplace. I can learn nothing from this man. And as regards cunning, I know far more about it than he. Now stop and translate no more."

22

WHEN genius has appeared in the figure of a king or an artist, the decadence which usually sets in with their sons, that exhaustion of nature after a great effort, at once undermines the security of newly founded dynasties. Old ruling houses, on the other hand, once these early dangers are overcome, are supported by their tradition, whatever the conduct of their individual members may be. In the struggle of years, Ali had secured the hereditary succession of his vassalage, and yet in spite of his ninety-five children he was duped by fate, for his first and best-born son did not come to the throne, and those who succeeded the Macedonian coffee-dealer in the Pharaonic mask were little men. A grandson and a son who, in the next fourteen years, quickly abandoned the stand against England abroad and Ali's state socialism at home, undermined the world's respect for a newly awakened Egypt, and accustomed the great powers to regard events on the Nile merely as another Napoleonic adventure, the consequences of which could quickly be smoothed out with the iron of legitimacy.

The reign of Ismail (1863–1879) might be compared with that of Wilhelm II. Both grandsons of powerful empire-builders, both were prematurely and unexpectedly called, at the age of thirty, to thrones which were not yet sufficiently well established to resist sudden or thoughtless movements. Both were unquestionably gifted and personally charming; they wasted the heritage of their fathers, not by ugly vices or ambitious wars, but because they were thrown off their balance by a power suddenly received and almost beyond control, and by that passion for amusement which Bismarck defined when he said: "The Kaiser would like to have a birthday every day." Two serious-minded men, who had fought their way in youth through revolutions, in age through the resistance of old established powers, who both maintained the simplicity of their early years in their private habits into their ripe old age, were succeeded by two wealthy grandsons who strove to conceal their inward uncertainty under a brilliant exterior and to command the world's respect by assuming imperial airs. Thus Ismail and Wilhelm, who shared a great talent for arranging processions, both squandered in exactly thirty years the great patrimony it was their duty to preserve, and were deposed by the decree of foreign enemies whose interests they were declared to have compromised. Both were to spend a serene and leisured old age in richly dowered exile without fame and without philosophy, as befitted their characters.

Ismail, who had been partly educated in Paris, and petted on political missions to the western capitals, seems to have taken as an example the least steady of European kings, Napoleon III, and to have determined to turn his own capital, which was very wealthy when he took it over, into a second and by no means African Paris. The new light, the new railways, squares and boulevards, the silk and decorations, above all the dazzling court-receptions, had gone to his head and obscured the business instinct he had inherited from Ali and had, at the beginning, displayed in his up-to-date administration of his possessions.

When he assumed the reins of government, everything seemed to smile on him. The American Civil War made Egypt, the young cotton country, suddenly rich by the stoppage of the American cotton export; the world, which had to be clothed, was ready to pay any price; fantastic figures created legends of fabulous wealth; engineers went to make their fortune on the Nile; France and England were competing for their standing in the country; the great canal then under construction was drawing all eyes to Egypt. Was it a wonder that the biggest banks offered their money to the happy child of fortune? And was it so frivolous of him to take it? In sixteen years Ismail borrowed $495,000,000 from Europe.

Not all was wasted. During his reign nearly 9000 miles of new canals were built; he constructed the Ibrahim Canal at Asyût, which turned an area said to cover a million feddan, which till then had lain fallow, into fertile lands. He multiplied the harbours, the lighthouses, and the sugar factories, and above all he increased the cotton crops, so that exports rose in value from

$20,000,000 to $70,000,000. He turned 200 schools into 5000, and spent $400,000 a year on this most vital work. His great museum in Cairo was, according to the taste of the time, a marvel, like the Gezira Bridge he built beside it.

Ismail, however, fell victim to the boom, to his vanity, above all to the pace he had set himself, which carried him on with increasing momentum. He was in exactly the same position as the poor fellah. By a scandalous law that in actual fact placed all foreigners out of the reach of native justice, he had made the Levantine financier the slave-owner of the fellah, who had to take up loans at usurious rates of 40 and 50 percent in order to pay the taxes on his crops. With the same usury, the most distinguished banking-houses in Europe profited by Ismail's greed and profligacy and thus cheated him with their interest, private commission, their committees and fictitious payments, and all the tricks of the Paris and London stock exchanges, in a way which would have sent a small man to prison. An Englishman of the time called the big bankers the scum of Europe, for they actually paid over to the cheerful king only 60 percent of his loans on paper.

If anyone is deserving of contempt in this affair it is the creditors and not the debtor. Nor has history any sympathy with those who later lost their money through the spendthrift on the Nile.

But things had not yet reached this pass when Ismail celebated the most brilliant event of his life, the opening of the Suez Canal.

A handsome and highly gifted Frenchman had, in his youth, given riding-lessons to Said, Ismail's mild predecessor. Owing to this friendship, he had got possession of a precious document which had till then been refused to everybody by Mehemet Ali and his successors, namely, a permit of two lines "to construct a canal suitable for ocean-going navigation between Suez on the Red Sea and the Gulf of Pelusium." While the world in general, and English commerce in particular, grasped the significance of the canal from the outset, while the Saint-Simonists in France led the movement and the figures of Goethe and Napoleon hovered in the background, one of the most famous politicians of his time, Lord Palmerston, made himself ridiculous by writing, as late as 1855: "It would cut off Egypt from Turkey, stop the advance of the troops of the suzerain power, and place Great Britain's interests in Egypt and India at the mercy of France." His fear of France was greater than his vision of the British Empire. When the French apostles of the Canal had partially replaced by machinery the *corvée* of the fellahin, which was suddenly revealed by English puritanism in an attempt to stop the Canal, the first steam-dredges began to clatter in the Red Sea.

The story of the Suez Canal belongs to human history and not to the history of the Nile, but the Canal is to a certain extent the Nile's enemy because it draws Egypt to the sea. With a tragic foresight which Ismail, in his cheerfulness, may have failed to realize, he said at the opening that the Canal had cut Egypt off from Africa and made it part of Europe. In actual fact the water that links this African country to the equator is more important than the water which was to make it European: today it is becoming clear that it is the Nile that determines Egypt's fate, and not the Mediterranean. While the whole world gained by the Canal, the only land to lose by it was Egypt. Ismail wanted the Canal for Egypt and not Egypt for the Canal, but his intentions were thwarted by his character, and he soon lost all his shares and all his profits.

On that November day of 1869, he was happy. The Emperor of the French and many princes were his guests, and the great Verdi conducted his new Egyptian opera in the new opera house in Cairo. It was all an opportunity to pour out money such as even this graceful spendthrift would never see again. But this king and this emperor, both grandsons of obscure citizens of forgotten places on the Mediterranean, the one looking like a schoolmaster, the other like a banker, would have merely looked ridiculous in their role of creators of new world conditions if it had not been the hand of the lovely Empress Eugénie which cut the symbolic ribbon, and thus raised the union of two seas into the sphere of the eternal feminine.

Ismail had paid the Sultan millions for the title of Khedive and the right to a still more stringent limitation of the succession. By the time the Canal was opened, however, he was determined to get rid of his powerless overlord at last and to startle the world with a speech declaring Egypt independent and himself King.

At the last moment this was prevented by the intervention of a foreign power.[1]

From that moment everything went wrong: a year after the great day, Napoleon was deposed and the Empress exiled; ten years later Ismail's turn came. While the Canal developed in world importance, while the number of vessels using it grew within fifty years from 500 to 6000, the number of people from 29,000 to 250,000, while the profits multiplied a hundredfold, the bankruptcy of the spendthrift Khedive approached with such rapid strides that he was forced to sell his Suez shares for $20,000,-000. This time it was the French who made a blunder, for they refused to buy, and even Disraeli had to take it on his own responsibility when, with a single collaborator sharing his secret, he acquired the priceless shares through Rothschild. The whole defeat of France in East Africa dates from this blunder in 1875.

Ismail was lost. His main plan, which was to involve England and France so deeply in Egypt that they would have to protect it, and to keep the Sultan quiet with shiploads of gold, was feasible only as long as he had money. Even when he received the beautiful Empress on the sumptuous ship, the guests were actually the hosts, for Ismail had taken up a new loan in Paris to pay for it. Then came the fall in cotton prices and two low Nile floods with bad harvests. Tradesmen had got into too bad habits in the course of ten years to be corrected now, for if one model gun was ordered, they would send a dozen, and in the general confusion not only did a Parisian dressmaker appear at the Khedive's palace to claim his 150,000 francs for the dresses of a single princess, but the barbers, camel-drivers, and donkey boys came for the piastres the court still owed them.

When the powers at last intervened, and sent a commission to Cairo to take possession of the state revenues, Ismail received his creditors in a silk tent at the foot of the pyramids and gave a brilliant public reception for the gentlemen whose business it was to confront him with his budget, so that thousands of fellahin in the neighbouring country might realize how well he stood with the European powers.

---

[1] Personal information given to the author by King Fuad I, according to which the relative documents are in Italian archives.

This Commission of the Debt—on which, in Gilbertian fashion, an Englishman checked the assets, a Frenchman the liabilities—laid hands on the nearest things they could find in order to have something to show to the creditors raging on the stock exchanges of Europe, and that was the fellah. It was the fellah who had to pay up. Even in the previous years, as Chirol reported:

The fellahin were dragged from their own fields in order to work on the huge estates the Khedive had stolen from them. Under the perpetual threat of the curbash they had to perform the *corvée* to keep the canals open for the use of others. Crowds of women and children would be begging for an ear of maize while Ismail was holding his courts, and his exploiters, Egyptian and European alike, were battening on his hospitality.

Since everything had to be scraped together to satisfy the bondholders in London, Paris, and Berlin, who had thought to get rich by looking on, no Egyptian official was paid at the proper time, and the only men whose profits swelled were the lawyers of the international courts. But the fellah went turbanless, clad only in his blue shirt, and any other clothes he had he hid, while many an old sheikh had to abandon his immemorial dignity and go without a cloak.

Once, when the Commission of the Debt discovered that, of their $25,000,000 interest due, $7,500,000 was missing, and that the government had simply not paid it over, two pashas were sent into the country with half a dozen usurers to force the fellahin to sell their harvest in advance for half its price, which was paid a month later on the pretext that it was not yet ripe. At the same time half their possessions, down to the gold coins on their women's veils, was seized as a tax. In this way the government was able to hand over its $7,500,000 a few hours before the time limit. But when an English consul ventured to plead the cause of the fellah in his reports, the famished creditors pushed him out of office.

What, after all, did the fellah know about the Parisian banks and the Congress of Berlin? And yet it was Bismarck who, in the course of the Congress, brought about a decision, for two years before he had practically advised the English to occupy Egypt, hoping that their administration would avert the danger of a war in the Near East. But when, on his instigation, the western powers demanded the deposition of the Khedive, the powerless suzerain, the Sultan, awoke at the last moment, and declared that the deposition of a Turkish vassal was his business. After looking on for fifteen years while his representatives on the Nile were governing on their own account, he suddenly pulled himself together, and since the west was threatening to forestall him in this dictatorial gesture, sent off a telegram addressed "To the Ex-Khedive of Egypt, Cairo."

Ismail carried it off brilliantly. An eye-witness relates that he started, then quietly opened the telegram, and read: "You will obey His Omnipotent Majesty the Sultan by transferring the Khediviate into the hands of Mohammed Tewfik, Khedive of Egypt." Then he carefully folded the paper, saying: "Send at once for His Highness Tewfik Pasha." When his son appeared, Ismail went the whole length of the hall to meet him, put his son's hands to his lips, and said: "Welcome to my lord." Then he kissed him on both cheeks, blessed him, wished him success, and without further discussion, quitted the astonished, rather diffident prince who had become a king overnight. He himself at once proceeded to his harem. The next day he drove to his son's house and was the first to enter his name on the visitors' list of the new ruler. Then he packed, took a few of his wives and friends and a trifle of three million francs, and ordered a ship for Italy.

His last night Ismail spent alone with his son.

23

_____

AT this deepest point of his bond-age, the Egyptian fellah awoke. Though he did not revolt him-self, like his fathers forty-five centuries before, for the first time he yielded to the agitation of his leaders. Egyptian nationalism, which Mehemet Ali, a foreigner, had developed from above, now arose for the first time from below. The silken tent under which the fellah had seen his king banqueting with his creditors was torn to ribbons in the gale of the catastrophe; when a few men moved from village to village, passionately declaiming against the foreigners, the fellah realized that the struggle must be taken up against the pashas too, who were growing rich through the foreigners. This was another case in which political revolution drew its strength from social resentment. A circle of malcontents in Cairo was already speaking of a republic on the Swiss pattern, which would be joined by Syria and the Hejaz. "I hope," said one of them, "that I shall not die before the Egyptian Republic is proclaimed. May we all live to see the saturnia regna."

The chief promoters of the movement were ulema from El Azhar, who revolted against the old tyranny of the Koran, and officers who revolted against the preferential treatment of Turks in the army: however different their mentality, they were all genuine Egyptians, full of hatred for the foreigners, and sons of the middle classes, who, having been raised to social equality by the will of Mehemet Ali, had again been suppressed under his successors. For the first time, even the Egyptian fellah had re-ceived a commission in the army. But the Mamelukes were not entirely conquered; two of them had even murdered Ali's suc-cessor, while the Viceroys, playing cat and mouse with the Sultan, often had Turks in their entourage. Among the rebellious officers who demanded "Egypt for the Egyptians," and nothing else, one stands out.

Arabi, born a fellah in a Delta village when Mehemet Ali was still alive, had been educated, as a son of the village sheikh, at one of his first schools. Later, at El Azhar, he had learned not only the Koran, but the new politics too, had entered the army and become an officer, and had been Viceroy Said's aide-de-camp on a pilgrimage. At that time he is said to have picked up an Arabic life of Napoleon, which the Pasha had flung out of his tent in a rage, and been fired by it. Every life of Napoleon has had dangerous consequences.

Arabi had reached the rank of captain when his patron died. But when Ismail, his successor, began to govern with the help of money and foreigners against the interests of the fellah and the Egyptians, Arabi, then in his middle twenties, joined the group of extremists who were even then proposing to depose Ismail. Once, when he had been delivering wild speeches under the windows of the palace, he was court-martialled, reduced to the ranks, and probably flogged; the same thing happened a second time in the Abyssinian war. Insulted as an officer, an Egyptian, and a fellah, he was now ripe to become a popular leader; all he needed was to be able to speak.

Tall and heavily built, slow-moving, more like a peasant than a soldier, chary of speech, with the eyes of a dreamer, he was a success neither as a politician nor as an officer. Arabi first began to produce an effect when he spoke in public. For when the fellahin heard one of themselves talking to them about their troubles in their own language, they felt as if a dream had come true, and as currents of enthusiasm radiated from this heavy, honest man, as he could quote the Koran and was as earnest a Moslem as he was an Egyptian, he gradually won the people. At all points, he seems in his simplicity to have been the opposite of that other leader who was at that time proclaiming himself the Expected Mahdi in the Sudan, whom we saw in all his humbug, in all his malice and hollowness, on the Upper Nile.

But Arabi saw daily with his own eyes what he had to point out to the mob to shake it out of its apathy. Ismail's extravagance and the fellah's distress, the privileges of the Turks, the fact that the Khedive was a foreigner and a Turk, words of loyalty to the Caliph, oaths on the Koran and the sword, and his regular signature "Arabi the Egyptian"—no more was needed to make him dangerous and popular. Soon he was called "El Wahid," the Only One; his house was full of suppliants and advisers; and while he never ceased to speak against those in power, demanding at the same time a great national army, all the people heard was that he was determined to expel the foreign, Greek usurer, and acclaimed him with enthusiasm. "We soldiers," cried Arabi on one occasion, "remember Caliph Omar who, in old age, asked his people whether he had governed them well. 'O Protector of the Faithful,' they replied, 'O son of Al-Khattab, thou didst take the right way, and we love thee. But thou knowest we were ever ready to slay thee with our swords if thou hadst taken to evil courses.'"

Given the hatred of the foreigners which the new Khedive, Tewfik, inherited from his deposed father along with his debts, his only possible course was to try to circumvent the dangerous tribune of the people. He therefore raised him to the rank of colonel. But even that did not help, and when Arabi refused to command his men to dig canals on the private estates of the Khedive, he was arrested and released by his men, and now Egypt had an Egyptian leader against Turkish tyranny, a national hero.

But he was only half a hero, and even if the Khedive was no hero at all, at least he was in a position to fall back on the Sultan and the great powers, who suspected nothing in the affair but a military revolt. On that September afternoon in 1881, when Arabi marched with 2500 men to the Palace to await the Khedive who was on his way home, when everything depended on the personal courage of the two men, a scene took place in which the Khedive, according to the account of his English aide-de-camp, was ridiculous, Arabi, according to his own, loyal instead of radical.

The Khedive, who was twelve years his opponent's junior, and not military-minded, asked the Englishman in a whisper what he ought to do. The Englishman whispered back that he should command the colonel to sit down and sheathe his sword. It was done, but the Khedive did not dare to follow the Englishman's next whispered suggestion and demand his sword, for he saw fifty threatening officers between himself and the gate. When Arabi stated his political demands, the Khedive, supported by the Englishman, declared: "I am master in this country, I shall do what I like."

"We are no longer slaves," retorted Arabi. "From now on we shall refuse to be treated as chattels." Exit Khedive, into the castle. The troops withdraw.

Such scenes, which have taken place on a much bigger scale in front of the palaces of other capitals, are unique in the six millenniums of Egyptian history. It was almost a royal defeat, like March 1848 in Berlin. But the revolutionaries in Cairo achieved more than those in Berlin, for on the same day the Khedive granted to the leader personally nearly everything his party demanded: the dismissal of his ministers, the reinforcement of the army, the appointment of a kind of senate, even the promise of a constitution. Arabi was made Minister of War, and the only thing his Khedive prohibited was a public procession through the streets with a band in the evening.

Neither, of course, trusted the other, the Khedive gave assurances in turn, to Arabi that he would support the rising, to the creditor states that he would suppress it, while the Sultan was playing the same double game with Arabi and the Khedive.

But meanwhile, over these Egyptians and Turks, the great gods were fighting in the drifting clouds, as once they fought at Troy, in the shape of the French and English governments, while still higher, like Fate, eternal Moira herself, throned the committee of creditors, hurling thunderbolts on gods and men alike, to rescue the spendthrift Ismail's loans—or at least 50 percent of them—from the rising will of the people. France, with the premonition of her Egyptian defeat, occupied the Turkish province of Tunis, at the same time joining her rival England in the promise of protection to the Khedive against all revolutionary movements. Their object was to irritate the leaders of the revolt; they demanded Arabi's dismissal, but this merely inflamed popular indignation against the foreigners, and plunged thousands into the dread of pogroms against the Christians, until the Sultan sent over a ship which landed, not guns, but a little chest; it contained

250 decorations, the highest being for Arabi, the revolutionary who had always stood by the Caliph. That was the way the old Seraglio imagined that revolutionaries could be appeased. The only men to make a firm stand were the shocked creditors, who became, so to speak, the religious movers of the opposition. They forced both their governments to dispatch a squadron to Alexandria. For the first time since 1807 foreign men-of-war appeared in June at the mouth of the Nile, and since the French quickly took their departure, the Union Jack flew alone.

Thus Arabi was forced into actions which a far stronger man could hardly have carried out. As the Khedive in his weakness went over with all speed to the foreigners and dismissed Arabi as a traitor while Arabi did exactly the same to the Khedive, any possibility of impartial judgment ceases. To the question, "What is high treason?" Schiller has given the only reply in his fine saying: "If it succeeds, it is forgiven."

As always happens when men would like to fire off a few guns to clear their heads, a spark was enough to produce a blaze: in a street in Alexandria, a Maltese came to blows with a donkey boy about his pay. An hour later the long repressed irritation of the town had broken out. Two hundred were killed, the English consul was wounded, and thousands lost all they had. The whole thing happened not in spite of the English warships, but on account of them, for their threatening presence could not but exasperate Egyptians of all classes. Arabi, strangely temperate at this time, warned the English that their first shot would free the Egyptian people from its debts. For that matter he hastily manned his forts, for he was uncertain whether the English warships would not be joined by others from the Sultan. Then he spent an evening with his friends, competing with them in verses and epigrams, for they were all hopeful, even though they had no fixed plan of campaign. Such foreigners as could fled in terror. Even the Turks packed up; 14,000 Christians are said to have left before the bombardment, and 30,000 to have fled to other parts of Egypt.

At the critical moment Arabi seems to have lacked determination. We may ask whether it was his guns or his feelings that failed him. Did he, as the English declared, set fire to the city himself remembering the fire of Moscow, or was the fire a symptom of the rising rage of the people? It is certain that the English bombarded Alexandria and entered a city in chaos. It is just as certain that for weeks the Egyptians resisted this foreign invasion with unprecedented passion and showed more strength and more popular feeling than in any foreign invasion in the whole long course of Egyptian history.

As regards the battle of the gods in the clouds, the English landed troops to "protect" the Suez Canal, while the French withdrew, and having lost their Suez shares, abandoned for the second time the vital isthmus. In these days, more was decided than the three powers probably realized.

Arabi fought, but he did not lead. It was the first battle of his life; he was no general, and on the warning of Lesseps and others, who could not but care more for their canal than for Egyptian freedom, he abstained from a blockade of the Canal when everything depended on holding up the English fleet. All the same, the Egyptian fellah army stopped the advance of the modern English army for two months. But when it was betrayed by bribed officers, it fled towards Cairo, and with it Arabi, who was, in the end, taken prisoner, condemned to death, reprieved, and deported to Ceylon.

Arabi was then forty-two. When he returned home at the age of sixty, to live in Cairo till he was over seventy (1911), poor as he had always been, a neglected, forgotten fellah, he saw the very England, whose landing he had resisted, ruling his country in all its power, and far more powerful than the Sultan had been before them. In this affair, the English had had a bad start. "A bad beginning on good ground is better than a good beginning on bad ground," as an English officer said later. They had no right to treat Arabi as a rebel, which he was not, for the Khedive had put him in charge of the army, or else they should have declared their protectorate at once, as they did in other countries. The middle way taken by Gladstone in his anti-imperialism could not but make the Egyptians suspect that what the English cared about was the Suez Canal and the Lancashire cotton spinneries, which required cotton grown under British supervision.

What must the aged Arabi have thought in his poor, lonely

room in old Cairo when he heard the clank of the English troops in the city, and saw the progress they had achieved a generation after establishing the peace and order they declared they had come to establish? Was it for the weal or woe of his country that he, Arabi the Egyptian, had furnished them with a pretext for landing? Was he, after all, rather a visionary than a soldier? Should he, in the days of Alexandria, have taken a firmer tone, have spoken as the master of Egypt, which he then was? And should he not have prevented the second landing of the English by closing the Canal? What he later told an English official was as sincere as his defence in prison, but it all sounds too visionary and too honest for him to be the man to cope with the tricks of the European banks. If Arabi was the first fellah to rule in Egypt, perhaps he was not fellah enough, and the many hours he spent in prayer in the field did the alumnus of El Azhar more honour than the soldier.

No one spoke more finely of him than General Gordon, the incorruptible Scot, who, even while the English troops were fighting, and before Cairo was taken, wrote: "As for Arabi, whatever may become of him individually, he will live for centuries in the people: they will never again be 'Your obedient servant.' "

24

THE English were established on the Nile, more like the Romans than the Greeks, who had both preceded them there. But though they had come more heavily armed than either, and had advanced through the Delta step by step as conquerors, shooting and killing, they did not, like their predecessors, claim to rule the Nile valley henceforth, did not hoist the British flag, but declared, and have continued to declare to this very day, that they had only come to establish order on the Nile and withdraw. They had lent their millions, not to the Egyptian people, but to a spendthrift Khedive of their own free will, and had done so simply in the desire to get a higher rate of interest for it than in the west; if they now came to save their money, since the awakening Egyptians were no longer disposed to pay for the frivolity of a foreign ruler, they could write neither Christ nor freedom on the banners of their campaign.

Alexander and Cæsar had advanced to these coasts, without a pretext, without an excuse, proclaiming their desire to treat the people well if they would hand over their grain and refrain from molesting the foreigners on the routes to Asia. Two thousand years later, Mr. Gladstone, who had studied the Romans and even translated the Greeks, in the same Delta wanted, like them, nothing but cotton and the road to Asia, but he lived too late and too early to make his demands in the tone which was called naïve before and dynamic after his time.

Mehemet Ali had foreseen it all. "Big fish eat little fish," he said. "One day, England will take over Egypt from the bankrupt Turkish Empire." Even the English politicians knew the truth, but at first they kept it to themselves, especially Lord Palmerston who, in 1859, wrote to his Ambassador in Paris that England wanted Egypt merely as a man who has an estate in the north of

England wants a good road with comfortable hotels to take him to his house in London.

Later, the wisest of the Englishmen who worked in or on Egypt, regretted this double dealing. Lord Zetland, Lord Cromer's biographer, wrote: "It may indeed be said without hesitation that in 1882, Mr. Gladstone's Government were looking in any direction except that in which they were moving. They were caught up in the tide and swept along in the direction of a military occupation, but they went protesting, and when they found themselves in possession of the country, they did so to their own dismayed astonishment and utterly against their will."

Such criticism by no means stands alone, and when, in the course of fifty years, we find many eminent English experts on the Egyptian situation taking the same tone, we begin to realize that a decision of such importance in the history of the world is not only the result of very serious consideration, but is actually dictated by a trait in the English character. We might define it by saying that the famous farsightedness of English politics, like that of the Vatican—for both are alleged to think in centuries— looked at more closely resolves itself into an unerring instinct which, at a given moment, does the right thing without foreseeing its remoter consequences. This reminds us of one of Goethe's observations. When he explained to Schiller, in that first, decisive conversation, his idea of the primeval plant as a concretion of experience, and Schiller objected that that was not experience, but an idea, Goethe replied: "All the better for me if I have ideas without knowing it and without wanting to."

If the English, in spite of all, continue to declare that they wished only to remain in Egypt as long as it was to Egypt's advantage, and forty-nine such official declarations have been counted in the first twenty years of the occupation, they are as sincere as a husband who will not let his beautiful wife out of his sight on the pretext that without him she would go to the bad. The truth is that this strange, island-like country, whose constitution remained a matter of such uncertainty throughout all the centuries of Turkish rule, has always attracted the strongest power on the Mediterranean, and that its importance has steadily increased, while its situation in the struggle for liberty has steadily deteriorated owing to the Suez Canal. The instinctive feeling that, as Napoleon had already declared, no power could remain in possession of India without holding Egypt, led England to lay her hands on the country, and in spite of endless difficulties, she had no reason to regret it. Where would the British Empire be today if England abandoned the Nile valley, or even if that great piece of English luck, the Great War, had never happened, to bring about within a few days the secession from Turkey which Mehemet Ali had never dared, Ismail never achieved, and which no great power had ever been able to bring about because the other great powers had always intervened?

The situation here arising between the conquerors and the conquered, which arises in every colonial enterprise, may be no tragedy but it is a drama. Whoever takes it upon himself to awaken a sleeping mass of coloured men must, in the end, be thrust aside by those who have awakened in dead earnest. Galatea comes to life, and flees from her master. In Egypt, where the mass is represented not by naked Negroes, but by the descendants of the oldest of civilized peoples, the struggle is rendered more interesting by the mutual respect of both parties, and, as in every good play, remains morally undecided. Among the protagonists, the most intelligent know what thanks are due to England, what consideration is due to Egypt, and yet, as education advances, the irritability of those who profit by it increases.

This marriage was fruitful, but it was never a good one, for the English do not love the Egyptians. With their habit of command, they are extremely patient with savages, as they are with their domestic animals: the savage is aware of it and is grateful to his master; and just as there are misanthropes who love their dogs the more, the better they know men, autocrats always get on better with their servants than with their collaborators unless they can force their collaborators into the position of servants. But in Cairo, it would often happen that the English would encounter some highly cultured Egyptian who was not at all impressed by these lords with their topees and ducks, and who, though he had to suffer their technical superiority, only fostered gloomier feelings towards them on that account.

At the same time, the Egyptian realizes perfectly clearly that the English are much more rarely true Christians than he and his like are true Mohammedans. The religious contrast which is of no great importance in the Sudan develops into a spiritual rivalry in the city of El Azhar. This city is so old, its culture so venerable, its records so long, that its present heirs may well regard this invading people from a northern island, with its foreign customs and faith, with the philosophically critical eye with which the latest star in vogue is observed by some venerable sage.

Only the most delicate tact could do equal justice to the superior wisdom of such sages and their sons' and grandsons' thirst for liberty, and only personality feel its way to a harmony by creating a condition which has no name, no legal title, and no umpire. It was England's good fortune to find such a man.

25

AT the beginning of the century, when Arabi, the old, forgotten, national hero, now a poverty-stricken half-fellah, would sometimes venture into the smart streets of the new Cairo, he might see a man of his own age, in a brilliant carriage, proclaimed by outrunners covered with gold and sweat, a man whom all knew and feared. He had never come into personal contact with this man, although both lived in Cairo for six years at the same time. It was the great enemy who had supplanted him, the man who had held in his hands for the twenty years since Arabi's collapse the power Arabi had once held for a few months, the man who incorporated that foreign power which Arabi had in vain struggled to keep away at the risk of his life, and which now ruled his country. It was the representative of Great Britain, Lord Cromer.

He was in everything the reverse of the fellah's son—once the restless dreamer, the flaming orator, who now stood embittered on the curbstone. The man in the carriage came of rich, middle-class business people, his family was descended from a Frisian family which had been English for two centuries. Broad, heavy, and reliable, he seemed to have developed by foresight, judgment, and deliberation that concentrated power which could be seen at a glance in his physical massiveness and his keen, inquiring eyes. Under fair hair tinged with grey, a fresh-complexioned, blue-eyed face looked out of the brilliant equipage, which the man on the curbstone watched with sad, dark eyes. The only thing these two neighbours in Egypt, who did not know each other, had in common was their military beginning, for Cromer had taken his commission at the same age as Arabi, had done a tedious period of service in Corfu, and seemed at that time to have less of a future before him than the protégé of the Khedive.

He had, however, a world-empire and his tradition behind

him, and while he was attracting attention in Parliament and foreign affairs, and, as the private secretary of the Viceroy of India, to whom he was related, making his mark there by his gifts, the destiny of the oriental revolutionary was running into confusion. After a short period of service on the Commission of the Debt, rotating in true imperial fashion between the War Office and Parliament, Jamaica and America, he had been summoned to Cairo immediately after the occupation of Egypt to solve a very delicate problem—namely to civilize a foreign country without governing it, to the advantage of both countries. For twenty-four years, he steadily developed this task: after the first few years he was in actual fact the secret Pharaoh of Egypt.

Three qualities seem to have raised him above the merely shrewd business man, and guided him to a success which, at that time, Curzon and Rhodes were the only Englishmen to attain: a sense of reality, sincerity, and an entire absence of vanity. He was fifty-three when he declined the office of Viceroy of India, the most brilliant the Empire has to offer, because his work on the Nile seemed to him more fruitful, and he found questions of irrigation "much more interesting than a novel."

A decided sense of the symbolic nature of his task, without which no man of action can become great, lent him strength in all hazards, and, having settled a hundred queries with a thousand figures, he wrote a long poem describing the happiness he found in this constructive work.

> Is it no profit when the slave
>   Who groaned beneath the tyrant's ban,
> Crushed from the cradle to the grave,
>   Has learnt the dignity of man?
> Is it no profit, no avail,
>   To stay the Pasha's ruthless hand,
> To hush the widow's piteous wail,
>   The children's curse throughout the land?

Devotion and endurance, the determination of a forthright, cool mind to perform the chosen task, are again shown in Lord Cromer by the fact that he won at thirty-five the woman he had fallen in love with at twenty-one. When, twenty years later, fate took from him what he had wrested from it, he left her deathbed, went to his office, and at once dispatched a long telegram to London on the subject of lighthouses in the Red Sea.

All he had to do, all he had to supervise, this greatest transformation that Egypt had known for a thousand years, had to be carried out under the jealous eyes of France, in perpetual friction with the creditors and banks of the European capitals. For what Lord Cromer had at heart was not the bondholder in Paris but the fellah in the Delta. England and England alone was to extend her power in Egypt, but she was to do so in harmony with the Egyptian and not at his expense. And yet at the same time he had to contend with perpetual changes of governments at home: he saw six or seven of them, each with a new policy.

What was he, then, in the great British hierarchy? A consul general, nothing more; but he should have been called First Consul. The officials in Cairo called him "El Lord." In his ill-defined position, which could be limited only by moral principles, he was forced to take the field at the end of the century in the Sudan campaign, and, as consul, to assume the responsibility for 25,000 fighting men. His prestige in England had risen to such a point that Lord Salisbury, having received a telegram from him when he himself was on leave and therefore not able to decode it, sent back an open telegram saying: "Do what you like."

In Cairo itself, surrounded by the rancour of the conquered, he had won the respect of the politicians by refusing any kind of personal profit where it was taken for granted that everybody was venal. In the country, his legend steadily grew among the fellahin. During the cholera, when an English officer was trying to force a fellah woman to remove the cesspool from the neighbourhood of her house, she screamed at him in her rage: "I shall go to Cairo, to the man Krumer; he will protect me against you."

And yet his work was by no means entirely beneficent. Much was left undone, many problems were solved in the interests of the Europeans and against those of the fellah whom he wished to protect. The problematic side of his mission arose from the profound contradiction which no colonial enterprise can quite overcome. What is done for the good of the community cannot be completely severed from the advantage of the colonizing power, even though its mission is in the hands of a man moved by pure love of mankind. What Cromer aimed at was a regeneration of the Egyptian people, and in 1883 he was already advising the evacuation; but in 1886, he advised against it, and yet nothing of moment had happened in these three years. As a Liberal, which he was all his life, he felt this conflict deeply, for he wrote in a private letter as early as 1884:

Surely it is a cruel fate that drives me with all my strong opinions against an extension of territory and the assumption of fresh responsibilities and with strong anti-Jingo convictions which deepen every year I live, to be constantly making proposals which, at all events at first sight, have a strong Jingo flavour. . . . In this uncongenial political atmosphere, I am always having to act and to speak in exactly the opposite way to what I should wish.

If we add this inward conflict to the outer one, we begin to realize that the man whose task it was to clear such a jungle, and yet take care that no snake should bite him in the heel, had need of a mighty ax. For what Lord Cromer found was at first stronger than what he brought with him.

He found Egyptian, Turkish, and European powers, hostile to him and to each other. There were Turkish ministers who, in the early days after the bombardment, had clung to the English hand to swing themselves up again and now hated them for it; there were rich pashas who, like Russian princes, turned the sweat of the peasants into dresses for their Parisian mistresses; ulema who lived by embezzling the funds of religious institutions; everyone, including the Khedive, could not but fear that the strangers would dock their revenues, and since, at the outset, they put no faith whatsoever in their social motives, but merely saw money vanishing from Egyptian into English pockets, the flame of their rancour was fed when they saw the fellah protected at their own expense.

In the towns, Lord Cromer found men who were neither educated nor uneducated, and in the country illiterates who were nevertheless not savages. He had not only to understand them, but to conceal the fact that he did. "Command what is to happen," said the cleverest, "but do not inquire how we carry it out." In actual fact the Egyptians, like hotel-keepers, had no object but to make a profit on their guests: it was gradually borne in upon them that they were themselves becoming guests in their own country, and were having to pay for all the protection and comfort the foreigners were offering them

At the same time, Cromer's omnipotence was more obvious in small things than in big, for as he brought only a few dozen officials with him, and nobody was disposed, in this government without tradition, to take any decision upon himself, everything was pushed onto the shoulders of the new Pharaoh. He had to decide on the form of a procession of the Abyssinian Church, the dismissal of an English coachman in the Khedive's service, the exhumation of an Egyptian saint, and the domestic troubles of a lady of the court, who had to be told that she could not box her husband's ears with her slipper; at the same time he had to point out to an English Egyptologist that the possession of a royal cartouche was hardly worth a war with France, and to a botanist that the conquest of a certain kind of clover on the Ghazal was hardly worth a fresh expedition to Nubia. But, as an Englishman, he could not carry out the great reforms—the Nile, the schools, the army—as quickly as he wished in his philanthropy, for he could not put an end too quickly to the confusion which justified the occupation.

He thought a great deal about the fellah.

The pasha who had oppressed the fellah from time immemorial had at first merely changed his form. When the fellah had set out on the war of liberation under his brother Arabi, it seemed as if the Syrian and Greek usurers had vanished; now they came back, for even the Englishman could not free the fellah from his debts. But why, the agitators asked them, must you bear the costs of the ruined streets of Alexandria, which the English shot to pieces to deprive us of our freedom?

Three great innovations, however, were made to relieve the fellah. The curbash had gone, and the dread of surprise by the tax-collectors had vanished too. Before, the fellah could never know when and how much he had to pay; now he could be sure of being told exactly. Whereas, before, he had to continue to pay taxes for a field that had long been washed away, now he was free of taxes if he could prove that even a corner of his field had not been watered. If the labourers on the neighbouring land of the pasha held up or diverted the water, the village could complain to the Englishman and the rich man was prevented from laying violent hands on the poor man's water. And while, in their youth, they had been whipped to the *corvée* on the canals, and, with their mud-laden hands, were kept there throughout the glowing day, to sleep at night on a sack, they were now paid, and only had to come in time of water-famine. Cromer practically abolished this army of slaves.

It may be that El Lord never knew how his orders were infringed far away in Upper Egypt, and how the mudir, here and there, re-established his ancient power, but for his part, the fellah never knew what the apparently omnipotent Lord had to contend with in Cairo in order to give the fellah in the Delta room to breathe. When he proposed using dredges instead of the *corvée*, the Debt Commission refused the $2,500,000 necessary; and when the affair was noised abroad, the powers agreed to the abolition of this kind of slavery only on condition that foreigners in Egypt should again live tax-free.

There was something else the fellah did not know—that round a big green table in the capital a dozen foreign gentlemen were sitting who could veto the new barrages, could even veto every single canal, for, as old creditors, they had in their hands the finances which, Milner declared, not ten other men in Cairo understood. The shadow of the profligate Khedive, the image of the silk tent under the pyramids, lay across the new century, and secured to the foreigners the continued right to recoup themselves for their losses. If the Sultan still had to receive nearly $5,000,000 yearly tribute because his forefathers had conquered Egypt four hundred years before and done nothing for it since, the English found no other solution than to deprive the fellah of his beloved pipe, for the tribute had to be squeezed out of the tobacco tax. Even in 1910, the fields and homes of the fellahin were seized for debts of less than $250.

Thus it was again a great event in the fellah's life when Lord Kitchener, who, on Lord Cromer's advice, took his place in 1911, secured to him by law as inalienable property, five feddan, his house, implements, and two draft animals: a similar measure had long since been introduced in France, and even in the Punjab.

As they are by nature grateful, the fellahin did not forget their benefactor, and years later, when Kitchener's name was mentioned, they would rise from their squatting position and lay their hands on their foreheads.

It must be said in justice that not everything could be accomplished. Everything that Cromer did, he had to do within the old framework. Above all, he had to start the new irrigation while the old was still working, he had to renew every canal before he closed an old one, and, so to speak, operate on the still beating heart. Even tradition was against him. Thus the fellah saw how the rich could buy exemption from military service by paying $200 before the drawing of lots, and $500 after it, while he had often to destroy an eye with silver nitrate to get free. But he saw too the courage and devotion of the English officers during the cholera. What the English doctors and sanitary experts have achieved in Egypt since that epidemic is one of the great deeds of humanity. It is enough to outweigh two omissions which might otherwise condemn them.

The first is the privileged position of Europeans in Egypt, which must be more difficult for a people's pride to bear than the presence of foreign troops. If the police have no power over a foreign thief, brothel-keeper, or opium-dealer simply because he is not an Egyptian, the hatred of the foreigner cannot but grow. The other concerns the schools.

Why, we must ask, did so powerful a man as Lord Cromer not threaten to resign when the Commission of the Debt refused the credits for new schools? He was no fool, like the dictators of today, to whom weapons are more vital than books because they understand the weapons and not the books. This crucial question, which lies at the root of the present Anglophobia of the Egyptians, who feel, quite justifiably, that they have been cheated of forty years of education, can be explained only by England's secret wish to make the Egyptian people healthy, to rule them more justly, but to keep them stupid. The alleged resistance of the Egyptians themselves stands revealed as their burning wish to have their children educated, thousands of whom were turned away because there were not enough teachers and schools. If Cromer is quoted as advocating a primary instead of a literary education, if the English point to the opposition from El Azhar, their own documents prove the contrary, nor was the lack of money decisive.

Here are figures: While Mehemet Ali and even Ismail educated and fed the scholars free, so that in 1879 only 5 percent were paying for their schooling, in 1898, under the English, the figure had risen to 86 percent. In 1897, 91 percent of Egyptian men and 99 percent of the women could neither read nor write. While under Ismail, 2 percent of all Egyptians were going to school, the number had sunk, in 1908, under the English, to 1.5 percent instead of rising to 20 percent. As the illiterate population of Egypt has not decreased in the course of the epoch, which, after all, was the epoch of schools all over the world, it must have enormously increased. But they do not learn even what they ought to learn. If, of 150,000 pupils in 1906, according to an English account, 90,000 could not write, 90,000 knew no arithmetic, and 70,000 could not read, the white power in charge of their education must be responsible.

The English, who, in the first twenty years of the occupation, paid 1 percent instead of 20 percent of their total expenses on education, and had their omnipotent advisers in every department, handed over the Education Department alone to Armenians and other foreigners. In this department, the care for the young must have been obscured by party politics, for in twenty-nine years there were twenty-nine changes of minister, and only the last, whom Cromer appointed himself, was a man—Zaghlul.

And yet all that Cromer did in Egypt, without recourse to war, burdened with debt, and faced with the antagonism of powerful natives, was admirable. For he gave the fellah, for the first time, the confident feeling that he was as good as the pasha in the sight not only of God but of the law. The danger that this self-confidence would turn against the protecting power lies in the very nature of this and similar enterprises. Thus even Cromer's last year in office was shadowed by an incident in which one member of a party of British officers shot a fellah's pigeons and lost his life for it, but the lives of six fellahin were exacted in retribution. With this highly imperialistic verdict, the career of the liberal friend of the people came to an end.

26

TWO struggles have determined the fate of Egypt since it has been in English hands—the struggle for the gold at the mouth of the Nile and the struggle for freedom: they may not be as old as the Nile, but they are as old as mankind. The Egyptians had never really fought for freedom. This is connected with the absence of revolution in their history, for the conquest of national freedom cannot be imposed on a nation from above, and therefore cannot be accomplished without grave disturbances to the class structure of society. Hence the Egyptian problem becomes complicated: the struggles for freedom and cotton, which means gold, do not run counter to each other, they are inextricably involved, and even though Egyptians of all classes would be glad to get rid of the English, and only a few gain by their presence, the Egyptian servants of the cotton-plant are more deeply bound up with its world-market than with the fate of the fellah.

A cotton-planter in the Delta, a dealer in Alexandria, the lawyer, the investor, the importer in Cairo—all these two million townsmen, who are involved, indirectly at any rate, in the cotton trade, have no thought, when they review their plans and prospects morning and evening, for the fellah's happiness and health, which are as indispensable to the cotton as the Nile. Even in their sleep, they are pursued by stock-exchange quotations, which decide their own fortunes according to the fluctuation of prices on the world-market. That Allah, in his mercy, should inflict the weevil on the cottonfields of the unbelievers in Mississippi, that a war in Central Asia should remove competition from that quarter, that the strike of weavers in Lancashire should be broken so that there is no danger of higher wages to reduce prices further, that the Nile should not rise too high and again threaten the old barrage—such are the dreams of a hundred thousand inhabitants of the great city on the Nile. For they may live on sugar and tobacco, rugs or building, but the price of Sakellarides cotton determines their income, and elements and crises which might force it down hover like apparitions of gloom in the clouds and can menace the life of a whole nation as profoundly as the loss of a battle on a distant coast.

Such is the strength of the Nile at its end, and just at its end; for the cotton crop depends on the vagaries of the Abyssinian rain and the work of the English engineers, without which the finest crisis in India would be of no use, but the men of the towns realize this as little as men who, continuously absorbed in their enterprises, notice the symptoms of the growing disease which may destroy them altogether. Only the fellah lives with the Nile; in the Nile he fears Hapis, the ancient god who can bless or destroy him. It is his hands, and the hands of his wife and children, which water and tend the little shrub, which pluck and clean, collect and deliver, and all his work is governed by the temper of the river and the spirit of those who have tamed it. But as for the world-market, he may, once in a lifetime, have heard of it as of some distant deity: if that deity is ill-humoured, he feels it, because his masters reduce his day's wages.

Thus the struggle for freedom, even in this country, takes on different forms among the rich and the poor. The fellah alone, whose life was not changed, whose fortune was not increased by the cotton, desires simply and solely the freedom of his country; he alone, the most dependent of all, is perfectly free to seek it. But meanwhile, those who represent him, and the spirit of the century, are fighting so that he shall not again fall victim to the pasha's curbash. The withdrawal of the English could deprive him of nothing; the Nile has provided for his apparently circumscribed life, even if a shift of the powers on the world-market should threaten the cotton prices on which the apparently great life of the rich depends. For since Mehemet Ali's first advance, which began, a hundred years ago, to transform the grainland of Egypt into a cotton-producing country, and hence to increase the national fortune, the fellah has remained in his poverty, and what English interests have given to, and taken from, his country has hardly changed his whitewashed house of Nile mud, his onion soup, and his blue jacket, which filled the daily life of his fathers under the Pharaohs.

The only thing he has gained is the alphabet, which the last Khedives and the first King imposed upon him with much more force than the English. With this dangerous key, he opened the gate of knowledge, and it is no mere chance, it is a symbol, that the first leaders of the nationalist movement, Arabi and Zaghlul were not pashas, but fellahin, born in Delta villages, educated in the new schools, which decipher for them the hieroglyphics of a foreign script, and hence the causes of their slavery.

In 1913, when the advance of this education had led to the convocation of a first representative parliament, it fell into confusion because it was not free to act, for under the pressure of foreign troops, it could be dissolved indefinitely, or compelled to illegitimate work. Hence, at every election, there have been overwhelming nationalist majorities, all demanding the evacuation of the English. The feeling against the foreigners in the country has been so strong for the last fifty years, and has so gathered strength in the last twenty, that no one dares to oppose it, even if he wishes to. Once, when the government proposed to extend the lease of the Suez Canal till the year 2008, the proposal was rejected by all votes but one, and a general riot of feeling accompanied the vote throughout the country. Even Kitchener, who had managed to win over the fellah by his law, alienated the crowd by behaving like an English resident at an Indian court, and they resented being treated with the paternal consideration which the English show to savage tribes.

The growing hostility which every protectorate must experience, has special reasons in this case: first, the bad start; secondly, the English character. The reiterated promise not to stay in the country could not but create, as the years went on, feelings similar to those of a business man disturbed by the visit of a lady who keeps her hat and coat on, repeatedly consults her watch, assuring him that she simply must go, but stays for hours and cannot be induced to go by her unhappy victim. Today not a single Egyptian really believes that England will ever give up the country voluntarily.

Nor can Cairo help comparing the exclusiveness of the English with the friendliness of the French, who will invite a colonial colleague to their homes, or even make him a minister in Paris. How can a subject foster friendly feelings when the foreign master displays his superiority by breaking off all association after office hours with the man he has worked with all day? The young Englishman in Cairo, who cannot be dismissed, does not pay taxes, and even stands outside of police jurisdiction, lives in the sight of the Egyptian, who is superior to him in experience and knowledge of the country, plays polo and tennis almost exclusively with his fellow-countrymen, and leaves the Egyptian aristocrat, whose home is a centre of Arab culture, standing at the gate of the Gezira Club, practically as he does his groom?

The objection that the harem system of the Egyptians is responsible for this state of affairs is nullified by the English custom of opening its clubs only to men; there are daughters of Egyptian grandees who are received at foreign courts in Europe, but not by the British High Commissioner in Cairo. Their fathers can race horses from their stables, but if their horse has won, they cannot give it a piece of sugar in the ring because they are not admitted. Much of the good that is done by the English in the administration of the country is undone in society, and yet the great men of Cairo would probably prefer things the other way round.

The great source of suspicion is the Nile. If it were an entirely Egyptian river, rising at Aswân! Everything connected with the Nile was planned by Ismail, but his plans were realized on the grand scale only under the English administration. With six dams, the English hammered their fame into the bed of the greatest and strangest river on earth; British energy and perseverance, measured according to the season, flow through several hundred sluices for all the world to see; and even though they were inspired by the technique with which our century tames other rivers, this great spectacle, its consequences, and hence the credit due are nowhere so great as on this single river which is the life of the country.

The Nile, however, flows from far distances, and there, on its steamers, the British flag waves beside the Egyptian: it is present, ghostly and invisible, even on its lower course. In the curious form of the condominion, both powers rule over both countries, *de jure* in the Sudan, *de facto* in Egypt, but in such a way that the weaker Egyptian, in both countries, feels overreached by the stronger Englishman. As fate has placed him on the lower course of the Nile, and has made the life of his fourteen millions absolutely dependent, at the risk of starvation, on a flood of the right height at the right time, he cannot but be profoundly disturbed when he sees his foreign protector ruling on the upper reaches, where the river is, so to speak, brewed like a drink. The foreigner up there cannot poison it, but what if he were to stop its flow by means of new dams?

The technical impossibility sketched in an earlier chapter does not dispose of the question of injury, for between the total stoppage of a river and its free flow there are as many shades as between the refusal and the yielding of a woman, who, like England, would like to enchant and dominate at the same time. Lord Milner, one of the highest of English officials, wrote, even before 1900:

It is an uncomfortable thought that the regular supply of water by the great river, which is to Egypt a question of life, must always be exposed to some risks, as long as the upper reaches of that river are not under Egyptian control. Who can say what might happen if some day a civilized power, or a power commanding civilized skill, were to undertake great engineering works on the Upper Nile, and to divert for the artificial irrigation of that region the water which is essential for the artificial irrigation of Egypt? Such a contingency may seem very remote, I admit that it is very improbable, but before it is laughed out of court, let us consider what would be the feelings of any ordinary country, our own, for instance, if there were even a remote possibility that the annual rainfall could be materially altered by the action of a foreign power.

This very balanced, official declaration, which is not unique among English writers on Egypt, reveals the danger, and the feelings, which must make the Egyptian outlook gloomy. In addition to the moral considerations put forward by the English, they instance the good quality of the cotton in the Delta—they would injure their own Lancashire mills if they were to reduce or retard the Nile in the Delta by dams above Khartoum. But what Lord Milner foresees as a possible political weapon in the hands of another power can also become effective under English rule as a threat in time of trouble. When the British Governor of the Sudan was assassinated in Cairo in 1924, the English demanded as indemnity an unlimited increase of the area to be irrigated in the Gezira between the Blue and White Niles instead of the territory limited by treaty as before, and even if they dropped so immoral a demand a few days later, it shows to what lengths an indignant opponent can go.

The man who, like Arabi before him, came into open conflict in our own times with the English as the leader of the Egyptians against foreign rule was only ten years younger than he; the difference between them was that Arabi's conflict began when he was forty, Zaghlul's when he was seventy. That is why the exile of two heroes of freedom of the same generation was separated by fifty years.

Zaghlul, a fellah from the Delta like Arabi, looked beside him like a Caucasian beside an Arab. Tall and angular, with his Mongolian cheek-bones, fair complexion, and genial, straightforward blue eyes, he was a living refutation of all the racial theories which seem to have become the parlour game of contemporary Europe. For in spite of the contrast between them, both were true Egyptians, the product of unknown mixtures in the racial melting-pot of Egypt: both drew the essence of their being from the soil and not from their descent. In his speeches, Zaghlul drew his most telling metaphors from the Nile.

Educated at El Azhar, rich by marriage, familiar by his origins with the distress of the fellah, by his career as a lawyer with the tricks of the pashas, Zaghlul appeared with and after Arabi as a moderate champion of freedom, but remained without influence till he was well on in the fifties. The man who first admitted him to office was Lord Cromer, who appointed him Minister of Education in 1905, in order to experiment for once with a moderate nationalist. He wrote once that Zaghlul had the qualities to serve his country: he was honest, competent, and courageous, and should go far. He went farther than Cromer would have liked if he had lived to see.

When, at the beginning of the war, Turkey joined the Central Powers, and the sympathies of the Khedive were directed to both, Egypt's dependence on foreign bread became obvious, since she did not produce enough to feed herself: to express it dramatically, we might call this situation the tragic consequence of the lust of gold which had exchanged grain for cotton.

For that part of the people which hated the English more than the Turks, and the actual rule of the Christians more than the legal rule of the Mohammedans, was faced with famine in case of a blockade; nor did anyone know what forms English irrigation at Aswân would take. England, who had protected Turkey, seventy years before, from the Egyptian secession under Mehemet Ali, now called on Egypt to secede from Turkey, appealing to the memory of that illustrious ruler, and forced her, after four centuries, into a struggle against her co-religionists, although the Sultan had proclaimed the Holy War.

Even here, England did not find the right form to express her power. In November 1914, three courses were open to her: to annex Egypt, to incorporate it into the British Empire as a dominion, or to declare it independent and demand its alliance. But she neither took over the Turkish position as the suzerain power, nor did she grant the autonomy which she had so long promised. On the contrary, she deposed one Khedive, appointed another with the title of Sultan, adjourned the Legislative Assembly indefinitely, and assured the people that they were not obliged to fight.

The threatening advance of the Turks to the Suez Canal forced the English, however, like the Mamelukes before them, to conscript the fellah in the form of a "Voluntary Labour Corps," and to commandeer his last camel, leaving him without a draft animal, even though they paid him, and then to hale him off to build a railway through the desert, the last great *corvée* in Egyptian history. Still graver was the fact that they later sent more than 100,000 free Egyptians to Syria, 8000 to Mesopotamia, 10,000 to France, and even made a collection for the Red Cross among these Moslems.

Nothing could do more harm to England's name than the omission of any recognition of Egyptian help after the victory.

When Zaghlul, in 1918, demanded autonomy as a reward, he was even refused permission to go to London. That was the signal for the storm to break. Look, cried the agitators, can you see now how you are being duped by the English? Why did you lay three miles of ties a day in the glowing desert to destroy your brothers in the faith in their struggle against the Christian dogs? Why did we not revolt, and help the Turks who came marching from Syria to drive the English out of the country? We helped to win the victory. Hussein and Feisal, our neighbours, are founding new empires on the plan of the American President, we alone have remained slaves. Soon they will turn off the water up there in Khartoum with their dams and thirst us out.

When Zaghlul too, embittered like the rest, had developed, contrary to the rule, from a moderate young politician into a radical old one, and began to use the same language, he was arrested out of hand by the English and deported, first to Malta, then to the Seychelles, like Arabi fifty years before. Wild riots, the murder of English officers, the destruction of dams, and the burning of houses proclaimed the fellah's indignation; the Wafd was created as the great national party; Moslems and Copts combined to fight England; and when the English officers were obliged to escort the mail on mules through the desert because the railway was torn up, they may have had their private thoughts about the Foreign Office in London.

Three years of false moves, of murders and their punishment, of the exile and martyrdom of the national leader, came to an end with the declaration of Egyptian independence, but the time for any real reconciliation was past and the independence was diminished by the retention of too many sovereign rights by the suzerain power.

Zaghlul, however, the popular hero who was now recalled, became still more radical in his old age, since he was, in particular, disappointed in MacDonald, and realized that England would not yield a step. When Lord Allenby, followed by a great military suite, presented his ultimatum to Premier Zaghlul after the murder of the Sirdar in Cairo, Zaghlul pointed out of the window and asked the English commander: "What is the meaning of all this? Does England want to declare war on Egypt?" To speak at such a moment in such a way to such a man is a sign of prouder fearlessness than most of contemporary history has to show.

When he died soon after, in 1926, Zaghlul was given a funeral such as no Egyptian had ever had before him—he was buried as a Pharaoh and a friend of the people. A fellah lay on the bier past which the nation defiled, a fellah born in a little, dark room of Nile mud, among fowls and pigeons, between the donkey and the camel, and doubtless furnished with the talismans of the wise-woman, which for once were worth the money. How high such a life towers above that of Cheops and his huge pyramid!

The King, too, who returned to Egypt from an official tour shortly after Zaghlul's death, gained in sympathy and popularity with his people, and deepened both in ten years of his reign by a host of new ideas. He parcelled out crown land and gave it to the fellah on payment down of a tenth of its value, letting him pay the rest in instalments; he built schools and hospitals and awakened European interest by great scientific enterprises.

But he could not haul down the British flag on the citadel. When an Egyptian passes by the railings of the English barracks near the great Gezira Bridge, he stops and watches the troops at their drill with the piercing bitterness of the conquered.

Now, finally, in the summer of 1936, an agreement has been reached. It does not fulfil all the aspirations of the Egyptians, for the English seem to require many years to build a few barracks elsewhere, and even the departure of the troops from Cairo does not mean that they will abandon the Canal. But here, as well as in the Sudan, Egypt has made some strides towards independence. Everything in the next few years will depend upon which of the two countries produces the better statesman; that man will also have to understand how to utilize the coming war in the solution of this problem.

27

ON the Gezira Bridge in Cairo, the Nile, in June, is hardly audible. This is the only big bridge in Cairo, and even this one is only a third as long as the bridge in Khartoum. For here, where the Nile flows through the last stretch of its course in majestic breadth and calm, it is split by the two islands just where all eyes are fixed upon it, and cannot display to its capital, the ancient city of Cairo, the full spectacle of its power. The eight bridges which connect its banks across the islands are short, and it is only because they have to be raised at times for the passage of steamers, stopping the traffic, that they reveal the greatness of the master commanding them from below.

In August, however, everyone crossing the bridge hears a great roar from below, for meanwhile the flood has come. In May, a strong swimmer can still swim against the current; in June, he would find it difficult; later, nobody attempts to swim up the Nile. The capital watches the rising flood with the feelings of a besieged city: how strong is the enemy, what forts will he storm tomorrow, when will relief come? For if everyone crossing the bridge in these critical August days wonders whether it is really the flood that has come, or only a wraith, an illusion, a fortnight later everyone is anxiously wondering whether the river is not going to rise too high. Not until the Nile has fallen steadily for several days in succession at the beginning of October does the general anxiety cease. Man's struggle with the Nile is like the struggle for a deeply loved woman; the man who masters the river is never sure of it, and never knows whether he will not himself be overcome in the end.

During the period of high flood, there is movement everywhere: sentries stand every fifty yards along the canals; at dangerous points detachments of up to a hundred men are posted to

579

watch the dams and report trouble; and late at night, when they
move about the Delta with their lanterns, they look like glow-
worms swarming in the hot night. Steamers and motor-cars stand
ready everywhere for the inspectors who spend these September
days like generals in battle, every nerve strained, placing or moving about boats with sandbags or stones and piling up cotton-
plants and maize-straw in readiness for any dam-burst. Everything
depends on the watchfulness of a dozen men, who may not sleep
and must be everywhere at the same time. Thus even today, in the
finely irrigated province of Girga on the Middle Nile, the story
is told of an English inspector who, in 1886, got the upper hand
of a catastrophic flood by throwing up an embankment in a single
day with the help of the whole village, and how the village invited
the Christian to take part in the service of thanksgiving at the
mosque, an unprecedented happening which throws a profound
light on the religious feelings of a people at the mercy of an
element.

Another time, in 1887, a dam burst which protected a village
north of Mansûra. As the men, women, and children carried up
all they had, their furniture, doors, and windows, to stop up the
gap, the Englishman in charge noticed that the most active of all
was a man whose strength belied his white hair. Later he heard
that this man, when on sentry duty in 1878, had been unable to
prevent a burst in the Delta, and that Khedive Ismail, in his rage,
had ordered him to be thrown into the Nile. On that night, when
he awaited death, his hair turned white. Later he was pardoned
because he was innocent, and now he was once more fighting a
burst, and, with his white head, did more than all the others.

Everything growing in the Delta, which means the major part
of all Egyptian cotton, depends on the Barrage du Nil, which lies
16 miles below Cairo where the Nile branches. This is the last
bridle man puts on the river, and its possibilities for defensive
purposes are so great that Viceroy Said developed the Barrage
into a genuine fortress in order to flood the whole Delta in case
of invasion. Even this reminder of the destructive power of the
Barrage has kept alive the Egyptian distrust of the English. Today
the Barrage is still an old-fashioned fort with its bastions and

galleries, drawbridges and casemates, and looks like an old engraving.

This is the point at which the Nile divides, and Plato was the first to conceive for it the beautiful image of a branching tree. The Delta, which, with its length of 155 miles and width of 135, is not as regular as its name implies, was watered up to a hundred years ago by basins, as the whole of Egypt was at that time, and it was by Mehemet Ali's enterprise that a first dam was designed for perennial irrigation. This was more difficult at this point, but more profitable, because here the cultivable land is not squeezed into the narrow valley, but spreads out like the Dutch marshes. The double purpose of all Egyptian irrigation—to irrigate all parts at all seasons—is particularly evident here.

It was not the fault of the French that their dam cracked, or that walls standing on shifting earth stored only two instead of fourteen feet of water: we can realize here the powerlessness of an agent of civilization in the east whose capacity is purely advisory. For while the Egyptian engineers, when the barrage was built, carried out the French plans badly, the English, forty years later, could build as they wanted to. Even today, when the English store fifty feet of water, the foremost experts declare that the Egyptians could not run their waterworks themselves if the English were to leave the country.

The two dams, which, though they differ in length, each have sixty-one arches and two sluices, are decorated with a relief from a statue of Ramses II which was discovered in Thebes; this relief, which once symbolized the union of the two Egypts, now gives superb expression to the union of the two branches of the Nile. The tongue of land formed by the two dams contains the most luxuriant garden in Egypt: probably no piece of land receives more water. It is indulged like the children of a hygiene expert who are fed according to the soundest principles of health he has discovered in his laboratory.

In addition to a second concrete barrage at Zifta, which crosses the eastern branch lower down, an earth dike must be thrown up every year across both branches of the Nile just before they discharge; thus the mouths of the Nile must be blocked to hold up the water trickling through the barrage. This is done exactly three weeks after the closing of the dam at Aswân, generally on March 19, when the last wave to pass through Aswân, which left Khartoum on February 10, arrives at the mouth. The life and safety of a dictator, or a multi-millionaire with his army of doctors, is not watched more carefully than the Nile. The general system of the Delta is regulated by six arteries with unpronounceable Arabic names.

This system, however, like the human body, is complicated by pumps, wheels, and siphons in order to reach the parts lying three feet higher. Here, where the cotton demands the utmost care, a network of drainage canals and an exact calculation of time are necessary. The summer storage water thus circulates like counters in a children's game: five days of water, then less or none for ten days; the total period is fifteen days for cotton, and eight to ten for rice, provided there is enough water.

And here, just before its end, the fettered river still hurls its strength against man, to remind him of the power of the element. The silt, without which the country could not live, becomes troublesome here in the Delta, and has to be removed: all canals are cleaned for forty days a year, generally in January, when the canals are closed for repair. As the perennial system requires less silt, and Egypt can manage at the present time with 28 million tons, the surplus of the 40 to 120 million tons of silt which comes down yearly is distributed more generously, for these great fluctuations are the result of the vagaries of the Abyssinian rains. What is not used for the dikes is given to the fellah free. If he does not want it, the government has to pay for its removal, and sometimes the fellah is faced with the question whether he should use the gift of the Nile on his fields or whether he will make more by destroying it, a momentous question which, in time of revolution, often decides the political colour of thousands, and sometimes decides the outcome of the revolution itself.

The second element that has to be dealt with here is the salt, since the sea-water, which is ten times too salty for the crops and twenty times so for drinking purposes, here enters the river. The exclusion of the salt is the second purpose of the earth dikes which are thrown up every year, and for which big steps of wood, later connected by boats and sacks, form a kind of permanent framework. When the dikes have advanced so far that only a gap of 65 feet remains in the middle, the salt water is expelled by a sudden release of Nile water up at the barrage, and the chemist, testing the water on the bank to arrive at the right proportion of salt, orders more or less water from the barrage by telephone.

All this water, the administration of which alone costs $2,500,-000 a year, is distributed free, here and throughout the country; the taxes are paid on the watered land. But how paltry these sums look compared with the cost of human destruction! The six barrages built in Egypt in our century at a cost of $60,000,000 came to less than the cost of a week of the World War. And yet these barrages on the Nile cannot, like those in other parts of the world, be used to produce light and power at the same time: the fluctuations of the river have permitted the installation of power-stations only at very few points. Here the Nile has remained almost unconquerable: like a genius, it works when it is in the mood, because it wishes to, but not steadily, because it must. And in the Delta it is navigable only in the flood months: only the lower reaches of the Rosetta Nile are navigable at other times.

Until the English came, no code of law governed the whole, and even if the Nile served man for thousands of years before the rights and duties of those living on it were defined in the "Canal Acts," the possibility of any abuse on the part of those in power has been considerably reduced since the hierarchy of the water was established. If the whims of the Nile played into the hands of the rich, since the land in Egypt actually changes as often as the land at the foot of a volcano, the fellah knows today that, if the Nile has retreated from his sakia, and formed a new island, he can dig a ditch and lead the water to his wheel without paying for it. He knows that even the pasha will be punished if he stops his poor neighbour's water with stones, if he closes a sluice too early, digs a hole in the bank, or has a dike removed. He knows that he will get a supplement of water from the inspector in April if his rice needs more than was estimated.

The oldest lesson the Nile taught man, to act in common, has been raised to a science by his six millenniums of experience, a science which makes use of everything offered by tradition, but can be more economical on the whole, juster in the detail, because neither the Pharaoh nor the Viceroy is the lord of the soil as he was in the time of Joseph or Mehemet Ali. The dams with their meticulous distribution, the transformation of a grain country into a cotton country, the abolition of the *corvée,* the great reduction in the number of foreign dealers, the schools, and the exemption of the smallest holdings from seizure for debt—all these things have once more united the Egyptians in state socialism, and in spite of all the regulations concerning what is to be cultivated and when and where, have enhanced the self-respect of the fellah who, till now, was a slave, not of water, but of man.

28

GREEN is the colour of the Delta, as it is of the whole Nile valley. But as it here covers a vast expanse, and not a mere strip, as it is a country and not an oasis, the desert yellow impinges only on its outer edges. While Upper Egypt was a harmony of green, yellow, and blue, the dominant chord in the Delta, with its pale sky, its houses, its sails, and the women's clothes, is green, white, and black. If, instead of palms, northern trees rose from the flat expanse, it might be a Dutch landscape: the water is everywhere, for a thousand little canals cross the big ones.

It is, however, only the general picture which recalls the dunes, and not the variety of its details. Everything that moves is Egyptian in its density and softness. When consuls were still poets, a French consul under Louis XIV wrote: "Egypt, silvery in September, is emerald in November and golden in August." But now it is October.

A camel, huge against the sky, strides slowly along carrying away a rocking mountain of dry cotton-leaves to be burnt. A man rides along the dam on his donkey with the new water-wheel he has bought in the town tied on behind. An antiquated little Ford rattles past with fourteen men, all laughing, sitting in it or hanging onto it, their robes fluttering. Slowly two white double sails ride before the north-west wind through the plain, and their burden is as white as the sails—mountains of foamy cotton. Two black women and five children are sticking yellow maize straw at equal intervals into the soil, ready for tomorrow's bean-planting. Two men, standing naked in the canal, lift lumps of Nile mud with their hands, beat them flat, and trundle them to the little white house on wheelbarrows—the glittering specks in it are crystals from Abyssinia, distant memories of an almost forgotten youth. A little hill tries to rise, and reaches a height of five feet, while above it, the wind sweeps in strange rings, for it is the highest point far and wide. The northern windmill stands perhaps as high, solitary, like an emigrant, with flapping wings, apparently working a pump.

Beyond, two black, rusty dredges tower: they are casting the silt on the fields. A thousand bright yellow pots lie in even heaps on the bank like old cannon balls. Three camels pass with long, waving tails like giant peacocks—they are carrying bundles of palm-leaves. Cranes fly low everywhere, knowing that everyone will spare them as the friends of the cows. A donkey takes a plucky leap over a canal; its rider seems to be a watchman, for he carries an old musket. A cloud of birds flutters up from an open heap of corn—nobody has stopped their depredations. An avenue of acacias leads to a fine house, the dome of a mosque shimmers yellow and blue behind it. Four high, red-brick buildings clash against the green; in front of them, a boy is grooming a magnificent horse, which softly paws the ground; the four buildings are racing-stables, the white huts of Nile mud beside them are fellah homes. Fifty men in long white shirts are loaded each with two stones in baskets, which they are carrying to the canal to build a new head. Beyond, long boats are carrying stones to the same place; they come from Cairo, there are no stones in the Delta. Two donkeys, tied to a canal stake, look on blinking, and rub their heads together. A black woman comes through the fields to the canal, her empty pitcher lying sidewise on her head; she fills it slowly, then returns with the pitcher upright on her head. More sails glide slowly through the fields; the black boats bear a light burden, but here it is a royal burden, it is the white, loose cotton. Beside the canal a boy is turning a wooden screw to reach the sakia on the other side. Both creak. There he stands and turns the livelong day, ten hours, to raise water—water.

29

NOW the towns come with their bustle and their factories: there are few mills in this cottonland, which works only 1 percent of its crop; few tobacco factories in the country that has produced the finest tobacco; few sugar-refineries which, in the country of the sugar-cane, do not produce enough to supply the country. Beside them the fellah's buffalo still turns a wheel that squeezes the cane with a cylinder and produces a kind of molasses; that is what they like, not the sugar from the factory.

At the farthest corner of the Delta, however, south-west of Alexandria, Faust's endeavour begins again—the struggle to reclaim a steppe country for the peasant and the gardener. There, close to the sea, towards the Libyan frontier, bedouins turn out their cattle to graze on the nomad steppe which receives a little rain in winter, and plant a little grain before the scorching summer comes, just as they did nearly two thousand miles up the Nile in Middle Nubia. But there are Egyptian and Roman ruins to show that this was once cultivated land; the ruins of a lighthouse lead to the conclusion that it was in the time of Cleopatra; and tradition says that it was densely cultivated grainland. Potsherds show Christian work, for on them a saint stands between two camels.

Here, where the wine of the Ptolemies grew, a Greek has once more brought olden times back to life. A little town which he built and a road he laid out bear the name of Gianaclis, and thus, after the Macedonian king and the Macedonian coffee-dealer who ruled here, a tobacco-planter came to awaken the sleeping land; he grew as old as Pharaoh. In this fine climate, helped by a cool breeze, by rain and a canal in the neighbourhood, he raised oranges, olives, and grapes for a new kind of wine on dunes of silt and sand. Thus the area of the Delta can be extended by one fifth and, to combat the growing cotton crisis, tobacco can be grown again, the fellah's delight, which was taken from him in order that a profit could be made on its import. For Egypt, with four cigarettes per day per head of the population, including the women and children, consumes $100,000,000 worth of imported tobacco yearly, more than any other country, instead of cultivating it in the country where the Nile water and perhaps the air also give it a delicacy it has nowhere else.

So great is the power of the white queen: cotton has supplanted everything. Egypt, which once supplied the Roman Empire with grain, now has to import flour from Australia, and when the dams open up new land, it is not given up to grain. While in 1900 there were still 1.2 million acres of wheat and .8 million of cotton, in 1926 the figures were already 1.2 million acres of wheat and 2 million of cotton. The population of Egypt had almost doubled, but the bread in the country was not allowed to increase, so that money might swell at the cost of independence, for it is cotton that rules, and not freedom. In 1925, $310,000,000 worth of cotton and cotton-seed was exported, but $60,000,000 worth of grain was imported, and even in 1930, after the crisis in cotton, its export was 87 percent of the total exports of Egypt. Now reason is returning: for 1935 the figures show 1.8 million acres of cotton and 1.4 million of wheat.

This speculation was profitable only for the best years. In the Delta, where the feddan of cotton yields $150, the clover, which only yields $50, can be cut five times a year, which means that it can be of great profit to the country. The soil, moreover, was exhausted by over-planting, for even before the war, cotton was planted every second year instead of every fourth, until it began to yield less and lose its quality. As much harm was done to the land as to a woman who is forced to bear a child every year.

Thus everything turns on the white queen, yet she is sent abroad; Egypt, which allowed so many foreign monarchs to grow rich in the country, sends this native queen away because the foreigners pay more. Instead of spinning the cotton here and then weaving the yarn, great ships carry it for hundreds of sea-miles to a distant island so that the cotton-mills of Lancashire need not buy from America, but can send the same cotton back in the form of material for clothing, and useless millions are wasted on freight. Having first compelled nature against her will to grow a plant where the rain it needed did not fall, the cotton was torn from the fields and carried off to a foggy island, to be sent out again into the world transformed. Zeus managed his metamorphoses more promptly and elegantly—he performed them on the spot.

Are the species so fine as is maintained? Then they ought to be exchanged by treaties. Is there no room in the Delta for mills? A single small mill could work the crop for miles round about just as a thin book on a table can contain a world of thoughts and visions. A man who wants to prevent something happening, and has the power to prevent it, always finds technical reasons for proving the undesirable impossible.

Has the fellah gained by the cotton?

During the first period of luck, when the cotton of the southern states was practically cut off for the four years of the American Civil War, the pashas had grown rich, but the fellah felt only the double burden of work in the fields, and the liberation of the slaves in America created new slaves in Egypt. After the World War, with the transformation of the social structure of Egypt, a few fellahin were able to make fortunes in the great boom: up to $200 per kantar was paid for cotton, and up to $5000 for good land. There are still fellahin in the Delta who acquired as many as a thousand palms out of the money they made then, and that means an income of $5000. The name of a fellah is known who one day bought land to a value of $200,000 from a bankrupt company and, when the time came for signing the agreement, made his appearance with a retinue of donkeys carrying the gold in sacks. The English traders laughed at the folly of the fellah who let his money sleep in his house of Nile mud, and did not make it work, but they themselves most likely lost their own a few years later in some splendid company with sumptuous offices and impressive notepaper.

As he is frugal, the fellah saves: a finer donkey, a prettier house, a gold necklace for his wife—that is all. He has faith only in the land that the Nile waters, and it is the land that he buys for himself and his children. An enriched fellah has never been seen squandering his money in Cairo or Paris, where the cotton-speculators parade in Pharaonic fashion for a few months. He has rarely been seen to lord it over his neighbour fellah who has remained poor. Every one of them knows the Arab story in which the rich fellah leads the poor one to the magnificent tomb of his father, but the poor one cries: "By the time thy father has raised the marble slab of his tomb, mine will have long been in Paradise."

For enigmatic reasons that no expert can explain, the fellahin, especially in the Delta, have developed a so-called vice that seems to run counter to their cheerfulness. Nowhere on the Mediterranean are drugs so widespread among the poor; they are familiar to the rich everywhere. The fellah has been systematically poisoned for decades, not only by factories in Eastern Europe, but by the highly moral European centres which sell philantropy and democracy cheap. Thousands of dealers, smugglers, and agents live on this prohibited traffic. It is open to question whether the manufacture of heroin, which gives men feelings of happiness and thrilling dreams, is more immoral than the manufacture of poison gas, which kills them. Some governments sanction the latter in order to conquer territory, but prohibit the other so that their citizens may not be weakened for that purpose.

When the fellah in the Delta buys the forbidden pellet or herb, in tobacco, in chocolate, in pepper, he often does so in the hope of reviving his sexual powers, but it is the contrary that happens. If he is merely dull and hopeless, he smokes some hashish in his nargileh until the leather pipe falls from his hands and he begins to dream. An energetic struggle in recent years had greatly reduced the discoverable quantity of drugs, but no one knows how much remains undiscovered. Since the drugs were detected in the soles of imported slippers, the dealers have devised all sorts of new, romantic hiding-places, such as the skin of the camel, which they slit, sew up, and open again in their hiding-places. Here, too, a complete injustice condemns every Egyptian smoker who is caught to years of prison, while the convicted Turkish dealer escapes with a few months. No state which allows so many thousands to lie in poverty and apathy has the right to punish them for spending a few piastres on dreams, sweet exhaustion, and oblivion.

It would be better for the cotton magnates, who would enjoy neither power nor wealth if it were not for the fellah, to protect him against the diseases which their dams brought into the country.

What man extorts from nature, he must pay for, but the man who pays is not always the man who profits. The Egyptians thought themselves blessed, and so they were, for the country was free from malaria, although the stretches of stagnant water ought to have bred it, and Herodotus and Cæsar write of mosquito nets. We know how nature could take her revenge for Alexander the Great's attempt to reclaim the marshes: he probably died of marsh-fever. What he lacked was clover, and it was the clover that protected the Nile valley and the Delta in spite of all the stagnant basins. Pure water was proved to be injurious, silt-laden water healthy, and when, in Bengal, the irrigation with silt was abandoned, and watering left to the rain, malaria arrived. Even during the war, the hundreds of infected refugees from Palestine did not bring it to Egypt.

Since the barrages were built, however, although Lord Cromer tried to guarantee their harmlessness with all kinds of reports by experts, a disease has come to Egypt, due, not to the Nile, but to the man who conquered the Nile.

One of the two greatest engineers who studied the Nile and built the dams—Willcocks and Murdoch MacDonald—and realized the great example of Faust, occupied his old age, as a true philanthropist, only with the harm done by what he had built. Willcocks never ceased to warn the ministers and cotton kings, the Egyptian and English potentates, who simply strove to conceal the dangers, instead of averting them. He showed why the ancient Egyptians, who had brought the clover from the Middle Nile, cut it repeatedly, so that it bloomed repeatedly, and kept off the mosquitoes with its blooms. The Pharaohs even forbade the fellah in the public service or in prison to eat uncooked vegetables.

The barrages and the new irrigation system have raised the ground water everywhere, and hence made the cesspools, in particular, the breeding-ground of a pest, a hook-worm, which produces eruptions and fever, and while it does not kill man, sometimes makes him desperate with pain and saps his strength with anæmia, rendering him an easy victim to other diseases. This bilharziasis appears everywhere where the perennial system has been introduced, both in Upper Egypt, where the canals are not allowed to drain off, since they carry drinking-water, and in the northern and eastern Delta, where the water lies and many canals are dirty. Those concerned strive in vain to conceal what independent medical men assert, namely that in the sugar-fields of Kom-Ombo, with their perennial irrigation, 66 percent of all the fellahin are attacked by the disease, while a few miles away, in the basin land of Edfu, only a few, and in the excellently irrigated province of Girga, also watered with basins, none at all fall victim. In the Delta, where it is most difficult to draw off the water, an allied disease, anchylostomiasis, due to an intestinal worm, has attacked 95 percent of the fellahin and bilharziasis 65 percent.

The more water is stored, the higher the ground water rises: in the Delta, it threatens to flood the houses. Yet there are remedies for this new plague in Egypt; they only have to be applied, to be paid for—public latrines must be built, village ponds filled up, main canals deepened so that they flow to their mouths as deep, wide rivers, and the ground water must be diverted into the Nile, where it would profit the land and the canal; drainage canals must be shut in winter instead of being used as a means of access, so that the level of the ground water would sink after the Nile flood, and all land must be drained before irrigation. These are complicated preventive measures which need time. There is, however, one remedy which, if applied quickly and on a large scale, could save the people. The worm attacks them as they stand working in the water, and since in Egypt two out of every three work standing in the water, their legs would have to be protected as the policemen protect theirs with their fine, high boots, especially where the papyrus luxuriates. If the policeman or the engineer is practically immune from both diseases owing to the protective rubber on his legs, a cotton company would only have to debit its budget with the million dollars which the 250,000 pairs of rubber boots would cost; they could, moreover, be lent out in a rotation of four. In this way, it could put into practice the teaching of Christ for the same amount of money it now spends to send its cotton missionaries into the jungle. But if it is not disposed to abandon the more profitable form of the battle with sin, it would have to enter these million dollars in its budget as a dead loss. If the dividend at the end of the year drops 2 percent, a million men have been saved from serious disease by it. That 2 percent, which the European, living on stock-exchange quotations, loses on his cotton shares, is the price of the boots which would save the Egyptian fellah from a disease which is eating at the vitality of the people, and be the ransom of the queen.

30

IN autumn, countless women and children crouch on the soil of the Delta picking cotton. The garb of the servants is black, the queen is white, a cloud hangs between them. Everything about her looks unreal, white and fleeting, a game played with down, a children's dream.

The shrub is capricious; in youth it is self-willed, wants to enjoy itself, lacks steadiness, seems born to a delicate life: it does not yet know what ordeals await it. Its fate will be harder than that of any other plant, for its transformation is not accomplished in its sap, but at its most sensitive spot, in its fibres, and it is accomplished with pain.

In March, the same women were sitting here, carefully transplanting the first seedlings behind ridges to protect them from the wind; then they weeded, continually loosened the earth round the roots, and always transplanted the little plants higher up the ridge, until they were on top and could grow freely. A thousand hours, the livelong summer, their brown, women's hands were busy about the tiny leaves to remove maggots, a training in patience and tenderness, such as their upbringing of their children. Meanwhile, the men were thinking all summer of how the tender shrub with the yellow flowers could best be watered.

When at last the seeds swelled in their cotton-wool bolls, all eyes were fixed on the long fields, for the finest cotton is obtained if it is cut, like asparagus, at the right moment, that is, when the brownish-black boll bursts. As this does not happen everywhere at the same time, and the crops are always sold all together, in this huge national enterprise the most vital work is quite personal, and its value can be increased by practice and patience more than is the case with any other plant, even tea and coffee. If the raw cotton is cream-coloured, the fellah is glad, for that is the best kind, and if he could see the staple under the microscope, he would recognize its toughness by its fine twist, and the quality of the cellulose, after chemical treatment, by the little barrel-shaped swellings.

The fellah knows very well that it is the "long staple" he lives on, and pronounces the word "Sakellarides" as his ancestors pronounced "Isis" or later "Demeter." But no one in the market knows that this name of the finest Egyptian strain is the name of a Greek farmer who first grew it in 1906; and when the American buyers first met the man in Alexandria, they were as startled by him as if a god had descended to earth, for they had regarded as something divine the name of the dearest cotton in the world. For it is by means of the long staple, which is excelled only by the cotton of South Florida and Arizona, which can grow it in small quantities, that Egypt can compete with the big cotton countries; for it produces no more than 7 percent of the world crop, and can hold its own between India and America only because Allah or Kyrios Sakellarides discovered the 40-millimetre staple and had dreamed of the silky sheen of women's chemises it was to produce before he grew the strain.

The cotton-gamble—for that is what it is in a little country which lives entirely on it—rules the fate of the Egyptians, quite apart from the ravages of pests, such as occurred in 1922, and the world-crises which this African island, without an army, subject to a world power, and threatened by competition on the Upper Nile, cannot influence. It is true that the world demand is increasing: the greed of the textile manufacturers persuaded mankind of so many new needs that the world consumption rose, between 1884 and 1904, from 7 to 15 million bales. Today the hopes of the moral millionaires are fixed on the abolition of the revolting nakedness of Africa, where it is alleged that only 2 percent of the population wear shirts.

The older fellah, it is true, knows nothing about all this, but his son has already read in the papers that in Texas the crop from a few million acres was ploughed under by the tractor while on the Indus the biggest dam in the world was opened in order to increase the cotton crop there by 23 percent, which was reduced by law in America by 25 percent. The fellah may not understand this contradiction, but he is no more foolish than those responsible for it. He feels only that he is the victim, for when distant gods in America make cotton prices fall from 18 to 7 cents per pound of cotton in the course of two years, when at the same time the red powers in Asia against which his paper warns him, grow new strains which bear 200 instead of 30 bolls, it all costs the fellah, in his hut of Delta mud, his hope of a new donkey, his boys' school fees, and maybe his few grammes of hashish.

In order to protect himself, he has become an expert salesman. But before the sale, it is again the women who, with their defter hands and unflagging patience, clear the white bolls of bad brown parts, beat leaves out of the cotton, clean it handful by handful, always working forward from the still uncleaned heaps at the back, while the children collect the waste in baskets. When the men have carried the crop on donkeys into the courtyard, the second cleaning comes; it is more thorough than the first, since the wind cannot here blow back the withered leaves. The whole Delta looks as if it were covered with groups of women in black draperies who move with nodding heads in the sun between the white hills, often with a child at the breast—figures of fate combing the last impurities out of the white robe of life's spoilt children. Strange altars, draped in black, have been set up among them: they are the gratings on which the cotton is beaten, and they are hung round with cloths to keep the withered leaves from falling back on it. At last it is all clean—the queen is white.

Only now does the fellah's great moment come, for now the buyer arrives from Alexandria: now he will examine and buy. The fellah, who was once cheated as a matter of course, can now read, every morning, the cotton-price telegrams, but the actual quality, which is now tested, can raise or lower the price, and that is what matters. As the first picking is always the best, it lies at the back and the bottom of the white heap, and the buyer must slowly work his way through, while the fellah plunges his brown hands into the white, downy world, shakes it up, makes it float and sink, and praises it as the purest cotton in the world—or at any rate in the Delta. Then Allah is called to witness, quantities of coffee are consumed, for every purchase is a risk, nobody can examine the whole crop, bit by bit, and as the buyer knows where the seller is trying to hide the inferior parts, he is always suspicious. Any number of neighbours stand round: the longer the bargaining, the better the deal, and as they all wear the fez and blue shirt, it is the buyer in his European garb and straw hat who looks like a savage captured by the others. Time and time again his offer is greeted with a roar of laughter, until at last it is accepted and the neighbours clap their hands—the play is over.

Now the village clerk appears—even today he looks like that Pharaonic statue in Cairo which was called the Omdeh because the fellahin who excavated it shouted that it looked like their mayor—and when he has written the agreement, generally with a reed pen on his flat left hand, the price for so many hundred-weight, one-third for pure cotton, two-thirds for oil and fodder from the seeds, is at once paid in banknotes, but the buyer has to sign the notes, because the fellah has no faith in the signature of the National Bank.

The stuffing of the sacks has already been going on for some time. Now the weigher arrives with a little caravan: three donkeys with the weigher and two assistants, the tripod on a fourth, the scales on a fifth, the weights and all the rest on a sixth. During these weeks, the tripod runs through the Delta like a huge spider, for here the scales follow the sacks, and not the sacks the scales. Finally, after further quantities of coffee and cigarettes, all the sacks have been weighed up and strapped onto donkeys and camels, for now the ginning begins. And as the sacks retreat along the dam on the backs of the animals, the fellah, his wife, and every child follow it silently with their eyes, perhaps mourning the disappearance of the white queen for whom they have laboured so many hundreds of hours in the sun. Of the notes which the man still holds in his brown hands, many will forthwith pass into those of his creditors. The strict necessary remains. Nobody imagines it means wealth.

In front of the ginning-machines, grown-up girls and twelve-year-old boys sit, pale and coughing, for everything is enveloped in white fluff, and the nimble fingers must feed the machines and protect themselves from wheels and gratings. The old, unventilated factories in the Delta, which ruin the lungs with flue, are slowly being improved, but this slavery is less evil than that in the compress in Alexandria. For in order to ship the cotton to that distant island where it is turned into fabrics, the freight must be reduced in bulk and the weight concentrated from five to seven hundredweight per bale. For this process, steam pressure is not enough, human arms and feet must set to work.

It is a bacchantic scene. Amid the roar of the machines, in open, corrugated iron sheds with huge sliding gates, among wire ropes, rollers, and iron plates, a hundred men and women shout and sing, waving their hands and feet in the air—all hurrying, pale with excitement, tense as man must be in the race with the machine, their hair full of white fluff, their shirts, sleeves, legs, one mass of downy powder. With swift hands, the women beat the last traces of leaves out of the flakes, but the men stand at the grating from which the loose cotton rolls like foamy white rivers on endless bands to a huge square hole. Before it can roll into the hole, the cotton must be stamped down to be compressed in readiness for the mechanical pressure of the machines. With their foreheads bound, the men in their blue shirts stamp without ceasing, singing an eternal refrain of two lines given out by their leader, to keep time even while they are waiting. They have been offered masks of damp cotton-wool; they do not want them, they want to sing as they swing, eight at a time, into the iron chest which stands in the middle of this downy world.

Then, under their hard brown feet, they feel the white down; they stand and stamp, singing, in the whirl of snow, fighting for their breath, and now they sink slowly as they dance, distressed by the dust of the whirling fibres, every aperture of their heads stopped up, coughing, blinking, rubbing their eyes, and still singing while, with their priestly fillets, they seem to be sinking into their grave like barbaric sacrifices to some invisible, unknown god who rules the fellah from far over the sea. Now that lot seems to be finished, for suddenly the eight men clamber out of their iron grave, vault over its sides, and stamp and sing on, till a few minutes later, a new sacrifice comes along. Ten times an hour, a hundred times a day, half-slaves, half-priests, they sink into their cloudy, foamy tomb.

In a great market hall not far from the compress, the buyers are waiting in white coats to protect their smart suits. There they find samples from the bales, feel about with knowing fingers, draw out the staples, throw them back—they know the strain. But of sowing, growth, and reaping they have seen nothing: they do not know, or have forgotten, that the labour of a whole family is compressed into that bale. Now the plants become strains, and just as the deeds of heroes, long after their life, are assembled in one name of legend, it seems to be the names of gods that ring through the hall: "Sakel (sakellarides)! Assili! Armuni! Casuli! Pilion! Zagora! Sakel!"

And voices ring through the hall, crying judgment: they might be the voices of the Judges of the Dead, not of cotton-dealers, as they cry: "Good colour, tinged, high-coloured. Good staple, strong staple, silky staple."

Here the first cycle in the history of the white queen comes to an end. But over on the exchange, the whole life of the plant, the meaning of the strains, the entire significance of the cotton, dies.

Under the dome a mob of a hundred or two roaring men seethes and rolls round a circle of open iron grilles enclosing a raised platform with two silent men standing on it; with cold, even contemptuous eyes, they look down on the human surge. These sworn brokers have seen this battle every weekday of their lives; they know how hollow all the excitement is; for years on end they have heard the roll of these breakers; they seem to have gone deaf in their perpetual roar. In actual fact, they are the only men who understand every shout that rises round about them.

With a careless hand, they chalk up figures and fractions on a big board. This contract exchange of Alexandria, this business in cotton futures, which no longer takes account of value, has driven these thieves of God's days here, today as every day of this century, and while they grasp each other's buttons or hair, while they struggle to catch one of the two mighty ones by the arm, they shout figures upon figures in a rising roar, and when the man in the middle beckons outward, it means: "You" (sale), but when he beckons towards himself, it means: "From you" (buy). And so the poor creature plays the new Ramses at the mouth of the Nile every morning from eleven to one.

None of these men has ever seen the yellow cotton flowers, none has seen the grating with its black cloths, the court with its white heaps, the scales with the tripod or the heavy-laden camels; none knows the man sinking in the press, nor even the strains with their godlike names. These are mere gamblers, hoping for high prices at closing-time if they wish to sell, low prices if they wish to buy; their chips are cottons that are not even ripe, have perhaps not even been sown yet. And it is these markets from which the great shocks come that affect the lives of whole peoples and classes.

All the plants and all the canals have vanished in the far distance; the dams, the sluices, which were devised to grow this cotton are no more; Egypt is a state lit by electric light; the world a network of cables from Liverpool to Bombay, with stock-exchange quotations quivering through the oceans—races and classes, calicoes and cloths, languages and peoples have vanished, and the Nile is a legend.

31

ABOVE the dome of the exchange, slanting up from Rosetta, a flock of flamingos whirs south-west, for on Lake Mareotis, in the marshes at the mouth of the Nile, they will find thousands of their kind. Coloured like a sunset, their slender necks hidden in their wings, they stand on one leg on the shores of the lake, looking over at the cranes which have just alighted by the water in beautiful curves from their flight to the stubble fields. Black moorhens, grave and sober, morosely observe the adventurous cormorants, and seem to be more akin to the sea-swallows and sandpipers, who never quit their strict formations. Above, white gulls swoop proudly, and over them all the fish-eagle hovers motionless, waiting, watching, till suddenly he drops like a lead plummet, then, with a flapping fish in his talons, again rises into the infinite.

Under the sycamores, great herons stand, each melancholy and alone, but the delicate ospreys perch, with indrawn head, like white blossoms in the almost leafless acacias. Suddenly, colours like jewels flash through the stillness, persicus, the bee-eater, the loveliest of all, flies low over the water, with his flashing wings and long beak.

The swallows have already arrived from the north; the northern lands have grown too bleak for them—they may have nested on the English coast. On steely wings, they flit through the air, for they will not stay even here, the south is calling them, and this very day they will set out on their second great flight from the coast of Egypt. They depart in softly twittering flight, always on the fringe of the green land, until the river has gathered itself together again, and is wide and commanding. Now the Nile shows them the way, for on both sides lies the terror of the hungry yellow desert.

Green covers the way of this flock of northern swallows; they can stop anywhere and find food and water—green the valley of the river, now wide, now narrowing again, bending here and there, but never much. And as they move over the Nile, they sweep twittering over the great city with its bridges and its palaces, and its lofty fortress; beyond at the desert's edge the sugar-loaves stand, and in front of the highest, the sphinx lies watching. Columns and chimneys rise out of the green valley, and hosts of boats with white sails, all carrying piles of yellow pitchers; camels trot in long files, but the donkey jumps ahead, and the children laugh. The sound of the sakia whines over the Nile valley, the yoked oxen turn a thousand water-wheels, and the men sing as they turn. Horus screams through the blue, startling the swallows from the north.

But below the flock from the north, the river begins to roar—it is the First Cataract that is foaming, for all the sluices are open and nature takes its course. It takes its course through the ugly stretch where palms and villages have sunk, till the black, dripping rocks of the Second Cataract divide into a thousand islands, and now, at the great bend, the groups of waterfalls are repeated, roaring through the days and nights. But the swallows follow the huge S in the yellow sand, here alone will they find what they need if they are going to escape still farther to the south. Not until the wilder brother of the Nile appears from the south-east, rushing down in virile fullness, not until Khartoum, will these seekers of the south find the second paradise of the birds on the Nile after the first one on the Delta.

Most of them stay here, where everything grows that they dreamed of up there. But a small group presses on, and now for more days and weeks they fly over the yellow steppe; now they see the crocodile motionless on the grey stone in the midday heat, in the evening they see the lion creep up to the bank out of the thicket, and where the course of the river grows confused, where the swamps begin with their labyrinth of channels, one morning, under the flying strangers, the elephant comes to the Nile, trotting slowly along with wife and child, incredible to the visitors from the north, who hasten on—to the south.

And there, at the end, huge lakes spread, an evergreen landscape opens, the fields widen into a garden again, as they did up on the Delta, and the rainy air fosters the growth and bloom of all vegetation, so that there is infinite food for the northern swallows. But one morning, their piping flock flits low over huge waterfalls. There, in a quiet creek, a gigantic maw yawns pink: puffing and sluggish, the hippo snorts and grunts as it raises its head to spout a jet of water from its nostrils. Terrified, the swallows fly into the thicket. They listen, look, and tremble. At their feet the Nile is born.

A roar heralds the river.

INDEX

Index